# The New York Times

► *Guide to* ◄

# RESTAURANTS

► *in* ◄

# NEW YORK CITY

► 1991-92 ◄

Also by the Author

*The Seafood Cookbook,*
with Pierre Franey

*Cuisine Rapide,*
with Pierre Franey

# The New York Times

# ▸ *Guide to* ◂
# RESTAURANTS
# ▸ *in* ◂
# NEW YORK CITY
# ▸ 1991-92 ◂

# *Bryan Miller*

TIMES BOOKS

RANDOM HOUSE

Copyright © 1987, 1988, 1989, 1991 by
The New York Times Company
Maps copyright © 1988, 1991 by David Lindroth
All rights reserved under International and
Pan-American Copyright Conventions. Published in the
United States by Times Books, a division of Random House, Inc.,
New York, and simultaneously in Canada by Random House
of Canada Limited, Toronto.

ISBN: 0-8129-1876-2

The restaurant reviews in this book appeared previously in *The New York Times* in a slightly different form. Copyright © 1986, 1987, 1988, 1989, 1990 by The New York Times Company. Reprinted by permission. All rights reserved.

Design by Beth Tondreau Design

Manufactured in the United States of America
9 8 7 6 5 4 3 2
Revised Edition

*To Mireille*

# ACKNOWLEDGMENTS

Putting together a book like this is a painstaking exercise that requires an energetic and professional support team, with which I am blessed. Many thanks to the editors at Times Books for all their patience and help, especially Ruth Fecych and Beth Pearson; also to my editors at *The New York Times*—particularly Annette Grant, John Montorio, Myra Forsberg, Don Caswell, Gladys Bourdain, Wade Burkhart, and many others in the Weekend section—who make it happen week after week. I would also like to thank my diligent researchers, Amy Albert and Joy Bindelglass-Klein.

# CONTENTS

**INTRODUCTION** xi

**EDITOR'S NOTE** xvii

**MAPS** 2
1. West 50s and north  4
   *(includes Lincoln Center, Central Park, and the Upper West Side)*
2. West 14th Street to West 49th Street  6
   *(includes Chelsea and the Broadway Theater District)*
3. Houston Street to 13th Street, west of Broadway  8
   *(includes the West Village)*
4. Below Houston Street  10
   *(includes SoHo, TriBeCa, Chinatown, Little Italy, Wall Street, and South Street Seaport)*
5. Houston Street east of Broadway to East 49th Street east of Fifth Avenue  12
   *(includes the East Village, Gramercy Park, and Murray Hill)*
6. East 50s and 60s  14
7. East 70s and north  16
   *(includes the Upper East Side)*

   Restaurants in the Boroughs  18

**STAR RATINGS** 19

**PRICE LISTINGS** 23

**TYPES OF CUISINE** 28
American ▸ Afghan ▸ Argentinian ▸ Brazilian ▸ Cajun ▸ Caribbean/Cuban ▸ Chinese ▸ French ▸ Ethiopian ▸ Greek ▸ Italian ▸ Indian ▸ Japanese ▸ Mexican ▸ Russian ▸ Scandinavian ▸ Thai ▸ Turkish ▸ Venezuelan ▸ Vietnamese

**SPECIAL OFFERINGS** 33
Breakfast ▸ Business Entertaining ▸ Carryout and Delivery ▸ Carryout Services ▸ Dining Alone ▸ Fun for Kids ▸ Large Groups ▸ Live Music ▸ Notable Wine List ▸ Open Until Midnight ▸ Outdoor Cafe ▸ Pretheater Menu ▸ Private Rooms ▸ Romantic ▸ Sunday Brunch ▸ Sunday Dinner ▸ A Taste of New York City for Out-of-Town Visitors

**RESTAURANT REVIEWS** 53

**DINER'S JOURNAL** 493

**BEST DISHES** 561

**RESTAURANT INDEX** 569

*(To locate the review and neighborhood map for each restaurant in this book, please consult the Restaurant Index.)*

# INTRODUCTION

What a difference three years make. When the last edition of this guide was published, New York City was riding the crest of an unprecedented restaurant boom. New places were opening at a dizzying rate, and New Yorkers, it seemed, couldn't race out fast enough to sample them.

The stock market crash of 1987 and its fallout on the financial industry helped puncture that balloon. Changing demographics played a role, too: the restaurant-going baby boomers started having babies themselves, and priorities shifted from making the scene to making the mortgage. Sticker shock has also affected the diner in the past few years. As we passed the $100 dinner-for-two plateau and headed toward $125 or more, diners balked. It didn't take restaurants long to get the message.

The buzzword in the restaurant world today is "downscaling." Dozens of restaurants, in an attempt to survive in a shrinking market, are lowering prices, simplifying menus, even changing names to reflect their new economical status. All this has made for a busy time trying to keep track of the changing restaurant scene.

The definition of a good guidebook such as this, I believe, is one that allows a reader to find precisely what he or she wants within three subway stops, assuming there are no track fires or stuck doors. For this reason the restaurant reviews are relatively short and to the point, and every entry in the book is easily identified on maps and thoroughly cross-referenced.

- ▶ If you're looking for a specific restaurant, see the Restaurant Index, beginning on page 569.
- ▶ If you're looking for a particular type of

> restaurant (Open Sunday, Broadway Theater, etc.) see Special Offerings, page 33.

▶ If you're looking for restaurants in a particular neighborhood, see the Maps, beginning on page 2.

▶ If you're looking for a particular dish, see Best Dishes, beginning on page 561.

The Diner's Journal selections, which appear every Friday in the Weekend section of *The New York Times*, grew out of a desire to fill the needs of younger and budget-minded readers. These are often restaurants that are too small or too narrowly focused to merit a full review, but for one reason or another are worth pointing out. Perhaps I found a place that makes a terrific couscous, or a storefront Italian spot that has a grandmother in the back turning out hand-rolled cannelloni that could bring tears to a Neapolitan's eyes.

A word about *The New York Times*'s system of restaurant reviewing is in order for those who may not be familiar with the newspaper's method. In the course of my work as food critic for the *Times* I visit restaurants anonymously every day. Each place reviewed is visited a minimum of three times with three or four diners. In the event I am known to the establishment—this is unavoidable in some cases—I reserve a table under a different name and send dining companions ahead of time to claim it. Frequently I send confederates to dinner before writing the review to determine how unknown patrons are treated.

Readers often ask me if it is possible to review a restaurant when the owner happens to know me. While it is always easier to work anonymously, such a circumstance does not obviate an honest assessment. I realized this during a year-long kitchen apprenticeship in a French restaurant seven years ago, during which time several local critics came in.

When the owners told us what was happening I realized there was little we could do. By this time all our sauce stocks had been prepared, the fish, meat, and vegetables purchased, and the desserts made. We could have given the critic extra-large portions, but that might well have backfired and caused a negative reaction. On any given day a

- ▶ Product knowledge. Those who serve food should have basic knowledge of the ingredients and cooking techniques used in each dish on the menu. Once I had a waiter describe a dish as "veal with some sort of brown sauce on top." Appetizing, isn't it?
- ▶ Wine. Those who serve wine should have at least minimal knowledge about grape varieties and general flavor characteristics.
- ▶ Table setting. The tableware should be clean and set in the proper fashion before customers are seated.
- ▶ Watchfulness. Waiters should always be within hailing distance of customers, close enough to respond to eye contact. This way, when guests are ready to order or need something, the waiter can come promptly. Diners, on the other hand, should never try to get a waiter's eye by snapping fingers or bellowing, "Waiter!"
- ▶ Ashtrays. Ashtrays should be cleared frequently, especially before food is brought to the table.
- ▶ Table clearing. The table should be cleared and crumbed before the serving of the entrée and the dessert.
- ▶ Serving. The old rule about serving on the left and removing on the right applies only to classic French-style presentation in which foods are served from platters. Having food arranged on plates in the kitchen has rendered that rule nearly obsolete. Food should be served on the side that is least disruptive to the diner.
- ▶ "Everything okay?" Waiters should never ask this question while customers are eating. It is annoying and reflects a lack of confidence about the food on their part. They should be nearby to respond to comments or complaints.
- ▶ "Who gets the chicken?" The service staff should never auction its food at tableside. It doesn't take a photographic memory to jot down on a pad who gets what.
- ▶ The check. Waiters should not present the check while guests are still drinking coffee unless it is

requested. This gives diners the impression of being rushed. When diners ask for the bill, it should be presented promptly to the person who made the request.

## Reservations

In fairness it must be pointed out that many problems in the flow of service can be attributed to inconsiderate diners who arrive late for their reservations without calling ahead and letting management know, or worse, failing to show up altogether. This has forced some restaurants to adopt the airline practice of overbooking to cover their losses. If everyone happens to show up, of course, a crisis ensues. Some top New York restaurants, including La Côte Basque and Le Cirque, report no-shows approaching 50 percent on weekends and holidays. Diners who change their plans should always give restaurants as much advance notice as possible.

## Gripes

If you have a complaint about the food, wine, or service, bring it up discreetly with the manager or owner. Too often diners vent their wrath on waiters, who may not be responsible for the problem—certainly not if the food is substandard. Never make a scene. That only exacerbates the situation and makes everyone defensive. You may be surprised at how much more you can accomplish by talking to management in a polite but firm tone. If you still do not get satisfaction, find out if there is a higher up, perhaps a major investor or absentee owner, and write a cogent, thoughtful letter. Take it from somebody who gets more than his share of irate letters, a smart-alecky tone only diminishes your chances of success.

If the problem involves sanitation in the dining room or kitchen, contact the New York City Department of Health (212-285-9503).

# EDITOR'S NOTE

A few words about the system of alphabetization used in this book are in order. A strict letter-by-letter approach has been followed, and spaces between words as well as punctuation marks have been disregarded. For example, Barbetta comes before B. Smith's; China Grill precedes Chin Chin. English articles *(A, An, The)* have also been disregarded, though foreign articles, such as *La* and *El*, have not, so that La Gauloise follows Lafayette. Numbers in restaurant names are alphabetized as if they were spelled out.

The index at the back lists all restaurants in the book following the same letter-by-letter system.

#### The New York Times

### Guide to
# RESTAURANTS
### in
# NEW YORK CITY
## ‣ 1991-92 ◂

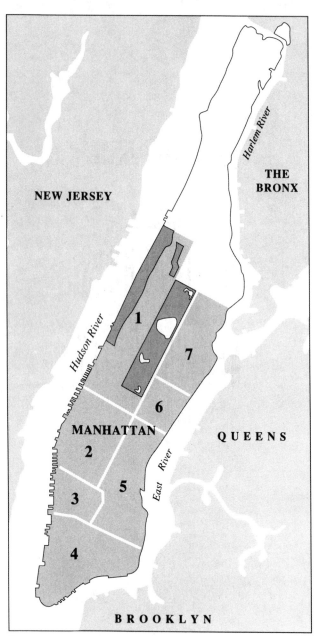

# MAPS

Every Manhattan restaurant in this guidebook appears on a map in this section. Those in the other boroughs of the city are listed on page 18. If you aren't sure which map carries the restaurant you are looking for, consult the restaurant index (see page 569). Each entry in the index is followed by a map number and the page(s) where the restaurant is described.

On the key facing each map, restaurants covered only in the Diner's Journal are followed by (DJ).

1. West 50s and north (includes Lincoln Center, Central Park, and the Upper West Side)
2. West 14th Street to West 49th Street (includes Chelsea and the Broadway Theater District)
3. Houston Street to West 13th Street, west of Broadway (includes the West Village)
4. Below Houston Street (includes SoHo, TriBeCa, Chinatown, Little Italy, Wall Street, and South Street Seaport)
5. Houston Street east of Broadway to East 49th Street east of Fifth Avenue (includes the East Village, Gramercy Park, and Murray Hill)
6. East 50s and 60s
7. East 70s and north (includes the Upper East Side)

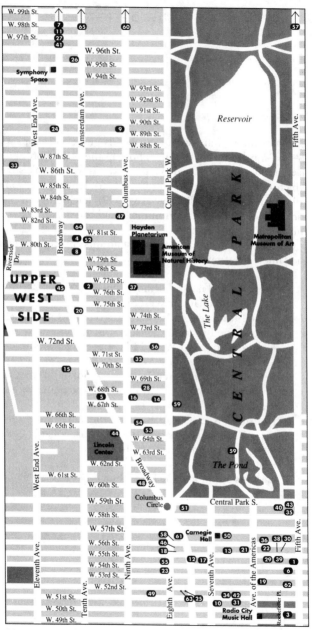

## MAP 1

### WEST 50S AND NORTH

*(Includes Lincoln Center, Central Park, and the Upper West Side)*

1. Adrienne, 700 Fifth Avenue.
2. Alcala, 349 Amsterdam Avenue.
3. American Festival Cafe, Rockefeller Plaza, 20 West 50th Street (DJ).
4. Amsterdam's Bar and Rotisserie, 428 Amsterdam Avenue.
5. Andiamo!, 1991 Broadway.
6. Aquavit, 13 West 54th Street.
7. Au Grenier Cafe, 2867 Broadway (DJ).
8. Baci, 412 Amsterdam Avenue (DJ).
9. Bella Luna, 584 Columbus Avenue (DJ).
10. Bellini by Cipriani, 777 Seventh Avenue.
11. Border Cafe, 2637 Broadway (DJ).
12. Broadway Diner, 1726 Broadway (DJ).
13. Cafe Between the Bread, 145 West 55th Street (DJ).
14. Cafe des Artistes, 1 West 67th Street.
15. Cafe Luxembourg, 200 West 70th Street.
16. Cameos, 169 Columbus Avenue.
17. Carnegie Deli, 854 Seventh Avenue (DJ).
18. Chantal Café, 257 West 55th Street.
19. China Grill, 60 West 53rd Street (entrance at 52 W. 53rd St.).
20. Coastal, 300 Amsterdam Avenue.
21. Corrado, 1372 Avenue of the Americas.
22. Darbar, 44 West 56th Street.
23. Da Tommaso, 903 Eighth Avenue.
24. Docks, 2427 Broadway.
25. Gallagher's, 228 West 52nd Street.
26. Indian Cafe, 201 West 95th Street (DJ).
27. Indian Cafe, 2791 Broadway (DJ).
28. La Boîte en Bois, 75 West 68th Street.
29. La Bonne Soupe, 48 West 55th Street (DJ).
30. La Caravelle, 33 West 55th Street.
31. La Cité, 120 West 51st Street.
32. La Kasbah, 70 West 71st Street (DJ).
33. La Mirabelle, 333 West 86th Street.
34. Le Bernardin, 155 West 51st Street.
35. The Manhattan Ocean Club, 57 West 58th Street.
36. Marie-Michelle, 57 West 56th Street.
37. Memphis, 329 Columbus Avenue.
38. Menchanko-Tei, 39 West 55th Street (DJ).
39. Michael's, 24 West 55th Street.
40. Mickey Mantle's, 42 Central Park South.
41. Ollie's Noodle Shop and Grille, 2957 Broadway (DJ).
42. Palio, 151 West 51st Street.
43. Palm Court, 59th Street and Fifth Avenue (DJ).
44. Panevino, 65th Street and Columbus Avenue, in Avery Fisher Hall at Lincoln Plaza (DJ).
45. Pasta & Dreams, 2161 Broadway (DJ).
46. Patsy's, 236 West 56th Street.
47. Poiret, 474 Columbus Avenue.
48. Punsch, 11 West 60th Street (DJ).
49. René Pujol, 321 West 51st Street.
50. The Russian Tea Room, 150 West 57th Street.
51. San Domenico, 240 Central Park South.
52. Sarabeth's Kitchen, 423 Amsterdam Avenue. (DJ).
53. Sfuzzi, 58 West 65th Street.
54. Shun Lee, 43 West 65th Street.
55. Siam Inn, 916 Eighth Avenue.
56. Sidewalkers', 12 West 72nd Street (DJ).
57. Sylvia's, 328 Lenox Avenue (DJ).
58. Symphony Cafe, 950 Eighth Avenue.
59. Tavern on the Green, Central Park West at 67th Street.
60. The Terrace, 400 West 119th Street.
61. Trattoria dell'Arte, 900 Seventh Avenue.
62. "21" Club, 21 West 52nd Street.
63. Victor's Café 52, 236 West 52nd Street.
64. Yellow Rose Cafe, 450 Amsterdam Avenue (DJ).
65. Zula, 1260 Amsterdam Avenue (DJ).

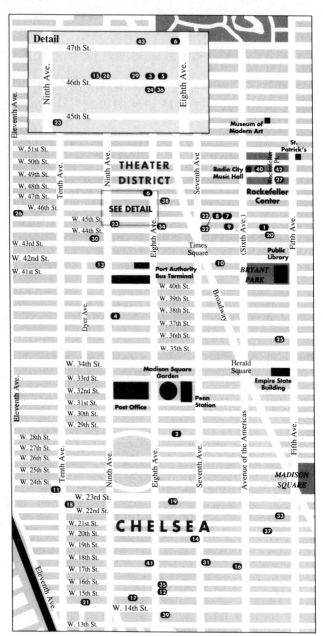

## MAP 2

### WEST 14TH STREET TO WEST 49TH STREET

*(Includes Chelsea and the Broadway Theater District)*

① Algonquin Hotel, 59 West 44th Street (DJ).
② The Ballroom, 253 West 28th Street.
③ Barbetta, 321 West 46th Street.
④ Bellevues, 496 Ninth Avenue.
⑤ Broadway Joe, 315 West 46th Street (DJ).
⑥ B. Smith's, 771 Eighth Avenue.
⑦ Cabana Carioca, 123 West 45th Street (DJ).
⑧ Cabana Carioca II, 133 West 45th Street (DJ).
⑨ Café Un Deux Trois, 123 West 44th Street.
⑩ Century Cafe, 132 West 42nd Street (DJ).
⑪ Chelsea Central, 227 Tenth Avenue.
⑫ Chelsea Trattoria Italiana, 108 Eighth Avenue.
⑬ Chez Josephine, 414 West 42nd Street.
⑭ Claire, 156 Seventh Avenue.
⑮ Crêpes Suzette, 363 West 46th Street (DJ).
⑯ da Umberto, 107 West 17th Street.
⑰ El Cid, 322 West 15th Street (DJ).
⑱ Empire Diner, 210 Tenth Avenue (DJ).
⑲ Eze, 254 West 23rd Street.
⑳ 44, at the Royalton Hotel, 44 West 44th Street.
㉑ Frank's, 431 West 14th Street (DJ).
㉒ Hamburger Harry's, 145 West 45th Street (DJ).
㉓ Jezebel, 630 Ninth Avenue.
㉔ Joe Allen, 326 West 46th Street.
㉕ Keen's Chop House, 72 West 36th Street.
㉖ Landmark Tavern, 626 Eleventh Avenue (DJ).
㉗ La Réserve, 4 West 49th Street.
㉘ Lattanzi, 361 West 46th Street.
㉙ La Vieille Auberge, 347 West 46th Street (DJ).
㉚ Le Madeleine, 403 West 43rd Street (DJ).
㉛ Le Madri, 168 West 18th Street.
㉜ Lotfi's Couscous, 135 West 45th Street (one flight up) (DJ).
㉝ Lola, 30 West 22nd Street.
㉞ Mamma Leone's, 261 West 44th Street.
㉟ Mary Ann's, 116 Eighth Avenue.
㊱ Orso, 322 West 46th Street.
㊲ Periyali, 35 West 20th Street.
㊳ Pierre au Tunnel, 250 West 47th Street.
㊴ Quatorze, 240 West 14th Street.
㊵ The Rainbow Room, 30 Rockefeller Plaza.
㊶ Rogers & Barbero, 149 Eighth Avenue.
㊷ The Sea Grill, 19 West 49th Street.
㊸ Trixie's, 307 West 47th Street (DJ).

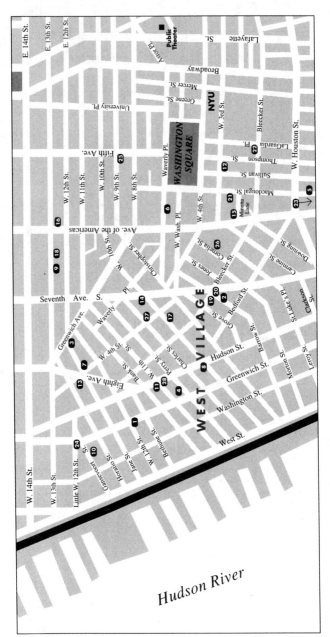

## MAP 3

### HOUSTON STREET TO 13TH STREET, WEST OF BROADWAY

*(Includes the West Village)*

1. Au Troquet, 328 West 12th Street.
2. Barrow Street Bistro, 48 Barrow Street (DJ).
3. Benny's Burritos, 113 Greenwich Street (DJ).
4. Caribe, 117 Perry Street (DJ).
5. Chez Momo, 48 Macdougal Street (DJ).
6. The Coach House, 110 Waverly Place.
7. Corner Bistro, 331 West 4th Street (DJ).
8. Cowgirl Hall of Fame, 519 Hudson Street (DJ).
9. Cuisine de Saigon, 154 West 13th Street.
10. Florent, 69 Gansevoort Street (DJ).
11. Harlequin, 569 Hudson Street.
12. Il Mulino, 86 West 3rd Street.
13. Jane Street Seafood Cafe, 31 Eighth Avenue.
14. John Clancy's, 181 West 10th Street.
15. La Bohème, 24 Minetta Lane.
16. La Gauloise, 502 Avenue of the Americas.
17. La Métairie, 189 West 10th Street (DJ).
18. La Tulipe, 104 West 13th Street.
19. Manhattan Chili Company, 302 Bleecker Street (DJ).
20. Pasta Presto, 37 Barrow Street (DJ).
21. Pasta Presto, 93 Macdougal Street (DJ).
22. Peculier Pub, 145 Bleecker Street (DJ).
23. Provence, 38 Macdougal Street.
24. Rio Mar, 7 Ninth Avenue (DJ).
25. Rose Cafe, 24 Fifth Avenue.
26. Sabor, 20 Cornelia Street.
27. Sevilla Restaurant and Bar, 62 Charles Street.
28. White Horse Tavern, 567 Hudson Street (DJ).

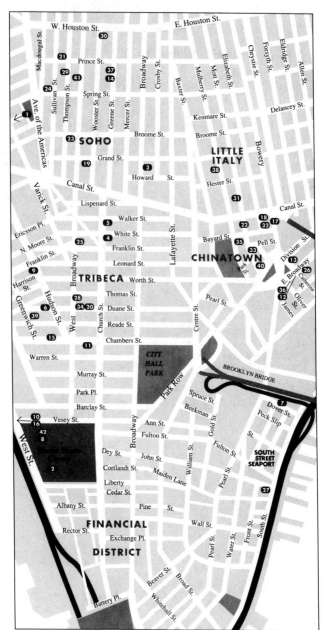

## MAP 4

### BELOW HOUSTON STREET

*(Includes SoHo, TriBeCa, Chinatown, Little Italy, Wall Street, and South Street Seaport)*

① Alison on Dominick Street, 38 Dominick Street.
② American Harvest, 3 World Trade Center (in Vista International Hotel).
③ Amsterdam's Grand, 454 Broadway.
④ Arquà, 281 Church Street.
⑤ Barocco, 301 Church Street.
⑥ Bouley, 165 Duane Street.
⑦ Bridge Cafe, 279 Water Street.
⑧ Cellar in the Sky, 1 World Trade Center (107th floor).
⑨ Chanterelle, 2 Harrison Street.
⑩ Donald Sacks, World Financial Center Courtyard, 220 Vesey Street (DJ).
⑪ Ecco!, 124 Chambers Street.
⑫ The Golden Unicorn, 18 East Broadway.
⑬ Great Shanghai, 27 Division Street.
⑭ Greene Street Restaurant, 101 Greene Street.
⑮ Hamburger Harry's, 157 Chambers Street (DJ).
⑯ Hudson River Club, 250 Vesey Street.
⑰ HSF, 46 Bowery (DJ).
⑱ King Fung, 20 Elizabeth Street.
⑲ Le Lucky Strike, 59 Grand Street (DJ).
⑳ Le Zinc, 139 Duane Street.
㉑ Madeline's, 177 Prince Street (DJ).
㉒ Mandarin Court, 61 Mott Street (DJ).
㉓ Manhattan Brewing Company, 40–42 Thompson St. (DJ).
㉔ Mezzogiorno, 195 Spring Street.
㉕ Montrachet, 239 West Broadway.
㉖ The Nice Restaurant, 35 East Broadway.
㉗ North Star Pub, 93 South Street (DJ).
㉘ The Odeon, 145 West Broadway.
㉙ Omen, 113 Thompson Street.
㉚ 150 Wooster Street, 150 Wooster Street.
㉛ Oriental Pearl, 103 Mott Street.
㉜ Oriental Town Seafood Restaurant, 14 Elizabeth Street.
㉝ Peking Duck House Restaurant, 22 Mott Street (DJ).
㉞ Rosemarie's, 145 Duane Street.
㉟ Saigon, 60 Mulberry Street (DJ).
㊱ Say Eng Look, 5 East Broadway.
㊲ SoHo Kitchen and Bar, 103 Greene Street (DJ).
㊳ Taormina, 147 Mulberry Street.
㊴ Tommy Tang's, 323 Greenwich Street.
㊵ 20 Mott Street Restaurant, 20 Mott Street.
㊶ Vuccirìa, 422 West Broadway (DJ).
㊷ Windows on the World, 1 World Trade Center (107th floor).

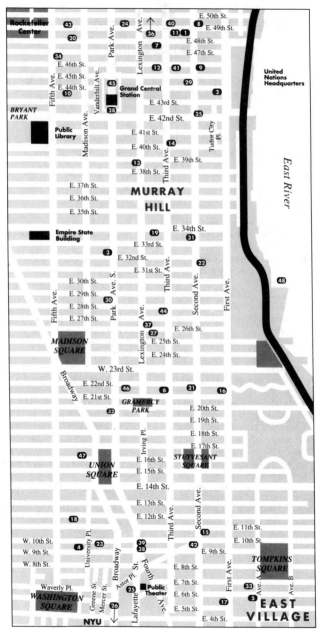

## MAP 5

### HOUSTON STREET EAST OF BROADWAY TO EAST 49TH STREET EAST OF FIFTH AVENUE

*(Includes the East Village, Gramercy Park, and Murray Hill)*

① Akbar, 256 East 49th Street.
② Ambassador Grill, One United Nations Plaza.
③ An American Place, 2 Park Avenue.
④ Arcobaleno, 21 East Ninth Street (DJ).
⑤ Benny's Burritos, 93 Avenue A (DJ).
⑥ Brandywine, 274 Third Avenue.
⑦ Bukhara, 148 East 48th Street.
⑧ Café de Paris, 924 Second Avenue (DJ).
⑨ The Captain's Table, 860 Second Avenue.
⑩ Chikubu, 12 East 44th Street.
⑪ Chin Chin, 216 East 49th Street.
⑫ Christ Cella, 160 East 46th Street.
⑬ Courtyard Café and Bar, 130 East 39th Street (DJ).
⑭ Docks on Third, 633 Third Avenue.
⑮ The "11" Cafe, 170 Second Avenue (DJ).
⑯ First Avenue Restaurant, 361 First Avenue (DJ).
⑰ Gaylord, 87 First Avenue.
⑱ Gotham Bar and Grill, 12 East 12th Street.
⑲ Harold's, 150 East 34th Street (in Murray Hill Hotel) (DJ).
⑳ Hatsuhana, 17 East 48th Street.
㉑ The Health Pub, 371 Second Avenue (DJ).
㉒ HSF, 578 Second Avenue (DJ).
㉓ Il Cantinori, 32 East 10th Street.
㉔ Inagiku, 111 East 49th Street (in Waldorf-Astoria Hotel).
㉕ Indochine, 430 Lafayette Street.
㉖ K-Paul's New York, 622 Broadway.
㉗ La Colombe d'Or, 134 East 26th Street.
㉘ The Oyster Bar and Restaurant in Grand Central Station.
㉙ Palm, 837 Second Avenue.
㉚ Park Bistro, 414 Park Avenue.
㉛ Pasta Presto, 613 Second Avenue (DJ).
㉜ Positano, 250 Park Avenue South.
㉝ Roettele A.G., 126 East 7th Street (DJ).
㉞ Rusty Staub's on Fifth, 575 Fifth Avenue (DJ).
㉟ Ryan McFadden, 800 Second Avenue (DJ).
㊱ Sette Mezzo, 969 Lexington Avenue (DJ).
㊲ Sido Abu Salim, 81 Lexington Avenue (DJ).
㊳ Siracusa, 65 Fourth Avenue.
㊴ Siracusa Gelateria, 65 Fourth Avenue (DJ).
㊵ Smith & Wollensky, 201 East 49th Street.
㊶ Sparks Steakhouse, 210 East 46th Street.
㊷ Sukhothai, 149 Second Avenue.
㊸ Sushiden, 19 East 49th Street.
㊹ Tatany, 388 Third Avenue.
㊺ Tropica Bar and Seafood House, 200 Park Avenue (DJ).
㊻ Umeda, 102 East 22nd Street.
㊼ Union Square Cafe, 21 East 16th Street.
㊽ The Water Club, East River at 30th Street.

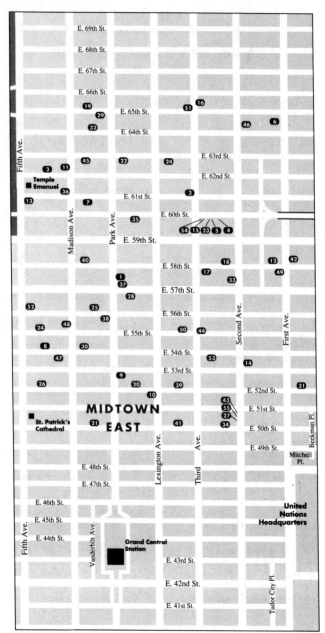

## MAP 6

### EAST 50S AND 60S

1. Akbar, 475 Park Avenue.
2. Alo Alo, 1030 Third Avenue.
3. Arcadia, 21 East 62nd Street.
4. Arizona 206, 206 East 60th Street.
5. Arizona 206 Cafe, 206 East 60th Street (DJ).
6. Auntie Yuan, 1191A First Avenue.
7. Aureole, 34 East 61st Street.
8. Bice, 7 East 54th Street.
9. Brasserie, 100 East 53rd Street (DJ).
10. Broadway Diner, 590 Lexington Avenue (DJ).
11. Ca'Nova, 696 Madison Avenue (DJ).
12. Cafe Nicholson, 323 East 58th Street (DJ).
13. Café Pierre, Fifth Avenue at 61st Street.
14. Chez Louis, 1016 Second Avenue.
15. Contrapunto, 200 East 60th Street.
16. David K's, 1115 Third Avenue.
17. Dāwat, 210 East 58th Street.
18. Felidia, 243 East 58th Street.
19. Ferrier, 29 East 65th Street (DJ).
20. The Four Seasons, 99 East 52nd Street.
21. Gloucester House, 37 East 50th Street.
22. Huberts, 575 Park Avenue.
23. Jane's Bar and Grill, 208 East 60th Street.
24. La Côte Basque, 5 East 55th Street.
25. Lafayette, 65 East 56th Street.
26. La Grenouille, 3 East 52nd Street.
27. La Méditerranée, 947 Second Avenue (DJ).
28. Le Chantilly, 106 East 57th Street.
29. Le Cirque, 58 East 65th Street.
30. Le Cygne, 55 East 54th Street.
31. Le Périgord, 405 East 52nd Street.
32. Le Régence, Plaza Athénée, 37 East 64th Street.
33. Le Steak, 1089 Second Avenue (DJ).
34. Lutèce, 249 East 50th Street.
35. Malvasia, 108 East 60th Street.
36. Maxim's, 680 Madison Avenue.
37. Mitsukoshi, 461 Park Avenue.
38. Mon Cher Ton Ton, 68 East 56th Street.
39. Nippon, 155 East 52nd Street.
40. Paper Moon Milano, 39 East 58th Street.
41. Paradis Barcelona, 145 East 50th Street.
42. Pasta & Dreams, 1068 First Avenue (DJ).
43. Pasta Presto, 959 Second Avenue (DJ).
44. F.J. Clarke's, 915 Third Avenue (DJ).
45. The Post House, 28 East 63rd Street.
46. Primola, 1226 Second Avenue.
47. Prunelle, 18 East 54th Street.
48. The Quilted Giraffe, 550 Madison Avenue.
49. Rosa Mexicano, 1063 First Avenue.
50. Shun Lee Palace, 155 East 55th Street.
51. The Sign of the Dove, 1110 Third Avenue.
52. Terrace Five, 56th Street and Fifth Avenue, Trump Tower, Fifth Floor (DJ).
53. Toscana Ristorante, 200 East 54th Street.
54. Yellowfingers di Nuovo, 200 East 60th Street (DJ).
55. Zarela, 953 Second Avenue.

## Upper East Side / Yorkville Map

**Streets (north to south):** E. 99th St., E. 98th St., E. 97th St., E. 96th St., E. 95th St., E. 94th St., E. 93rd St., E. 92nd St., E. 91st St., E. 90th St., E. 89th St., E. 88th St., E. 87th St., E. 86th St., E. 85th St., E. 84th St., E. 83rd St., E. 82nd St., E. 81st St., E. 80th St., E. 79th St., E. 78th St., E. 77th St., E. 76th St., E. 75th St., E. 74th St., E. 73rd St., E. 72nd St., E. 71st St., E. 70th St., E. 69th St., E. 68th St., E. 67th St.

**Avenues:** Fifth Ave., Madison Ave., Park Ave., Lexington Ave., Third Ave., Second Ave., First Ave., York Ave.

**Neighborhoods:** YORKVILLE, UPPER EAST SIDE

**Landmarks:**
- ICP (27)
- Jewish Museum
- Guggenheim Museum
- Metropolitan Museum of Art
- Whitney Museum
- Frick Collection
- Asia House

16 ◁

## MAP 7

### EAST 70S AND NORTH

*(Includes the Upper East Side)*

1. Al Amir, 1431 Second Avenue (DJ).
2. Anatolia, 1422 Third Avenue.
3. Azzurro, 1625 Second Avenue.
4. Bangkok House, 1485 First Avenue.
5. Border Cafe, 144 East 79th Street (DJ).
6. Cafe Greco, 1390 Second Avenue.
7. Cafe San Martin, 1458 First Avenue.
8. City Cafe, 1481 York Avenue.
9. East, 1420 Third Avenue.
10. Erminia, 250 East 83rd Street.
11. Fleming's, 232 East 86th Street (DJ).
12. Fu's, 1395 Second Avenue.
13. Girasole, 151 East 82nd Street (DJ).
14. Istanbul Kebap, 303 East 80th Street (DJ).
15. La Petite Ferme, 973 Lexington Avenue.
16. Le Refuge, 166 East 82nd Street.
17. Lusardi's, 1494 Second Avenue.
18. Mezzaluna, 1295 Third Avenue (DJ).
19. Mortimer's, 1057 Lexington Avenue.
20. Pamir, 1437 Second Avenue.
21. Paola's, 347 East 85th Street (DJ).
22. Parioli, Romanissimo, 24 East 81st Street.
23. Pasta & Dreams, 1675 Third Avenue (DJ).
24. Pig Heaven, 1540 Second Avenue.
25. Primavera, 1578 First Avenue.
26. Rathbone's, 1702 Second Avenue (DJ).
27. Saranac, 1350 Madison Avenue (DJ).
28. Ten Twenty-two, 1022 Lexington Avenue.
29. Trastevere, 309 East 83rd Street.
30. Voulez-Vous, 1462 First Avenue.
31. Wilkinson's Seafood Café, 1573 York Avenue.

# RESTAURANTS IN THE BOROUGHS

Adele, 501 11th Street, Park Slope, Brooklyn.
Aunt Sonia, 1123 Eighth Avenue, Brooklyn (DJ).
Dominick's, 2335 Arthur Avenue, Bronx (DJ).
Gage & Tollner, 372 Fulton Street, Brooklyn (DJ).
La Fusta, 80-32 Baxter Avenue, Elmhurst, Queens (DJ).
Moroccan Star, 205 Atlantic Avenue, Brooklyn (DJ).
New Prospect Cafe, 393 Flatbush Avenue, Brooklyn.
Peter Luger, 178 Broadway, Brooklyn.
The River Café, 1 Water Street, Brooklyn.
Roumeli Taverna, 33-04 Broadway, Astoria, Queens.
Water's Edge, East River Yacht Club, 44th Drive at East River,
    Long Island City, Queens

# STAR RATINGS

## The Star System

The *Times*'s star system rates restaurants on the following scale:

| | |
|---:|:---|
| ★ ★ ★ ★ | extraordinary |
| ★ ★ ★ | excellent |
| ★ ★ | very good |
| ★ | good |
| no stars | poor to satisfactory |

Stars are intended as a quick visual clue to the overall quality of a restaurant. I assign the stars based on a formula that breaks down like this: roughly 80 percent for food quality, 20 percent for service and atmosphere. These factors are evaluated without regard to price. That means that an "excellent" restaurant costing $40 per person and an equally good one for $60 per person would receive the same three-star rating. This does not mean I am unconcerned about price. If I feel the food or wine is excessively costly, that is always pointed out in the review. Keeping price out of the star formula simply allows me to compare apples to apples without the complication of adding various price levels to the equation. (For a breakdown of restaurants by price, see page 23.)

Bouley
Lafayette
Le Bernardin

Le Cirque
Lutèce
The Quilted Giraffe

★ ★ ★

Arizona 206
Café des Artistes
Darbar
The Four Seasons
Gotham Bar and Grill
Huberts
La Colombe d'Or
La Réserve
Le Cygne
Le Périgord
Le Régence
Montrachet
Park Bistro
The River Café
San Domenico
The Sign of the Dove
Union Square Cafe


★ ★

Adrienne
Alcala
Alison on Dominick Street
An American Place
Andiamo!
Aquavit
Arcadia
Arquà
Auntie Yuan
Aureole
Azzurro
Barocco
Bellini by Cipriani
Bice
Brandywine
Bukhara
Cafe Greco
Cafe Luxembourg

(★ ★)

Cellar in the Sky
Chanterelle
Chelsea Central
Chelsea Trattoria Italiana
Chez Josephine
Chikubu
Chin Chin
Claire
Coastal
David K's
Dāwat
Docks on Third
Eze
Felidia
44
Fu's
Greene Street Restaurant
Hatsuhana
Hudson River Club
Indochine
Jane's Bar and Grill
Jezebel
John Clancy's
La Caravelle
La Côte Basque
La Gauloise
La Tulipe
Le Chantilly
Le Madri
Le Refuge
Marie-Michelle
Maxim's
Mezzogiorno
Michael's
Mitsukoshi
Mon Cher Ton Ton
  (Japanese)
The Nice Restaurant
Nippon
The Odeon

(★ ★)

Omen
Oriental Pearl
Orso
Palio
Pamir
Paper Moon Milano
Parioli, Romanissimo
Periyali
Pig Heaven
The Post House
Primola
Provence
Prunelle
Quatorze
The Rainbow Room
Rosa Mexicano
The Sea Grill
Shun Lee
Shun Lee Palace
Siracusa
Sparks Steakhouse
Tatany
The Terrace
Tommy Tang's
Toscana Ristorante
Trastevere
"21" Club
Umeda
Voulez-Vous
The Water Club
Wilkinson's Seafood Café
Zarela


★

Adele
Akbar (Park Avenue)
Ambassador Grill
American Harvest

(★)

Amsterdam's Bar and Rotisserie
Amsterdam's Grand
Anatolia
Au Troquet
The Ballroom
Bangkok House
Bellevues
Bridge Cafe
Café Pierre
Café Un Deux Trois
Cameos
Chantal Café
Chez Louis
China Grill
The Coach House
Contrapunto
Corrado
Cuisine de Saigon
Da Tommaso
Docks (Broadway)
East
Erminia
Gage & Tollner
Gaylord
The Golden Unicorn
Great Shanghai Restaurant
Harlequin
Il Cantinori
Il Mulino
Inagiku
Jane Street Seafood Cafe
Joe Allen
Keen's Chop House
King Fung
K-Paul's New York
La Bohème
La Boîte en Bois
La Cité

▷ 21

(★)

La Grenouille
La Mirabelle
La Petite Ferme
Lattanzi
Le Zinc
Lola
Malvasia
The Manhattan Ocean Club
The Oyster Bar and Restaurant in Grand Central Station
Palm
Peter Luger
Pierre au Tunnel
Poiret
Positano
Primavera
René Pujol
Rose Cafe
Rosemarie's
Roumeli Taverna
The Russian Tea Room
Sabor
Sevilla Restaurant and Bar
Sfuzzi
Siam Inn
Smith & Wollensky
Sukhothai
Symphony Cafe
Taormina
Tavern on the Green
Ten Twenty-two
Trattoria dell'Arte
20 Mott Street Restaurant

Victor's Café 52
Water's Edge at the East River Yacht Club
Windows on the World

## SATISFACTORY

Akbar (49th Street)
Alo Alo
Barbetta
B. Smith's
Cafe San Martin
The Captain's Table
Christ Cella
City Cafe
da Umberto
Gallagher's
Lusardi's
Memphis
Mickey Mantle's
Mon Cher Ton Ton (French)
Mortimer's
150 Wooster Street
Oriental Town Seafood Restaurant
Paradis Barcelona
Patsy's
Rogers & Barbero
Say Eng Look
Sushiden

## POOR

Ecco!
Gloucester House
Mamma Leone's

# PRICE LISTINGS

The information box at the top of each review gives an idea of the restaurant's price range. Based on the cost of a three-course dinner with tax and 15 percent tip (no drinks), the price range is as follows:

| Inexpensive | less than $30 |
| Moderate | $30 to $40 |
| Moderately Expensive | $40 to $55 |
| Expensive | $55 or more |

## EXPENSIVE

Adrienne
An American Place
Aquavit
Arcadia
Barbetta
Bellini by Cipriani
Bouley
Café Pierre
The Captain's Table
Chanterelle
Felidia
The Four Seasons
Gloucester House
Gotham Bar and Grill
Huberts
Il Mulino
K-Paul's New York
La Caravelle
La Côte Basque
Lafayette
La Grenouille
La Réserve
La Tulipe
Le Bernardin
Le Cirque
Le Cygne
Le Périgord
Le Régence
Lutèce
Maxim's
Mitsukoshi
Mon Cher Ton Ton (French)
Mon Cher Ton Ton (Japanese)
Palio
Palm
Palm Court
Parioli, Romanissimo
The Post House

## (EXPENSIVE)

Primavera
The Quilted Giraffe
The Rainbow Room
The River Café
The Russian Tea Room
San Domenico
The Sea Grill
The Sign of the Dove
Sparks Steakhouse
The Terrace
"21" Club

## MODERATELY EXPENSIVE

Adele
Algonquin Hotel
Alison on Dominick Street
American Harvest
Arizona 206
Arizona 206 Cafe
Auntie Yuan
Aureole
Au Troquet
The Ballroom
Bice
Brandywine
Café des Artistes
Cafe Greco
Cafe Luxembourg
Cafe Nicholson
Cafe San Martin
Ca'Nova
Cellar in the Sky
China Grill
Chez Louis
Chikubu
Chin Chin
Christ Cella
The Coach House

## (MODERATELY EXPENSIVE)

da Umberto
Ecco!
Erminia
Eze
44
Fu's
Gallagher's
Girasole
Greene Street Restaurant
Hatsuhana
Hudson River Club
Il Cantinori
Inagiku
Indochine
Jane's Bar and Grill
John Clancy's
Keen's Chop House
La Cité
La Colombe d'Or
La Métairie
La Petite Ferme
Le Chantilly
Le Madri
Le Refuge
Lola
Lusardi's
Malvasia
Mamma Leone's
The Manhattan Ocean Club
Marie-Michelle
Memphis
Mezzaluna
Michael's
Montrachet
Mortimer's
150 Wooster Street
Orso

## (MODERATELY EXPENSIVE)

The Oyster Bar and Restaurant in Grand Central Station
Paola's
Paper Moon Milano
Paradis Barcelona
Park Bistro
Patsy's
Peter Luger
Positano
Primola
Prunelle
Punsch
René Pujol
Rosa Mexicano
Rosemarie's
Sfuzzi
Shun Lee
Shun Lee Palace
Siracusa
Smith & Wollensky
Tatany
Tavern on the Green
Ten Twenty-two
Toscana Ristorante
Trastevere
Trattoria dell'Arte
Umeda
Union Square Cafe
The Water Club
Water's Edge at the East River Yacht Club
Wilkinson's Seafood Café
Windows on the World

## MODERATE

Akbar (49th Street)
Akbar (Park Avenue)

## (MODERATE)

Al Amir
Alcala
Alo Alo
Ambassador Grill
American Festival Cafe
Amsterdam's Bar and Rotisserie
Amsterdam's Grand
Anatolia
Andiamo!
Arcobaleno
Arquà
Aunt Sonia
Azzurro
Baci
Bangkok House
Barocco
Barrow Street Bistro
Bellevues
Border Cafe
Brasserie
Bridge Cafe
Broadway Joe
B. Smith's
Bukhara
Cabana Carioca I
Cabana Carioca II
Cafe Between the Bread
Café Un Deux Trois
Cameos
Carnegie Deli
Chelsea Central
Chelsea Trattoria Italiana
Chez Josephine
City Cafe
Claire
Coastal
Contrapunto
Corrado
Courtyard Café and Bar

## (MODERATE)

Crêpes Suzette
Cuisine de Saigon
Darbar
Da Tommaso
David K's
Dāwat
Docks (both locations)
Dominick's
Donald Sacks
East
El Cid
Ferrier
Florent
Frank's
Gage & Tollner
The Golden Unicorn
Great Shanghai
  Restaurant
Harlequin
Harold's
The Health Pub
HSF
Jane Street Seafood Cafe
Jezebel
Joe Allen
La Bohème
La Boîte en Bois
La Fusta
La Gauloise
La Kasbah
La Méditerranée
La Mirabelle
Landmark Tavern
Lattanzi
La Vieille Auberge
Le Lucky Strike
Le Madeleine
Le Zinc
Mezzogiorno
Mickey Mantle's
New Prospect Cafe
The Nice Restaurant
Nippon
North Star Pub
The Odeon
Omen
Panevino
Pasta & Dreams
Peking Duck House
Periyali
Pierre au Tunnel
Pig Heaven
Poiret
Provence
Quatorze
Roettele A.G.
Rogers & Barbero
Rose Cafe
Roumeli Taverna
Rusty Staub's on Fifth
Sabor
Sarabeth's Kitchen
Saranac
Sette Mezzo
Sevilla Restaurant and
  Bar
Sidewalkers'
Siracusa Gelateria
SoHo Kitchen and Bar
Sukhothai
Sushiden
Sylvia's
Symphony Cafe
Taormina
Terrace Five
Tommy Tang's
Trixie's
Tropica Bar and Seafood
  House
20 Mott Street Restaurant
Victor's Café 52
Voulez-Vous

## (MODERATE)

Vucciria
Yellowfingers di Nuovo
Yellow Rose Cafe
Zarela

## INEXPENSIVE

Bella Luna
Benny's Burritos
Broadway Diner
Café de Paris
Caribe
Chantal Café
Chez Momo
Corner Bistro
Cowgirl Hall of Fame
The "11" Cafe
Gaylord
Hamburger Harry's
Indian Cafe
Istanbul Kebap
King Fung
La Bonne Soupe
Le Steak

## (INEXPENSIVE)

Lotfi's Couscous
Madeline's
Mandarin Court
Manhattan Brewing Company
Manhattan Chili Company
Mary Ann's
Menchanko-Tei
Moroccan Star
Ollie's Noodle Shop and Grille
Oriental Pearl
Oriental Town Seafood Restaurant
Pamir
Pasta Presto
Riazor
Rio Mar
Saigon
Say Eng Look
Siam Inn
Sido Abu Salim
Zula

# TYPES OF CUISINE

## AFGHAN

Pamir

## AMERICAN

American Festival Cafe
American Harvest
Amsterdam's Bar and Rotisserie
Amsterdam's Grand
An American Place
Arcadia
Arizona 206
Arizona 26 Cafe
Aunt Sonia
Aureole
Border Cafe
Bridge Cafe
Broadway Diner
Broadway Joe
B. Smith's
Cafe Between the Bread
Cafe Luxembourg
Cafe Nicholson
Cameos
The Captain's Table
Century Cafe
Chelsea Central
Christ Cella
City Cafe
Claire
The Coach House

## (AMERICAN)

Coastal
Corner Bistro
Courtyard Café and Bar
Cowgirl Hall of Fame
Docks (both locations)
Donald Sacks
44
The Four Seasons
Gage & Tollner
Gallagher's
Gloucester House
Gotham Bar and Grill
Greene Street Restaurant
Hamburger Harry's
Harold's
The Health Pub
Huberts
Hudson River Club
Jane Street Seafood Cafe
Jezebel
Joe Allen
John Clancy's
Keen's Chop House
Landmark Tavern
Manhattan Brewing Company
Manhattan Chili Company
The Manhattan Ocean Club
Memphis
Michael's

## (AMERICAN)

Mickey Mantle's
Mortimer's
New Prospect Cafe
North Star Pub
The Odeon
150 Wooster Street
The Oyster Bar and
  Restaurant in Grand
  Central Station
Palm
Palm Court
Peculier Pub
Peter Luger
The Post House
The Quilted Giraffe
The River Café
Rogers & Barbero
Rose Cafe
Rosemarie's
Rusty Staub's on Fifth
Sarabeth's Kitchen
Saranac
The Sea Grill
Sidewalkers'
Smith & Wollensky
SoHo Kitchen and Bar
Sparks Steakhouse
Sylvia's
Symphony Cafe
Tavern on the Green
Ten Twenty-two
Terrace Five
Trixie's
"21" Club
The Water Club
Water's Edge at the East
  River Yacht Club
Wilkinson's Seafood Café
Windows on the World
Yellow Rose Cafe

## ARGENTINIAN

La Fusta

## BRAZILIAN

Cabana Carioca I
Cabana Carioca II

## CAJUN

K-Paul's New York

## CARIBBEAN/CUBAN

Caribe
Sabor
Victor's Café 52

## CHINESE

Auntie Yuan
China Grill
Chin Chin
David K's
Fu's
The Golden Unicorn
Great Shanghai
  Restaurant
HSF
King Fung
Mandarin Court
The Nice Restaurant
Oriental Pearl
Oriental Town Seafood
  Restaurant
Peking Duck House
Pig Heaven
Shun Lee
Shun Lee Palace
20 Mott Street
  Restaurant

## ETHIOPIAN

Zula

## FRENCH

Adele
Adrienne
Alison on Dominick Street
Ambassador Grill
Au Troquet
Barrow Street Bistro
Bellevues
Bouley
Brandwine
Brasserie
Café de Paris
Café des Artistes
Café Pierre
Café Un Deux Trois
Cellar in the Sky
Chantal Café
Chanterelle
Chez Josephine
Chez Louis
China Grill
Crêpes Suzette
Eze
Ferrier
Florent
La Bohème
La Boîte en Bois
La Bonne Soupe
La Caravelle
La Cité
La Colombe d'Or
La Côte Basque
Lafayette
La Gauloise
La Grenouille
La Méditerranée
La Métairie

## (FRENCH)

La Mirabelle
La Petite Ferme
La Réserve
La Tulipe
La Vieille Auberge
Le Bernardin
Le Chantilly
Le Cirque
Le Cygne
Le Lucky Strike
Le Madeleine
Le Périgord
Le Pistou
Le Refuge
Le Régence
Le Steak
Le Zinc
Lutèce
Madeline's
Marie-Michelle
Maxim's
Mon Cher Ton Ton
Montrachet
Park Bistro
Pierre au Tunnel
Poiret
Provence
Prunelle
Punsch
Quatorze
The Rainbow Room
René Pujol
Roettele A.G.
The Sign of the Dove
The Terrace
Voulez-Vous

## GERMAN

Roettele A.G.

## GREEK

Periyali
Roumeli Taverna

## INDIAN

Akbar (49th Street)
Akbar (Park Avenue)
Bukhara
Darbar
Dāwat
Gaylord
Indian Cafe

## ITALIAN

Alo Alo
Andiamo!
Arcobaleno
Arquà
Azzurro
Baci
Barbetta
Barocco
Bella Luna
Bellini by Cipriani
Bice
Cafe Greco
Ca'Nova
Chelsea Trattoria Italiana
Contrapunto
Corrado
Da Tommaso
da Umberto
Dominick's
Ecco!
Erminia
Felidia
Frank's
Girasole
Il Cantinori

## (ITALIAN)

Il Mulino
Lattanzi
Le Madri
Lusardi's
Malvasia
Mamma Leone's
Mezzaluna
Mezzogiorno
Orso
Palio
Panevino
Paola's
Paper Moon Milano
Parioli, Romanissimo
Pasta & Dreams
Pasta Presto
Patsy's
Positano
Primavera
Primola
Roettele A.G.
San Domenico
Sette Mezzo
Sfuzzi
Siracusa
Siracusa Gelateria
Taormina
Toscana Ristorante
Trastevere
Trattoria dell'Arte
Union Square Cafe
Vucciria
Yellowfingers di Nuovo

## JAPANESE

Chikubu
East
Hatsuhana
Inagiku

## (JAPANESE)

Menchanko-Tei
Mitsukoshi
Mon Cher Ton Ton
Nippon
Omen
Sushiden
Tatany
Umeda

## KOSHER

La Kasbah

## MEXICAN

Benny's Burritos
Mary Ann's
Rosa Mexicano
Zarela

## RUSSIAN

The Russian Tea Room

## SCANDINAVIAN

Aquavit

## THAI

Bangkok House
Siam Inn
Sukhothai
Tommy Tang's

## TURKISH

Anatolia
Istanbul Kebap

## VENEZUELAN

The "11" Cafe

## VIETNAMESE

Cuisine de Saigon
Indochine
Saigon

# SPECIAL OFFERINGS

## BREAKFAST

Adrienne
Algonquin Hotel
Ambassador Grill
American Festival Cafe
American Harvest
Brasserie
Bridge Cafe
Broadway Diner (both locations)
Café Pierre
Carnegie Deli
Chanterelle
Courtyard Café and Bar
Cowgirl Hall of Fame
Florent
44
The Golden Unicorn
Harold's
HSF
King Fung
Le Lucky Strike
Le Régence
Madeline's
Mamma Leone's
Mandarin Court
Nice Restaurant, The
Ollie's Noodle Shop and Grille
Oriental Pearl
Oriental Town Seafood Restaurant
Palm Court
Rusty Staub's on Fifth
Sarabeth's Kitchen
Sylvia's
Ten Twenty-two
20 Mott Street Restaurant
Windows on the World

## BUSINESS ENTERTAINING

Adrienne
Akbar (49th Street)
Algonquin Hotel
Ambassador Grill
American Harvest
An American Place
Aquavit
Arcobaleno
Aureole
Au Troquet
Barbetta
Bice
Bistro d'Adrienne
Bouley
Brandywine
Bridge Cafe
Café de Paris
Café Pierre
Café Un Deux Trois
Ca'Nova
The Captain's Table
Century Cafe

▷ 33

## (BUSINESS ENTERTAINING)

- Chanterelle
- Chelsea Trattoria Italiana
- Chikubu
- Chin Chin
- Christ Cella
- Corrado
- Courtyard Café and Bar
- Crêpes Suzette
- Da Tommaso
- David K's
- Dāwat
- Docks (both locations)
- Felidia
- 44
- The Four Seasons
- Fu's
- Gage & Tollner
- Gallagher's
- Gotham Bar and Grill
- Great Shanghai Restaurant
- Harlequin
- Huberts
- Hudson River Club
- Inagiku
- Jane's Bar and Grill
- John Clancy's
- Keen's Chop House
- La Bonne Soupe
- La Caravelle
- La Cité
- La Colombe d'Or
- La Côte Basque
- Lafayette
- La Gauloise
- La Grenouille
- La Méditerranée
- La Réserve
- Lattanzi
- La Tulipe
- La Vieille Auberge
- Le Bernardin
- Le Chantilly
- Le Cygne
- Le Madri
- Le Périgord
- Le Refuge
- Le Régence
- Lutèce
- The Manhattan Ocean Club
- Marie-Michelle
- Maxim's
- Menchanko-Tei
- Michael's
- Mitsukoshi
- Mon Cher Ton Ton (Japanese and French)
- Montrachet
- Nippon
- Orso
- Palio
- Paradis Barcelona
- Parioli, Romanissimo
- Periyali
- Pierre au Tunnel
- The Post House
- Primavera
- Primola
- Prunelle
- The Quilted Giraffe
- René Pujol
- Rosemarie's
- The Russian Tea Room
- Rusty Staub's on Fifth
- San Domenico
- The Sea Grill
- Shun Lee
- Shun Lee Palace
- The Sign of the Dove
- Sparks Steakhouse

## (BUSINESS ENTERTAINING)

Sushiden
Symphony Cafe
Taormina
Toscana Ristorante
Tropica Bar and
 Seafood House
"21" Club
Umeda
Union Square Cafe
The Water Club
Windows on the World
Zarela

## CARRYOUT AND DELIVERY

Akbar (49th Street)
Akbar (Park Avenue)
Amsterdam's Bar
 and Rotisserie
Amsterdam's Grand
Anatolia
Auntie Yuan
Barocco
Bellevues
Benny's Burritos
Border Cafe
Brasserie
Bukhara
Cafe Between the Bread
Cafe Greco
Carnegie Deli
Century Cafe
Coastal
Corrado
Cuisine de Saigon
David K's
Dāwat
Donald Sacks

## (CARRYOUT AND DELIVERY)

East
Florent
Frank's
Fu's
Gaylord
Hamburger Harry's
The Health Pub
HSF
Indian Cafe
Istanbul Kebap
Lotfi's Couscous
Manhattan Chili
 Company
Mitsukoshi
Moroccan Star
Ollie's Noodle Shop
 and Grille
Oriental Pearl
Oriental Town Seafood
 Restaurant
Paradis Barcelona
Pasta & Dreams
Pasta Presto
Peter Luger
Pig Heaven
Positano
Prunelle
The Quilted Giraffe
Sarabeth's Kitchen
Shun Lee
Sido Abu Salim
Tatany
Trixie's
20 Mott Street
 Restaurant
Umeda

# CARRYOUT SERVICE

Akbar (49th Street)
Akbar (Park Avenue)
Al Amir
Amsterdam's Bar and Rotisserie
Amsterdam's Grand
Anatolia
Aquavit
Arcadia
Arcobaleno
Auntie Yuan
Azzurro
Baci
The Ballroom
Bangkok House
Barocco
Bellevues
Benny's Burritos
Bice
Border Cafe
Brasserie
Bridge Cafe
Broadway Diner (both locations)
Bukhara
Cabana Carioca (I and II)
Cafe Between the Bread
Cafe Greco
Cafe San Martin
Caribe
Carnegie Deli
Century Cafe
Chez Louis
Chin Chin
City Cafe
Coastal
Corrado
Courtyard Café and Bar
Cowgirl Hall of Fame
Cuisine de Saigon
Darbar
David K's
Dāwat
Dominick's
Donald Sacks
East
Florent
Frank's
Fu's
Gage & Tollner
Gaylord
The Golden Unicorn
Great Shanghai Restaurant
Hamburger Harry's
Hatsuhana
The Health Pub
HSF
Indian Cafe
Istanbul Kebap
Jane Street Seafood Cafe
John Clancy's
King Fung
La Bonne Soupe
La Gauloise
La Méditerranée
Landmark Tavern
Le Madeleine
Lotfi's Couscous
Mandarin Court
Manhattan Chili Company
Mary Ann's
Menchanko-Tei
Mezzaluna
Mitsukoshi
Moroccan Star
Mortimer's
The Nice Restaurant
Nippon
North Star Pub

## (CARRYOUT SERVICE)

Ollie's Noodle Shop and Grille
Omen
Oriental Pearl
Oriental Town Seafood Restaurant
Palm
Paradis Barcelona
Pasta & Dreams
Pasta Presto
Patsy's
Peking Duck House
Peter Luger
Pig Heaven
Positano
Provence
Prunelle
The Quilted Giraffe
Riazor
Rio Mar
Roettele A.G.
Rogers & Barbero
Roumeli Taverna
Sabor
Saigon
Sarabeth's Kitchen
Sevilla Restaurant and Bar
Shun Lee
Shun Lee Palace
Siam Inn
Sidewalkers'
Sido Abu Salim
Siracusa Gelateria
SoHo Kitchen and Bar
Sukhothai
Sushiden
Taormina
Tatany
Tommy Tang's
Toscana Ristorante
Trattoria dell'Arte
Trixie's
20 Mott Street Restaurant
Umeda
Wilkinson's Seafood Café
Yellowfingers di Nuovo
Yellow Rose Cafe
Zarela
Zula

## DINING ALONE

Alcala
Arizona 206 Cafe
Baci
The Ballroom
Bellevues
Brasserie
Broadway Diner (both locations)
Cabana Carioca I
Café de Paris
China Grill
Crêpes Suzette
Docks (both locations)
El Cid
Florent
Hamburger Harry's
The Health Pub
HSF
Inagiku
La Bonne Soupe
La Vieille Auberge
Mandarin Court
Menchanko-Tei
Mezzogiorno
Ollie's Noodle Shop and Grille

## (DINING ALONE)

The Oyster Bar and
   Restaurant in Grand
   Central Station
Sido Abu Salim
Terrace Five
Union Square Cafe

## FUN FOR KIDS

American Festival Cafe
Amsterdam's Grand
Arizona 206
Arizona 206 Cafe
Baci
Bellevues
Benny's Burritos
Border Cafe
Broadway Diner
Bukhara
Café Un Deux Trois
Caribe
Coastal
Contrapunto
Cowgirl Hall of Fame
David K's
Dominick's
East
The "11" Cafe
Florent
Hamburger Harry's
HSF
K-Paul's New York
La Bonne Soupe
La Kasbah
Mandarin Court
Manhattan Chili
   Company
Mary Ann's
Mickey Mantle's
The Nice Restaurant

## (FUN FOR KIDS)

Ollie's Noodle Shop
   and Grille
Palm Court
Pasta & Dreams
Pasta Presto
Peking Duck House
Pig Heaven
Saranac
Shun Lee
Sidewalkers'
Tavern on the Green
Trattoria dell'Arte
Trixie's
The Water Club
Water's Edge at the East
   River Yacht Club
Windows on the World
Yellow Rose Cafe

## LARGE GROUPS

Adrienne
Akbar (49th Street)
Alcala
Algonquin Hotel
Alo Alo
Ambassador Grill
American Festival Cafe
American Harvest
Amsterdam's Bar
   and Rotisserie
Amsterdam's Grand
An American Place
Anatolia
Andiamo!
Aquavit
The Ballroom
Bangkok House
Barbetta
Barrow Street Bistro

## (LARGE GROUPS)

Border Cafe
Brasserie
Bukhara
Cabana Carioca (I and II)
Cafe Greco
Cafe Nicholson
Café Un Deux Trois
Caribe
Century Cafe
Chelsea Central
Chez Josephine
Chez Momo
China Grill
Chin Chin
Courtyard Café and Bar
David K's
East
Felidia
Frank's
Fu's
Gage & Tollner
Gallagher's
Gaylord
Gloucester House
The Golden Unicorn
Gotham Bar and Grill
Great Shanghai Restaurant
Greene Street Restaurant
Harlequin
Hatsuhana
The Health Pub
HSF
Huberts
Hudson River Club
Inagiku
Indochine
Jane Street Seafood Cafe
Jezebel
Keen's Chop House
K-Paul's New York
La Cité
La Fusta
La Kasbah
La Méditerranée
Landmark Tavern
La Réserve
Le Bernardin
Malvasia
Mamma Leone's
Mandarin Court
Manhattan Brewing Company
The Manhattan Ocean Club
Maxim's
Memphis
Michael's
Mickey Mantle's
Mitsukoshi
Mon Cher Ton Ton (French)
Montrachet
Mortimer's
The Nice Restaurant
Nippon
Omen
Oriental Pearl
Oriental Town Seafood Restaurant
The Oyster Bar and Restaurant in Grand Central Station
Palio
Palm Court
Pamir
Paper Moon Milano
Park Bistro
Pasta & Dreams
Pasta Presto
Patsy's
Peking Duck House
Periyali
Pig Heaven

## (LARGE GROUPS)

The Rainbow Room
René Pujol
Riazor
Rio Mar
Rosa Mexicano
Rose Cafe
Roumeli Taverna
Rusty Staub's on Fifth
Sabor
The Sea Grill
Sevilla Restaurant
  and Bar
Sfuzzi
Shun Lee
Shun Lee Palace
Sidewalkers'
The Sign of the Dove
Smith & Wollensky
SoHo Kitchen and Bar
Sushiden
Taormina
Tavern on the Green
The Terrace
Tommy Tang's
Trattoria dell'Arte
Tropica Bar and
  Seafood House
20 Mott Street Restaurant
"21" Club
Union Square Cafe
Victor's Café 52
The Water Club
Windows on the World
Zarela

## LIVE MUSIC

Algonquin Hotel
Ambassador Grill
American Harvest

## (LIVE MUSIC)

Arcobaleno
The Ballroom
Border Cafe
Bukhara
Café Pierre
Cafe San Martin
Cameos
Cellar in the Sky
Chez Josephine
Gaylord
Greene Street Restaurant
Jezebel
Mamma Leone's
Manhattan Chili Company
Maxim's
Palm Court
The Rainbow Room
Riazor
Rio Mar
The River Café
The Sea Grill
Sidewalkers'
Tavern on the Green
The Terrace
Trixie's
Umeda
Victor's Café 52
The Water Club
Water's Edge at the East
  River Yacht Club
Zarela

## NOTABLE WINE LIST

Adele
Adrienne
Alcala
Ambassador Grill
An American Place

# (NOTABLE WINE LIST)

Andiamo!
Arcadia
Arizona 206
Arquà
Bouley
Brandywine
Bridge Cafe
Café des Artistes
Cafe San Martin
Cellar in the Sky
Chanterelle
Chelsea Central
Chez Louis
Docks (both locations)
Felidia
The Four Seasons
Gage & Tollner
Gotham Bar and Grill
Huberts
Hudson River Club
Il Cantinori
La Cité
La Côte Basque
Lafayette
La Grenouille
La Réserve
Le Bernardin
Le Cirque
Le Madri
Le Périgord
Le Régence
Malvasia
The Manhattan Ocean Club
Mezzogiorno
Michael's
Mickey Mantle's
Montrachet
New Prospect Cafe
The Odeon
The Oyster Bar and Restaurant in Grand Central Station
Palio
Paradis Barcelona
Park Bistro
Periyali
The Post House
Provence
The Quilted Giraffe
The Rainbow Room
The River Café
Rusty Staub's on Fifth
San Domenico
Saranac
The Sea Grill
The Sign of the Dove
Siracusa
Smith & Wollensky
SoHo Kitchen and Bar
Sparks Steakhouse
Symphony Cafe
The Terrace
Terrace Five
"21" Club
Union Square Cafe
The Water Club
Wilkinson's Seafood Café
Windows on the World

# OPEN UNTIL MIDNIGHT*

Alcala
Algonquin Hotel

---

* It is advisable to call ahead, for hours may change depending on the day of the week.

## (OPEN UNTIL MIDNIGHT)

Alo Alo
Amsterdam's Bar and Rotisserie
Amsterdam's Grand
Arizona 206 Cafe
Auntie Yuan
Azzurro
The Ballroom
Bellevues
Benny's Burritos
Bice
Border Cafe
Brasserie
Bridge Cafe
Broadway Diner
Broadway Joe
B. Smith's
Café des Artistes
Cafe Luxembourg
Cafe San Martin
Café Un Deux Trois
Cameos
Carnegie Deli
Century Cafe
Chelsea Central
Chez Josephine
Chez Momo
China Grill
Claire
Contrapunto
Corner Bistro
Cowgirl Hall of Fame
Da Tommaso
David K's
Dock's (both locations)
The "11" Cafe
Felidia
Ferrier
Florent
Fu's
Gallagher's
Gaylord
Girasole
The Golden Unicorn
HSF
Indian Cafe
Indochine
Istanbul Kebap
Jane Street Seafood Cafe
Joe Allen
La Bohème
La Bonne Soupe
La Cité
La Fusta
Landmark Tavern
Le Lucky Strike
Le Madeleine
Le Madri
Le Zinc
Lotfi's Couscous
Lusardi's
Madeline's
Mamma Leone's
Mandarin Court
Manhattan Brewing Company
Manhattan Chili Company
The Manhattan Ocean Club
Maxim's
Menchanko-Tei
Mezzaluna
Mezzogiorno
Mickey Mantle's
Mortimer's
The Odeon
Ollie's Noodle Shop and Grille
150 Wooster Street
Palm Court

## (OPEN UNTIL MIDNIGHT)

Paper Moon Milano
Paradis Barcelona
Pig Heaven
The Post House
Primavera
Primola
Provence
Punsch
The Rainbow Room
Riazor
Rio Mar
Rogers & Barbero
Rosa Mexicano
Rose Cafe
Roumeli Taverna
Sette Mezzo
Sevilla Restaurant
  and Bar
Sfuzzi
Shun Lee
SoHo Kitchen and Bar
Sylvia's
Symphony Cafe
Trattoria dell'Arte
Trixie's
20 Mott Street Restaurant
"21" Club
Umeda
Victor's Café 52
Voulez-Vous
Vucciria
Yellowfingers di Nuovo
Zarela
Zula

## OUTDOOR CAFÉ

Akbar (49th Street)
American Festival Cafe

## (OUTDOOR CAFÉ)

Andiamo!
Arcobaleno
Arizona 206 Cafe
Aureole
Barbetta
Barrow Street Bistro
Bella Luna
Benny's Burritos
Bice
B. Smith's
Cafe Between the Bread
China Grill
Courtyard Café and Bar
David K's
Ferrier
Harold's
La Bonne Soupe
La Kasbah
La Petite Ferme
Le Madeleine
Le Zinc
Mezzaluna
Mezzogiorno
Mickey Mantle's
Mortimer's
Paradis Barcelona
Pasta & Dreams
Pasta Presto
Provence
The River Café
Roettele A.G.
The Sea Grill
Symphony Cafe
Tavern on the Green
Ten Twenty-two
The Terrace
Terrace Five
The Water Club
Water's Edge at the East
  River Yacht Club

▷ 43

## PRETHEATER MENU

Adrienne
Algonquin Hotel
Alo Alo
Ambassador Grill
American Festival Cafe
Anatolia
Andiamo!
Aquavit
Barbetta
Bellini by Cipriani
Café de Paris
Cafe Greco
Cafe Luxembourg
Café Pierre
Cafe San Martin
Chantal Café
Chez Louis
Darbar
Eze
Ferrier
The Four Seasons
Greene Street Restaurant
Huberts
La Boîte en Bois
La Caravelle
Lafayette
La Gauloise
La Méditerranée
La Réserve
La Tulipe
Le Chantilly
Marie-Michelle
Palio
San Domenico
The Sea Grill
Sfuzzi
Symphony Cafe
Tavern on the Green
Toscana Ristorante
Tropica Bar and Seafood House
"21" Club
Voulez-Vous

## PRIVATE ROOMS

Adrienne
Akbar (49th Street)
Akbar (Park Avenue)
Alcala
Algonquin Hotel
Ambassador Grill
American Harvest
An American Place
Arcadia
Arcobaleno
Auntie Yuan
Bangkok House
Barbetta
Barrow Street Bistro
Bellevues
Bice
Bistro d'Adrienne
Brandywine
Brasserie
Broadway Joe
B. Smith's
Cabana Carioca (II)
Cafe Between the Bread
Cafe Nicholson
Carnegie Deli
Chez Josephine
Chin Chin
Christ Cella
City Cafe
Courtyard Café and Bar
Cowgirl Hall of Fame
Crêpes Suzette
Darbar
David K's
Dāwat

## (PRIVATE ROOMS)

East
Felidia
The Four Seasons
Frank's
Gage & Tollner
Gallagher's
Gaylord
Gloucester House
The Golden Unicorn
Great Shanghai Restaurant
Greene Street Restaurant
Hamburger Harry's
Harold's
Hatsuhana
The Health Pub
HSF
Huberts
Hudson River Club
Inagiku
Indochine
John Clancy's
Keen's Chop House
La Bonne Soupe
La Cité
La Colombe d'Or
La Côte Basque
Lafayette
La Grenouille
La Kasbah
La Mirabelle
Landmark Tavern
La Petite Ferme
La Réserve
Le Bernardin
Le Chantilly
Le Cirque
Le Cygne
Le Madeleine
Le Périgord
Le Refuge
Le Régence
Le Zinc
Lotfi's Couscous
Lutèce
Malvasia
Mamma Leone's
Manhattan Brewing Company
The Manhattan Ocean Club
Marie-Michelle
Maxim's
Mickey Mantle's
Mitsukoshi
Mon Cher Ton Ton (Japanese)
Montrachet
Moroccan Star
Mortimer's
The Nice Restaurant
Nippon
Oriental Pearl
Palio
Palm
Palm Court
Park Bistro
Pasta & Dreams
Patsy's
Periyali
Peter Luger
Primavera
Punsch
The Rainbow Room
René Pujol
Roettele A.G.
Rogers & Barbero
Roumeli Taverna
The Russian Tea Room
Rusty Staub's on Fifth
Saigon
San Domenico

▷ 45

## (PRIVATE ROOMS)

The Sea Grill
Sfuzzi
Shun Lee
Sidewalkers'
The Sign of the Dove
Smith & Wollensky
SoHo Kitchen and Bar
Sukhothai
Sushiden
Symphony Cafe
Tavern on the Green
The Terrace
Toscana Ristorante
Trattoria dell'Arte
Trixie's
20 Mott Street Restaurant
"21" Club
Umeda
Victor's Café 52
The Water Club
Water's Edge at the East River Yacht Club
Windows on the World

## ROMANTIC

Adele
Adrienne
Aquavit
Arcobaleno
Auntie Yuan
Au Troquet
Barbetta
Bouley
Brandywine
Bukhara
Café des Artistes
Cafe Nicholson
Café Pierre
Cellar in the Sky

## (ROMANTIC)

Chanterelle
Chez Josephine
Chin Chin
Courtyard Café and Bar
Crêpes Suzette
Erminia
The Four Seasons
Gage & Tollner
Huberts
Hudson River Club
Jane's Bar and Grill
La Caravelle
La Colombe d'Or
La Côte Basque
Lafayette
La Gauloise
La Grenouille
La Métairie
La Petite Ferme
La Réserve
La Tulipe
Le Bernardin
Le Cirque
Le Cygne
Le Madeleine
Le Périgord
Le Refuge
Le Régence
Lutèce
Maxim's
Palio
Palm Court
Parioli, Romanissimo
Prunelle
The Rainbow Room
The River Café
The Russian Tea Room
San Domenico
The Sea Grill
The Sign of the Dove

## (ROMANTIC)

Tavern on the Green
The Terrace
Toscana Ristorante
Trastevere
"21" Club
Victor's Café 52
The Water Club
Water's Edge at the East River Yacht Club
Windows on the World
Zarela

## SUNDAY BRUNCH

Adele
Adrienne
Akbar (49th Street)
Al Amir
Algonquin Hotel
Alo Alo
Ambassador Grill
American Festival Cafe
Amsterdam's Bar and Rotisserie
Amsterdam's Grand
Andiamo!
Auntie Yuan
Aunt Sonia
Baci
The Ballroom
Barrow Street Bistro
Bella Luna
Benny's Burritos
Bice
Border Cafe
Brasserie
Bridge Cafe
Broadway Diner
Broadway Joe
B. Smith's

## (SUNDAY BRUNCH)

Bukhara
Cabana Carioca (both locations)
Café des Artistes
Cafe Greco
Cafe Luxembourg
Café Pierre
Cafe San Martin
Cameos
Caribe
Carnegie Deli
Chelsea Central
Chez Momo
City Cafe
Claire
Coastal
Contrapunto
Corner Bistro
Courtyard Café and Bar
Cowgirl Hall of Fame
Darbar
David K's
Docks (both locations)
Dominick's
Donald Sacks
East
The "11" Cafe
Ferrier
Florent
44
Fu's
Gage & Tollner
Gallagher's
Gaylord
Girasole
The Golden Unicorn
Great Shanghai Restaurant
Greene Street Restaurant
Hamburger Harry's

## (SUNDAY BRUNCH)

Harlequin
Harold's
The Health Pub
HSF
Indian Cafe
Istanbul Kebap
Joe Allen
King Fung
La Bohème
La Bonne Soupe
La Cité
La Fusta
La Gauloise
La Kasbah
La Métairie
Landmark Tavern
Le Lucky Strike
Le Madeleine
Le Refuge
Le Régence
Madeline's
Mandarin Court
Manhattan Brewing Company
Manhattan Chili Company
Mary Ann's
Menchanko-Tei
Mezzaluna
Mezzogiorno
Michael's
Mickey Mantle's
Moroccan Star
Mortimer's
New Prospect Cafe
The Nice Restaurant
North Star Pub
The Odeon
Ollie's Noodle Shop and Grille
150 Wooster Street
Oriental Pearl
Oriental Town Seafood Restaurant
Orso
Palm Court
Panevino
Paradis Barcelona
Pasta & Dreams
Pasta Presto
Peking Duck House
Peter Luger
Pig Heaven
Poiret
Provence
The Rainbow Room
The River Café
Rogers & Barbero
Rose Cafe
Roumeli Taverna
The Russian Tea Room
Rusty Staub's on Fifth
Saigon
Sarabeth's Kitchen
Saranac
Sette Mezzo
Sevilla Restaurant and Bar
Sfuzzi
Shun Lee
Shun Lee Palace
Sido Abu Salim
The Sign of the Dove
SoHo Kitchen and Bar
Sylvia's
Taormina
Tavern on the Green
Ten Twenty-two
Trattoria dell'Arte
Trixie's
20 Mott Street Restaurant
Victor's Café 52

## (SUNDAY BRUNCH)

Voulez-Vous
Vucciria
The Water Club
Water's Edge at the East River Yacht Club
Windows on the World
Yellowfingers di Nuovo
Yellow Rose Cafe
Zula

## SUNDAY DINNER

Adele
Akbar (49th Street)
Akbar (Park Avenue)
Al Amir
Alcala
Algonquin Hotel
Alison on Dominick Street
Alo Alo
Ambassador Grill
American Festival Cafe
Amsterdam's Bar and Rotisserie
Amsterdam's Grand
Anatolia
Andiamo!
Arcobaleno
Arizona 206
Arizona 206 Cafe
Auntie Yuan
Aunt Sonia
Azzurro
Baci
Bangkok House
Barrow Street Bistro
Bella Luna
Bellevues
Benny's Burritos
Bice

## (SUNDAY DINNER)

Border Cafe
Brasserie
Bridge Cafe
Broadway Diner
Broadway Joe
B. Smith's
Bukhara
Cabana Carioca (I)
Café de Paris
Café des Artistes
Cafe Greco
Cafe Luxembourg
Café Pierre
Cafe San Martin
Café Un Deux Trois
Cameos
Ca'Nova
Caribe
Carnegie Deli
Chelsea Central
Chez Louis
Chez Momo
China Grill
Chin Chin
City Cafe
Claire
The Coach House
Coastal
Contrapunto
Corner Bistro
Corrado
Courtyard Café and Bar
Cowgirl Hall of Fame
Cuisine de Saigon
Da Tommaso
Darbar
David K's
Dāwat
Docks (both locations)
Dominick's

▷ **49**

## (SUNDAY DINNER)

Donald Sacks
East
Ecco!
El Cid
The "11" Cafe
Erminia
Ferrier
Florent
44
Fu's
Gage & Tollner
Gallagher's
Gaylord
Girasole
The Golden Unicorn
Gotham Bar and Grill
Great Shanghai
   Restaurant
Greene Street Restaurant
Hamburger Harry's
Harlequin
Harold's
The Health Pub
HSF
Il Cantinori
Inagiku
Indian Cafe
Indochine
Istanbul Kebap
Jane Street Seafood Cafe
Jezebel
Joe Allen
John Clancy's
King Fung
La Bohème
La Boîte en Bois
La Bonne Soupe
La Cité
La Fusta
La Kasbah
La Méditerranée
La Mirabelle
La Tulipe
Le Lucky Strike
Le Madeleine
Le Refuge
Le Régence
Le Steak
Lotfi's Couscous
Lusardi's
Madeline's
Mamma Leone's
Mandarin Court
Manhattan Brewing
   Company
Manhattan Chili
   Company
The Manhattan Ocean
   Club
Marie-Michelle
Mary Ann's
Memphis
Menchanko-Tei
Mezzaluna
Mezzogiorno
Michael's
Mickey Mantle's
Moroccan Star
Mortimer's
New Prospect Cafe
The Nice Restaurant
North Star Pub
The Odeon
Ollie's Noodle Shop and
   Grille
Omen
150 Wooster Street
Oriental Pearl
Oriental Town Seafood
   Restaurant
Orso
Palm Court

## (SUNDAY DINNER)

Pamir
Panevino
Paola's
Paper Moon Milano
Paradis Barcelona
Park Bistro
Pasta & Dreams
Pasta Presto
Patsy's
Peking Duck House
Peter Luger
Pig Heaven
Poiret
The Post House
Primavera
Primola
Provence
Prunelle
Punsch
Quatorze
The Rainbow Room
Riazor
Rio Mar
The River Café
Roettele A.G.
Rogers & Barbero
Rosa Mexicano
Rose Cafe
Roumeli Taverna
The Russian Tea Room
Rusty Staub's on Fifth
Sabor
Saigon
San Domenico
Saranac
Sette Mezzo
Sevilla Restaurant and Bar
Sfuzzi
Shun Lee
Shun Lee Palace
Siam Inn
Sidewalkers'
Sido Abu Salim
The Sign of the Dove
Smith & Wollensky
SoHo Kitchen and Bar
Sukhothai
Sylvia's
Taormina
Tatany
Tavern on the Green
Ten Twenty-two
Trastevere
Trattoria dell'Arte
Trixie's
20 Mott Street Restaurant
Umeda
Victor's Café 52
Voulez-Vous
Vucciria
The Water Club
Water's Edge at the East River Yacht Club
Wilkinson's Seafood Café
Windows on the World
Yellowfingers di Nuovo
Yellow Rose Cafe
Zarela
Zula

## A TASTE OF NEW YORK CITY FOR OUT-OF-TOWN VISITORS

American Festival Cafe
Café des Artistes
Carnegie Deli
Cellar in the Sky

## (A TASTE OF NEW YORK CITY FOR OUT-OF-TOWN VISITORS)

The Coach House
The Four Seasons
Gage & Tollner
Hudson River Club
Keen's Chop House
La Côte Basque
Le Bernardin
Le Cirque
Lutèce
The Oyster Bar and Restaurant in Grand Central Station
Palm
Peter Luger
P.J. Clarke's
The Rainbow Room
The River Café
The Russian Tea Room
The Sea Grill
Sylvia's
Tavern on the Green
The Terrace
"21" Club
The Water Club
Water's Edge at the East River Yacht Club
Windows on the World

# RESTAURANT REVIEWS

# ADELE

★

*501 11th Street, Park Slope, Brooklyn, (718) 788-4980.*

*Atmosphere: Romantic former carriage house with fireplace and candlelight.*

*Service: Low-key and attentive.*

*Wine: Well-chosen, unusual list with reasonable prices.*

*Price range: Moderately expensive.*

*Credit cards: All major cards.*

*Hours: Brunch, 11:30 A.M. to 3 P.M., Sunday; dinner, 6 to 10:30 P.M., Wednesday through Saturday, 5 to 9 P.M., Sunday.*

*Reservations: Requested.*

*Wheelchair accessibility: Everything on one level.*

Adele, an alluring little restaurant in a former carriage house in Park Slope, Brooklyn, is the creation of John Sielski, an experienced restaurant manager who started at Huberts when it was still in Brooklyn (it is now on Park Avenue in Manhattan), and Jim Dozmati, who was a garden designer by profession. Their nineteenth-century carriage house—a blacksmith and carpenter were still toiling there when they took over—seats forty with room to spare under the high, pressed-tin ceiling. A crackling fireplace, candlelight, flower-patterned wallpaper, and classical music contribute to the amorous mood.

The chef, Melicia Phillips, who came from a three-year stint at Chanterelle, turns out a wisely limited but diverse menu with Italian and French accents. Starters can be as simple as blood-warming duck consommé with al dente julienned vegetables, or as urbane as a velvety and well-seasoned foie-gras-and-avocado terrine. Soups are taken seriously here. Cream of leek, squash, and carrot is lusty and delicate at the same time; cream of mussel soup is on the rich side, but so scintillating with saffron that it is hard to be temperate.

If the squab salad with a compote of butternut squash and apples is available, go for it. The lightly bound terrine of lobster and shrimp is another good starter. Wild-mushroom cannelloni has double-barreled flavor, boosted by its mushroom broth. And for two-fisted eaters, there is a pancakelike fritter of potato and bacon set over a sweet-sharp abundance of red cabbage, a harmonious combination.

For a small, relatively new restaurant, Adele has a varied and uncommon wine list.

Entrées have a clean and unfussy appeal. Roasted guinea hen, meatier and more flavorful than so-called free-range chicken, is paired with cabbage, green beans, and carrots. Shell steak has a deep-aged flavor and comes out nicely blackened yet moist under a slab of garlicky herb butter. Braised venison with spaetzle and brussels sprouts had a wonderfully mellow red-wine sauce, but the meat was on the dry side. Roast duck was better in its faintly sweet apple-cider sauce, accompanied by sautéed watercresss and gratin of turnip.

Sea scallops arrive under an avalanche of deep-fried leeks and are ringed with a pleasantly sour-edged sorrel sauce. Salmon is nicely broiled, but the sauce of cucumber juice and fish stock tasted about as pallid as it sounds. On another visit, a leek-and-butter sauce did the fillet justice.

Don't expect ginger ice cream here to be like the lean, palate-cleansing scoops doled out at Japanese restaurants. If it weren't for the ginger, this could be spread on toast at breakfast. Brandy-soaked cherries nestled in pastry cream over puff pastry is a less cloying winner, as are cinnamon-dusted apple fritters with prune-and-currant compote. Among the lightest offerings are a lovely mille-feuille of strawberries with strawberry purée, and pear poached in red wine with cinnamon.

# ADRIENNE

★ ★

*Peninsula Hotel, 700 Fifth Avenue, at 55th Street, 903-3918.*

*Atmosphere: Luxurious Art Nouveau dining room.*

*Service: Amateurish and inattentive.*

*Wine: Quality selection, mostly French, wide price range.*

*Price range: Expensive (pretheater dinner prix fixe, $45).*

*Credit cards: All major cards.*

*Hours: Breakfast, 7 to 10:30 A.M., daily; brunch, noon to 3 P.M., Sunday; lunch, noon to 2:30 P.M., Monday through Friday; pretheater dinner, 6 to 7 P.M., Monday through Saturday; dinner, 6 to 10:30 P.M., Monday through Saturday.*

*Reservations: Requested.*

*Wheelchair accessibility: Two flights of stairs to restaurant level. Restrooms downstairs.*

When the Hong Kong–based Peninsula Hotel chain took over the Hotel Maxim's de Paris on Fifth Avenue at 55th Street in 1988, it inherited a somewhat prissy Old World French dining room called Adrienne that, despite its quality food, never really caught on among New Yorkers. Diners in New York City still need compelling reasons to enter a hotel restaurant for a meal, especially one without a separate street entrance.

Yet there is ample reason to give Adrienne another try. You will be enthralled by the dazzling cross-cultural cooking of Gray Kunz, a Swiss acolyte of the famed Fredy Giradet. Mr. Kunz, in his mid thirties, has worked in Hong Kong, where he learned to weave East-West culinary tapestries threaded with ginger, lemongrass, cardamom, and curry. Many novelty-chasing young chefs attempt similar amalgams these days, but few have the solid grounding of Mr. Kunz.

Adrienne could be a thoroughly enjoyable dining experience if it were not for the often dim-witted service. Waiters have a knack for lollygagging around when you don't need them and disappearing when you do.

The sumptuous Art Nouveau dining room has not been altered, a harmonious, fabric-lined space with beveled mirrors, soft rose-tinted banquettes, period sconces, deep armchairs, and explosions of fresh flowers. A casual bistro on the other side of the dining room serves good, earthy fare.

Mr. Kunz's Oriental influence is immediately evident in stellar starters like crispy little crimped ravioli filled with strands of leeks and ginger in a cream-enriched vegetable broth, and more buttery sautéed leeks on the side. Packets of silvery smoked salmon hold well-herbed diced vegetables and are garnished with a mound of crabmeat and an olive-oil-and-lime dressing that plays nicely off the saline fish. Gently warmed oysters are sprinkled with a confetti of crisped shallots and sesame seeds in an oceanic chervil-flecked sauce and then gratinéed before serving.

Not everything is so harmonious, particularly soups. At lunch one day two appealing-sounding cold versions were disappointments: a pallid jellied shellfish consommé with tarragon, and a lightly gelled, beautifully presented but underseasoned fish broth with chunks of salmon throughout.

Mr. Kunz must have an early rising saucier to turn out distinctly different sauces for a dozen or more entrées daily. Salmon filled braised with romaine lettuce is wonderfully embellished by a champagne butter sauce with a snappy edge of watercress; little monkfish fillets combined with a small baby sea bass showed their best in a light tomato sauce bound with a touch of butter and emboldened with pepper and fresh thyme.

Surprises abound on meat entrées. Saffron-scented triangles of pasta and batons of crunchy celery root enliven succulent veal loin; mignonettes of lamb are fanned over a ragout of eggplant with a light oregano cream sauce, and sweetbreads, firm and crisply sautéed, have a supporting cast of firm steamed asparagus and a faintly citric veal-stock sauce.

The French-dominated wine list starts off gently with quality offerings in the $20 neighborhood.

For dessert, try the chocolate mousse cake with bittersweet icing, or the opulent opera cake.

# AKBAR (49TH STREET)

**SATISFACTORY**

*256 East 49th Street, 755-9100.*

*Atmosphere: Contemporary and trim with white walls, brass, and glass.*

*Service: Polite but scattered.*

*Price range: Moderate.*

*Credit cards: All major cards.*

*Hours: Brunch, noon to 3 P.M., Saturday and Sunday; lunch, 11:30 A.M. to 3 P.M., Monday through Friday; dinner, 5:30 to 11 P.M., Sunday through Thursday, until 11:30 P.M., Friday and Saturday.*

*Reservations: Suggested.*

*Wheelchair accessibility: Two stairs at entrance, restrooms upstairs.*

The Indian restaurant Akbar opened its third outlet in 1988, on 49th Street near Second Avenue (the others are at 475 Park Avenue, near 58th Street, and in Garden City, L.I.). The newest location has an inviting setting: a two-level, glass-walled front and a clean, modern look of white walls, brass, and wood. A small open-air terrace in the back can be pleasant on a summer evening—that is, if you don't pay attention to the plastic flowers, aluminum kitchen vents, and the backs of apartment houses overhead.

It appears, though, that Akbar has overextended its resources with this new establishment, for much of the food is second-rate. And the service staff, while exceedingly polite, is confused and listless, often disappearing for long stretches.

You get an inkling that something is wrong when you sample the assorted appetizers, most of which taste like reheated leftovers. A more reliable starter is the well-seasoned mulligatawny soup, rich with lentils and mixed vegetables.

Indian breads, which can be so light and delicious at the Park Avenue Akbar, are for the most part dreary here. The puffed bread poori was greasy and deflating by the time it arrived at the table, and both nan and chapati were stiff and dry. The only superior bread was laccha paratha, a flaky layered dough swathed with melted butter.

Among entrées, such casserole dishes as the moderately spicy lamb vindaloo and sag (lamb cooked in creamed spinach and assorted spices) are the best bets. Meats and fish cooked in the tandoori oven never had a chance; the tandoori chicken was shriveled and dry, and fish tikka (tilefish on skewers) suffered the same fate. Something called a vegetable sizzler should be renamed the vegetable incinerator: a cube of cottage cheese blackened from the inferno was combined with lifeless cauliflower, carrots, and other vegetables.

Rice dishes were the most appealing part of the menu, especially the vibrant Banarasi pillau (long-grain rice with clove, peas, sliced almonds, and a touch of saffron). Some of the vegetarian dishes are good, too, such as the aloo baingan (eggplant and potatoes cooked in a cumin-laced gravy) and bhurta (baked spicy eggplant).

The best and most unusual dessert is a carrot pudding called gajar halwa, which is minimally sweet, moist, and laced with nuts and raisins.

# AKBAR (PARK AVENUE)

*Park Avenue, above 57th Street, 838-1717.*

*Atmosphere: Spacious, comfortable, dimly lighted room.*

*Service: Sluggish and minimally communicative.*

*Price range: Moderate.*

*Credit cards: All major cards.*

*Hours: Lunch, 11:30 A.M. to 2:45 P.M., Monday through Saturday; dinner, 5:30 to 10:45 P.M., daily.*

*Reservations: Suggested.*

*Wheelchair accessibility: Everything on one level.*

Akbar, the decorous Indian restaurant on Park Avenue (a sister establishment is on East 49th Street), is a reliable spot for Mogul cuisine, the refined and highly seasoned northern fare that is most common in this country. Mogul cooking is characterized by yogurt-marinated meats, butter-and-cream-enriched sauces, and the intoxicating perfume of saffron and tandoor-roasted meats. Revisits have found that many of Akbar's benchmark dishes still challenge the palate with a complex alchemy of herbs and spices while others inexplicably fall flatter than a punctured poori.

The spacious dining room is decorated in dark reds and white with crepuscular lighting, ornate white pilasters separating wall mirrors, a back-lighted stained-glass ceiling, and snug little alcoves along the walls. The service is occasionally sluggish, and getting dish descriptions from waiters beyond "very good" and "pretty spicy" is like trying to chat about the weather with a New York Telephone operator.

The kitchen has a tendency to be heavy-handed with red peppers, which suits me fine, but if you are sensitive to heat, let them know. The weakest part of the menu is probably appetizers. Indian fritters called pakora, filled with either chicken or vegetables, used to be delightfully light and cleanly fried here. Now they tend to be oily and heavy; likewise the vegetable patties called samosas.

The minced-lamb patties called shami kebab are dry and mushy, with so much ginger the meat is camouflaged. If you want to start out with lamb, try splitting an entrée portion of seekh kebabs: juicy minced lamb, onions, and fresh coriander molded around skewers and roasted in the tandoor. Another good option is chicken pakora, deep-fried squiggles of well-seasoned chicken. Mulligatawny soup is pleasing, mildly peppery, and redolent of clove.

Seafood tends to be overcooked, like the shrimp bhuna. It's a shame, because the sauce is sensational, layered with garlic, ginger, coriander, and pepper. Fish tikka, a tandoor-roasted dish that features cubes of red snapper rubbed with a peppery blend of spices, is preferable, as are the large prawns similarly cooked.

The tandoor method is most successful with kalmi kebabs, or marinated chicken legs, and chicken ginger kebab, in which the chicken is moistened with yogurt and ginger before roasting. The standard tandoori chicken, however, can have a dry and reheated texture. Much better is a nontandoor dish called chicken jalfrezi, in which the meat is slowly braised with firm cubes of fresh cheese in a lovely sauce sweetened with onions and peppers. Vindaloo of lamb, a fiery dish from the southwestern state of Goa, is still recommended for its skillful blending of heat and counterbalancing spices, specifically cinnamon and ginger.

All the Indian breads are well turned out here. Particular favorites are the onion-filled nan called kulcha and the hot unleavened whole-wheat paratha tossed with melted butter.

Vegetarians can always find solace in Indian restaurants, and Akbar has a dozen options, including bhurta (mashed, garlicky eggplant), mattar paneer (cubes of fresh cheese with firm fresh peas in a tingling hot sauce) and aloo gobi (cauliflower with lots of fresh ginger and coriander). The house special biryani, a traditional basmati rice dish combining chicken (both dark and white meat), saffron, and other spices, is moist and aromatic.

To Western tastes, Indian dessert is sort of like new-age music: you find it either wonderfully soothing or exasperatingly dull. To my taste, rose ice cream tastes like soap, an opinion shared by most of the people at my table. Mango ice cream met universal approval, though, as did the kheer, a rice pudding flavored with cardamom.

# ALCALA

★ ★

*349 Amsterdam Avenue, between 76th and 77th streets, 769-9600.*

*Atmosphere: Warm and inviting, with a long marble-topped tapas bar and elevated, brick-walled dining room.*

*Service: Pleasant and helpful; kitchen can be slow.*

*Wine: A fine, extensive selection of Spanish wines from various regions. Many good buys.*

*Price range: Moderate.*

*Credit cards: All major cards.*

*Hours: Dinner, 5:30 to 11 P.M. (tapas bar open until midnight), Tuesday through Saturday, 2 to 10 P.M., Sunday.*

*Reservations: Suggested.*

*Wheelchair accessibility: Bar-area tables on ground level; restrooms downstairs.*

In the limited world of authentic Spanish restaurants in New York, Alcala ranks among the best. The owner, Rufino Lopez, a native of Galicia in northwestern Spain, attempts to offer a sampling of Iberian specialties from several regions in this casual, affable spot.

The set-up dining room has a warm, friendly feeling—polished wood floor, brick and whitewashed walls, gentle lighting, and a pretty little backyard garden café. A large dining area downstairs is for private functions.

It's fun to start off at the long marble-topped bar up front and choose from an assortment of cold and hot appetizers. If it is true, as some medical reports contend, that olive oil lowers cholesterol levels, then Alcala should accept Blue Cross/Blue Shield cards for payment, for nearly everything on the menu has some. Among the more intriguing tapas (the selection varies daily) are fresh anchovies in a vinegar-laced marinade; morsels of chewy octopus in a similar dressing with pimientos; tender golden rings of friend calamari; rosy smoked trout over sliced cucumbers with dill; a zesty salad of artichoke hearts, sliced beef tongue and chickpeas in a cumin-perfumed olive-oil dressing, and shellfish salad (tiny squid, scallops, shrimp) in an herby vinaigrette dressing. Try a few slivers of Serrano, the buttery cured Spanish ham, along with rough-textured bread and a glass of robust red wine.

Speaking of wine, the Spanish selection here is perhaps the best in New York, with many remarkable bargains to be had if you are adventurous. In white, you can't go wrong with the clean and crisp Ermita Despiells from the Penedès region, or the equally pleasing Marques de Griñon; more than forty reds are stocked, starting at less than $15. Waiters are good about walking you through the selections. The sherry selection is impressive, too.

If you don't go overboard with tapas, consider the roasted suckling pig as an entrée. A slab of pale, savory pork hides under a brittle, caramel-colored sheet of skin, all in a clear, rich broth perfumed with rosemary. A gutsy occasional special is the wide earthenware casserole holding morcilla (blood sausage), smoked pork, chicken, beef brisket, peas, and spinach. All the meats are well cooked and authoritatively seasoned.

Other alluring preparations include the pepper-dusted fresh grouper ringed by a tasty assortment of eggplant, zucchini, tomatoes, and squash; juicy broiled lamb chops with stewed vegetables; and crisply sautéed salmon steak, rosy rare in the center, flanked by two sauces: a lemony olive-oil-and-garlic emulsion and a faintly piquant granular purée of dried peppers and almonds. Unfortunately the paellas are undistinguished.

The service staff here, mostly Spaniards, is as congenial and well meaning as one could ask, but sometimes the kitchen can't keep up with the rush of orders on a busy night.

For dessert, the thick, rich almond tart is splendid, if weighty, paired with apple purée vitalized with lemon zest. The Catalonian cream—a Spanish crème brûlée—is ultra light and tinged with cinnamon. Pass up the flossy rum cream roll called brazo de gitano for the exhilarating orange flan ringed with crème anglaise and shredded coconut.

Whether you are "just grazing through" or settling in for a while, Alcala is a spot with considerable charm and Latin spirit.

# ALISON ON DOMINICK STREET

★ ★

*38 Dominick Street, between Varick and Hudson streets, 727-1188.*

*Atmosphere: Comfortable, unpretentious dining room with soft lighting. Can be loud.*

*Service: Competent and good-natured.*

*Wine: Well matched with food; moderately priced.*

*Price range: Moderately expensive.*

*Credit cards: All major cards.*

*Hours: Lunch, noon to 2:15 P.M., Monday through Friday; dinner, 6 to 11 P.M., Monday through Thursday, until 11:30 P.M., Friday and Saturday; 5:30 to 9:30 P.M., Sunday.*

*Reservations: Necessary.*

*Wheelchair accessibility: Dining on main level; restrooms downstairs.*

The mirthful Manhattan parlor game of "find the restaurant" has a formidable new challenger—Alison on Dominick Street. Even if you are lucky enough to get a cabbie who knows the Hudson from the East River, chances are he will need your help ferreting out Dominick Street, an easy-to-miss spur off Varick Street just north of the Holland Tunnel. The quest should be worth it, though, for this unpretentious little outpost is serving some of the most seductive southwestern French fare around. The eponymous Alison is Alison Price, a former actress turned restaurant owner who has appeared in such gastronomic productions as Gotham Bar and Grill and Rakel. She has teamed up with Thomas Valenti, a gifted chef whose eclectic résumé includes Gotham Bar and Grill and Guy Savoy in Paris.

The setting is harmonious and comfortable: pastel-colored walls holding black-and-white photographs, royal-blue banquettes, indirect lighting, low-key jazz.

Southwestern French cuisine typically evokes images of rough-hewn country fare and artery-clogging foie gras and confit. Mr. Valenti's style is surprisingly light yet faithful to the lusty flavors of the region. Fine starters include deliciously blackened slices of rare lamb with lentils and mixed greens; a salad of fresh mussels in a lemony vinaigrette with chicory and artichoke hearts; and a seductive terrine of rabbit, duck foie gras, and mushrooms. A nice summery selection is the individual tart of herby eggplant, zucchini, tomato, and caramelized onions perfumed with basil. The only disjointed starter was a Japanese-looking roulade of cabbage, salmon, and tuna that, while fresh, needed more than dime-size dollops of herbed crème fraîche to unify the flavors.

Two of the favorite house entrées seem to be the hefty braised lamb shank, intensely flavorful, tender, and gelatinous, with a parsley-and-roasted-garlic sauce, wilted chicory, and fava beans. Guinea hen, more firm and flavorful than chicken, is delicious with its pan juices and a risotto of black olives, tomatoes, and fresh thyme. Loin of rabbit is wrapped in bacon to impart moisture and flavor (the leg needs no such help) and served with nutty roasted barley, mushrooms, and tiny pommes soufflés. Breast of Muscovy duck was returned to the kitchen for further cooking, and came back fine with sweet onions inside a flower of sliced turnips.

Seafood is prepared with gusto but does not lose its delicacy. Consider the firm, moist halibut steak over lentils, diced bacon, and turnips with a roasted shallot sauce, and crisply sautéed bass served swimming in the lightest tarragon-infused tomato broth with olives, leeks, artichokes, and shallots. Couscous is a wonderful sauce sponge.

The assault does not let up with desserts. Recommended are the serious chocolate-hazelnut ice cream, crème brûlée, and a quivering and ripe cantaloupe bavarois glazed with

Beaumes de Venise, a dessert wine from the Rhône, in a pool of vanilla-bean sauce. The individual lemon-meringue tart is a winner, but blueberry sorbet cream is a bizarre companion for it.

---

# ALO ALO

**SATISFACTORY**

*1030 Third Avenue, at 61st Street, 838-4343.*

*Atmosphere: Grand café setting; colorful, convivial but loud.*

*Service: Can be slow and inattentive.*

*Wine: Moderate size wine list at fair prices.*

*Price range: Moderate.*

*Credit cards: All major cards.*

*Hours: Brunch, noon to 3 P.M., Sunday; lunch, noon to 3 P.M., Monday through Saturday; light dishes, 3 to 6 P.M., daily; dinner, 6 to 11:45 P.M., daily.*

*Reservations: Suggested.*

*Wheelchair accessibility: Everything on one level.*

When Alo Alo opened in 1985 it was an animated and amusing spot that drew a dashing international cast of patrons. Moreover, the cooking was consistently pleasing, sometimes exceptionally so, under the Italian-born chef, Francesco Antonucci. The owners were the movie producer Dino de Laurentiis and a partner from Brazil, Ricardo Amaral. Recent visits found the clientele to be less flashy Milaneses and more frenetic Manhattanites. The food has lost some of its vitality, too. (Mr. Antonucci is now the chef and a co-owner of Remi; Mr. de Laurentiis has sold his interest to Mr. Amaral, who is rarely there.)

The playful grand café setting is still fun, though: the glass-wrapped, high-ceilinged room has cartoonlike papier-mâché characters perched on overhead ledges and pastel murals on the walls. The bar buzzes nightly with a young crowd sipping wine or caipirinhas, the Brazilian national cocktail made with fresh lime and sugarcane liquor. The room echoes loudly with conversation, and the overlay of pulsing background music makes communication even more difficult.

Many invigorating appetizers from the early days are gone. The grilled vegetable plate I used to love has been replaced by bland steamed carrots, zucchini, and artichoke hearts with roasted garlic cloves. The shrimp-and-avocado salad is pallid and served too chilled, and the warm carpaccio is unappetizingly gray (served with anemic winter tomatoes). Bresaola, or thinly sliced cured beef, has much more appeal, the lean, pleasantly salty meat complemented with hot mustard. You would do well with the simple grilled red and yellow peppers glossed with olive oil, or the endive salad with a disk of herb-crusted goat cheese.

The waiters, once nimble and capable, have lost their snappy efficiency. They often seem over their heads, which could be a result of understaffing.

The kitchen still produces some engaging pastas. Among the best are orecchiette, or ear-shaped noodles, in a smoky sauce of bacon, broccoli, and provolone cheese; fettuccine in a shrimp-and-fennel sauce, and a wonderful Sicilian dish combining spaghetti with chunks of canned tuna, spinach, and a rich seafood-stock-based sauce. Risotto, on the other hand, is a disaster, reminiscent of unseasoned boiled rice scattered with flakes of salmon.

I did not have much luck with seafood, either. Sautéed tuna was dry, and poached salmon was lackluster. Veal chop Milanese was woefully overcooked. Go instead for the moist braised chicken breasts with a zesty mustard sauce, or simply sliced sirloin with rosemary. Also good are chocolate mousse and tiramisù, rich with espresso flavor.

# AMBASSADOR GRILL

★

*1 United Nations Plaza, First Avenue at 44th Street, 702-5014.*

*Atmosphere: Cool, glassy, and modern urbane setting. Piano nightly.*

*Service: Professional and congenial.*

*Wine: Interesting regional French list with moderate prices.*

*Price range: Moderate (pretheater dinner prix fixe, $24).*

*Credit cards: All major cards.*

*Hours: Breakfast, 7 to 11 A.M., Monday through Sunday, 7:30 to 10:30 A.M., Saturday and Sunday; brunch, 11:30 A.M. to 2 P.M., Saturday and Sunday; lunch, noon to 2 P.M., Monday through Friday; dinner, 6 to 10:30 P.M., daily; pretheater dinner, 6 to 7 P.M., daily.*

*Reservations: Suggested.*

*Wheelchair accessibility: Several steps down to dining room; everything on main level.*

The Ambassador Grill is a cool, urbane restaurant in the United Nations Plaza Hotel that became somewhat the unofficial gastronomic embassy for Gascony in the southwest of France, the glorious region of ducks, geese, foie gras, confit, and truffles. That emphasis has been much diminished in the past year, but many Gascon dishes are still offered.

Several times a year a trio of leading chefs from that region comes to the restaurant to put on Gascon food festivals, and during the year regional specialties are offered on the menu. Half of the menu offers Gascon specialties throughout the year while the rest of the menu is a mix of French and American fare. The Gascon dishes are the most compelling reason to visit this surprisingly inexpensive dining room.

The subterranean room is striking with its interplay of dark walls, smoky glass panels, and starry lighting. Overhead the illusion of a skylight is created by the angling of many glass trellises that seem to reflect lights out to infinity. In a small open kitchen three cooks in white toques tend to the sizzling grills. Service is for the most part proper and prompt.

Upon being seated you can begin excavating a ramekin of well-seasoned duck rillettes with toasted croutons. If you are in an experimental mood, try the special Gascon cocktail called a pousse rapière—roughly translated as a thrust sword—a French sparkling wine tinted with a regional orange-flavored liqueur. The wine list also carries some moderately priced regional labels, such as the fresh and easy-drinking Colombard, an André Daguin label, a white, and the young, faintly tannic Madiran.

The unqualified best starter is the warm duck foie gras salad, which is on the Gascon side of the menu. It has strips of rare-grilled salmon paired with a meltingly rich slice of the foie gras, seared just enough to form a micro-thin crust, set over a bouquet of mixed greens in a mild wine-vinegar dressing ($3 supplement). Soft nuggets of mellow garlic confit add a heady rustic accent.

Recommended appetizers from the other side of the menu are the peppery rockfish chowder, which is actually more like a stew, made with an assertive shellfish stock, tomato, and fillets of rockfish, and a lovely dish of lightly poached shrimp served in a buttery shellfish stock blushed with sweet Sauternes.

Magret, the meaty breast of a fattened moulard duck that is raised to produce foie gras, is competently prepared—sliced, sautéed to rare, and glossed with a red-wine sauce ($3 supplement). The restaurant's cassoulet with duckmeat may be less rich and complex than it could be, but it is flavorful nonetheless. On Fridays the kitchen turns out a generous and oceanic bouillabaisse spiked with a garlicky aïoli ($4 supplement).

An unusual preparation that succeeds is lean Black Angus steak poached to medium rare in beef stock and an emulsion sauce melding egg yolks, mustard, and just a hint of vanilla that comes through moments after you swallow.

High spots of the dessert tray are lush plum tart with a

cracker-thin crust, a first-rate crème brûlée, and a fabulous mille-feuille made with sugar-dusted puff pastry disks floating on layers of whipped cream with fresh respberries.

The Ambassador Grill has one of the more lavish Sunday brunches in town. The staggering buffet seems endless, and the food is better than average for these affairs. You start out with a cold half a lobster and move on to entrées on the buffet: roast beef, delicious fennel sausage and boudin blanc with lentils, cheese-filled ravioli, roast turkey, mixed winter vegetables, scalloped potatoes, and eggs Benedict with a good hollandaise (the muffins tend to get dry on a hot plate though). The cold table holds all sorts of shellfish as well as smoked salmon, terrines, and cold meats. Fruits and assorted pastries round out dessert. The cost is $35, which includes unlimited champagne. A Saturday French buffet brunch features assorted terrines, smoked fish, stews, and homemade sausages. Wine is included in the $25 price.

# AMERICAN HARVEST

★

*3 World Trade Center, in the Vista International Hotel, 432-9334, 938-9100.*

*Atmosphere: Quiet and spacious dining room decorated in a traditional American theme.*

*Service: Mannered, but lacking in finesse.*

*Wine: Well-balanced California-oriented list at fair prices.*

*Price range: Moderately expensive (prix-fixe lunch, $23–$29, prix-fixe dinner, $35).*

*Credit cards: All major cards.*

*Hours: Breakfast, 7 to 10 A.M., Monday through Friday; lunch, noon to 2:30 P.M., Monday through Friday; dinner, 6 to 10 P.M., Monday through Thursday.*

*Reservations: Suggested.*

*Wheelchair accessibility: Everything on one level.*

American Harvest, the showcase restaurant at the Vista International Hotel in the shadow of the World Trade Center, waves the flag of American cuisine throughout its changing monthly menu. While some of the seasonal ideas are appealing, the execution continues to be a bit wobbly.

Many straightforward preparations are reliably satisfying —steaks, chops, and grilled seafood in particular—while some of the more thematic dishes are silly. Take the charcoal-broiled fillet of salmon, for example. It is rosy pink in the center and delicious on its own, so why gussy it up by embedding the flesh with harsh-tasting juniper berries? Moreover, the lemon mayonnaise is bland. Rack of lamb, three juicy double chops, is abused with a coating of acrid raw mustard seeds.

An all-American theme extends to the décor of the three dining rooms, featuring an old-fashioned hanging quilt, glass display cases filled with colorful folkloric wooden carvings, and a giant oil painting of fruits and vegetables. Tables are well separated and the noise level is low, making this a good spot for business entertaining.

The kitchen does not stint on quality of ingredients. Florid slices of lean tenderloin combine with mixed greens and a mustard vinaigrette to make a tasty starter, and the bluepoint oysters are icy and fresh. Poached shrimp and sea scallops are impeccable, too, although they could use some herbs to brighten up the cucumber-and-sour-cream dressing. Two of the best starters are the fluffy smoked-salmon mousse over leaves of endive and crisply sautéed sweetbreads atop a bed of chicory. Caesar salad is watery and tasteless.

Among the more satisfying entrées are tender medallions of veal stuffed with julienne of carrots and zucchini, set in a brassy oregano cream sauce, and the mild pink calf's liver with onions and avocado. Soft-shell crabs, a seasonal delight well worth celebrating, are described as "pan-fried with macadamia nuts." I assumed that they were breaded with crushed nuts, which sounded good; instead, the chef sautés them in butter then opens a jar of macadamia nuts and scatters some around the plate. Roast duck with rhubarb, moist and full-flavored, is a nice twist on the standard orange sauce. Vegetables are served family style.

The California-oriented wine list is reasonably priced and well balanced.

One expects serious down-home desserts at an all-American restaurant, but except for the lusty thick-crusted apple pie à la mode and a rich, brownielike Derby chocolate pie, most selections are sugary and commercial tasting.

# AN AMERICAN PLACE

★ ★

*2 Park Avenue, entrance on 32nd Street, 684-2122.*

*Atmosphere: Spacious, softly lighted room with large, well-separated tables.*

*Service: Well informed about menu; efficient if sometimes awkward.*

*Wine: Broad selection of quality American wines.*

*Price range: Expensive.*

*Credit cards: All major cards.*

*Hours: Lunch, 11:45 A.M. to 3 P.M., Monday through Friday; dinner, 5:30 to 10 P.M., Monday through Saturday.*

*Reservations: Recommended.*

*Wheelchair accessibility: Everything on one level.*

In early 1988 Larry Forgione, the celebrated American chef, moved from his small town-house restaurant on upper Lexington Avenue to much larger quarters on Park Avenue near 32nd Street. Those who have followed Mr. Forgione's cooking from the River Café in the early 1980s will recognize his distinctive repertory at this airy new spot, formerly Ritz Café and La Coupole.

Postmodern accents on the mahogany-sheathed columns and sponged yellow walls are mirrored in the contemporary furnishings. Tables are well spaced and (how rare in New York!) generous with elbow room; flexible wooden armchairs look forbidding but actually fit well.

Mr. Forgione has carried many of his signature dishes downtown, including the diverting three-smoked-fish terrine, featuring layers of salmon, whitefish, and sturgeon garnished with their caviars. One of the most splendid combinations is plump baked oysters, their pristine brininess boosted by sea-urchin roe in a chive-butter sauce (though stiffly priced at $10.50 for three oysters). Smoked-fish chowder is marvelously subtle, better than the monochromatic lentil-and-tomato soup with a slick of mint cream.

Two duck concoctions are worth trying: the zesty duck sausage combined with spoon-bread griddlecakes flecked with scallions, and cornmeal pancakes rolled around shreds of spicy roasted duck explosive with cilantro and surrounded by grilled red onions.

The (all-American, naturally) wine list is well chosen, neither bargain priced nor extortionate.

When Mr. Forgione reaches into the home cupboard for ingenuous American fare, he is one of the best cooks around. But sometimes histrionics supplant harmony, as in the perfectly fine roasted salmon encased in granitic cracked wheat, or the pretty but pale combination of sea bass with steamed mussels and wilted spring greens. Two free-range chicken dishes are enticing: the grilled boneless version with ham, scallions, and mushroom hash browns, and the sautéed breast of chicken with apple-cider vinegar sauce and sautéed apples. The charred Black Angus steak with a caramelized onion sauce, grilled leeks, and soothing potato gratin is a delight, as is the lamb encrusted with goat cheese and herbs along with sautéed fennel and whipped potatoes.

Among seafood entrées, mahi-mahi in a nubbly, semi-sweet corn-and-red-pepper relish is scintillating; so, too, is a special of buttery pompano in a shrimp-stock sauce with pasta.

The superior Betty Crocker assortment of desserts includes snappy lemon meringue tart, wonderful bread pudding under a sweet bourbon sauce, double-rich chocolate pudding, clove-scented apple pandowdy, and superb homemade ice creams. Devil's food cake was as dry as newspaper one evening, better the next time, and strawberry shortcake, which I have always swooned over here, was vitiated by a gummy, undercooked biscuit.

# AMSTERDAM'S BAR AND ROTISSERIE

★

*428 Amsterdam Avenue, between 80th and 81st streets, 874-1377.*

*Atmosphere: Frenzied café and bar; back room preferable when restaurant is busy.*

*Service: Able, casual, and harried.*

*Wine: Small, well-chosen selection at very reasonable prices.*

*Price range: Moderate.*

*Credit cards: All major cards.*

*Hours: Lunch, noon to 5 P.M.; dinner, 5 to midnight, Sunday through Thursday; 5 P.M. to 1 A.M., Friday and Saturday.*

*Reservations: Not accepted.*

*Wheelchair accessibility: Dining available in front room; men's room on same level, ladies' room up five steps.*

When Amsterdam's Bar and Rotisserie opened in 1984 on the Upper West Side, it created a feeding frenzy of uniquely Manhattan proportions, resulting in a nightly mob scene that made Saturday afternoon at Zabar's seem like a serene stroll through the Cloisters. The formula for success was as ingenuous as it was ingenious: serve comforting American food—rotisserie-cooked chicken, fish, and beef—at moderate prices in a gregarious setting.

That strategy still packs them in, although visits in the past year indicate that food quality has slipped and that the staff at times has a complacent, take-it-or-leave-it attitude. The no-reservations policy makes it risky to venture there hungry, especially on weekends, when waits of forty-five minutes are not uncommon. On such frenzied evenings it is insufferably loud at the tables in the front room between the bar and the open rotisserie section. The elevated back room, with its whitewashed brick walls, black tin ceiling, and tightly assembled café tables under red-and-white tablecloths, is marginally more accommodating.

For a restaurant that serves a limited, simple repertory, it is difficult to understand how quality can be so uneven. Marinated shrimp salad with watercress can be fresh and tasty in its garlic-and-lemon vinaigrette at lunch, insipid and stale at dinner. Even the roast chicken—and the kitchen goes through three thousand pounds a week—is hit or miss. At peak dinner hour, when the chickens are spinning off the rotisserie nonstop, the meat arrives moist and with a nice blistered skin that only this cooking method can impart; if you go at off hours, the bird may have been cooked in advance and left on a holding table to get flabby and dry. Moreover, the green herb sauce that comes with it, redolent of basil, sometimes arrives icy from the refrigerator.

Soups are good, such as creamy butternut squash and chicken-and-barley strong with mushroom flavor. The sesame-and-ginger-swathed noodles are a vivid starter, as is the subtle and silken gravlax with capers, brown bread, and a tangy mustard vinaigrette.

Whole Norwegian salmon is cooked on the flaming rotisserie, too, and the result can be pleasing. The rich pink fillet is enhanced with a light lemon, arugula, and cream sauce and accompanied by green beans and french fries. French fries, which accompany many dishes, are clean and crisp, as are roasted new potatoes. One of the best rotisserie-cooked items is the shell steak, which comes out nicely seared, pink in the center and succulent, along with a caper-mustard sauce. The wine list helps keep the tab down, with twenty well-chosen, inexpensive selections.

Desserts to try include a belt-stretching but irresistible chocolate mascarpone mousse layered with praline and vanilla custard and equally rich Mississippi mud cake.

# AMSTERDAM'S GRAND

★

*454 Broadway, at Grand, on the east side of Broadway, 925-6166.*

*Atmosphere: High-ceiling, two-tier restaurant done in black and white. Open rotisserie kitchen and long, comfortable bar. Informal.*

*Service: Pleasant young staff, generally efficient. Service tends to be better in rear dining room.*

*Wine: Good basic wine list, well priced.*

*Price range: Moderate.*

*Hours: Brunch, noon to 5 P.M., Saturday, 1 to 5 P.M., Sunday; lunch, 11:30 A.M. to 5 P.M., Monday through Friday; dinner, 5 to 9 P.M., Sunday and Monday, 5 to 11 P.M., Tuesday and Wednesday; 5 to midnight, Thursday, 5 P.M. to 1 A.M., Friday and Saturday (kitchen closes around midnight).*

*Credit cards: All major cards.*

*Reservations: Suggested.*

*Wheelchair accessibility: Restrooms downstairs.*

This downtown branch of the original Amsterdam's on the Upper West Side is a long, two-tier space done in sharp-edged shades of black and white, with a bar along one side and an open rotisserie grill on the other. This is a good place to stop for a fire-blistered and moist roast chicken, superior french fries, or simple salads. One of the appealing aspects of Amsterdam's is that you can drop in for a glass of wine and eat just an appetizer or an entrée, and get away for under $30 a person.

The house salad's ingredients vary slightly from day to day, but foraging usually turns up roasted red and yellow peppers, Black Forest ham, rotisserie-grilled chicken, sirloin strips, sun-dried tomatoes, zucchini, smoked Gouda, duck, and anything else within arm's reach of the chef.

Like the food, the wine list is straightforward and priced for the average financially overextended New Yorker. You can expect more attentive service in the back dining room than in the front one near the bar. Waiters and waitresses are efficient in a peremptory sort of way.

The short roster of lighter dishes (there is no distinct appetizer list) includes a meatloaf-thick slab of smooth-textured duck-liver mousse that could use a bolstering of seasonings; pretty red-tinted Swedish shrimp—they are pleasantly saline though not as fresh-tasting as those at the uptown restaurant—and delicious, glossy gravlax with a dill-mustard sauce.

Desserts are intended not to dazzle but to delight, and they succeed, particularly the sharp gooseberry tart and lustrous chocolate velvet mousse cake.

# ANATOLIA

★

*1422 Third Avenue, between 80th and 81st streets, 517-6262.*

*Atmosphere: Pastel-and-neon casual dining room; can be loud.*

*Service: Prompt and congenial.*

*Wine: Small wine list exceptionally well priced.*

*Price range: Moderate (pretheater dinner prix fixe, $19.50).*

*Credit cards: American Express, MasterCard, and Visa.*

*Hours: Lunch, noon to 2:30 P.M., Monday through Saturday; dinner, 5:30 to 11 P.M., Monday through Thursday, 5:30 to 11:30 P.M., Friday and Saturday, 5 to 10:30 P.M., Sunday, pretheater dinner, 5:30 to 7 P.M. Closed Sundays after Independence Day until the end of August.*

*Reservations: Suggested.*

*Wheelchair accessibility: Front dining room on main level; ramp to second level. Two steps down to restrooms.*

Anatolia offers a colorful rendition of cuisine from Turkey and the Middle East in an upbeat setting. The formula succeeds up to a point, but repeated visits indicate that inconsistency remains a problem.

The pastel-washed dining room sets a lighthearted tone with its lavender ceiling, simulated stone walls, faux Doric columns, streaking neon tubes, and spacy, saucer-shaped lights. Waiters glide around in their billowing costumes patiently describing the exotic cuisine to customers.

Cold appetizers come on a giant tray; many look more impressive than they taste. A purée of grilled eggplant boosted with garlic and parsley is unpredictable, fresh and deliciously smoky or bitter with raw garlic. White bean salad flecked with red onions and doused with a lemony vinaigrette is invigorating, as are pan-fried eggplant under a piquant garlic-yogurt sauce, pristine baby octopus salad, and grape leaves stuffed with rice, currants, and pine nuts.

A classic Turkish preparation called Circassian chicken is made by smothering shredded chicken meat with a walnut-and-garlic purée: at one sampling it is peppery and bright, another time drab. One of the recommended beef dishes is called "ladies thigh" kofte, a dill-infused meat patty topped with grated kasseri cheese (a salty sheep's or goat's milk cheese).

Anatolia has an exceptionally well-priced little wine list. Beer also goes well with this food.

Lamb is a staple in Turkey, and among the renditions offered here are succulent lamb shanks braised in vegetable broth and served with a light lemon sauce (the shank is prepared in tomato sauce occasionally) and sultan's bliss, a tender pan-seared lamb steak in a light tomato sauce accompanied by eggplant purée. The most compelling dish on the menu is boneless quail wrapped in grape leaves and grilled over charcoal, accompanied by rice with currants and pine nuts.

Among seafoods, skewered swordfish is dry and bland. The best is red snapper fillet that had been marinated with

Turkish raki (an ouzolike liqueur) and sautéed with onions, olives, peppers, and tomatoes.

If you can get over the psychological hurdle of a dessert pudding that contains shredded chicken, it might be worth trying the kazandibi, which is light, semisweet, and caramelized on top: it tastes nothing like chicken. Other choices are the delicious orange-scented baklava with its brittle pastry crust (walnut and pistachio versions are available, too), fresh chocolate-yogurt tart or, for fiber fans, a honey-drizzled baked dish of shredded wheat.

# ANDIAMO!

★ ★

*1991 Broadway, near 67th Street, 362-3315.*

*Atmosphere: Dramatic loft space with abstract art and track lighting. Moderate noise level. Completely nonsmoking restaurant.*

*Service: Professional and pleasant; timing sometimes slow.*

*Wine: Impressive selection, particularly from Italy, at reasonable prices.*

*Price range: Moderate (pretheater dinner, table d'hôte, prix fixe, $26–$32).*

*Credit cards: American Express, MasterCard, and Visa.*

*Hours: Brunch, 11:30 A.M. to 3 P.M., Saturday and Sunday; dinner, 5:30 to 11:30 P.M., Monday through Saturday, 4 to 9 P.M., Sunday.*

*Reservations: Suggested.*

*Wheelchair accessibility: Dining on ground level; restrooms downstairs.*

I must admit to having been skeptical, indeed almost cynical, upon seeing Andiamo! for the first time. It had all the trappings of yet another overdesigned underachieving Upper West Side pasta house: the silly name, the soaring loft space, striking oversize artwork, self-promotional newspaper blowups outside. But in this case the hype has some substance behind it.

Andiamo!, just two blocks north of Lincoln Center, lost its chef, Frank Crispo, in late 1990, so it is yet to be seen whether the new team can keep pace. The menu as of this writing is more or less the same.

You have to search to find Andiamo! for it is tucked away down a corridor behind a casual street-front spot called Cafe Bel Canto with the same ownership. Inside you encounter an airy loft with a balcony reached by an iron staircase. Track lighting shows off the abstract paintings, and on a makeshift stage a papier-mâché saloon pianist is frozen in mid-melody. Tables are comfortably spaced, and noise dissipates into the stratosphere.

Appetizers are little more than palate teasers, but they are vibrantly executed. Start with springy fresh smoked mozzarella with roasted peppers, or excellent lean carpaccio of beef under flakes of sharp Parmesan and sparkling caponata. Baked eggplant-and-mozzarella fritters are light and clean tasting, as are sautéed shrimp over lettuce and cucumbers slickened with a lemon-and-oregano vinaigrette.

Pastas are an engaging way to start, and virtually all are good. Top billing goes to an occasional special that combines a sheet of raw salmon under fettuccine tossed in a dill cream sauce. The hot pasta barely cooks the salmon in the plate, and the combination is sublime. Other memorable combinations are the crab-meat-filled tortelli (a variation of ravioli) in sweet carrot butter flecked with black pepper, spinach raviolini filled with minced veal in a sage cream sauce, and angel hair awash in a rich seafood broth touched with saffron along with salmon, shrimp, baby octopus, mussels, and scallops.

Three cheers for the low-key waiters and waitresses who present your meal along with a small pepper grinder and say, "It's here if you need it." Let's hope this becomes a trend. The service staff is well informed and diligent, although the kitchen seems to get thrown off pace at busy times. Nonsmokers will delight in the absolute ban on smoking on the premises, including the restrooms.

For entrées, you can choose something as straightforward as a nicely seared shell steak with golden rosti potatoes or picture-perfect lamb chops with a balsamic-vinegar-sharpened stock sauce. Rabbit confit can be alternately dry and moist, the result of uneven cooking. Seafood is nicely prepared, whether it is fillet of snapper under a lobster-thyme butter sauce or roasted monkfish in a lovely fish-broth-based sauce with addictive garlic chips and a mélange of vegetables.

Andiamo! has compiled an impressive collection of wines, especially from Italy. Selections in the $20 category are more than adequate.

For dessert, ice creams and sorbets are splendid. A trademark presentation here is a trio of ice creams with respective sauces—chocolate mint with crème anglaise, espresso with chocolate sauce, pistachio with caramel sauce—separated on the plate by strips of meringue. Slices of ripe pears form a tower with layers of brittle pastry, incredible mint chocolate ice cream, and caramel sauce. Chocolate ganache torte with vanilla sauce is no slouch either.

# AQUAVIT

★ ★

*13 West 54th Street, 307-7311.*

*Atmosphere: Sleek café and bar; dramatic eight-story atrium dining room.*

*Service: Laconic and workmanlike; kitchen slow.*

*Wine: Wide-ranging, expensive list with decent buys among Loire and Alsace whites.*

*Price range: Expensive.*

*Credit cards: All major cards.*

*Hours: Lunch, noon to 2:30 P.M., Monday through Friday, (until 3 P.M. upstairs); dinner, 5:30 to 10:30 P.M., Monday through Saturday.*

*Reservations: Necessary for the main dining room. Not accepted in the upstairs café for lunch only.*

*Wheelchair accessibility: Difficult steps at the entrance and to the downstairs dining room. Special arrangements can be made for patrons who call in advance.*

Lightheartedness is not a trait that comes to mind when one thinks of sun-starved, hard-working Scandinavians. So I'm never surprised upon entering Aquavit, the Nordic palace on West 54th Street, to encounter an impassive hostess at the door who whispers, "Reservations?"

"Thank you, we're happy to be here, too," I want to say, but decline for fear it would draw a blank stare. I find much about Aquavit cool and mechanical. It's not a place I would go to celebrate a promotion or birthday, but that's not to say it lacks appeal. The setting is dramatic and accommodating, much of the food beguiling, and the aquavit selection—if you are a fan of this potato-distilled liquor—is, well, heady.

This bi-level establishment, in the former John D. Rockefeller town house, is owned by SSRS, a Swedish hotel and restaurant chain. At the upper-level café and bar you can sample eight varieties of flavored aquavit along with light meals, including smorrebrod, savory Danish open-faced sandwiches with such combinations as velvety smoked salmon swathed with horseradish cream on rye pumpernickel bread; liver pâte, bacon, aspic, and horseradish; and a gravlax club sandwich on seven-grain bread with a green salad.

More formal meals are served downstairs in a towering eight-story glass-walled atrium with colorful mobiles overhead, a sloping gray-tile waterfall, and diffused lighting. One vexing problem is the oil-fueled lanterns on the tables. When you are downwind of one, the odor resembles choice stretches of the New Jersey Turnpike.

Most of the starters are various cold combinations of fish and caviars. Gravlax is de rigueur here. Made with farm-raised Norwegian salmon, it is sublimely buttery, infused with dill, and dusted with white peppercorns. A waiter mixes the condiment of fresh dill and mustard at the table.

The smorgasbord plate is a sparkling diorama of bleak roe, shrimp, smoked salmon, several kinds of herring, gravlax, and boiled potatoes: a fine assortment, but it hardly justifies a $6 supplement to the $60 prix-fixe menu. The mustard herring is particularly good. A dish called Swedish West Coast salad ($5 supplement) is a bore, reminiscent of a delicatessen party platter: bland mussels, cold lobster tail, decent crabmeat, sweet shrimp, peas, tomatoes, mixed greens, and asparagus. Scandinavian potato cakes, thin and crusty, are delightful with bleak roe, sour cream, and red onions.

The laconic waiters and waitresses will explain unusual foods if you ask, and otherwise are marginally attentive. It's the kitchen, not the staff, that seems unusually sluggish, which is surprising since most of the food is uncomplicated. The wide-ranging, generally expensive wine list has a few more reasonably priced wines than before. Look to Alsace, the Loire, and domestic sauvignon blancs for the best buys.

Game aficionados should home in on two superior entrées. Loin of Arctic venison is far more distinctive than domestic venison, with an earthy, aged flavor. Here it is served rare and is exquisitely tender, moistened with a mild apple-juniper sauce and accompanied by celery-root purée. Hazel grouse, which is found in the Arctic Circle, also has a gamy but not high taste, served with a thick stock sauce touched with juniper essence, and a fried potato basket holding mushrooms and pickled pears.

Among seafood entrées, well-executed classics include sautéed halibut with a brown butter sauce and capers, and poached turbot with the same brown butter glaze, horseradish, and boiled potatoes—fine, but nothing you couldn't get in a decent French bistro. More indigenous is the house favorite, salmon fillet sautéed on one side until crispy, and presented over a blend of black beans and black-eyed peas, tomatoes, and peas. The exuberant composition is ringed by a light red-pepper purée. Also recommended is the rare-baked salmon dotted with toasted almond slivers and set over a bed of spinach. The only disappointment was juniper-smoked salmon, which was excellent in all respects except for its lack of juniper flavor.

Desserts as a rule are simple and satisfying. Sliced apples baked in parchment paper sizzle under an advancing glacier of vanilla ice cream; thin crêpes come with excellent rum ice cream, and apple cake—exceptionally moist and chunky—is given new life here with crème anglaise. And brambleberry sorbet is astonishingly smooth, tart and sweet at the same time.

# ARCADIA

★ ★

*21 East 62nd Street, 223-2900.*

*Atmosphere: Cozy, attractive dining room with wraparound sylvan mural; bar dining area is loud and cramped.*

*Service: Forgetful and sloppy in the bar; better in the dining room.*

*Wine: Exceptionally well chosen, limited list; fair prices.*

*Price range: Expensive.*

*Credit cards: American Express, MasterCard, and Visa.*

*Hours: Lunch, noon to 2 P.M., Monday through Friday; dinner, 6 to 10 P.M., Monday through Saturday.*

*Reservations: Necessary.*

*Wheelchair accessibility: Everything on one level.*

Anne Rosenzweig is back full time in the kitchen of this highly successful American restaurant after a stint splitting her time as consulting chef at the "21" Club. Revisits have confirmed that the food at Arcadia still has homey, full-flavored appeal.

Arcadia is one of the most charming dining rooms in town, with its wraparound sylvan mural by Paul Davis, soft peripheral lighting, and burgundy banquettes. The only problem is that the space gets stuffy and clamorous when full. Don't get stuck in the two aisle tables unless you want to be jostled by waiters coming and going.

Alluring starters include penne in a creamy smoked-salmon sauce; grilled quail set atop cinnamon-tinted couscous; corn blini with sour cream and caviar; and exceptionally well blended Caesar salad. Black bean soup is still an unqualified winner, thick and hammy, zesty with hot pepper, and garnished with a sliver of goat cheese.

Rarely do I see diners agonize over menu orders as they do at Arcadia. Something as simple as roast chicken can be sublime, its skin golden and puffed, the meat remarkably moist, along with a delicious combination of spinach and sweet potatoes assembled in layers. Roasted cod is excellent, as are sea scallops in rich-flavored shellfish broth with a crouton swathed with spicy rouille.

A house specialty is called chimney-smoked lobster. The lobster is smoked and grilled at the same time over a wood-fired grate and served with aromatic tarragon buttter. The smoke-tinged meat is precut and served in the shell, accompanied by deliciously crunchy deep-fried celery-root cakes. Equally good are grilled sea scallops over a fricassee of Jerusalem artichokes, scallions, and tomatoes. Buttery sautéed spaetzle adds a soothing touch.

The wine selection, while relatively limited, is first-rate and fairly priced across the board.

Arcadia loyalists will steer you to the ineffably soothing chocolate bread pudding with brandy custard sauce. For an undiluted chocolate fix, try the bittersweet chocolate terrine with whipped cream and almond tuiles. Warm banana dumplings with caramel sauce, however, are achingly sweet. Go instead with the homemade espresso ice cream in a tuile cookie or the prunes poached in red wine with sharp cinnamon ice cream.

# ARIZONA 206

★ ★ ★

*206 East 60th Street, 838-0440.*

*Atmosphere: Adobe cavelike look with rough-beamed ceiling and natural wood tables.*

*Service: Casual but vigilant and professional.*

*Wine: Broad and well-priced selection of American labels.*

*Price range: Moderately expensive.*

*Credit cards: All major cards.*

*Hours: Lunch, noon to 3 P.M., Monday through Saturday; dinner, 6 to 11 P.M., Monday through Saturday, 6 to 10:30 P.M., Sunday.*

*Reservations: Necessary.*

*Wheelchair accessibility: Three small steps down into restaurant; special seating available in the bar (call ahead); restrooms downstairs.*

Any cook with a bag of jalapeños can ladle out the fiery dishes; it takes finesse to create an exciting and harmonious balance. No place does it better than Arizona 206, the Southwestern-style restaurant in the shadow of Bloomingdale's.

Brendan Walsh, who brought the restaurant to national prominence, left in early 1989 and was replaced by his longtime second, Marilyn Frobuccino. The transition was seamless. Not only has the food reached a new level of refinement and consistency in the last few years, but the staff, too, has finally learned to handle the nightly stampede with aplomb and grace. Don't be put off by the nonchalant waiters in blue denim shirts and string ties. They patrol the room constantly with eagle eyes, swooping down unobtrusively whenever needs arise.

The dining room's Southwestern setting is achieved with undulating molded plaster walls, bare wooden floors and tables, and clusters of desert flowers and braided peppers. Some of the tables are too neighborly for comfort, and conversations tend to echo off the cavelike walls. (A small adjacent annex called Arizona 206 Cafe serves a different menu featuring appetizer-size portions.)

The current menu is wisely limited in size. Buckwheat blini topped with minced smoked salmon, minced poblano peppers, sour cream, and osetra caviar are a zesty American twist on the Russian Tea Room signature dish. Oysters dusted with blue corn are delightfully crunchy, even better with their serrano-and-lime-tinted butter and sweet shallots on the side. At $35 a pound, barbecued foie gras is not something you are likely to see Dad flipping on the hibachi at summer picnics, so sample it here. Blistered and slightly charred outside, pink and silken within, it is an extraordinary taste sensation along with a sweet, fibrous cactus pear salad.

Next to such kinetic starters, the gorditas—dense tortillas topped with a blend of peanuts, pork, veal, scallions, and green tomato salsa—seem common, although they probably suffer only by comparison. Beer is appropriate for this rodeo of the palate, but the wine list carries a well-priced selection of domestic labels, many of which have the requisite staying power.

There is not a weak link among the entrées. Rib eye of lamb is exquisitely smoky, rare as requested, along with a smoldering tomato-chili sauce and ratatouille tossed with crumbled goat cheese. Roast quail is superb, crisp and succulent, with buttery polenta and green beans; equally good is the pan-roasted baby chicken with masked rutabagas and potatoes.

Pistachio-coated rabbit is another entrée to watch for. The firm, moist meat is fork-tender and enclosed in a carapace of sweet, crushed nuts. Mole poblano, a spicy, dark red sauce with a hint of desert aridness, enhances the combination; the creamy greens douse the fires.

Among seafood selections, there is an excellent grilled salmon with pulpy smoked tomatoes and a flanlike corn pudding sharpened with minced poblano peppers. The paella for two rivals that of any Spanish restaurant in town. The rice has just the right resiliency and is explosive with the flavors of andouille sausage, garlic sausage, green chilies, mussels, clams, and chicken.

Desserts are relatively traditional but well executed. Apple-cranberry crisp is fresh and crunchy from the addition of toasted pumpkin seeds. White chocolate ice cream is not so cloying as it usually is elsewhere, and simple vanilla custard is cleansing and delicious with tangerines and raspberries on top.

Arizona 206's growth under Mr. Walsh fortunately has not diminished with his departure. Today, as before, it has no peers when it comes to Southwestern cuisine.

# ARQUÀ

★ ★

*281 Church Street, corner of White Street, 334-1888.*

*Atmosphere: Large, airy minimalist space with soft ocher-colored walls. Loud at times.*

*Service: Genial and knowledgeable.*

*Wine: Well-chosen, small list.*

*Price range: Moderate.*

*Credit cards: American Express.*

*Hours: Lunch, noon to 3 P.M., Monday through Friday; dinner, 5:30 to 11 P.M., Monday through Thursday; 5:30 to 11:30 P.M., Friday and Saturday.*

*Reservations: Necessary.*

*Wheelchair accessibility: Several stairs at the entrance; restrooms downstairs.*

This airy and animated restaurant, one of the best places for pasta downtown, is housed in a towering former industrial space that is given warmth by its ocher-toned walls, which evoke ancient sandstone churches aglow at sunset. Large circular Art Deco sconces ricochet soft light across the tables.

Arquà is named after a village in northeastern Italy that was the home of the fourteenth-century poet and philosopher Petrarch. Leonardo Pulito, the young Italian-born chef, has a highly developed sense of balance when it comes to flavors and textures. The cold antipasto plate, for example, includes slices of rolled veal paired with a sweet-hot mustard aspic, as well as roasted red peppers, onions, and a sprightly bean salad. I could make a lunch of that alone with some of the excellent thick-crusted country-style bread. Another good starter is the pretty arrangement of artichoke leaves slathered with olive purée and crowned with bacon strips and a dusting of Parmesan. Grilled radicchio leaves are enhanced by melted nutty taleggio cheese.

Parties of four or more might nibble on two or three appetizers to leave room for half orders of pasta before the entrée. You might start with pappardelle del dogi, long flat strips of resilient homemade noodles layered with ricotta cheese, radicchio leaves, and Italian sausage—it just needed a few shakes of salt to bring out the subtle flavors. Agnolotti, little spinach-filled pasta curls, are wonderfully light and tasty in their fresh tomato sauce thickened with creamy mascarpone cheese, as are mattonella d'Arquà, thin sheets of pasta layered with artichoke purée and topped with béchamel and grated Parmesan cheese, and fettuccine all'anatra in a gutsy duck sauce.

The Holy Trinity of North Italian cuisine—gnocchi, risotto, and polenta—is beautifully executed here. The feathery little gnocchi are superb; the preparation changes daily, usually bathed in some variation of light tomato sauce with sage, basil, rosemary, or other fresh herbs. Risotto, which also comes in various disguises, is outstanding. Polenta is creamy and lusty, blended with sausage and wild mushrooms. The limited wine list is well chosen, offering some bright and fresh selections.

Other good bets are calf's liver with onions, flanked by triangles of toasted polenta, and chicken al Prosecco (the sparkling wine from Veneto), in which the breast is combined with a Prosecco-and-cream sauce bound with olive paste and mushrooms.

A standout entrée that is occasionally offered as a special is salmon steak wrapped in radicchio leaves and braised in white wine and fish stock, then sprinkled with balsamic vinegar to add an invigorating touch before serving.

Desserts are appropriately light—and irresistible. Ricotta cheesecake has a lively lemony touch; cocoa-dusted tiramisù, made with espresso-drenched ladyfingers and sweetened mascarpone cheese, is habit-forming; and the world's lightest napoleon should come under glass to keep the pastry from blowing away.

# AUNTIE YUAN

★ ★

*1191A First Avenue, near 65th Street, 744-4040.*

*Atmosphere: Dramatic all-black dining room with pinpoint overhead lighting.*

*Service: Knowledgeable and efficient.*

*Wine: Small list, well suited to Chinese food.*

*Price range: Moderately expensive.*

*Credit cards: American Express and Diners Club.*

*Hours: Lunch, noon to 4 P.M., daily; dinner, 4 P.M. to midnight, Monday through Saturday, noon to 11 P.M., Sunday.*

*Reservations: Suggested.*

*Wheelchair accessibility: Everything on one level.*

Auntie Yuan, the midnight-cool, elegantly modern Chinese restaurant on First Avenue, is the most enduring and consistent member of the David Keh clan (Pig Heaven, David K's). Lighting in the coal-black dining room approximates that of a movie theater at intermission. Overhead spotlights illuminate solitary pink orchids on the well-spaced tables, and the black fabric banquettes would be ideal for napping. Tuxedo-clad captains run the prompt, helpful service staff.

It is surprising to see Auntie Yuan so quiet at lunch though busy at dinner. Perhaps it's the dark room. I must admit that re-entering sunlight after lunch there caused retinal shock that had me doing Bela-Lugosi-at-sunrise impersonations for two blocks.

Auntie Yuan has a strong core menu of regional dishes with a few nods to Western tastes: Oriental-style salmon dishes, for example, wines by the glass, and sorbets for dessert. It is still the place I go when a yearning for Peking duck strikes. The skin is always potato-chip thin and sweetly glazed, with a layer of fat underneath to impart richness; the meat is pink and flavorful. Orange beef, a potential source of interminable indigestion when poorly prepared, is a paragon here: slightly crunchy outside, fibrous but tender inside, with its sweetness foiled by pungent flecks of orange rind, garlic slivers, and hot peppers.

Chicken is prepared with zest if you get it sliced with hot peppers waiting in ambush, or the home-style version with spinach and garlic; less interesting but satisfying are chicken with snow peas and chicken with walnuts. Most of the seafood sampled was recommendable. Sliced sea scallops get a needed boost from a saline black-bean sauce, along with scallions and broccoli.

Cleanly fried strips of flounder are appealing on their own; not so when combined with a glutinous sweet sauce garnished with peas and raisins. A side order of well-seasoned poached spinach saved the day.

Auntie Yuan still offers a small wine list and about six wines by the glass. Chablis and Gewürztraminer seem to work well with this food, as does sparkling wine.

Nibbles at the start of the meal are sometimes the most engaging part. Bite into a delicious steamed-shrimp-and-scallop dumpling and watch your dining mates duck for cover as the juice spurts out. Shanghai-style steamed pork dumplings are vibrant with ginger, while crescent-shaped vegetarian dumplings are packed with spinach brightened with grated ginger. Barbecued quails are still a house favorite, and with good reason: they are moist, appealingly crunchy, and sweet. Chicken soong, those lettuce packets filled with rice noodles and squiggles of meat, is helped by a dip in soy sauce. Another good starter is the salad of sliced duck tossed with crinkly rice noodles and sesame seeds.

Desserts, like the commercial-tasting sorbets, are mundane. Stick with fresh fruit.

# AUREOLE

★ ★

*34 East 61st Street, 319-1660.*

*Atmosphere: Airy, cream-and-beige-colored dining room with mezzanine area. Noise moderate.*

*Service: Efficient, knowledgeable.*

*Wine: Moderately priced list well suited to the food.*

*Price range: Moderately expensive.*

*Credit cards: American Express, MasterCard, and Visa.*

*Hours: Lunch, noon to 2:30 P.M., Monday through Saturday; dinner, 6 to 10:30 P.M., Monday through Thursday, 6 to 11 P.M., Friday and Saturday.*

*Reservations: Necessary.*

*Wheelchair accessibility: Three steps down at entrance; also steps down into the dining room. Restrooms downstairs.*

The star attraction at this studiously unpretentious East Side spot is Charles Palmer, who made his mark dazzling customers with eclectic French-American cooking at Brooklyn's River Café. His partners in Aureole (it means halo in French) are Nicolette Kotsoni and Steve Tzolis, who also own Il Cantinori on West 10th Street and Periyali on West 20th Street. From its successful but hectic beginning two years ago Aureole has been getting stronger with maturity.

From the street through a two-story window you can see the cream-colored walls adorned with plaster representations of sundry wildlife, not all of which is on the menu. The dining rooms, including the upholstered banquettes, are done in soft beiges, with clusters of flowers here and there to brighten the scene. Tables are fairly close, but the towering space, with its more private mezzanine, diffuses noise well. In keeping with Mr. Palmer's rural, easygoing background, Aureole shuns the pomposity of so many ambitious restaurants. Waiters are well schooled and efficient yet just familiar enough to be likable.

One of the surprises among appetizers is a "sandwich" of sea scallops in which a brittle lid of sautéed potatoes rests atop the meltingly tender scallops glossed with a citric-edged shellfish stock—a rousing textural contrast. Tuna carpaccio gets a much-needed rejuvenation with the sheet of glistening fillet laid over mixed greens and wild mushrooms moistened with a lemony vinaigrette. Mr. Palmer is at his best with straightforward fare, like his splendid onion soup, a special, to which confit of duck and a hint of fresh thyme have been added.

Aureole's wine list is more impressive for its strength than its length: like the food, the wines are unconventional, with many surprises, especially among whites, that stand up to the abundance of citric sauces on the menu.

One example of Mr. Palmer's style is grouper, its snowy, crisp-skinned flesh glossed with sevruga caviar butter and paired with wonderfully crunchy noodle cake. However, venison with spaetzle came out tasting like slightly overcooked beef, surrounded by a jarring wine sauce harsh from nutmeg and garnished with mandarin plums and orange rind. Tea-smoked squab has lovely nuances of flavor from the tea, and it is cooked to pink perfection and enhanced with a balsamic vinegar sauce enriched with essence of foie gras. Roast chicken is sublime, its plump, firm meat larded with strips of Parma ham and served with a lovely ragout of artichokes and cloves of roasted garlic.

If you want to indulge in just one dessert, my suggestion is the remarkable mascarpone cheese torte, aptly called silken on the menu, cut with a double espresso sauce; lemon tart is refreshing, but pairing it with grapefruit sorbet seems like overkill. The incredibly intense jasmine tea ice cream is recommended only for hard-core tea lovers, while a leaning-tower mille-feuille is layered with unpleasantly bitter vanilla custard. On a plate the size of a hubcap comes a cylinder of bittersweet chocolate filled with ultra-rich chocolate mousse, garnished with chocolate truffles: consume at your own risk.

# AU TROQUET

★

*328 West 12th Street, corner of Greenwich and 12th streets, 924-3413.*

*Atmosphere: Cozy and comfortable, with moderate noise level.*

*Service: Inattentive and occasionally slow.*

*Price range: Moderately expensive.*

*Credit cards: All major cards.*

*Hours: Dinner, 6 to 11 P.M., Monday through Saturday.*

*Reservations: Necessary.*

*Wheelchair accessibility: One small step down; everything on one level.*

Au Troquet is everyone's idea of a romantic little French restaurant in Greenwich Village. It's a cozy, low-key spot with white-framed windows and lacy curtains, subdued lighting, and a young, discreet French staff.

The moderately priced menu carries an enticing-sounding roster that emphasizes Provence. This is the kind of place you really want to like, and while there are enough alluring dishes to win your affection, inconsistencies limit the restaurant's appeal.

A good way to begin is with the lean, pepper-dusted gravlax or the rough-textured and highly seasoned rabbit terrine. Seafood terrine, a special worth watching for, has scallops, salmon, and monkfish seasoned with basil. Not so the mussels in a shallot-sweetened broth, which smelled rank from over-the-hill mussels.

The dining room has considerable charm, but that doesn't necessarily mean I want to spend nearly three hours there at dinner, which occurred on two of three visits. Service can be exasperatingly slow: it's not clear whether the fault lies with the kitchen or the dining-room staff.

Main courses, especially the simplest ones, are better than

appetizers. You can get a gutsy steak au poivre with a piquant stock sauce; blood-warming pot-au-feu is nearly a soup, but the flavors meld beautifully. Other recommendations are the thick and tender veal chop with chanterelles and Madeira sauce, and marinated grilled swordfish with garlic and oregano.

Several dishes fall just shy of the target. For example, chicken legs stuffed with chicken mousse were attractive and interesting texturally, but the mousse was bland; shrimp Provençale was bright and herby, but the shrimp were overcooked. A better option is a special of sautéed sea bass, crisp-skinned and moist, in a delicate Bordelaise sauce. Snapper is equally appealing, paired with a zesty aïoli sauce. Both fish dishes, however, come with the same dried-out purées, one of carrots, the other of peas, and a limp twirl of pasta. The wine list is limited and undistinguished.

For dessert, frozen chestnut terrine on a pool of crème anglaise tops the list, followed by a good crème caramel. Forget the soggy profiteroles.

# AZZURRO

*1625 Second Avenue, at 84th Street, 517-7068.*

*Atmosphere: Cheerful if cramped little dining room. Can be loud.*

*Service: Friendly and concerned young staff does a first-rate job.*

*Wine: All-Italian wine list; good choices at fair prices.*

*Price range: Moderate.*

*Credit cards: American Express and Diners Club.*

*Hours: Dinner, 5:30 to 11 P.M., Monday through Thursday, 5:30 P.M. to midnight, Friday through Sunday.*

*Reservations: Necessary.*

*Wheelchair accessibility: Everything on one level.*

This minuscule, family-run place continues to turn out some stellar Sicilian-style pastas, salads, and seafood. Azzurro, as well as a newer sister restaurant, Baci on Amsterdam Avenue, are run by two personable young men, Marcello and Vittorio Sindoni, and their mother, Maria Maddalena Sindoni.

The dining room of Azzurro is a narrow rectangle with brick walls, a white tile floor, and tables along each wall. Overhead a dusk-blue ceiling is sprinkled with tiny inset lights that resemble stars.

The food is fresh, pure, and unpretentious. An appetizer of tart charred fresh endive, tied in little bundles with scallion strips and slickened with olive oil, is a delight. Homemade mozzarella that is so fresh that it is still warm is encased in a translucent slice of prosciutto and presented with ripe tomatoes and fresh basil. Caponata is among the best I have had, a chunky mélange of sweet eggplant, garlic, roasted red peppers, and basil.

The cold seafood salad, a special, features a cast of sparkling fresh bay scallops, shrimp, and squid in a mild olive-oil-and-garlic dressing. Minestrone, based on a good chicken stock, is lighter than most versions and explosive with the flavors of fresh vegetables.

Pastas are the highlights of the menu. The portions are so large they are best split between two if ordered as a middle course. Mrs. Sindoni performs magic with lowly cauliflower, blending its florets with pine nuts, raisins, basil, and Parmesan cheese to create a remarkable sauce for al dente rigatoni, an occasional special. Bucatini tossed with shredded sardines, raisins, wild fennel, and pine nuts, a Sicilian specialty, is another combination that prompted applause at my table. The combination is saline and faintly sweet at the same time. Other winners include thin noodles in a snowy ricotta cream sauce and penne with delicious roasted eggplant and salty sun-dried tomatoes.

The waiters remain admirably high-spirited and energetic as they weave their way dextrously among the tight tables. The all-Italian wine list is organized by courses, with suggestions for each. Good choices exist for under $25.

Entrées are not as uniformly superior as the first two courses. The best are grilled tuna Sicilian style, pan-sautéed and scattered with sweet red onions, basil, roasted peppers, and tomatoes (a special); grilled swordfish glistening under a coating of olive oil; grilled red snapper done the same way; and succulent baby lamb chops.

There are only two desserts, and they are a must: an espresso-rich tiramisù lathered with whipped mascarpone cheese and dusted with cocoa powder, and an airy napoleon constructed with the most fragile puff pastry.

# THE BALLROOM

★

*253 West 28th Street, 244-3005.*

*Atmosphere: Rustic, colorful tapas bar; main dining room spacious and comfortable. Classical guitarist. Cabaret room. Free parking available for dinner guests.*

*Service: Generally efficient.*

*Wine: Overpriced international list.*

*Price range: Moderately expensive.*

*Credit cards: All major cards.*

*Hours: Brunch, noon to 4 P.M., Sunday; lunch, noon to 3 P.M., Tuesday through Friday; dinner, 5 P.M. to midnight, Tuesday through Thursday, 5 P.M. to 1 A.M., Friday and Saturday.*

*Reservations: Suggested.*

*Wheelchair accessibility: Dining on ground level. Restrooms down a flight of stairs.*

At the Ballroom, the Chelsea restaurant and cabaret, the tapas bar does a fairly brisk business. Felipe Rojas-Lombardi, the Peruvian-born chef and owner, turns out a varied and generally tasty assortment of Iberian tidbits. It is always fun to have a drink and tapas before dinner at the long wooden bar under a curtain of garlic ropes, dried red chilies, Serrano hams, and dried salt cod.

Among the best tapas are the lemony seviche of bay scallops with a hot pepper afterburn; earthy snail-and-red-bean casserole; a moist, eggy tortilla made with potatoes, onions, and artichokes, and salty slices of Serrano ham.

Some of the best tapas are those cooked to order, which I suppose makes them appetizers and not tapas. Deep-fried squid rings are delectably light and golden. Seared cubes of quickly marinated swordfish are extraordinarily moist and tasty, as are the grilled jumbo shrimp. Among the more unusual starters are the tapas soups, coffee-cup portions of puréed vegetable soups—carrot, eggplant, or green pea—each with distinct seasonings. A lunch buffet of many of the tapas plus a cheese course is a good deal at $18.50.

Main courses can be ordered at tables flanking the bar or in the larger downstairs dining room, which is dominated by a giant mural of an artsy crowd in the original Ballroom in SoHo. A classical guitarist on an overhead platform plays at lunch and dinner.

Many customers order the paella here, and there are three to choose from. Don't count on the service staff to enlighten you on the differences. While waiters are personable and reasonably efficient, their knowledge of the food is sketchy.

The best is the saffron version, combining mildly spicy chorizo, rabbit, plump shrimp, clams, black mussels, and squid rings with moist, aromatic rice. The paella verde is potent with zesty coriander, giant New Zealand green mussels, sweetwater prawns (overcooked), pheasant (dry), and morcilla, a blood sausage. The negra version, tinted with squid ink, is fresh and nicely seasoned.

Two seafood dishes are deftly prepared: grilled salmon with sautéed onions, spaghetti squash, and quinoa, a Peruvian grain like barley with a faintly nutty flavor; and poached cod with aïoli and a searingly hot pepper sauce.

The Ballroom's wine list is overpriced across the board, most notably among the wines from California, Bordeaux, and Burgundy. I suggest the decent house red or white.

Desserts are displayed on a buffet table, and some look better than they taste. Pass up the achingly sweet chocolate raspberry cake and the oversugared flan. Better options are the rich, dark pecan pie, cheesecake, and moist orange poundcake. Fruit tarts, which change daily, are usually good bets, too.

# BANGKOK HOUSE

★

*1485 First Avenue, near 78th Street, 249-5700.*

*Atmosphere: Dark and sleek with mirrors and pastel walls. Moderately high noise level.*

*Service: Gracious and hard-working but often rushed.*

*Price range: Moderate.*

*Credit cards: American Express, MasterCard, and Visa.*

*Hours: Dinner, 5 to 11:30 P.M., nightly.*

*Reservations: Necessary.*

*Wheelchair accessibility: Dining room on street level; restrooms downstairs.*

Thai restaurants are the Benettons of the New York food scene: they are all over the place, they look distinctive from the outside, yet they all peddle virtually the same wares. Bangkok House on First Avenue near 78th Street is a notch above the pack, an energetic and engaging place where you can leave recalling more than just low prices.

One enters a long, shadowy room with a startling backdrop of lavender, green, and blue walls, tall mirrors, and dark carpeting. Clusters of pretty gladioli and mums soften the hard edges. The place is usually packed with extroverted young East Siders who consume formidable quantities of Singha, the Thai beer, with their meals. The decibel level can make conversation a challenge.

The encyclopedic menu is divided into food groups (chicken, beef, for example) and is simplified with a code borrowed from Bingo: you order B-2 for beef with coconut, N-1 for noodles with shrimp, and so on. While purists may find this a touristy gimmick, what would you rather ask for, F-18 (frogs' legs) or ka-gop gra-tiem prik-Thai?

Stimulating starters include the cigar-shaped rolls of ground shrimp in thin bean-curd skin, deep fried until golden and served with a sweet plum sauce, and zippy barbecued beef strips paired with a ground chili, lime, and onion sauce. The spring rolls—bean-curd-wrapped cabbage, bean sprouts, and ground pork—lack flavor; moreover, they were fished out of the oil too late, leaving them nearly burned. Two soups are soothing and brightly seasoned: the lemongrass broth holding shrimp and straw mushrooms, and tom ka gai, a hot and sweet marriage of chicken with coconut milk, onions, and chili. Two dishes listed as house specialties are letdowns: the fatigued and dry roast duck with hot sauce, and the classic deep-fried whole fish with a garlic-and-chili sauce called pla lad prik, which also was on the dry side.

Better options are perfectly sautéed shrimp set over pleasantly bitter Chinese cabbage, and the lovely sea scallops powered with lots of fresh ginger, scallions, and onions. Waiters here are good-natured and hard-working, although they don't offer much help when it comes to choosing dishes or filleting a whole fish.

The traditional Thai method of cooking beef and pork is to skewer slices of the meat, grill or sauté them, and serve them with an assortment of sauces on the side. This is performed reasonably well here with nur yang, in which beef is marinated in an aromatic spice mix, then grilled and offered with a hot garlic sauce (the meat itself has little flavor, but with the sauce it is delicious); a similar preparation with pork using garlic and white pepper is good, too.

Vegetable side dishes to consider are the terrific eggplant with black-bean sauce, and sautéed bitter cabbage with oyster sauce. Seven noodle and rice dishes are available, including a fresh and clean version of pad Thai, blending shrimp, egg, bean sprouts, and ground peanuts. Desserts are sticky sweet to my taste, including the coconut custard and fried banana with honey.

# BARBETTA

**SATISFACTORY**

*321 West 46th Street, 246-9171.*

*Atmosphere: Plush and baronial dining room; enchanting outdoor café.*

*Service: Sloppy and forgetful.*

*Wine: Substantial list, but sloppy and outdated in some areas.*

*Price range: Expensive (pretheater dinner prix fixe, $39).*

*Credit cards: All major cards.*

*Hours: Lunch, noon to 2 P.M., Monday through Saturday; pretheater dinner, 5 to 7 P.M., Monday through Saturday; dinner, 5:30 to 11:30 P.M., Monday through Saturday.*

*Reservations: Suggested.*

*Wheelchair accessibility: Three steps at the entrance; everything else on main floor, including restrooms.*

If the food quality lived up to the setting at Barbetta, the sumptuous Italian restaurant on West 46th Street, it would be one of the hits of the Broadway theater district. Lamentably that is not so.

The setting is palatial, with its pale yellow walls, the rococo sconces and regal chandeliers, and it boasts one of the prettiest outdoor gardens in New York. It is possible to have a pleasant experience at Barbetta, especially if you sit in the garden on a clement evening and order the right dishes. Of more than thirty dishes sampled, however, fewer than a third can be recommended.

Here's a winning strategy: start with some roasted peppers or the salad of tomatoes, mozzarella, and basil. The assorted antipasto carries the same peppers but is otherwise unexciting. And the house mixed salad is so drenched in vinegar it is inedible.

Next try one of the risottos, which are skillfully prepared

—full flavored and with just the right resilient texture. I had the savory version with wild mushrooms and morsels of chicken liver. If you want to try pasta, go with the tagliatelle, folded flat noodles, in a satiny tomato-cream sauce enlivened with basil. Linguine in pesto sauce is fresh but needs salt to bring out the flavors.

For the main course, the best bet is the simple but compelling pollo al babj, which is a pan-roasted chicken with a blistered golden skin emboldened by pepper. Another satisfying choice is the veal chop al verde, an extra-thick slab rich in flavor and combined with a white-wine-and-parsley sauce.

Broiled Dover sole remains a good seafood choice. Cold poached salmon with lemon mayonnaise can be exceedingly dry, while the tasteless cold trout has the texture of papier-mâché. Vegetables have steam-table texture and little seasoning.

For dessert, look for the fruit tarts of the day, which can be splendid, or the poached peach in a dense, concentrated zabaglione. One dessert on the menu is a terrific summer cooler, the granita of espresso crowned with whipped cream—for caffeine hounds only.

# BAROCCO

★ ★

*301 Church Street, at Walker Street, 431-1445.*

*Atmosphere: Airy, minimally disguised industrial loft; can be loud.*

*Service: Pleasant and competent, but not attentive to details.*

*Wine: Well-chosen list, moderately priced, but lacks enough inexpensive bottles.*

*Price range: Moderate.*

*Credit cards: All major cards.*

*Hours: Dinner, 6:30 to 11:30 P.M., Monday through Thursday, until midnight Friday and Saturday.*

*Reservations: Necessary.*

*Wheelchair accessibility: Several steps up at entrance; everything on one level. Too narrow for wheelchairs.*

Chances are you won't share a banquette with Sean Penn or Mikhail Baryshnikov at Barocco, a minimally camouflaged industrial space in TriBeCa. But you will eat well, and at prices that will allow cab fare home and maybe an Off-Broadway show.

The four-year-old Barocco is a relaxed trattoria that attracts a colorful cross section of downtowners. The barebones setting belies some stout yet refined cooking by Sandro Prosperi, one of the owners. The airy space has a casual bar up front, a high ceiling swathed in warehouse gray, glass-block windows, a peeling wooden floor, and white columns that actually have a structural purpose. One side door is resourcefully concealed with what looks like an old patterned bed sheet—not the Adam Tihany approach, but it does the job. Black banquettes and a cluster of tables in the center fill up quickly after 8:30 P.M., and the decibel level soars, so I prefer to dine there early or very late.

You can get off to a lusty start with either fettunta—small bricks of grilled country bread rubbed with garlic and doused with olive oil—or bruschetta, the same bread under minced tomatoes and fresh basil. Minestrone is a motherly delight, thick and boldly seasoned, as is the lentil-and-pea soup fortified with ham bone. Perhaps the best starter is the fried calamari, which is light as tempura and well seasoned.

The kitchen turns out some wonderfully orchestrated pastas, which can be split as appetizers. Most memorable is the unlikely sounding combination of pappardelle with tender morsels of rabbit and squab, along with black olives and sun-dried tomatoes in a well-herbed tomato sauce.

Another enticing dish was the fettuccine with firm, fresh artichoke hearts, tomato, pancetta, and shredded basil. Oddly enough, one of the simplest pastas missed the mark: penne with tomato, basil, and ricotta, which, at least relative to the others, tasted flat and undistinguished. The homemade ravioli are a paragon of refinement. One is filled with shredded duck, spinach, and a touch of sage under a light mixed-vegetable sauce. A spinach ravioli is filled with ricotta and Swiss chard, served with a well-seasoned fresh tomato-and-basil sauce.

Judging from the tables near mine, I would call the whole roasted red snapper a big mover. (The fish may change with market availability.) I sampled it twice, and both times it was moist and fragrant with fresh herbs. Rosemary-seasoned roasted potatoes and garlicky sautéed spinach made fine sidekicks. The last time I had it, I requested that the fish be deboned. The waitress replied, "No problem," then served it on the bone. This kind of thing can happen at Barocco, which is not exactly the Quilted Giraffe when it comes to service.

The staff gets the food to you promptly but don't expect much in the way of food or wine counsel, or little extras like wine pouring. Besides the red snapper, another good seafood choice is rare-grilled Norwegian salmon with a slightly acidic parsley-and-caper sauce that is a perfect foil for the rich fish. The same garlic-strewn spinach came with it, but this time the garlic had burned, leaving a harsh flavor. The chef has an affinity for rosemary, as it shows up everywhere, including the excellent rack of lamb. Strip steak is richly flavored and well charred, and the simple grilled chicken is moist and subtly flavored with an olive-oil-and-basil marinade. The homiest dish of all is the wonderfully mellow roast loin of pork with splendid mashed potatoes and spinach. Talk about Mom Food. Desserts can be excessively sweet, particularly the chocolate napoleon and the ultra-rich tiramisù, so I suggest you stick with the textbook crème caramel, poached pears with Marsala-flavored whipped cream, or the superb raisin-studded bread pudding.

# BELLEVUES

★

*496 Ninth Avenue, at 38th Street, 967-7855.*

*Atmosphere: Clean, white-tiled, dinerlike setting. Mobbed at night.*

*Service: Can be slow and distracted at night; better at lunch.*

*Wine: Well chosen and inexpensive.*

*Price range: Moderate.*

*Credit cards: None.*

*Hours: Lunch, 11:30 A.M. to 2:30 P.M., Monday through Friday; dinner, 6 P.M. to midnight, Monday through Saturday, until 11:30 P.M., Sunday.*

*Reservations: Necessary.*

*Wheelchair accessibility: Everything on one level. Room often cramped.*

The sparkling little white-tile-and-Formica French bistro is unexpected along the squalid stretch of Ninth Avenue south of the Port Authority Bus Terminal. "This is like Les Halles of New York!" exclaimed a lunch companion, one of those eternal urban optimists who could liken the IND Coney Island line to the Orient Express.

Inside, perched on stools at a long counter, is a cross section of midtown west: a young woman in a white tank top and leopard-skin shorts, a dark-suited man reading *The Wall Street Journal,* a pair of dressed-for-success businesswomen poking at salads, and a swatch of carrot-colored hair attached to a body of indeterminate gender. That's Bellevues.

One wants to love this place. It seems so indigenous, so uncalculated, from the aqua banquettes to the Formica tables and gallery of amateur photographs on the walls. The problem is, the food, once lusty and assertive, has lost some of its pizazz.

Salads and soups can be good—rich gratinéed onion or a rouille-enhanced seafood broth—and the subtly smoked chicken that comes with mixed greens and horseradish cream on the side is excellent. But charcuterie is decent commercial quality, nothing more: duck mousse is creamy but nondescript, pork rillettes are unevenly seasoned, and the pork terrine is bland. The boudin noir (blood sausage) with apples and onions, which I have enjoyed here in the past, tasted oddly anemic this time. Garlic sausage has some zip, though.

The kitchen still turns out top-notch french fries and real mashed potatoes. Both are lusty matches for the bavette (grilled flank steak), a juicy cut of meat that gives your choppers a good workout. Calf's liver is buttery and mild, smothered in sautéed onions. Cornmeal coating and a shrimp-bisque sauce do well by a sautéed tilefish with well-seasoned sautéed zucchini and squash, and grilled tuna with basil butter is nicely executed.

Two dishes one expects to shine in a humble bistro are bores: a dryish rabbit with mustard sauce and a veal paillard that is overly thick, underseasoned, and further abused by bitter burned shallots in the sauce. Grilled half chicken, nicely herbed, is always pleasing. Hold the side order of gloppy, oversauced gratinéed leeks, though. Bellevues keeps its limited, well-chosen wine list in line with food prices, with most bottles under $20. The nonchalant service staff does a better job at lunch than at dinner, when the mob can be too much for it.

Desserts are largely routine. Tarte Tatin is fresh but lacks caramel, crème brûlée is so thick it fights back, and blueberry cheesecake is run-of-the-mill. If you are into serious chocolate, the chocolate hazelnut torte is almost fudgelike, set off with crème anglaise. "We are pleased to accept cash only," the menu states. Glad to hear it. Les Halles this is not, but for a cheap, satisfying meal on the fringes of midtown, Bellevues is worth noting.

# BELLINI BY CIPRIANI

★ ★

*777 Seventh Avenue, at 51st Street, 265-7770.*

*Atmosphere: Stylish European cafe feeling; good sound muffling.*

*Service: Much improved; professional and watchful.*

*Wine: Undistinguished list at high prices.*

*Price range: Expensive.*

*Credit cards: All major cards.*

*Hours: Lunch, 11:45 A.M. to 3 P.M., Monday through Friday; dinner, 5:30 to 11:30 P.M., Monday through Saturday, until 9 P.M., Sunday.*

*Reservations: Suggested.*

*Wheelchair accessibility: Dining room on ground level; restrooms downstairs.*

When Bellini by Cipriani, an American version of the renowned Harry's Bar in Venice, opened in early 1987 on Seventh Avenue, it had little of the class associated with the original. The menu was reminiscent of Harry's Bar, as was the setting. And Harry Cipriani himself, the urbane, magnetic host, cosseted the jet-set crowd as smoothly as ever. But something was missing.

The food, for one, ranged from merely passable to dismal. And Mr. Cipriani's charms notwithstanding, service was slipshod if not outright clownish. So it is pleasing to report improvements in both areas, making Bellini by Cipriani a reliable, though pricey, theater-district dining option.

The main dining room has a cosmopolitan café aura, with its little nibbling bar near the entrance, beige print fabric on the walls, dark wood wainscotting and green marbleized borders, antique sconces, soft leather chairs, and semiopen kitchen. Tables—still tacky and annoyingly wobbly at times—draped in starched pale yellow linen, are well separated for easy conversation.

I don't usually drink cocktails, but a Bellini is a must here, a stimulating, if sneakily alcoholic, blend of peach juice and sparkling wine. Among starters, the carpaccio of Norwegian salmon with asparagus is superbly buttery and flavorful. Various cannelloni are offered on the changing menu. The one stuffed with salmon mousse with shrimp garnish was particularly well done, the pasta firm to the tooth as it should be, and with a restrained sauce of melted cheese and tomato. Another sampled, stuffed with ground veal and garnished with sweet peppers and mozzarella, was equally good.

Two other veal dishes can be recommended: veal-stuffed ravioli in a sage-perfumed meat-and-mushroom sauce, and tagliatelle in a rich and subtle veal ragù. One of the few clunkers, on the other hand, was the house's traditional fish soup, which suffered from a lifeless stock base.

The captains here are good about describing all the daily specials, and they attend to all the fine points. It is surprising to see a perfunctory wine list at a place of this stature. Only Italian reds are fairly well represented, and prices are high.

Seafood, which was so maladroitly prepared the last time Bellini by Cipriani was reviewed, in 1987, is now the kitchen's strength. One exceptional dish is a salmon fillet poached in white wine and encrusted with thin nickel-size slices of fried zucchini. It comes draped in an herb-brightened zucchini sauce. Another felicitous combination is a sautéed halibut fillet with a delicate orange sauce garnished with orange sections. Red snapper is lovely with its mildly sassy curry sauce.

There are few places in town to get competently prepared risotto, but this is one. Those we enjoyed included the shrimp version—the shrimp are flambéed in brandy to add a haunting sweet flavor—and another with ripe end-of-summer tomatoes. Only the vegetable risotto lacked seasonings. Extra-light semolina gnocchi, the size of big checkers, were pleasantly cheesy in a good tomato sauce.

Rounding out the menu are juicy baby lamb chops with shiitake mushrooms and a sweet balsamic vinegar sauce; fork-tender roasted duck in a long-simmered red-wine sauce along with fall vegetables; and crisply roasted chicken in an herb and vinegar sauce with grilled polenta on the side.

Desserts are outlandishly rich, and hard to resist. The house special mocha cake, sublime layers of coffee-soaked genoise and mocha cream, is suggested. A runner-up is the dense and intense chocolate layer cake, which tastes less sugary than it did the last time I had it here. On the other end of the sweets spectrum is the helium-light sabayon cake. If you want a real pyrotechnics show, order the Grand

Marnier crêpe with vanilla ice cream. The result is heady, and splendid.

# BICE

★ ★

*7 East 54th Street, 688-1999.*

*Atmosphere: Handsome, softly lit room with moderate sound muffling.*

*Service: Brisk and efficient.*

*Wine: Well-chosen Italian list. Average prices.*

*Price range: Moderately expensive.*

*Credit cards: All major cards.*

*Hours: Lunch, noon to 3 P.M., daily; dinner, 6 to midnight, Monday through Saturday, until 11:30 P.M., Sunday.*

*Reservations: Necessary.*

*Wheelchair accessibility: Bar dining area on street level; main dining room two steps up; restrooms downstairs.*

Never have I seen an enterprise take off the way this Milan restaurant spinoff did three years ago. And today, right in the middle of a downturn in the food industry, it is cruising along as if no one had bothered to tell it that times are tough.

What is Bice's recipe for success? In the early days, when I found the food to be satisfying but nothing exceptional, I chalked it up to the chic, cosmopolitan scene there. Unknowns, even with reservations, were greeted with the warmth usually accorded to census takers. But nobody seemed to mind waiting in the bar, further enriching the coffers by downing a Bellini or two. Today, though, the more mature Bice is more accommodating, better about honoring reservations and, best of all, turning out some splendid dishes.

Bice is one of the handsomest Italian restaurants in town.

At this time of year, the glass-paned wooden doors that form the street-side wall of the restaurant are swung open, creating a semioutdoor cafe in the bar. The main dining room, done in beige and wood with brass sconces and recessed, indirect lighting, has a multipeaked ceiling crisscrossed by wood beams. The room can become loud when the convivial late-dining set moves in about 9 P.M., but not distractingly so.

The best dishes here by a long shot are the pastas and risottos. Gossamer broccoli-filled ravioli come with a clean, light sauce of olive oil, garlic, and sun-dried tomatoes; another, filled with ricotta and a purée of asparagus, has a sublime sauce of fresh crayfish and a fresh crayfish stock. Tortelloni, a plump raviolilike pasta, have a lusty filling of puréed potatoes and pancetta seasoned with fresh rosemary.

The chef has extremist views on the issue of al dente pasta, which once led to the return of a dish and at other times left us chewing more than we should have. After the rigatoni with eggplant and mozzarella came back from the kitchen further cooked, it was delightfully subtle. If you yearn for a fine linguine with clams, Bice's version, an occasional special, is superb: sweet baby clams are tossed in a sauce of strong olive oil, parsley, and clam broth. Two risottos sampled had a perfect resilient texture and creamy consistency: one with fresh spinach and Parmesan cheese, the other generously seasoned with saffron and holding bits of Italian sausage.

The pastas (but not risotto) may be ordered in half-portions as an appetizer. Other worthwhile starters include the crostino of mozzarella and tomato seasoned with oregano and basil; marinated goat cheese with fresh asparagus and mushrooms; and warm carpaccio of beef with marinated vegetables. The most unusual starter was a special one evening called gelato di Parmigiano, which is aged Parmesan cheese mixed with whipped chilled cream and egg yolks, served with sliced pear—rich, but a startling and delicious contrast of flavors and textures. The brisk waiters here are not big on chatter, thank heaven, but they go about their work with dispatch. The wine list, mostly Italian, is well chosen; no bargain by any standard, but not extortionate.

Main courses are essentially uncomplicated trattoria fare. Grilled butterflied baby chicken with rosemary is reliably pleasing (but the potatoes with it are bland), as is paillard of chicken with herb butter. Roasted guinea hen, a special, was particularly well executed, the sliced leg and breast meat moistened with a lively sauce of balsamic vinegar and honey—just enough honey to blunt the sharp vinegar. The Black Angus sirloin served with mixed roasted peppers had exceptional flavor, even though overcooked. Swordfish was dry on two occasions, although an herb-crusted salmon was moist and vibrantly seasoned, served with asparagus. My seafood odds were 50–50 on another evening, when grilled red snapper covered with wilted Vidalia onions was pleasantly sweet, and unseasoned tuna steak garnished with sautéed bean sprouts was a bore.

If you try just one dessert here, it has to be the remarkably moist and citric orange cake with chocolate frosting. Chocolate polenta is a good idea, light and minimally sweet, with white chocolate sauce; and espresso granita can both cool and recharge your batteries on a sultry summer day. Bice's tiramisù is too sweet for my taste, so I would opt instead for any of the homemade gelati, or maybe a pear sorbet spiked with pear brandy.

# BOULEY

★ ★ ★ ★

*165 Duane Street, 608-3852.*

*Atmosphere: Romantic country-French setting with arched ceilings and soft indirect lighting.*

*Service: Seasoned and knowledgeable about the food and wine.*

*Wine: Extensive French-oriented list, strong in regional selections; prices average.*

*Price range: Expensive.*

*Credit cards: All major cards.*

*Hours: Lunch, noon to 3 P.M., Monday through Friday; dinner, 6 to 11 P.M., Monday through Saturday.*

*Reservations: Necessary, often a week or more in advance.*

*Wheelchair accessibility: Dining room on main level; restrooms downstairs.*

When Bouley was first reviewed in 1987, shortly after it opened in TriBeCa, I noted that the restaurant had the potential for greatness. Overstriving and wobbly execution, though, resulted in too many near misses and a two-star rating. Today, though, Bouley displays remarkable poise and self-confidence.

David Bouley's rabid zeal for fresh regional ingredients, his cerebral approach to textures and flavors, and his obvious delight in wowing customers make this one of the most exciting restaurants in New York City. Add to these attributes a refined and unobtrusive service staff, and Bouley is now elevated to four-star status.

The immense hand-carved wooden door imported from Provence leads into a serene country-French setting: a graceful vaulted ceiling, romantic lighting reflecting from cream-colored walls, lace curtains, bucolic Impressionist paintings, and a profusion of wildflowers. Outside the dining room is a too-small waiting area and bar. Inside, the tables are well separated, but not enough to prevent an obstreperous scene at peak hours.

The gazetteer-style menu may be intimidating at first ("Orient Point potatoes," "Camden, Maine, lobsters," "Hurley Mountain chives"). Not only is it long and meticulously detailed; the poorly photocopied list of specials is difficult to read. It looks as if third graders were hired to run it off on their classroom mimeograph machine.

Once you get it all sorted out, two of the more delicate starters are a stratified grilled eggplant terrine, with a lid of goat cheese and a vernal parsley sauce, and superb fresh Maine crabmeat garnished with thin asparagus with a leek-and-chive vinaigrette. A particularly dazzling Bouley creation is sautéed salmon fillet coated with toasted sesame seeds and served in an incredibly flavorful pool of tomato water. If sweet Maine lobster is your passion, Bouley is the next best thing to a weekend in Bar Harbor, offering cold lobster meat over sliced yellow potatoes with a sauce of basil and truffle oil; lobster morsels in a stock with paprika and port wine, surrounded by tiny pasta shells, and roasted lobster tail and claw served in heady lobster consommé faintly flavored with peppermint. (The combination sounds odd, but the subtle dose of peppermint is wonderful.)

One of the very few dishes that didn't work is called cured sashimi-quality tuna, which comes with a vinegary red sauce that bullies the pristine fish. If fresh sardines are in, don't miss them: grilled, presented with an honor guard of baby mussels (unnecessary, really) and a sauce of balsamic vinegar and herb oil. Creamless asparagus soup, the color of a putting green in June, is intense yet light.

The servers at Bouley are much more polished and less solemn than they were several years ago. They are also well schooled in the involved menu. The French-oriented wine list has considerable depth, both in major growing areas and the lesser-known regions. Prices are average for a luxury restaurant.

Main courses may sound overembellished, but tasting reveals how strategically conceived they are. For example, sweetbreads are dusted with clove powder for pungent sensation and cooked with sweet red onions for contrast. They are enhanced with a minimally sweet white Madeira sauce and garlic. An extraordinarily flavorful pigeon is cooked two ways: the breast is layered with foie gras and rolled in savoy cabbage, then steamed and served with a sauce of pigeon stock bound with foie gras, while the leg is roasted and served with a pigeon-stock sauce scented with sweet garlic.

Seafood is Mr. Bouley's metier. Seared black sea bass is seasoned with a complex medley of spices including cumin, nutmeg, ginger, and curry. It is presented over a julienne of vegetables and glazed with a sauce of white Madeira, mushroom juice, and herbed oils. Deftly roasted halibut comes over sweet rhubarb, red onions, and mustard seeds, with braised ramps and little yellow beets on the side. Roasted monkfish is prepared simply and smashingly, combined with savoy cabbage, roasted garlic and a light tomato-coriander sauce.

Desserts alone could compel one to investigate co-op possibilities in the Duane Park neighborhood. The pastry chef, Peter Sioti, turns out a chocolate soufflé with hot chocolate sauce that makes you tremble: as if that were not enough, it comes with maple ice cream and a little banana tart. The hot raspberry soufflé paired with a chocolate pear soufflé is not far behind on the emotion meter. Raspberries are also used in a stellar individual tart with an almond-paste base, ringed with blackberries and served with caramel ice cream. The tart of glazed shredded apples is memorable, too, with cleansing apple sorbet and blackberry sauce.

# BRANDYWINE

★ ★

*274 Third Avenue, between 21st and 22nd Streets, 353-8190.*

*Atmosphere: Cozy steakhouse with cherry-wood paneling and leather banquettes.*

*Service: Knowledgeable and efficient.*

*Wine: Good selection of Alsatian wines at fair prices.*

*Price range: Moderately expensive.*

*Credit cards: American Express, MasterCard, and Visa.*

*Hours: Lunch, 11:30 A.M. to 2:30 P.M., Monday through Friday; dinner, 5 to 10:30 P.M., Monday through Saturday.*

*Reservations: Recommended.*

*Wheelchair accessibility: Dining on one level; restrooms on same level, but doors are too narrow for wheelchairs.*

In mid-1989 the owners of Brandywine decided to give their American steakhouse a new spin. They hired as consultant the four-star chef of Lafayette, Alsace-born Jean-Georges Vongerichten, who suggested adding a menu of rustic specialties from his home region. He even brought his mother, Jeannine Georges, to New York to help with recipes and sent over one of his cooks, Michael Mandato, to run the kitchen. This may seem a strange hybrid, but if you have never experienced lusty Alsace cuisine, this is a fine place to do it.

The main dining room is as warm and snug as a down coat, with its dark cherry-wood paneling, antique brass sconces, black tufted leather banquettes, candlelight, and equestrian art. An intimate back room can be used for private parties.

The menu has two sections, one Alsatian, the other American steakhouse. Upon being seated, you are given a tapenade-style black olive purée and slabs of good sourdough bread. Titillating starters from the Alsatian section include joue de porc, or pigs' cheeks, which are among the tenderest parts of the animal. Cut into rounds the size of a half-dollar, they are lightly breaded, coated with mustard, and sautéed, and served with warm potato salad in a light vinaigrette that cuts the richness of the meat. Foie gras bolstered with Armagnac is luxurious in its cushion of moist brioche, and mussels benefit from steaming in sweet-tinged Riesling wine with shallots. Diners at my table voted the huge terrine of marinated herring in cream too salty and assertive, while moist roast quail over green lentils was so good we were tempted to order it again as an entrée.

Two good options from the steakhouse page are tender little squid in a creamy, well-seasoned polenta, and a delightful roulade of goat cheese wrapped in a thin potato crust.

This kind of food calls for wines with real backbone: whites with high levels of acid (naturally, most Alsace whites are ideal), and bold reds. The list here provides an adequate selection of both at affordable tabs. The French maître d'hôtel is helpful in making successful combinations.

Main courses are gargantuan. Choucroute garnie comes in a deep ceramic casserole, a grand assembly of smoked pork chops, potatoes, bratwurst, veal sausage, and sauerkraut. My favorite is the civet d'oie Parmentier, a sublime casserole of rich shredded goose meat with red cabbage under a layer of mashed potatoes. Tripe stewed in Riesling, shallots, and garlic with spaetzle needed zest. And what was labeled—in French—palette of pork (upper shoulder) with horseradish and potatoes was really cut from the loin: tasty, but dry.

From the other side of the menu you can get a moist, thick slab of swordfish with basil butter, a delicious partly blackened salmon with a vinegar-tart sauce, squash and braised scallions (the menu says leeks), or a monstrous porterhouse steak.

Chocolate cupcakes may not sound like an exciting dessert, but don't miss them: they ooze with warm chocolate mousse in the center and come with vanilla ice cream. A faithful version of kugelhopf, the Alsatian yeast cake with almonds and currants, is served fresh and soft here, not slightly dry from age the way the French like it. As for beer sorbet, it has a stale smell that reminded me of Sunday morning after a college beer bash. I needed some of the thinly sliced quince with a thin pancake on top to purge the unpleasant sensation.

# BRIDGE CAFE

★

*279 Water Street, corner of Dover Street, 227-3344.*

*Atmosphere: Old waterfront tavern with tin ceiling, wood bar, and linoleum floor.*

*Service: No-nonsense efficiency.*

*Wine: Small but quality list, fair prices. Good selection of wines by the glass.*

*Price range: Moderate.*

*Credit cards: All major cards.*

*Hours: Breakfast, 7 to 11:30 A.M., Monday through Friday; brunch, 11:45 A.M. to 4 P.M., Sunday; lunch, noon to 5 P.M., Monday through Friday; dinner, 5 to midnight, Monday through Saturday, 5 to 10 P.M., Sunday.*

*Reservations: Recommended.*

*Wheelchair accessibility: Dining room and restrooms on ground level. Narrow entryway.*

Seven years after the opening of the redeveloped South Street Seaport, distinguished restaurants are still as scarce as surfboards on the lake in Central Park. Sloppy Louie's became unsloppy (and mediocre) through gentrification, and even the venerable Sweets churns out fast-paced tourist grub. If you are combining a trip to the seaport with lunch or dinner, it would be worthwhile to walk several blocks north, almost under the Brooklyn Bridge, to Bridge Cafe.

Mercifully unrestored and without an Ann Taylor or Williams-Sonoma in sight, Bridge Cafe resembles the waterfront watering hole it was for the better part of this century.

The dining room, with a long, well-elbowed bar, looks as if no interior designer has ever sailed within ten miles of it. The ancient linoleum may have been a color at one time, but decades of shuffling longshoremen and fishmongers have erased any evidence. The old pressed-tin ceiling has been painted brown, and the yellow wooden-slat walls are adorned with posters, photographs, and maritime art. Gingham-covered tables, soft piped-in jazz, and pleasant, no-nonsense waitresses in T-shirts and sneakers reinforce the casual tone.

The food befits the unmannered setting. Two good seafood choices are the tender sautéed sea scallops with wide ribbons of carrots and a mustardy herb sauce, and fillet of flounder with a perfumed combination of lemongrass, tarragon, and nasturtium.

In the spring, soft-shell crabs are the big seller, and they are superlative: plump, cleanly fried, and sweet, with boiled potatoes, green beans, and broccoli. Grilled Norwegian salmon is perfectly cooked, set over a balsamic vinegar sauce with tomatoes and endive.

Nonseafood options are not so reliable, including a gummy pasta with a sauce of smoked duck, red beans, and rosemary cream, and dry chicken breast stuffed with spinach, tahina paste, and lemon.

Bridge Cafe has a decent and fairly priced wine list, as well as a daily selection of a half-dozen wines by the glass. Waitresses know more about the food than about the wine. They also manage to keep admirably cool and composed at frenzied lunchtimes when Wall Streeters blaze in and out.

Best bets among appetizers include the soup specials—

thick, sweet corn chowder or refreshing and light cream of cucumber with dill—herbed fried calamari, and a shrimp-and-watercress salad zestily seasoned with curry and coriander.

For dessert, pear-and-ginger tart is sprightly, and rhubarb pie has a nice crumbly crust and pleasant tart-sweet sensation. Pecan pie and lemony cheesecake are runners-up.

# B. SMITH'S

**SATISFACTORY**

*771 Eighth Avenue, at 47th Street, 247-2222.*

*Atmosphere: Stylish and spacious soft-pastel dining room with Art Deco accents. Loud.*

*Service: Haphazard and forgetful.*

*Wine: Adequate wine selection, generally overpriced.*

*Price range: Moderate.*

*Credit cards: All major cards.*

*Hours: Lunch, noon to 4 P.M., daily (brunch specials on Sunday); dinner, 5 P.M. to midnight, daily.*

*Reservations: Suggested, especially on weekends.*

*Wheelchair accessibility: Everything on one level.*

As tawdry Eighth Avenue in the Forties and Fifties inexorably undergoes gentrification, restaurants follow as surely as high rents. B. Smith's, named after a former model, Barbara Smith, was a pioneer when it opened several years ago on the fringe of Times Square. Despite a too-cute-for-its-own-good menu, it has endured.

Ms. Smith's corporate backer is Michael Weinstein and company, owners of Ernie's on Upper Broadway and America on East 18th Street.

In familiar Weinstein style, the décor received first priority, no expense spared, in hopes of creating an immediate sensation. To that end, B. Smith's succeeded. The airy postmodern interior sports a gleaming stainless-steel bar up front that attracts a stylish clientele. In the back is a softer-edged dining room dabbed in peach tones and with Art Deco touches. A colorful abstract mosaic covers one wall. One design element not addressed is noise, which can be deafening.

The overly ambitious menu makes for tempting reading, but the execution is something else. The problem here is obvious: the kitchen's wide-angle lens attempts to take in every voguish type of cooking—Cajun, new American, Deep South, Italian—and winds up with very little in focus.

Appetizers and desserts are the most reliable; in fact, it wouldn't be a bad strategy to load up on both ends and leap-frog the middle. Soups are quite good, at least when they arrive hot—the odds are a coin's toss that they will. A thick and garlic-bolstered purée of roasted tomatoes brightened with fresh basil is a fine way to start.

Among the regular appetizers, shrimp poached in an herby shellfish stock loaded with garlic are light and flavor-packed; by contrast, sparkling fresh bluepoint oysters are bullied by an overly citric beurre blanc and garnish of grapefruit and orange sections. B. Smith's menu also carries a selection of entrée-sized salads that could be split if ordered as appetizers, as well as "light plates," sort of in-between portions for the grazing herds. The plain green salads are fine, but steer away from such fatuous creations as duck salad under a syrupy raspberry sauce that belongs on ice cream.

A notable light plate is grilled lean duck sausage infused with fennel along with warm potato salad. In the same category, vermicelli with lobster, onions, tomato butter, and mascarpone is a frumpy and bland mess, while potato-and-leek pancake was sodden and missing the promised caviar garnish.

The asparagus-green waiters and waitresses, ranging from spike-haired to straitlaced, seem perpetually in a fog and tend to disappear for long stretches. The wine selection is adequate but generally overpriced by several dollars a bottle.

Among entrées, overcooking vitiates some otherwise decent preparations; three examples are the chicken paillard, grilled salmon (a special), and grilled shrimp. The last was described enthusiastically by Ms. Smith as shrimp under a mango glaze. On two occasions the thick, bright yellow sauce had a cloying flavor that could best be described as melted vanilla ice cream. Even the accompanying banana fritters tasted reheated. The simplest entrées are the most satisfying: grilled lamb chops in Madeira sauce, steak with french fries, and grilled duck breast flanked by good duck sausage in a heavily reduced red-wine sauce.

The scenario brightens with dessert. Except for an overly sugared sweet-potato-pecan pie, other options are worthwhile: dense triple chocolate torte surrounded by a moat of raspberry sauce and crème anglaise, coconut tuiles with white chocolate ice cream, and lavish profiteroles.

# BUKHARA

★ ★

*148 East 48th Street, in the Helmsley Middletowne Hotel, 838-1811.*

*Atmosphere: Handsome and low-key with sandstone-colored walls and soft lighting.*

*Service: Low-key, polite, helpful.*

*Wine: Small list available.*

*Price range: Moderate.*

*Credit cards: All major cards.*

*Hours: Lunch, noon to 3 P.M., daily; dinner, 6 to 10:45 P.M., daily.*

*Reservations: Suggested.*

*Wheelchair accessibility: Two steps down to dining room; restrooms two more steps down.*

There is something wonderfully primordial about watching Madison Avenue moguls roll up their shirtsleeves and tear into slabs of roasted lamb with their hands, then lick their fingers and snag a clump of cauliflower along with some barbecued shrimp. This peculiar scene unfolds daily at Bukhara, the Indian restaurant that specializes in what is called frontier cooking. While it may not be the most appropriate place for a business lunch to review scripts for the new advertising campaign, Bukhara has a lot going for it as an exotic dining spot serving some provocative food.

Absent are the usual curries, milk-based sauces, and buttery gravies found in conventional Indian restaurants, leaving the food exceptionally clean and light. Eating with the hands makes Bukhara a diverting place to take children: where else can they have such wicked fun doing exactly what their parents have been lecturing them not to do for years? Tableware is provided upon request. The cavernous dining room is stately and comfortable. It has rough sandstone-colored walls holding gleaming hammered-brass-and-copper trays and colorful embroidered rugs, gentle, indirect lighting, and stout teakwood tables and chairs. Behind a glass partition is a sparkling slate-walled kitchen where chefs tend the tandoors. The noise level is low even when the room is full.

The offerings are limited to about a dozen entrées, with a handful of appetizers and four desserts. Since appetizers are not particularly compelling—chicken kebabs are dry and beef brochettes are humdrum—I like to order an entrée and split it among two or four as a starter. One appetizer worth trying, however, is chicken chunks marinated in tart pomegranate juice and served with black-peppercorn-and-yogurt dressing.

In this frontier style of cooking, based on that of the Pathan people of Peshawar in Pakistan, primary ingredients are marinated in yogurt (or another moistening agent), herbs, and spices, then seared to seal in moisture and finished in the superhot tandoor. This technique does wonders for lamb. Barah kebab is the name for cubes of yogurt-marinated lamb aromatic of cumin and ginger. Seekh kebabs are incredibly juicy cigar-shaped rolls of minced lamb spiked with hot red pepper and cumin.

Large groups might consider a house specialty called sikandari raan, an entire leg of lamb that has been marinated in dark rum, braised in the oven, then finished in the tandoor. The rum flavor is not evident, but the meat literally tumbles off the bone and is exquisitely succulent. Jumbo prawns, which are more fragile than meat, came out of the oven mealy and overcooked. Chicken is vulnerable to drying out, too, as in the murgh Bukhara, a spicy chicken kebab. Much better was murgh malai kebab, a cream-moistened dish of chicken cubes infused with ginger, garlic, and potent fresh coriander.

The tandoors turn out a host of fabulous breads: nan, a fluffy white-flour disk; roti, a flat, earthy whole-wheat round, and khastra roti, a toasted whole-wheat bread sprinkled with cuminseed. The best is the puffed and charred whole-wheat bread that is dusted with dried mint. Nan Bukhara, described on the menu as communal nan, is the size of a small surfboard. There is a limited wine list, and Indian and domestic beers are available.

After your palate runs this gauntlet of spices, you will be ready for something refreshing and cool. Kulfi is a sprightly orange-perfumed frozen cream served in orange peel (spoons are provided with dessert).

# CAFÉ DES ARTISTES

★ ★ ★

*1 West 67th Street, 877-3500.*

*Atmosphere: Romantic, elegant room with bucolic murals. Moderate noise level.*

*Service: Well-informed and professional.*

*Wine: Well-chosen selection; daily specials available.*

*Price range: Moderately expensive (prix-fixe lunch, $19; prix-fixe dinner, $32.50).*

*Credit cards: All major cards.*

*Hours: Brunch, noon to 4 P.M., Saturday, 10 A.M. to 4 P.M., Sunday; lunch, noon to 3 P.M., Monday through Friday; dinner, 5:30 P.M. to midnight, Monday through Saturday, 5 to 11 P.M., Sunday.*

*Reservations: Necessary well in advance.*

*Wheelchair accessibility: Ramp to dining room; restrooms downstairs.*

With its burnished-wood walls, lead-paned casement windows, bursts of flowers, and Howard Chandler Christy's sylvan murals of frolicking nymphs, Café des Artistes has the warmth of a venerable old café in Vienna or Budapest. The main room, dominated by a prodigious buffet, is more neighborly and louder than the intimate tables that ring the bar on the second level.

The cooking in recent years has become bolder, more soulful, even sassy. One can start with something as rustic as the platter of cochonnailles (charcuterie of pork), which includes a well-seasoned jambon persillé (ham-and-parsley terrine), a rough-textured terrine of pork studded with walnuts, unremittingly rich but delicious rillettes of pork, and earthy garlic sausage. With the banner of homey peasant food flying high these days, you may be tempted to try the superb sweetbread headcheese bound with a full-flavored gelatin.

Garlic-perfumed sausage is tasty, but its wrapping of pastry is soggy. Cold mussels under dabs of a curried mayonnaise made a tantalizing starter at lunch one day, as did a house special called "salmon four ways": smoked, poached with tartar sauce, gravlax, and dill-seasoned tartar-style.

Café des Artistes has a well-chosen little wine list with prices starting around $25. While you scan that selection, a waiter will come around toting a bargain basket of daily specials, each bottle $16. There are usually some good buys among them from the Côtes-du-Rhône and lesser-known regions of Burgundy or California.

The staff is enthusiastic and well-schooled about entrées. One tip that paid off was the bourride, a Provençale specialty that is a cross between a soup and a stew in which the seafood stock is thickened with aïoli, a garlic mayonnaise. There are many variations of bourride in France, and this commendable rendition includes mussels, swordfish, and scallops in a silken, garlic-bolstered sauce carrying a hint of anise. Other good seafood choices are moist paillard of swordfish with a light mustard-and-butter sauce; chunky, well-peppered salmon cakes with broccoli and rice, and that much-abused New England staple, scrod, which is nicely browned and garnished with deep-fried capers, red potatoes, and acorn squash purée.

If you are devouring protein in preparation for the New York Marathon, several entrées here are just what the trainer ordered. A special one evening of roasted veal breast came out the size of a throw pillow, stuffed with onion-sweetened pork and chestnuts—delicious and overwhelming. The kitchen's twist on cassoulet, made with lentils rather than white beans, loses nothing but heaviness in the process. It is moist and complex with the flavors of lamb, duck, and garlic sausage. Duck confit with white beans, two generous legs and thighs, has just the right balance of salt and herbs, and the meat is sinewy yet succulent.

Pot-au-feu, which threatens to become the carpaccio of the '90s as restaurateurs scramble to rusticate their menus, is a paragon here. The assembly—gelatin-rich beef in a sturdy, clear broth with leeks, carrots, and red potatoes—arrives in a ceramic crock big enough to feed the busboy staff. Cornichons and mustard come on the side, as well as a silver marrow knife for excavating what to many is the whole reason for ordering this homespun dish. And if suspender-stretching casseroles like these are not on your agenda, you can still get a pungent pepper steak, deftly grilled sweetbreads, or rack of lamb with red cabbage and carrots.

If Mr. Lang is making the rounds of the dining room, he is likely to encourage you to experience his beloved Ilona torte. "Ten eggs in it!" he declares with an impish smile. Rich? It goes without saying, but the sweet mocha filling is anchored by a sharp espresso flavor. Linzer torte is too dense and was served too cold, but toasted orange pound cake was heavenly. The kitchen here has always turned out a fine dacquoise, and still does. And the rate at which the intense hazelnut mousse cake was devoured was rivaled only by the disappearance of the glazed macadamia nut tart.

# CAFE GRECO

★ ★

*1390 Second Avenue, between 71st and 72nd streets, 737-4300.*

*Atmosphere: Cool, clean, and informal, with high ceilings, tall windows, and lots of natural wood.*

*Service: Friendly and competent.*

*Wine: Interesting multinational selection, reasonably priced.*

*Price range: Moderately expensive.*

*Credit cards: All major cards.*

*Hours: Brunch, noon to 4 P.M., Saturday and Sunday; lunch, noon to 4 P.M., Monday through Friday; dinner, 5 to 11 P.M., daily.*

*Reservations: Suggested.*

*Wheelchair accessibility: Dining facilities in front room; restrooms downstairs.*

Cafe Greco was one of the first Manhattan restaurants to ride the Mediterranean wave three years ago. The kitchen turns out a sunny mélange of cuisines under an umbrella called Mediterranean, including dishes from Sicily, the Greek Islands, southern France, and Morocco.

This is a cool and casual spot, with a pretty little bar and café up front that spills out onto Second Avenue; the interior is subdued and restrained by today's aggressive design standards—ocher walls, high ceilings, brass and wood, and tall arching windows that look out on a lighted backyard garden.

The menu is intelligently balanced and wisely limited in size. You can warm up with the sprightly giveaway ratatouille and assortment of intriguing breads, perhaps along with a glass of lovely peach-flavored sparkling wine, a house special. Carpaccio of salmon is a pristine winner, glossed with good olive oil and fresh basil, as is the herb-perfumed little tart holding layers of eggplant, tomato, and zucchini. From Greece comes the excellent phyllo pastry stuffed with spinach and cheese, called spanakopita. The North African contribution, skewered chunks of chicken in tahina—a purée of sesame seeds—is a palate teaser.

An Italian-inspired soup is splendid, combining a clear, richly flavored beef stock with orzo, Swiss chard, and fava beans. A pasta special one day, cappellini with mussels in a fresh tomato-and-basil sauce, was delicious but marred by grit.

Grilled salmon is bolstered with a zesty sauce of roasted red peppers, black olives, and fresh tarragon in a dish I would row across the Mediterranean for. The salmon is exquisitely charred outside, ruddy within, and was presented over braised endive with spinach on the side. Two other fish dishes excel: charred halibut steak with a beautifully balanced basil beurre-blanc sauce, and expertly sautéed swordfish with a rosemary-scented mayonnaise and buttery baby zucchini.

On the meat side of the menu, you can't go wrong with the rosy medallions of lamb with a light but intense stock sauce, marinated white beans, and Swiss chard, or the simple roasted veal chop with sage leaves and roasted cloves of garlic. Roast chicken with couscous and grilled leeks is a soothing combination, along with some roasted whole shallots for good measure. Grilled rib steak with deep-fried shallots is satisfying but pales next to some other entrées. Finally there is the crisp roast squab, mild and juicy, in a vermouth-edged stock sauce. The accompanying fried polenta is absolutely addictive.

If all this sun and fun on the Mediterranean coast puts you in the mood for serious desserts, go with the thick and custardy raspberry napoleon, superbly rich chocolate-and-hazelnut sabra cake, anisette-spiked cheesecake, or an assortment of regional pastries. Gelati tastes like conventional ice cream.

# CAFE LUXEMBOURG

★ ★

*200 West 70th Street, 873-7411.*

*Atmosphere: Stylish and lively Art Deco room; can be loud.*

*Service: Upbeat and energetic.*

*Wine: Small but quality list at fair prices.*

*Price range: Moderately expensive (pretheater dinner prix fixe, $34).*

*Credit cards: American Express, MasterCard, and Visa.*

*Hours: Brunch, 11 A.M. to 2:30 P.M., Sunday; dinner, 5:30 P.M. to 12:30 A.M., Monday through Thursday, until 1:30 A.M., Friday and Saturday, 6 to 11:30 P.M., Sunday; pretheater dinner, 5:30 to 6:30 P.M., daily.*

*Reservations: Necessary.*

*Wheelchair accessibility: Everything on one level.*

The Lincoln Center area still suffers from a relatively lackluster cast of restaurants, considering the demand for quality dining before and after performances. Several promising places have opened in the neighborhood over the past few years, but none so far rivals seven-year-old Cafe Luxembourg for its consistently appealing fare and kinetic ambiance.

The Art Deco room has a timeless and indigenous appeal, with its cream-colored tile walls, black-and-white terrazzo floor, period sconces, and café tables. Patrons cluster at the long zinc-topped bar in the early evening. The dining room, a tightly arranged maze of red banquettes and rattan-style chairs, can be loud when conversation ricochets off the tiles and mirrors. About 9 P.M., a romantic on the staff dims the lights, and suddenly the room becomes soft and seductive.

The seasonal menu—a little French brasserie style, a little contemporary American—is cleverly orchestrated to offer everything from simple salads and steaks to more refined creations, such as a crisply sautéed mahi-mahi in a light, faintly sweet Sauternes sauce offset by piquant strands of ginger. A worthwhile bargain is the daily pretheater prix-fixe dinner.

Based on my experiences, the young, upbeat staff here is good about getting you out to catch a performance. The scene can become frenzied later in the evening, but in the best brasserie tradition, waiters and waitresses take it all in stride. Two enticing starters are the salad made with chicory, cubes of bacon, garlic croutons, and Roquefort cheese, all in a peppy mustard vinaigrette; and the lemony salad of marinated red snapper brightened with cilantro. The crab cakes have been winners here for years: meaty, golden brown, just peppery enough to enhance the sweet crabmeat, and paired with a rouille, a red-pepper hot sauce. There was an exceptional special one evening of nicely browned sweetbreads sprinkled with sesame seeds and garnished with shiitake mushrooms and threads of carrot and zucchini in a vinaigrette.

Aside from the mahi-mahi entrée, another recommended choice is the grilled red snapper in a light champagne vinaigrette. Grilled vegetables served on the side, however, were nearly raw. Among the most consistently good options are the well-aged strip steak, cooked precisely to order, with either sautéed red potatoes or good french fries; thick, tender veal chop with red-pepper-and-tarragon sauce, and delicious calf's liver in a mustard sauce speckled with pink peppercorns and fried leeks. Grilled loin of lamb could not be more flavorful or juicy, with thyme-scented pan juices and a terrific garlic flan; roast veal was equally well done, except for the leathery reheated spaetzle on the side.

Desserts are generally on the light side. Lemon tart is worth seeking out, as is the perfect crème brûlée. The most intriguing, though, is the quivery grapefruit Bavarian, essentially a citric custard base blended with whipped cream and meringue. Departing from the light theme are the velvety, rich white and black chocolate mousses.

# CAFÉ PIERRE

★

*Fifth Avenue at 61st Street, 940-8185, 838-8000.*

*Atmosphere: Plush, warm, and elegant room. Low noise level.*

*Service: Professional and attentive, but the kitchen seems laggardly at times.*

*Wine: Moderate-size French and American list.*

*Price range: Expensive (prix-fixe dinner, $37).*

*Credit cards: All major cards.*

*Hours: Breakfast, 7 to 10:45 A.M., daily; brunch, noon to 2:45 P.M., Sunday; lunch, noon to 2:30 P.M., daily; dinner, 6 to 10:30 P.M., daily; prix-fixe dinner, 6 to 7 P.M., daily; supper, 10:30 to 11:15 P.M., daily.*

*Reservations: Suggested.*

*Wheelchair accessibility: Several steps down at main entrance; stairless side door can be used on request; restrooms on same floor.*

Cafe Pierre is a sanctuary of privilege in the Pierre Hotel where the ladies appear to have emerged from *Town and Country* magazine, and the men wear year-round tans and European suits. For years the café was known as a glorified tea room, but as other hotels began to upgrade their restaurants in recent years, the Pierre followed suit.

The old menu was jettisoned and replaced by one carrying many food fashions of the day, from duck ravioli and prettily composed salads to lemon mousse. The Old World dining room also got a facelift. But it is still soft and opulent, all done in soothing gray and white, with cloud murals overhead and swagged fabric draping ornate mirrors. Tables are tightly arranged but the noise level is well muted. A cozy piano bar lounge up front attracts a late-night cognac-sipping crowd.

The veteran service staff, looking so distinguished and worldly in black tie, is attentive and sophisticated, but the pace of the meal is unaccountably slow—delays seem to originate in the kitchen.

Among the stylish appetizers are a bright, light terrine of scallops, salmon, and spinach broccoli with a tart watercress sauce; sautéed fresh foie gras paired with artichoke slivers and a delicate sherry-vinegar glaze, and sautéed shrimp freckled with black pepper in an Oriental-style sweet-and-hot sauce.

Not everything works so well. A potato crêpe filled with smoked salmon and caviar is dry as dust, while the cold foie gras terrine is undercooked in the center.

Entrées are similar at lunch and dinner, supplemented by five daily specials. Simple dishes are the best: grilled fillet of veal in a rich stock sauce flanked by an asparagus flan, a special; tender, thick medallions of veal in the same sauce enlivened with chives; juicy saddle of lamb with braised endive; and noisettes of beef in red-wine sauce with basil.

One outstanding offering is a perfectly steamed fillet of sea bass set over a bed of fennel and tomatoes. Baked black bass with baby artichokes, by contrast, was well cooked but lacked seasoning. Duck breast is tender and appealing in a mildly sweet sauce laced with orange confit. The sweet-potato fries with it, however, were limp.

Desserts are uniformly superior, among them pears Hélène under a glazed crème anglaise sauce ringed with warm chocolate; ethereal Amaretto layer cake; buttery apple tart with whipped cream; terrific lemon mousse with raspberry sauce, and potent chocolate terrine. If you really want to splurge, try the profiteroles oozing with mint ice cream, all slathered in chocolate sauce.

# CAFE SAN MARTIN

**SATISFACTORY**

*1458 First Avenue, near 76th Street, 288-0470.*

*Atmosphere: Breezy and casual if somewhat cramped and loud.*

*Service: Good-natured but sometimes sloppy.*

*Wine: Impressive Spanish selection.*

*Price range: Moderately expensive.*

*Credit cards: American Express, MasterCard, and Visa.*

*Hours: Brunch, noon to 4 P.M., Sunday; dinner, 5:30 P.M. to midnight, Monday through Saturday, 4 to 10:30 P.M., Sunday.*

*Reservations: Required.*

*Wheelchair accessibility: Three steps up to the dining room: restrooms downstairs.*

Cafe San Martin, the glittery Spanish restaurant on First Avenue near 76th Street, has an air of prosperity and good times, which is part of its appeal. Diners in search of genuine Spanish food, however, can't help but be suspicious upon seeing a menu cluttered with such non-Iberian fare as duck pâté and Waldorf salad, fettuccine Alfredo and crêpes suzette. Culinary ecumenism at times can succeed, but it takes a special talent to pull it off, which this restaurant lacks. All three cuisines embraced here—Spanish, French, and Italian—are feebly done.

The dining room, run by the ever-vigilant and genial Ramon Martin, is smartly casual. The service staff is pleasant and informed, although sometimes too lazy to walk around a table to clear, instead reaching over diners' heads to fetch a plate. The whitewashed brick back dining room, adjacent to an exposed kitchen, has a towering skylight festooned with greenery; the peach-toned front room has a pianist who entertains nightly. Both rooms are loud and slightly cramped, with tables too small for the oversize dishes.

The appetizers are not exactly a publicity campaign for Spanish gastronomy. Black bean soup is anemic, lacking spices and ham flavor; watery gazpacho is no better; a dish described as Spanish sausage cooked in red wine is just that —mildly spicy sausages doused with wine and heated in aluminum foil.

The best choices are the simplest, such as garlic-seasoned shrimp or the carpaccio of Nova Scotia salmon. Any restaurant that claims Spanish heritage should be able to make tripe madrileño. The version here is so loaded with salt as to be nearly inedible.

Among entrées, only the most rudimentary fare can be recommended: rack of lamb with green beans and little crenelated fried potatoes; entrecôte with a lively garlic sauce and, when available as a special, moist and crisp-skinned roast suckling pig (it can also be ordered twelve hours in advance). Another Spanish specialty, paella for two, is a letdown. The only real flavor comes from the assertive garlic sausage; the rest—lobster, shrimp, mussels, clams, and chicken—is dry. A Basque specialty, monkfish in green sauce made with parsley and garlic, is fresh and attractively presented if not as well-seasoned as it could be. Another dish, called Mediterranean Delight, is slightly better, combining shrimp, lobster, mussels, clams, scallops, and monkfish in a more vivid version of the same sauce.

Desserts are elaborately displayed on a cart in the dining room, but the kitchen has such a sweet tooth that it makes most of them too cloying for my taste, including the apple tart and chestnut cake. Bread pudding with orange-rind garnish is moist and good, as is the crème caramel.

# CAFÉ UN DEUX TROIS

★

*123 West 44th Street, 354-4148.*

*Atmosphere: Big, bustling brasserie with colorful tongue-in-cheek décor.*

*Service: Articulate and energetic.*

*Wine: Limited list with reasonable prices.*

*Price range: Moderate.*

*Credit cards: American Express, MasterCard, and Visa.*

*Hours: Lunch, noon to 4 P.M., Monday through Friday; dinner, 4 P.M. to midnight, Sunday through Friday, 4 P.M. to 12:30 A.M., Saturday.*

*Reservations: Accepted only for parties of five or larger.*

*Wheelchair accessibility: Four steps up at the entrance; restrooms down a flight of stairs.*

Café Un Deux Trois continues to be one of the better bets for Broadway theater-district dining. This cavernous brasserie can be loud—very loud indeed—at peak hours before and after theater, as the din amplifies off the bare walls and tile floor. This is not the sort of place to hammer out final details on the big new account, but it's a great spot to argue about a play or movie you have just seen —and you can even illustrate your points on the paper tablecloths with crayons set out in a glass.

The vast open dining room is a visual pun of sorts, with its faux marble columns, mustard-colored walls painted to look as if they are peeling, sky murals wrapped in trompe-l'oeil frames, deliberately chipped moldings, and playful mismatched colors. Waiters and waitresses are extremely well-poised and diction-conscious—they even sing "Happy Birthday" in five-part harmony. The service is snappy and efficient under fervid conditions.

The short regular menu is supplemented by many daily

specials. The most reliable appetizers are the creamy and well-seasoned duck-liver mousse that goes well with French bread, and a good grilled boudin blanc (a special)—chicken-and-veal sausage served with sautéed onions and apples. The house pork-based terrine is satisfying if not exceptional. A gutsy grilled steak with french fries is de rigueur at a rollicking brasserie like this—the steak is well cooked and pleasing, but the french fries are woefully limp. The same steak with a green-peppercorn sauce is too timid for my taste, but might be suitable for those who shun hot foods.

Goujonettes of chicken (breaded and deep-fried strips of white meat), are addictive; keep them a safe distance from the cloying sweet-hot dipping sauce. Roast chicken is competently prepared, too.

On the entrée list, one old reliable is the simple breaded chicken breast with a mild mustard sauce and julienne of buttery carrots and zucchini. Along with a mixed salad, it makes a satisfying late supper. Steak tartare is competently prepared—studded with saline capers—but paired with the same soggy french fries.

Café Un Deux Trois has the least success with seafood. A special of shrimp in a green-peppercorn cream sauce was bland, while another—sole cooked in a foil pouch with parsley, tomato, zucchini, carrots, and summer squash—was soupy and overcooked.

Desserts are straightforward and satisfying. Among the best are crème caramel laced with orange zest, poached pears with chocolate sauce and whipped cream, and a ripe strawberry charlotte.

# CAMEOS

★

*169 Columbus Avenue, between 67th and 68th streets, 874-2280.*

*Atmosphere: Pastel and Art Deco second-story dining room with a lively piano bar.*

*Service: Somewhat lax and confused.*

*Wine: Moderate-sized international list at average prices.*

*Price range: Moderately expensive.*

*Credit cards: American Express, MasterCard, Transmedia, and Visa.*

*Hours: Brunch: 11:30 A.M. to 2:30 P.M., Saturday, 11:30 A.M. to 4 P.M., Sunday; lunch, noon to 3 P.M., Monday through Friday; dinner, 5:30 P.M. to midnight, Monday through Saturday, 5:30 to 10 P.M., Sunday.*

*Reservations: Necessary at dinner.*

*Wheelchair accessibility: Long flight of stairs to entrance.*

You climb a long, narrow stairway to this second-level establishment, then enter a cheerful bar flanked by a white grand piano where a well-groomed fellow plays show tunes. The dining room is long and compact, brightened with sprays of flowers and Art Deco touches. The tight dimensions of the room combined with all the hard surfaces amplify conversation to a distracting level; overlay some Cole Porter tunes, and you wind up conversing nose to nose with your dining partner.

The eclectic menu—a little Italian, a little French, a little American—is characterized by clean, clear flavors, and the chef has fun with his eye-catching presentation. Premium ingredients are used, although occasional underseasoning fails to do them justice.

Top vote getter among appetizers is the superlative fillet of bass in a carapace of golden puff pastry sprinkled with poppy seeds and set over a good sharp beurre blanc. Another winner is the pepper-coated fillet of beef, three thin, ruddy slices enlivened with a caper-mustard sauce. Grilled skewered vegetables escort a pair of sweet freshwater prawns, and a minced salmon-and-scallop seviche is fresh and nicely presented, although it needed more of its lime-and-sesame dressing. And a warm salad of Brie and goat cheese with tart greens was abused by bitter, overvinegared dressing.

Among the entrées, neither of the two pastas sampled

was memorable. Primavera sauce one evening tasted like something you would get at a militant health-food restaurant that eschews seasonings; fettuccine weighed down with ungainly boulders of lamb and duck sausage is a near miss —the sausage alone is delicious, but the rest is insipid. A better option is the deftly grilled tuna steak slathered with onions and in a peppery sauce. Swordfish is admirably done, too, in a chive beurre-blanc sauce vibrant with lemon; at lunch it comes in a subtly sweet ginger-and-orange sauce bound with sesame oil. Chicken breast in a balsamic-vinegar sauce with minced herbs is a lively and light lunch entrée, too, ringed with baby vegetables. On the debit side, fresh, firm red snapper cooked in parchment has little flavor other than a few sprigs of thyme.

The chef's grilled Black Angus rib-eye steak is terrific, brushed with a little maple syrup blended with orange rind and soy sauce—the sweet blackened crust imparts an irresistible extra dimension to the lusty beef. Veal chop is excellent, too, sweetened with roasted shallots and perfumed with fresh rosemary; whole medallions of venison are tender and engaging in a sharp green-peppercorn-and-shallot sauce.

Desserts are not up to par here. Soupy vanilla mousse with a core of rum chocolate is achingly sweet, as is the dense chocolate torte. Pecan pie with chocolate sauce is the best of the lot.

# THE CAPTAIN'S TABLE

**SATISFACTORY**

*860 Second Avenue, at 46th Street, 697-9538.*

*Atmosphere: Kitsch-galore dining room.*

*Service: Amiable and competent.*

*Wine: Overpriced list.*

*Price range: Expensive.*

*Credit cards: American Express, MasterCard, and Visa.*

*Hours: Lunch, noon to 3 P.M., Monday through Friday; dinner, 5:30 to 11 P.M., Monday through Friday, 5 P.M. to midnight, Saturday.*

*Reservations: Suggested.*

*Wheelchair accessibility: Everything on the ground floor; restrooms two steps up.*

The Captain's Table is one of those overpriced, underwhelming East Side fish houses. The dining rooms feature gaudy hanging lights in the form of grape clusters, multicolored chandeliers, flower-patterned synthetic tablecloths (soiled to boot), ceramic birds dangling overhead, little plaster animals on wall shelves and, in the back, a giant green ceramic peacock.

As you inspect the menu and nibble on the dry, stale bread, a waiter comes by with a large tray holding specimens of the day's seafood selection. He runs through the list, patting his wares like a used-car salesman to emphasize quality. (This unsanitary practice notwithstanding, most waiters and waitresses we met were amiable and attentive.) The seafood at the Captain's Table cannot be faulted for freshness; the kitchen, however, often manages to diminish its appeal by overcooking and underseasoning.

The best appetizers are fresh and saline cherrystones and oysters on the half shell presented over ice. The baked clams, though, are overbreaded. A special one evening, small lobster tails from Australia, were tasty and fresh tasting; jumbo tiger shrimp, on the other hand, were cooked to rubbery stiffness. The kitchen makes a first-class clam chowder, light and generously seasoned. If fresh shiitake mushrooms are available, get them sautéed with garlic.

The large seafood selection is prepared either broiled or sautéed, usually accompanied by unseasoned vegetables on the side. Broiled whole grouper and red snapper were fresh and served with sautéed fennel; fresh lemon was all they needed. Both tuna steak and swordfish were dry, the latter coming with a good garlic sauce. The remaining broiled or sautéed fish had a 50 percent success rate at best.

Red snapper fillet cooked "en papillote" (in aluminum foil, actually) was a sorry sight, the fish and its accompanying shrimp were stiff and tasteless, the scallops and mussels just salvageable, all in a light tomato broth. Those who have never tried blowfish might sample it here—the firm, fibrous fillet is slightly browned outside and served with a tasty garlic butter. Sautéed soft-shell crabs are recommended when in season.

The wine list is remarkable only for its overpricing. The few desserts are nearly a total loss save for the ice cream and crunchy, semisweet pecan pie.

# CELLAR IN THE SKY

★ ★

*1 World Trade Center, 107th floor, 938-1111.*

*Atmosphere: Tranquil cellarlike ambiance with classical guitarist.*

*Service: Attentive and efficient.*

*Wine: Wines included with meal.*

*Price range: Moderately expensive (prix-fixe dinner, $80, including wine).*

*Credit cards: All major cards.*

*Hours: Dinner, one seating at 7:30 P.M., Monday through Saturday.*

*Reservations: Required.*

*Wheelchair accessibility: Restrooms on entrance level; several steps up into dining room. Arrangements can be made ahead of time to use service corridor.*

Cellar in the Sky is the small, wine-oriented restaurant in the larger complex known as Windows on the World. The Cellar seats only thirty-six, and offers a leisurely preset five-course meal built around an aperitif and four wines for $80. If you don't mind surrendering personal choice to fate, Cellar in the Sky can be one of the more enchanting and delectable experiences in town.

The dimly lit, romantic dining room has a cavelike motif sporting wine racks along glass walls. It does not offer the celestial views of the main restaurant, although what you gain in the trade-off is more varied and refined food that is artfully presented and paired with intelligently selected quality wines. A classical guitarist plays nightly. The $80 prix fixe might sound stiff, but considering that no supplements are levied and wine is included, it is really no more expensive than many other first-class establishments in New York City.

The menu changes about twice a month. Typical dinners might begin with such finger foods as silken foie gras mousse on toast, bite-size vegetable tartelettes, caviar on buttered brown bread, and buttery smoked sea scallops set over a tangle of julienned leeks. The wines for starters: a zesty Trimbach Riesling on one occasion, a bright and dry Wente Chardonnay another time.

Subsequent courses are gracefully orchestrated to embrace a range of flavors and textures. It might be a terrine of fresh foie gras (not as flavorful as it could be) served with brioche and assorted greens, or a superb dish of fresh and mild calf's liver set over wilted sweet onions with veal stock. The summertime soups are always light and delicate—I preferred the sweet oyster bisque redolent of oyster brine to the cream of sole with chives.

The service staff is attentive and accommodating. Waiters make certain your wine well never goes dry.

Both fish courses excelled: a perfectly cooked, meaty fresh turbot brightened with the lightest of cream sauces, one colored with parsley, the other with carrots. Lobster out of the shell in a truffle beurre blanc was as prettily arranged as it was delicious, surrounded by spokes of asparagus and flecked with black truffles. A luscious Pommard from one of the region's premier vineyards, Rugiens, set the stage for tender squab in a pinot-noir-based sauce flanked by red and white cabbage; rare roasted strips of duck breast were surrounded by lively fettuccine flecked with fresh sage and shards of crisped duck skin.

A small but well-chosen cheese course follows with an appropriate wine. Desserts are satisfying though not memorable—lime tartelette paired with lemon mousse and pale lime sherbert one day, and somewhat dense profiteroles encasing coconut ice cream surrounded by fresh berries another time.

Cellar in the Sky is a celebratory sort of place where decisions are few and the wine flows freely from a regal fountain. For any lofty occasion, it is well worth the ascent.

# CHANTAL CAFÉ

★

*257 West 55th Street, 246-7076.*

*Atmosphere: Small, cheerful, brick-lined space with a skylighted back room.*

*Service: Affable but inexperienced and sometimes confused.*

*Price range: Inexpensive (pretheater dinner prix fixe $19).*

*Credit cards: All major cards.*

*Hours: Lunch, 11:30 A.M. to 3 P.M., Monday through Friday; dinner, 5:30 to 10:30 P.M., Monday through Thursday; until 11:30 P.M., Friday and Saturday; pretheater dinner, 5:30 to 7 P.M., Monday through Friday.*

*Reservations: Suggested.*

*Wheelchair accessibility: Several steps down to the dining room; restrooms on the same level.*

While the straightforward French repertory at this theater district bistro occasionally hits a flat note, diners who get to know the menu are fairly assured of a pleasing experience among the tourist traps in this part of town.

The long narrow space has a brick-walled front room with a row of tables along one side. You pass the little open kitchen to reach a skylighted back room, a makeshift-looking affair with timbered beams, overhead fans, hanging plants, a chalkboard menu, and wedding-reception rental chairs.

The key to satisfaction is to stick with house standards

like the rack of lamb with rosemary, a well-cooked steak with crisp french fries, and paillard of chicken with fresh tarragon sauce. When the kitchen is on, the navarin of lamb can be appealing, its red-wine sauce mellowed with lamb juices. Lean, rosy steak tartare is a particular bargain at lunch for $8.95.

Simple seafood preparations are satisfying, like the grilled salmon with dill sauce, grouper with a sweet-tinged beurre blanc and fish-stock sauce, and grilled swordfish with tomato and ginger. Waitresses and waiters here are good-natured, and they try hard; at these prices one tends to be less demanding about fine points. The wine list is sorely in need of reworking. The selection is paltry and undistinguished, with some white wines sampled already over the hill.

For starters, big tender leeks vinaigrette are always well turned out, as are the warm goat cheese salad and beefy onion soup gratinée. The house terrine is moist and mildly livery, but cold broccoli soup is a roll of the dice: bright and tasty one day, anemic the next.

Desserts are not a high point here. You can get a decent crème brûlée and a light, thin-crusted apple tart, but pass up the forgettable chocolate cake and the sodden tarte Tatin.

# CHANTERELLE

★ ★

*2 Harrison Street, at the corner of Hudson Street, 966-6960.*

*Atmosphere: spacious, handsome room with well-spaced tables and moderate noise level.*

*Service: Well trained and efficient.*

*Wine: Exceptionally well-chosen selection.*

*Price range: Expensive.*

*Credit cards: All major cards.*

*Hours: Breakfast, 7:30 to 9:30 A.M., Tuesday through Friday; lunch, noon to 2:30 P.M., Tuesday through Friday; dinner, 6 to 10:30 P.M., Tuesday through Saturday.*

*Reservations: Necessary well in advance.*

*Wheelchair accessibility: Everything on one level.*

In their first eight years as restaurateurs, the publicity-shy Wunderkinds, the Waltucks (David is in the kitchen; Karen, his wife, tends the front), honed their ten-table act to four-star precision. To food-obsessed New Yorkers, their move to slightly larger quarters (fifteen tables) on Harrison Street in 1989 after a four-month closing was the biggest boon to TriBeCa since the subway. My first revisit was befuddling—overcooked steak, flaccid sweetbreads—but I wrote it off to reopening jitters. Three more dinners and nearly fifty dishes later, puzzlement turned to dismay. The new Chanterelle still has its soaring moments, but they are not so frequent as before. Maybe larger crowds have overburdened the kitchen, but the sublime integration of flavors and textures that once marked Mr. Waltuck's cooking is not always evident. In some dishes, ingredients on the plate seem awkwardly introduced at the last minute, like freshmen college roommates. And there is the overall feeling: brisker and less personal.

The airy dining room in the landmark Mercantile Exchange Building is an expanded version of the original: soft pale yellow walls, decorative wood columns, brass chandeliers, a forest of rhododendrons, spacious tables.

The menu is limited to five appetizers and eight entrées (with daily specials). The signature grilled seafood sausage with beurre blanc is as good as ever, as is foie gras with chanterelles and cèpes in a subtly sweet balsamic-vinegar sauce. A buttery cold foie gras terrine comes with onions cooked in Campari: it is jarring at first, but it grows on you. Less interesting is a tuna carpaccio under strips of scallions, briny little pearls of flying-fish roe, and sea urchin sauce.

Memories of the old Chanterelle swirl around such multidimensional delights as braised guinea hen with fennel and truffles under a lid of puff pastry. The current entrées seem to be more bistrolike: halibut with mustard-dill sauce and haricots verts; veal chop with morel cream sauce; red snapper with red-wine butter sauce, asparagus and baby carrots; swordfish in red-pepper purée and sugar snap peas. They are all skillfully prepared, but nothing you could not find at a half-dozen other places in town for half the price. Several dishes come to the table with the same vegetables.

One exceptionally refined dish, reminiscent of the old days, is squab in a terrific sauce infused with anise and fresh herbs. Soft-shell crabs are heavenly in a lime-and-coriander sauce. Sweetbreads are firm and fresh one evening in sherry-vinegar sauce with cèpes, flabby and poorly cleaned of membrane a second time in a bland morel sauce.

Chanterelle's wine list is exceptionally well chosen, not unexpectedly skewed toward big-name, big-price labels. The splendid cheese plate, served with dense and crusty Tom Cat bread, deserves a fine Burgundy. The service staff is exceptionally knowledgeable about the cheeses (and all the food) and attends to all the fine points.

Highlights among the dessert list include bursting ripe blueberry tart, Tupelo honey ice cream, ineffably light and potent chocolate mousse cake (much better than the dry chocolate pavé with coffee sauce), and fruit sorbets. An apple mille-feuille one evening had leathery pastry and hard apples, while strawberry tart with lemon custard had a crust that should have been served with a chisel.

# CHELSEA CENTRAL

★ ★

*227 Tenth Avenue, between 23rd and 24th streets, 620-0230.*

*Atmosphere: Charming saloon ambiance with brick walls and soft lighting.*

*Service: Amiable and knowledgeable about food, but pacing can be slow.*

*Wine: Well-chosen limited list with fair prices.*

*Price range: Moderate.*

*Credit cards: American Express, MasterCard, and Visa.*

*Hours: Brunch 11:30 A.M. to 3 P.M., Sunday; lunch, 11:30 A.M. to 3 P.M., Monday through Friday; dinner, 5:30 to 11 P.M., Monday through Thursday, 5:30 to midnight, Friday and Saturday; 5:30 to 10 P.M., Sunday.*

*Reservations: Suggested.*

*Wheelchair accessibility: Three steps up to dining room; restrooms on same level.*

While it is geographically within the bounds of Chelsea, this inviting saloon-style restaurant on Tenth Avenue is not likely to be discovered by neighborhood strollers—unless you happen to be strolling to a muffler repair shop down by the Hudson River.

I had not returned to Chelsea Central for more than a year until word got around that a promising new chef had arrived, Stephen Meyers, who came up the ranks via La Caravelle, Le Bernardin, and the Sign of the Dove.

Chelsea Central has a well-worn charm, with its long mahogany bar, stamped tin ceiling, tile floor, ceiling fans, and café tables with bentwood chairs. Tulip sconces diffuse soft light on the brick walls and white napery. Somehow, the more refined food has prompted patrons to dress up, although you still see neighborhood regulars in pullovers and khakis.

Mr. Meyers's pure and motherly food is just what you need to revitalize the system after a week of urban aggravation and gastronomic abuse. Crusty loin of pork with braised cabbage, confit of shallots, and garlic mashed potatoes; pink and juicy leg of lamb with carrots and broccoli; roast chicken with celery purée and an herby vinegar sauce: they all brought table conversation to an abrupt halt. This is dig-in food.

Mom may not have been a big confit maker back in the 1950s, but if she had been, hers would have tasted like this. A duck leg is superbly moist and infused with spices, teamed with sliced wood-grilled breast, a faintly peppery port sauce, wild rice, and deep-fried turnip chips.

A well-aged steak, cooked precisely to order, comes with fried shallots and dauphin potatoes, also known in France as doormat potatoes, because they are flat potato pancakes that are sautéed, then baked. A recommended seasonal special is the mild-flavored loin of New Zealand venison, served with a punchy pepper sauce, cranberry relish, and cylinders of polenta garnished with more relish.

On the seafood side is salmon grilled to just pink in the center and set over braised leeks with a subtle red-wine sauce; seared tuna steak, coated with black pepper, came with delicious orzo colored with tomatoes and Swiss chard.

Several pastas are offered daily. My favorite was a lusty combination of penne with lots of crumbled fennel sausage, tomato, black olives, and arugula. The tartness of the arugula and the salinity of the olives plays off the sausage in a compelling way. The well-scrubbed young waiters and waitresses wearing long white aprons are full of enthusiasm for the food but have little to offer in the way of wine tips. Service can get bogged down—probably the fault of the kitchen—on busy nights. The wine list is limited but particularly well chosen and fairly priced.

A terrific way to begin is with the butternut-squash-filled ravioli in a reduced chicken broth with pine nuts and Swiss chard.

A flourless chocolate marquise is a fitting finale, rich, semisweet, and irresistible; also superior are the deep-dish apple pie with cinnamon crumb topping and the thin sweet-sour lemon tart.

# CHELSEA TRATTORIA ITALIANA

★ ★

*108 Eighth Avenue, between 15th and 16th streets, 924-7786.*

*Atmosphere: Brick and whitewashed walls; casual and friendly.*

*Service: Extremely eager to please; efficient.*

*Wine: Moderate-size Italian list, at fair prices.*

*Price range: Moderate.*

*Credit cards: All major cards.*

*Hours: Lunch, noon to 3 P.M., Monday through Friday (the kitchen remains open between lunch and dinner for light meals); dinner, 5 to 11:30 P.M., Monday through Saturday.*

*Reservations: Suggested.*

*Wheelchair accessibility: Dining facilities on one level; restrooms downstairs.*

Upon walking into this homey Chelsea establishment, your urban stress meter immediately drops to a more healthful range. The brick-and-whitewashed dining room is soothing, tidy, and calm. A cheerful crowd of neighborhood regulars clusters at the bar before dinner, and the tuxedo-clad maître d'hôtel greets you as one of the inner circle, even if it is your first visit.

Chelsea Trattoria Italiana is a friendly and easygoing restaurant that serves some top-notch pastas at affordable prices. It is owned by the Bitici brothers (Sergio, Michael, John, and Joseph), who also run Minetta Tavern on Macdougal Street, the Grand Ticino Restaurant on Thompson Street, and Toscana on Third Avenue at 54th Street.

The menu is not notable for bold innovation but rather for the chef's pure and understated approach. Ingredients are unassailably fresh, and pastas are authoritatively seasoned but not oversauced. You could start off with zesty mussels or clams in an herby tomato broth, or the rather thickly sliced but flavorful carpaccio with pesto sauce (the mixed antipasto is nothing special). Considering the felicitous choice of pastas, however, I recommend starting with half portions of those.

The chef prepares several daily specials. One evening they included terrific whole-wheat-flour-and-spinach ravioli, called cappelletti, filled with minced mixed vegetables in a cold fresh tomato purée; another is aromatic linguine with pesto sauce and tender young string beans. Fettuccine tossed with wild mushrooms and sun-dried tomatoes is a brassy delight, as is another special, cappellini, glossed with garlic-scented olive oil and al dente broccoli. Tortellini Bolognese misses the mark slightly from oversalting. If you yearn for something to jolt the taste buds, try the tagliolini in a light tomato-based arrabbiata sauce spiked with garlic and hot green peppers.

Risotto, too, is masterfully prepared, especially the one studded with squid, shrimp and clams, crabmeat, scallions, parsley, and just enough hot pepper to keep you on edge.

The service staff combines polite efficiency with refreshing candor. One evening I was in the mood for a steak and ordered the beef Fiorentina. Our captain lowered his notepad, shook his head, and said, "If you want a steak, get a real steak, not one with all that stuff on it." The pan-sautéed fillet that came out was superb, beefy, tender and juicy. Veal chop with sage would have been better cooked the same way rather than broiled. The veal was top grade and tasty but came out nearly raw in the center and slightly dry outside.

Among seafood dishes, look for the occasional special of sautéed red snapper embellished with black olives, tomatoes, capers, and white wine. Sweetbreads are prepared to the customer's specifications. One of my dining companions asked for them sautéed with white wine, and they were a marvel of subtlety—firm textured, golden, and delicious. Even a lowly chicken breast sautéed with white wine, mushrooms, and sun-dried tomatoes was memorable, for the meat was perfectly cooked and the sauce well balanced.

Desserts are acceptable but nothing to swoon over. I suggest the moist and semisweet orange layer cake and the dense chocolate cake; tiramisù is rich and creamy but lacks the sharp espresso edge it should have, and ricotta cheesecake would be better without the thick, heavy crust.

# CHEZ JOSEPHINE

★ ★

*414 West 42nd Street, 594-1925.*

*Atmosphere: Lively theatrical atmosphere; piano players nightly.*

*Service: Diligent about getting pretheater customers out on time; generally efficient.*

*Wine: Limited but well-rounded list with fair prices.*

*Price range: Moderate.*

*Credit cards: American Express, MasterCard, and Visa.*

*Hours: Dinner, 5 P.M. to midnight, Monday through Saturday.*

*Reservations: Suggested, especially for weekends and pretheater.*

*Wheelchair accessibility: Dining on main level; restrooms up long flight of stairs.*

If stars were awarded for exuberance, Chez Josephine would have few rivals. On some nights at this ebullient production you see more colorful characters, crazy plot twists, and dramatic flourishes than at most plays on nearby Off Broadway. Sundry musicians drop in to play the grand piano, a beaming French tap dancer brings the house down when she leaps onto the zinc-topped bar, a fortune teller charms customers upstairs, and Jean-Claude Baker, the incessantly entertaining owner, manages to be everywhere at once.

Mr. Baker has made his theatrical bistro an homage to Josephine Baker, the exotic chanteuse who was the toast of Paris in the 1920s. All over the place you see images of Miss Baker in various stages of undress. And at the drop of a napkin, Mr. Baker—one of the singer's many adopted children—will regale customers with stories about her illustrious and tragic life.

You can start with something as simple as a well-seasoned and mildly livery pork terrine or a peppery lobster bisque rich with lobster-stock flavor and generous with sweet white meat. A typical rustic French starter is the warm mussel casserole made with tiny tender mussels, red potatoes, pearl onions, herbs, and white wine. Another appetizer that is hardly French but appealing nonetheless is crimped ravioli filled with goat cheese in a light veal-stock sauce with fresh dill and pine nuts.

The young service staff is diligent about getting pretheater customers out on time. They also manage to work around Mr. Baker's dining-room antics with good humor.

Mr. Teulade's daily specials represent some of his best efforts. One evening we had a wonderful pot-au-feu with veal shank, vegetables, and duck-confit sausage accompanied by coarse salt, cornichons, and grainy mustard. Another was juicy roasted loin of pork, sliced and served over smoky lentils and bacon. Osso buco was succulently gelatinous, and the vegetable couscous with it was a good match. A little more sauce would have been welcome, though.

On the regular menu, reliable options include earthy boudin noir (blood sausage) with red cabbage, apples, onions and good french fries; rosy calf's liver with sherry-wine vinegar and shallots; rack of lamb over mashed potatoes with carrots; and a snappy steak au poivre with pommes coin de rue, which are cubed, sautéed potatoes.

Mr. Teulade has a passion for desserts; thus, the selection here rises above typical bistro fare. Cherry clafouti is light, custardy, and minimally sweet, while le délice Josephine, a chocolate mousse cake, is dark, unrepentantly rich, and addictive. One of the most alluring desserts is called warm apple-and-rhubarb crêpe cake made with layers of thin crêpes sandwiching sweet apples and faintly tart rhubarb. There is also an intense cappuccino mousse and good praline bombe, with layers of praline, genoise and ice cream.

# CHEZ LOUIS

★

*1016 Second Avenue, between 53rd and 54th streets, 752-1400.*

*Atmosphere: Spacious, casual dining room decorated in florid red with French posters.*

*Service: Amiable and competent.*

*Wine: Fine selection at exceptionally low prices.*

*Price range: Moderately expensive.*

*Credit cards: All major cards.*

*Hours: Lunch, 11:45 A.M. to 3 P.M., Monday through Friday; dinner, 5:30 to 11:30 P.M., Monday through Saturday, 5 to 10 P.M., Sunday.*

*Reservations: Suggested.*

*Wheelchair accessibility: Several steps down at entrance and up to dining room; restrooms downstairs.*

When this two-fisted bistro came along in 1985, it presaged what has by now become a full-scale revolt against overstylized food served in tea-party portions. David Liederman (of David's Cookies) set out to emulate Chez L'Ami Louis in Paris, a glorious hovel on the Right Bank that features game and poultry roasted over wood fires. For the first few years, New York's Chez Louis turned out some soulful and seductive fare, but recent visits indicate that the fires have dimmed somewhat. Chez Louis bears no resemblance to its Parisian icon. It has a spacious bar in front and an elevated dining room in the back that faces an urban courtyard. The room is done in florid red wallpaper with framed French posters all about.

Some of the dishes I have enjoyed in the past now seem carelessly assembled and erratically seasoned. Take, for example, a hallmark dish here, the herbed roast chicken for two. On my first visit, the bird had been cooked so long that the breast meat was papery-dry, and even the thigh was slightly overcooked; on a second sampling it was right on target. The herb-infused chicken-stock sauce and roasted garlic were delicious both times.

When the weather turns warm, there may not be a big demand for cassoulet, which may be just as well; this one lacks a deep, long-cooked richness, and the pork is dense and tough. A better choice is coq au vin, another blood-warmer, which is savory in its herb-perfumed red-wine sauce. At lunch, two other chicken dishes were well turned out: a pecan-breaded chicken breast was deliciously crunchy and came with a mustard-sharpened sour-cream sauce; and grilled baby chicken.

A monstrous veal rib emerges from the fires nicely seared and remarkably juicy (though you have to season it), along with roasted onions, yellow squash, and zucchini.

I have never liked the hubcap-size potato pies here. Because of their bulk, they are always pasty in the middle and lack seasoning except for some minced garlic on top. The smaller version, which is served with single-portion entrées, is at least cooked throughout, though not necessarily more flavorful. Lightly fried onion rings or roasted vegetables are better side dishes.

Seafood sampled was uneven. Grilled salmon with a sassy green-peppercorn sauce was inedibly dry one evening, moist and buttery another time. A special called sea scallops with red peppers and ginger sauce with brown rice was cooked well, but evidence of ginger was not easy to find. A better choice was a lunch special one day, moist grilled swordfish with a honey-mustard sauce and saffron rice. Lobster fans might consider the grilled two-pounder, glossed with tarragon butter.

Chez Louis has an exceptionally well-priced, French-oriented wine list.

Since main courses are so copious, one is advised to go lightly on starters. Freshly shucked, well-iced bluepoint oysters are a fine way to start, as are the fresh mussels under a zesty lemon-coriander sauce. Onion soup is almost viscous from long simmering, and arrestingly sweet. Spring vegetable soup was an oddity, for it was filled with winter vegetables—carrots, leeks, potatoes—and timidly seasoned. White-bean-and-leek salad could have used a boost from herbs. If you opt for something more substantial, the wonderfully silken foie gras terrine studded with green peppercorns awaits.

For dessert, there is a creation aptly named Super-Duper Brownie Sundae that is an adolescent's dream, heaped with ice cream, whipped cream, and chocolate sauce. Deep-dish apple-and-raisin pie with a walnut-cookie crust is for serious eaters, too. Pecan squares are achingly sweet, but lemon crème brûlée is not a bad idea. And, of course, there are David's Cookies.

While Chez Louis can still be recommended for some of its clean, homespun fare, its overall performance has slipped from two stars to one.

# CHIKUBU

★ ★

*12 East 44th Street, 818-0715.*

*Atmosphere: Soft gray and natural-wood dining rooms; low noise level.*

*Service: Prompt and pleasant, but not always helpful in explaining dishes.*

*Price range: Moderately expensive.*

*Credit cards: American Express and Diners Club.*

*Hours: Lunch, 11:30 A.M. to 2 P.M., Monday through Friday; dinner, 5:30 to 10 P.M., Monday through Saturday.*

*Reservations: Requested.*

*Wheelchair accessibility: Everything on one level.*

Chikubu is the kind of low-key place that makes living in New York tolerable to the homesick Japanese business executive: a demure, homey, and personable restaurant that is largely uncompromised by tempura-crunching Americans, at least at dinner. At lunchtime, though, the scene is more international as midtowners stream in for light, salubrious fare and fast-paced service.

Chikubu specializes in the cuisine of Kyoto, which is known for its broiled seafood and casseroles. A wide sashimi selection is available, but sushi is served only at lunch.

The long, narrow front dining room is spare and trim with light gray walls and blond-wood tables. A sushi bar in the back is usually packed at lunch with regulars, Japanese all, and upstairs are four private tatami rooms (one with pits below the table for those whose toes turn blue after sitting cross-legged on a mat for an hour).

The lunch menu has a box lunch—bento box, that is—that you can inspect on the way in: a sample is on display under cellophane. The box usually has a main course surrounded by rice, sashimi of tuna, two types of pickled seaweed, tamago (the sweetened, omeletlike tidbit), rice noodles with chopped eggs, and more. On one occasion, the main course was excellent broiled fresh eel glazed with a sweet blend of soy sauce and mirin. Another time it was delicious cutlets of tender pork in a brittle, light rice flour breading.

Sashimi is better sampled at the sushi bar, where the selection is wider than indicated by the soft-spoken waitresses. The standard sushi assortment is top grade, the rice appropriately seasoned with vinegar and sugar. The selection varies if you state no preference, usually including tuna, squid, cuttlefish, fluke, and the like.

Among the cooked fare, tempura can be bright and light one day, floury the next. Broiled dishes are far superior to fried ones. Shioyaki flounder is a house special in which the skin is lightly salted and broiled until parchment crisp. Similar renditions are done with salmon and fluke. The hot-stone method of cooking is often more flash than flavor in Japanese restaurants, but Chikubu's is an exception: a beef fillet is well seasoned and seared outside, cooked medium rare within, and served with a soy sauce flavored with garlic and onions. When the weather turns cold, Japanese clients turn to yosenabe, a heady seafood-and-cabbage soup cooked at the table.

A new dessert that is as unexpected as it is delightful is called pumpkin pudding, which is essentially a dome of fibrous, minimally sweet pumpkin topped with whipped cream.

# CHINA GRILL

★

*60 West 53rd Street, entrance at 52 West 53rd Street, 333-7788.*

*Atmosphere: Towering and loud block-long restaurant with an extended bar, open kitchen, and lively crowd.*

*Service: Usually energetic and friendly, but haphazard kitchen system leads to awkward delays.*

*Wine: Heavy on big-name Bordeaux and expensive French whites.*

*Price range: Moderately expensive.*

*Credit cards: All major cards.*

*Hours: Lunch, noon to 2 P.M., Monday through Friday; dinner, 5:30 to 11 P.M., Monday through Thursday, until midnight, Friday and Saturday, 6 to 10 P.M., Sunday.*

*Reservations: Necessary.*

*Wheelchair accessibility: Dining on ground floor; restrooms downstairs.*

At times, especially after 9 P.M., China Grill resembles a restaurant in which the adult proprietors have gone home and the teenagers have taken over. One Thursday evening, the sound system was cranked up until the percussive artillery of a Sting song hammered the towering marble walls; an animated young woman dressed in black hunched over the reservations desk, giggling on the telephone; a busboy dropped a service of coffee all over the Marco Polo inscription on the marble floor; and the bartender was so distracted he asked us for our order three times.

This may sound like the first salvo in a devastating review, but it is not, for some of the food at this three-and-a-half-year-old Oriental-California hybrid is provocative and well executed. It's only that the place tends to come unglued late in the evening; lunch and early evening are less chaotic.

The grandly proportioned setting is dramatic: a soaring block-long space with jade walls, dangling eggshell-colored light shades, a marble floor inlaid with (coffee-splotched) quotations from the journals of Marco Polo, and a long bar bordering the open kitchen, where the sizzling action is nonstop.

Among entrées, grilled squab is a standout, its glossy skin holding moist, faintly gamy meat, with a caramelized black vinegar sauce. It comes with a nubbly rice pancake holding sliced shiitake mushrooms. Honey-glazed duck is equally well done. You are served sliced breast meat, cooked medium rare, and two legs, all with a sweet plum purée. Another sure-fire winner is Shanghai lobster. In this, lobster meat is nestled among a fragile forest of brittle rice noodles, deep-fried spinach, and ginger in a lovely curry sauce. Sizzling whole red snapper is monstrous but lacks the promised ginger marination flavor and is overcooked.

Barbecued salmon with a subtle Chinese mustard sauce is satisfying but not special, and steamed fillet of halibut in cucumber broth is as insipid as it sounds. A savory if architecturally flawed lunch special is veal loin sandwich. Exceptionally succulent slices of veal are piled between thick layers of brioche and served with a ginger-and-soy dipping sauce. A German shepherd would have a chore getting its jaws around this assembly.

You may be perplexed at the haphazard way dishes are brought out one at a time from the kitchen. Our waiter called it "Chinese style," which means the dishes arrive one by one when the kitchen gets around to them. That may work fine in family-style Chinatown restaurants, but for an à la carte midtown place that caters to a time-pressed business crowd at lunch, it can be exasperating. Except for the dizzy folks at the front desk (I was cut off two out of three times I called for reservations), the service staff is good natured and at times energetic.

Among scintillating appetizers to sample are little rolls of sake-cured salmon in cabbage leaves, garnished with ribbons of cucumber and filaments of raw beets. Two gargantuan salads make fine lunch entrées: shreds of roasted chicken are tossed with toasted sesame seeds, mixed greens, crispy rice noodles, sesame oil, and a touch of hot pepper oil. Peking duck salad is on the sweet side, combining red cabbage, sweet peppers, and an orange-tangerine sauce.

The often spicy and highly acidic dishes here call for crisp, clean white wines, but the list here, heavy on big-name Bordeaux and expensive French whites, is more appropriate to a French or Italian restaurant.

At the end of the meal, even the coffee is served Chinese style, which is to say whenever the staff feels like bringing it to you, before, with, or after dessert. Among the best of the sweets is moist poundcake covered with tart cranberries and adrift in a hot caramel sauce with vanilla ice cream. A combination platter of cinnamon-dusted wontons with coconut and chocolate ice creams is fun, but cinnamon-raisin pudding is nondescript. And the Zany Dessert of the Month Award goes to a plate of anemic coffee gelatin, rescued only by decent espresso ice cream.

China Grill represents a good idea in an ideal location, but its lack of discipline in the dining room and the kitchen reflects a one-star performance, down from the two stars it received in 1987.

# CHIN CHIN

★ ★

*216 East 49th Street, 888-4555.*

*Atmosphere: **Handsome and refined front dining room in soft peach and wood tones; back room more whimsical.***

*Service: **Highly professional and friendly.***

*Wine: **Impressive list at sensible prices.***

*Price range: **Moderately expensive.***

*Credit cards: **All major cards.***

*Hours: **Lunch, 11:30 A.M. to 5 P.M., Monday through***

*Friday; dinner, 5 to 11:30 P.M., Monday through Saturday, 5 to 11 P.M., Sunday.*

*Reservations: Suggested.*

*Wheelchair accessibility: Two steps at the entrance; all facilities on the same level.*

Chin Chin is among the most stylish and enticing Chinese restaurants in town. If you have a flash of déjà vu there, chances are you are familiar with Auntie Yuan on First Avenue near 65th Street, where James Chin worked as manager for five years. The other half of the eponymous duo is his brother, Wally.

The Chin brothers, sincere and engaging professionals both, stuffed their backpacks with some choice goodies from Auntie Yuan before blazing their own trail, and many of them have reappeared on the menu at Chin Chin—the terrific cold noodles in fiery sesame sauce, crackling barbecued quails, the pepper-laced orange beef, a host of excellent wines. At the same time, Chin Chin is a highly personal effort, reflecting the brothers' dedication to fulfilling what they call their "lifelong dream."

The two dining rooms are dramatically different. The rectangular front room, with its warm pale peach walls and burnished woodwork, could be mistaken for a tasteful American restaurant were it not for the gallery of charming sepia-toned portraits of the extended Chin family on the walls. Tables along rust-colored banquettes are comfortably sized and conversation is well muffled. The step-down back room could be another restaurant altogether, this one a blizzard of white—walls, ceiling, tablecloths—interrupted only by colorful Oriental pottery perched on wall ledges.

The Chins are keenly attuned to the difference between "uptown" and "downtown" Chinese food aficionados, and they have cast their lot with the former. Chin Chin's food is scintillating but never startling. (If you have a hankering for braised cod tongue or crunchy ducks' feet, hop the downtown IRT.) Steamed vegetable dumplings are light and fresh, although my dining crew unanimously preferred the pan-fried pork-filled version brightened with fresh ginger. You can't go wrong with the golden puffed tendrils of fried squid or the succulent shredded duck salad on a bed of crispy rice noodles with tomato and coriander.

A starter called vegetable duck pie is an intriguing deception. A mock duck skin is made by deep frying strips of rice-flour dough embedded with black mushrooms and water chestnuts, which is then served like Peking duck inside a rice pancake along with scallions and hoisin sauce. The combination has the texture of Peking duck, if not the rich flavor. If given the choice, I would go for the real thing, which, by the way, is excellent here—generous with rosy duckmeat. Velvet corn soup, a soothing crab-laced concoction, is just the thing for a frosty fall evening.

The Chin brothers work the dining room like a political advance team, welcoming guests, setting the mood, answering questions, and then standing back to monitor the proceedings. Unlike so many downtown restaurants, which insist upon dumping eight courses on the table at once, meals here are paced to your request. If you like wine with Chinese food—indeed, many sprightly whites go well with it—the impressive and sensibly priced selection here offers a good chance to experiment. Two whites I highly recommend with this food are the Château Ste. Chapelle Johannisberg Riesling from Idaho and the 1986 Tocai Friulano, Ronco del Gnemiz from northern Italy, both under $20.

Main courses worth exploring are the crispy whole sea bass, which is impeccably fresh and glazed with a piquant sauce; fleshy prawns prepared Sichuan style with ginger and hot pepper; shredded pork laced with hot and sweet peppers and black mushrooms; and lovely Chinese broccoli swathed in oyster sauce bolstered with garlic. Sautéed mussels in black bean sauce were a good idea, but the mussels were muddy tasting and gritty. I was surprised to see curried lamb stew on the menu, but not surprised to find it starchy and uninteresting.

Chicken with walnuts and leeks is rather tame and nondescript tourist fare. Go instead with the dish called three-glass chicken, in which the meat is braised in an aromatic mélange of white wine, water, and soy sauce, along with garlic, ginger, and coriander. Ten-ingredient rice—packing everything from shrimp to cubes of Smithfield ham—makes a vivid side dish.

Ice cream and fruit are the only desserts.

# CHRIST CELLA

**SATISFACTORY**

*160 East 46th Street, between Lexington and Third avenues, 697-2479.*

*Atmosphere: Drab and colorless dining rooms with a masculine feeling.*

*Service: Perfunctory, informal.*

*Wine: Outdated international list.*

*Price range: Moderately expensive.*

*Credit cards: All major cards.*

*Hours: Lunch and dinner, noon to 10:30 P.M., Monday through Thursday, noon to 10:45 P.M., Friday, 5 to 10:45 P.M., Saturday.*

*Reservations: Recommended.*

*Wheelchair accessibility: Elevator between two dining rooms. Restrooms accessible.*

Revisits to this once-venerable but now moribund steakhouse indicate that Christ Cella has a long way to go if it is to catch up with the midtown competition. The dowdy downstairs dining rooms could probably be described as "homey" if the food were better. The front room upstairs, the largest of all, at least benefits from sunlight and a street view.

Menus are superfluous. Steaks, chops, and several fish entrées are rattled off so quickly in a rote manner that you may have to ask your waiter to repeat the list. Service is perfunctory, nothing more.

Lamb chops continue to be among the best bets, char-blackened outside and buttery within. Veal chops are cooked to order and relatively tender but pale tasting. New York strip steak can be rich and beefy, or overcooked and dry, depending on the luck of the draw. Broiled snapper dusted with paprika has all the flavor of typing paper. It comes with a cereal bowl full of tartar sauce, but even that fails to rescue it.

The anachronistic wine list offers no specific names for Bordeaux châteaux but rather describes them as merely St. Emilion, St. Julian, Médoc, and so on.

The biggest letdown is the famous Christ Cella lobster, which for years has been renowned for its size. On one occasion ours was indeed a hefty critter—about three pounds—but its mushy texture hinted that it had passed on to lobster heaven some time before the chef made its acquaintance. Another time a 2½-pounder was better.

Considering the limited number of side dishes served, one would think the kitchen could do a better job. Not so with the leathery hash brown potatoes, soggy premade Caesar salad, and assorted salad greens with gloppy blue cheese dressing. The crabmeat salad, which is the best of the lot, comes with the same cliché ketchup cocktail sauce that you find at Peter Luger.

After the meal, a waiter comes to your table lugging a tray holding a giant napoleon the weight of a barbell. Actually, it is pretty good, in a gooey sort of way. Rum cake with chocolate filling is vastly enhanced by a dousing of rum.

# CITY CAFE

**SATISFACTORY**

*1481 York Avenue, near 78th Street, 570-9810.*

*Atmosphere: Clean and comfortable café done in white brick and tile. Moderately noisy.*

*Service: Chummy but generally competent.*

*Wine: Moderate American list at fair prices.*

*Price range: Moderate.*

*Credit cards: All major cards.*

*Hours: Brunch 11:30 A.M. to 3 P.M., Saturday and Sunday; dinner, 5:30 to 10 P.M., Sunday through Tuesday, 5:30 to*

*10:30 p.m., Wednesday, 5:30 to 11 p.m., Thursday through Saturday.*

*Reservations: Suggested.*

*Wheelchair accessibility: All facilities on ground level. Restrooms small for wheelchairs.*

City Cafe is one of those sparkling, antiseptic Upper East Side dining spots that have such an air of camaraderie and élan that one is compelled to try them. Unfortunately, the café's antiseptic quality extends to the food, which too often is untouched by seasoning.

The wide, open dining room is done in whitewashed brick and tile with well-spaced café tables draped with paper, and bentwood chairs. A garden in the back opens in warm weather. The walls look like a gallery of who's who in the restaurant world, festooned with framed menus from such diverse establishments as the Quilted Giraffe in New York, Tour d'Argent in Paris, and the Fog City Diner in San Francisco.

Waiters in striped sport shirts are chummy and opinionated but generally perform their jobs with care.

The meal gets off to a good start if you try the wonderfully moist and nubbly cornbread. The menu sounds beguiling, which heightens the frustration when something comes out as insipid as a special of angel-hair pasta with grilled shrimp and scallops: the pasta is limp and tasteless, ringed by the well-cooked shellfish and pale tomatoes. Grilled shrimp alone, a regular appetizer, are rubbery (although the red cole slaw on the side is good).

Two starters can be recommended. You will not find more delicate fried calamari in town (served with a spicy tomato-based tarter sauce). Salads are bright and fresh, too.

The best entrée is the simplest: roast chicken with mashed potatoes and chutney. Sautéed lemon sole is the runner-up, enlivened with capers, lemon, and a liberal dose of garlic. Veal chop is pleasing, too, thick and tender with a rich stock sauce and assorted winter vegetables.

When the kitchen falls flat it is either from overcooking, as in the case of the double-thick pork chop with excellent onion-laced mashed potatoes, or from lack of seasoning, which mars a grilled tuna special.

Desserts are heavy duty and exceedingly rich. Brownies with ice cream and hot fudge are as good as they are nostalgic; chocolate pecan pie, though, is cloyingly sweet.

# CLAIRE

★ ★

*156 Seventh Avenue, near 20th Street, 255-1955.*

*Atmosphere: Tropical-theme dining room with paper-covered tables.*

*Service: Casual and pleasant but occasionally slow.*

*Wine: Small but adequate list, well matched to the food and fairly priced.*

*Price range: Moderate.*

*Credit cards: All major cards.*

*Hours: Brunch, noon to 4:40 P.M., Saturday and Sunday; lunch, noon to 4:30 P.M., Monday through Friday; dinner, 5:30 P.M. to 12:30 A.M., Sunday through Thursday, 5:30 to 1 A.M., Friday and Saturday.*

*Reservations: Suggested.*

*Wheelchair accessibility: Dining on one level; restrooms in basement.*

In recent years, seafood prices have jumped higher than dolphins at a Florida marine park. Almost extinct are the clattering old-fashioned fish houses, where simple, grilled fillets (usually dyed with paprika) were served up with a salad, boiled potatoes, and cole slaw. Today's seafood restaurants are more likely to be genteel places with French or Italian accents and princely prices.

Six-year-old Claire in Chelsea is a happy exception. Modeled after a restaurant of the same name in Key West, Florida, it is a big, aqua-toned place with bare wood floors, paper-covered tables, skylights, wood latticework room dividers, and palms. The hard-edged room reflects noise, making it loud at peak lunch and dinner hours. The crowd ranges from local business types at lunch to casually clad neighborhood regulars at dinner.

The cooking by Thai-born Dhanit Choladda has improved notably since earlier visits. One example from his improved repertoire is Caribbean triggerfish, a species with firm, mild white flesh. It is broiled and draped with a Thai-style coconut-curry sauce that packs plenty of heat but is balanced with sweet onions. Another fiery selection is the wonderfully fresh "Sichuan style" tilefish enlivened with a pepper-kindled black bean sauce. Even the meaty crab cakes carry an invigorating blast of cayenne along with a bright cilantro sauce. Not much effort goes into side dishes, though, as just about everyone gets the same white rice and sautéed vegetables (bok choy one day, Chinese broccoli the next).

If your tastes run to tamer fare, try the snowy broiled pompano accompanied by chopped tomato and basil, or the clear, oceanic linguine with white clam sauce. The other pasta sampled had a Cajun flair: farfalle with spicy tasso ham, sweet little rock shrimp from Florida, and scallions. Two fish suffered from overcooking: the inedibly dry sautéed skate and a blacktip shark in a sherry, dill, and mushroom sauce. While Claire is primarily a seafood house, you can get a respectable hamburger here as well as an exceptionally buttery filet mignon.

The service staff, clad in khaki pants and white shirts, is good natured and casual in style. Sometimes the pace is too casual, though. The wine list is small and functional, with adequate selections well matched in price to the entrées, in the $15 to $25 range.

Recommended starters include the excellent conch chowder, creamy but light, loaded with resilient chopped conch and potatoes, and fired up with a dash of pepper. An attempt at a Cajun-Oriental amalgam, blackened tuna sashimi, flopped, however. The tuna was neither sashimi nor cooked but rather unappetizingly gray. The seviche of tuna with dill and capers was appealing, as were the intriguing soft-shell Louisiana crayfish and little rock shrimp sautéed in garlic and lemon with a touch of cilantro. The chef's affinity for Cajun fare arises again in the sausage appetizer of lusty andouille from Louisiana with a grainy mustard sauce.

Chocolate desserts are a house favorite, and I especially liked the fudgelike chocolate-macadamia-nut torte and the Mississippi mud cake with a two-fisted whiskey sauce.

# THE COACH HOUSE

★

*110 Waverly Place, west of Washington Square, 777-0303.*

*Atmosphere: Charming former coach house, spacious and relaxing.*

*Service: Genteel if not always prompt.*

*Wine: Spotty list without vintages or producers listed.*

*Price range: Moderately expensive.*

*Credit cards: All major cards.*

*Hours: Dinner, 5:30 to 10:30 P.M., Tuesday through Saturday, 4:30 to 10 P.M., Sunday.*

*Reservations: Suggested.*

*Wheelchair accessibility: Dining on ground level; men's restroom upstairs, women's restroom downstairs.*

Be wary when a restaurant is described as an institution, which often signifies that its main attribute is being old. Usually the food reminds me of another institution that played a pivotal role in my life: high school.

The Coach House, circa 1948, certainly has the pedigree and ambiance to qualify as an institution, but fortunately there are reasons to go there other than for sentimentality. Under the curatorship of Leon Lianides, the Coach House has peaked and waned over the years. Recent visits found the Coach House to be neither at its most spirited nor its most feeble, but rather somewhere comfortably in the middle.

The setting retains an old New York charm. This high-ceilinged former stable has brick-and-paneled walls adorned with Early American and French still lifes, a beamed ceiling, red leather banquettes, spindly brass chandeliers, and pretty flower arrangements. The formally attired waiters have a gentility about them, although service is not always as attentive as it once was. An upstairs dining room, used for overflow and parties, has an appeal of its own with a similar color scheme.

The traditional American menu has changed little over the years, which is the way its devoted regulars like it. Start out nibbling on some of the warm corn bread, which is notable for its minimal sugar. Starters you can still rely on include the tasty and fresh eggplant Provençale, lean sausage atop cold lentils in vinaigrette, and the peak quality well-iced oysters (varieties change with market availability). Black bean soup, the house signature dish, came tepid and lacking flavor one evening, steaming hot and gutsy with essence of ham bone another night. Crab cakes are still well made, but the unembellished demiglace that serves as a sauce is insipid.

The Coach House, which used to pride itself on a fine American wine list, has little to crow about today. Nearly half of the wines I ordered from the California section were out of stock. No vintages are listed, and for French wines, producers are not identified.

Meat and potatoes are the way to go here. The steak au poivre is still snappy and tender, with good sautéed potatoes on the side. Rack of lamb was poorly trimmed of fat but succulent, and hulking prime ribs of beef were satisfying. Sirloin steak was overcooked on two occasions, but with a good beefy flavor and well-cooked carrots and spinach on the side. The chicken potpie is not the most appetizing-looking creation—it comes ladled onto the plate cafeteria style—but it is full of moist, fresh chicken and firm vegetables. Veal medallions were tasty, too, sautéed with lemons and herbs.

Of the fish offered, you are better off with the roasted snapper with dill sauce or the shrimp in a pleasant lemony mustard sauce than with the exceedingly dry and underseasoned roasted salmon.

Desserts still excel, whether it is the sublime sugar-dusted chocolate cake, the luxurious Grand Marnier bavaroise, the rich chef's custard, or the crusty pecan pie.

While the Coach House is not up to its two-star level of 1985—one star is now more appropriate—it still has palpable appeals aside from nostalgia.

# COASTAL

★ ★

*300 Amsterdam Avenue, at 74th Street, 769-3988.*

*Atmosphere: Contemporary glass-fronted dining room with coastal mural covering the walls. Extremely loud.*

*Service: Polite and eager; sometimes too eager, resulting in rushed service.*

*Wine: Eclectic list with some unusual selections; very well priced.*

*Price range: Moderate.*

*Credit cards: American Express.*

*Hours: Brunch, 11:45 to 3 P.M., Sunday; dinner, 6 to 11 P.M., Monday through Thursday, 6 to 11:30 P.M., Friday and Saturday, 5:30 to 10 P.M., Sunday.*

*Reservations: Accepted for six or more.*

*Wheelchair accessibility: Everything on one level.*

A major drawback at this otherwise meritworthy seafood house is the crashing noise, which was so loud one evening it nearly knocked me back onto the street when I opened the door. Conversation ricochets off the wraparound windows, stainless-steel bar, wooden floor, and aqua-colored walls covered with a coastline mural.

If you can take the decibels, the rewards are considerable.

Somebody in the kitchen knows how to cook fish and season it deftly. Broiled halibut is sublimely moist, with a good lemony hollandaise (the sauce also goes well with the rare-cooked yellowfin tuna). Snowy red snapper is equally pristine under a concassé of plum tomatoes, scallions, and fresh basil. Broiled grouper is elevated by its vibrant Provençale sauce combining olives, capers, and onions.

Several of the seafood pastas need a jolt of seasoning, such as the broiled shrimp over linguine with steamed asparagus, and angel hair entwined with lobster and mussels in light tomato-cream sauce touched with saffron and Parmesan. The kitchen's attempt at Tex-Mex redfish is a rousing success. Redfish fajitas are made by combining the peppery-coated fillets with grilled onions, warm tortillas, spicy rice, and three ramekins of garnishes: avocado, sour cream, and coriander-tomato salsa. The same formula is a winner with chicken, too.

Cioppino, a fish stew usually associated with San Francisco, tastes as if the overworked kitchen rushes it—the combination was so loaded with tomato that I could hardly find the fish, and garlic slices were almost raw. If you are a lobster fan, the steamed one-and-a-half-pounder is fresh and good.

The wine list is intriguing and well-priced, offering selections from California, the Pacific Northwest, Virginia, New York State, and even Texas. A half dozen are sold by the glass.

Among the appetizers worth trying are the trio of vibrant little seviches, each in a large mussel shell: salmon nuggets in tomato concassé, citrus-marinated tuna with red pepper, and red snapper paired with matchsticks of fresh coconut, scallions, and Tabasco. The four-pepper gravlax is alive with fresh dill and moderately hot, while lovely slices of rare-grilled tuna are superb over succotash. Lobster bisque is light in texture but potent with the shellfish flavor, and New England clam chowder is the real thing.

With such care lavished on the fresh fish, I was surprised to find the oysters tasting rinsed and musty. If you like calamari, the deep-fried pinky rings here are terrific, served with a peppery dressing. Crab cakes, on the other hand, were served cold one evening, then were watery and bland the next.

The best desserts are crumbly apple betty, coconut crème caramel, and thin sugar cookies with vanilla ice cream and fresh strawberries.

# CONTRAPUNTO

★

*200 East 60th Street, 751-8616.*

*Atmosphere: Informal, all white, open kitchen.*

*Service: Confused and haphazard when busy, not very professional.*

*Wine: Moderate-size list; reasonable prices.*

*Price range: Moderate.*

*Credit cards: All major cards.*

*Hours: Lunch, noon to 5 P.M., daily; dinner, 5 to midnight, Monday through Saturday, 4 to 10 P.M., Sunday.*

*Reservations: Not accepted.*

*Wheelchair accessibility: Two flights of stairs to dining room.*

Contrapunto is an upbeat, informal pasta restaurant at 60th Street and Third Avenue that is well worth keeping in mind if you are venturing over to Bloomingdale's territory or one of the movie clusters in the neighborhood.

The menu begins with four appetizers, all good: a mixed green salad with a walnut-oil dressing; grilled mushrooms with garlic; air-dried beef with Parmesan cheese; and a salad of Italian cheeses and roasted peppers. Following are twenty pastas, both fresh and imported, and a handful of specials. There isn't a real clunker among them.

Almost anything with seafood is a safe bet. Try the capelli marina piccola, strands of al dente angel-hair pasta flecked with dried tomatoes, shallots, leeks, and basil, all crowned with a diadem of littleneck clams in the shell; or the fettuccine with chunks of sweet fresh lobster in a mild sage-and-butter sauce.

One of the best dishes is brodetto, a souplike mélange of red snapper, half a lobster, sea scallops, squid, clams, garlic, and fresh herbs. The seafood is served atop flaxen strands of angel-hair pasta swathed in a strong fish stock.

The only seafood dish that doesn't make the grade is malfatti aragosta, large pasta squares filled with paltry bits of lobster in a lackluster sauce. Most of the artistically presented vegetable and cheese pastas are bright and flavorful. Among the more intriguing offerings was the fusilli tossed with dandelion leaves, arugula, watercress, fennel, tomato, garlic, and a generous dusting of hot pepper. The heat of the peppers playing off the cool sensation of the fennel is a delight. There are many vegetable variations—some with mushrooms, or leeks, or varied herbs—and most work well.

Another good choice is the giant ravioli stuffed with mascarpone cheese, spinach, watercress, sage, and Parmesan glistening under a sauce of white wine, butter, and olive oil. The fresh pasta is resilient and the stuffing wonderfully herbaceous.

The wide-open, slightly cramped dining room, all white with spotlit tables, can be deafening at peak hours. Service sometimes resembles a Keystone Kops routine. One white-aproned waiter dashes over breathlessly to take your order, another delivers it ("Who gets the capelli?"), and yet a third tends to wine and other matters. Keep this in mind if you plan to go to a movie or catch a sale at nearby Bloomingdale's.

Most of the cakes and tarts for dessert taste like decent commerical quality—a bit heavy-handed with sugar. The homemade gelati also were too sweet. A better choice is the homemade sorbet, particularly strawberry or orange.

# CORRADO

★

*1373 Avenue of the Americas, near 55th Street, 333-3133.*

*Atmosphere: Clean and bright room done in white with sky-blue trim. Can be loud.*

*Service: Reserved and generally efficient.*

*Wine: Adequate list at reasonable prices.*

*Price range: Moderate.*

*Credit cards: All major cards.*

*Hours: Lunch, 11:30 to 4 P.M., Monday through Friday; dinner, 5 to 11:30 P.M., daily.*

*Reservations: Necessary at lunch, suggested at dinner.*

*Wheelchair accessibility: Dining on ground level; restrooms downstairs.*

In several ways, Corrado, on the Avenue of the Americas near 55th Street, is just what midtown Manhattan needs. In a neighborhood that is frenetic, congested, and sooty, this handsome trattoria is relaxed, airy, and sparkling clean. What's more, the food fits the bill for the average hyperkinetic luncher: light, fresh, and undemanding.

The original owner, Corrado Muttin, has moved on to open another restaurant, but the menu remains essentially the same. The setting, like the food, eschews gimmickry. The glass-fronted dining room is audacious in its simplicity, all white with sky-blue accents, a pattern that is repeated on the tableware. Tables are well separated, although when the place is packed at lunchtime, conversation can amplify in the stark, hard-surfaced room.

Appetizers are simple and appealing. You won't find a better-quality bresaola. The tissue-thin dried beef is meltingly tender and just salty enough to keep you coming back for more; all it needs is a drizzle of olive oil, lemon juice, and some black pepper. The mayonnaise-and-tuna sauce on the veal tonnato is more interesting than the dryish thin slices of veal.

A good way to start here is by splitting the wonderfully creamy yet firm-textured risottos. One I enjoyed immensely was flavored with red wine and white truffles, bolstered by a sturdy veal stock; another was explosive with the flavor of meaty porcini. Pastas are generally on target, too. The foundation of this chef's cooking is an exceptionally ripe and well-herbed tomato sauce. This boosts the al dente ravioli stuffed with minced veal under a tomato-and-basil sauce; also good is the tagliolini with a ripe, Parmesan-sharpened pesto sauce, and the linguine with shrimp in a flavor-packed marinara sauce. One dish that failed to excite was the farfalle with Bolognese sauce: the pasta was just short of al dente, leaving it a bit starchy, and the sauce had a peculiar sweet flavor that no one at my table liked. Gnocchi is deftly made, slightly resilient, with the same tomato-and-basil sauce.

The service team here is reserved and generally efficient, although at times the kitchen seems to bog down, resulting in long waits. The wine list is adequate and fairly priced.

Among entrées, I have had good luck with seafood. Shrimp in a subtle mustard cream sauce is delightful (although the carrots on the side were woody); sautéed swordfish on two occasions was remarkably moist and aromatic of fresh rosemary. The same good swordfish is obscured, however, when cut into cubes and mired in marinara sauce. Another worthy light entrée is the moist morsels of chicken in a lovely lemon sauce (a similar preparation works well with veal, too). Veal chops and lamb chops are top quality, as is the fillet of beef with a tame green-pepper sauce.

The best desserts include a changing assortment of light and ripe fruit tarts and a well-made tiramisù.

# CUISINE DE SAIGON

★

*154 West 13th Street, 255-6003.*

*Atmosphere: Faded southeast Asian ambiance; low-key, harsh lighting.*

*Service: Halting and slow; occasional language problems.*

*Price range: Moderate.*

*Credit cards: All major cards.*

*Hours: Dinner, 5 to 11 P.M., Sunday through Thursday, 5 to 11:30 P.M., Friday and Saturday.*

*Reservations: Requested weekends.*

*Wheelchair accessibility: Two stairs down at entrance; everything on ground level.*

Cuisine de Saigon is situated on the ground floor of an old brownstone, and the restaurant has been minimally disguised in Southeast Asian attire. As you enter, you pass through a dark bar–waiting room into the dining area with its arched ceiling painted dark red, faded blue-gray walls reminiscent of an old classroom, Oriental paintings, harsh overhead lighting, and simply appointed tables. Waiters are slow and may pretend they understand English better than they do. I recommend going on less crowded weeknights if possible.

The four-page menu is tempting to read, but don't be deceived by its size—in many cases you face a Hobson's choice. Two or three of the chef's basic sauces go by several aliases and show up unexpectedly.

For example, the crispy bass features a nicely fried and meaty whole fish sprinkled with shredded ginger and scallions. It is set in a sweet and salty sauce based on nuoc mam, a saline fish condiment, soy sauce, and seasonings. We experienced a flash of déjà vu, however, when the shrimp Saigon style (shrimp blended with bits of pork and scallion) arrived in the same sauce. Chicken Saigon style played

▷ 173

nearly the same tune; so did a dish called crispy chicken, which was satisfying but not crispy.

The two barbecued selections—beef and pork—are tasty variations on the same theme, served with lettuce for making little rolls, julienne of vegetables for garnish, and hoisin sauce.

The kitchen's strong suit is broiling; its weakest is frying. Try the shrimp with sugarcane, an engaging combination of shrimp paste molded to a stalk of sugarcane before broiling and served with translucent rice paper, lettuce, coriander sprigs, fresh mint, and pickled onions. The idea is to make cigar-shaped rolls with the ingredients and swab them with sweet hoisin sauce.

The Vietnamese have an insatiable sweet tooth. Only if you have one, too, would I suggest the aromatic duck, cut-up pieces of meat on the bone in a honey-and-hoisin sauce.

Lemongrass, a long, thin herb that resembles scallions, is a staple in Vietnamese cooking. I have a passion for it, so it was disappointing to find barely any in the lemongrass chicken, which was overpowered by a sharp, peanut-laced curry sauce.

Another standard in Vietnamese cooking is the spring roll, which at its best is extraordinarily light, crisp, and exploding with the flavors of fresh mint and vegetables. On a scale of 1 to 10, these are about 7—the pork-and-shrimp filling is well seasoned and the roll is skillfully fried, but it lacks zip.

For dessert try the steamed banana cake, a resilient and quivering specimen garnished with coconut milk and peanuts.

# DARBAR

★ ★ ★

*44 West 56th Street, 432-7227.*

*Atmosphere: Comfortable two-level establishment with warm, orange fabric-covered walls adorned with tapestries and hammered brass.*

*Service: Attentive and hard-working.*

*Wine: Small international wine list, moderate prices.*

*Price range: Moderate.*

*Credit cards: All major cards.*

*Hours: Lunch, noon to 3 P.M., Monday through Friday; buffet only, Saturday and Sunday; dinner, 5:30 to 11 P.M., Sunday through Thursday, until 11:30, Friday and Saturday.*

*Reservations: Suggested.*

*Wheelchair accessibility: Several stairs down to main dining room; restrooms upstairs.*

Darbar is a remarkably reliable Indian restaurant in midtown, as solid as the Taj Mahal and as unchanging. The kitchen offers mostly northern cuisine, with some scorchers from Goa added to the pot. Beware of dishes described as hot, like the lamb stew, gosht vindaloo, and the chicken dish called murgh Madras, for they can burn a hole in the tablecloth. No compromises for Western palates are made here unless you ask.

The two-level restaurant has a bar downstairs and magnificent hammered-copper hangings on fabric-covered walls. Upstairs the tables often seem too small for the quantities of food that arrive, but aside from that the setting is essentially comfortable and soothingly illuminated. The main dining room, done in warm orange, also has handsome tapestries and hammered-brass wall decorations. Darbar is a good place to take large groups because the staff happily combines tables and helps you order a suitable family-style menu.

Appetizers to start with include crisp and clean fresh vegetable-filled samosas; chicken pakora, tender squiggles of chicken marinated in yogurt and spices, then battered and fried; shrimp pakora, made with shrimp marinated in sour cream then dusted with mixed herbs and lightly fried; and a combination of chickpeas, potatoes, and onions seasoned with tamarind sauce and black Indian salt—it comes on mild but has a delayed spicy undercurrent. Mulligatawny, the classic south Indian soup made with lentils, tomatoes, and spices, is nicely turned out.

Waiters at Darbar are quietly efficient and accommodating. One evening we were a party of seven, and our waiters effortlessly remembered every dish and who got what. The restaurant has a small international wine selection. Indian beer is the beverage of choice with this food, though.

Among entrees, we did not come across a seriously flawed dish. The choices among chicken preparations are varied. Mughlai korma is a traditional Mogul recipe in which chunks of boned chicken are infused with sweet coconut and yogurt during cooking and finished with assorted spices and nuts. Yogurt is the main ingredient in the tandoor-cooked chicken Darbar, in which boneless chicken is marinated in yogurt, garlic, and spices before roasting. The meat emerges exceptionally juicy and mildly hot. I am particularly fond of reshmi kebab, exceptionally moist dark meat of chicken seasoned and grilled in the tandoor.

Many good lamb options are available, too. Among the best are shahi lamb chops, which are marinated in yogurt, ginger, and garlic, then roasted in the tandoor until succulent. It is delicious with saffron-perfumed Basmati rice studded with minced vegetables, raisins, and nuts. Other lamb dishes to consider are rogan josh, bite-size morsels cooked in a sweet onion sauce with yogurt, cream and almonds, and tandoor-roasted lamb (tikka masala) served in a sauce of onions, butter, and tomato. The one goat dish sampled, goat rogan josh, was on the dry and tough side.

Lobster is not something I traditionally associate with Indian food. A dish called lobster malai khasa, however, was a standout: the sweet tail meat was cooked in coconut cream, a sublime combination. Speaking of shellfish, crab Malabar is equally alluring, the shredded meat simmered in a sauce of onions and tomatoes for sweetness and fennel seed for its sharp aroma.

Breads are exceptionally well made here. Always fun to share are the crinkly hot-air balloons of poori, which are greaseless and delicious. Tandoori roti, a round whole-wheat bread baked in the tandoor, has an earthy and nice charred flavor. A favorite at my table was onion kulcha, which is a baked pocket of bread stuffed with sweet onions and fresh coriander. All the breads are wonderful accompaniments to the creamy lentil dish, dal, and the restorative yogurt-based mixture called raita.

Superior vegetarian dishes include the grilled eggplant mixture called baingan bhurta, blended with onions, tomatoes, and spices; and shag paneer, fresh white cheese enhanced with spinach, coriander, and spices. Many of Darbar's best dishes are offered on the $19.95 prix-fixe lunch special and the $26.95 pre- and post-theater menu.

The cardamom-flavored rice pudding called kheer is a refreshing semisweet finale, as is nutty kulfi ice cream perfumed with rose water. Gulab jaman, the dry milk honey pastry, is mercifully less sweet than most versions, and fig ice cream is the best of the offerings.

# DA TOMMASO

★

*903 Eighth Avenue, near 54th Street, 265-1890.*

*Atmosphere: Simple, comfortable, with well-spaced tables.*

*Service: Extremely accommodating and warm.*

*Wine: Limited Italian list; average prices.*

*Price range: Moderate.*

*Credit cards: American Express, MasterCard, and Visa.*

*Hours: Lunch, noon to 3 P.M., Monday through Friday; dinner, 4:30 P.M. to midnight, Monday through Saturday, 3 to 11 P.M., Sunday.*

*Reservations: Necessary.*

*Wheelchair accessibility: Everything on one level.*

Amid the dizzying cacophony of the Broadway theater district, Da Tommaso is a snug and tranquil little place that offers reasonably good food at modest prices. If you feel a sense of déjà vu there, it is because the dining room suggests so many suburban family-run Italian restaurants, the ones that generally take root near a train station.

The largely traditional menu has few surprises—and the food is fresh and wholesome, which is more than can be said for some of the mass-feeding corrals in the theater district.

The setting is functional and tidy, a wood-partitioned room with a little bar near the entrance, pale yellow walls, coral curtains, smoky mirrors, and fresh carnations on adequately spaced tables. The obeisant maître d'hôtel and partner, Rosario Carvelli, has a way of making his presentation of the daily specials seem like an invocation. He stands at the table, hands clasped, head bowed, and recites the day's culinary liturgy, pausing reverentially between selections.

Pastas are the high points here. Among the best are angel hair with tender, meaty clams and a bright garlic-fueled broth; fettuccine with shrimp, radicchio, and shallots; and simple but clean-tasting penne with tomato and basil. One of the more assertive selections is penne in a sweet-edged tomato sauce with vodka (caviar is optional and unnecessary). The house pasta primavera has a colorful cast—fresh peas, zucchini, squash, mushrooms—but was overcooked. If you crave greens, get the linguine with perfectly cooked broccoli and zucchini in a light garlic-and-olive-oil sauce. The pasta labeled "top secret" on the menu is worth uncovering, a gratifying seasonal combination of spaghetti tossed with lots of garlic, broccoli florets (or broccoli di rape when in season), shrimp, and olive oil.

While seafood cannot be faulted for freshness, preparations tend to be banal, like the dryish tuna with capers and mixed vegetables, and the attractively presented red snapper in an underseasoned broth with cauliflower, broccoli, endive, and potatoes. One good lunch choice is moist grilled swordfish in a champagne, shallots, and caper sauce. Other dependable options are the generous lamb chops in white wine, cognac, and sage or the plain but tender double-cut veal chop.

Among starters, stay with simple selections like roasted peppers with balsamic vinegar, spiedino alla romano (deep-fried mozzarella with capers and anchovy sauce) or grilled oyster mushrooms with firm, moist polenta.

I rarely had room for dessert here but was cajoled into having a wonderful pear sorbet molded into the shape of the fruit, flanked by pear slices and fresh berries, which was much better than the cakes and tarts sampled.

# DA UMBERTO

**SATISFACTORY**

*107 West 17th Street, 989-0303.*

*Atmosphere: High-ceilinged, tri-partitioned space done in sponged ocher walls; very loud.*

*Service: Frazzled and confused.*

*Wines: Moderate-size Italian list at reasonable prices.*

*Price range: Moderately expensive.*

*Credit cards: American Express.*

*Hours: Lunch, noon to 3 P.M., Monday through Friday; dinner, 5:30 to 11 P.M., Monday through Thursday, 5:30 to 11:30 P.M., Friday and Saturday.*

*Reservations: Necessary.*

*Wheelchair accessibility: Restrooms downstairs.*

A Florentine-style restaurant called Ristorante da Umberto appeared on a drab block in the eastern reaches of Chelsea in early 1988, and before you could say tiramisù, it was mobbed. Early raves brought even more pastaphiles, making the towering echo chamber (called a dining room) so loud it could wilt your radicchio.

I don't doubt that da Umberto was an interesting, perhaps even special, spot when it opened. But its apparent decline from sheer exhaustion or incompetence underscores the danger of rushing out too soon to review a new place. Many well-intentioned restaurateurs are naïve about pacing. They burn out early, like those marathon runners who sprint to the head of the pack at the outset, then collapse before the midway mark. Three recent visits reveal that da Umberto, while capable of turning out a few good gutsy north Italian dishes, has become inconsistent and fatigued.

The first warning of a breakdown was the greeting, or lack of one. We stood in the shatteringly loud foyer, huddled with other diners next to the long marble-topped bar, waiting for a nod of recognition. The entire place is done in sponged ocher walls with wine racks serving as room dividers and with exposed heating ducts. Finally a wilted-looking host shuffled over and led us through two semipartitioned dining rooms into a third room adjacent to the glass-enclosed kitchen.

Some of the best food can be found on the cold buffet table: chunky and boldly seasoned caponata, smoky roasted peppers, refreshing slices of fennel, white-bean salad, grilled artichokes, snowy fresh mozzarella, and more. If you order white wine, it will come frigid and be poured into frosted glasses, the way fancy pubs like to serve beer.

Half-orders of pasta were not available, our waiter told us on a frenetic Saturday night, "because the chef will start throwing pots and pans at me if I ask for that now." At least he's honest. The Italian waiters here have frazzled looks and, most likely, significant hearing loss from the constant din. It's self-service when it comes to pouring wine, and not much else gets done without a lot of wild gesticulating by the diner.

Of the pastas we sampled, fusilli with mixed seafood was pleasing, made with cubes of good smoked tuna, black olives, and garlic; fettuccine with salmon in a light cream sauce was a winner, as was the farfalle with pesto. It was difficult to warm up to the pasta with lobster sauce because shell shards had me worried about some expensive recent dental work. Gnocchi all'arrabbiata was forgettable, too: gummy little pellets in a standard red sauce stoked with hot pepper flakes.

The best entrées are the homiest ones: a special of roast pork infused with garlic, or moist roasted quail stuffed with zesty sausage (although the accompanying polenta had solidified into dry sponges). The veal chop is simple and excellent, and if your taste runs to tripe, the tomato-and-olive-based stew here does it justice. Unaccountably, the kitchen makes a mess of veal paillard: it is bland and soggy from its soupy rosemary-and-wine sauce. A special of veal with artichoke hearts and tomato was utterly tasteless, too.

Among seafood options, salmon with mustard sauce was satisfying on two occasions, and a special of grouper was a mixed bag: the garlicky tomato sauce was good, but mussels and clams ringing the plate were rubbery. Soft-shell clams suffer the same fate as veal paillard, arriving in a lack of broth.

Except for a good moist cheesecake, desserts are dreary: a cloying and rubbery concoction misidentified as profiteroles (actually a white-chocolate mousse cake of sorts), inedibly sweet raspberry cake, oversugared poached pears, and gluey napoleon.

# DAVID K'S

★ ★

*1115 Third Avenue, at 59th Street, 371-9090.*

*Atmosphere: Spacious, comfortable, and uncluttered setting; flattering lighting and good sound muffling.*

*Service: Knowledgeable and efficient.*

*Wine: List well matched with the food.*

*Price range: Moderate (three-course Peking chicken menu, prix fixe $19.50; three-course lobster menu, prix fixe $24.50).*

*Credit cards: All major cards.*

*Hours: Brunch, noon to 3:30 P.M., Saturday and Sunday; lunch, noon to 3 P.M., Monday through Friday; dinner, 5 to 11 P.M., Sunday through Thursday, until midnight, Friday and Saturday.*

*Reservations: Suggested.*

*Wheelchair accessibility: Special entrance must be requested to avoid the revolving door. Three small steps to the restroom level.*

In the fall of 1987 David Keh ripped out the leopard-skin banquettes at the old Safari Grill, toned down the spacy pink neon columns, and installed a team of Chinese cooks behind the open kitchen's grills. The revamped establishment was called David K's. The front room, with its glass wall facing busy Third Avenue, is more bustling than the larger back room, with its colorful fabric-covered banquettes, dun-colored rug, and easy lighting. Commodious wicker chairs in both rooms, as well as pretty china and heavy silverplate table service, make for an elegant setting.

As Mr. Keh and his wife, Jean, tell first-time customers, the food at this new restaurant has a salubrious bent, with hardly any deep frying, a minimal use of fats and oils, no MSG and, as the health-food companies like to say, "no artificial anything."

Indeed, the food on the whole is pure and clean tasting, and some dishes excel. One example is the appetizer of airy Chinese noodles tossed with chunks of cool lobster in a bright ginger sauce. Spicy chicken dumplings are engrossing in their warm peanut-butter-and-sesame-paste sauce, while shredded beef combined with crackling rice noodles and scallions are delicious in their mustard-and-peanut dressing.

Only two appetizers were a little two austere: the dried-out slices of swordfish in scallion sauce and the vegetable hand rolls, an idea borrowed from the Japanese, a lifeless mass of egg whites and bland julienne of vegetables rolled in iceberg lettuce. A much better alternative is called jumping shrimp, succulent and sweet shrimp cooked in the shell with scallions and garlic. Several of the vegetable dishes make bright starters, especially the flash-cooked broccoli loaded with shards of garlic.

David Keh was one of the first Chinese restaurateurs to consider wine seriously, and his list has many fresh dry whites that go particularly well with the food. I usually have the fresh and spicy Hugel Gewürztraminer ($18).

One of the more usual dishes on the menu is called Peking Chicken, which is designed as a leaner and lighter alternative to Peking Duck. A 6½-pound chicken is sectioned and deep fried—it is the only fried dish on the menu

—until the skin is brittle and golden and the meat still moist. It is then served with the traditional hoisin sauce, scallion, and pancakes. In this version, the pancakes are made with whole wheat, and, to my taste, they are more flavorful than those made with rice.

Although Mr. Keh is credited with introducing Sichuan cuisine to New York, there are few firecrackers on this menu. About as hot as it gets is a preparation of pork with cashews, leeks, and hot peppers—the meat is extraordinarily tender and the sauce mildly zippy. Another, spicy lamb with scallions, probably could benefit from a bit more spark in the pepper department, for I found it rather flat. Three seafood dishes can be highly recommended: braised sea bass in a garlic-and-ginger sauce garnished with scallions and fresh coriander; sweet prawns cooked simply but lovingly with white wine and garlic; and lobster cooked in a light lemon sauce strewn with lemon rind to impart a nice tart edge.

Befitting a healthful menu, desserts are played down, with only ice creams, sherbets, and fresh fruit featured.

"This," says Mr. Keh, making the rounds of the dining room in his characteristic dark blue suit and bright red tie, "is the kind of food I personally love to eat." Chances are, you will agree.

# DĀWAT

★ ★

*210 East 58th Street, 355-7555.*

*Atmosphere: Streamlined pink-and-pale-green room with flattering lighting, comfortable setting, and low noise level.*

*Service: Extremely well mannered and efficient.*

*Price range: Moderate.*

*Credit cards: All major cards.*

***Hours:*** *Lunch, 11:30 A.M. to 3 P.M., Monday through Saturday; dinner, 5:30 to 11 P.M., Sunday through Thursday, until 11:30 P.M. Friday and Saturday.*

***Reservations:*** *Suggested.*

***Wheelchair accessibility:*** *Everything on one level.*

When Dāwat opened in late 1985 with a menu devised by Madhur Jaffrey, the actress and cookbook author, it was one of the more stylish and unusual Indian restaurants in town. The culinary script was more ambitious than most: the only shortcoming was inconsistency. Recent revisits indicate, though, that the kitchen has sharpened its act.

The long rectangular dining room is done in shades of peach and blue-green with clusters of wooden folkloric figurines spotlighted on the walls. The restaurant was packed every time I went, and the exceedingly polite service staff, directed by a team of captains in dark suits, handled affairs with grace and efficiency. Even when the dining room is crowded, the noise level is tolerable.

Many of the best dishes from the early days remain. Subtlety is not in the vocabulary of this chef, so if you want a mild dish, make it known.

Tantalizing appetizers include shami kebab, bite-size disks of moist ground lamb brightened with mint; a blend of brittle little wafers tossed with potato cubes and chickpeas in a spicy yogurt-and-tamarind sauce (dahi aloo poori), and light, crisp fritters of spinach, onions, and potato skins that you dip in a tamarind chili sauce (bhaja). One of my favorite dishes here has always been the bhel poori, an Indian snack that combines puffed rice, wheat chips, fresh coriander, mango powder, and assorted chutneys, blitzing the palate with sensations of sweet, hot, and sour. Baghari jhinga, shrimp with garlic, mustard seed, and curry, was tasty but rubbery from overcooking.

The entrée list is daunting. Curiously, some of the more elaborate dishes succeed while simple preparations, such as the tandoor-cooked mixed grill (shrimp, chicken, lamb kebabs, and chicken), are occasionally overcooked. The best entrée this time around by far was chicken badami, in which the boned meat came in a creamy sauce of ground almonds. It is good with any of the superior Indian breads.

Two seafood dishes from Madhur Jaffrey's repertory are superior. One called Kerala-style konju pappaas combines shrimp with coconut milk flavored with mustard seeds and hints of curry and tamarind; another features salmon fillet swathed with an invigorating coriander chutney and steamed to pink succulence in a banana leaf. Side dishes to consider are the excellent creamy kali dal, combining two types of beans laced with ginger, and okra with browned onions and dried mango called bhindi masala. Dāwat serves a wonderful carrot pudding for dessert, slightly crunchy threads of carrot in a mildly sweet sauce, as well as a super-rich pudding aromatic of cardamom.

Dāwat offers one of the best lunch deals on the East Side. Five exotic and delicious prix-fixe menus are offered, all under $12. And you certainly won't leave hungry. I counted nine dishes on my table as part of the $10.95 chef's menu: rogan josh (baby goat in cardamom sauce), farasvi bhaji (green beans with grated coconut), paneer bhurji (crumbled fresh cheese with peppers, tomatoes, and onions), paratha (whole-wheat tandoori-cooked bread), vegetable biryani (rice, almonds, yellow raisins, and spices), raita (yogurt with mint and tomato), chutney, papadum (spicy chickpea wafers), and cucumber-onion salad. With a drink and tax, the tab came to $15.

# DOCKS (BROADWAY)

★

*2427 Broadway, between 89th and 90th streets, 724-5588.*

*Atmosphere: Clean, bright black-and-white tile oyster bar with an elevated informal dining room.*

*Service: Expect to wait for your table on busy nights; the staff is well-informed about seafood and effective under pressure.*

*Wine: Good list at fair prices.*

*Price range: Moderate.*

*Credit cards: All major cards.*

*Hours: Brunch, 10:30 A.M., to 2:45 P.M., Sunday; lunch, 11:30 A.M. to 3:00 P.M., Monday through Saturday; dinner, 5 to 11 P.M., Sunday through Thursday, 5 to midnight, Friday and Saturday.*

*Reservations: Required.*

*Wheelchair accessibility: One small step at the entrance to lower level of the dining room; restrooms are downstairs.*

Some patrons used to complain about the cavalier attitude among the harried staff at this black-and-white tiled fish house on upper Broadway. That problem has pretty much been solved. Overall, this is still a satisfying sleeves-up, oyster-slurping, lemon-squirting spot with a lively scene every night. It offers an ever-changing assortment of fish—everything from fresh tuna and mako shark to jackfish and Mediterranean rouget—as well as a broad sampling of clams and oysters.

Frying is one of the kitchen's strong points. Those who harbor fond memories of crunchy fried clams and oysters at the boardwalk will be delighted with the light and greaseless renditions here. Grilling has improved at Docks since earlier visits, and the fish selection changes daily according to market availability.

The long tile bar with its glass-enclosed shellfish display is a diverting place to have a glass of white wine and an assortment of oysters that may include assertive and saline Belons, tender Wellfleets, mild Apalachicolas, bluepoints, and Chincoteagues. Clams, either on the half shell or "steamers," are delightful, too. Because of the crowds at Docks, you may have to spend fifteen minutes or so at the bar waiting for a table, even with a reservation.

A long list of daily specials is listed on a blackboard over the open kitchen. An exuberant fellow who served us one evening was impressively knowledgeable about every kind of fish and shellfish, and he was not abashed about peppering his commentary with, "Now this is a really great choice" and "These just came in this afternoon."

Aside from all of the good fried seafood, which might be shared by a group as an appetizer, and the raw clams, other superior choices are the light and crisp calamari rings served with a smoky cumin-laced hot sauce, and steamed giant New Zealand mussels, a special, in a splendid saffron-perfumed cream broth. Two occasional specials that do not make the grade are a seafood boudin that is bready, dry, and tasteless, and "tuna fingers," which are battered and deep-fried strips of tuna that come out tasting like generic fish substances.

Lobster fans will be happy with the freshness of the steamed monsters here, ranging in size from two pounds up (prices vary). Entrées come with crunchy fresh coleslaw and a choice of potatoes (french-fried yams are terrific) or dill-flavored rice. Swordfish, thick tuna steak, and mako shark all were dry to my taste, and fried catfish was undistinguished.

When special bouillabaisse-type dishes are featured, I suggest you try them. A rouget casserole one evening holding lobster, clams, scallops, and whole rouget was heady with oceanic aromas and deftly assembled so each ingredient was properly cooked.

Desserts are surprisingly good, especially the peerless chocolate mud pie that is creamy, unremittingly rich, and exquisitely lumpy with nubbins of semisweet chocolate. Apple crumb cake, Key lime pie, and chocolate chip ice cream are exceptional, too, while only a cloying raspberry pie should go back to the galley for reworking.

Docks has a terrific Sunday brunch. You can get a breakfast of scrambled eggs and lox—not side by side, but all mixed up, and with some onions tossed in for good measure.

# DOCKS ON THIRD

★ ★

*633 Third Avenue, at 40th Street, 986-8080.*

*Atmosphere: Large brasserie setting with well-spaced tables and moderate noise level.*

*Service: Pleasant and functional if not refined.*

*Wine: Well-chosen selection at good prices.*

*Price range: Moderate.*

*Credit cards: All major cards.*

*Hours: 11:30 A.M. to 11 P.M., Monday through Thursday, 11:30 A.M. to midnight, Friday; dinner, 5 to midnight, Saturday, 5 to 11 P.M., Sunday; brunch, 10:30 A.M. to 3 P.M., Sunday.*

*Reservations: Necessary.*

*Wheelchair accessibility: Dining on ground level; restrooms up a winding staircase.*

The midtown Docks is a spinoff of the popular original on Broadway at 89th Street. While the formulas are virtually identical, the setting here is more stylish and comfortable. This 275-seat, two-level expanse has a big arching wood-and-brass bar in the center, on which are displayed all manner of iced shellfish. In the evening, Art Deco sconces combined with candles and strategically placed overhead spotlights create a cool, urbane mood. For such a big, crowded place, Docks rarely gets too loud.

Appetizers run from assorted oysters of the day, which are always freshly shucked and in fine condition, to excellent rings of lightly breaded fried calamari with a cumin-laced hot sauce, and excellent clam chowder. The chowder is creamy but light, generous with clams, potatoes, and smoky bacon. It goes nicely with the grainy house bread. Steamers in beer broth were big, plump, and tender, although I would prefer to have the broth on the side for dipping rather than under all the shells; a special one day of clams with a tangy ginger-and-scallion sauce was tasty, but sandy. And crab cakes, while beautifully browned and well seasoned, were overblended, perhaps in a food processor, so they had a mushy texture.

The service staff could use some tips on fine points. More than once a waiter lurched over our table to serve or pick up plates rather than walk several steps around the table, and wine pouring is hit and miss. Speaking of wine, the selection here is exceptionally well thought out and overflowing with bargains. Roughly half the wines are under $25.

Daily entrées are supplemented by a blackboard list. If your tastes run to exotic species, you may from time to time sample such items as deep-fried blowfish tails, which, while not the most appetizing sounding, actually are very good. Roughly the size of a prawn, they have firm, mild flesh and a little bone running down the middle, so don't chomp down on one like I did, but nibble along each side. They are slightly breaded and cleanly fried, accompanied with a good aïoli.

Among regular entrées, grilled salmon could not have been better, nor could the simple but pristine red snapper fillet. The barbecued seafood grill—skewered shrimp, mako shark, tuna, peppers, and onions—is nicely cooked, too. All fried foods are light and excellent, especially the clams, oysters, and scallops. Entrées come with snappy homemade coleslaw and either baked potato or rice (the rice I sampled, with pecans, was limp and bland).

While the entrées are generally light and salubrious, one of the desserts could sink a tugboat. The mud fudge comes in a barge-sized crock overloaded with deadly rich chocolate, ice cream, and whipped cream; Key lime pie is just the opposite—light, bright, and refreshingly citric. Good ice creams and sherbets round out the selection.

# EAST

★

*1420 Third Avenue, between 80th and 81st streets, 472-3975.*

*Atmosphere: Handsome Japanese country setting. Low tables where guests sit on the floor. Deep pits allow legs to dangle below.*

*Service: Confused and inattentive.*

*Price range: Moderate.*

*Credit cards: American Express, MasterCard, and Visa.*

*Hours: Lunch, noon to 2:30 P.M., daily; dinner, 5 to 10:45 P.M., Sunday through Thursday, 5 to 11:15 P.M., Friday and Saturday.*

*Reservations: Recommended.*

*Wheelchair accessibility: Low tables unsuitable for the handicapped; several stairs lead to dining room.*

Upon entering East, the handsome, countrified Japanese restaurant on the Upper East Side, you are stopped at an alcove of little wooden lockers and asked to remove your shoes. You are then ushered into the dining room, which has two sections of low-slung tables separated by a center aisle that is as shiny as a new bowling lane from constant sock buffing. Under each communal table is a knee-deep pit for those who consider sitting in a lotus position for two hours about as relaxing as doing one-arm pushups.

East, which has two other branches in Manhattan—on Third Avenue near 26th Street and on East 44th Street—may not serve the most exciting Japanese food in town, but it is an entertaining setting with more than enough good dishes to please the crowd. It is a popular spot among the young and limber East Side set—so much so that the man who takes reservations warned me that tables are held only fifteen minutes beyond the appointed hour.

A few suggestions to get the proceedings off on a high note include the broiled halved eggplant swathed with sweet miso sauce, cold spinach dusted with fish meal in a sesame-accented soy sauce, and cold bean curd with chopped scallions and ginger. The kitchen is not very adroit at frying, as evidenced by the leathery deep-fried tofu and the heavy, inelegant vegetable tempura (also available as an entrée). And negimaki, that benchmark dish of grilled scallions rolled in sliced beef that is found in nearly all Japanese restaurants, is thick and chewy.

An alternative way to start is with an assortment of sushi or other raw-fish specialties. The sushi deluxe plate features a nicely balanced variety of sushi and sashimi: tuna, salmon, crab, surimi, fluke, yellowtail, and mackerel. All were pleasingly fresh and well presented; some were spiked with hot wasabi mustard that shot straight to the nasal cavity. The standout sushi was yellowtail, a thickly sliced, flapping-fresh fillet that was extraordinarily buttery and oceanic. The maki rolls wrapped in seaweed sheets, while fresh, were not as crisp as they should have been. Your luck should be better at the sushi bar, where they are prepared in front of you and served immediately.

Waiters and waitresses at East skid along the polished floors wearing elfin red socks. However, during my three visits, they often seemed to be skidding past our table to someone else's. When things get busy in the dining room, busboys sometimes resort to the unsightly practice of scraping leftovers onto a platter right at your table, cafeteria style, instead of carrying them one by one into the kitchen.

Main courses comprise some lovely grilled seafood items. Salmon teriyaki, a beautifully grilled plank of fillet, is arresting with its pickled ginger garnish—just go lightly on the exceedingly sweet sauce. Ditto for the otherwise good chicken teriyaki. The careful grilling here makes any of the daily grilled fish specials worth trying.

East may not be the place for assiduous sushi mavens who scrutinize fish textures the way numismatists study coins, but for a lighthearted evening in a convivial setting, it can fit the bill.

# ECCO!

**POOR**

*124 Chambers Street, 227-7074.*

*Atmosphere: Charming old bar and restaurant with tile floor and handsome old wood.*

*Service: Rude and inept.*

*Wine: Moderately priced Italian list.*

*Price range: Moderately expensive.*

*Credit cards: American Express.*

*Hours: Lunch, 11:45 A.M. to 3 P.M., Monday through Friday; dinner, 5:30 to 11 P.M., Monday through Friday, 5:30 to 11:30 P.M., Saturday, 5:30 to 10:30 P.M., Sunday.*

*Reservations: Necessary.*

*Wheelchair accessibility: Dining room on street level; restrooms downstairs.*

Rude and slow service, combined with indifferent food, leaves little to recommend at this downtown Italian restaurant. The first evening, a captain wearing a bow tie and a look of exasperation suddenly appeared and, without even saying hello, started barking the daily specials. He had an air of impatience as we ordered, and when one guest hesitated to reconsider a dish, he grumbled, "Yeah, yeah, be right back," then disappeared. When he returned, I asked for a pinot grigio, to which be barked, "Don't have it. You'll have the Gavi." He then shouted the order at one of his minions, who promptly forgot about it. It's that kind of place.

The mixed antipasto plate, for which we waited a half hour (wineless), combined cold, bready mussels; good garlicky ribbons of marinated eggplant; pallid tomato salad; and tasty shrimp with artichokes. The kitchen will not make half orders of pasta but will split full orders. Penne with a creamy tomato sauce cut with vodka was al dente and tasty although tepid; spicy spaghetti with scallops, calamari, mussels, and shrimp came in a good, peppery tomato sauce, and tortellini with peas and mushrooms in a cream sauce was tasty. Fusilli in a smoky tomato, onion, and pancetta sauce, however, had telltale signs of having been reheated in mixed batches: some of the pasta was undercooked, the rest overcooked.

During all my visits, we waited much too long for entrées, but one night when it ran to more than forty minutes, we asked one of the captains about it. He contended it was our fault because we had not ordered our entrées at the same time as our appetizers—which we had—and walked away. Several entrées were not worth the wait: salmon in white wine was overcooked one evening (better a week later), steak "alla Ecco!" with garlic and rosemary was tough and bland, and veal with artichoke, a special, was forgettable. Better choices were the thick, tender veal chop (light on seasoning but top-quality meat) and lamb chops with garlic cloves and rosemary.

For dessert, there are a good heavy-duty cheesecake, a flaky napolean, and a fudgelike chocolate cake that would sate most chocolate fiends.

# ERMINIA

★

*250 East 83rd Street, 879-4284, 517-3410.*

*Atmosphere: Small romantic room; rustic décor, candlelight, soft music.*

*Service: Professional and low-key.*

*Price range: Moderately expensive.*

*Credit cards: American Express.*

*Hours: Dinner, 5 to 11 P.M., daily.*

*Reservations: Required.*

*Wheelchair accessibility: One small step at the entrance.*

Erminia is an enchantingly romantic little spot, a snug Upper East Side hideaway of barn board and brick, dried flowers, rustic bric-a-brac, candlelight, and soft music. It attracts an urbane and self-possessed clientele, the type of diners who eschew the fervid fishbowl scene in favor of soft intimacy. Some couples even hold hands there.

The traditional Italian food, like the setting, is safe and familiar. On a gastronomic bar graph, neither the highs nor the lows are dramatic. If everything clicks, however, you can enjoy a tranquil evening with straightforward food and discreet service and return home without a ringing in your ears from the clamor.

Two suggested starters are the crisply sautéed baby artichokes flecked with garlic and glazed with good olive oil, and terrific fresh mozzarella, faintly nutty and silken-textured, alongside roasted red peppers and billowy leaves of vibrant basil. The carpaccio of smoked filet mignon is rather thick and chewy, although flavorful. Steamed clams and mussels are presented in a zesty tomato sauce.

With a bowl of pasta costing $16 or more, one might resent being charged an extra dollar for sharing a portion as an appetizer. We paid up to try as many as possible. My favorites are the least elaborate: briny pasta with white clam sauce that is redolent of garlic and fresh basil, and pappardelle tossed in a lovely ricotta cheese sauce. Vermicelli pizzaiola, described as having a sauce built with garlic, tomato, olives, and julienne of veal, is overly sweet to my taste; to find the alleged veal requires sharp vision at tight focus. A special one evening, angel-hair pasta with shellfish, was remarkable for its tastelessness.

Wood-fire grilling is a specialty, and is generally executed with care. If you prefer meat on the rare side, though, make sure to speak up or it will come our the far side of medium. Baby lamb chops, veal chops, and a mixed grill including beef, lamb, chicken, and fennel-perfumed sausage all benefit from the open-fire cooking. Each comes with little mounds of tasty polenta strewn with strips of prosciutto. Among the nongrilled items, both chicken dishes—one sautéed with lemon and wine, the other with sausage in a vibrant vinegar-edged sauce—are pleasing.

On the seafood side, zuppa di pesce, served inside a large halved lobster shell, is 80 percent squid and can have an acrid burned-garlic sensation; thick rings of squid in a rugged tomato-herb sauce are better.

Desserts are limited to a respectable chocolate mousse, rich tartufo, oversugary napoleon, and berries with pallid zabaglione.

While Erminia has some rough spots, it still holds appeal to those seeking a special ambiance and undemanding fare.

# EZE

★ ★

*254 West 23rd Street, 691-1140.*

*Atmosphere: Comfortable and tranquil town-house setting.*

*Service: Formal and well trained.*

*Wine: Interesting and unusual selection from Mediterranean France.*

*Price range: Moderately expensive.*

*Credit cards: American Express, MasterCard, and Visa.*

*Hours: Dinner, 6 to 10:15 P.M., Tuesday through Saturday.*

*Reservations: Suggested.*

*Wheelchair accessibility: Flight of stairs up to the entrance. Restrooms down a flight of stairs from the dining room.*

Eze is the name of a town on the French Riviera, which reflects the Provençale-Mediterranean cooking of Gina Zarrilli, the chef and owner. I have never warmed up to the solemn town-house setting, a colorless, high-ceilinged L-shaped space with a service bar up front, lace curtains over tall windows, and expanses of naked white walls. High-backed chairs are better for your posture than comfort, adding to a formality that is reinforced by the mannered staff.

But there is nothing stuffy about the food. The menu, which changes every two weeks, carries sunny starters like the fillets of salted codfish alternating with layers of sliced potatoes in a bright blend of tomatoes, olives, garlic, herbs, and saffron. Tear off a chunk of the excellent yeasty rolls and sop up the sauce. Fettuccine comes in an explosively fresh pesto sauce; equally good is the pasta tossed with salmon and taragon.

When fresh sardines are available, Ms. Zarrilli simply grills them with olive oil and herbs, and sets them out with boiled new potatoes and roasted peppers; ditto for the meaty mussels in a garlic-and-parsley broth. Cream of ratatouille soup, lumpy with black olives, is redolent of a Provençale garden in June. The only appetizers that fell short were the mealy marinated trout in a clashing orange vinaigrette, and the undistinguished gingered chicken wings with granitic undercooked chickpeas. The wine list shows off a few uncommon selections from Mediterranean France worth noting.

Among entrées, a light-handed Provençale approach works best with such specials as grilled squab, which, though farm-raised, has a rich, gamy flavor counterbalanced with a sweet-edged beet sauce, along with yellow squash and creamy mashed potatoes freckled with chives. Cornish hen infused with garlic and marjoram was extraordinarily succulent (although the corn on the cob accompanying it tasted like the frozen variety), as was thyme-flecked rack of lamb cooked to blood pink, garnished with a sweet garlic-and-onion jam. Loin of pork was trimmed lean but wonderfully moist in its reduced pan juices and was aromatic of maple and rosemary.

The most impressive seafood entrée is the whole braised red snapper for two, which is presented ringed with good couscous and a red-pepper purée. Seafood stew is a winner: a pastiche of mussels, clams, shrimp, and calamari bolstered with a tomato-tinted shellfish stock flavored with fennel and Pernod.

Nothing is more reminiscent of the Mediterranean than fresh figs, and at Eze they are used as the mortar between layers of airy puff pastry and vanilla ice cream; another evening the pastry sheets were bound by a clean and tart lemon custard ringed by a moat of raspberry coulis. And if there were an Olympics for chocolate cake, the flourless version here, crowned with caramel ice cream, would cruise to the semifinals with ease. Only a gummy raspberry torte was left unfinished.

# FELIDIA

*243 East 58th Street, 758-1479.*

*Atmosphere: Handsome wood bar and rustic dining room downstairs; skylit room upstairs.*

*Service: Generally professional, although the pace is slow.*

*Wine: Wide-ranging Italian list.*

*Price range: Expensive.*

*Credit cards: All major cards.*

*Hours: Lunch, noon to 3 P.M., Monday through Friday; dinner, 5 P.M. to midnight, Monday through Saturday.*

*Reservations: Recommended.*

*Wheelchair accessibility: Dining on ground level. Restrooms down one flight of stairs.*

There have been many changes in recent years along restaurant-packed East 58th Street, but throughout it all, Felidia has thrived. Every night the elegant two-story restaurant is buzzing with a well-heeled crowd, and chances are you will have to kill some time at the bar, reservation or not.

That's not so bad, really, especially if the staff sets out some of the excellent golden-fried calamari to tide you over. Felidia, owned by Lydia and Felix Bastianich, specializes in food from the northern Adriatic area. It is expensive —count on about $70 a person with wine—and while the extensive menu has a few weak spots, the food is generally very good, particularly the regional specialties.

You enter via a long, burnished-wood bar, beyond which is a tightly arranged dining room with rustic touches and leafy foliage; the skylit balcony upstairs is more attractive. The service staff, led by several captains in black tie, manages to keep on top of things, but you should not go to Felidia unless you have time for a leisurely meal.

The best way to start is with a half order of one of the pastas. Fuzi, little twists of homemade pasta, are enticing with eggplant, basil, and a hint of fresh mint. Pasutice, a thin, diamond-shaped pasta that is another specialty from the Istria region, comes with a vibrant combination of clams, shrimp, scallops, tomatoes, and herbs. Equally stellar are pasta with tender baby clams in the shell, and tortellacci, large triangles of pasta stuffed with Swiss chard and ricottone (a slightly drier form of ricotta) glossed with butter and fresh sage. It is rare to find a distinctive vegetarian plate in restaurants, but the one here is splendid, combining al dente broccoli, peas, carrots, beets, fava beans, and more in a bright vinaigrette.

Felidia has one of the widest-ranging Italian wine lists in New York, but three wines I ordered were out of stock.

When it comes to entrées, the kitchen excels with lusty, rustic fare, such as the meltingly tender osso buco, rich with bone marrow; roasted pheasant in a wine-and-stock reduction, and a monstrous veal chop Valdostana style, oozing with fontina cheese. Sweetbreads fans would do well with the firm, fresh sautéed version here, enhanced with lemon and capers (with a side of unseasoned green beans and cauliflower).

Two disappointments came in the seafood category. A dish called halibut peperonata was described by our captain as spicy, but in fact the timidly seasoned fillet came out with a latticework of roasted peppers combined with spinach and a bland carrot-and-potato purée. The other was the pasutice with a lobster sauce that reeked of iodine. Better choices were the nicely grilled red snapper, and a lovely, moist swordfish steak cooked with balsamic vinegar, white wine, and capers.

Balsamic vinegar also adds a delicate extra dimension to a dessert plate of strawberries and pineapple. Raspberry tart is flaky and ripe, and chocolate mousse cake is unrepentantly rich. The cheese selection is exceptionally good, too.

# 44

★ ★

*Royalton Hotel, 44 West 44th Street, 944-9415, 944-9416.*

*Atmosphere: Futuristic lobby of Royalton Hotel; comfortable with acceptable noise level.*

*Service: Can be exasperatingly slow.*

*Wine: Small, well-chosen list with fair prices.*

*Price range: Moderately expensive.*

*Credit cards: All major cards.*

*Hours: Breakfast 7:30 to 10 A.M., daily; Continental breakfast, 10 A.M. to noon, daily; brunch, noon to 2:30 P.M., Saturday and Sunday; lunch, noon to 2:30 P.M., Monday through Friday; dinner, 6 to 11 P.M., Sunday through Wednesday, until 11:45 P.M., Thursday through Saturday.*

*Reservations: Necessary.*

*Wheelchair acccessibility: Several steps up into the lobby. Dining and restrooms on one level.*

Dining in a busy hotel lobby on lime-green chairs under hot pinpoint lights and decorative sconces that look like truncated steers' horns might not be everybody's idea of elegance. But when the food is as absorbing as that at 44 in the Royalton Hotel, one's architectural sensibilities mellow quickly.

The refurbishing of the Royalton by Ian Schrager and the late Steve Rubell in 1988 included a bar and restaurant in the ten-thousand-square-foot lobby, which stretches from 43rd to 44th Street. The designer, Philippe Starck, turned the frumpy, threadbare expanse into a futuristic corridor done in bold colors and winsome design accents. Once you recover from the visual surprise, though, the restaurant is actually quite comfortable.

The kitchen's inventive and well-focused cooking is familiar. It dabbles in various international cuisines, remolds a few classics, and usually comes up with beguiling combinations. With an appetizer of duck à l'orange, he takes confit of Muscovy duck leg and thigh, glazes it with a little honey, and sets it over shredded apples with a sauce of duck broth flavored with orange and cloves. It's a sublime combination. Other such starters are vibrant anise-cured salmon served with brioche and a wasabi paste sweetened with poached pears; lightly charred broccoli in a pool of curry vinaigrette; and four big firm pieces of seared sweetbreads over mixed greens with candied walnuts and a vinegar-sharpened veal-stock sauce.

At lunch, a salade Niçoise was copious, with sliced eggs, potatoes, and well-seasoned mixed greens, but the grilled tuna on the side was dry. Typical of Mr. Zakarian's style is a rough-textured terrine of veal and potatoes stippled with bacon.

The combination of a novice service staff and a sometimes sluggish kitchen can lead to inexcusable delays. One evening we could have taken a tour of the hotel, watched the late television news in one of the rooms, and had a drink at the bar in the time it took our entrées to appear. Service at lunch is better than at dinner.

Roast chicken served over lentils with pan juices and braised curly chicory on the side is a homey dish. I would go back in a flash for the superb veal chop with pearl onions, spinach, and carrots, or the crusty Black Angus fillet with rosti potatoes. And the nemesis of every youngster—brussels sprouts—showed up with a succulent roasted squab, sautéed potatoes, and rosemary-scented cabbage.

Among the seafood offerings, fillet of grouper in a horseradish crust was delicious on its own, but when served atop rigatoni in an eggplant-and-tomato sauce it caused a head-on collision of flavors that could be heard in Times Square. More harmonious is the nearly blackened salmon, still rosy in the center, perched on sliced cucumber with a garnish of dates.

Desserts are terrific. Try the trifle of lemon and yogurt served with a stem glass, or the relatively light and intense sweet-potato pie. Profiteroles are not done by the book—these are filled with ice cream—but they are fresh and delicious with a Jackson Pollock smattering of chocolate.

# THE FOUR SEASONS

★ ★ ★

*99 East 52nd Street, between Park and Lexington avenues, 754-9494.*

*Atmosphere: Palatial scale that affords the luxury of privacy at well-spaced tables. The rosewood-paneled Grill Room is masculine and trim, while the glittering Pool Room is romantic and plush.*

*Service: The huge platoon of captains, waiters, and busboys works as a crack team.*

*Price range: Expensive.*

*Credit cards: All major cards.*

*Hours: Pool Room, dinner, 5 to 9:30 P.M., Monday through Thursday, 5 to 11:30 P.M., Friday and Saturday; Grill Room, dinner, 5 to 11:30 P.M., Monday through Saturday ($41.50 prix-fixe in Pool Room, 5 to 6:15 P.M. and 10 to 11:15 P.M.)*

*Reservations: Required; two weeks in advance for weekend evenings.*

*Wheelchair accessibility: Elevators available for handicapped.*

The Four Seasons has had a tough few years as the economy has contracted and lavish expense-account dining has been cut back. Still, it remains the main lair of powers that be in the publishing and financial worlds. The palatial scale of the place, which fairly exudes power and money, is one reason. Another is the light, clean food, which is now being served by a new team in the kitchen. The longtime chef, Seppi Renggli, left in 1989. He was replaced by Christian Albin, the former sous chef, and Stefano Battistini, former chef at the Sea Grill in Rockefeller Center. As of this writing the menu had not been totally implemented, but it seems that the new team's style follows in spirit that of Mr. Renggli.

Dining at the Four Seasons differs dramatically according to when you go and where you sit. The legendary Grill Room, with its Astrodome ceiling, rippling copper chain curtains, and dark, masculine rosewood walls, is the ultimate power-lunch spot, an unrivaled arena of high-rolling executives.

The menu in the Grill Room has been updated to emphasize lighter and more healthful fare, dubbed spa cuisine. Typical of the kitchen's approach is moist baked swordfish enhanced with olives and scallions, escalope of veal in a faintly hot soy-and-Wasabi-mustard sauce, and excellent tuna carpaccio under threads of ginger and minced chives.

In contrast to the importunate Grill Room, where almost no one eats dessert, the lavish Pool Room with its graciously appointed tables, lofty foliage, and gurgling illuminated marble pool is for romance and extravagance. A laundry list of all the dishes tasted could run on forever, so the following is a representative sampling.

Terrines are consistently superior, especially the one combining pheasant, quail, and mallard duck served with cranberry relish. Cold breast of pigeon with tart red currants is another winner.

The hot appetizers are unqualified successes. The mildly spicy and generous crab gumbo is loaded with shards of sweet white meat, okra, celery, and green and red peppers; another good choice is the oversize ravioli stuffed with minced lobster spiked with jalapeño peppers and root vegetables mired in a bracing lobster cream sauce. It is ringed by speckled pieces of lobster meat sautéed in black butter. Game fanciers will not be disappointed with the pappardelle swathed in a winy venison ragout sauce.

The roster of superior dishes is extensive: blackened sweetbreads with morels and Swiss chard, tender young roasted rabbit with polenta and spinach, snapper baked in a crust of sea salt and pepper with two sauces—a rich tarragon or a lighter blend of lemon, olive oil, and parsley—scallops of veal with ginger, and breast of pheasant with golden Gorgonzola polenta. Desserts are justly renowned. The Gilbraltar-like "fancy cake" soaked with curaçao is a must. Hazelnut layer cake is outstanding, too, as are all of the homemade sorbets and soufflés.

The Four Seasons is extravagantly expensive for non-expense-account types (count on $70 to $80 per person at dinner, about $60 at lunch), but prices are more reasonable at pre- and posttheater hours, with prix-fixe dinners at $41.50.

# FU'S

*1395 Second Avenue, at 73rd Street, 517-9670.*

*Atmosphere: Modern and softly lighted contemporary room.*

*Service: Friendly and helpful, although the kitchen can be slow.*

*Wine: Limited list well matched to the food.*

*Price range: Moderately expensive.*

*Credit cards: All major cards.*

*Hours: Noon to midnight, daily; dim sum brunch, noon to 4 P.M., Saturday and Sunday.*

*Reservations: Recommended.*

*Wheelchair accessibility: Main-level dining room is accessible. Restrooms are on the same level.*

For all the clamorous charms of Chinatown, there are times when one is in the mood for Chinese food served in a more relaxed setting. A half dozen or more uptown Chinese restaurants offer food that equals the best found downtown—at uptown prices, of course. Fu's remains one of the best of this lot.

The menu pays homage to the major regional cuisines: from Beijing, Sichuan, Hunan, Shanghai, and Canton. Fu's is the creation of Gloria Chu, a compact, fast-talking dynamo who excels at cajoling and cosseting the well-heeled crowd that fills the dining room nightly. Her staff is well trained and knowledgeable, so you might want to let your waiter know your preferences, especially if you like spicy Sichuan, which is served on the tame side here unless otherwise specified. On the whole, Fu's is not a place for adventurous Chinese eaters (East Siders don't normally come looking for sea cucumber or ducks' feet).

Fu's has a sleek little black-lacquer bar near the entrance facing Second Avenue. The multilevel dining area is done in gray felt wallpaper with comfortable cranberry banquettes around the perimeter, potted palms, indirect lighting, fresh flowers, and crisp linen.

A refreshing starter is the chicken soong, a pleasing textural contrast of minced chicken, celery, peppers, and carrots in a pocket of iceberg lettuce (about the only worthwhile use for this tasteless American vegetable). Fried dumplings are still winners, crisp and clean little crescents filled with pork and shrimp and seasoned with fresh coriander and ginger. They are particularly good with the dipping sauce of vinegar, fresh coriander, scallions, ginger, sugar, and hoisin. I am less enthusiastic about a special called Grand Marnier shrimp, which sounds and tastes like happy-hour hors d'oeuvres in a Fort Lauderdale hotel. Better choices are the simple if unadventurous cold hacked chicken, sparkling sesame noodles, or hot-and-sour cabbage. Spareribs are meaty and nicely charred.

A good selection of domestic and imported beers is available, and there are some assertive wines that stand up to the spectrum of food flavors encountered here. One that I like with Chinese food is the Gewürztraminer from Hugel (about $15).

Among main courses, two house specials are outstanding: Peking duck is wonderfully moist, brittle-skinned, and sprightly with its traditional garnishes; pan-fried flounder is a meaty giant that is deboned at tableside and served with a zesty coriander-and-soy sauce. Crispy sea bass Hunan style—that is, deep fried—is fresh and well cooked, with a mildly piquant Hunan sauce made with tomato, vinegar, chili sauce, and scallions.

Orange beef here is still one of the better versions in town, the strips of meat tender and moist and the sauce deftly balanced between hot and citric sweet. The lemon chicken, however, is syrupy sweet. A better chicken dish is the fresh and bright mélange of chicken breast, water chestnuts, red peppers, and black mushrooms. The best side dishes sampled were the garlic-loaded eggplant family style and the equally garlicky sautéed string beans. String beans also work well in a moderately peppery entrée called crispy dry shredded beef Sichuan style.

Fu's is one of the few Chinese restaurants that offer special steamed dishes for customers on low-cholesterol, low-sodium, or low-carbohydrate diets.

# GAGE & TOLLNER

★

*372 Fulton Street at Jay Street, Brooklyn, (718) 875-5181.*

**Atmosphere:** *Turn-of-the-century dark mahogany dining room with gas-fueled lamps.*

**Service:** *Polite and sincere.*

**Wine:** *Well-chosen American selection.*

**Price range:** *Moderate.*

**Credit cards:** *American Express, MasterCard, and Visa.*

**Hours:** *Brunch, noon to 4 P.M., Sunday; lunch, 11:30 A.M. to 3 P.M., Monday through Friday; dinner, 5 to 10:30 P.M., Monday through Friday, 4 to 11 P.M., Saturday, 5 to 9 P.M., Sunday.*

**Reservations:** *Suggested. (Free parking evenings and weekends.)*

**Wheelchair accessibility:** *Dining room on ground level; bathroom accessible but small.*

The 110-year-old Gage & Tollner stands with defiance and dignity amid the dispiritingly tacky Fulton Mall in Brooklyn. The future didn't look promising for this landmark seafood house a few years ago when the Dewey family, which had owned it since 1919, put out a for-sale sign. Along came Peter Aschkenasy, who had the unenviable distinction of presiding over the final demise of another city landmark restaurant, Luchow's on 14th Street. He then opened a Luchow's on Broadway, which did not last. Nor did a later venture called Uncle Sam's on West 52nd Street.

Mr. Aschkenasy took over Gage & Tollner in November, 1988, and brought in Edna Lewis as chef. She is the renowned Southern cook and author who was chef at the short-lived Uncle Sam's. (Stay with me, the plot improves.) While Gage & Tollner's obituary was being prepared, a funny thing happened. Customers started returning. Much of the revival can be attributed to the boyish enthusiasm of Mr. Aschkenasy.

The long, dark mahogany dining room is delightfully democratic: no good tables, no bad tables, just long rows of symmetrically arranged white linen, like a college dining hall. Arched mirrors along the felt-covered walls make the space seem ever larger than it is. From the fifteen-foot-high ceiling hang gas-fueled brass chandeliers. The waiters, many of whom have played long supporting roles in Gage & Tollner's drama, are unfailingly polite and sincere.

Befitting her culinary tradition, Mrs. Lewis cooks with full-throttle gusto. Subtlety—whether in salt, sugar, or herbs—is not in the Southern vocabulary. Mrs. Lewis turns out an extraordinary braised brisket of beef, the sinewy, fork-tender meat infused with herbs and concentrated meat juices. Pan-fried quail with julienne of ham is well browned and crisp—the slightly burned edges are terrific—with eggy spoon bread and green beans cooked in ham stock. Smithfield ham, which is extremely salty, is not helped by the accompaniment of the salty ham-flavored beans. Sweet corn pudding, though, is a fine foil.

Less assertive specialties of Mrs. Lewis include the crusty and generous crab cakes with red rice and sharp, fresh coleslaw, and the mildly spicy shrimp-and-crab gumbo rich with crabmeat, okra, and green peppers and served over rice. Two fine soups are the Charleston she-crab, creamy and peppery with a good base of crab stock and sherry, and the summery, ripe cold tomato and basil.

Some of the plain broiled fish, while fresh, is unaccountably bland. The best fish is poached Norwegian salmon with a basil sauce, sugar snap peas, and red rice.

Gage & Tollner has a wide range of shellfish preparations. The soft-belly broil is a delectable platter of broiler-charred Ipswich clams in lightly seasoned breading with lemon wedges and tartar sauce; clams and oysters Casino are faithfully rendered, not overcooked. Hefty cornmeal-coated fried oysters, too, are cleanly and skillfully executed. A well-chosen, mostly American wine list offers reasonable value.

Rhubarb pie and blackberry pie are the best desserts, ripe and with old-fashioned flaky crusts. Lemon meringue is a pale cousin. You won't go wrong with fresh, minimally sweet pecan pie or the orange soufflé garnished with orange zest. Poached pear comes with an exceedingly sweet vanilla sauce.

# GALLAGHER'S

**SATISFACTORY**

*228 West 52nd Street, 245-5336.*

*Atmosphere: Vintage steakhouse with wood-paneled walls, sports photographs galore, and exposed wood-burning grills.*

*Service: Routine and reasonably efficient.*

*Wine: Short, virtually all-California list; eighteen big name reds, four whites.*

*Price range: Moderately expensive.*

*Credit cards: All major cards.*

*Hours: Noon to midnight daily.*

*Reservations: Recommended, especially weekends.*

*Wheelchair accessibility: Everything on one level.*

Sixty-year-old Gallagher's is a remarkably well-preserved time capsule in the heart of the Broadway theater district, a virile steak house devoted to hearty American food and heated sports badinage. Lamentably, the conversation is more lively than the food, based on repeated visits.

Gallagher's is the sort of restaurant I wanted to love, for it has a wonderful unvarnished charm and nostalgia as thick as a double lamb chop. There is the grand old mahogany bar presided over by a wise-cracking chap with an endless repository of anecdotes on any given topic, the smoke-tinted pine walls covered with photographs depicting sports legends of the two- and four-legged variety (the owner breeds horses upstate) and the glowing open kitchen where steaks sizzle over wood fires.

The old-time waiters sometimes seem to be on autopilot as they go through their nightly paces, but the job gets done. The best strategy at Gallagher's is to begin with something as simple as the cherrystone clams or bluepoint oysters on the half shell, which were well iced and fresh (our waiter steered us away from the broiled oysters, which he candidly described as "terrible"), or the winter elixir of oxtail soup, a beefy broth replete with winter vegetables and beef.

Vichyssoise was insufficiently chilled and had a sour taste; gazpacho was pallid, too. The major problem with entrées is overcooking, which ruined a perfectly good pork chop one evening, a veal chop two out of three times, and most of the seafood—particularly salmon steak and swordfish. Moreover, some food comes to the table tepid. The only seafood I recommend is the two-and-a-half-pound steamed lobster.

Of course, most patrons come here for steak, and the broiled sirloin is nicely charred over hickory fires and reasonably tasty. Get a side order of lyonnaise potatoes, or hash browns; baked potatoes were tired and appeared to have been reheated, perhaps more than once. Broiled mushroom caps glazed with butter were fresh and flavorful, while creamed spinach needed a good jolt of salt and pepper to bring it to life. Other meat suggestions are the prime ribs of beef, a juicy monster, and the succulent double rib lamb chops.

Cheesecake, if you can handle it after all this, is the preferred macho dessert—and it is the real thing here. Deep, cinnamon-spiked apple pie is a winner, too. A brick of frozen chocolate mousse comes under a glacier of whipped cream and chocolate sauce—not bad, and the kind of dessert a twelve-year-old would love. Other offerings were humdrum, and coffee is still watery and lukewarm.

# GAYLORD

★

*87 First Avenue, between 5th and 6th streets, 529-7990.*

*Atmosphere: Cheerful pastel-colored dining room with multicolor ceiling lights.*

*Service: Scattered on weekends, considerably more attentive on weeknights.*

*Price range: Inexpensive.*

*Credit cards: American Express, MasterCard, and Visa.*

*Hours: Lunch, noon to 3:30 P.M., daily; dinner, 4 P.M. to midnight, daily.*

*Reservations: Recommended on weekends.*

*Wheelchair accessibility: Dining room on one level; restrooms downstairs.*

This colorful, one-hundred-seat restaurant that looks as if it belongs on Columbus Avenue rather than the Lower East Side has a little bar up front flanked by a platform where a couple of musicians sit cross-legged and play traditional Indian music on weekends. Inside, the arched ceiling is lined with lights that cast a rainbow of purple, pink, yellow, blue, and aqua. Faux windows along one wall open toward an illusory subcontinental sun, while along the back wall two large portholes offer views of the chefs at work.

The staff is generally attentive and helpful, except when the place fills up on weekends, when things can get confused. Two tasty starters are the small dishes of shrimp swathed in a piquant sauce made with onions, hot peppers, bell peppers, and coriander, or the less fiery dish of lump crabmeat sautéed with mixed spices and tomato. Both come with puffed and golden-blistered poori bread. Keema nan, the carbon-speckled tandoori bread, is delicious stuffed with spicy minced lamb. Skip the assorted hors d'oeuvres, which include some doughy and leaden fritters, and choose instead either the sprightly fried chickpeas spiked with chili powder and coriander, or the chicken chat, a hot-cool dish combining shredded meat with cucumber in a tamarind sauce.

I have had little success with tandoori chicken, which can be chokingly dry. Fish tandoori, though, is terrific. Cubes of mako shark are marinated in hot-edged mixed spices and roasted in the tandoor oven. The firm-fleshed fish emerges unbelievably succulent. A good accompaniment is the saffron-perfumed rice with nuts and dried fruit, called kacchi biryani.

Indian desserts are typically quite sweet, but some of these exceed even normal sucrose levels—gulab jamun (honey-dipped fried cheese balls) and kheer (cardamom-scented rice pudding). Less cloying are the frothy Indian ice creams, called kulfi; gajar halwa, shredded carrots cooked in milk and honey; and firni, a semisweet milk pudding brightened with rosewater.

# GLOUCESTER HOUSE

**POOR**

*37 East 50th Street, 755-7394.*

*Atmosphere: Dated-looking dining room on two levels.*

*Service: Supercilious and inattentive.*

*Price range: Expensive.*

*Credit cards: All major cards.*

*Hours: Lunch, noon to 3 P.M., Monday through Friday; dinner, 5:30 to 10 P.M., Monday through Friday. All-day menu on Saturday, noon to 10 P.M..*

*Reservations: Recommended.*

*Wheelchair accessibility: Dining facilities on ground level; restrooms downstairs.*

Gloucester House has been a fixture in midtown Manhattan since 1935, for many of those years as a haunt of the expense-account lunch crowd and known for its legendary prices. I had never been there, but my curiosity was piqued upon hearing that the restaurant charged $16.25 for a crab cake appetizer and $33.50 for a piece of broiled swordfish. (Does the fisherman who caught it join you to recount the spirited fight he had bringing it in?) The main dining room has a dated 1950s look done in sky blue with off-white walls and a speckled blue-and-white acoustical-tile ceiling. Stairs lead to a balcony room that is used for overflow and parties. Tables are fairly well spaced and the acoustical tile keeps noise to a minimum, which makes it suitable for business lunches.

A dubious extra feature for the power luncher is the food, which is so drab it never distracts from the task at hand. Upon being seated, you are presented a tray of delicious little muffins, a house tradition. I suggest you eat them quickly and often. Appetizers are remarkably dreary, especially the royally priced crab cake, which is filled with cartilage and underseasoned. Billi bi, the French cream-of-mussel soup, is as pale as dishwater, while New England clam chowder is starchy and filled with potatoes. Oysters on the half shell were bland, as if the brine had been rinsed out.

Never have I encountered a restaurant captain more supercilious than the one here who tried to persuade us to order one of the house's more expensive wines. When I asked him for the Trefethen Riesling, a fresh, dry (unusual for Riesling) white from California, he grimaced and shook his head.

"You really want that?" he asked, offering instead a chardonnay for about $5 more. When I insisted, he shrugged, warned me that I would be sorry, and left. When it came to ordering a second wine, I chose a simple Mâcon-Villages for $16. This time, to my astonishment, he broke out laughing. The rest of the service staff is more polite but hardly professional, with wine left unpoured and used dishes left on the table.

Main courses are no better than appetizers. Broiled fish is devoid of seasoning and cooked until bone dry, ruining fillets of salmon, snapper, and pompano. They come with waterlogged boiled potatoes. Swordfish can be had broiled (also dry) or cut up into little cubes and swathed in an undistinguished mustard sauce. Sautéed sole was the least dry but was untouched by seasonings. Considering this record, I was not tempted to spend $43.50 to $59.50 for lobster (price varies with size).

Overcooked salmon could not be rescued by a decent béarnaise sauce, nor could anything help a trout almondine that arrived, boneless as promised, looking as if someone had taken an ax to it. A stack of soggy french fries on the side offered no relief.

Gloucester House has been praised over the years for its signature blueberry slump, but all I tasted were cloves strewn throughout. Pecan pie was superior but minuscule for the $6.

# THE GOLDEN UNICORN

★

*18 East Broadway, at Catherine Street, 941-0911.*

*Atmosphere: Sprawling and sparkling two-story restaurant with relatively well-spaced tables and moderate noise level.*

*Service: Polite and efficient, though not too helpful about menu questions.*

*Price range: Moderate.*

*Credit cards: American Express, MasterCard, and Visa.*

*Hours: Lunch and dinner, 11 A.M. to midnight, daily; dim sum menu available 8 A.M. to 5 P.M., daily.*

*Reservations: Suggested.*

*Wheelchair accessibility: Elevator access to dining room. Restrooms on the same level.*

When you enter the marble-and-glass lobby of the building at 18 East Broadway in Chinatown, an official-looking woman, wearing a dark blue uniform and holding a walkie-talkie, trots over and inquires, "Are you here for dinner?" "Well, yes, we are." "Take this elevator," she beckons, barking orders in Chinese to a command post upstairs. On the second floor, we enter an expansive sparkling banquet hall of marble and chrome with chocolate-brown rugs, pink curtains, white tablecloths, and potted plants. Captains wearing dark suits and little gold name tags usher us to a table. (On subsequent visits, we were dispatched to a similar room on the third floor, featuring a glass-fronted display case holding brandies and cognacs and two giant shark fins.)

The Golden Unicorn, a branch of a Cantonese restaurant by the same name in Hong Kong, is more opulent—and expensive—than the average spot in Chinatown. Some of the food is superior, although a tour of the voluminous menu uncovered a fair number of run-of-the-mill offerings that could be found for a lot less money at any one of three dozen neighborhood restaurants.

The Golden Unicorn actually has two menus, an encyclopedic main document and a smaller one featuring house specialties. I suggest you concentrate on the latter and in general stay away from fried foods, which tend to be heavy and greasy.

Appetizers are the least interesting of all, so you may want to skip them and share an extra main course or two. From this special menu, sliced chicken comes out sizzling on an iron serving platter with sweet onions, ginger, and black pepper, a clean and well-balanced combination that works. From the same menu, scallops are prepared in an unusual way, set atop cubes of bean curd, cooked in a bamboo steamer, and daubed with a thick, salty black-bean sauce, garnished with scallions; other fine options are the shrimp, chicken, and squid combination with a chili-laced hot sauce, and the baked crabs in a mildly hot curry sauce dotted with sweet peas. The crabs are recommended for those who have no aversion to rolling up their sleeves and attacking food with their hands. There is no other way to excavate the sweet, sinewy meat. (Ample hot towels are offered for cleanup.)

No one at my table was enthusiastic about a dish called beef roll with golden mushrooms and ham, although the waiter recommended it. The cigar-shaped rolls were exceedingly salty and stringy. If you want meat, try the sliced beef with minced vegetables and black mushrooms.

Waiters here are generally helpful and vigilant. They are not, however, very helpful when it comes to ordering. And, as in most Chinatown restaurants, everything comes cascading out of the kitchen at once, no matter how many dishes have been ordered.

Among seafood offerings, cubes of flounder combined with good hefty prawns and crabmeat come in a lovely scallion-flecked shellfish sauce. Salt-baked shrimp, with lots of black pepper, are invigorating. A dish called Sichuan-style squid is insipid. A better seafood option is the steamed flounder with chives and ginger. And vegetable dishes are generally well prepared, especially the Chinese-style mustard greens with a thick, tasty crabmeat sauce.

# GOTHAM BAR AND GRILL

★ ★ ★

*12 East 12th Street, 620-4020.*

*Atmosphere: Cavernous postmodern room that can be very loud.*

*Service: Casually dressed staff is exceptionally knowledgeable about food; pace can be slow.*

*Wine: Many fine high-priced wines but also a decent selection under $25.*

*Price range: Expensive.*

*Credit cards: All major cards.*

*Hours: Lunch, noon to 2 P.M., Monday through Friday; dinner, 6 to 10:30 P.M., Monday through Thursday, 6 to 11:15 P.M., Friday and Saturday, 5:30 to 9:45 P.M., Sunday.*

*Reservations: Necessary.*

***Wheelchair accessibility: Stairs impede easy access to dining area; restrooms downstairs.***

If stars were awarded for the food's altitude on the plate, Gotham Bar and Grill would have no serious rivals. Alfred Portale, the I. M. Pei of contemporary American cooking, brings new meaning to the term haute cuisine with his skyscraper salads, towers of twirled pasta, high-rises of french fries, and soaring desserts. A lesser talent might use such diversions to disguise substantive shortcomings, but for Mr. Portale, one of the most accomplished young chefs on the American scene, this is just his whimsical signature.

The six-year-old Gotham Bar and Grill remains one of the most dynamic restaurants downtown.

Food is not the only part of Gotham Bar and Grill that soars. The five-thousand-square foot postmodern setting in a former warehouse evokes this bigger-than-life vertical city and there is even a Statue of Liberty overseeing the hungry masses. The multilevel room, with its neoclassical columns and parapets, is dramatically illuminated through the use of billowy parachutelike fabrics that filter much of the overhead light.

A high point, literally, among appetizers can be the seafood salad, a gravity-defying stack of greens mixed with squid rings, lobster, scallops, octopus slices, and mussels, all tossed in a lemony vinaigrette. Warm skate salad is a blissful introduction to this underappreciated fish, its thin, tender flesh sautéed to golden with a touch of salinity from capers, garnished with mixed greens. Two excellent fall dishes are the pan-browned quail over shiitake mushrooms with new potatoes in a sherry vinaigrette, and a foie gras terrine encased in tender breast of guinea hen.

Smoked foods here in general are too intense for my taste, especially an acrid linguica sausage served with a leek-and-goat cheese tart. When Mr. Portale tinkers with pasta, the results are usually as surprising as they are delightful: penne with chorizo, clams, and tomatoes is one such combination that harmonizes unexpectedly.

Waiters in khakis, white shirts, silk ties, and sneakers have an informal demeanor but are sharp and knowledgeable. The pace of dinner here is leisurely, so be prepared to spend two or more hours at the table.

Startlingly good entrées abound: crisp little squab on a bed of cubed eggplant and red pepper alongside sweet parsnip-filled ravioli; mustard-swabbed rack of lamb in a silky, rich lamb stock sauce with flageolets and terrific garlic flan; extraordinarily tender loin of rabbit with white beans, baby fennel, spinach, and a marjoram-scented sauce. Roasted red snapper benefits from its earthy accompaniment of smoked tomatoes, braised leeks, and saffron-shallot flan, and tuna steak is invigorating in its peppery shellfish-and-red-wine sauce, along with a ziggurat of lemon-chive pasta.

There is no shortage of pedigreed, pricey wines on the list here, but at the same time good selections can be had for under $25. A decent variety of half bottles is available, too.

If I had to recommend a single dessert, it would be the warm nectarine strudel made with crimped, brittle phyllo dough with toasted almond cream. Warm chocolate cake with brandied cherry ice cream comes in a close second, followed by the lush sorbets (cantaloupe, muscat grape) and sky-high profiteroles.

# GREAT SHANGHAI RESTAURANT

★

*27 Division Street, at Market Street, 966-7663.*

*Atmosphere: Clean and trim room in gray and white; well-spaced tables.*

*Service: Businesslike and low-key but lacking personality.*

*Price range: Moderate.*

*Credit cards: American Express.*

*Hours: Lunch and dinner, 11:30 A.M. to 10 P.M., Sunday through Thursday, until 11 P.M., Friday and Saturday.*

*Reservations: Necessary.*

*Wheelchair accessibility: Dining facilities on ground level; restrooms downstairs.*

The maritime cuisine of southern coastal China, called Soo-Hang, is the specialty of Great Shanghai Restaurant. The extensive menu carries a little of everything, however, from the familiar to the exotic—and the overall quality is impressive.

The dining room, recently redecorated, is clean and contemporary, all light gray and white with a tile floor, saucer-shaped sconces, and tables that are relatively well spaced (at least for Chinatown). A handsome, glass-enclosed private room in the back can be requested for special parties.

Among the best appetizers are the ginger-packed pork dumplings, fried to golden brown on one side; bright and fresh steamed vegetable dumplings; and squiggly homemade noodles coated with sprightly sesame paste. An unusual preparation worth trying is called assorted meat with mung bean sheet. These translucent and slightly gelatinous sheets provide a neutral base for the lively mélange of shredded vegetables, chicken, beef, and pork in a light, tasty wine sauce.

Many Chinese restaurants have adopted the pretentious practice of calling old-fashioned egg rolls "spring rolls," which in fact bear little resemblance to the Chinese counterpart. The "spring rolls" at Great Shanghai are simply decent egg rolls—seasoned pork and minced vegetables in a thick hide of fried dough. One of the cold starters, called pigeon with wine sauce, had an odd chemical aftertaste, perhaps from the marinade.

The waitresses at Great Shanghai are taciturn and businesslike. Once your food is delivered, you are on your own. If you want extra rice or water, you have to flag them down. And at 10 P.M., whether you are finished or not, the waitresses sit down to dinner.

Seafood entrées are, on the whole, the strongest choices. The fried whole sea bass is one of the better versions in Chinatown, crisp and meaty in a sweet-edged sauce studded with garlic cloves. Sautéed prawns in ginger sauce, one of the Soo-Hang specials, is extraordinarily delicate, garnished with julienne of carrots and scallions. Shrimp in garlic sauce and snow peas is a scorcher but good if you can take the heat. A dish called scallops, shrimp, and seafood stick is a tame but pleasing Cantonese-style casserole loaded with firm-cooked vegetables—seafood stick is a euphemism for surimi, the sweetened processed fish.

On the meat side, double sautéed pork with chili sauce is not so fiery as it sounds; it is combined with tofu and black mushrooms. Sliced beef with orange sauce, however, is tough and dry, while chicken with cashew nuts is tender and mildly seasoned. Get a side order of the excellent sautéed green beans with nubbins of pork and fistfuls of garlic scattered throughout.

Great Shanghai's owners, the Wu brothers, also have six Peking Duck Restaurants in Manhattan, so one would expect a good rendition of this specialty. It's not the best I've had in town—the skin is not as crisp as it could be—but the meat is moist and the garnishes fresh and attractively presented.

Great Shanghai has always been a dependable spot in Chinatown, and now, with its spiffed-up dining room, it is more appealing than ever.

# GREENE STREET RESTAURANT

★ ★

*101 Greene Street, 925-2415.*

*Atmosphere: Theatrical multitiered SoHo loft with a bandstand.*

*Service: Pleasant and competent.*

*Wine: Extensive wine list with wide range of prices.*

*Price range: Moderately expensive (pretheater dinner prix fixe, $31.50).*

*Credit cards: All major cards.*

*Hours: Pretheater dinner, 6 to 7:30 P.M.; noon to 8 P.M., Sunday; dinner, 6 to 11:30 P.M., Monday through Thursday, until 1 A.M., Friday and Saturday.*

*Reservations: Suggested, especially on weekends.*

***Wheelchair accessibility:** Restaurant is multitiered and the restrooms are up a long flight of stairs. Arrangements can be made for those who call in advance.*

This dramatic breakthrough loft, with its brick walls, shadowy theatrical lighting, and sixty-foot-high mural, has a bandstand in the center where jazz is featured nightly. Waiters and waitresses in black tie put on a lot of mileage crisscrossing the vast space, and they do a creditable job with good humor. The Chinese-born chef, Shao Kwoan Pang, offers a well-rehearsed medley of American, French, and Italian dishes at fair prices.

Safe and familiar starters include the goat cheese and mixed greens, and sautéed sea scallops in a bright lemon-butter sauce with spinach. The Oriental influence can be seen in the pretty tableau of smoked salmon rolls set over a fan of sliced cucumbers with a crème-fraîche-and-cucumber salad alongside. And even if lobster ravioli has the ring of a cliché these days, this rendition is still worth trying. The pasta is exceptionally light and the filling redolent of fresh tarragon. Two dishes that need more rehearsal are the rich lobster sausage paired with an inappropriately rich herb mayonnaise and the underseasoned fettuccine with asparagus and salmon.

The music at Greene Street—either piano or light jazz—adds a soothing backdrop during the week; on weekends, however, it can be rattling.

The entrée selection is wisely orchestrated to offer adequate options but not overextend the kitchen on busy evenings. Reliable choices include the beefy grilled sirloin steak with a mild green-peppercorn sauce, roasted potatoes and carrots, and the lovely rack of lamb in a rosemary-perfumed red-wine reduction along with slices of roasted eggplant and herbed tomatoes. Another straightforward winner is the moist chicken breast surrounded by roasted garlic cloves and baby vegetables (the baby carrots and zucchini were nearly raw, however).

Dover sole, a special, was filleted at the table and served with a good caper-and-butter sauce. It's a shame the staff took so much care to serve a fine fish, then plopped down unseasoned vegetables on the side. Other specials were veal chop, tender and well cooked, in a lusty wild-mushroom sauce with roasted potatoes and spinach; firm, rich sweetbreads in a Madeira-and-wild-mushroom sauce; and pink slices of duck breast in a brandy sauce flavored with lingonberries, along with wild rice and sautéed apples. Red snapper fillet, cooked to a turn, came in a parsley-and-white-wine sauce that could have used a pinch of herbs but was pleasing nonetheless.

Greene Street has an exceptionally deep wine list with a wide range of prices and a changing selection available by the glass. Among desserts, the crème brûlée and white chocolate mousse will hardly inspire you to break into song: both are pale and boring. Chocolate mousse cake and the cappuccino mousse with raspberries, however, are uplifting. Fruit tarts are as pretty as they are delicious, and sorbets are pure and ripe.

The overmiked singing notwithstanding, Greene Street offers a harmonious blend of good food and genial service in a rakish SoHo setting.

# HARLEQUIN

★

*569 Hudson Street, corner of West 11th Street, 255-4950.*

*Atmosphere: Sophisticated and distinctive all-gray décor.*

*Service: Professional and efficient.*

*Wine: Good Spanish list, reasonably priced.*

*Price range: Moderate.*

*Credit cards: All major cards.*

*Hours: Brunch, noon to 3 P.M., Saturday, noon to 4 P.M., Sunday; lunch, noon to 3 P.M., Monday through Saturday; dinner, 5:30 to 11 P.M., Monday through Saturday, until 10:30 P.M., Sunday.*

*Reservations: Suggested.*

*Wheelchair accessibility: Four steps up at entrance; dining room on one level; restrooms down a flight of stairs.*

The owners of this inviting Spanish restaurant, Ileana and Jose Barcena, remain as gracious and enthusiastic as ever; they seem genuinely grateful that you have chosen their restaurant, which is rare today. The well-trained service staff reflects their attitude, endearing Harlequin to its cadre of regulars. Throughout the year, the Barcenas put on ambitious Spanish wine and food events.

When Harlequin opened in Greenwich Village in 1985, it showed great promise of offering New Yorkers a non-clichéd version of Spanish cuisine, particularly the little-known foods from the northern coastal areas of Galicia and Asturias. While the restaurant offers some intriguing regional specials from time to time, the promise has not been entirely fulfilled.

The dining room hardly looks Spanish, all cool gray with well-separated tables and dishware carrying the frolicking Harlequin logo. On one side of the dining room is a sparkling little bar and on the other a glass display case filled with Lladro porcelain statuettes.

One of the best appetizers is still the shrimp in cream of garlic, a half-dozen grilled shrimp arranged atop two sauces: one an aggressive blend of garlic, cayenne, white wine, lemon, and brown stock; the other a thick and heady combination of garlic, white wine, fish stock, and cream. Brandada de bacalao—what the French call brandade de morue—is terrific here, a garlic-powered purée of dried, salted cod and potatoes that is eaten with toasted black bread. The snowy purée is passed under the broiler before serving to give it a golden-brown, crisp surface.

Spanish food aficionados may want to watch for occasional specials of angulas, the bean-sprout-size white eels that are prepared in the traditional manner: placed in a little earthenware crock and cooked in sizzling olive oil flavored with shards of fresh garlic.

Harlequin has one of the strongest Spanish wine lists in the city, and prices are reasonable. The paella for two here is still a winner. In Spain, there are as many recipes for this national dish as there are provinces: some with meat, some with shellfish, some with neither. Mr. Barcena does not take sides. He throws in everything—chunks of lobster, shrimp, sausage, clams, mussels, scallops, and sometimes pork and chicken—all fresh and well-cooked. The yellow rice is moist and complex with a blend of saffron, garlic, crushed tomatoes, and chicken stock. Another good choice was a special of merluza (hake), a fairly meaty and mild white fish, presented in a garlicky wine broth with tender clams and herbs. A dish called pixin al eneldo (Asturian monkfish with dill sauce) was well cooked and enhanced by a bright, slightly tart sauce; it was much better than the dolphin fish (sometimes called mahi-mahi) surrounded by a bitter red-pepper purée.

Among the meat dishes, honey-glazed rack of lamb for two is always satisfying, as are the firm and rich lamb sweetbreads paired with medallions of veal and wild mushrooms. A homespun preparation called aguja de res—Spanish pot roast, really—came off lame from lack of seasoning.

For dessert, fruit tarts are anything but light and delicate, but I liked them nonetheless; flan, or crème caramel, is on the mark, but frozen raspberry soufflé is just adequate. On a sweltering summer evening fruit sorbets are a good choice.

Overall, Harlequin is still one of those engaging, family-run restaurants that you naturally want to like, despite the occasional lapses. With a few refinements in the kitchen, Harlequin could become an object of high passion.

# HATSUHANA

*17 East 48th Street, 355-3345.*

*Atmosphere: Bright, clean, and trim dining rooms on both of two levels, each with long sushi bars.*

*Service: Waiters can have a rushed and indifferent attitude.*

*Price range: Moderately expensive (prix-fixe dinner, $25).*

*Credit cards: All major cards.*

*Hours: Lunch, 11:45 A.M. to 2:30 P.M., Monday through Friday; dinner, 5:30 to 9:30 P.M., Monday through Friday, 5 to 10 P.M., Saturday.*

*Reservations: Necessary.*

*Wheelchair accessibility: Several steps down to dining room. Ground-level restrooms available for the handicapped.*

Twelve-year-old Hatsuhana is one of the city's premier (and pricey) Japanese restaurants, mobbed daily by Japanese and Americans alike. While high volume assures that the seafood does not languish, it also leads to frenzied, impatient service and certain shortcuts in preparation.

There are dining rooms on both of the two levels, each with long sushi bars flanked by rows of tightly packed wooden tables. The sushi bar selection is exceptional. Many of the more exotic treats never make it to the tables—at least those of non-Japanese-speaking customers—so if you are an adventurous aficionado the bar is the only place to be. One such delight sampled recently was the exquisitely buttery and sweet meat from the fluke fin. Other times you might find tiny fried Japanese crabs, about the size of a quarter, that you pop in your mouth like candies. The crunchy texture and salty essence are delightful. The Japanese mackerel, which is far more delicate than the Spanish type, is another treat, as is the sea-urchin roe, which is ineffably oceanic here.

From the regular menu, the sushi Hatsuhana assortment is a good basic sampler. You are given a slip listing options and asked to check off ten. Among them are tuna, toro (the fatty flesh from tuna belly), shrimp, giant clam, mackerel, flounder, eel, and crab. The sashimi assortment has a similar lineup with the addition of excellent octopus mantle. The touchstone of a sushi bar, aside from freshness of the fish, is the subtle seasoning of the rice with vinegar and sugar. This adds a clean, sharp edge to the sushi. On two out of three visits, both hectic lunches, the rice was well cooked but tasted unseasoned.

Some of the special appetizers are titillating: negihamachi, chopped yellowtail flounder flecked with scallions; negitoro, chopped belly of tuna, which is more assertive and rich, prepared the same way; and sabagarimaki, slices of silver-skinned mackerel blended with pickled ginger and wrapped in Japanese white radish. Tairagai-yaki, described as broiled sea scallops in salt, were disappointing. Some of the scallops on the plate appeared to be little calicos, not big sea scallops, and all were dry and stringy. The vegetarian California roll is nothing special, either, mainly avocado wrapped in sesame-dotted rice.

Some of the cooked dishes are superior, including moist, sweet chicken teriyaki, and rare-cooked salmon teriyaki. Tempura of shrimp, fish, and vegetables, though, is just run-of-the-mill. The batter is crumbly and slightly oily.

When the restaurant is going full tilt, service can get bogged down at the tables, so the sushi bar is a better bet if you are on a tight schedule. At a recent lunch, the staff was so rushed we never received hot towels or water. It is advisable to make dinner reservations no later than 8:30 P.M. since the kitchen closes at 9:45.

# HUBERTS

★ ★ ★

*575 Park Avenue, entrance on 63rd Street, 826-5911.*

*Atmosphere: Elegant, roomy, with soft filtered light.*

*Service: Competent and discreet.*

*Wine: Intelligent list, well matched to the food; fair prices.*

*Price range: Expensive (pretheater dinner prix fixe, $27).*

*Credit cards: All major cards.*

*Hours: Pretheater dinner, 6 to 6:30 P.M., Monday through Saturday; dinner, 6 to 10 P.M. Monday through Saturday.*

*Reservations: Preferred.*

*Wheelchair accessibility: One step at entrance to main dining room; restrooms on ground level.*

Like upwardly mobile immigrants, Huberts restaurant has followed each surge of its success with a move to a better neighborhood. Karen Hubert and her chef and husband, Len Allison, started in 1976 with a Victorian-style nook in Boerum Hill in Brooklyn. In 1981, they crossed the East River and settled on East 22nd Street, near Gramercy Park, where their ingenuous charm and ecumenical cooking continued to win followers. In 1988, they reached the summit: a Park Avenue address.

Their new residence, designed by Adam Tihany—of Bice, Remi, and Metro, among others—has a handsome Australian-ash bar, which flanks the main dining room. The serene and soft-edged main dining room evokes a Japanese mood. Artificial light is filtered through amber window panels, tables are well spaced, and the acoustics are kind to conversationalists. A second dining room at the other end of a long hallway reflects the same mood.

The Oriental accent is no accident, for the owners are enamored of Japanese aesthetics and cuisine (in fact, two of the chefs are Japanese), which is evident in such intriguing appetizers as soft-shell crab marinated in a cool combination of ponzu (a Japanese citrus vinegar), soy sauce, sake, and lime juice, as well as a bright shrimp salad embellished with threads of daikon (a Japanese radish), cucumbers, black seaweed, and a piquant rice-vinegar dressing.

Mr. Allison's Cook's Tour then moves on to the American bayou with grilled shrimp in an invigorating beer-based sauce stoked with Cajun spices. Another zippy starter, a Huberts standard, is lean, well-seasoned rabbit sausage with a smoky Mexican mole sauce.

Japanese handiwork is evident in presentation, with each dish a little diorama of colors and textures. Huberts has always boasted one of the more intelligent wine lists in town, not showy and encyclopedic but in harmony with the food and full of surprises. Prices are reasonable, too.

Some of the more compelling dishes include pink-roasted duck with haricots verts, poached pear, and a crunchy vegetable strudel bulging with shredded leeks, cabbage, celery root, carrots, and ginger. Pan-blackened salmon is the real thing here: peppery and crisp outside, blush pink within, served with cornmeal-dusted okra and roasted potatoes.

Rack of lamb comes with a soothing goat-cheese lasagna, and country captain chicken is an exuberant orchestration of spices, curry being dominant, with couscous on the side.

A fine selection of cheeses rolls your way before dessert, although some people may resent paying $10 for it on top of a $60 prix-fixe dinner (the surcharge is not added if you skip dessert).

The sweets are winners all, especially the frozen espresso mousse with pear sorbet, blood orange tartlets with ginger-cherry-blossom ice cream, peach sorbet in the shape of a rose, and blueberry tartlets with kirsch-and-cinnamon ice cream.

# HUDSON RIVER CLUB

★ ★

*250 Vesey Street, in the World Financial Center, 786-1500.*

*Atmosphere: Handsome, three-tiered dining room with sweeping view of New York Harbor.*

*Service: Can be laggard and forgetful.*

*Wine: Well-priced list offering some unusual samplings from around the country.*

*Price range: Moderately expensive.*

*Credit cards: All major cards.*

*Hours: Lunch, noon to 2:30 P.M., Monday through Friday; dinner, 5:30 to 10 P.M., Monday through Saturday.*

*Reservations: Necessary at lunch.*

*Wheelchair accessibility: Elevator to restaurant; ramp to restrooms.*

New York City's relatively paltry selection of quality restaurants on the waterfront has been substantially enhanced with the arrival in early 1990 of the Hudson River Club, a handsome and comfortable dining room facing New York Harbor with the Statue of Liberty and Ellis

Island off in the distance. The food can be as inspiring as the setting.

The Hudson River Club is in the imposing World Financial Center, which also houses offices, shops, and a spectacular glass-enclosed public atrium. At midday, the complex buzzes with the financial-industry crowd; after sunset, though, janitors seem to outnumber visitors. The challenge facing the Hudson River Club is to lure diners this far downtown at night. After four samplings of the regional American menu by Waldy Malouf, a chef who was recruited from La Crémaillère in Banksville, N.Y., I'd say the odds are better than ever that it can be done.

The Hudson River Club, designed by Philip George (he also did Le Bernardin), is a long, three-tiered space in light oak paneling with brass accents, subtle fabric-covered banquettes, and handsome art from the Hudson Valley school. Befitting a place that caters to discreet bankers and brokers, conservations are well muffled. At lunch, the room is filled with dark-suited Wall Streeters, many with beepers, cellular telephones, and hand-size computers on the tables.

Mr. Malouf's cohesive and well-rounded menu emphasizes foods and wines from the Hudson River Valley. A fine example among starters is the magnificent pumpkin-apple soup, a fine balance of earthy and sweet, garnished with croutons, crumbled bacon, and cinnamon. Another personal favorite is the dome-shaped fritter of lump crabmeat encased in golden potatoes and slices of toasted almonds. The most refined—and fought over—appetizer at my table was the ethereal sea-urchin custard: three halved urchin shells filled with the powerfully oceanic roe whipped with brandy, cream, and egg, garnished with a white butter sauce and caviar.

Like most new restaurants, the Hudson River Club had difficulty getting its service crew shipshape. Some of the waiters seemed to be in a fog—we had to ask for water four times at lunch—and little details like wine-pouring, table-clearing, and knowledge of food were hit and miss. More recent revisits found their performance to be improving.

The restaurant makes an admirable effort to introduce regional American wines at fair prices, from not only California and the Hudson River Valley, but also such diverse places as Texas, the Pacific Northwest, and Michigan. It would be helpful, though, if someone on the staff would take the initiative to describe some of the lesser-known wines to customers.

Among the superior main courses are perfectly cooked salmon wrapped in a webbing of thin fried potatoes with a bright parsley-and-dill sauce; a meaty roasted veal shank embellished with orange rind, rosemary, baby turnips, and carrots (I just wish a marrow knife were provided), and succulent squab, moist and distinctive, with a sauce enriched with foie gras.

Mr. Malouf's cooking is impressive not just for its cleanly orchestrated flavors, but also for his attention to complementary textures and flavors. No two dishes have the same garnish. One of the highlights is roasted chicken that is coated with a mixture of crushed walnuts and maple syrup. It is then deboned and served with pan juices along with a potato basket holding celery-root purée. Surprisingly, the juices are only faintly sweet with maple flavor, and the assertive celery root is a perfect foil. Veal steak cut from the loin is superb, too, wrapped in caramelized leeks and served with winter squash and potato pancakes.

A few of Mr. Malouf's creations seemed conceptually flawed. A thick cornmeal coating on sea scallops obscures their flavor, and a sauce of hard apple cider with sliced apples further muddies the waters. A filet-mignon-shaped tuna steak as thick as an almanac—the faddish way to prepare tuna these days—is, as so often is the case, unevenly cooked: dry outside, medium-rare in the middle.

I have not seen any banana plantations along the Hudson River, but that would not stop me from ordering a dessert of banana mousse under a lid of crinkled phyllo dough with mango sorbet and sliced bananas. Steamed gingerbread is outrageously good, garnished with slices of ripe pears and a light caramel sauce. Other rousing options are maple custard with orange and apple slices, apple tart with an excellent buttery crust and walnut ice cream, and lemon-meringue tarts.

# IL CANTINORI

★

*32 East 10th Street, 673-6044.*

**Atmosphere:** *Enchantingly rustic Tuscan farmhouse setting. Back dining room more tranquil and spacious than front.*

**Service:** *Knowledgeable and professional, though sometimes overwhelmed by the crowds.*

**Wine:** *Moderate-size well-priced list.*

**Price range:** *Moderately expensive.*

**Credit cards:** *All major cards.*

**Hours:** *Lunch, noon to 2:45 P.M., Monday through Friday; dinner, 6 to 11:15 P.M., Monday through Thursday, 6 to 11:45 P.M., Friday and Saturday, 6 to 11 P.M., Sunday.*

**Reservations:** *Necessary, preferably several days in advance.*

**Wheelchair accessibility:** *One step at entrance; restrooms downstairs.*

Il Cantinori is an enchanting Tuscan-style restaurant in Greenwich Village that serves moderately expensive but uneven food. It is the kind of place you want to love, with its stucco walls, wood-beam ceiling, glazed tile floor, handsome country furniture, and skylighted back room. And many people do, for it is mobbed nightly.

The kitchen can turn out some exceptional pastas and risottos, but at the same time many other dishes, particularly game and seafood, tend to be overcooked and underseasoned. This seems to be a result of the kitchen trying to grapple with an unrealistically large repertory. The written menu is varied enough: eleven appetizers, eight pastas and risottos, and eleven main courses. Just as you are absorbing all this, a waiter comes by and drones on about all the daily specials, most of which you forget by the time he finishes.

Among starters to try are the colorful cold antipasto plate, an assemblage of roasted peppers, roasted whole shallots, cauliflower, and slices of grilled zucchini swathed with tomato sauce and capers.

Tuscan pot roast over polenta sounded irresistible. Alas, what came out was a tasty stew of shredded beef and vegetables mired in a quicksand of pale cornmeal reminiscent of Cream of Wheat. Several superior pastas can be had in half portions as starters, including tagliolini in a bracing lamb sauce, rigatoni in Bolognese sauce nicely sweetened with carrots and onions, and penne in a beautifully balanced sauce of smoked salmon, brandy, and cream. Ravioli stuffed with spinach and ricotta is delightful in a sauce of crumbled lean sausage, tomato, and herbs.

It's a shame that such finesse does not follow through to the main courses. Sweetbreads, for instance, were flops on two occasions: the first time flaccid and bland in a sauce of white wine, onion, and carrots; on a second try ruined by acrid burned butter sauce and charred sage. Pheasant was overcooked, as was a special of rabbit with rosemary and garlic (but served with wonderful roasted potatoes).

The scenario improves if you opt for the broiler-crisped rack of lamb; thick, juicy veal chop with mashed potatoes and peas flecked with prosciutto, or pounded fillet of veal with shiitake mushrooms and Marsala sauce. Although game is touted here, the only dish that can be recommended is the crisply roasted quails seasoned with thyme.

Waiters here know the menu well and work hard, although the crowds can bog them down at times. They also know the moderately sized, well-priced wine list well, which is a plus.

For dessert, there is rich hazelnut or ricotta gelati with biscuits, a ripe plum-and-apricot tart, a Granny Smith apple tart, and one of the best renditions of tiramisù in town: light, sharp with espresso flavor, and minimally sweet.

# IL MULINO

★

*86 West 3rd Street, 673-3783.*

*Atmosphere: Lively bar where customers wait for tables in the crowded, dim dining room.*

*Service: Perfunctory and somewhat careless.*

*Price range: Expensive.*

*Credit cards: American Express.*

*Hours: Lunch, noon to 2:30 P.M., Monday through Friday; dinner, 5 to 11:30 P.M., Monday through Saturday.*

*Reservations: Necessary.*

*Wheelchair accessibility: Can accommodate if notified in advance.*

Il Mulino has such fervid partisans that criticizing any part of it could lead to a parking-lot brawl. It's not that this expensive, homespun place does not have charm, but just that the imagery clouds the reality.

Regulars love the routine whereby waiters start piling food in front of you before the menu is presented. Il Mulino makes one feel like a scrawny G.I. on a weekend furlough at Mom's. First comes a plate of peppery fried zucchini, followed by delicious slabs of toasted Italian bread under a pile of minced garlic, chopped basil, and tomatoes; then slices of richly marbled salami.

As if that were not enough, the waiter lugs over a wheel of Parmesan the size of a Fiat's tire and gouges out a big chunk. "Too many people leave restaurants hungry these days," volunteers the proprietor, rubbing his midsection.

It doesn't take long to realize that this largess is part of a larger sales pitch—the equivalent of getting free whitewall tires with your $32,000 BMW. When we got down to business at lunch, it was a very expensive affair indeed.

Il Mulino has a sizable and nearly evangelical following that lines up three deep at the small front bar every night waiting for an open pew. Management must have a policy of not honoring reservations at night. In revisits for this edition of the guidebook, I waited forty-five minutes one evening, twenty-five minutes on another.

You don't go to Il Mulino for the atmosphere. The drab little dining area, pressed between the kitchen and the bar, seems to be illuminated by a few near-dead flashlights. The menu is just a formality. A captain comes by and runs off an impossibly long list of specials, by which time you are so mellow from your extended happy hour and sated from all the tidbits on the table that you would just as soon order espresso and call it a night.

If you stick it out, a few dishes are worth trying. Skip such run-of-the-mill starters as clams Casino and go for one of the better pastas. Half orders are not allowed—You don't want to go home hungry, do you?—so the portion of angel hair tossed with a peppery sauce replete with fresh clams, mussels, and squid should be shared. The trenette with pesto is tasty, as is the rich and meaty spaghetti Bolognese, although mired in enough sauce for three portions.

Oversaucing is the rule rather than the exception here. Two particularly unfortunate examples were a special of pappardelle in a champagne cream sauce with truffles, a swampy, oversalted mess (and hardly grazed by truffles), and fillet of red snapper, which came under such a deep sea of garlicky tomato sauce that it never surfaced. A $40 rubbery lobster was beyond rescue from its potent garlic sauce. The menu carries no fewer than a dozen veal preparations. The juicy, softball-size veal chop garnished with brittle leaves of sage had to be sent back because it was raw in the center—but it was good on the rebound. Chicken dishes range from satisfying—morsels sautéed with garlic and wine—to deadful, such as the special of chicken with sausage and peppers in a gelatinous sauce reminiscent of Chinese fast food. Both mammoth steaks on the menu are winners, one simply broiled, another aromatic of shallots, sage, and wine.

While Il Mulino partisans speak lovingly of the warm personal service, my three dinners (lunch was much better) found waiters who brokered food at the table, or, if not, often served it to the wrong person.

After such a food assault, fruit is the most appropriate

dessert. You can get a terrific zabaglione with fresh strawberries or raspberries here, or a lovely poached pear.

# INAGIKU

★

*111 East 49th Street, 355-0440.*

*Atmosphere: Opulent Japanese ambiance with pagoda-theme tempura bar.*

*Service: Friendly and eager although sometimes slow.*

*Price range: Moderately expensive.*

*Credit cards: All major cards.*

*Hours: Lunch, noon to 2:30 P.M., Monday through Friday; dinner, 5 to 11 P.M., daily.*

*Reservations: Necessary.*

*Wheelchair accessibility: Dining room has several levels separated by small steps; restrooms on the same level.*

Inagiku, the opulent Japanese restaurant in the Waldorf-Astoria Hotel, has always been my favorite spot for tempura. A large circular wooden bar under a pagodalike roof surrounds white-frocked chefs who make all sorts of sizzling and crisp tempura—shrimp, lobster, beef, vegetable, and more that is served just seconds out of the deep fryer along with a dipping sauce. It took me a long time to sample the rest of the menu—and while some of it is fine, I think I'll stick to the tempura bar from now on.

The dining area behind the bar at Inagiku is richly appointed in gold-patterned wallpaper and deep red rugs. Tables are well separated, and the noise level is low. The restaurant attracts an army of dark-suited Japanese businessmen at lunch and a well-heeled mixed clientele at dinner. Those seeking even more privacy can reserve the handsome tatami rooms in advance.

The menu is relatively unadventurous. Sushi, either as

an appetizer or an entrée, features slices of tuna, fluke, salmon, and shrimp—all unquestionably fresh, although the rice lacks vinegar flavor. Ikura (salmon roe) and uni (sea urchin) are good, too. Sashimi features more or less the same cast.

When it comes to cooked items, the kitchen frequently overdoes it. Dinner appetizers of grilled shrimp on bamboo skewers were tough and so was the chicken yakitori prepared the same way. Stick with appetizer tempura, which was as fresh and light as ever.

The Inagiku seafood special is rather paltry. It combines small pieces of broiled lobster that, though well cooked, arrive nearly cold, and salmon stuffed with lobster meat in a light creamy sauce along with a soy-based dipping sauce. One evening I tried a special, called seafood cooked on a stone. It rated high marks for theatrics but made little sense from the culinary standpoint. The roaring hot rock came out covered with scallops on skewers, salmon steak, Alaskan crab claws, clams, and lobster in the shell. No matter how fast you wolf down your meal, the items that sit on the stone longest overcook. All came with a soy-and-seaweed sauce.

At lunch one day I tried the beef cooked over stone, which can be superb if the meat is top quality—which this wasn't. A better choice was the shikki no bento, or special lunch box. One of the pretty black lacquer boxes contained sashimi of fluke and tuna, pickled vegetables, and something that could best be described as chicken meatballs (they were mildly seasoned and moist). The second box held a dried-out piece of cooked salmon and pickled lotus root, and the third a big rice ball, tamago (the sweet egg-based sushilike dish), and pineapple. The assorted hot platter on the lunch menu, an appetizer, was the best part of the meal: tender negimayaki (broiled strips of beef and scallions), grilled shrimp and scallops on skewers, and chicken teriyaki with sweet sauce. Miso soup is superior, too, filled with little white mushrooms.

The traditionally garbed waitresses are extremely gracious and warm-hearted, although sometimes services is slow.

Inagiku is one of those narrowly focused restaurants that do one thing very well. For tempura, its lively bar can't be beat.

# INDOCHINE

★ ★

*430 Lafayette Street, south of Astor Place, 505-5111.*

*Atmosphere: Large and airy dining room with vaguely tropical theme; can be exceedingly loud.*

*Service: Indifferent. Expect to wait for a table. Once seated, the pace is prompt.*

*Price range: Moderately expensive.*

*Credit cards: All major cards.*

*Hours: 6 P.M. to 12:30 A.M., daily; closed Christmas Day.*

*Reservations; Necessary.*

*Wheelchair accessibility: Several steps up at entrance, otherwise on one level.*

Indochine's service has become frenetic and sometimes supercilious in recent years, and overbooking continues to be a problem. (You can avoid many annoyances by going early on weeknights.) But on the brighter side, the amalgam of Vietnamese and Cambodian food here is as dynamic as ever.

The long rectangular room flirts with a tropical theme: palm fronds painted on the walls, greenery scattered here and there, dark green banquettes and white tablecloths. Tables are too close, conversation is too loud, and some of the preening artsy types who strut around the place look like refugees from an old Andy Warhol movie.

But then there is the food, which for me makes it all worthwhile. Nowhere in New York, for example, will you find a more vivid and authentic version of the much-abused Vietnamese spring roll. Actually, several versions are served here: one combines morsels of shrimp, vermicelli, bean sprouts, coriander, and fresh mint rolled in translucent sheets of rice paper; another has shredded crabmeat instead of shrimp. Both are remarkably light and have a delightful crunchy texture. The Vietnamese dipping sauce nuoc mam, made with salted anchovies and vinegar, comes on the side. Steamed Vietnamese ravioli filled with ground chicken, bean sprouts, and black mushrooms, however, has little flavor on its own without the dipping sauce. Deep-frying is clean and light here, as in the spring rolls called cha-gio, which are golden deep-fried tubes of rice pancakes stuffed with seasoned pork, carrots, and vegetables.

One of my favorite dishes over the years at Indochine has been the sweet-and-sour shrimp soup, an incredible yin-yang combination of taste sensations. The orange-tinted broth, generous with perfectly cooked shrimp, gets its sweetness from slices of pineapple and its tartness from chunks of tomato and tamarind seasoning. This combination attacks the palate first with sweetness, then with a slightly sour sensation, and reaches a finale with the smooth, long aftertaste of a good fish stock.

Other spirited dishes for starters or main courses are the pristine steamed shrimp salad brightened with fresh mint and lemongrass; a salad of lean, tender beef slices that comes on fiery hot at the outset then cools off with the sensations of the lemongrass and shallots; and grilled eggplant in a lime-and-ginger vinaigrette.

Despite management problems that lead to overbooking tables and overtaxing the staff, food manages to come out of the kitchen promptly. Don't expect much help from the waiters or waitresses when it comes to choosing dishes. They have little time for conversation.

Several seafood dishes are worth seeking out. One is the aromatic fillet of gray sole steamed in a banana leaf with coconut milk and lemongrass. I also liked the simple but invigorating sautéed shrimp with scallions, tomato, and basil. Sticky rice sweetened with cinnamon, clove, and anise is a good foil to the highly seasoned cooking here.

Another entrée that always surprises and delights those who try it for the first time is the boned deep-fried chicken wings stuffed with vermicelli, bean sprouts, carrots, lemongrass, galanga (in the ginger family), and diced chicken: the skin is golden and crisp, the stuffing multitextured and delicious, especially with nuoc mam or the peanut dipping sauce. Spareribs with lemongrass are better than the average Chinese restaurant rendition but light on the lemon flavor. Roast duck with ginger sauce and carrots is a better choice, as are the fresh, tender frogs' legs in ginger sauce.

Desserts have improved slightly in recent years. Creamy hazelnut mousse cake and lemon tart are the real things, and coconut sorbet is excellent (better than pale raspberry). Skip the supermarket-quality blueberry tart.

# JANE'S BAR AND GRILL

★ ★

*208 East 60th Street, 935-3481.*

*Atmosphere: Urbane and inviting dining room done in black and white; moderate noise level.*

*Service: Amiable and attentive.*

*Wine: Limited list skewed toward moderately expensive bottles.*

*Price range: Moderately expensive.*

*Credit cards: All major cards.*

*Hours: Lunch, noon to 2:30 P.M., Monday through Friday; dinner, 6 to 11 P.M., Monday through Thursday, 6 to 11:30 P.M., Friday and Saturday.*

*Reservations: Suggested.*

*Wheelchair accessibility: Three steps down into restaurant; dining on one level; restrooms downstairs.*

The former rustic-looking Chatfield's has been turned into an urbane and inviting spot called Jane's Bar and Grill, done primarily in black and white with framed photographs on the walls, brass sconces, black leatherette banquettes, and lone red roses on each table. Table settings are diverting too, right down to the snazzy monogrammed plates and the flatware. The room can get loud at peak hours, but not excessively so.

The chef, Daniel Baylis, formerly of Aurora and the

Odeon, has designed a menu that is light and attractively presented using Mediterranean-style sauces based on vegetable purées and olive oil. Typical of his style are the vegetable tart, a disk of puff pastry heaped with well-seasoned roasted eggplant, red peppers, zucchini, mushrooms, and tomatoes, and a mixed salad surrounded by morsels of fresh lobster with an intensely ripe sorbet of tomato and basil. Another exceptional starter is lobster-filled cannelloni seasoned with coriander and presented over a fresh tomato sauce garnished with fava beans. The pasta is firm and fresh —not overcooked as so many restaurant cannelloni are— and the coriander gives the whole dish a zesty freshness.

Pepper-coated slices of rare grilled tuna are appealing, but a sauce of capers, tomato, and cubes of unripe avocado does not help the cause. The lobster-and-corn soup is made with a good ripe lobster stock, and crab cakes, while perhaps in need of a pepper boost, are crispy and moist. Rich homemade duck sausage comes atop a bed of lentils sweetened with shallots and bacon, along with a snappy watercress salad.

Jane's wine list is adequate for the average diner, but one would like to see more selections at the lower price end.

Most entrées are homey and well balanced, like the roasted baby chicken with bacon and onions. A wonderfully textured gratin of potatoes, just shy on seasonings, comes on the side. Tuna is nicely seared outside and rare in the center, cooled by a gazpacho sauce made with tomato, diced peppers, and vinegar. A good grilled shell steak is garnished with tomato chutney, and an excellent rack of lamb is encursted with aromatic pesto along with ratatouille and airy little quennelles of garlic. A thin fillet of salmon is deftly cooked and spread over a lively mixture of corn, spinach, tomato, and coriander.

Except for a lemon tart with an overly thick and burned crust, desserts are appealing. Frozen caramel soufflé is a ziggurat of egg whites and caramel, not too sweet, and ringed by marinated oranges. Warm chocolate cake with praline ice cream is definitely for sucrose fiends, while the napoleon of strawberries is sublimely light and brittle. For the insouciant dessert lover, there are pecan waffles with warm chocolate sauce and bourbon ice cream. The more abstemious can opt for a lovely Tupelo honey sorbet.

# JANE STREET SEAFOOD CAFE

★

*31 Eighth Avenue, corner of Jane Street, 243-9237.*

*Atmosphere: Friendly neighborhood spot in rustic, tavernlike setting.*

*Service: Congenial but often too rushed to tend all the tables effectively.*

*Wine: Extensive wine list well matched to the food, reasonably priced.*

*Price range: Moderate.*

*Credit cards: All major cards.*

*Hours: Dinner, 5:30 to 11 P.M., Monday through Thursday, 5:30 P.M. to midnight, Friday and Saturday, 4 to 10 P.M., Sunday.*

*Reservations: Not accepted.*

*Wheelchair accessibility: One step at the entrance; everything on one level.*

It's easy to sail right by the Jane Street Seafood Cafe on lower Eighth Avenue without ever noticing it, as I have done dozens of times. The weathered-wood façade clings to the bow of a big brick apartment house, and the lack of a conspicuous sign leaves the impression it is just a neighborhood watering hole with New England pretensions. Inside, however, is a neighborly, sleeves-up fish house that prepares a staggering variety of fish and shellfish.

Despite its effective camouflage, the restaurant is usually packed, and reservations are not accepted. The lack of a sit-down bar or waiting area forces patrons to line up in the cramped foyer. Tables are tightly arranged in the tavernlike setting with its brick-and-natural-wood walls, low lighting, and blackboard menus. The casually dressed service staff is sometimes hard to distinguish from the casually dressed patrons.

The kitchen prepares fish in a light and salubrious manner, with few cream sauces or elaborate garnishes. Sometimes the result is too timidly seasoned for my taste, or in some cases not seasoned at all.

Bowls of good creamy coleslaw are set out on the table for starters. Some of the better appetizers are the brittle fried zucchini sticks, succulent sweet littleneck clams, and cleanly fried bluepoint oysters with tartar sauce. Mussels steamed in wine and sherry with shallots and garlic had good flavor but were sandy; baked clams oreganato were run-of-the-mill and chewy. On a recent revisit the Manhattan clam chowder scored high marks for flavor and the clams were not overcooked.

You will need the help of the staff to decipher some of the dishes, such as squid Rudolfo and monkfish mahnken. Waiters and waitresses are chatty and cooperative, although the fervid pace of the dining room keeps them on the run, perpetually lunging from one table to another. The extensive wine list is well matched to the food, and prices are fair. Plenty of good whites that complement the fish are available for less than $20—for example, the Mâcon-Blanc Villages from Jadot and the Torre di Giano white from Lungarotti. Chalkboard wine-by-the-glass specials are available daily.

Frying is still performed well here, so you can usually rely on the crispy golden-brown fried fillet of sole or, when they are available, the fried soft-shell clams. Other winning options are the poached fillet or ruddy king salmon enhanced with a mild dill sauce and the oversize portion of red snapper under a profusion of sautéed onions, tomato, and basil —tasty, if hardly dainty. Most of the entrées come with the same supporting cast, insipid brown rice and a vegetable of the day, such as baked acorn squash.

One of the frequent specials is called sole Portuguese, a fresh, firm fillet riding a garlic-loaded crest of tomatoes and mushrooms. Another house special is dubbed Jane Street sole, seasoned with mixed herbs, dusted with Parmesan cheese, and crowned with a slice of broiled tomato. The mysterious monkfish mahnken turned out to be a pleasant surprise, the meaty medallions sautéed in butter with florets of broccoli and onions, then combined with a sherry sauce spiked with Tabasco.

Among the dishes to skip are the boring sautéed shrimp with mushrooms and the underseasoned and slightly fishy fillet of bluefish cooked in wine and garlic, both the sort of seafood preparations you expect to find at the Sandpiper Room of a highway motel chain. Whole rainbow trout is engaging on the plate and perfectly cooked, but looks are not everything. It cries out for seasoning. A better choice is the moist grilled swordfish aromatic of oregano.

Some of the desserts have sweetness going for them but little else, such as the dryish chocolate truffle cake and the achingly sweet chocolate pie. The zesty and fresh apple-raisin pie, made without sugar, is a refreshing way to end the meal, as are the good assorted sorbets. If your tastes run to more serious sweets, go with the intense chocolate mud cake or the frozen mocha pie.

# JEZEBEL

★ ★

*630 Ninth Avenue, corner of 45th Street, 582-1045.*

*Atmosphere: A large room cluttered with antiques and bric-a-brac. Stylish late crowd.*

*Service: Congenial, but slow and confused.*

*Wine: Small wine list.*

*Price range: Moderate.*

*Credit cards: American Express.*

*Hours: Dinner, 6, 8, and 10 P.M. seatings, Monday through Saturday, 6, 8, and 9 P.M., Sunday.*

*Reservations: Necessary.*

*Wheelchair accessibility: Everything on one level.*

Jezebel is a marvelously cluttered expanse, a cross between a leafy nightclub and a vintage clothing boutique. You enter the dining room at Jezebel and find yourself amid palms and assorted foliage swaying under the breeze of big room fans. Lacy, multicolored shawls hang from ceiling pipes; eccentric old lamps flicker in every corner; antique furniture mixes with white wicker chairs and porch swings suspended from the ceiling. Add to this potpourri Oriental rugs, vintage posters, lace-covered tables, and crystal chandeliers and you have one of the most intriguing settings in New York—just a short walk from the Broadway theater district. Jezebel, a black-owned soul-food restaurant, is noteworthy not only for its authentic food but also for its ultra-stylish mixed crowd

Jezebel is the creation of Alberta Wright, a former antiques dealer who swapped sideboards for Southern-fried chicken. When she decided to open the restaurant and had to choose a décor, it seemed only natural to bring her treasures with her.

Even the waitresses have a period look about them—although sometimes it's difficult to figure out what period—decked out in everything from slinky cocktail dresses to flowing peasant skirts. Too bad they are not as efficient as they are attractive. Service can be absentminded and exasperatingly slow, especially when the place fills up at the evening seatings. (If you have theater tickets, though, they make a point of getting you out in time.) I have never seen so many birthday parties in a restaurant—one evening I counted seven—and the staff spends an inordinate amount of time serenading revelers at their tables. Perhaps they should allow the piano player to sing "Happy Birthday" and let the waitresses tend to more pressing business.

The soul-food menu is as unalloyed as anything you will find uptown, and much of it is inviting. Start with the superior corn bread, which is moist and crumbly and minimally sugared, and the fresh baking-powder biscuits. Smothered garlic shrimp is one of the better appetizers, the shrimp cooked to a turn and the zesty red sauce crackling with hot pepper. Rib bits, little hacked-up morsels of sweetly coated pork ribs, are habit-forming.

Among the soups sampled, my favorite was the Pinesville (peasant) cow pea made with small beans resembling lentils and a richly flavored stock. Charleston she-crab soup was unusual but appealing, a frothy broth packing lots of fresh crab flavor and lightened with cream.

Main courses are portioned for field hands, so go lightly on appetizers and bread. You can get a fine fried chicken here, crisply fried outside, succulent and mildly peppery, flanked by deliciously fresh collard greens and run-of-the-mill potato salad—I preferred that to the spiced honey chicken, which, while competently cooked, was a little too sweet for my taste. Yet a third poultry preparation is chicken with waffles, a late-night Harlem tradition harking to the Jazz Age: late-night revelers would stop at such all-night haunts as Wells on 133rd Street for a plate of this sobering combination. At Jezebel, it is smashing: a portion of good roast chicken under pan-dripping gravy alongside fluffy, golden waffles with butter. I held back on the maple syrup, however.

Curried goat is not something you will find in the postmodern yuppie palaces around town. The falling-off-the-bone braised meat comes in a brassy sauce generous with cayenne pepper, along with rice, beans, and collard greens. Smothered pork chops tasted as if they had been cooked a bit too long, for the meat had a flabby, bready texture under its thick gravy; the accompanying okra was good but the grits were mushy, as if they had been reconstituted. Two shrimp dishes were worth trying: one an aggressively spicy Creole recipe, the other featuring a fiery garlic sauce with rice, cauliflower, and zucchini.

Jezebel has a small, standard wine list. Beer and bourbon go well with this type of food.

One would expect first-class sweet-potato pie here, but what came out was a loosely bound and soggy crusted wedge under whipped cream. Bread pudding was the unequivocal dessert winner—crusty, studded with raisins, and sweetened with Grand Marnier. Light and creamy chocolate cheesecake is satisfying, and strawberry shortcake, made with those light fresh biscuits, is the real thing.

# JOE ALLEN

★

*326 West 46th Street, 581-6464.*

*Atmosphere: Lively bar and brick-walled dining room decorated with theater posters.*

*Service: Amiable but not always professional.*

*Wine: Limited list at remarkable prices.*

*Price range: Moderate.*

*Credit cards: MasterCard and Visa.*

*Hours: Noon to midnight daily (except Wednesday and Saturday, when the kitchen opens at 11:30 A.M.).*

*Reservations: Necessary.*

*Wheelchair accessibility: Two stairs down at the entrance; all facilities on one level.*

The cast of dining spots along Restaurant Row in the Broadway theater district (West 46th Street between Eighth and Ninth avenues) has changed dramatically in recent years. Once primarily a collection of family-run French bistros, it has become a medley that also features Italian, regional American, and Oriental spots, some of which change identities as frequently as Broadway marquees. One establishment that has endured for twenty-three years and helped maintain the street's distinctive show-business character is Joe Allen. (There are also Joe Allen restaurants in London, Toronto, and Paris.) This brick-walled tavern-restaurant has always been known more for its animated scene than for ambitious cooking.

The long bar at Joe Allen is decorated with framed Broadway posters and other theater memorabilia. The dining area, separated from the bar by brick arches, is done in a similar theme, with an open kitchen and skylight at one end.

You could drop in here, as I did late after a Broadway

show, and have a salad of grilled sea scallops over arugula and red peppers in a mild vinaigrette, or perhaps strips of lean, lightly smoked salmon with sour cream paired with a delicious thin pancake studded with corn and leeks. For entrées, there might be a reasonably tasty grilled sirloin with steak fries and undercooked squash and zucchini. Pan-fried boneless chicken is light and moist (served with the same woody vegetables).

The kitchen turns out a gutsy, moderately spicy black-bean soup and a cooling, chive-flecked vichyssoise. At lunch, an appetizer of sautéed salad greens with shrimp and sausage was inelegant and bland; tabbouleh, the Middle Eastern salad made with bulgur wheat and parsley, onions, tomatoes, and olives, was a good idea badly executed: the mountainous portion was more filling than flavorful.

Stick to simple dishes like fried chicken wings or the satisfying onion-and-mushroom pie and you will be all right.

Reliable entrées include the mixed grill (fennel-scented sausage, lamb chops, and thick slabs of bacon), grilled chicken and baked beans (too sweet to my taste), and the hefty house hamburger (curiously not on the menu but always available). Sautéed calf's liver is a winner, too, accompanied by well-seasoned sautéed spinach. I have little success with seafood here: grilled salmon is competently cooked but unseasoned and served with a nondescript ginger-lime sauce.

Joe Allen is renowned for its extensive beer selection, but if you are a wine drinker, some remarkable bargains can be found. The list is small, only seven reds and six whites, but virtually all are reputable.

Most desserts are heavy hitters, not the kind of food recommended if you hope to remain conscious for a play afterward: creamy cheesecake, overly sweet apple crisp with raisins, and a daunting mountain range of something called hot fudge pudding cake under an avalanche of ice cream and chocolate sauce. Fresh fruit and ice cream are less weighty alternatives.

# JOHN CLANCY'S

★ ★

*181 West 10th Street, 242-7350.*

*Atmosphere: Graceful and stylish Greenwich Village ambiance; upstairs quieter than downstairs.*

*Service: Highly professional and congenial.*

*Wine: Substantial French-American list, fairly priced.*

*Price range: Moderately expensive.*

*Credit cards: All major cards.*

*Hours: Lunch, noon to 3 P.M., Monday through Friday; dinner, 6 to 11:30 P.M., Monday through Saturday, 5 to 10 P.M., Sunday.*

*Reservations: Necessary.*

*Wheelchair accessibility: Four steps down to the dining room. Women's room on same level; men's room downstairs.*

Fresh, deftly grilled seafood is the specialty at this comfortable Greenwich Village institution. The step-down main dining room and bar is done in whitewashed brick walls and pearl gray, with pastel garden prints on the walls; the upstairs, done in similar colors, is more intimate.

Among the occasional specials that can be recommended are a grilled yellowfin tuna with ginger-lime vinaigrette; sautéed soft-shell crabs with a sauce combining sherry, soy, ginger, and scallions; red snapper with grilled eggplant; and grouper with a light tomato-and-olive sauce accompanied by delicious spinach-ricotta pancakes.

It is refreshing to see fish served whole on the bone, as most are here, for the flavor and texture are undeniably better this way.

Lobster Américaine is a classic (and time-consuming) preparation that many restaurants try to simulate using shortcuts. The rendition here, however, is more authentic tasting than most, a bracing red sauce redolent of lobster essences with hints of garlic, cayenne pepper, cognac, and lots of tarragon. The lobster meat is partly cooked out of the shell, then returned to it before serving.

The well-trained service staff is particularly vigilant and agreeable, always willing to accommodate special requests.

Portions are large here, so you may want to opt for a light starter, such as oysters on the half shell, which vary from day to day but are always icy and fresh, or the subtle, delicately flavored gravlax under a dollop of caviar-freckled crème fraîche. Lobster bisque is the real thing, fired up with a belt of sherry; a special of corn chowder one day, though, was floury and bland.

John Clancy's is one of the few restaurants in town that serves the dessert English trifle, a wide-mouth goblet layered with sherry-soaked génoise, raspberry pureé, crème anglaise, and whipped cream—deadly but good. Crème brûlée is too dense and thickly encrusted with sugar; try instead the chocolate roll oozing with whipped cream and drizzled with warm chocolate, or the seductive caramelized black-walnut pie. The diet smasher's award goes to the embarrassingly large portion of Grand Marnier chocolate mousse cake wrapped in génoise and smothered in whipped cream.

The demand for quality seafood houses is greater than ever, so it is no surprise that John Clancy's is filled most nights while many other restaurants in the neighborhood languish.

# KEEN'S CHOP HOUSE

★

*72 West 36th Street, 947-3636.*

*Atmosphere: Clubby and masculine, dripping with mementos from the turn of the century.*

*Service: Amateurish and slow.*

*Wine: Strong American list; moderate prices.*

*Price range: Moderately expensive.*

*Credit cards: All major cards.*

*Hours: Lunch, 11:45 A.M. to 3 P.M., Monday through Friday; dinner, 5:30 to 11 P.M., Monday through Friday, 5 to 11 P.M., Saturday. Pub menu of lighter fare—including oysters, mussels, and chowder—in the barroom from lunchtime to 9:30 P.M., Monday through Friday.*

*Reservations: Recommended.*

*Wheelchair accessibility: Four steps at entrance; restrooms on same level as main dining room.*

This landmark steakhouse, dating from 1885, is a bustling lunch spot among the Garment District crowd, and a popular spot for private parties in the evening. It can be relied upon for good steak, chops, and shellfish.

The four main dining rooms and the gleaming old bar still have the look and aroma of a creaky old men's haunt (in 1905, the actress Lillie Langtry broke the sex barrier by successfully suing Keen's for discrimination). Thousands of numbered clay pipes hang from the ceiling. One could spend a day perusing the vintage photographs, newspaper clippings, and posters covering the walls. While the food has improved significantly under the current chef, service remains amateurish and slow.

Appetizers include many old standards—shrimp cocktail, smoked salmon, and escargots—as well as some more alluring selections. Oysters—plump and tasty Chincoteagues while they're in season—are prepared differently every night. Sometimes they are dredged in flour and briefly sautéed, then napped with a subtle red-wine-and-butter reduction laced with julienne of leeks and tiny cubes of baby yellow beets. A similar preparation pairs oysters with a light Riesling sauce studded with scallops.

Ragout of wild mushrooms with cabbage and parsley in a buttery red-wine sauce is a good starter, as is scallop-carrot-and-potato chowder. Grilled rabbit sausages, though, are skinny and dry, and cold poached salmon with horseradish sauce (an appetizer for two or an entrée) is served too cold and on the dry side.

The cynosure of the menu is still mutton chop, a massive

section of double cut loin that is thoroughly charred outside and succulently pink in the center as requested. The flavor is surprisingly tame for mutton.

Broiled filet mignon, rack of lamb, and a thick, crusty veal chop smothered in wild mushrooms are all skillfully grilled.

Ordinarily I steer away from seafood in a chophouse, but the chef here makes a concerted effort. Whole spicy sizzling fish is prepared by rolling a black bass in chestnut flour and spices, then sautéeing it. While I could not detect any spices, the fish was moist and flavorful nonetheless. It was presented over wild rice with a bizarre blend of applesauce and wasabi, which tasted as strange as it sounded.

On Saturday evening, which is the slowest night of the week in this part of town, diners are invited to have coffee and dessert in front of a crackling fire in the Bull Moose Room. Warm gingerbread with whipped cream and an unrepentantly rich hazelnut meringue cake with layers of chocolate ganache and butter cream are the recommended choices. Sitting in snug leather chairs under the watchful eye of a massive bull moose mounted above the hearth, one feels like old J.P. himself wheeling and dealing with his cronies. All that's missing is the pipe, so bring your own.

# KING FUNG

★

*20 Elizabeth Street, just south of Canal, 964-5256.*

*Atmosphere: Enormous dining room with well-spaced circular tables and harsh lighting. Family atmosphere.*

*Service: Good-natured and energetic.*

*Price range: Inexpensive.*

*Credit cards: MasterCard and Visa.*

*Hours: Daily from 8 A.M. to 11 P.M.*

*Reservations: Accepted.*

▷ 249

***Wheelchair accessibility:** One step at entrance; all facilities on one level.*

Sunday night at King Fung, a sprawling, harshly lighted establishment in Chinatown, is about as close as you get to the feeling of a boisterous and colorful family restaurant in Hong Kong. Large circular tables are occupied by three or four generations; adults belt down water glasses of Johnnie Walker Red with their prawns and spicy pork (alcoholic beverages are not served, but customers may bring their own) while spring-loaded children with kidneys the size of lentils race back and forth to the restrooms, dodging nimble waiters carrying oversize platters.

King Fung can be an amusing place if you are in the right mood. Moreover, some of the dishes on the budget-priced menu are first-rate. You would have a hard time finding a better Peking duck in town. The version here is presented whole at the table, the honey-gold skin brittle and delicious with just enough fat to moisten the succulent meat. The accompanying pancakes are fresh and almost translucent, making for a light and elegant combination. By contrast, the plain roast duck is fatty and tastes steamed.

Starting with the appetizers, steamed pork dumplings are light and well seasoned, while fried dumplings tend to be gummy inside. Dry scallop soup, thick with black mushrooms and shredded vegetables, also is intensely flavorful. Sliced chicken with bamboo shoots, which sounds prosaic, is in fact a paragon of subtle Cantonese-style cooking. Each vegetable—scallions, carrots, and bamboo shoots—is cooked to a turn, and the faintly salty seasoning brings out the best in the chicken.

Most of the seafood dishes sampled were superior. Baked lobster Chinese style was delivered sectioned in the shell and glossed with a combination of light soy sauce, egg, scallion, and black beans.

King Fung is foremost a Chinese restaurant for Chinese customers, as evidenced by the host of strange and intimidating dishes that I politely passed up: duck webs, fish lips, sea cucumber, and preserved egg. I do have a weakness for tripe, but the preparation here was too austere for my taste: bright and fresh but plain and unsauced, with only scallion and shards of ginger to help it.

The good-natured and forever hustling service staff does a good job, and most waiters can explain the food relatively well. The restaurant offers a dim sum menu for breakfast and lunch as well, starting at 8:00 A.M.

For Peking duck and lobster I would return eagerly—and if you go on Sunday the sideshow is included.

# K-PAUL'S NEW YORK

★

*622 Broadway, south of Bleecker Street, 460-9633.*

*Atmosphere: Casual, spacious place with long, open kitchen.*

*Service: Ingenuous and hardworking.*

*Wine: Decent house white and red.*

*Price range: Expensive.*

*Credit cards: All major cards.*

*Hours: Dinner, 5:30 P.M. to 11 P.M. Monday through Friday.*

*Reservations: Suggested.*

*Wheelchair accessibility: One small step at entrance; restrooms on ground level.*

Just when everyone thought the Cajun craze had been interred in that gastronomic Woodlawn where all such fads return to dust, here comes Paul Prudhomme, bounding out of the bayou with his magic spices and magnetic personality. His New York outpost caused quite a feeding frenzy for a few months, but now that the novelty has faded so, too, have the crowds.

If you have never eaten real Cajun food in Louisiana this is still as close as you can get. No imitators match the master chef's intellectual approach to blending peppers and balancing textures. But Mr. Prudhomme is not always in the kitchen here—he shuttles between New York and his New

Orleans establishment—and my visits indicate that when he is missing the food can lose something.

You start right off here with a basket of irresistible breads, including Cheddar-jalapeño rolls, muffins, and bran rolls. The only alcoholic beverages served are beer, house wines served in Mason jars, and eye-watering Cajun martinis, made with pepper-laced vodka or gin, that are offered in two sizes, pint and quart. Gumbo and jambalaya are typical starters. The former is a turgid broth chunky with andouille (highly seasoned smoked pork sausage) and rice that tricks your palate into perceiving it as sweet with onions and bell peppers. Two seconds later, firecrackers start flashing as it washes over the palate, finally reaching full-blown detonation in the aftertaste and bringing a flush to your cheeks. This is not superficially searing food, as lesser cooks are prone to serve, but rather a tightly stitched quilt of flavor sensations. Jambalaya, on the other hand, has the same complexity but is cranked up several notches on the pepper meter. In it, andouille is allied with rice, crawfish, and a sweet-hot tomato sauce that, as a fellow diner put it, "is so hot you have to wear tie shoes because it could blow loafers right off your feet."

Other musts are the Cajun popcorn, cleanly fried puffballs of battered crayfish with sherry sauce; a terrific similar dish called fish tidbits, bite-size pieces of wonderfully seasoned (but not hot) flounder or catfish with tartar sauce; crunchy coconut-dusted, beer-battered shrimp with a tangy sweet sauce; and roasted sweet andouille, which is lean and milder than the regular type, with mustard sauce. One evening when the chef was absent, a nouvelle-looking platter of dryish sliced tenderloin of rabbit came with a zesty Creole mustard sauce. That same evening, a crawfish enchilada with green chili sauce and melted cheese was the kind of nondescript creation one could find at any number of second-rate taco parlors.

An added pleasure at K-Paul's is the ingenuous waiters and waitresses who truly appear to enjoy working here. They can help you navigate the main courses, some of which have puzzling names like eggplant pirogue, and swordfish with hot fanny sauce. A pirogue is a dugout canoe in the bayou, and this dish was made with a dug-out eggplant deep fried and filled with a delicately seasoned seafood mixture in a Creole sauce and topped with shrimp. Bronzed swordfish with hot fanny sauce is a golden-sautéed fillet with a sauce of chopped pecans and diced jalapeños, paired with don't-ask-how-much-butter-is-in-them mashed potatoes.

Shrimp etouffée, in a cayenne-enriched seafood sauce with shrimp and rice, was one-dimensional the evening the chef was absent. When he was there a week later, it was splendid. The blackening technique of cooking fish and meat here is a revelation to those used to carbon-encrusted replications so often served in other restaurants. Mr. Prudhomme's blackened tuna is lively with black pepper and seared to dark golden, not at all burned. His blackened prime rib is something I still dream about, a pepper-coated, exquisitely tender, rib of beef in a dark, rich pepper sauce.

Considering portion sizes here, desserts like warm bread pudding with raisins and whipped cream seem not only excessive, but indeed immoral. And delicious. Pecan pie is on the sweet side but well made. Pecan-and-sweet-potato pie is better, garnished with Grand Marnier whipped cream. The moist pecan-layered spice cake with thick layers of icing is like a birthday cake you know you should not eat, but you have two pieces of anyway.

# LA BOHÈME

★

*24 Minetta Lane, near Avenue of the Americas, 473-6447.*

*Atmosphere: Faux-barn look with whimsical test-tube lights overhead; crowded.*

*Service: Hardworking but overtaxed.*

*Wine: Limited and unremarkable list.*

*Price range: Moderate.*

*Credit cards: American Express.*

*Hours: Brunch, noon to 4 P.M., Sunday; dinner, 5:30 P.M. to midnight, Tuesday through Friday, 5 P.M. to midnight, Saturday, 4 to 11 P.M., Sunday.*

*Reservations: Necessary.*

*Wheelchair accessibility: Restrooms downstairs.*

Many Greenwich Village diners have an on and off affair with La Bohème, the rough-hewn bistro on Minetta Lane that is convenient to several Off Broadway theaters. While the culinary production can be provocative, the staging and cast could use some reworking. Even so, I return there often for the seductive roasts, lovingly prepared seafood, and thin-crusted pizzas.

The long rectangular dining room has a converted-barn-in-Vermont look, with plank floors, wood-and-stucco walls, and close tables the size of cutting boards that are draped with Provençale fabric and butcher paper. Test-tube-shape lights dangling from looped wires in the ceiling add a playful touch. Overbooking is not a problem; it seems to be a policy. On busy nights, customers overflow the bar and queue up along one wall.

Prices are moderate, so it's possible to be self-indulgent without having to hitchhike home. I can't get enough of the zesty eggplant purée slathered over toasted French bread and topped with layers of melted mozzarella and tomato sauce: the eggplant has a haunting aftertaste that comes from dried mint. The French staple, saucisson chaud, or garlicky country sausage, is terrific with warm sliced potatoes in a perfectly balanced vinaigrette (a rare commodity in restaurants). Other good choices are rustic pork terrine, tasty braised endive with prosciutto, and a sparkling watercress-and-goat-cheese salad.

The pizzas that come whizzing out of the brick oven have thin, deliciously blistered crusts and well-orchestrated toppings. Among those I favor are the unlikely combination of shrimp, scallops, mussels, and olives dappled with mozzarella and tomato; and the eggplant, leeks, and spinach.

Most of the staff, as well as the owner, Paris DuLac, are cheerful and accommodating under the often-strained conditions.

The kitchen turns out some fine bistro standards, like roast duck, crisp and rendered of all but just enough fat to add succulence, along with well-seasoned carrots, broccoli, eggplant, and roasted potatoes; a respectably fiery and tender steak au poivre with good french fries; and leg of lamb with a coarse mustard sauce and spinach flecked with snowy goat cheese (a special). Grilled Cornish hen gets intriguing treatment, moistened with a sauce that combines potent saffron lightened with lemon (too bad the hen was overcooked). Roast chicken was no less eccentric, dressed up with a green-peppercorn sauce counterbalanced with, of all things, cantaloupe. Oddly enough, the combination of piquant and sweet in the sauce works splendidly, although the sliced cantaloupes for garnish remind me of a motor inn brunch.

On the seafood side, there is a zippy and fresh monkfish au poivre and an even hotter (though slightly dry) Cajun-style mako shark with carrots, zucchini, and spinach. It's nice to see that vegetables here are not merely a cosmetic addition, as is so common elsewhere, for each is cooked just right and seasoned with care.

Dessert portions are hefty, but if you can go the extra distance, I can suggest the satiny chocolate mousse with fresh strawberries, better-than-average profiteroles, and apple tart with puff-pastry crust.

# LA BOÎTE EN BOIS

★

*75 West 68th Street, 874-2705.*

*Atmosphere: Minuscule, attractive country French setting.*

*Service: Poised and competent.*

*Wine: Pricey French list, well matched to the food.*

*Price range: Moderate (prix-fixe dinner, $27).*

*Hours: Dinner, 5:30 to 11:30 P.M., Monday through Saturday, 5 to 10 P.M., Sunday.*

*Credit cards: None.*

*Reservations: Necessary.*

*Wheelchair accessibility: Very small restaurant, with steps down to dining room.*

La Boîte en Bois is the creation of Alain Brossard and Jean-Claude Coutable, a seasoned team of restaurateurs. Running the dining room and kitchen respectively, they still offer traditional bistro fare at reasonable prices. The brick-and-barn-board dining room, adorned with antique farm tools and bucolic paintings, is as claustrophobic as ever. It is so neighborly, in fact, that one evening when someone at my table sneezed, a customer three tables away turned and said, "God bless you."

There are no dramatic changes to report about the style or quality of the food over the years. The leeks vinaigrette are still winners, fresh and with a good homey dressing and crumbled egg white on top; terrines are generally well made and seasoned judiciously; and pea soup is wonderful on a piercingly cold winter night. But I am disappointed with the chicory-and-bacon salad (called frisée aux lardons in French), which is excessively greasy from too much untrimmed bacon. Likewise, French-style saucisson is too fatty for my taste and lacks garlic flavor, but the lentils with it are delicious.

Even at busy times the waiters keep cool, going through their ministrations with professional aplomb—and some nimble acrobatics while weaving through the tight confines. The wine list is well matched to the food, with a good selection of Rhône and Beaujolais, but priced on the high side.

One of the most popular dishes from the restaurant's inception in 1985 is salmon cooked in parchment paper with a subtle, creamy mustard sauce. Red snapper, an occasional special, is excellent when sautéed with fresh tarragon and presented with boiled potatoes and spinach. Duck fanciers will find two lusty renditions: roasted duck with a heady Armagnac sauce, and slices of breast in a sweet and tart sauce made with stock and raspberry vinegar. Such bistro staples as entrecôte with mustard sauce and steak au poivre are not tamed for the tourist trade.

Crème brûlée remains the star among desserts, with frozen praline soufflé a distant second. White chocolate mousse in a big goblet suffers from the sweets. The kitchen turns out some nice fruit tarts, and a good rendition of that old French classic, oeufs à la neige.

# LA CARAVELLE

★ ★

*33 West 55th Street, 586-4252.*

*Atmosphere: Old World charm in mural-wrapped room; good noise control.*

*Service: Experienced, genial professionals.*

*Wine: An extensive and prestigious selection, but lacking moderately priced choices.*

*Price range: Expensive (pretheater dinner prix fixe, $37).*

*Credit cards: All major cards.*

*Hours: Lunch, noon to 2:30 P.M., Monday through Friday; pretheater dinner, 5:30 to 6:30 P.M., Monday through Saturday; dinner, 5:30 to 10:30 P.M., Monday through Saturday.*

*Reservations: Recommended.*

*Wheelchair accessibility: Everything on one level.*

Just a few years ago, La Caravelle was suffering an advanced case of culinary senescence, and it seemed destined for that big banquette-lined dining room in the sky where it would join former Manhattan luminaries like Le Pavillon, the Colony, and Luchow's. A transfusion of new blood in the kitchen and the dining room kept the patient breathing, but many still believed the outlook was dim for this icon of a more decorous era.

Today, the feisty Caravelle approaches its thirty-first anniversary with a new aura of vitality. The classically inspired French fare has been streamlined, the softly upholstered dining room is as comforting as ever, and even the waiters seem to have an extra lilt in their step.

The rejuvenation program at La Caravelle had a setback when the resourceful young chef, Michael Romano, left in late 1988 to run the kitchen at Union Square Cafe. The toque was handed to Mr. Romano's second, David Ruggiero. He in turn left, in 1990, for Maxim's, and was replaced by Franck Champely, who came from the Regency Hotel on Park Avenue. Menu changes were going into effect as of this writing, so some of the dishes described below may be replaced or revised.

You enter La Caravelle via a corridor lined with bright red banquettes where many of the longtime habitués can size up all who come and go. The main room, dominated by cherry murals of Parisian street scenes, has a warm, civilized feeling. Well-distanced tables, carpeting, and acoustical tiles allow intimate conversation even when the place is full.

Don't expect to find the overflow crowd from 150 Wooster Street here. At lunch, huddles of dark-suited corporate types lend the room an importunate New York ambiance. On any given night among the generally older, well-heeled patrons are a few couples who seem to have been coming here since the Kennedy administration. André Jammet, the owner (his partner and the founding chef, Roger Fessaguet, retired in 1988), is deft at balancing the needs of both types of patrons.

Typical of the lighter dishes here these days is a starter of crab ravioli set over spinach and topped with a light shellfish-stock sauce emboldened with fresh ginger. The accompaniment of shredded turnips and carrots tossed in butter makes for a lively flavor contrast. Sweet, perfectly cooked shrimp are served at room temperature over mixed greens tossed in a good herby shrimp-stock emulsion. Sliced scallops with a garnish of black truffle are delightful over buttery minced leeks and a half-dollar-size disk of puff pastry: the chive-butter sauce around this is overkill, though. One of the house classics, a silken, well-seasoned gratin of lobster that arrives in a pretty silver casserole, is diminished only by a mound of rubbery pasta in the center.

Shreds of duck confit marry well with sliced beets and

mixed greens in a good vinaigrette, and sautéed foie gras makes an empyreal sandwich between thin slices of apple.

The experienced French staff pretty much pampers customers. As for the elitist wine list, you have to hunt diligently to find good bottles under $30. And I'm still curious about why the staff pours white wine into red-wine glasses, and vice versa. Is this a new trend?

Seafood entrées to look for are the moist, meaty halibut steak garnished with shredded deep-fried leeks and a tomato vinaigrette. The kitchen smokes its own fresh salmon, which is terrific grilled medium rare and surrounded by wild mushrooms moistened with a subtle vinaigrette. Monkfish over cabbage leaves is appealing, too, in a vinegar-sharpened lobster-butter sauce.

Fillet of lamb is exceptional with tart cranberries and chestnut purée. Sweetbreads are prepared in a sensuous manner: first blanched, then dredged in minced truffles and sautéed. A light asparagus purée adds color but not much flavor. If you are looking for a two-fisted cassoulet before winter's end, the Wednesday special here is outstanding, replete with tender lamb, duck confit, and pork. Top votes for dessert go to the seductive raspberry flan, green apple sorbet with purée of Granny Smith apples, and the caramelized pear version of tarte Tatin. Or if you want to go all the way, try the chocolate-drenched slices of ripe pear in puff pastry with raspberry sauce. It's always gratifying to discover a restaurant on the rebound. It would be premature to say La Caravelle is on the way to recapturing its former glory. At the same time, it seems to have postponed a trip to that big banquette in the sky.

# LA CITÉ

★

*120 West 51st Street, 956-7100.*

*Atmosphere: Big, bright, and delightfully garish brasserie; grill room more sedate and tranquil.*

*Service: Can be slow at lunch, otherwise professional.*

*Wine: Expertly chosen but lopsided toward expensive bottles.*

*Price range: Moderately expensive.*

*Credit cards: All major cards.*

*Hours: Continual service noon to midnight Monday through Friday, 5 P.M. to midnight, Saturday and Sunday; grill serves 11:30 A.M. to 2 A.M., daily.*

*Reservations: Necessary.*

*Wheelchair accessibility: Dining available on ground level. Restrooms for handicapped.*

La Cité, the rococo extravaganza on West 51st Street, bills itself as a brasserie, but those who have been to places like Vaudeville and Bofinger in Paris will see several obvious differences. Whereas real brasseries are inexpensive, casual, drop-in places, La Cité is pricey, self-conscious, and formal. *Brassaurant* might be a better term for this creation of Alan Stillman, who also owns Smith & Wollensky, the Manhattan Ocean Club, and the Post House.

The grand, multilevel setting has two main dining arenas and a cozier grill room, which serves essentially the same food at slightly lower prices. The main rooms evoke all the festive garishness of grand European brasseries: Art Deco molding, immense cylindrical chandeliers, tall mirrors, red velvet banquettes, and waiters in spiffy black jackets and long white aprons.

Some attempts at typical brasserie cooking succeed; others don't. And prices are all over the board, from $16 for rubbery-skinned blood sausage and mashed potatoes to $29.50 for excellent sirloin steak and french fries. Count on $100 for two, especially if you dip into the astutely chosen but lopsided wine list (of more than 150 labels, only eight are under $20; even the humble Bourgeuil and Chinon from the Loire are $25). And considering that brasseries are historically built around beer—the word means brewery in French—it is surprising that no beer list is offered.

The much ballyhooed choucroute, made with quality ingredients, has improved over the course of my visits, but it still lacks a deep, integrated flavor. The same goes for the decent if shallow-tasting cassoulet. One of the best entrées is the golden-skinned, spit-roasted chicken with raisins, pearl onions, and button mushrooms. Grilled salmon with a fresh dill vinaigrette is better than the roasted monkfish, which comes overpowered with green peppercorns. At lunch in the handsome grill room, a huge juicy lamb steak comes with delicious white beans cooked in chicken stock with basil. As for our side dish, I don't know whether to call it mashed potatoes with butter or butter with mashed potatoes—whatever, it is unrepentantly good. A thick slab of swordfish is deftly turned out, too, embellished with tissue-thin homemade potato chips. Thursday's special is duck confit with sautéed apples and lentils. The crispy-skinned leg is tasty and tender for sure, but not at all complex and buttery like a real confit.

For starters, shellfish of all sorts, especially oysters and intensely oceanic sea urchins, are excellent. A salad pairing confit of chicken with sun-dried cherries is a felicitous combination. I would go back to the grill room just for a sizzling batch of small, incredibly sweet mussels served in a skillet.

The service staff is well schooled, but lunch service can be slow so you should make it known if you are on a tight schedule.

Desserts are the most consistent course: prune Armagnac ice cream with walnut cake and fruit compote, sublime banana ice cream crowned with a light chocolate mousse and thin coconut cookies, intense chocolate torte with vanilla ice cream and raspberry sauce. If you only try one, get the cappuccino mousse topped with granité of espresso.

# LA COLOMBE D'OR

★ ★ ★

*134 East 26th Street, 689-0666.*

*Atmosphere: Cozy and rustic Provençale setting.*

*Service: Welcoming and efficient.*

*Wine: Good regional French selection, particularly strong in wines from Provence and Rhône.*

*Price range: Moderately expensive.*

*Credit cards: All major cards.*

*Hours: Lunch, noon to 2:30 P.M., Monday through Friday; dinner, 6 to 10:30 P.M., Monday through Thursday, until 11 P.M., Friday and Saturday.*

*Reservations: Necessary.*

*Wheelchair accessibility: Two steps down to dining level. Women's room on same level; men's room up a flight of stairs.*

La Colombe d'Or, a snug Provençale-style French restaurant that for more than a decade had been an unassuming neighborhood spot in the Gramercy Park area, shot into the forefront of haute dining under its former chef, Wayne Nish, who earned his culinary stripes at The Quilted Giraffe. Mr. Nish left in mid-1990 to open his own place, called March, on East 58th Street.

With Mr. Nish's longtime second now calling the shots, the kitchen can still turn out an impressive range of dishes that evoke the fragrant cuisine of southern France. The twenty-five-seat main room, two steps below street level, has an inviting, provincial charm with its little wooden bar up front, terra-cotta floor, colorful fabric-covered banquettes, whitewashed brick walls, and gentle lighting. A second, slightly larger room is done in a similar motif, as is a private room upstairs. The restaurant is owned by George and

Helen Studley (he is Belgian-born, she German), who decided to open a restaurant here in 1976 after living a year in Provence.

I knew there was some serious cooking going on here on the first visit as soon as I tasted the house-smoked salmon salad. A thick slice of buttery-textured, lightly smoked fish was served next to a slice of ripe tomato and lamb's lettuce. Another interesting starter was the escargots served with a cream reduction imbued with the refreshing essences of fennel and radish.

A notable special one evening was goat-cheese-stuffed grilled quail paired with a wedge of sautéed angel-hair pasta flavored with Parmesan cheese and chives. Another was sautéed scallops and chanterelle mushrooms in a light butter emulsion with vermouth under a nearly translucent blanket of fresh pasta imprinted with fresh herbs.

Two typical Provençale entrées worth seeking out are the poached fresh cod presented over a bed of sliced fennel and arugula with a potent garlicky aïoli sauce, and the perfectly cooked salmon glazed with sweet mustard and olive oil set over a light butter-and-chive sauce. Another ingenuous winner is rosemary-flecked grilled chicken in a red-wine reduction with olives. Baby lamb chops were wonderfully seasoned but a tad overcooked; conversely, calf's liver with glazed carrots and onions was too close to raw for my taste. A well-aged sirloin steak came with terrific matchstick potatoes.

In cool weather, confit is a welcome addition to menus, and the duck confit served here is outstanding: moist, full of flavor, and crisply sautéed. A house specialty is bouillabaisse, and this one is as gutsy and delicious as you will find in town, a thick red broth replete with lobster, clams, mussels, shrimp, and monkfish. It is served in a cast-iron casserole with slabs of toasted French bread smeared with aïoli.

The chef's affinity for bold seasoning can be seen in desserts, too. I liked his ginger-spiked custard topped with crumbled pralines, although some people at my table said the flavor was so strong it made their eyes water. A walnut-caramel brownie with vanilla ice cream disappeared in seconds, as did a moist double-chocolate mousse cake and a ripe strawberry tartlet.

# LA CÔTE BASQUE

★ ★

*5 East 55th Street, 688-6525.*

*Atmosphere: Old World charm in a comfortable dining room wrapped in seaside murals.*

*Service: Experienced professionals keep a steady cadence.*

*Wine: Extensive list, especially among Bordeaux, but pricey. Many whites lack vintages and producers.*

*Price range: Expensive (lunch prix fixe $32, with several supplements; dinner prix fixe $55, with supplements).*

*Credit cards: All major cards.*

*Hours: Lunch, noon to 2:30 P.M., Monday through Saturday; dinner, 6 to 10:30 P.M., Monday through Friday, until 11 P.M., Saturday.*

*Reservations: Necessary.*

*Wheelchair accessibility: One small step up at entrance; everything on one level.*

After four recent visits to La Côte Basque, still one of New York City's most sumptuous dining spots, I came away with several lingering memories. One is of an awestruck young couple (my guess was high-school-prom age) trying to act worldly as they struggled with the all-French menu and puzzled over the surfeit of silverware. It was one of those terrifyingly wonderful evenings they surely will never forget. Another is the timeless charm of the dining room with its seaside murals, red leather banquettes, and profusion of fresh flowers. A third is a splendid bottle of Meursault enjoyed one evening.

You may notice that food is not one of the top three impressions, a fact that is disturbing. The cooking these days at Jean-Jacques Rachou's thirty-two-year-old restaurant is pleasing overall, sometimes uplifting, but too rarely memorable. La Côte Basque has never been a place to go for culinary revelation. Its strength was its faithful execution of classic French cuisine in this era of gastronomic free-for-alls. In this role, however, it seems to have slipped a notch.

A wide-ranging sampling of the current menu found that while a little more than half of the dishes continue to uphold French tradition proudly, the rest are flawed. A .500-plus average may keep a baseball team on top of the league, but not a restaurant.

A striking example is La Côte Basque's once-splendid assortment of cold shellfish with vegetables. On two recent occasions, the crabmeat was ice cold and tasteless. The lobster was pleasing, but the garnish was more appealing to look at than to taste. Vegetables here are a problem across the board, but especially with entrées, where they often have the limp appearance of having come from a steam table.

Among the recommended starters is a ballotine of salmon, studded with lobster, carrots, and peas, and surrounded by pretty turned cucumbers and sweet peppers in a sparkling parsley sauce. Another good choice is roasted sea scallops, a special, which are set over tart sautéed endives in a lemony herb-butter sauce. And one day the chef proposed delicious quails stuffed with forcemeat, mushrooms, and caramelized onions, with a clean, sharp sauce of lingonberries and Madeira. One preparation I have enjoyed over the years is the regally presented casserole of shellfish—in this case scallops and lobster—in a light ginger-spiked, cream-thickened shellfish stock. It was well cooked this time, but unbalanced, tasting mostly of ginger.

It takes a large crew of captains and waiters to run this sprawling ship, and the experienced professionals here have it down to a poised routine. Several captains are knowledgeable about the well-stocked wine list and can be helpful, at least among reds, of which Bordeaux is best represented (at fairly elevated prices). A restaurant of this caliber, however, should not omit the vintages of whites like Meursaults, Chablis, and all Alsace selections.

La Côte Basque has always turned out picture-perfect classics like grilled Dover sole meunière, roasted chicken with herbs, and rack of lamb—and it still does. Cassoulet is still a winner, too—crusty, rich but not too heavy, and replete with buttery duck confit, garlic sausage, and pork. A hint of cinnamon and cumin in the sauce does wonders for rosy lamb medallions, which come with raisin-flecked couscous. Venison, though, came out gray and bland, although the peppery sauce with roasted chestnuts was invigorating. Fans of sweetbreads should be satisfied with the big, firm, and well-browned version here, accompanied by a sturdy sauce of veal stock, mushrooms, and cauliflower.

Overall, seafood was less successful. A special of three fillets—snapper, salmon, and sea bass—arrived well cooked, but the salmon and bass needed seasoning. So, too, did the insipid mound of pasta in the center, garnished with chopped tomatoes. Another time a salmon steak, said to be cooked with thyme, came out devoid of any seasoning; only the good hollandaise saved it. One evening when the kitchen did turn out a fine grilled snapper, perfectly cooked and flavorful, the deep-fried parsley promised on the menu was missing.

One area in which La Côte Basque has not lost pace is desserts. Individual apple tarts are superb, especially with vanilla ice cream ringed by a coulis of apricots and Calvados. Soufflés are heavenly, too, whether made with Grand Marnier or seasonal fruits, and île flottante comes under a dome of spun sugar that resembles a bird cage. Another visual stunner is the green apple of lacquered sugar that holds whipped cream flavored with applejack brandy.

La Côte Basque, which received three stars in 1986, is still one of the grandest of the old-guard French restaurants, and regulars who know the menu can have a transcendent experience there. Others run a small but significant chance of being disappointed—and that is not the definition of a three-star restaurant. Two stars seems more fitting for La Côte Basque today.

# LAFAYETTE

★ ★ ★ ★

*65 East 56th Street, 832-1565.*

*Atmosphere: Plush and civilized. Well-spaced tables, quiet.*

*Service: Low-key and excellent.*

*Wine: Fine international wine list at wide-ranging prices.*

*Price range: Expensive.*

*Credit cards: All major cards.*

*Hours: Lunch, noon to 3:00 P.M., Tuesday through Saturday; pretheater dinner, 6 to 6:30 P.M., Tuesday through Saturday; dinner, 6:00 to 10 P.M., Monday through Saturday.*

*Reservations: Required at least a week in advance.*

*Wheelchair accessibility: Everything on one level.*

Jean-Georges Vongerichten is arguably the brightest young chef on the American scene today, and his ever-evolving food at this sumptuous hotel dining room continues to startle and delight. Mr. Vongerichten earned his stripes under the tutelage of Louis Outhier, an international consultant who had a Michelin three-star restaurant on the French Riviera. Mr. Vongerichten's assignments took him to France, Bangkok, Singapore, London, and Boston before coming to New York.

Cream is virtually absent in Mr. Vongerichten's kitchen; instead, fresh vegetable juices or herb-infused oils are the foundations of many sauces. The young chef's repertory is exquisitely refined yet never fussy, and the galaxy of flavors found on the menu reflects Mr. Vongerichten's cosmopolitan background.

Lafayette's dining room is plush and spacious, done in soothing shades of beige and cream. Tables are widely spaced, and extraneous sound is well-muffled. The gleaming kitchen can be seen, but not heard, through a glass wall.

In addition to the $65 prix-fixe dinner menu ($45 pre-theater; $25 and $35 at lunch), one can order from a $95 tasting menu.

You can begin with such light offerings as tomato tart with tomato water. It is made by slashing a ripe tomato, seasoning it with salt, and hanging it in cheesecloth for six hours. The water, seasoned with basil leaves, is served in a little ceramic bowl accompanied by a tartlet made with the leftover tomato pulp, goat cheese, and puff pastry. It truly is tomato heaven. In the fall Mr. Vongerichten takes a thin puff pastry disk, and places on top a mild white cheese and caramelized onions; next to it is served a little cup filled with intense onion broth scented with cuminseed.

Another fall delight is pigs' cheeks coated in cornmeal, an Alsace specialty. They are meltingly tender inside and crunchy outside, paired with seared foie gras over cool black beans moistened with vinaigrette.

Another winning starter is a carpaccio of tuna and black bass molded together to create a marbled effect, ringed with minced sweet pepper, eggplant, zucchini, and olives glossed with a saffron-and-basil vinaigrette. Sea urchin is given a new dimension here. The saline roe is the base for a terrific cold soufflé ringed by fresh periwinkles, Belon oysters, and clams in a shellfish stock enhanced with lemongrass.

A provocative starter that borrows from Asian cooking is called crab and Swiss chard cannelloni. Fresh crabmeat and Swiss chard are enveloped in sheets of fresh pasta and set over a pale yellow sauce made with reduced vegetable bouillon and carrot juice, then seasoned with cardamom and bound with a little butter—an extraordinary fusion, just faintly sweet from the carrots.

The service staff at Lafayette is as refined as the food. They never hover, never fawn, yet when you need something, they magically appear. The international wine list has fine selections in every price range. Temperature-controlled rooms assure that the reds are always cellar temperature.

Mr. Vongerichten's entrées are organized according to the cooking method: for example, those prepared with vinaigrette sauces, those with herb-perfumed oils, and those based on vegetable juices. The results are stunning: spit-roasted sweetbreads with chestnut-and-pomegranate vinaigrette; saddle of venison with cranberry oil and tart/sweet quince pancakes; roast pheasant with ginger oil and beets; and shrimp poached in orange juice, ginger, and Sauternes with fried lotus root.

The pastry chef, Jean-Marc Burillier, turns out some sublime desserts. Toasted-almond Amaretto soufflé with a poached pear is a heavenly combination. Others to watch for are the exceptionally light Bavarian cream pie, the two-layered cake of passion-fruit mousse and chocolate over a bright citric sauce, gratin of wild raspberries, and hazelnut anisette layer cake.

# LA GAULOISE

★ ★

*502 Avenue of the Americas, between 12th and 13th streets, 691-1363.*

*Atmosphere: Comfortable and unpretentious bistro setting.*

*Service: Generally professional.*

*Wine: Mostly French list with many higher-priced bottles; adequate selection from $20 to $25.*

*Price range: Moderate (pretheater dinner prix fixe, $19.50).*

*Credit cards: American Express, MasterCard, and Visa.*

*Hours: Brunch, noon to 3 P.M., Saturday, noon to 4 P.M., Sunday; lunch, noon to 3 P.M., Tuesday through Sunday; pretheater dinner, 5:30 to 6:45 P.M.; dinner, 5:30 to 11:30 P.M., Monday through Saturday.*

*Reservations: Suggested.*

*Wheelchair accessibility: Everything on one level.*

For more than a decade, long before French bistros became the rage in Manhattan, La Gauloise has been quietly and competently serving up such homespun fare as mussels marinière, pepper steak and french fries, roasted rabbit, roast chicken, and crème brûlée. This handsome and genial spot on the northern rim of Greenwich Village is still doing so today and at prices that make it worth a detour for those seeking a civilized business lunch or a pretheater dinner.

Speaking of pepper steak, the one here is nicely executed, tender and mildly spicy. Creamy dauphinoise potatoes served with it are terrific. Sweetbreads are particularly well turned out, nicely browned and served with a tart/sweet vinegar-based sauce. I also like the crispy confit of duck. Roast chicken, the other touchstone of bistro fare, is prepared with motherly love as well.

In this era of unremittingly chic restaurant design. La Gauloise is as comforting as a down pillow. Polished dark-wood trim and mirrored panels combine with etched-glass room dividers and benevolent lighting to provide an authentic French setting. Jacques Alliman, one of the original partners—the other, Camille Dulac, left several years ago to run Le Chantilly in midtown—is a likeable fellow and vigilant host.

Appetizers are the weakest players in the lineup. Rillettes of salmon are dry and uninteresting; confit of duck, in a pretty green bean salad, is properly rich-textured but needs more seasonings; and smoked trout, a special, was mealy and paired with a thin, pale raifort sauce. Tasty and fresh pâté de campagne is a reliable starter.

The wine selection is thoughtfully attuned to the menu, although you will be hard-pressed to find many bargains.

The chef's major strength is sauces, which are concentrated and harmoniously seasoned. The delicately seared sheet of salmon paillard, for example, is paired with a refined basil butter that lets the luxurious fish shine through. That would have been the case with grilled tuna steak, under a vinegar-edged white-wine-and-horseradish sauce, had the fish not been dry from overcooking. The accompaniments were better: couscous, carrot purée, and a vibrant ratatouille.

Lamb chops were somewhat scrawny and pallid the last

time I sampled them here, and sole meunière was an oily bore. If you like rabbit, try the beguiling preparation of tender white medallions bolstered with a mild tarragon-mustard sauce. While soft-shell crabs are in season they are worth getting, simply sautéed in butter until crackling and golden outside.

The dessert cart carries familiar bistro regulars. The best bets are the excellent crème brûlée with a lid of translucent burnt sugar, pears poached in red wine, custardy bread pudding with coffee sauce, and classic oeufs à la neige. Don't risk the guilt for puny and oversauced profiteroles or the grainy and overly sweet charlotte of pears.

There is something reassuring and warm about La Gauloise that goes beyond a laundry list of dishes. It may be the unpretentious setting, the neighborly crowd it attracts, or the genial pampering by Mr. Alliman. A real French bistro is a place that puts one at ease. On that account, La Gauloise continues to succeed.

# LA GRENOUILLE

★

*3 East 52nd Street, 752-1495.*

*Atmosphere: Plush and soft-edged dining room resplendent with flowers.*

*Service: Generally efficient, if colorless and routine.*

*Wine: A few reasonable buys, but mostly high-priced list.*

*Price range: Expensive (lunch prix fixe, $37.50, dinner prix fixe, $68).*

*Credit cards: American Express, MasterCard, and Visa.*

*Hours: Lunch, noon to 2:30 P.M., Tuesday through Saturday; dinner, 6 to 11:30 P.M., Tuesday through Saturday.*

*Reservations: Necessary.*

***Wheelchair accessibility:*** *Dining room and restrooms on one level (management requests advance notice to reserve the most accommodating tables).*

La Grenouille, still run by the Masson family that started it, has been on a regrettable slide for the past few years, partly the result of staff defections and inconsistency in the kitchen. The current chef, Gerard Chotard, joined the team in late summer of 1987, but so far he has not enlivened the sometimes stodgy, high-priced food.

The capacious, richly upholstered dining room is partitioned in two—the front reserved for celebrities and regulars, the equally accommodating back, ringed by soft crimson banquettes, for the rest. Prodigious clusters of seasonal flowers tower in the corners. Unfamiliar patrons run the risk of being sentenced to a Gallic purgatory along the back wall, hard against the kitchen door, where the clatter and chatter can be unnerving.

Seasoned French waiters, with a few notable exceptions, are efficient but lack the vitality and spirit one expects at this level of restaurant. Among the appetizer specials, a lobster terrine was attractively arranged on the plate, fresh and brightly seasoned—our waiter arrived with the accompanying toast just as I was taking a last bite ("I guess it's too late for this," he said). For a $16 supplement, you can get a slab of rosy duck foie gras along with a thin, commercial-tasting gelatin purportedly made with Sauternes. The same foie gras shows up in a nice green salad sprinkled with black truffles that, too, have lost their punch.

Crab cakes are plump and deliciously sinewy; another special, lobster mousse, sweet and light, was set in a compelling sweet-edged Port sauce. Such menu standards as baked littleneck clams are rubbery, and the purée of pea soup called St. Germain is anemic. Lobster bisque, though, is the real thing, velvety and intense. I don't know where La Grenouille gets its dense whole-wheat raisin rolls, but they are more suited to a delicatessen than an haute French establishment.

The wine list has a few reasonable buys that begin in the mid $30s, but prices shoot up quickly to the $70-and-higher range.

The best entrées include a snappy steak au poivre with a delicious celery purée, rack of lamb with a tarragon-perfumed stock sauce, and grilled sole with a mild mustard sauce (and limp haricot verts). Braised sweetbreads were lusty in their morel sauce on the first visit, yet on a second try the morels were pale-tasting and the sauce watery. Chicken in a champagne cream sauce had more richness than flavor. A better option is the pot-au-feu, an occasional special, a savory combination of oxtail, duck confit, and winter vegetables.

The lunch menu offers something called jardinière of seasonal vegetables. The season must be winter, for everything tastes frozen: soggy broccoli and turnips, pale plum tomatoes, waterlogged baby corn—all heaped unceremoniously on the plate without seasoning. Another special, described by our waiter as "braised veal in brown sauce," was so dry it tasted like overcooked turkey breast. Lobster is delicately prepared, however, served out of the shell in a herbaceous clear sauce along with chives, tomato, and potatoes.

As for desserts, the soufflé for two—we opted for raspberry with raspberry sauce—was so sugary we could not finish it. Another night, chocolate soufflé was excellent. Bread-and-butter pudding was less impressive looking but a winner, all crusty and moist. Chocolate mousse was sublime.

La Grenouille still carries the prices and trappings of a first-class French restaurant, yet in recent years the food quality has dropped from four stars to one. You can't eat the flowers.

# LA MIRABELLE

★

*333 West 86th Street, 496-0458.*

*Atmosphere: Quaint and simple cluster of simply appointed dining rooms. Moderate noise level.*

*Service: Welcoming and efficient.*

*Wine: Well-priced selection, especially among French whites.*

*Price range: Moderate.*

*Credit cards: All major cards.*

*Hours: Dinner, 6 to 10 P.M., Monday through Thursday, 5:30 to 10:30 P.M., Friday and Saturday, 5 to 9 P.M., Sunday. Closed Sunday in July and August.*

*Reservations: Suggested weekdays; necessary weekends.*

*Wheelchair accessibility: Two steps from sidewalk to dining room; restrooms on same level.*

La Mirabelle, a comforting French bistro in the former coffee shop of a residential hotel on far West 86th Street, is the kind of place you can drop into after a harrowing day at the office and soothe your nerves over a bottle of inexpensive Bordeaux, a restorative plate of lamb stew, and maybe a crème caramel. The irrepressibly cheerful owner, Annick le Douaron, always has a kind word, and the gentle waitresses do not seem inconvenienced by your presence.

The tiny dining room has more than doubled in size with the annexation of a former dentist's office. The setting is still charming in a low-key manner. The entrance, with its frosted glass wall, icicle chandeliers. lace curtains, and Florida-pink walls, still looks like a small-town beauty parlor. A main room has a little bar with Naugahyde stools and high ceilings with elaborate trim typical of prewar buildings.

The menu carries a small roster of bistro fare as well as daily specials that include cassoulet (Thursday) and navarin of lamb and bouillabaisse (both on Friday). And what is a bistro without onion soup? This one is bolstered with a good beef stock and encased in molten Gruyère cheese; pea soup, a special, was light and creamy, with firm peas bobbing throughout. The classic coquilles St. Jacques preparation is shamelessly rich, the well-cooked scallops mired in a well-seasoned Mornay sauce and gratinéed with Gruyère cheese. Seafood crèpes, on the other hand, have a surfeit of cheese and Mornay sauce that suffocate the seafood. There are some light starters, too, best among them the curly chicory salad with crusty bacon, a seasonal special; and the Bibb lettuce salad with creamy goat cheese.

La Mirabelle's wines are aptly matched to the ingenuous food, with many good selections under $20.

If you go on a Saturday evening, couscous is the special, and it is exceptionally good, moist and replete with well-seasoned lamb, chicken, carrots, and chickpeas. Another favorite of mine is sautéed loin of lamb infused with garlic and mixed herbs and accompanied by roast potatoes and carrots. Sole à la meunière is lifeless by comparison, lacking enough lemon in the butter.

Anytime I see a stew on the menu here, I go for it. The lamb stew, a special, is sublimely sweet from onions, carrots, and turnips, and a rabbit stew with prunes is equally succulent.

Desserts are right out of the original *Larousse Gastronomique*. Crème caramel, neither too dense nor too sweet, is the best option, followed by mini fruit tarts of the day or the monstrous ice cream and chestnut parfait (coupe aux marrons).

# LA PETITE FERME

★

*973 Lexington Avenue, between 70th and 71st streets, 249-3272.*

*Atmosphere: Cozy and romantic Provençale setting.*

*Service: Casual and easygoing.*

*Wine: Small, standard list.*

*Price range: Moderately expensive (prix-fixe brunch, $14.95).*

*Credit cards: All major cards.*

*Hours: Brunch, noon to 2:30 P.M., Saturday; lunch, noon to 2:30 P.M., Monday through Saturday; dinner, 6 to 10:30 P.M., Monday through Saturday.*

*Reservations: Recommended.*

*Wheelchair accessibility: Two flights of narrow steps make it difficult for wheelchairs.*

Few Manhattan restaurants are as casually enchanting as La Petite Ferme. This little nook resembles a doll house, with its stucco walls, farmhouse shutters, rough-hewn beams, stenciled wallpaper, and glazed earthenware plates. The once-spirited country food, however, has wilted a little.

It is not that the provender is of inferior quality, but rather that too often seasonings are in short supply, resulting in dishes that are fresh but flat. This is all the more frustrating because expectations are higher when the restaurant's daily chalkboard menu carries only four changing entrées and a handful of appetizers.

As you peruse the wine selection, a plate of golden homemade potato chips is placed on the table along with dense-crusted French bread. If game terrines are available, I suggest you try one. The rabbit-and-duck terrine is richly flavored and faintly peppery, served with hot mustard and cornichons. Steamed asparagus glossed with butter is soothing if hardly provocative; a more distinctive starter is creamy and aromatic mushroom soup. Mussels are a house special, big meaty monsters in a snappy mustard vinaigrette —one evening they tasted old and limp, another night resilient and fresh.

The casual waiters and waitresses have an easygoing attitude about service that might be nettlesome elsewhere but seems appropriate in this tranquil setting—except when our waiter inadvertently served two of our entrées to an adjacent table.

A French restaurant does not come to mind when one yearns for a good poached lobster, but the sweet and meaty two-pounder here, slickened with a shallot-flecked red-wine-vinegar sauce, equaled that served at most of the better fish houses in town. Fillets of sole rolled around an underseasoned salmon mousse with beurre blanc, however, were bland.

Meat entrées suffer less from the blands: entrecôte with maître d'hôtel herb butter stands well on its own, full-flavored and tender; chicken in a classic chasseur sauce, combining mushrooms and shallots, is ruggedly enjoyable; while a moist chicken breast in a pallid wine-and-herb sauce falls flat.

La Petite Ferme is one of those soothing spots where you tend to linger longer than usual before facing the shrill of the real world. The uniformly good desserts make it even more tempting to dally. Fruit tarts are winners all, especially the brittle-crusted, glistening raspberry; the dense fudgelike chocolate terrine benefits from its pool of crème anglaise; and fruit sorbets—passion fruit, papaya, kiwi, and raspberry—are smooth textured and vibrant.

# LA RÉSERVE

★ ★ ★

*4 West 49th Street, 247-2993.*

*Atmosphere: Comfortable room with oversize murals of wildlife; soft light, low noise.*

*Service: Generally vigilant and professional.*

*Wine: Well-rounded selection at average prices.*

*Price range: Expensive (lunch prix fixe, $31; pretheater dinner prix fixe, $40; dinner prix fixe, $49).*

*Credit cards: All major cards.*

*Hours: Lunch, noon to 3 P.M., Monday through Saturday; pretheater dinner, 5:30 to 7 P.M., Monday through Saturday; dinner, 7 to 10:30 P.M., Monday through Thursday, 7 to 11:30 P.M., Friday and Saturday.*

*Reservations: Necessary.*

*Wheelchair accessibility: Everything on one level.*

Amid the hubbub and hustle of Rockefeller Center, La Réserve, as the name implies, is a sedate sanctuary. Colorful murals in the dining room depict a marshy wildlife reserve, and indeed, the gastronomic game warden here, Jean-Louis Missud, keeps a vigilant eye on his well-feathered flock.

The main dining room is cozily upholstered, relatively spacious, and softly lighted. Even when the house is full, the clamor is well muted.

From the kitchen's repertory you may start with a brilliant tidbit like duck foie gras layered with slices of ginger-speckled apple and garnished with truffles, or a comforting soupe au pistou (Provençale-style vegetable soup) fragrant with chervil and basil and served with an aïoli-swathed crouton. Succulent grilled quails brushed with hazelnut vinaigrette make a lovely salad, garnished with poached quail eggs and mixed greens.

The wine list has a fairly wide range, but prices are erratic —$28 for a St. Veran? Since I am known to the staff here, my table was never without the company of an eager waiter. Acquaintances who have visited recently, though, report that the staff is not always so accommodating.

The entrée lineup, like a good ball team, has power and depth. Roasted squab with turnips, bacon, and a sweet fresh-corn-and-cream flan is a serendipitous combination. Crisply browned sweetbreads are excellent, along with firm-cooked asparagus, truffles, and a little endive package filled with mushrooms. Another well-crafted combination is slices of juicy magret of duck over a slab of duck foie gras and a roasted quail atop wilted cabbage. Also appealing are the veal kidneys in a dark, sweet-edged Burgundy sauce offset by a snap of black pepper.

Seafood choices are uniformly delicate: sea bass under a buttery crust of sliced potatoes with chervil; halibut in a light vermouth-and-watercress sauce on a palette of baby vegetables, and poached Dover sole with a custardy artichoke mousse (or grilled with grainy mustard sauce). Only a salmon with purée of cucumber and coriander sauce was diffidently seasoned.

La Réserve recently signed on a hot-shot young pastry chef named Didier Berlioz, formerly of the Hotel Negresco in Nice. If premeditated diet subversion were a crime, he could be deported solely on the basis of his insidious velvety chocolate charlotte. Glistening caramelized tarte Tatin would rank at least as a misdemeanor.

In summer, try the white peaches fanned around a cleansing rosemary granité, or the pear granité in a bittersweet chocolate cone.

# LATTANZI

★

*361 West 46th Street, 315-0980.*

*Atmosphere: Comfortable brick-walled grotto; low noise level.*

*Service: Brusque and occasionally inattentive.*

*Price range: Moderate.*

*Credit cards: American Express.*

*Hours: Lunch, noon to 2 P.M., Monday through Friday; dinner, 5 to 10 P.M., Monday and Tuesday, 5 to 11, Wednesday and Thursday, until midnight Friday and Saturday.*

*Reservations: Recommended.*

*Wheelchair accessibility: Three steps down to dining room; Restrooms on same level.*

Lattanzi, the cozy, brick-lined grotto on Restaurant Row, is a solid, comfortable, family-run spot in the Broadway theater district. The extended Lattanzi family has become a culinary conglomerate in recent years with four other restaurants in Manhattan: Trastevere, Trastevere 84, Erminia, and Va Bene. All the cooking has similar roots, but the twist at Lattanzi is a menu of cuisine from the ancient Jewish ghetto in Rome. The special menu is available at lunch and after 8 P.M.

The below-ground dining room with its cloth-draped hanging lamps, painting of ancient Pompeii, and reasonably spaced tables is a pleasant place to spend a relaxing hour before a show. For a family-run establishment, though, the service is anything but homey. Captains can be gruff and at times pushy. No one knows (or seems to care) who gets which order.

All this is an advisory to order quickly if you are on a tight schedule. The best-known dish from the Roman Jewish tradition is carciofi alla giudea, or artichokes Jewish style. The dish has several variations, depending on where you have it and the type of artichoke used. Lattanzi presses tender baby artichokes into a pan and sautées them with garlic and parsley until they are crisp.

Another interesting starter from the Jewish menu is a combination plate of eggplant that is first fried then marinated in a sweet combination of vinegar, sugar, olive oil, and tomatoes. The plate also includes excellent fresh mozzarella and a Roman specialty called suppli al telefono that is essentially a dense and bland ball of mozzarella coated with a risottolike rice mixture, then rolled in breadcrumbs and fried.

Rank mussels on one visit have dissuaded me from trying them again. I also have had several disappointments among pastas. Some have been al dente to the point of toughness, including an otherwise nicely made bucatini all'amatriciana with bacon, onion, and tomato, and tortelloni filled with ground veal and sausage with a bright marinara sauce. The two best pastas are linguine in a vibrant and herby white clam sauce, and orecchiette, small shell pasta, tossed in olive oil, garlic, fresh tomatoes, and tuna.

Grilled meats are a good way to go here, whether they are lamb chops scented with rosemary and garlic with sautéed mushrooms or the tender grilled veal chops. Most entrées come with the same vegetables, like roasted sliced potatoes, onions, and sautéed spinach. Veal scaloppine with artichokes, garlic, and onions are tender but underseasoned. An unusual fish dish from the Jewish menu is red snapper with raisins and vinegar. This unlikely combination has an invigorating balance, with the sweet raisins playing off the tart vinegar. You can get a nicely roasted chicken here seasoned with rosemary and garlic, or chicken capriccioso, in which the meat is cut into pieces and cooked with sweet peppers, onions, and marinara sauce.

The rich desserts require more than a short walk to the theater to work off. Chocolate mousse is dense and potent but not overly sweet, zabaglione with strawberries packs a serious dose of Marsala, and the napoleon is an oozing tower of brittle browned pastry and thick sweet cream. You also can't go wrong with the moist and sugar-dusted ricotta cheesecake.

# LA TULIPE

★ ★

*104 West 13th Street, 691-8860.*

*Atmosphere: Intimate town-house dining room; can be loud.*

*Service: Generally inattentive; long wait for entrées.*

*Wine: Average selection.*

*Price range: Expensive (pretheater dinner prix fixe, $40; dinner prix fixe, $62).*

*Credit cards: All major cards.*

*Hours: Pretheater dinner, 6 to 6:30 P.M., Tuesday through Sunday; dinner, 6 to 10 P.M., Tuesday through Sunday.*

*Reservations: Recommended.*

*Wheelchair access: Several steps down at entrance; everything on one level.*

While there is virtue in consistency, a static act can become fatigued over the years. The performance at La Tulipe has also lost some of its homey charm. Some of the food now tastes as if it is prepared by rote, not by a loving cook.

The setting still has appeal. There is a little Parisian-style bar in the front room of this renovated brownstone where customers patiently sip champagne while waiting. John Darr, the schoolmasterly co-owner, escorts you to the back where a cluster of tables is arranged in a chocolate-colored room with pretty tulip sconces, dainty flower arrangements, and strategically placed mirrors to give the illusion of more space. The noise level can be distracting at peak hours.

In all the years I have been going to La Tulipe, I have never seen Sally Darr, the chef, enter the dining room. This is certainly no criticism, for she was presumably overseeing every last detail of the kitchen. Certain dishes sampled in recent months cause me to wonder whether that is still the case. Take, for example, a house standard since 1979, one that I remember enjoying more than once: red snapper fillet cooked in parchment paper with fennel, potatoes, and carrots. On two recent visits, the fish was woefully overcooked and devoid of seasonings save a lonely sprig of thyme. Another house specialty, described on the menu as roast lobster with vegetables in a saffron-seasoned seafood broth, was equally insipid, the claw meat mealy and dry and the lusterless sauce separating before our eyes as it was served.

Yet some of Mrs. Darr's homey fare is as alluring as ever. Tender little bay scallops are flash sautéed, nested over spinach, and drizzled with sizzling brown butter; a meaty and succulent squab is set over braised cabbage and bacon, along with al dente carrots and haricots verts; and the roast chicken—aromatic of garlic cloves and leaning against a snowdrift of buttery mashed potatoes—is still worth trudging through a blizzard for. One evening, a baby chicken was deboned and stuffed with foie gras of duck, moistened with a sauce of chicken stock, morels, and cèpes: it is as luxuriant as it sounds.

Service has always been distractingly slow at La Tulipe, the price one supposedly pays for a highly personalized dinner prepared by the owner. The pacing has not improved over the years. Nor has the service, which still leaves you often pouring your own wine and waving for bread or water. At these prices, customers deserve better. Except for a drab duck terrine and the overvinegared salads, appetizers are pleasing, especially the regal Parmesan soufflé in a crust of phyllo dough, and the sparkling leek terrine with mustard sauce. Zucchini fritters are still as light and brittle as ever, presented in their little picnic basket garnished with parsley, and the tomato soup with basil and mint manages to remain ripe and bright year round. The wine selection has never been exceptional.

Apple tart is still the strongest contender among desserts, moist and sweet with a remarkably light crust; lemon soufflé is inedibly sour, and the apricot soufflé arrived one evening only three-fourths cooked. Two old standbys are still winners: the fragile tulip-shaped tuiles filled with vanilla ice cream, toasted almonds, and hot chocolate sauce (La Tulipe Marie-Louise), and a classic rendition of île flottante with praline sauce.

# LE BERNARDIN

★ ★ ★ ★

*155 West 51st Street, 489-1515.*

*Atmosphere: Luxurious and spacious room with well-spaced tables and low noise level.*

*Service: Knowledgeable and efficient.*

*Wine: Excellent French selection at fairly high prices.*

*Price range: Expensive.*

*Credit cards: All major cards.*

*Hours: Lunch, noon to 2:15 P.M., Monday through Friday; dinner, 6 to 10:15 P.M., Monday through Thursday, 5:30 to 11 P.M., Friday and Saturday.*

*Reservations: Necessary.*

*Wheelchair accessibility: Special access for wheelchairs; everything on one level.*

One question often posed to a restaurant critic is, "What is the difference between a three-star and a four-star restaurant?" Indeed, it is a fine distinction. A succinct explanation would be: a three-star establishment must excel; a four-star must excel and inspire. Le Bernardin, the all-seafood restaurant that received four stars in 1986 shortly after it opened, is a paradigm of a restaurant that does both.

Le Bernardin's near-fanatical regard for fresh seafood

and its revolutionary style of preparation—at least in this country—have been emulated from coast to coast. Even home chefs, who for generations followed the credo "cook fish until it flakes," are now serving rare-pink tuna steaks at backyard barbecues. Rarely has a restaurant had such a pervasive influence on a nation's cuisine.

Aside from its historical stature, Le Bernardin is still a glorious place to dine. Gilbert and Maguy Le Coze, the dashing siblings who are chef and manager respectively, have not lost a step in their sprint to fame over the last three years. In late 1986, they closed their renowned Paris restaurant to concentrate on the New York venture.

Miss Le Coze, lanky and angular with dark fluttering eyes and a strobelike smile, is the omnipresent hostess: suggesting a wine here, sharing a laugh with a customer there, straightening a tablecloth. Her staff is well schooled in the food, highly professional and polite, although some readers have written about their abrupt and too-fast-for-comfort service.

The room is striking for its size and subdued elegance: a soaring teak ceiling, gray-blue walls, well-spaced tables, capacious armchairs, and larger-than-life oil paintings of, naturally, fishermen and their catch. Even when the restaurant is packed, which is virtually every day, the room absorbs extraneous noise, making civilized conversation possible.

As for the food, under Mr. Le Coze and his exacting lieutenant, Eberhard Muller, it has, if anything, become even more refined and certainly lighter. I recall vividly the first time I tasted a scallop at Le Bernardin, the translucent slivers having a texture close to firm custard, with a frothy oceanic flavor. The same quality scallops—they are alive when they hit the poaching liquid—are still served, enhanced by a subtle tomato fondue touched with lime and sharpened with hot pepper.

That same degree of freshness is evident in other starters: silvery strips of fresh cod fillet that have been marinated in juniper-berry oil, salt, and sugar, served with a sprinkling of fresh thyme and rosemary—an intriguing combination—and beignets of basil-wrapped shrimp.

Belon oysters from Maine are superb raw, or seared quickly, returned to the shell, and moistened with a white-wine sauce and the oyster brine, all topped with caviar.

Broiled Louisiania shrimp arrive looking like a high-kicking chorus line, their seared tails extended in unison. They come with a lustrous parsley-and-shallot butter. Strips of glistening skate are draped over a green salad and bathed in a perfectly balanced vinaigrette.

Le Bernardin has an excellent French wine list, especially among white Burgundies. Prices at one time were scandalously high, but they have come down somewhat in the past year.

Among entrées, the sea scallops that are so seductive as appetizers are equally so whether served with a truffle vinaigrette garnished with black truffles or in a sorrel-and-tomato sauce. Shrimp pressed into ground black pepper and fresh thyme are sautéed quickly and served with a pure, faintly sweet shrimp-stock sauce. One of my favorite dishes on the current menu is called herb-crusted codfish with rosemary vinaigrette: the firm, snowy fillet is crisp outside, explosively flavorful with herbs, and intoxicatingly aromatic. The list of superlatives goes on.

Desserts have not changed as much as the rest of the menu. My least favorite is a special, combining harsh cinnamon ice cream with a rice pudding soufflé (an unnecessarily dandified version of a gutsy American classic). Mille-feuille of green apples and raisins is a lovely combination of tart and sweet. An occasional special from the old menu is still one of the best: the trio of pears, which combines a cinnamon-tinged poached pear, a warm tiny pear tart, and pear sorbet. And for caramel fans, there is still the dazzling if daunting marathon of caramel ice cream, crème caramel, oeufs à la neige, and caramel mousse.

# LE CHANTILLY

★ ★

*106 East 57th Street, 751-2931.*

*Atmosphere: Plush and comfortable Old World dining room with generously separated tables.*

*Service: Professional and vigilant.*

*Wine: Good selection, especially among Bordeaux; expensive.*

*Price range: Moderately expensive (pretheater dinner prix fixe $31.50).*

*Credit cards: All major cards.*

*Hours: Lunch, noon to 3 P.M., Monday through Saturday; pretheater dinner, 5:30 to 6:45 P.M., Monday through Saturday; dinner, 5:30 to 11 P.M., Monday through Saturday. Closed Saturday for lunch in summer.*

*Reservations: Suggested.*

*Wheelchair accessibility: Everything on one level.*

Le Chantilly is a restaurant in transition. In mid-1990 the longtime chef, Roland Chenus, ended his partnership with Camille Dulac. The sous-chef was about to take over at this writing.

The dining room was spruced up several years ago, with newly reupholstered banquettes and a few more dreamy murals of the famous château that is the restaurant's namesake. The result is one of the more serene and civilized settings in town, with amply separated tables that allow for privacy.

Those with an archaeological bent will be able to unearth a few artifacts from the old menu. Instead of serving snails the traditional way, in a ramekin with garlic butter, the kitchen now gift wraps them in thin ravioli along with wild mushrooms and tomatoes and sets them adrift on a satiny cream sauce. The success of this dish rests in the restrained garnishes that allow the snails' flavor to come through. A similar approach using crayfish just misses the mark because of oversalting.

One of the more compelling menu innovations is called beignet of wild salmon, which involves coating one side of the fillet in a crêpelike batter and sautéeing it. It is presented over wilted spinach with a beurre-blanc sauce tinged with blackberry vinegar. Not every success is so laboriously crafted. Sweet freshwater prawns from Hawaii, a special, are simply grilled and garnished with ginger-and-herb butter; a light and spirited alternative is excellent gravlax paired with anise-infused tuna and black bass marinated with (insufficient) dill—all displayed over julienne of leeks in a vinaigrette sauce. A fish soup is based on a deep rich stock, and the ingredients are well cooked, but unaccountably the end result is lacking—perhaps it just needs a last-minute adjustment of seasonings.

Service has seen a dramatic turnaround at Le Chantilly; it is much more animated and attentive. The wine list, too, has been bolstered, especially among Bordeaux; prices are on the high end all around.

As for main courses, the performance is considerably stronger among meat dishes than seafood. You can get a good broiled Dover sole here at lunch, and one of the dinner highlights is a tableau of sea scallops and shrimp over a glistening ginger-cream sauce flecked with tomato—just don't chomp down on one of the big anise seeds. However, disappointments include a naked slab of poached halibut in a pallid tomato sauce, and a special grilled tuna steak that is so dry a bucket of ginger vinaigrette could not have revived it. Grilled lobster would please most aficionados, although I find little evidence of promised Thai herbs in the butter sauce.

The winner at my table one evening was the superb roasted squab—the pink-cooked breast meltingly tender and flavorful and the crisp-skinned leg meat dark and rich. It came with warm chicory salad tossed in a light sesame oil. Roast Muscovy duck likewise was falling-off-the-bone tender, and its pleasingly pungent sauce, combining lime and bitter oranges, was a rousing surprise.

The classic French desserts are as uncompromisingly delicious as ever, especially the airy charlotte anchored with passion-fruit mousse, pear tart with a sublime buttery crust, and a light and semisweet pear clafoutis. Only mocha layer cake is too sweet and a bit dry. Soufflés in every color float across the dining room all evening long. Of those sampled, chocolate with crème anglaise surpasses the grainy lemon with raspberry sauce.

# LE CIRQUE

★ ★ ★ ★

*58 East 65th Street, 794-9292.*

*Atmosphere: Plush, densely packed room done in a rococo style. Good acoustics despite large crowds.*

*Service: Unflappably seasoned European staff, highly professional and cordial.*

*Wine: Superlative international list at fair prices.*

*Price range: Expensive.*

*Credit cards: American Express, Diners Club, and Carte Blanche.*

*Hours: Lunch, noon to 3 P.M., Monday through Saturday; dinner, 6 to 10:30 P.M., Monday through Saturday.*

*Reservations: Necessary well in advance.*

*Wheelchair accessibility: Dining room on one level; restrooms four steps down into an adjacent hotel lobby.*

Le Cirque has emerged as arguably the preeminent restaurant in New York City, one that combines consistently titillating food, expert service, superb wines, and world-class people watching. Le Cirque's unparalleled spirit springs from the staff and customers who fill it. On any evening the celebrity scorecard overflows, and overseeing it all is the ineffably charming workaholic owner, Sirio Maccioni.

Daniel Boulud, the young Burgundian who has been in charge of the kitchen since late 1986, is awesomely versatile —with the help of the city's largest kitchen brigade.

One starter that has become one of Mr. Boulud's signature preparations is called sea scallops fantasy in black tie, an individual silver casserole dish of exquisite sliced sea scallops layered with black truffles, moistened with buttery vermouth and truffle juice. Next to that you can find something as unabashedly earthy as a cold terrine of beef shanks with leeks in a faintly piquant raifort sauce speckled with diced vegetables, or tissue-thin carpaccio of red snapper glossed with truffle oil under a cover of arugula and fresh chervil. Foie gras comes in no fewer than two dozen costumes, depending on Mr. Boulud's whim (sautéed with Concord grapes and cranberries was inspired).

Since I am known to the staff and can't objectively judge the service, I resorted to sending first-timers there three times and asked them to report their impressions. The unknowns said they were always greeted politely, although twice they had to wait fifteen minutes for a table. Once seated, they were always treated courteously.

Trying to describe Mr. Boulud's vast lunch and dinner entrée repertory in this space would be like itemizing the fall exhibitions at the Metropolitan Museum of Art on a postcard. We'll have to browse. One world-class dish is the roasted black sea bass wrapped in diaphanous sheets of sliced potatoes, all golden crackling, set in a concentrated Barolo wine sauce brightened with shallots and fresh thyme. Simpler but also sublime was the grilled salmon atop a sward of fennel studded with walnuts and bathed in a walnut-oil vinaigrette. Mr. Boulud, who stalks the markets of Brooklyn's Atlantic Avenue to sate his passion for the best spices, has flushed more than a few highly powdered cheeks in the dining room with his brassy lobster in curry sauce. However, a special of rouget, the delicate Mediterranean fish, was lost under its rich lobster and wild asparagus sauce. Much better was the fat fillet of grouper over sautéed cabbage and shiitake mushrooms in a sublime white-wine sauce infused with rosemary.

The new selection of roasts and game is stellar, and the distinctive sauces with each, passed through Mr. Boulud's alembic, emphasize purity and accessibility over elaborateness. Take, for example, his navarin of lamb. It may be lighter and daintier than a thick-sauced home version, but the verdant flavors come rolling through.

A frequent special is five-hour braised lamb, a wondrous twist on the navarin redolent of garlic, fresh tomato, cardamom and coriander, served with cinnamon-perfumed couscous and raisins. On Thursdays you may find the best pot-au-feu (or the Italian version, bollito misto) on this side of the Atlantic (elevated from peasant status with slabs of foie gras). Pasta primavera was introduced to this country at Le Cirque, so you should try this lustrous version if for nothing other than historical purposes.

Magret of duck is cooked to a perfect blush, touched with plum-sweetened stock; fork-tender venison has a diadem of autumnal purées (chestnut, spinach blended with pear, and pumpkin) and a juniper-honey sauce.

Equal to the menu in breadth and quality is Mr. Maccioni's international wine list, one of New York's greatest—over five hundred bottles on the regular list, and at fair prices for a luxury establishment.

Some of the leading pastry chefs in the country have waved their wands at Le Cirque, and the newly assembled team under the Austrian-born Farbinger Markus is more than carrying on the tradition: three-tiered raspberry napoleon that is so light it should come with fishing weights to hold it down, mango curls paired with ripe mango ice cream and mixed berries, a brittle web of spun sugar holding luscious fresh figs and vanilla ice cream, splendid chocolate sorbet served in a porcelain egg, and the signature crème brûlée—much mimicked but still the paragon.

# LE CYGNE

★ ★ ★

*55 East 54th Street, 759-5941.*

*Atmosphere: Elegant and colorful two-level town house. Moderate noise level.*

*Service: Excellent.*

*Wine: Adequate selection though not impressive.*

*Price range: Expensive (lunch prix fixe, $37; dinner prix fixe $58).*

*Credit cards: All major cards.*

*Hours: Lunch, noon to 2 P.M., Monday through Friday; dinner, 6 to 10 P.M., Monday through Friday, 5:30 to 10 P.M., Saturday.*

*Reservations: Required.*

*Wheelchair accessibility: Two steps at the entrance; restrooms downstairs.*

Le Cygne is a serene and civilized refuge in midtown that since its opening in 1969 has quietly maintained a remarkably high level of food and service. In 1988 it had a changing of the guard in the kitchen when Pierre Baran, the chef for three years, moved on to the Knickerbocker Club and was replaced by Jean-Michel Bergougnoux, formerly of Le Régence and Lutèce. The transition has been so smooth that most patrons probably didn't notice any difference. Such consistency is not surprising, for Le Cygne is lovingly guided by its founding owners, Gérard Gillian and Michel Crouzillat.

The restaurant is in a two-story town house with a sunny postmodern décor. The main dining room is done in cool tones of gray and blue highlighted by white columns and ceiling trim; Impressionistic flower murals are softly illuminated, adding color and an aura of fantasy. Even when the restaurant is crowded, the noise level remains low.

Mr. Bergougnoux's style is classically rooted, yet wisely attuned to the desires of his clients, who include a large percentage of waist-watching business lunchers during the day and older, affluent couples at dinner. The chef employs butter and cream judiciously in combination with vegetable purées and intensely reduced stocks.

An excellent introduction to the Bergougnoux style is an appetizer of oysters wrapped in spinach leaves and set over a chilled layer of balsamic vinegar, cream, and aspic. A whimsical autumn special is baby pumpkin hollowed out and layered with ginger-scented pumpkin mousse, chunks of lobster meat, and black trumpet mushrooms, surrounded by a lobster-stock sauce: a culinary trick that is indeed a treat. Another lobster starter did not work as well, this one combining steamed chunks of lobster over a sward of blanched cabbage with an orange-butter sauce that was overly acidic.

Fois gras is sublime here, whether in a cold terrine layered with artichokes, or sautéed with apples and a splash of wine vinegar. The service team at Le Cygne continues to be a paragon of efficiency and class. Waiters and captains are never overbearing—and never hover—but they have that sixth sense of knowing when their presence is needed. The wine list is adequate, though hardly impressive in depth or quality. Captains are usually reliable when asked for suggestions.

Mr. Bergougnoux has some magnificent seafood entrées on the fall menu. One example is rosettes of blush-pink salmon, ringed with strips of crisped skin and paired with green lentils swathed in veal stock with Italian parsley and tomatoes; another is the purée of dried cod that is redolent of garlic, garnished with golden homemade potato chips and surrounded by a fish-stock sauce aromatic of fresh thyme. Snapper is memorable, too, dusted with coarse pepper and broiled, then set atop sautéed cabbage with an excellent beurre blanc made with champagne vinegar.

On the other side of the menu, you can find such lusty fall fare as tender veal medallions encased in a thin sheet of potatoes, then a strip of bacon, all surrounded by seasonal vegetables, or squab wrapped in lettuce leaves and cooked in a pastry crust with a truffle-enriched stock sauce. One game dish that disappointed was the dry and tasteless pheasant with cèpes.

Self-disciplined business lunchers will need to exercise every ounce of self-restraint to turn down desserts, which are extraordinarily good. The lofty lemon soufflé with raspberry sauce, a house standard, is still terrific, as are the mille-feuille of pears with pear sorbet, and the chestnut mousse charlotte. Thin-crusted, buttery apple tart is exquisitely delicate and delicious, the best in New York.

Fortunately for fans of Le Cygne, the changes there have been barely perceptible, and if anything, for the better.

# LE MADRI

★ ★

*168 West 18th Street, 727-8022.*

*Atmosphere: Spacious, comfortable (but loud) Tuscan-style dining room with wood-burning pizza oven and outside patio.*

*Service: Generally efficient and knowledgeable.*

*Wine: Well-chosen list with good price range.*

*Price range: Moderately expensive.*

*Credit cards: American Express.*

*Hours: Lunch, noon to 3 P.M., Monday through Friday; dinner 6 to 10:30 P.M., Monday through Saturday. From 10:30 P.M. to 12:30 A.M. a pizza and salad menu is offered.*

*Reservations: Necessary, sometimes several days in advance for dinner.*

*Wheelchair accessibility: Dining on one level; restrooms downstairs.*

At Le Madri, or The Mothers, Pinot Luongo said he would import revolving trios of nonprofessional Italian mamas from Tuscany to cook alongside his full-time professional chef. It made for a public-relations bonanza when the restaurant opened in May 1989: no matter that two of the women were neither married nor mothers and that one lived in Brooklyn where she ran a catering business.

There are no gimmicks in the design of the place, however. The big main dining room is splendid and comfortable, though piercingly loud when full. Pale yellow walls, a vaulted ceiling supported by columns, a tiled wood-burning pizza oven, strategically aimed lights on overhead scaffolding, well-spaced tables—all contribute to a smart north Italian setting.

While most of the cooking is exceptionally good, a few

dishes are just elegantly packaged commercial-tasting fare. Dungeness crab salad, for instance, is overrefrigerated and underseasoned; the cold antipasto plate at lunch was routine except for the delicious white beans and the steamed baby beets marinated in olive oil and lemon juice. Three of the better starters are a heaping bowl of tender deep-fried baby squid and crunchy deep-fried parsley, sweet fresh prawns and more of those delicious tarragon-scented white beans, and thin, light pizzas with nicely charred crusts (tomato, excellent mozzarella, and basil; wild mushrooms and oregano; and shellfish with herbs).

Several pastas were big hits at my table. Foremost among them was a special called pezzoccheri, flat buckwheat noodles tossed with cubes of potatoes, cabbage, sage, and tart taleggio cheese—now that's food from the hearth. Spaghetti with tomato and basil may not win any creativity awards, but when the ingredients are as splendid as these and lovingly balanced, the dish is heavenly. A Ligurian specialty called panzotti alle noci, ravioli triangles stuffed with ricotta and spinach, glistening with butter and sprinkled with grated pine nuts and walnuts, is another high point.

Not so thrilling were the Sicilian rendition of fusilli with a one-two punch of salt (anchovies and capers) insufficiently counterbalanced by olives and tomatoes. The women make a mean risotto, though: try the earthy arborio rice in a rich stock with heady porcini.

The amiably garrulous service staff has a good grasp of the food as well as the wine list, which is well rounded and intelligently priced, starting in the high teens.

A fine white wine would be sublime with the perfectly roasted whole striped bass infused with the flavors of rosemary and fennel, or with the wonderfully delicate and moist halibut served in a light pan broth with fresh thyme sprigs and sweet onions and green beans. Two visually alluring dishes were disappointments: unseasoned tuna steak over julienne of vinegared cucumbers; and broiled medallions of salmon over spinach, garnished with red pepper and chervil (well cooked but without an integrated flavor).

The best dessert tried was chocolate-hazelnut tart, chewy and intense, with honey gelato. The winy zabaglione with fruit is an alternative, much better than the blueberry-and-raspberry tart with a leathery frangipani, and the dry, grainy polenta pound cake.

# LE PÉRIGORD

★ ★ ★

*405 East 52nd Street, 755-6244.*

*Atmosphere: Plush, comfortable, and quiet dining room.*

*Service: Congenial professionals, among the best in New York; kitchen pace can be slow.*

*Wine: Weighted toward big-name producers.*

*Price range: Expensive (lunch prix-fixe, $28; dinner prix fixe, $48).*

*Credit cards: All major cards.*

*Hours: Lunch, noon to 3 P.M., Monday through Friday; dinner, 5:30 to 10:30 P.M., Monday through Saturday.*

*Reservations: Recommended.*

*Wheelchair accessibility: One step down at entrance; restrooms downstairs.*

Le Périgord marked its twenty-fifth anniversary in 1989, the last seven under the culinary tutelage of Antoine Bouterin, a master of classical and Provençale cooking. While many old-school French dining rooms are struggling, Le Périgord seems to be flourishing. Mr. Bouterin's scintillating food is certainly one reason. Equally important, though, is the exemplary service team under the owner, Georges Briguet. It performs with the precision of a trapeze troupe. Not only are the people polished professionals, but they also genuinely care about their customers.

The dining room is soft and spacious, with beige-and-pink-flowered wall fabric, indirect lighting, leather chairs, and bursts of fresh flowers.

Mr. Bouterin's cooking, while classically rooted and opulent, is generally light and herb-infused. Consider the French summer vegetable soup called pistou, an occasional special, which is as heady as a stroll through a Provençale garden. Another worthy special is the tart of buttery smoked salmon over sautéed leeks. The tartar of fresh salmon is rich and bold with garlic, cumin, and curry, but the herb mayonnaise is unnecessary.

Brandade de morue, the southern French specialty of puréed cod, olive oil, and milk, is heavenly here, much lighter and more herbaceous than most versions. The same cannot be said for the garlic soup, which was served tepid and which needed salt. Instead, watch for the shellfish soup, another special, which is exquisitely fresh, faintly sweet from onions and carrots, and redolent of saffron.

Le Périgord's wine list is weighted toward big-name producers at big prices, but affordable bottles can be found among Mâcons and Côtes-du-Rhônes. As sharp and congenial as the service staff is, the pace of the kitchen can be a little too leisurely at times.

Outstanding seafood dishes include the skate with a potent aïoli and red cabbage (although a side plate of unseasoned vegetables adds nothing but color), and steamed halibut in a basil sauce with asparagus and haricots verts. Also appealing are seared salmon steak in a light cream sauce with spinach and fresh clams, and monkfish in an assertive curry sauce.

Sweets worth the indulgence include a good sharp lemon meringue tart with raspberry sauce, crisp and light cherry crêpes soufflés, a fluffy lemon custard roulade in a moat of vodka-spiked crème anglaise, and exceptionally ripe pear soufflé.

# LE REFUGE

★ ★

*166 East 82nd Street, 861-4505.*

*Atmosphere: Romantic, intimate, and friendly.*

*Service: Well trained, only occasionally overburdened.*

*Wine: Modest and somewhat eccentric list with fairly high prices.*

*Price range: Moderately expensive.*

*Credit cards: None.*

*Hours: Lunch, noon to 3 P.M., Monday through Saturday, noon to 4 P.M., Sunday; dinner, 5:30 to 11 P.M., daily.*

*Reservations: Necessary.*

*Wheelchair accessibility: Dining room on one level; restrooms downstairs.*

Le Refuge is a beguiling French restaurant just a short walk from upper Madison Avenue shops and the Metropolitan Museum of Art. This romantic spot still has a subdued neighborhood feel, if your neighborhood happens to be the affluent East Eighties. The food is neither avant-garde nor from the school of Old Masters: it's simply an agreeable mix of updated French home cooking by the chef and owner, Pierre Saint-Denis.

The three dining rooms are smartly rustic: the front with white walls, tasteful antiques, and a small service bar; the small middle alcove trimmed in country tiles; and the back room all brick with pretty tapestries, timber beams, well-worn wooden tables, and soft lighting.

Appetizers are exceptionally appealing. You can start with a verdant vegetable terrine combining minced carrots with artichoke hearts and red pepper floating on a refreshing coulis of red peppers and tomato, or a lovely green salad with warm, pleasantly tart goat cheese. The house veal-and-duck-liver terrine studded with pistachios is moist and richly flavored, as are the deftly assembled warm oysters atop blanched leeks and gratinéed with hollandaise. Only the icy carpaccio of tuna with a listless vinaigrette is lacking.

Service varies depending on the circumstances—it gets scattered in the front room when busy—but overall is vigilant and professional. The wine list is modest and somewhat eccentric, with many selections by lesser-known producers, and prices are on the high side.

Mr. Saint-Denis's regulars cherish consistency over creativity, so many dishes stay on the menu throughout the year. One is the excellent lamb chops embellished with a rosemary, garlic, and lamb-stock sauce along with homey potatoes à la dauphinoise. An occasional special of lamb medallions stuffed with spinach is delicious, too. Underseasoning marred the lobster and shrimp in basil cream sauce with bland green and white pasta.

Other seafood dishes to look for are swordfish in a light, aromatic Provençale sauce with an intriguing purée of turnips, beets, and potatoes, and salmon in a silken red-wine butter-and-shallot sauce (the chef, however, should add the salmon caviar garnish after cooking the fish, so the eggs do not congeal).

Two desserts excel: the ineffably light chocolate cake potent with a lingering, faintly dry aftertaste; and layered chocolate praline mousse with vanilla cream and a pear poached in red wine. After those, the rest seem ordinary, although the mini strawberry tart and chocolate mousse airy with egg whites are pleasing as well.

Whether you are a Rembrandt fan or just a fair-weather stroller, it is nice to have Le Refuge in the neighborhood.

# LE RÉGENCE

★ ★ ★

*Hôtel Plaza Athénée, 37 East 64th Street, 606-4647, 606-4648.*

*Atmosphere: Plush, hushed, and ultra-French.*

*Service: Professional and congenial.*

*Wine: Impressive but expensive selection.*

*Price range: Expensive (Lunch prix fixe, $25.50; dinner prix fixe, $59.50).*

*Credit cards: All major cards.*

*Hours: Breakfast, 7 to 10 A.M., daily; lunch, noon to 2:30 P.M., daily; dinner, 6 to 9:30 P.M., daily.*

*Reservations: Necessary, especially at dinner.*

*Wheelchair accessibility: Ramp access to dining room and restrooms.*

Le Régence, the opulent, Old World French restaurant in the Hôtel Plaza Athénée, got a new lease on life in 1987 when a new team of French restaurateurs took over the kitchen after the defection of Daniel Boulud and several of his lieutenants to Le Cirque.

The hotel hired as consultants the estimable Rostang clan from France, the Flying Wallendas of French cuisine—father Jo and son Philippe, who own La Bonne Auberge in Antibes, a Michelin two-star restaurant, and another son, Michel, whose namesake restaurant in Paris also has two stars. One or more of the Rostangs visit Le Régence monthly to oversee the menu.

The setting is indeed regal, a soft and stately den done in turquoise and white trim, with velvet banquettes, soft leather armchairs, ornate mirrors, and benign lighting. The gentle art of conversation can be pursued here without a megaphone, and the European-style staff is meticulous and proper without being stuffy.

The Rostang style of cooking is generally contemporary and light, emphasizing flavor over flair, and is sometimes unpredictable—soy butter may show up with grilled fish, or vinegar and honey in a scallop preparation. Among the starters, two arresting dishes are the corn pancake studded with bits of smoked salmon, set over a lustrous curry sauce —the sweet kernels of corn play off the salty salmon, while the zesty sauce adds just the right fillip to bring it all together; less complex but equally compelling is the luscious onion tart over mixed greens.

If you haven't had your fill of baby raviolis by now, the lobster-stuffed little pouches here are as light and fresh as can be, glossed with an olive-oil-and-lobster-coral sauce; more original is the sublime salmon-and-scallop tart. Sheets of raw salmon envelop sweet sea scallops, onions, and cream sauce aromatic of dill, all framed in a crust that is so thin it resembles matzoh.

Le Régence takes its wine seriously, but some of the prices on the impressively stocked list are way out of line.

Several seafood entrées excel. Thin slices of black bass were presented over a crêpe and enhanced with a caviar-freckled sauce, beautifully grilled red snapper came with charred scallions and a lovely soy-butter sauce, and skate-fish was paired with braised cabbage leaves in a subtle sweet-and-sour sauce.

Mustard is put to good use to enliven the sauce with slices of rosy beef fillet. Lemon adds a diverting sharpness to the sauce for duck breasts, which come with good corn pancakes. Veal chop was plump and succulent at dinner, while paillard of veal at lunch was equally flavorful, although the sorrel sauce was a bit timid to my taste.

Not all desserts are worth the guilt—particularly a flossy and tasteless pear soufflé and a bizarre almond-and-pineapple tart with coconut sauce, the kind of cloying dessert you expect at a pseudo-Polynesian establishment. The sorbet assortment is stunning, presented under a web of spun sugar. Cold chestnut soufflé is splendid, as is the ultra-light and ripe mango mousse. A Rostang specialty is the pear poached in red Burgundy wine with black currants, under a dome of pastry—the only way to improve it would be with a scoop of vanilla ice cream.

Le Régence has bounced back with style. For a civilized business lunch or a self-indulgent special-occasion dinner, it is a place to be pampered in the loftiest French style.

# LE ZINC

★

*139 Duane Street, 732-1226.*

*Atmosphere: Authentic and lively bistro feeling in a room that resembles a Victorian-era parlor car.*

*Service: Occasionally rushed, but competent.*

*Wine: Limited French list at reasonable prices.*

*Price range: Moderate.*

*Credit cards: American Express, MasterCard, and Visa.*

*Hours: Lunch, noon to 3 P.M., Monday through Friday; dinner, 6 P.M. to midnight, Monday through Thursday, 6 P.M. to 12:30 A.M., Friday and Saturday.*

*Reservations: Suggested.*

*Wheelchair accessibility: Two small steps at the entrance; dining rooms on one level, restrooms downstairs.*

The local competition has heated up considerably since Le Zinc opened in 1983 on Duane Street. The food here got off to a slow start, but trendy downtowners didn't seem to mind. Only when other hip competitors with better food arrived did Le Zinc upgrade its food—for a while. Recent visits indicate that it is on the slide again.

The dining room is reminiscent of a cavernous Victorian-era railroad car, with its barreled ceiling, dark wood trim, brass chandeliers, zinc-topped bar, and red banquettes. The slow and easy ambiance accelerates as the evening wears on and the inappropriate, thumping pop music amplifies to a crashing level. Service, however, is confused and slow.

Best bets as starters include the frisée au lardon, or chicory-and-bacon salad with a poached egg; a rough-textured, gamy terrine; or duck-liver mousse with a port-wine aspic. Seafood soup is nothing more than a humdrum clam chowder, and even salads are nondescript. Both shellfish starters are winners: the clear and icy Virginia oysters on the half shell with a tart migonnette sauce and meaty fresh steamed mussels in a nice oceanic broth.

The small wine selection starts with a decent house wine, Beaujolais Villages, although for a few dollars extra you can get the superior cru Beaujolais called Brouilly. Decent whites from the Loire and Burgundy are available for under $25. Among whites the Muscadet for around $15 is a solid choice, especially with seafood.

Among the fish main courses that harmonize with the Muscadet are the thick fillets of roasted monkfish in an assertive fresh dill sauce, and delicate sea bass over a vivid fennel coulis ringed with carved vegetables, both specials. A winning seasonal lunch entrée is the cold poached coho salmon in a spirited basil sauce. Less successful was poached trout in a flat-tasting basil sauce.

Two dishes that once excelled, osso buco and cassoulet, were disappointments on recent revisits—the former mired in an undistinguished tomato sauce, the latter dryish and in need of more seasoning. Chicken breast stuffed with a chicken mousse and sun-dried tomatoes was moist and flavorful.

Fruit sorbets are the best bet among desserts. Skip the gelatinous tiramisù and the dense, rubbery crème caramel.

# LOLA

★

*30 West 22nd Street, 675-6700.*

*Atmosphere: Elegant café ambiance with pastel-colored walls adorned with attractive prints and drawings and soft lighting. Annoyingly loud when full.*

*Service: The comely young staff is outgoing and helpful but occasionally awkward.*

*Wine: Well-priced, eclectic list.*

*Price range: Moderately expensive.*

*Credit Cards: American Express.*

*Hours: Brunch, noon to 4 P.M., Sunday; lunch, noon to 3 P.M., Monday through Friday; dinner, 6 P.M. to 2 A.M., Tuesday through Saturday; 6 to midnight, Monday.*

*Reservations: Suggested.*

*Wheelchair accessibility: Everything on one level.*

Lola is a stylish restaurant with a Caribbean accent in the blossoming Madison Square neighborhood. On paper, at least, the menu lineup is enticing. In reality, though, some dishes fail to excite. Moreover, the noise level can be numbing. There is barely a soft surface in the house, so when conviviality peaks, usually about 10 P.M., the dining room becomes a huge echo chamber.

While perusing the menu, you can be priming your palate with sharp little cayenne-spiked shortbread cookies made with cheese and pecans. And when choosing, keep in mind that on the whole, the appetizers are better than the entrées. Bermuda seafood chowder is consistently pleasing, a rich, sweetish broth chock-full of fresh tuna and vegetables; sweet-potato vichyssoise, which is served hot, is another winner. West Indian potato-and shrimp fritters sound intriguing, but upon first sampling they were a letdown, undercooked and 90 percent potato; several nights later, they were a pleasant surprise—crisp, well seasoned, and amply filled with shrimp. Even the accompanying chopped-tomato-and-basil garnish came to life.

The outstanding appetizer is grilled calf sweetbreads, which are firm, fresh, and infused with a faint smoky flavor. They come with a tart salsa of parsley, garlic, capers, and olive oil. Skip the watery and tasteless grilled polenta and try instead the mountain of ultra-thin cayenne-laced onion rings.

The service team, led by the ebullient Miss Bell, is long on personality though occasionally short on finesse. No useful help is offered regarding the wine list, which is fairly priced but includes several clunkers. Play it safe with well-known producers and you'll do fine.

If you'd like to try something with a West Indian accent, you might choose the sharp shrimp-and-chicken curry served with rough-textured wild-rice waffles. As for the so-called 100-spice Caribbean fried chicken, it sounds more ominous than it is. What you get is perfectly acceptable fried chicken coated with mildly hot dried spices and a Chinese-inspired three-cabbage salad.

Even the most humble West Indian restaurant should be able to turn out a creditable shellfish gumbo; the rendition here, though—with shrimp, clams, mussels, ham, and rice—is lackluster. So are the ersatz osso buco, the dried-out veal paillard, and the colorless tenderloin of pork roasted in milk and garlic. Simple grilled dishes fare better, such as the lovely lamb chops with golden-fried shoestring potatoes, and the swordfish steak enhanced with a caper-dill crème fraiche sauce.

The ricotta-flavored gelato, while not exactly a staple of Jamaican cuisine, is still worth trying. So, too, is the light and creamy Frangelico pumpkin cheesecake.

Keep Lola in mind for Sunday brunch when Gospel singers shake the house.

# LUSARDI'S

**SATISFACTORY**

*1494 Second Avenue, at 78th Street, 249-2020.*

*Atmosphere: Clubby and inviting room with a well-attired clientele.*

*Service: Sometimes forgetful and inattentive.*

*Price range: Moderately expensive.*

*Credit cards: All major cards.*

*Hours: Lunch, noon to 3 P.M., Monday through Friday; dinner, 5 P.M. to midnight, Monday through Saturday, 4 to 11 P.M., Sunday.*

*Reservations: Necessary.*
*Wheelchair accessibility: Everything on one level.*

The setting here is indeed beguiling: creamy yellow walls, brass lamps, wood-framed windows behind gossamer white curtains, and a wall rack loaded with wines. As for the service, waiters have a professional mien but are lazy about refilling glasses and removing dirty plates; and they never seem to know who ordered what dishes—at $18 for a bowl of risotto with vegetables, it's the least one can expect.

Among appetizers, the assorted grilled vegetables are a safe option—radicchio, endive, zucchini, and red peppers. Tuna carpaccio, however, was a sodden mess, tasting as if it had been recently defrosted (and lacking any of the promised truffle oil); bruschetta was nothing more than pale out-of-season chopped tomatoes and onions heaped on toasted bread. Two starters that can be recommended are the sheets of lean air-cured beef over arugula with olive oil and lemon that were pleasantly salty, and the firm and fresh sliced mushrooms and artichokes under olive oil and shavings of Parmesan cheese. Cold seafood salad—calamari and scallops with olives—is fresh and lively.

None of the pastas sampled left a deposit in my memory bank. Penne in tomato sauce with basil and black olives was fine if ordinary, as was tortelloni in a four-cheese sauce. Ravioli filled with riccota and spinach, a special, barely rose above pizzeria fare, and paglia e fieno, the thin two-toned pasta tossed in a cream sauce with peas and prosciutto, was bland.

The quality of veal here is excellent, especially the thick, juicy chop garnished with fresh sage; the medallions of veal under melted Fontina cheese are tender and flavorful, too. Not much can be said for seafood. Swordfish was over the hill and flaccid; salmon purportedly cooked in cognac, white wine, and lemon was fresh and well cooked but devoid of those flavors. The only plate that went back to the kitchen empty was the fried seafood platter (calamari, scallops, and shrimp). Several chicken dishes sampled were well cooked—pollo Abruzzese (tomato, rosemary, white-wine sauce), pollo Valsugana (shallots, pepper, tomato cream)—yet one dimensional.

We were in the mood for some wonderfully corrupting desserts when the waiter came by and ran off eight choices. After we ordered, he returned from the kitchen with a chagrined expression to say, "We only have two left, tartufo and strawberries with zabaglione." The former was ordinary, the latter insipid, the sauce lacking Marsala flavor. Another evening, we had a good, coffee-infused tiramisù served in a wine goblet, and sufficiently corrupting flourless chocolate cake.

# LUTÈCE

★ ★ ★ ★

*249 East 50th Street, 752-2225.*

*Atmosphere: A town house with an airy and cheerful garden dining room, an intimate anteroom, and a pair of formal, old-fashioned rooms upstairs.*

*Service: Highly professional staff, knowledgeable and correct.*

*Wine: Lean pickings in lower price range; good selection of older vintages.*

*Price range: Expensive (lunch prix fixe, $35; dinner prix fixe, $58, with some supplements).*

*Credit cards: All major cards.*

*Hours: Lunch, noon to 2 P.M., Tuesday through Friday; dinner, 6 to 10 P.M., Monday through Saturday, except from Memorial Day to Labor Day, when the restaurant is closed Saturdays.*

*Reservations: Necessary well in advance.*

*Wheelchair accessibility: Two steps down at the entrance; restrooms are upstairs.*

The premier classical French restaurant in New York, if not the country, Lutèce keeps rolling on. Much of the restaurant's appeal centers on André Soltner, the affable, self-effacing host who wouldn't leave his cherished restaurant unless under subpoena.

First-timers at Lutèce are invariably surprised by its unassuming setting. Lutèce is not a "designed" or "conceptualized" environment; it is simply a comfortable place, enhanced by the intangible ornamentation of countless memorable times.

You enter the charming pint-size barroom with its zinc-topped bar, marble café tables, and framed posters of Paris. Down a narrow hallway, past the partly exposed kitchen, you find a cozy anteroom, then beyond it the cheerful main garden room with its green slate floor, white wood trim, and a high Quonset-hut-like ceiling that light filters through during the day, casting a soft glow. Upstairs are two small, more formal rooms with crystal chandeliers, oil paintings, and subdued lighting.

The classic French menu is merely a formality, for Mr. Soltner and his staff conjure up a host of daily specials that should be considered carefully. In the spring you might start with a light and vibrantly seasoned vegetable terrine, layers of spinach and carrot ringed by sliced scallops in a lovely vinaigrette. A slice of fresh salmon, lightly smoked in the kitchen, is seared until its skin side is crisp, the flesh still deep pink, and is presented over a shallot-infused vinaigrette; the smoky fish and sweet shallots play off each other beautifully.

In cooler weather you might sample the superb Alsatian onion tart, sautéed foie gras with apples and vinegar, or the chausson, a golden turnover stuffed with crabmeat, scallops, and minced vegetables with a tarragon-loaded sauce choron. If Mr. Soltner comes to your table and sizes you up as an adventuresome eater, he may offer some of his more rustic offerings: a cold terrine of eel bound with an excellent gelatin made with bones and herbs, or onglet, a sinewy yet full-flavored cut of beef favored by the French but rarely served in this country. (It was indeed exceedingly chewy to American tastes.)

The wine list at Lutèce has improved in recent years, with more good selections at the lower end of the scale. Some of the best bargains, especially among whites, continue to be from Alsace. The depth in Bordeaux and Burgundy is impressive. Several captains can be relied upon for sound advice.

The highly professional French service staff at Lutèce has a reputation for sometimes being haughty with unknown customers. I receive letters occasionally from diners who complain about indifferent treatment. In my experience—at first incognito, although later I was known to the staff—this has not been the case. Whether these are isolated incidents or a pattern of behavior is difficult to assess.

The food at Lutèce is classic but not static, intensely flavorful yet not weighty. My idea of a transcendent Lutèce meal is something like baby lamb—real baby lamb, succulent and buttery—roasted to perfection with fresh herbs and paired with sautéed potatoes, mellow duck confit over mixed greens, or flawless golden sweetbreads with morels, lots of them. Roasted rabbit, which is so often dry and bland in restaurants, is incredibly tender here, the slowly simmered sauce robust with a vegetable and stock reduction. Roast duck with a subtle cherry sauce is sublime, too.

At lunch a baby chicken is served split and partly boned,

with cubes of buttery polenta and a splendid asparagus sauce. One of the few failures was a dry roulade of veal stuffed with Gruyère in a banal brown sauce. I'm also not wild about Alsace-style escargots in brioche—sort of a snail submarine sandwich—in which the escargots are lost in their garlicky log of brioche. Sautéed John Dory fillets, firm and mild, are extraordinarily good in a creamy red-pepper purée, as were all fish preparations sampled. For dessert, tarte Tatin is wondrously light and delicious. Pineapple in puff pastry with crème anglaise sounds suspicious but actually works, crème caramel with orange rind is simple and good, and the chocolate mousse terrine is downright dangerous.

You dine at Lutèce not to ride the latest wave in French cuisine, but rather to stroll leisurely through familiar terraine, sniffing the flowers along the way. And how sweet they can be.

# MALVASIA

★

*108 East 60th Street, 223-4790.*

*Atmosphere: Pretty, comfortable room in Mediterranean colors. Moderate noise level.*

*Service: Competent overall; kitchen can fall behind when busy.*

*Wine: Well-chosen, mostly Italian list with fair prices.*

*Price range: Moderately expensive.*

*Credit cards: All major cards.*

*Hours: Lunch, noon to 3 P.M., Monday through Saturday; dinner, 6 to 11:30 P.M., Monday through Saturday.*

*Reservations: Suggested.*

*Wheelchair accessibility: Three steps down to dining room; restrooms upstairs.*

Malvasia is the name of a grape that makes an apricot-perfumed sweet wine on the island of Lipari, just north of Sicily. Gennaro Picone, the chef and owner, is a native of the island, thus the name. He collaborated with the architect Adam Tihany on a witty setting that blends Mediterranean colors.

Malvasia's three-story town house with a twenty-foot ceiling has an expansive, airy feeling. The sandstone-yellow walls are offset by vibrantly hued banquettes covered with geometric patterns of beige and blue and red. Table arrangements are cozy but not cramped.

Mr. Picone has all the right moves to please lean, deal-making business lunchers; at dinner, his clean, herb-infused cooking can delight those once-more-around-the-reservoir types who eschew anything heavier than their credit cards. Olive oil, lots of greens, abundant vegetables, grains, grilled fish and meat—all characterize his cooking. Sometimes flavor does, too.

At lunch, we started with herb-bolstered marinated grilled quail with mixed greens. (On a second sampling, at dinner a week later, the quail was on the dry side and bland.) Seafood carpaccio was a fine palate-primer, slices of tuna, salmon, and sea bass with a sheen of oregano-scented vinaigrette. A cast of well-seasoned vegetables—fennel, zucchini, eggplant, tomato, peppers—was refreshing, as were simple sautéed shiitake mushrooms.

The fiber meter scores higher than the flavor meter when it comes to a salad of raw baby artichokes, grilled shrimp, grilled tomato, and what tasted like hothouse basil. (I can't imagine regular basil so bland.) Perhaps the best starter is a warm salad of tender baby octopus, clams, calamari, langoustine, and shrimp with white beans and potatoes, all moistened with a shellfish broth.

The chef's passion seems to be pastas and risottos. Orecchiette with tomato and broccoli di rape; rigatoni under slivers of eggplant, tomato, and grated ricotta cheese; linguine in a meaty lamb ragù with slivers of al dente eggplant: all are delightful. The resilient, nubbly texture of arborio rice and just the right amount of stock make for a memorable risotto of spinach. Shrimp-and-radicchio risotto is buttery and tart at the same time.

Waiters decked out in colorful striped vests are generally

efficient and good-natured, although the kitchen can become bogged down at busy lunch hours. The mostly Italian wine list is priced intelligently to match the food.

Among entrées, you can't go wrong with straightforward fare like brittle, crusted grilled Cornish hen with spinach, zucchini, and potatoes, and grilled lamb chops with an eggplant compote studded with pine nuts. Among seafood dishes, grilled tuna with arugula and oregano vinaigrette is light and pure, better than the bland snapper with caper sauce, and the dry Provençale-style swordfish. Sea bass is done similarly but better, with a sauce of capers, herbs, and tomatoes. It succeeds here because the fish itself is well seasoned and marries nicely with the sauce; in the former the swordfish is bland, the sauce assertive. One of the chef's more interesting creations is breast of duck with a mildly sweet Malvasia wine sauce enhanced with green olives and dates on top.

Gelato—hazelnut and vanilla—is a wonderful punctuation. Lemon tart has a real bite, but I found it cleansing and good. A sweet tooth would be sated by the excellent pecan-loaded caramel tart. Of course, a glass of Malvasia dessert wine is a felicitous ending.

# MAMMA LEONE'S

**POOR**

*261 West 44th Street, 586-5151.*

*Atmosphere: Touristy Neapolitan grotto look. Enormous open room upstairs.*

*Service: Slow and indifferent.*

*Wine: Overpriced Italian list.*

*Price range: Moderately expensive.*

*Credit cards: All major cards.*

*Hours: Breakfast, 5:30 to 10:30 A.M., daily; lunch, 11:30 A.M. to 2:30 P.M., Monday through Saturday; dinner, 4 to*

*11:30 P.M., Monday through Friday, 4 P.M. to midnight, Saturday, 2 to 9 P.M., Sunday.*

*Reservations: Suggested.*

*Wheelchair accessibility: Two flights of stairs to restrooms.*

In 1988 Mamma Leone's moved to 44th Street at Eighth Avenue, four blocks from its former home. For years this six-hundred-seat Neapolitan tourist haunt has been considered little more than a garish sideshow in the Broadway theater district, hardly worth serious scrutiny. Yet so many out-of-towners are lured there by its advertising that I decided to give it a try.

The *Playbill*-toting customers who wander in are met by a host and escorted past white plaster nymphs, leafy grottoes, brick arches, and Chianti-filled wine racks into one of the downstairs dining rooms or upstairs to a sprawling open room overlooking West 44th Street.

Upon being seated you are presented with a platter of Italian breads strewn with cottony cubes of pale tomato and garlic, which they call bruschetta; a rubbery brick of tasteless mozzarella the color of old soap; a dish of olives; slices of pepperoni; and a basket of breadsticks.

As for the service staff, I have had warmer encounters with people serving me traffic summonses. The weary veterans I encountered, all wearing gold badges with their tours of duty—"Mamma Leone's Since 1954"—trudge around their defined stations with the apparent goal of exerting the least possible energy on an eight-hour shift. When I made the unpardonable mistake of asking a waiter assigned to the adjacent territory for a clean fork—mine was smudged and encrusted—he grunted and pointed to another waiter at the far end of the room.

We waited fifteen minutes for a bottle of wine from the arrogantly overpriced list, only to have our waiter plop it down at the table unopened, then disappear—not to fetch a corkscrew, however, but to take a dessert order from another table. Ten minutes later he returned, desserts and corkscrew on his platter. Why make two trips when one will do?

As for the food, it is scarier than anything conjured up at *The Phantom of the Opera* at the Majestic Theater next door. When I asked our waiter what was in the appetizer called stuffed tomato and zucchini, he muttered something incomprehensible, flashed an exasperated look, then finally said, "Bread crumbs, you know, bread crumbs." Bread crumbs they were, over a fibrous halved tomato and a woody hollowed-out zucchini. Stuffed clams had even more bread crumbs, sodden and sticky ones, with barely a hint of clams. Minestrone Leone put canned soup in a favorable light, and sheets of prosciutto did little for a hard, over-chilled, unripe melon.

Forget any of the pastas that come with industrial-grade tomato sauce. One mildly satisfying addition to the updated menu is fettuccine with salsa aurora (tomato, cream, and porcini). Fusilli puttanesca, on the other hand, is a bland and soupy mess. Roasted leg of veal with grilled polenta, for $29.95, features two anemic slices of dry meat lying in a puddle of watery juice, along with a pale yellow slab that tastes like day-old Cream of Wheat.

Roast chicken, for $24.95, arrived looking like one of those shriveled delicatessen birds after about nine hours on the rotisserie—and it tasted even drier. One dish that survived the kitchen relatively undamaged was osso buco, a tender braised veal shank with an inoffensive vegetable sauce. Seafood? Don't even ask.

For dessert, you can attack a wedge of the Sahara called cheesecake or get a sugar rush from an awful rendition of tiramisù. As a final insult, they try to trick tourists into tipping on the tax as well as the food by combining the two on credit-card receipts.

Mamma Leone's is to Italian cuisine what lambada is to classical ballet—but not half as amusing.

# THE MANHATTAN OCEAN CLUB

★

*57 West 58th Street, 371-7777.*

*Atmosphere: Handsome and soothing dining rooms with hand-painted ceramics on display.*

*Service: Competent and genial.*

*Wine: Intelligent list well matched to food at sensible prices.*

*Price range: Moderately expensive.*

*Credit cards: All major cards.*

*Hours: Noon to midnight, Monday through Friday, 5 P.M. to midnight, Saturday and Sunday.*

*Reservations: Recommended.*

*Wheelchair accessibility: Six steps down to the dining section in the bar; restrooms downstairs.*

The name Manhattan Ocean Club summons images of an exclusive wood-paneled enclave festooned with navigational charts and nautical art, where Montauk Magellans repair to sip Scotch and swap sea yarns of high adventure on Long Island Sound. In fact, it is neither a club nor does it look particularly maritime; rather, it is a handsome and sophisticated midtown seafood house where the food, which for years was one notch above galley grub, has been gradually improving.

The main dining room, two flights below street level, is done in unaggressive creams and pastels. Pretty hand-painted reproductions of Picasso ceramics are mounted in the walls behind glass. This clean, tasteful setting is muddled only by the pretentious Doric finials on the building's rectangular support columns—sort of like putting a Rolls-Royce hood on a Volkswagen Beetle. A twisting stairway leads to an upstairs room adorned with Picasso prints.

The Manhattan Ocean Club is owned by Alan Stillman, a restaurateur and wine aficionado who also runs two of the city's most popular steak houses: the Post House and Smith & Wollensky, as well as La Cité, a midtown brasserie. It is no surprise that the wine list is intelligently assembled and fairly priced, especially among domestic selections. The service staff is competent and amicable, although someone should be on hand to offer help with wines.

As for the food, serious piscivores will be pleased with a good deal of the daily catch. A fine way to start is with a creation dubbed tonno con vitello (tuna with veal sauce), a tongue-in-cheek twist on the Italian classic vitello tonnato (veal with tuna sauce). Surprisingly, it works beautifully: a thick rectangle of tuna steak is coated with ground black pepper and seared until blackened outside and sushi-cool in the center. It is garnished with a light veal mousseline seasoned with capers. Clams baked with crushed filberts and pesto are a bore; go instead with the selection of five oysters baked five ways: one with anise-flavored Pernod, others with a sharp curry, a sweet compote of peppers, bright pesto (minus nuts), and oregano.

If you have a yearning for crab cakes, these two hefty patties are better than average and nice and peppery. Clam chowder gets off to a promising start: it smells like the real thing, is nicely seasoned and chunky with potatoes, but, alas, there is little evidence that any clams dropped in for a visit. A special one evening of fettuccine with smoked shrimp and tomatoes sorely needed a boost of salt to bring out the flavors.

Daily fish offerings are highlighted by fish drawings on the menu. You might check the mahi-mahi, a Pacific dolphin fish with a meaty mild flavor, delicious with a glaze of citrus butter and crispy spaetzle. Tuna steak is charred outside and rare within, brightened with a tomato-and-mint vinaigrette, and farm-raised striped bass is enhanced by a basting of soy sauce, ginger, and garlic. Halibut is cooked to a turn, too, ringed with an excellent beurre-blanc sauce enriched with fish stock and garnished with crushed tomatoes. The shoestring potatoes could become addictive; unseasoned sautéed spinach, on the other hand, should be eaten only because it's good for you.

On the negative side are a flaccid sautéed Dover sole that had been out of the English Channel a day or so too long, dried-out swordfish au poivre, and heavy, overly breaded soft-shell crabs with Brazil-nut butter. Most vegetables come à la carte.

Desserts, like everything else here, are copious. A condominium of puff pastry is mortared with light chocolate mousse and banana slices, all in a pool of dry-edged chocolate sauce. Plum cake tasted rancid one evening—I couldn't force myself to try it again. I can recommend the nutty crusted raspberry-and-peach torte as well as the house special chocolate basket, a little shopping bag of molded chocolate filled with white chocolate mousse and surrounded with strawberry sauce. A triple-header dessert combines beguiling pot de crème, grainy crème brûlée, and ripe raspberry mousse.

# MARIE-MICHELLE

★ ★

*57 West 56th Street, 315-2444.*

*Atmosphere: Contemporary and comfortable, with Art Deco touches.*

*Service: Pleasant and efficient.*

*Wine: Modest selection; fair prices.*

*Price range: Moderately expensive (pretheater dinner prix fixe, $29.50).*

*Credit cards: All major cards.*

*Hours: Lunch, noon to 3:30 P.M., Monday through Friday; pretheater dinner, 5:30 to 6:30 P.M., daily; dinner, 5:30 to 11 P.M., daily. (Free parking after 5:30 P.M.)*

*Reservations: Suggested.*

*Wheelchair accessibility: Several steps at the entrance. All other facilities on the same level.*

Marie-Michelle is an urbane and comfortable spot, done in shades of rust and dusty rose with a smoky mirrored wall on one side and gentle lighting. Villeroy and Boch china in a spiffy Art Deco pattern and pretty flower clusters around the room contribute to the polished scene.

The eponymous owner is a kinetic, sophisticated hostess who in 1987 took over a compact Continental restaurant on West 56th Street, stenciled her name on the front door, and began charming the midtown business crowd with her magnetic personality and pleasing French fare.

The food is generally light and well seasoned. My last lunch there began with shrimp over steamed spinach leaves in a nice shellfish-stock sauce. Artichoke and crabmeat salad came with an overpowering sesame dressing, and the salad was too cold. Whether or not Ms. Rey suggests the appetizer called plateau du pecheur, or seafood plate, I suggest you try it; it's a tasting plate of excellent icy Belon oysters, cherrystone clams on the half shell, marinated sea scallops, and lustrous gravlax with anise sauce. Lean, tasty duck terrine is cushioned on rich-flavored aspic. I have always felt that such prissy preparations as asparagus in a dome of puff pastry with lemon-butter sauce were gilding the lily; the ingredients here are good, although I would prefer more asparagus and less fluff.

Among main courses the kitchen turns out a succulent roast chicken in pan juices with dauphinoise potatoes and simple lamb chops accented with a whiff of thyme. Among seafood dishes, the rule of thumb is the simpler the better. Dover sole meunière is nicely done, served with diced tomatoes, carrots, and broccoli. Steamed snapper over leeks and cubed potatoes came in an overly citric sauce. Norwegian salmon in a clean, light Beaujolais sauce is a winner, as is baby salmon with a lemony butter sauce cut with capers.

Ms. Rey, who orbits the room fielding questions and making suggestions, some of which have already been made by her well-trained service staff, creates a lively and sociable scene. Her wine list lacks the muscle to support the diverse menu, although a cadre of French standards are available at fair prices.

Desserts hold their own in this impressive lineup. Crème brûlée is thicker than most versions but delicious under a burnished sugar crust, fruit tarts are beautifully presented and delicate, and sorbets (especially cassis and passion fruit) are refreshing and ripe. Don't miss the apple napoleon, a caramel-varnished lid of brittle pastry over apple slices and pastry cream garnished by puffs of whipped cream holding mint leaves.

# MAXIM'S

★ ★

*680 Madison Avenue, at 61st Street, 751-5111.*

*Atmosphere: Lavish belle époque dining rooms with bucolic murals, stained glass, and ornate woodwork. Live music nightly. Black tie required for men on Saturday.*

*Service: Excellent.*

*Wine: Top heavy with prestigious, expensive labels.*

*Price range: Expensive.*

*Credit cards: All major cards.*

*Hours: Dinner, 6 to 11 P.M., Tuesday through Saturday. Music begins at 7 P.M., dancing at 9.*

*Reservations: Necessary.*

*Wheelchair accessibility: Elevator to dining room; two steps to restrooms.*

Since opening in late 1985, Maxim's, a clone of Paris's legendary nightspot, has had a rough time. This extravagant French dowager fluttered into town amid much fanfare only to find few courters along the boulevard Madison. High prices, a haughty image, and heavy, outmoded French food conspired to make Maxim's one of the prettiest empty dining rooms in New York.

A thriving banquet operation kept it going while management changed strategies. Just as it seemed that Pierre Cardin, the owner, might be forced to design a leisure line for Caldor to keep his restaurant afloat, Maxim's came to life. A total revamping of the menu under a new chef, Marc Poidevin, formerly of Le Cirque, worked wonders. Add to that the stunning desserts by the pastry chef, Jean-Marc Burillier, excellent service, and nightly dance music, and Maxim's has become a contender in this competitive East Side neighborhood. In mid-1990 Mr. Poidevin and Mr. Burillier left to take jobs at Tavern on the Green. Maxim's then recruited David Ruggiero from La Caravelle. Thus, some of the menu is in transition.

The multilevel dining rooms shine with burnished rosewood walls adorned with vines of hammered brass, elaborate wall moldings, sylvan murals, stained glass, plush banquettes, and tables holding pink roses.

You can start with something as simple as frothy butternut squash soup enriched with duck confit and wild mushrooms, or a superbly subtle terrine of duck foie gras infused with port wine. Tuna carpaccio, which has become as common as bottled water, is so attractively presented it takes on another dimension: the glistening sheet of fresh tuna is garnished with asparagus spears, colorful salad greens, fresh herbs, and caviar.

Maxim's wine list is top heavy with prestigious high-priced wines, although there are some relative values to be had.

Among the best seafood dishes is braised red snapper over a thick slice of fennel, which imparts a faint anise flavor to the flesh. It is served with golden celery chips and a light star-anise sauce spiked with Pernod. A close second is the buttery salmon in a balsamic-vinegar sauce with braised endives and lima beans.

Lobster could not be fresher or more skillfully cooked, decorated with fried laces of ginger and roasted garlic cloves. It is set over a slightly sweet creole sauce made with reduced tropical fruits, vanilla, and rum combined with a packet of spinach holding lentils. Veal chop can be leathery tough, so I suggest you go with the delicious roast baby chicken aromatic of fresh tarragon and flanked with pearl onions, braised endive, and a square of grilled foie gras, or grilled baby lamb chops with tomatoes and zucchini slices over eggplant caviar.

Unless you have an iron will when it comes to the waistline, it would be best to stay on the dance floor when the dessert cart rolls around. Warm apple charlotte with a bitter almond flavor is sublime, as is the buttery chestnut mousse (although I did not detect any of the promised bourbon sauce). Sorbets (lemon, raspberry, and mango) are bright and intense. Frozen lemongrass parfait lacked the exotic flavor of lemongrass, although it tasted like a good lime mousse. One of the more unusual selections is the Curaçao chocolate layer cake with semisweet orange sauce, a lovely match.

About 11 P.M., the lights go down, the combo heats up, and turn-of-the-century Paris comes alive. Maxim's is very expensive (count on $80 to $100 a person with wine), but with so few places around where couples can dance and find food this appealing, it is worth noting.

# MEMPHIS

**SATISFACTORY**

*329 Columbus Avenue, between 75th and 76th streets, 496-1840.*

*Atmosphere: Towering postmodern café; shatteringly loud.*

*Service: Casual, pleasant, able.*

*Price range: Moderately expensive.*

*Credit cards: American Express, MasterCard, and Visa.*

*Hours: Dinner, 6 to 11 P.M., Monday through Thursday, 6 to 11:30 P.M., Friday and Saturday, 6 to 10 P.M., Sunday; late night menu, lighter fare, 11:30 to 1:30 A.M., Friday and Saturday.*

*Reservations: Suggested.*

*Wheelchair accessibility: Dining room on ground level; restrooms downstairs.*

How a Louisiana Creole-Cajun restaurant came to be called Memphis is only the first of many puzzling aspects of this popular and shatteringly loud Upper West Side dining spot. You would do well to memorize the exact address before going, for there is no sign on the smoky glass exterior (chic perhaps, but supercilious). Inside you encounter a crepuscular, postmodern echo chamber of bare cement walls, palm trees, decorative columns, glass-brick windows, and closely arranged tables: the overall effect is dramatic by night, but in blazing daylight it would probably resemble a futuristic gas station.

The food is baffling, too. Quality ingredients are used, and a sincere effort is evident, but somehow the majority of dishes would be unrecognizable to anyone who has spent a weekend in New Orleans. The major problem is sweetness, which is pervasive: in salads, soups, and sauces.

The sugar assault begins with the gumbo, a faintly piquant swamp of crabmeat, shrimp, andouille sausage, and crayfish. Ravioli filled with smoked duck is mired in a gluey tarragon-cream sauce that is likewise blasted with sugar. Crab cakes are one of the safer starters, mildly spicy and light, accompanied by a green salad drenched in sweet dressing. The best appetizers sampled were two soups: a rich and smoky corn-and-shrimp chowder, and a strange-sounding but surprisingly harmonious duck-and-crayfish chowder stoked with cayenne.

The road to satisfaction among entrées bypasses the bayou and heads straight into Middle America: a rack of lamb swabbed with Chinese mustard and sautéed turnips is fine; grilled swordfish with tarragon beurre blanc, new potatoes, and a corn-and-okra side dish called maque chow is pleasing, too.

The trip gets a little risky when you head south. The New Orleans barbecued shrimp come piled high atop scallion-flecked rice, under brittle shards of bay leaf and enough acrid filé powder to season the Mississippi. The shrimp on the seafood sampler plate is boiled in a good spicy broth and comes with a meaty crab cake, flabby overcooked crayfish, and a chilled half lobster.

Rounding out this Tennessee-Louisiana joy ride is a dish called roasted and grilled duckling, a nicely cooked, lean and moist specimen assaulted with a dark rum and plantain sauce that is both sweet and harsh at the same time. It came with a red-beans-and-rice side dish and pickled okra. The unfussy Southern fried chicken with mashed potatoes is preferable to the bland roasted free-range chicken served with a jalapeño corn-bread stuffing.

Desserts are by far the best course. Pecan pie is an unqualified winner, with a crust of crunchy toasted pecans and a light filling that is (amazingly) not too sweet. Chocolate cake is hauntingly rich with a lingering afterglow, and the apple-and-cranberry bread pudding is absolutely addictive.

# MEZZOGIORNO

★ ★

*195 Spring Street, 334-2112.*

*Atmosphere: Playful trattoria with long marble-topped bar and café tables.*

*Service: Excellent and genial young staff.*

*Wine: Italian list well matched to food, reasonably priced.*

*Price range: Moderate.*

*Credit cards: None.*

*Hours: Lunch, noon to 3 P.M., Monday through Friday; dinner, 6 P.M. to 1 A.M., Monday through Friday; open noon to 1 A.M., Saturday and Sunday. Pizza served noon to 4 P.M. and 10 P.M. to 1 A.M.*

*Reservations: Recommended.*

*Wheelchair accessibility: Everything on one level.*

Mezzogiorno is typical of the new breed of buoyant northern Italian trattorias that have been sprouting all over New York—only here, the food is considerably better than most.

You encounter a long marble-topped bar at the entrance flanked by café tables along the white-paned windows (for smokers); the playful back room has a long tan banquette along one wall and tables surrounding a faux marble column. Nearby, behind the bar, is a giant ceramic mask whose mouth is the opening for the pizza oven. The walls are full of glass-covered boxes holding bizarre three-dimensional collages. Music and conversation ricochet off all the hard surfaces, so when the place fills up it can be clamorous.

The food, fortunately, is more disciplined than the art. All eleven meat carpaccios can be highly recommended. Among my favorites are the cold beef version scattered with crunchy shards of raw artichoke hearts and slivers of sharp Parmesan cheese, all speckled with good olive oil and black pepper. The one seafood carpaccio offered on the regular menu, made with swordfish, had a mealy texture.

Arresting appetizers include a light and crumbly flan made with ricotta cheese set in a shredded-lettuce sauce brightened with lemon, and bresaola, diaphanous slices of dry salted beef, layered over lamb's-lettuce salad and morsels of creamy goat cheese. Risotto is unusual but delicious. The rice is cooked with a potent dose of saffron, cooled, then molded into pancakes and sautéed until lightly charred on the bottom.

Salads can be ordered as starters or main courses. They are excellent, from the curly endive with pancetta and a poached egg (a nice Sunday brunch) to shrimp with slivers of zucchini sautéed in olive oil.

The young Italian waiters in their jaunty yellow-striped shirts and blue aprons are the type of easygoing professionals you rarely find on this side of the Atlantic. They exude a passion for the food and pride in their métier that is contagious. The wines are well matched to the food, starting with refreshing northern Italian whites in the $20-to-$30 range.

Beguiling pastas include orecchiette, "little ears" in Italian, with sausage and batons of fennel in a light tomato sauce; fazzoletti (folded thin sheets) with wild mushrooms; and tagliolini with shrimp, arugula, and tomato. The only letdown was gummy black linguine, made with squid's ink, in a hot-pepper-and-tomato sauce.

Four or five specials are offered daily. Pink-tinted gnocchi, made with potato and tomato, are supple and light, bathed in fresh tomato sauce and garnished with shredded basil. Lasagna is compelling, too, sheets of al dente pasta holding cubed eggplant and tomatoes, bound with a cheesy white sauce.

The pizza chef tends the wood oven at lunch and after 10 P.M. The thin crusts are nicely charred, with toppings ranging from potato and sun-dried tomato to pancetta and onion, mixed vegetables and wild mushrooms.

Dozens of Italian restaurants make the dessert of ladyfingers and sweetened mascarpone cheese called tiramisù, but Mezzogiorno's is one of the best. Other happy endings are the faintly chewy hazelnut-and-chocolate torte with intense vanilla ice cream, and assorted fruit under a foamy avalanche of zabaglione that has been passed under the broiler until browned and bubbling. A fine selection of Italian dessert wines and grappas are offered by the glass.

# MICHAEL'S

★ ★

*24 West 55th Street, 767-0555.*

*Atmosphere: Cheerful, sunny room with well-spaced tables, fine contemporary artwork, and good noise control.*

*Service: Casual and familiar, but vigilant.*

*Wine: Well-chosen selection, especially among California labels, with average prices.*

*Price range: Moderately expensive.*

*Credit cards: All major cards.*

*Hours: Brunch, 11:30 A.M. to 3 P.M., Saturday and Sunday; lunch, noon to 2:30 P.M., Monday through Friday; dinner, 6 to 11:30 P.M., daily.*

*Reservations: Necessary.*

*Wheelchair accessibility: Several steps down to dining level from entrance. Restrooms near entrance.*

The eponymous Michael McCarty made his mark in the seminal days of California cooking with Michael's in Santa Monica. In the last year, he has packed up his arugula and hit the road, opening restaurants called Adirondacks in Denver and Washington.

In Manhattan he has taken over the site of the long-somnolent Italian Pavilion and turned it into a bright and cheerful setting. Heavy drapery was torn down to allow sunlight in from street-level windows and from a courtyard in back. Eggshell-toned walls are adorned with a heady collection of contemporary art from the likes of Jasper Johns. Tables are well spaced, and noise rarely seems intrusive even when the room is full. Mr. McCarty, donning boxy designer suits, his hair slicked back as if he has just dashed out of the surf, is a relentlessly chatty host. He likes to hold your shoulder while talking to you.

It's easy for know-it-all New Yorkers to make fun of the affectations at Michael's—the menu, for example, which reads like a Rand McNally Road Atlas ("Chicago sweetbreads" and "San Fernando Valley greens")—but behind the pretension is a serious, disciplined kitchen.

There is no shortage of roughage among starters. Among the serendipitous combinations are the curly endive with crisp nuggets of Iowa bacon in a mustard-chive vinaigrette, and goat cheese with radicchio, Belgian endive, and watercress with a subtle walnut-oil vinaigrette. Grilling is done with finesse. Grilled quails are nicely charred along with sweet-onion confit, wild rice, string beans, and (pale) tomatoes. Little rare-grilled fillets of lamb are excellent with the same supporting cast.

The best pasta appetizer is a pristine assembly of fettuccine with batons of grilled salmon, tomatoes, Parmesan, garlic, and top-grade olive oil; the same pasta with prosciutto, Parmesan, pecorino, tomatoes, and basil has a complex flavor from the interplay of cheeses, but it was oversauced and too heavy for an appetizer.

Michael's has assembled a diverse playground for wine buffs, especially fans of California labels. Prices are not out of line, considering the quality.

If I were to return to Michael's without my reviewer's cap, my top choice among entrées would be the least elaborate: perfectly grilled chicken with tarragon butter and a stack of brittle, firm french fries; beefy dry-aged prime steak with the same potatoes; or classic sautéed sweetbreads with lemon, capers, and parsley.

Grilled duck, rare in the center and deliciously blackened outside, is enhanced by a rich stock sweetened with Grand Marnier; squab, cooked the same way, comes in a fruity yet tart-edged pinot noir sauce (without evidence of the promised ginger, though); and extraordinarily tender seared lamb is perfumed with a cognac-lamb stock and black truffles. Two reliable seafood choices are moist swordfish with tomatoes and basil beurre blanc, and big, pearly sea scallops sharpened with watercress and surrounded by squiggles of lean bacon.

If you want a real California experience for dessert, dare to try the Heath Bar torte: layers of caramel custard, caramel mousse, and caramel with a bittersweet icing. It sounds appalling, but it's terrific: not nearly as cloying as expected. Custard with blackberries was nondescript, but most fruit tortes and the tarte Tatin are superior.

# MICKEY MANTLE'S

**SATISFACTORY**

*42 Central Park South, 688-7777.*

*Atmosphere: Contemporary, blond-wood sports bar; back room more tranquil.*

*Service: Friendly and eager.*

*Wine: Small list, but exceptionally well chosen and moderately priced.*

*Price range: Moderate.*

*Credit cards: All major cards.*

*Hours: Serves same menu from noon to midnight (kitchen closed from 4 to 5:30 P.M.), Monday through Saturday, until 11 P.M., Sunday.*

*Reservations: Suggested.*

*Wheelchair accessibility: Special access doors available (call ahead) to back dining room; restrooms on same level.*

What could be more wholesome and all-American than a restaurant named after old No. 7, the booming Bronx Bomber himself, Mickey Mantle? This is a fun place for children, with its lively, action-packed ambiance, friendly and gregarious service, and familiar (although uneven) food. To the average wide-eyed ten-year-old, Mickey Mantle is probably some vague Hall of Fame icon as remote as Ty Cobb, but that's not important, for the delicious scent of cowhide and freshly mowed outfields clings to this place, and the effect on children is magical.

The contemporary and informal space, with a big bar up front overlooking Central Park South, is filled with sports memorabilia, including the uniforms of Mantle, Babe Ruth, and Joe DiMaggio; autographed photos; paintings; posters; and even nonstop videos replaying old World Series film and interviews with Mantle. The main-level dining room has soft pillow-lined booths and bare pine tables; a step-down back room is more tranquil, removed from the cacophonous bar. Young, bouncy waiters and waitresses, wearing floppy baseball shirts, are enthusiastic as a Little Leaguer on opening day.

The food can be satisfying, but you have to know your way around the ball park. Recommended starters include the crisp, golden calamari rings with spicy red sauce; smoked trout with horseradish cream; or one of the soups: French onion or, if available, the chunky and flavorful turkey gumbo. Caesar salad is made far in advance and contains soggy croutons, and crab cakes are nondescript, garnished with over-the-hill tomatoes.

One welcome feature at Mickey Mantle's is a children's menu, offering lower-priced, smaller-portioned entrées. Hamburgers are superior, lean and juicy, although french fries are sometimes soggy. Southern-fried chicken fingers with creamy mashed potatoes are sure to please little sluggers. One of the best dishes, available in children's and adult portions, is the chicken potpie, replete with chunks of fresh chicken, carrots, peas, and okra.

Meats from the hickory smoker tend to be overwhelming, so smoky as to obscure the flavor of the ingredients. I have had little luck with pasta here, whether it is the bland fusilli with olive oil, garlic, and basil, or the humdrum seafood pasta with a tomato cream sauce. Stick with all-American food, like the soothing pot roast with pan gravy and buttered noodles, or the rare-grilled loin of lamb with eggplant and black-eyed-pea relish.

Youngsters will like the commercial-tasting, sugary apple pie, or the Key lime pie with a texture suitable for caulking windows, but adults are advised to have either ice cream, brownies, or an old-fashioned hot fudge sundae.

# MITSUKOSHI

★ ★

*461 Park Avenue, at 57th Street, 935-6444.*

*Atmosphere: Main room harshly lighted, smaller room more comfortable. Tatami rooms tranquil and elegant.*

*Service: Charming and well meaning if occasionally hampered by overburdened kitchen.*

*Price range: Expensive.*

*Hours: Lunch, noon to 2 P.M., Monday through Saturday; dinner, 6 to 10 A.M., Monday through Saturday.*

*Credit Cards: All major cards.*

*Reservations: Recommended; necessary at lunch.*

*Wheelchair accessibility: Elevator to below-ground dining room, restrooms on dining room level.*

A Japanese proverb says that if you enjoy a food you have never had before, your life will be lengthened by seventy-five days. By frequenting the gleaming sushi bar at Mitsukoshi, an elegant (and expensive) Japanese restaurant on Park Avenue at 57th Street, an adventurous eater could probably rack up a few extra seasons in the Hamptons. Not so in the dining rooms, however, which feature mostly familiar—though generally superior quality—fare.

Mitsukoshi runs on overdrive at lunch as Japanese and American executives swarm in for a quick meal. The evening is more tranquil—so much so that customers are discouraged from coming in later than 8:30 P.M., presumably so the staff can head home early. Aside from the sushi bar, which is often full, especially at lunch, there are three dining areas. The overilluminated main room has garish gold fabric wallpaper and Lucite chandeliers. I prefer the more tranquil ambiance in a nook between the stairs and the bar. Handsome tatami rooms accommodate four to twenty diners.

In the main dining room, traditionally garbed waitresses could not be more charming or patient, although service can be slow at peak lunch hours. A good way to start is with the sushi assortment. The seafood is unfailingly fresh, although I have invariably found that food at lunch is brighter and prepared with more care.

The sushi assortment may include lightly smoked salmon, fresh salmon, tuna, yellowtail, and fluke. If you are a fan of sea urchin, called uni, it should not be missed here. The orange roe arrives chilled and glistening in a seaweed roll. Its oceanic flavor refreshes and delights. Sashimi has a similar cast of characters, perhaps with some mackerel or toro (tuna belly, which has a richer texture). The selection at the sushi bar is far greater, depending on daily specials. I have had some superb sea eel (anago), octopus (tako), and scallops (hotategai) in recent visits.

Negimaki, the grilled sheets of beef rolled around scallions and served with teriyaki sauce, is particularly well prepared here: the meat is succulent, tender, and cooked rare. Two other good choices are the deep-fried tofu with tempura sauce and the exceptionally clean and light tempura of shrimp and vegetables, which comes with a tangy ginger dipping sauce.

A diverting communal main course is shabu shabu, which is excellent here. A caldron of simmering broth is heated at the table and diners cook their own food. The colorful selection includes deliciously marbled slices of beef, Chinese cabbage, mushrooms, spinach tofu, scallions, carrots, and rice noodles. It comes with two sauces, one a lemon-and-soy combination, the other sesame and soy. Several entrées that I used to like here are disappointing now. Filet mignon, this time unseasoned and pale in flavor, arrives on a sizzling black platter along with broccoli, carrots, onions, and cauliflower. Another, toban-yaki, which was fresh and deftly cooked the last time we had it, now is an austere assortment of grilled salmon, scallops, shrimp, and Alaskan King crab.

Ice cream here is terrific, especially the sharp and creamy ginger. Runners up were potent green tea and red bean. The fresh fruit assortment is generous but so cold we had to wait fifteen minutes to eat it.

# MON CHER TON TON (FRENCH)

**SATISFACTORY**

*68 East 56th Street, 223-7575.*

*Atmosphere: Plush and comfortable room, with low noise level.*

*Service: Well-meaning, professional staff, seemingly hampered by a slow kitchen.*

*Wine: Extensive but expensive list focusing on California and France.*

*Price range: Expensive.*

*Credit cards: All major cards.*

*Hours: Lunch, noon to 2:30 P.M., Monday through Friday; dinner, 5:30 to 10 P.M., Monday through Saturday.*

*Reservations: Suggested.*

*Wheelchair accessibility: Entrance ramp. Two steps up to dining room. Restrooms on main level.*

There is a good deal of Japanophobia around town these day as nothing seems safe from the voracious yen, including real estate, banks, motion-picture companies, and even cultural icons like Rockefeller Center. It was no surprise, then, that one of the most lavish and expensive new restaurants to open in 1989 was Japanese-owned: Mon Cher Ton Ton, on East 56th Street.

Actually, it is two restaurants under the same roof, one French, the other a Japanese grill. Visits to the former suggest that the Japanese find interpreting French cuisine more challenging than shrinking microchips. In late 1989 the restaurant hired as a consultant Marc Meneau, the chef and owner of a three-star restaurant in Burgundy. The menu should be changing dramatically.

Mon Cher Ton Ton (a play on a French child's expression for "My Dear Uncle") is part of a Japan-based restaurant chain that also owns Seryna on East 53rd Street. The French dining room is spacious, softly upholstered, and serene, with dark blue rugs, deep armchairs, high-backed fabric-covered banquettes, and hurricane lamps casting gentle light. It is a fine setting for a business lunch or an intimate dinner. The only startling design element is a pair of bizarre wall sculptures of broken colored glass and floating gold bars that could be a high-school science project depicting what drugs can do to your brain cells.

The menu is conceptually fuzzy and unevenly executed. The cooking is not really a synthesis of the two cuisines, but rather a patchwork of French and Japanese creations assembled in no particular order.

Starting in the Eastern Hemisphere, there is a cold crabmeat-and-avocado ravioli that is essentially a gussied-up Chinese dumpling with little flavor. The assortment of glistening sashimi is appealing, as is a pretty lobster salad formed into a mountain peak with grated radish, zucchini, asparagus, and ribbons of cucumber in a sprightly vinaigrette. Moving westward, there is an insipid combination of angel-hair pasta tossed in a light sesame-soy dressing garnished with shrimp tempura, and richly marbled beef carpaccio that arrives half frozen. Tartar of tuna is unassailably fresh and garnished with sevruga caviar.

One of the more daring starters is sautéed halibut steak with a layer of foie gras in the center, a marriage that seemed risky, to say the least. Surprisingly, the flavors and textures harmonize, the sliver of foie gras adding richness and a touch of sweetness to the neutral-tasting halibut. A light chervil vinaigrette with bits of tomato and capers provides a unifying touch of salt.

The laggard pace of service can be irksome. Waits between courses are aggravatingly long. Since the well-meaning service staff seemed as exasperated as we were about it, the kitchen may have been at fault. The wine list, well represented in California and France, is priced high across the board. For the best buys, look to the Loire selections among whites and to West Coast merlots in reds.

Several main-course dishes are worth trying. A pink fillet of salmon comes under balloons of puff pastry with a mild mustard sauce along with leeks and spinach; crisp-sautéed red snapper is done to perfection, too, glossed with olive oil and basil and served with a tangle of deep-fried turnips and carrots. A tempura of sea bass is not as alluring, for its green-peppercorn sauce is paltry and the deep-fried vegetables are redundant. It comes with a nice sweet-corn flan on the side. One of the best entrées is rosy loin of lamb fanned over sautéed zucchini and shredded potatoes, even if the promised tarragon is missing from the lamb. You can order fish simply grilled with tempura of vegetables.

Desserts are nothing out of the ordinary: poached pear with vanilla ice cream, orange sorbet on a tuile cookie, and a ring of white chocolate around a rich dark chocolate mousse center that is inexplicably called chocolate cake. Ice creams are the best bet, particularly the intense praline.

# MON CHER TON TON (JAPANESE)

★ ★

*68 East 56th Stret, 223-7575.*

*Atmosphere: Cozy individual rooms with private grills; large dining bar.*

*Service: Attentive and personal.*

*Wine: Same as in French room (see review above).*

*Price range: Expensive.*

*Credit cards: All major cards.*

*Hours: Lunch, noon to 2:30 P.M., Monday through Friday; dinner, 5:30 to 10 P.M., Monday through Saturday.*

*Reservations: Suggested, particularly at lunch.*

*Wheelchair accessibility: Entrance ramp. Dining room and restrooms on main level.*

The Japanese dining room at Mon Cher Ton Ton is sort of a Benihana for the expense-account crowd: urbane, opulent, and minus all that silly pseudoceremonial knife slashing. Meals are cooked in front of customers on gleaming stainless-steel burners by individual chefs. The Japanese staff here is understandably more self-assured in this setting than in the French restaurant, and while the menu is exceedingly simple, attention to quality ingredients is obvious.

The dining room is divided into rooms for four to eight people by tall teak posts reminiscent of cactuses—don't ask me to explain that theme—each with its own grill. The overhead exhaust fans are strong enough to suck up a toupee, but you'll be grateful for them when the sizzling begins. In the front of the room is a sixteen-seat marble counter attached to a wide grill. This is a good place to drop in for a quick, casual lunch.

Seafood is exhilaratingly fresh, whether it is the tartar of tuna with caviar (the same appetizer offered in the French restaurant) or the rich, ruddy marinated salmon in a sparkling rice-vinegar-and-herb vinaigrette. Crabmeat-and-avocado salad is pure and refreshing, as is the glistening salad of halibut sashimi over curled ribbons of cucumber and laces of celery with mustard vinaigrette.

Beautiful Japanese ceramics add to the stunning presentations. Another visual knockout is a ring of lightly browned scallops under ribbons of zucchini, cucumber, and carrots, with a drizzling of rice-wine-vinegar sauce and a dollop of intense sea-urchin roe. The lobster-filled vegetable terrine is well seasoned and fresh, but served too cold.

This is not a place to discuss confidential business transactions or have a discreet romantic meal, for the staff is always next to you either cooking or clearing. A demure woman in a crisp white outfit and chef's toque prepared our entrées with little conversation or fanfare. Seafood is cooked on the grill with some safflower oil and finished with butter, shallots, and white wine. Fillet of salmon is delicious, seasoned with salt and pepper, seared on the hot grill, and laced with a lemon-butter white-wine sauce. Red snapper is excellent, too.

Among meat entrées, sirloin of beef for two is tender and tasty, though not well charred the way a steakhouse serves it, and accompanied by a mild chili sauce. Many entrées come with a bright mélange of bean sprouts, zucchini, and lettuce cooked on the grill. Small, pink lamp chops are similarly good, served with fat cracklings that are irresistible.

Desserts are similar to those served in the French room. The apple tart here is better than anything I had next door, deliciously ripe and with a fragile crust. A combination mousse—half lemon, half cassis—is pleasing with a puddle of crème anglaise, as are assorted ice creams.

# MONTRACHET

★ ★ ★

*239 West Broadway, between White and Beach streets, 219-2777.*

*Atmosphere: Spare but comfortable and unpretentious.*

*Service: Amicable and efficient.*

*Wine: Superior selection with many unusual regional wines from France; good prices.*

*Price range: Moderately expensive (prix-fixe dinners $25, $29, and $45).*

*Credit cards: American Express.*

*Hours: Lunch, noon to 3 P.M., Friday; dinner, 6 to 11 P.M., Monday through Saturday.*

*Reservations: Necessary on weekends.*

*Wheelchair accessibility: Everything on one level.*

Montrachet's unpretentious style, excellent Provençale food, and modest prices make it well worth a trip from anywhere in town. The current chef, Debra Ponzek, is finally gaining the recognition that is her due.

You don't go to Montrachet to be wowed by the latest Adam Tihany boffo interior design. It's a comfortable but somewhat stark space in a former industrial loft. The smaller front dining room, dominated by a polished mahogany-and-onyx bar, has pale aqua-gray walls, rust banquettes, and closely clustered tables. A back room is more spacious.

Like her predecessors in the kitchen, Ms. Ponzek has a light touch and symphonic sense of seasoning. In the Provençale tradition, fresh herbs, olive oil, and refined stocks are favored over butter and cream. The seasonal menu, carrying about ten entrées, is supplemented by plenty of inventive specials. One example was a starter of angulas, the tiny, spaghetti-thin eels from Spain. Simply marinated in a garlic-and-olive-oil vinaigrette and served over a fresh artichoke heart, they are wonderful. A vivid summer appetizer is the layered terrine of red peppers, eggplant, zucchini, goat cheese, and spinach enveloped in strands of fettuccinelike pasta, enhanced by a warm dill-scented tomato sauce. Fans of the classic Provençale soup called pistou (the term actually comes from Italian cooking and translates as pounded basil) will swoon over the rendition here, a richly flavored broth explosive with basil essence and replete with firm-poached string beans, white beans, carrots, and other vegetables.

Other highly recommended starters include the salad of roasted thyme-perfumed squab breast with garlic and lentils, superb sautéed foie gras paired with sweet glazed shallots and wild mushrooms, and a beguiling bouillabaisselike shellfish mélage—lobster, baby clams, mussels—in a tarragon-scented broth with fennel and leeks.

The waiters, wearing black pants and black shirts (all they need are stockings over their faces to complete the cat-burglar outfit), are a bright, informed bunch. It's not easy to keep up with the kinetic owner, Drew Nieporent, but they make a valiant effort. The wine list is a little jewel, not voluminous, but lovingly chosen and fairly priced. Daniel Johnnes, the sommelier, always has a few surprises up his sleeve for those who express curiosity.

If I had to pick a favorite dish from the alluring repertory, it would be the sheer sheets of salmon fillet draped over a sward of lentils flavored with bacon and red wine. The salmon is seared for less than a minute under the broiler—so it nearly melts into the lentils—then garnished with fresh chervil. Right up there, too, are succulent thyme-seasoned loin of lamb with vegetable-flecked couscous and the extraordinarily moist roast chicken with pan juices, surrounded by whole garlic cloves and mashed potatoes that could bring nostalgic tears to your eyes.

Another winning dish is snowy red-snapper fillet with roasted red peppers, spinach, and asparagus in a pool of lemon-brightened fish broth. Black sea bass with a saffron vinaigrette and a colorful palette of summer vegetables could have used a touch more in the seasoning department.

It's hard to resist the waiter's seductive description of the house signature dessert: two individual soufflés, one with raspberries, the other chocolate with raspberry sauce and vanilla ice cream. Give in. They are worth it.

# MORTIMER'S

**SATISFACTORY**

*1057 Lexington Avenue, at 75th Street, 517-6400.*

*Atmosphere: Dark, candlelit, brick-walled tavern feeling.*

*Service: Uneven. Better in main room than annex.*

*Wine: Short, mundane list with good prices.*

*Price range: Moderately expensive.*

*Credit cards: All major cards.*

*Hours: Brunch, 12:15 to 4:30 P.M., Saturday and Sunday; lunch, noon to 3:30 P.M., Monday through Friday; dinner, 6 P.M. to midnight, daily.*

*Reservations: Necessary for parties of five or more only.*

*Wheelchair accessibility: Everything on ground level.*

In Tom Wolfe's *Bonfire of the Vanities*, there is a clubby, bibulous East Side restaurant where a booze-soaked journalist hangs out and mooches free meals from celebrity-struck acquaintances. He has a particular fondness for the paillard of chicken. These scenes leapt to mind upon entering the dark, cool dining room at Mortimer's. If this is indeed the model for the book, I would change only one detail: the journalist should have ordered rack of lamb.

There are really two Mortimer's. One is for the well-connected regulars, a very East Side, very Hamptons clique, who are embraced warmly and cosseted by the suave owner, Glenn Bernbaum. Then there is the Mortimer's for everybody else. If my three visits were typical, unrecognized walk-ins can expect a greeting normally accorded bill collectors.

Chances are that unknowns will be dispatched to a table in a side room where regulars would no sooner dine than they would atop a cardboard box on Lexington Avenue. There is nothing wrong with the pleasant side room, and indeed, regular customers rightfully deserve the best tables in the main area. It's just that considering the inattention given to walk-ins, and the country-club quality of the food, it's difficult to recommend Mortimer's.

The main room, flanked by a long busy bar, resembles a classy tavern, with brick walls, gas lanterns, wood floors, and candlelight. The side room, with its own small bar, is similar but more subdued.

The menu is as timeless and undemanding as a Disney movie. You can start with good gravlax aromatic of dill, with brioche; a sweetish chicken-liver terrine, or too-lemony Caesar salad. Artichoke vinaigrette is fine, but one soup sampled, vichyssoise, was watery and dull. Waiters, who scurry about in floor-length white aprons, range from amiable and hard working in the main room to amiable and slack in the side room, forgetting tableware, wine, water, and dessert menus.

Regulars probably know that red meat is the safest route among entrées. The rack of lamb with a rich stock-based sauce, crispy shallots (several burned), and broiled tomato was cooked to order and well seasoned; entrecôte could not be faulted, served with greaseless matchstick potatoes and a good béarnaise sauce. A special on one evening, old-fashioned beef stew with carrots and peas, was solidly satisfying. So, too, was the simple grilled chicken. I can't say the same for the dry veal Milanese with nutmeg-blasted spinach, and a superficially spicy but intrinsically bland chicken curry. Mortimer's is not for wine aficionados: the list is short and commonplace, although it is fairly priced.

Among seafood offerings, fat little crab cakes were nicely done and served with sprightly fresh coleslaw. Dover sole, requested on the bone, was served filleted, and had too little brown butter to enhance it. Scallops in butter and lemon were reminiscent of fish day at a school cafeteria.

I ate more of the dense cheesecake than I should have because of lingering hunger after those scallops. Pecan chocolate pie is better than most, minimally sweet and loaded with fresh pecans, and chocolate mousse cake is moist and intense.

# THE NICE RESTAURANT

★ ★

*35 East Broadway, near Catherine Street, 406-9776, 406-9510.*

*Atmosphere: Expansive, bright, and festive. Large circular tables and comfortable bentwood chairs. Noise level moderate.*

*Service: Good-natured and generally efficient waiters. Some have difficulty speaking English.*

*Price range: Moderate.*

*Credit cards: American Express.*

*Hours: 8 A.M. to 11 P.M., daily.*

*Reservations: Suggested.*

*Wheelchair accessibility: Ground-floor dining room with restrooms on same level.*

When the Nice Restaurant opened five years ago on East Broadway in Chinatown, it was among the first of a new wave of cavernous, glittery Hong Kong–style Cantonese restaurants in the area. These are festive places to be sure. On any evening at this two-level, five-hundred-seat extravaganza, you might encounter sprawling tables of ten or more family members celebrating a birthday, a gaggle of schoolchildren and their chaperons clattering in another corner, and even a mirthful wedding reception complete with choral singers accompanied by dozens of wineglass percussionists. Romantic dining this is not. If you are in the right mood, though, the Nice offers ample treats on its copious menu.

The upstairs dining room has a party motif with its shiny gold columns, bright lighting, and red-felt-covered walls on which golden dragons and serpents cling. The good-natured waiters make up in hustle and congeniality what they lack in communication skills. Trying to elicit useful menu tips from them can be as fruitful as asking a subway conductor to hold the train while you search the platform for a lost mitten. Every dish a diner mentions brings a "very good" or "people like it." One especially civilized touch here is the presentation of hot towels three or four times during the meal.

The menu does not follow the traditional pattern of appetizers, main courses, and desserts; it simply lists everything together, which is the way dishes arrive, too.

A fine way to start is with minced squab, diced Chinese bacon, and sour preserved vegetables that you wrap in lettuce and eat with your hands. One house specialty that is not always available but is worth asking for is roast suckling pig. Only one pig is cooked each night, the manager says, and it goes fast. Its brittle skin, rubbed with a combination of bean paste and soy, is insulated with a thin layer of fat and sits on slices of juicy pork. The meat rests on a base of sweet-cooked soybeans that counterbalance the salt in the skin. Fans of barbecued pork ribs will relish the version here. These are actually hefty pork chops hacked into finger-size portions. Brushed with a honey glaze, they are strictly for the sweet-toothed.

Aside from a well-executed roast duck, two other duck

preparations can be recommended. In the duck with winter melon, the rich, moist meat, which is in a crock, has a faintly smoky flavor and comes in a mild sauce holding cubes of sweet melon and mushrooms. Braised duck is more distinctive, infused with a tealike essence, along with bamboo shoots, mushrooms, and other Oriental vegetables.

One favorite dish from previous visits that did not delight this time is called soybean-sauce squab in a pot. A whole squab, head and all, is sectioned and cooked in a small ceramic crock with soy sauce, wine, vinegar, sugar, and spices. When prepared well, it is ineffably tender and imbued with the heady marinade. Unfortunately, it was woefully overcooked during recent visits.

One house specialty that has held up is salt-baked chicken. The technique of cooking chicken in a salt crust, which is not unique to China, leaves the meat juicy and falling off the bone. The chicken is removed from the crust and passed under a broiler to brown the skin before serving. On a list of house specialties is another winner, chicken with black-bean sauce, dried scallions, and lots of fresh ginger.

Deep frying is not a strength of this kitchen, as evidenced by the gummy shrimp-and-scallop rolls. A better way to go is with the sautéed squid with black-bean sauce and green peppers. The squid is first charred in a wok, which imparts a toasty edge, then quickly tossed with well-seasoned vegetables. Pan-fried flounder is crisp and greaseless served with shredded scallions; steamed flounder, however, could have used a minute more in the heat.

Those hot towels come in handy when a dish called crabs with bean threads come around. The crabs are served in the shell, covered with a light soy-based sauce, and entangled in rice noodles. It's tough, messy work, and the rewards are marginal at best.

At lunch, the dim sum selection is better than most in Chinatown. I had only a limited sampling, but memorable items included pan-fried leek dumplings, barbecued pork bun, and steamed shredded chicken roll.

The Nice now serves beer and wine, so brown bagging is no longer necessary. You might want a bag, however, to take home some of that salt-baked chicken.

# NIPPON

★ ★

*155 East 52nd Street, 758-0226, 688-5941.*

*Atmosphere: Low-key and relatively quiet traditional Japanese setting.*

*Service: Friendly and efficient.*

*Price range: Moderate.*

*Credit cards: All major cards.*

*Hours: Lunch, noon to 2:30 P.M., Monday through Friday; dinner: 5:30 to 10 P.M., Monday through Thursday, 5:30 to 10:30 P.M., Friday and Saturday.*

*Reservations: Recommended.*

*Wheelchair accessibility: Dining room on ground floor; restrooms four steps up.*

Twenty-five-year-old Nippon is the granddaddy of Manhattan Japanese restaurants, dating from an era when all but the most adventurous Americans would sooner swim to Japan than bite into a chunk of raw fish. Today, of course, sushi has become the fast food of the executive set, and the competition is intense.

Over the years, Nippon has managed to remain as fresh and high-spirited as its food, making it a favorite among Japanese businessmen at lunch and a more diverse clientele at dinner.

The two-tier dining room, with a wide, comfortable sushi bar on the upper level—a good place to spread out a newspaper or magazine if dining alone—is pretty and low-key, done in blond wood and shades of beige and tan. Tables are rather tightly arranged, although the noise level is well muffled. Private tatami rooms should be reserved several days in advance.

Waitresses in traditional garb range from the seasoned no-nonsense veterans who happily order for you if you display the slightest hesitation ("Get the tuna, you will like it") to diffident young women with inexhaustible patience.

The menu seems endless, but closer inspection reveals that many dishes show up in various preset banquets. Tempura is offered as a starter. The deep-fried morsels of shrimp, broccoli, and eggplant were a bit greasy one evening at dinner, much better several days later at lunch. Yamakake, cubes of glistening fresh tuna along with scallions in a sweetish mustard sauce, was invigorating, as was a house special, aigamo-hasamiyaki, slices of rare-cooked duck coated with a sweet glaze. A rousing Japanese ponzu sauce (vinegar, hot peppers, and grated radish) failed to revive the rinsed cherrystone clams, and an artistic arrangement of raw beef in a flower was fresh and tasty, although icy cold from the refrigerator.

Sushi and sashimi are available in all sorts of combinations. One good way to sample the day's bounty is with the special assortment dish, a moderate-size portion of tuna, fluke, shrimp, squid, salmon eggs, and sea urchin. The seafood was uniformly fresh and attractive; just as important for sushi is the rice, which was adhesive without being gummy and was nicely flavored with vinegar and sugar. Japanese beer or sake enhance both. The wine selection is spotty and overpriced.

Grilled entrées, particularly the salmon and porgy, are skillfully cooked but unseasoned. I dabbed them with some mustard-stoked soy sauce and did just fine. On the meat side of the menu, grilled chicken teriyaki is delicious in its sweet-edged glaze, served with broccoli and bean sprouts. Negimayaki, the scallion-stuffed beef rolls, are soggy and oversauced, lacking the crisp grilled texture they should have.

Often I find the Japanese seafood casseroles that are prepared at the table more entertaining than flavorful, but the yosenabe here is subtle and wonderfully saline. It combines clams, shrimp, lobster, tuna, and salmon with cabbage and translucent rice pasta.

If you are in a serious fish-eating mood for lunch, try the colorful combination special called makunouchi-bento, served in a compartmented platter. Aside from sashimi and assorted sushi, there is a refreshing little watercress-and-

and more. There appears to be a logical progression in eating this mini-buffet of contrasting flavors, moving gradually from hot to sweet. Judging from the bemused look of the tempura chef as he watched me leap-frog through the courses haphazardly, I didn't even come close. It sure was good, though.

# THE ODEON

★ ★

*145 West Broadway, at Thomas Street, 233-0507.*

*Atmosphere: No-frills Art Deco cafeteria; lively late-night scene.*

*Wine: Fine selection of moderately priced bottles.*

*Service: Young, friendly, and competent staff.*

*Price range: Moderate.*

*Credit cards: All major cards.*

*Hours: Brunch, noon to 3:30 P.M., Sunday; lunch, noon to 3 P.M., Monday through Friday; dinner: 7 P.M. to midnight, Sunday through Thursday, until 12:30 A.M., Friday and Saturday; late supper, until 2 A.M., Sunday through Thursday, until 3 A.M., Friday and Saturday.*

*Reservations: Recommended.*

*Wheelchair accessibility: Dining on ground level; restrooms downstairs.*

It is a sign of these ephemeral times that a restaurant just a decade old is called an institution. Yet the Odeon, a no-frills Art Deco cafeteria on lower West Broadway, is considered the virtual Fraunces Tavern of trendy TriBeCa.

One element that fosters the Odeon's pioneering image is its stylishly threadbare appearance. The place looks as if it has been there since Jimmy Walker's administration, with its speckled linoleum floor, faded vinyl banquettes, steel-framed Formica tables, and overhead fans. The American-bistro-style fare has fluctuated in quality over the years as chefs have come and gone. The current chef, Stephen Lyle, earned his stripes at Quatorze, the solid French bistro on West 14th Street, and later Man Ray in Chelsea.

The Odeon is still one of my favorite spots for a snappy steak au poivre with frail, golden french fries. The steak with black-and-green-peppercorn sauce has a nice bite to it, too. Another pleasing preparation, an occasional special, is grilled flank steak. The sinewy yet tender meat is well-charred and moistened with an assertive red-wine sauce. An especially comforting choice is the roast chicken redolent of fresh herbs with spinach and mashed potatoes.

Seafood is generally reliable. Two examples recently were the grilled salmon steak under a summery tomato-and-basil vinaigrette with sliced fennel and asparagus, and grilled mahi-mahi marinated in a vinaigrette made with soy sauce, lime, and cilantro, along with well-seasoned spinach and potatoes. Roast duck with ginger and scallions is a tempting concept, but unfortunately the duck arrived dry from overcooking, as did the veal paillard. The one pasta sampled, radiatore, came in a lopsided Mediterranean-style sauce of basil-roasted red peppers and too many green olives.

The service staff manages to maintain a brisk pace fairly well, but it's strictly self-service when it comes to such fine points as refilling wineglasses. Speaking of wine, the selection here is in perfect pitch with the food, and prices are right.

Appetizers are uniformly tasty. It required fast reflexes and a threatening tone with fellow diners to salvage some of the superb cornmeal-coated calamari with a roasted-pepper-and-garlic mayonnaise. Two exuberant starters are the lightly smoked tuna over cold lentils and scallions; and a salad of fennel, white beans, and tomatoes in a tart yogurt-and-mint dressing paired with asparagus vinaigrette that is a sprightly marriage, too. Cold black-bean soup may sound off-putting, but this relatively light-textured purée was delicious with an underpinning of hot pepper that was countered by a cooling garnish of coriander, sour cream, and tomatoes.

Some improvements are evident in desserts. The slender-crusted apple tart, prodigal profiteroles with mint and vanilla ice creams, and coffee parfait are first rate. On the debit side are a curdled crème brûlée and a great-looking but pallid-tasting frozen peach soufflé.

# OMEN

★ ★

*113 Thompson Street, between Prince and Spring, 925-8923.*

*Atmosphere: Comfortable brick-and-wood multilevel dining rooms suggesting a Japanese country inn.*

*Service: Gracious and sincere, if occasionally slow on busy evenings.*

*Price range: Moderate.*

*Credit cards: American Express and Diners Club.*

*Hours: Brunch, 11:30 A.M. to 4:30 P.M., Saturday and Sunday; dinner, 5:30 to 10:30 P.M., Tuesday through Sunday.*

*Reservations: Suggested.*

*Wheelchair accessibility: Several steps at entrance; everything on one level.*

The casual charm of a restaurant in rural Japan is evoked by the brick-and-wood interior of Omen, a four-year-old local favorite in SoHo that continues to turn out high-quality, distinctive fare at reasonable prices. In contrast to the sleek and minimalist uptown sushi bars, which are designed for speed, Omen is a place for winding down with a sake and a steaming bowl of fish soup. Oriental lanterns hang from a timbered ceiling, spacy electronic music pulses from above, and striking calligraphy adorns the walls.

Omen is family-run, with two sister outlets in Kyoto. According to Mikio Shinagawa, the young owner, all three restaurants serve essentially the same fare, which is an eclectic and wholesome interpretation of recipes from around Japan.

The restaurant's signature dish, Omen, is a beguiling soup that I rely upon in winter when my internal antifreeze level drops to critical. The broth is made by steeping seaweed in chicken stock and spiking it with soy sauce, sake, and mirin, a sweet and syrupy rice wine. It is accompanied by a pretty ceramic plate holding a fresh and colorful array of partially cooked vegetables including white radish (also known as daikon), lotus root, broccoli, carrots, and burdock root, as well as raw spinach and scallions. All of the vegetables are plunged into the broth followed by the long, white wheat-flour noodles, called udon. The crowning touch is a sprinkling of crunchy sesame seeds.

Although the obliging young waiters and waitresses are a little shaky in the English department, they make a valiant effort to explain unusual dishes.

Surprisingly, sushi is not served at Omen, yet a wide range of uncompromisingly fresh sashimi is available. A good sampling is the assorted sashimi plate, which holds pieces of florid and smooth tuna and cool thin slices of octopus, as well as squid, giant clam, and fluke. One of the more intriguing preparations is raw tuna with Japanese yam. Deep-red tuna cubes rest in a pool of soy sauce and are covered with matchstick strips of Japanese yam and crowned with a quail egg. The neutral-tasting yam has a texture that suggests egg whites. The combination is a singular sensation that took me two samplings to begin to appreciate.

Two other uncommon preparations worth trying are the avocado and shrimp with miso sauce, and the spinach and scallops with peanut cream. The former consists of a ripe avocado half stuffed with marinated cucumber slices and topped with whole shrimp. The savory sauce combines egg yolks, rice vinegar, salt, and sugar. The second dish, one of my favorites, features scallops and blanched spinach swathed in a peanut-cream sauce tinged with mirin, sake, and soy sauce.

There is no logical progression to this menu, which does not distinguish between appetizers and entrées. A good way to start is with a light soup. Both the miso and clear soups are subtle and soothing. One could make a meal of the chirinabe, a stewlike mélange of chicken slices, broccoli, mussels, fluke, tofu, and cabbage in a richly flavored chicken stock. The solid ingredients are plucked out with chopsticks. To savor the broth, you must abandon Western reserve and slurp it from the bowl Japanese style.

The three chicken dishes on the menu are superior—all are variations of deboned roasted meat marinated in a sweetish soy sauce cut with sake and mirin. The sansho chicken is extraordinarily buttery and moist, with what tastes like hints of orange (I was told later that this was the effect of sake). It comes with hair-thin strands of carrot and white radish. The others are chicken with grated radish (tori-mizore), and cold chicken with cucumber (tori-tosazu).

Japanese beer is the best accompaniment to these salty flavors. A nice way to clear the palate at the end is with some ice cream: the dry-edged green tea or the creamy red bean.

# 150 WOOSTER STREET

**SATISFACTORY**

*150 Wooster Street, 995-1010.*

*Atmosphere: Former garage brightened with trompe l'oeil and palms.*

*Service: Arrogant at front desk; staff can be friendly and helpful.*

*Wine: Well-chosen, reasonably priced selection.*

*Price range: Moderately expensive.*

*Credit cards: All major cards.*

*Hours: Brunch, 11:30 to 3 P.M., Saturday and Sunday; dinner, 6:30 to 11:30 P.M., daily.*

*Reservations: Necessary, sometimes several days in advance.*

*Wheelchair accessibility: Dining on ground level; restrooms downstairs. Bathroom available for handicapped.*

If attitude is the social currency of SoHo, then superhip 150 Wooster Street is the Federal Reserve Bank of superciliousness. We arrived one evening fifteen minutes late because of a torrential rainstorm and were sent to the bar for another fifteen minutes. A hostess then approached and admonished us that because we were now a half hour late we'd better eat fast because she needed the table soon.

The disappointments of 150 Wooster Street are perplexing, for up to now Brian McNally, the owner (of Indochine and the Odeon) has created one exemplary restaurant after another. To make matters worse, the food is mediocre here. Mr. McNally seems to be a victim of his own success. I have read for months about the restaurant's sizzling celebrity scene: Richard Gere, Carolina Herrera, Ron Darling, and Paloma Picasso are among those who can't stay away; Diane Von Furstenberg and Calvin Klein hold court in the banquettes, and Bianca Jagger practically dragged in a cot for the opening of the summer season.

The setting, in a graffiti-smeared former garage, is bare bones but comfortable. The off-white walls with barn-board wainscotting are accented with trompe l'oeil windows depicting tropical scenes (this was originally designed to be a Brazilian restaurant). The floor is covered in a wavy blue-and-white tile pattern. Although guests can receive an icy reception here, once you are seated the young waiters and waitresses can be welcoming and eager to please.

Starters include gummy gnocchi with none of the promised fennel-seed flavor in a decent sauce of prosciutto, cognac, and cream; a boring little tart of Gruyère, tomato, and thyme over a cakey crust; bland, mealy seafood sausage with pesto; and pallid chowder of scallops and clams.

Pasta is better: penne with asparagus, cream, lemon zest, and tangy pecorino romano cheese is a tantalizing combination, as is fettuccine with crispy pancetta, white wine, tomato, and olive oil. A version of risotto made with barley is a diverting variation, nutty and delightfully chewy, fueled with spicy merguez sausage, roasted peppers, and sharp Parmigiano-Reggiano. But of all the entrées sampled over three visits, only three can be recommended: a good sirloin steak with marjoram butter, mashed potatoes, and fried endive; veal chop with tempuralike fried onion rings; and sautéed red snapper with saffron cream sauce and crunchy diced potatoes.

The kitchen makes a picture-perfect crème brûlée and a fine thin-crusted apple tart served with cinnamon ice cream.

In a fitting final gesture, on my last visit a busboy lugging a wet dishwasher rack through the crowded room dripped water on my sister's head. I wonder what Bianca would have done.

# ORIENTAL PEARL

★ ★

*103 Mott Street, between Hester and Canal streets, 219-8388.*

*Atmosphere: Big, bright, bustling spot. Loud.*

*Service: Friendly, helpful, and prompt.*

*Price range: Inexpensive.*

*Credit cards: MasterCard and Visa.*

*Hours: 8 A.M. to 11 P.M., daily.*

*Reservations: Necessary on weekends.*

*Wheelchair accessibility: Everything on one level.*

You have to be in a festive mood to appreciate Oriental Pearl, a sprawling five-hundred-seat Chinese party palace on Mott Street. I have never been there when there wasn't a wedding, birthday party, family reunion or straight-A's-in-seventh-grade party rattling the house. Major celebrations are partitioned off from other diners by a long pink curtain, which is sort of like insulating a ski chalet with a screen door. When chopsticks clink against glasses, beckoning the bride and groom to kiss, the din can create waves in your tea cup.

These matters aside, I can recommend Oriental Pearl for the same reason Chinese families flock there for weddings:

the food is very good and the service is prompt. This six-month-old establishment, which has an ownership connection with Oriental Town Seafood on Elizabeth Street, serves predominantly Cantonese food, with a little Sichuan and Beijing fare sprinkled in.

The main dining room is a carnival of ceramic statues, dragons with flashing eyes, and colored lights. Waiters in pink jackets are personable and helpful, even if their English is shaky.

A good way to start is with one or more of the special appetizers, including the cleanly fried jumbo shrimp (sometimes available with scallops, too) with walnuts and Chinese broccoli in a light, tasty cream sauce, or spareribs Peking-style, which have a slightly sweet glaze and arrive inside a deep-fried potato next with broccoli.

While the menu appears daunting in size, a closer look reveals that many sauces are listed over and over. If, for example, you like the black-pepper sauce, your options are numerous. Tender braised shrimp with zingy black-pepper sauce are worth trying, as are the jumbo salt-baked shrimp with a piquant aftershock of pepper. Other seafood selections to look for are the superlative steamed flounder in a light soy-based broth brightened with chopped scallions and fresh coriander, and the sea bass in the same broth.

Some of the vegetable side dishes lack seasoning, like the sautéed mixed vegetables and the sautéed mustard greens. One evening our waiter recommended asparagus, an off-menu special, and it was delicious, garnished with a sweet ground-pork sauce. String beans with heaps of garlic are good, too, cooked until just barely firm.

When I asked to sample a dish called steamed chicken with mustard greens, our waiter waved me off and said: "You will like crispy chicken." We were delighted with the juicy meat and the brittle skin, not unlike that of a good roast duck. Deep-fried squab is done equally well. A zesty unfried alternative is chicken slices in black bean sauce laced with a generous dose of hot pepper.

We did not have much luck with the house-special pan-fried noodles, which contained nearly raw shrimp, straw mushrooms, and Chinese broccoli; likewise, the seafood fried rice could have used more seasoning. An off-menu delicacy that I have heard about from a habitué of Oriental

Pearl is called snow pea leaves, which are the wonderfully delicate shoots of snow peas that are sold seasonally in Oriental markets. When our group asked a waiter for some, his eyes lighted up in surprise and he broke into a conspiratorial grin. Ask to have them simply sautéed or steamed rather than smothered with crab sauce, which masks their fragile flavor.

For dessert, there is the traditional semisweet red-bean soup or fruit. Oriental Pearl serves superior and wide-ranging dim sum from morning through lunch hour. What this clattering place lacks in tranquillity it makes up for in fresh and tasty food. If you want to have your wedding reception there, though, I suggest you call well in advance.

# ORIENTAL TOWN SEAFOOD RESTAURANT

**SATISFACTORY**

*14 Elizabeth Street, south of Canal Street, 619-0085.*

*Atmosphere: Crowded, bright, and loud.*

*Service: Routine and rapid.*

*Price range: Inexpensive.*

*Credit cards: None.*

*Hours: Breakfast: 9 A.M. to noon, daily; lunch, noon to 3 P.M., daily; dinner, 3 to 11 P.M., daily.*

*Reservations: Suggested.*

*Wheelchair accessibility: Everything on one level.*

"Excuse me! Going fishing," exclaimed the Chinese waiter, a small net in hand as he lifted the lid of a deep fish tank near the restaurant's front door.

Inside were half a dozen carp in various states of lethargy, seemingly unconcerned about who among them was next in line for that great wok in the sky. The waiter scooped one of the fish out of the milky water and plopped it nonchalantly on the floor as he replaced the lid. The fish just lay there, barely flapping a tail, which indicated that if the chef didn't do him in soon, another affliction would. I did not order "fresh" carp at Oriental Town Seafood Restaurant.

This bright and bustling Cantonese restaurant is always jammed with large tables of Chinese families, which, according to conventional wisdom, is an encouraging sign. Three excursions into the vast and sometimes forbidding menu left me less than overwhelmed. A handful of dishes rise above the mediocre, but few compel one to race back downtown.

The dining room is one of those compact megawatt affairs with rows of bare light bulbs along a reflective gold ceiling. Big round tables are as tightly packed as a midtown parking garage. If you arrive around 7 P.M., chances are you will have to line up at the door, next to the fish tank and tall cellophane bags of carryout shark fins.

The menu goes on forever, although variety is not so great as it seems. Seven or eight standard sauces mate with chicken, beef, pork, seafood, and vegetables, so a little tasting goes a long way. Beer is the only alcoholic beverage. Waiters are a harried lot, ricocheting from one table to the other, so don't get fancy and start asking lots of questions. One evening I asked if it would be possible to have dishes served several at a time rather than all at once. "No," our waiter replied emphatically, ending the discussion.

A good light way to warm up is with the golden bean-curd cubes holding morsels of shrimp in the middle. They are delicious with some of the coriander-flecked soy sauce. Every Chinese family in the house seemed to be eating a special, giant steamed oysters smothered in black-bean-and-ginger sauce. This creation might not be for oyster purists —the boldly salty sauce masked all the briny oyster flavor—but the combination had appeal in its own right.

Another dish on the specials list was better than average, too: shrimp braised with black pepper over sautéed Chinese broccoli. Although the pepper level could have been cranked up a few notches for my taste, the sauce was appealing, redolent of fresh ginger, and the shrimp well cooked. Shrimp Sichuan, on the regular menu, was not so compelling. The medium-size shrimp had made a touch-and-go landing on the wok, leaving them just this side of raw, and the sauce was timid. Another listlessly seasoned dish was a special, shredded chicken with sesame.

When the waiter drops a plate of quartered oranges on your table, don't be silly and ask for a dessert list. Suck on an orange and go home.

# ORSO

★ ★

*322 West 46th Street, 489-7212.*

*Atmosphere: Bright, sunny, and casual setting with open kitchen and skylight.*

*Service: Good-natured and generally efficient.*

*Wine: Excellent list priced to match the food.*

*Price range: Moderately expensive.*

*Credit cards: MasterCard and Visa.*

*Hours: All-day menu, noon to 11:30 P.M., Monday, Tuesday, Thursday, and Friday, 11:30 A.M. to 11:45 P.M., Wednesday and Saturday, noon to 11:45 P.M., Sunday.*

*Reservations: Necessary.*

*Wheelchair accessibility: Several steps down into the dining room; restrooms are downstairs.*

In a little over five years, Orso, the breezy Italian trattoria on West 46th Street, has earned cachet as Broadway's leading theatrical hangout. If after-theater dinner is planned at Orso, chances are the crowd will resemble the roster from a current *Playbill.*

Orso is owned by Joe Allen, whose namesake bar and restaurant next door is another Broadway institution. Orso's step-down main dining room is framed by a high arching skylight that makes for a sunny setting at lunch; at night it adds an illusion of spaciousness. The restaurant is done in clean ocher tones and wood and is lined with photographs of sports and entertainment celebrities. An open tile-and-steel kitchen in the rear buzzes practically nonstop from noon to midnight. The rustic, colorfully painted plates are showing signs of heavy use and should be replaced.

Orso's frequently changing menu carries about a dozen starters, a selection of small pizzas, and a blend of north Italian pastas and entrées. The pizzas are light enough to sample without spoiling the appetite. They have thin yeasty crusts and sprightly toppings, among them tomato, mozzarella, prosciutto, and Parmesan; and Swiss chard, prosciutto, black olives, mozzarella, and Parmesan. Shards of thin, brittle pizza bread infused with garlic and olive oil are also available.

Among the other appetizers, shrimp grilled in their shells are well seasoned, and a bowl of lentil-and-potato soup is fresh and lustily seasoned. Another good choice is steamed mussels served in a deep bowl in their broth and garnished with crumbled Italian sausage and sliced potatoes.

Two dishes that need some reworking are warm spinach-and-prosciutto salad topped with sweetbreads, which was ruined by too much vinegar in the dressing, and undercooked grilled eggplant paired with overmarinated raw salmon with green-peppercorn sauce.

Pastas rotate daily, and among the best of the regular repertory are tagliatelle (flat noodles) tossed with cubes of grilled eggplant, radicchio, and Parmesan, and ravioli filled with spinach, sausage, and creamy ricotta in a light tomato-and-basil sauce. Taglierini (thin noodles) is delicious in a bright sauce of olives, capers, oregano, and tomatoes along with cubes of succulent swordfish.

The poised and self-assured waiters and waitresses are energetic but lack sophistication in the fine points of service. Wine bottles are plopped on the tables for customers to sample and pour, and little things, like refilling water glasses and replenishing bread, are done sporadically, if at all. The wine list is excellent and priced to match the food. Many simple fresh whites and reds are under $20.

Based on my experiences, seafood is the best bet among entrées. You can't go wrong with the grilled tuna steak in a clean and lively Mediterranean sauce of black olives, tomatoes, and capers, or with the grilled swordfish with a pleasantly salty sauce of black-olive butter. Pan-fried perch was moist and flavorful with sage garnish and thin sautéed potatoes. Game, which was one of my favorites in Orso's early days, was not so compelling this time around. Quail with porcini and pancetta was garnished with some thyme sprigs, but you had to gnaw on the sprig to get any flavor. The polenta with it was gummy and bland. I had better luck with the roast chicken, which was aromatic of rosemary and garlic and was accompanied by grilled leeks and lean sausage.

Not many restaurants serve tripe, but if you are a fan of this assertive rustic specialty, Orso does it as well as any place in town. The tripe is wonderfully tender and mild in a garlic-loaded sauce that has a nice salty edge from pancetta and Parmesan. Two dishes more in the mainstream are also pleasing: the veal scaloppine with a lemon, caper, and veal-stock sauce, and the excellent calf's liver with onions.

Try the eye-opening espresso gelato for dessert (pistachio and cappuccino are good, too) or the intense chocolate mousse cake. For those without a sweet tooth, various cheeses—Parmesan, goat, Gorgonzola, and mascarpone—make nice finishing touches with a glass of red wine. The ricotta-filled tart with strawberry sauce is flaccid and uninteresting.

# THE OYSTER BAR AND RESTAURANT IN GRAND CENTRAL STATION

★

*Grand Central Terminal, lower level, 42nd Street and Vanderbilt Avenue, 490-6650.*

*Atmosphere: Three rooms: a sprawling main dining room with vaulted ceiling and high noise level; marble-topped counters in an adjacent area; a more intimate wood-paneled tavern room.*

*Service: Hosts can be snooty and indifferent; the staff is friendly if not entirely professional.*

*Wine: Excellent selection of American whites; expensive.*

*Price range: Moderately expensive.*

*Credit cards: All major cards.*

*Hours: 11:30 A.M. to 9:30 P.M., Monday through Friday.*

*Reservations: Recommended.*

*Wheelchair accessibility: Everything on one level.*

In the halcyon days of rail travel, when a train whistle signaled escape and adventure in a grand style, a fitting place to begin a journey was the Oyster Bar and Restaurant in majestic Grand Central Terminal. Rail travel has lost much of its romance over the years; so, too, has this once-classy landmark restaurant.

The decline is evident upon arriving. I have had warmer welcomes by train conductors on the 5:45 to New Haven. In three of four visits, we shuffled around the reception area while a harried host tried to cope with the inconvenience of our arrival: his strategy sometimes involved disappearing for several minutes, perhaps in hopes we would go away. Once we were seated, however, the rest of the staff was friendly and helpful.

The three dining areas are distinctly different. A sprawling outer room under the great vaulted tile ceiling is bustling and clamorous. On the other side of the entrance are long S-shaped marble counters where I like to stop for a quick lunch of oysters on the half shell and a seafood pan roast. The clubby tavern room has a long bar, softer lighting, and wood-paneled walls adorned with old ship prints.

Any discussion of the Oyster Bar must begin with the wide selection of oysters on the half shell. At a recent dinner, a selection of Belons and Chincoteagues were glistening fresh, well iced, and briny. On another occasion, bluepoints that came with a cold shellfish medley were watery and tasteless; the platter also included mussels in a mustardy vinaigrette, tasteless clams, and dry old prawns. At lunch, a bowl of foul-smelling steamed mussels had to be returned. Oysters Rockefeller had so much spinach purée in them that the shellfish flavor was undetectable.

The best shellfish dish is the pan roast. It's a misnomer, actually, for the shellfish is neither roasted nor cooked in a pan. Made with oysters, sea scallops, shrimp, lobster, clams, mussels, or a combination of these, it is a special treat. Cooks behind a counter in the main room pour a mixture of light cream and clam juice into big stainless-steel steamers. They then toss in some tomato paste, a soupçon of Worcestershire sauce, and seasonings. The seafood goes in last and is cooked in the superheated broth for less than a minute. The finished product, faintly spicy and infused with shellfish essence, is poured over a slab of toast in a large white bowl. It can be split as an appetizer or ordered as an entrée.

The Oyster Bar has one of the finest American whitewine selections in New York City, but you could get dizzy trying to read the tiny, single-spaced list. Prices are on the high side across the board.

Main courses are unpredictable. One day you will have an unassailably fresh fillet of tautog with fiddlehead ferns and boiled potatoes, or a summery salad of mixed greens holding strips of red-snapper fillet under a lively tarragon dressing; the next day it might be a plank of tuna so dry your cat would be insulted if you took it home. Swordfish was nearly as dry, too. Mediterranean striped bass with chanterelles is insipid, and fried oysters with french fries are underseasoned and heavy.

Desserts are surprisingly good, whether light and tart Key lime pie, a deep-dish apple pie with an earthy wholewheat crust, chocolate mousse cake with a layer of white chocolate mousse, or the fresh fruit salad.

# PALIO

★ ★

*151 West 51st Street, 245-4850.*

*Atmosphere: Splendid, spacious room offering comfort and low noise level.*

*Service: Formal and informed but not always attentive to details.*

*Wine: Copious international list with wide price range.*

*Price range: Expensive (pretheater dinner prix fixe, Monday through Friday, $43; Saturday, $45).*

*Credit cards: All major cards.*

*Hours: Lunch, noon to 2:30 P.M., Monday through Friday; pretheater dinner, 5:30 to 6:30 P.M., Monday through Saturday; dinner, 5:30 to 11 P.M., Monday through Saturday. Bar serves light fare from 5:30 P.M. to midnight.*

*Reservations: Suggested.*

*Wheelchair accessibility: Elevator access to dining room, where everything is on one level.*

Palio, the splendiferous Tony May creation in the Equitable Assurance Tower on West 51st Street, came on the scene in 1986 when it seemed restaurants could not be big enough, lavish enough, or expensive enough for self-assured, free-spending New Yorkers. Financed by Equitable, it was and is one of the most luxuriant settings in town. The chef, Andrea Hellrigl, was lured from the resort town of Merano in Italy's Alto Adige region, where he has a hotel and restaurant of local renown.

For all its blandishments, Palio had one unsettling flaw: Mr. Hellrigl's kitchen was as unpredictable as the Mets in September. The food could be inspired one day, insipid the next. In July, Mr. May turned control of Palio over to the chef, and there was hope that the pride of proprietorship would lead to more consistency on the plate. Three recent visits, however, failed to find evidence of that.

The restaurant is named for the Palio, the ancient horse race in the central plaza of Siena. The equine theme is most dramatically evoked in the magnificent ground-level bar, dominated by a brash wraparound Sandro Chia mural of the wild and woolly annual competition. The bar remains an enchanting spot for pretheater drinks and snacks. A tuxedoed culinary customs inspector checks your credentials ("Name? Time of reservation? Everyone in your party present?") before clearing you for the elevator ascent to the second-floor dining room.

The dining room is a grand space: a high, coffered ceiling, walls adorned with flags from the Palio competition, trellised woodwork, deep armchairs, and well-separated tables set with shimmering brass plates. Color-coordinated waiters swoop down with baskets of irresistible olive-oil breadsticks and superb bread. The mannered service staff is quick to pull out chairs and fold napkins but can't always be bothered with such minor details as replacing tableware and pouring wine.

Several of the appetizers are conceptually interesting but lose something in the execution. Take, for example, the baby shrimp nested in an artichoke heart under a tangle of deep-fried threads of leeks: the texture is delightful, the flavor is lacking. Or the tender little squid over a cube of polenta with an underseasoned tomato broth.

Tuna tartar had a nice peppery edge, although the basil sauce over it was more of a distraction than an enhancement. An invigorating starter is stracchino, a fresh, tangy cow's-milk cheese from Lombardy, placed on a slab of warm polenta and glazed under the broiler until golden and bubbly. The wine list is not a bargain bin, but plenty of fine selections can be found for under $25.

Mr. Hellrigl is the product of a region in Italy that, because of its strong links with Austria and Switzerland, has less of the Mediterranean influence in its cooking than regions farther down the boot. For example, juicy breasts of squab in a crust of shredded artichoke over a bed of spinach with béarnaise sauce is hardly Italian, but it is an engaging match. Well-herbed lamb chops encased in rösti-style potatoes is another dish that belies the chef's pedigree, as do mildly gamy quail thighs stuffed with goose liver.

Among the pastas that can be recommended are spaghetti alla chitarra with a lustrous fresh seafood sauce, and the spaghetti with sun-dried tomatoes.

I was glad to see that my favorite dessert from several years ago is still going strong: the warm chocolate polenta pudding with white chocolate sauce. Other fine punctuations are the poppy-seed-freckled semifreddo with blackberries and a dark, sweet cherry sauce, rich chocolate almond cake with vanilla sauce, and—eureka!—a tiramisù that actually has sharp espresso flavor.

In short, the change of ownership at Palio has yet to yield palpable changes. For the moment, it is still a three-star setting with two-star food.

# PALM

★

*837 Second Avenue, near 45th Street, 687-2953.*

*Atmosphere: Sawdust-covered floors, wooden chairs, caricature-covered walls. Loud and bustling.*

*Service: Veteran waiters are affable and generally efficient.*

*Price range: Expensive.*

*Credit cards: All major cards.*

*Hours: Lunch, noon to 5 P.M., Monday through Friday; dinner, 5 to 11:30 P.M., Monday through Saturday.*

*Reservations: Necessary for lunch; accepted at dinner only for four or more.*

*Wheelchair accessibility: Two steps at entrance; restrooms downstairs.*

It is impossible to be dispassionate about Palm, the archetypal New York steakhouse that opened as a restaurant and speakeasy in 1926. Judging from the clamorous, standing-room-only crowds at the bar nightly, one might think these fervid Palmists somehow missed news of the Twenty-first Amendment that made it possible to have cocktails before dinner elsewhere.

To love Palm one has to be the type who revels in a Pamplona-like atmosphere with sawdust-strewn floors, smoke-smudged walls festooned with celebrity caricatures, wham-bam service, and lumberjack-size portions. I get a kick out of steakhouses like this—that is, assuming the food is equally engaging. At Palm, unfortunately, that is no longer the case. The quality of steaks and seafood that earned Palm a four-star rating ten years ago has gradually sagged to one-star level. You can still get a first-rate sirloin here, and if luck is on your side, good brittle cottage fries. The rest, however, is as unpredictable as the stock market.

The seventeen-ounce sirloin steak that made Palm famous is still a winner—seared under a super-hot broiler to impart a blackened crust while remaining juicy and succulent within. Although Palm dry-ages its own beef rather than relying on the vacuum-packed provisions most restaurants use today, I found that the steak, while enjoyable, lacked characteristic intensity of flavor. The thin disks of cottage fries and tangle of deep-fried onion can be fresh and crunchy one night, tepid and leathery on another from sitting in the kitchen too long. Other vegetables range from acceptable to cafeteria-style. The wine list is thin and undistinguished.

Another of Palm's erstwhile favorites is called steak à la stone, featuring sliced strips of sirloin steak over a mound of sautéed onions and pimientos. Once again, the meat languished in the kitchen too long and began to turn steam-table gray from the heat and moisture of the onions. Three double-cut lamb chops were right on target, plump, charred, and pink-fleshed; the veal chop was equally good. Filet mignon, a blackened mass roughly the size of a baseball, would have been hard to identify if eaten blindfolded, so lacking was it in flavor.

As for the four-pound lobsters that come to the table split, broiled, and with melted butter, they are less succulent than steamed lobsters but delicious in their own right with a nice smoky tinge. I have never tasted broiled red snapper as enormous as the one reeled in to the Palm kitchen—nor as bland.

If there is room for dessert, try either the top-notch creamy cheesecake or the awesomely rich chocolate mousse cake.

The similar if more subdued Palm Too across the street serves more or less the same fare. Although the original Palm has lost its edge as an all-around restaurant, I can still recommend it for a stiff drink and a slab of sirloin—which, after all, is what the place is really all about.

# PAMIR

★ ★

*1437 Second Avenue, between 74th and 75th streets, 734-3791.*

*Atmosphere: Dim, nightclublike feeling with candlelit tables and Oriental rugs on the walls.*

*Service: Eager—sometimes too eager—and helpful.*

*Price range: Inexpensive.*

*Credit cards: MasterCard and Visa.*

*Hours: Dinner, 5:30 to 11 P.M., Tuesday through Sunday.*

*Reservations: Necessary.*

*Wheelchair accessibility: Front dining room on one level; restrooms downstairs.*

Pamir is a long, dimly lighted place with a Middle Eastern nightclub feeling to it. Oriental rugs, sundry wall hangings, and soft music contribute to its mysterious charm. The candlelit tables are closely arranged to accommodate an avid clientele nightly. Polite waiters in white shirts and black vests are eager to please and happy to order tasting meals for those who want to experience a wide range of dishes. Because the dining room is so busy, they are sometimes overzealous when it comes to clearing plates, so it is advisable not to leave the table for any reason until you are finished; you might come back to find another party enjoying appetizers.

Afghan food is a blend of Middle Eastern cuisine with spicy Indian accents, emphasizing lamb, chicken, and vegetables. This can be seen in such appetizers as sambosa goushti, puffed triangles of light and well-fried pastry stuffed with a mixture of ground beef and chickpeas redolent of cumin and cinnamon; bulanee gandana, thin turnovers filled with scallions and herbs that are eaten with a yogurt sauce; bulanee kachalou, another turnover, somewhat dry though, stuffed with mashed potatoes, ground beef, and spices; and aushak, flat scallion-filled raviolis sauced with a combination of yogurt, ground meat, and mint. Try the turnovers with some blazing-hot cumin-and-coriander sauce.

Afghan soup, called aush, is a tasty combination of noodles, mixed vegetables, and spiced ground beef in a mint-laced meat broth. House salads, which come with the dinner, must be an affectation meant for Americans—iceberg lettuce and anemic winter tomatoes. Beer goes well with this earthy food, which is just as well, because the wine list is mundane.

Entrées include various marinated lamb kebabs, which are grilled nicely just to medium rare, as well as highly seasoned kofta kebabs, balls of ground beef or lamb. The most intriguing main courses, though, are the rice-based dishes, norange palaw and quabilli palaw. The former is a circular mound of saffron rice laced with almonds, pistachios, and thin strips of orange zest. Underneath the rice is an aromatic lamb stew that when mixed with the rice yields a complex and subtle mélange of flavors and textures. Quabilli palaw is made with brown rice and has for garnish almonds, pistachios, carrot strips, and raisins that give it extra sweetness.

Portions are large, so it is fun to have everyone order something different and share. Other good choices are sabsi-chalaw, chunks of tender lamb in a garlic-flavored spinach sauce, and skewered lamb chops with brown rice. Several side dishes are worth trying. Sautéed pumpkin with a dollop of yogurt is exceptionally pleasing; so is sautéed eggplant served the same way.

The only dessert worth going out of the way for is firnee, a semifirm custard brightened with rosewater.

# PAPER MOON MILANO

★ ★

*39 East 58th Street, 758-8600.*

*Atmosphere: Smart, stylish room in black and white; can be cramped when full.*

*Service: Brisk and generally professional.*

*Wine: Adequate selection well matched to the food.*

*Price range: Moderately expensive.*

*Credit cards: American Express, MasterCard, and Visa.*

*Hours: Lunch, noon to 3 P.M., Monday through Saturday; dinner, 6 P.M. to 12:30 A.M., Monday through Saturday, 6 P.M. to midnight, Sunday.*

*Reservations: Necessary.*

*Wheelchair accessibility: Ramp access to dining room; restrooms on main floor.*

The Milanese may be best known for their prowess as fashion pacesetters, but they are proving equally deft at tailoring restaurants that capture the public fancy. The invasion began several years ago with Bice in midtown Manhattan, which from the day it opened has made Armani fashion previews look sparsely attended. Imitation trattorias in various shades and sizes have popped up all over town, the latest and most ambitious of which is Paper Moon Milano on East 58th Street.

Paper Moon Milano is a smart and snappy environment, built for speed and style but not legroom, like a Lamborghini. It is part of a chain that owns restaurants in Milan and Tokyo. Starker and cooler than Bice, Paper Moon Milano attracts the same self-assured, crisply attired, polyglot crowd. Except for the tan tablecloths and some wood-and-brass accents, black and white is the leitmotif, from the tiled floor and moody photos of Milan to the stylish outfits on the women dining here. The restaurant can get a bit close and clamorous at times, but I like the brisk, confident cadence of the room. And the good-looking waiters in long white aprons glide through the premises with the agility of figure skaters.

Upon being seated, you are given a lagniappe of savory strips of herbed focaccia. This presumably softens you up to absorb the prices of the appetizers, many of which are $10 or more. The selection here is first-rate, though: buttery prosciutto di Parma with ripe melon, a superior Niçoise salad, and a delicious combination of white beans, tuna, and onions. Sandy arugula diminished an otherwise tantalizing salad of shrimp in a mild mustard vinaigrette. The grilled vegetable plate here is better and more varied than at most other restaurants, as is the ultra-thin and earthy bresaola under shredded basil, shards of sharp Parmesan, and fragrant olive oil.

Half orders of pasta are not served, so you either split one order or go for an entrée portion. I didn't encounter a dud in three visits, for the kitchen understands balance and clean flavors. Among the best are penne tossed with eggplant, mozzarella, fresh basil, and a touch of oregano; a simpler but equally satisfying penne in a delicate and creamy tomato sauce with basil; and farfalle in a pink tomato sauce with slivers of smoked salmon. Penne all'arrabbiata hs a gentle kick to it and a strong underpinning of garlic. And the seafood pasta is masterfully executed, with baby squid, clams, and shrimp in a subtle bath of chopped tomato and olive oil. The red risotto sampled, also with mixed seafood, benefited from the same light-handedness.

Paper Moon Milano carries a few fresh and light pinot biancos and verdicchios for about $24, and among reds there are ample good choices that fit the style of food, including the 1987 Rosso di Montalcino (Altesino) for $22.

Main courses are not as consistent as starters, but a few stand out. The mixed grill offers meltingly tender charred fillet of beef, baby lamb chops, lusty pork sausage, well-seasoned veal, endive, and eggplant. The sliced sirloin with green peppercorns and rosemary is a winner; so, too, is the grilled veal chop. Sliced swordfish with arugula and marjoram sounded enticing, but the carpaccio-thin fish was dry and tasteless. And the grilled Cornish hen had been fired to a papery texture.

A good bet for a light meal is one of the fragile-crusted pizzas, particularly the one with creamy ricotta cheese, tomato, and sausage.

Aside from several appealing fruit tarts and a better-than-average tiramisù (it had a good espresso jolt), desserts are ordinary. Speaking of espresso, it's the real thing here, which is no small find in this town.

Paper Moon Milano is fueled by brio and a buoyant style. While not every dish is a winner, when it comes to scintillating pastas this moon shines brightly.

# PARADIS BARCELONA

**SATISFACTORY**

*145 East 50th Street, 754-3333.*

*Atmosphere: Airy, spacious dining room with well-separated tables.*

*Service: Well-schooled waiters, generally efficient.*

*Wine: Good selection of Spanish wines in the $20-to-$25 category.*

*Price range: Moderately expensive.*

*Credit cards: All major cards.*

*Hours: Brunch, noon to 3 P.M., Sunday; lunch, noon to 3 P.M., Monday through Friday; dinner: 6 to 10:30 P.M., daily (tapas served until midnight).*

*Reservations: Requested.*

*Wheelchair accessibility: Dining on main level; restrooms on same level.*

Since most Spanish restaurants in New York are oriented toward Castile or Andalusia, the opening of Paradis Barcelona in 1989 promised an opportunity to sample seaside Catalan cuisine. It turned out, however, to be a promise not entirely fulfilled.

Housed in the Kimberly Hotel building on East 50th Street, Paradis Barcelona is an American outpost of a big Barcelona-based restaurant and catering chain. While a few dishes here are vividly rendered, by and large this is Catalonia for the tour-bus crowd: safe, cozy, and deodorized.

The 145-seat dining room is lavishly, if eccentrically, appointed. The spacious, contemporary room has tan walls with polished wood wainscotting, mirrored columns, and a handsome Spanish tile floor.

Catalonia's proximity to France is evident in the regional cuisine, which includes dishes like goose-liver terrine, Dover sole amandine, turbot with spinach and tarragon, and duck-filled cabbage packets with truffles. These are not the kind of dishes for which New Yorkers are starved. The more indigenous food is alluring but, lamentably, not always appealing.

Rabbit is a specialty of Iberian cooking, so we went for that first. A paella-style casserole of artichokes, rabbit, and rice was on the dry side, and the rabbit had little flavor, although the saffron-tinted rice with sweet peppers was moist and tasty. Another evening, the Costa Brava paella parellada was based on the same rice foundation (this time a little dry) with a fresh and well-cooked assembly of octopus, mussels, clams, and chicken. The lobster paella was a letdown, essentially the same mixture with a split lobster on the plate. Monkfish, called rape in Spanish, is stewed in a good shellfish stock with potatoes and clams; sea bass came with a different green-pepper sauce and two twirls of noodles, one green, one white. Trubot set over spinach was fresh and well cooked, but none of the advertised tarragon sauce was evident. The Dover sole amandine came with the usual sliced almond garnish and a sweet sauce of ground almonds and olive oil. If you are a fan of the coveted and expensive ($35) saltwater baby eels called angulas, they are classically prepared here in sizzling olive oil with garlic and hot pepper.

The Spanish can do wonders with goat meat. What is

described here as roasted baby goat actually appeared to have been braised, which left the meat exceptionally tender. Its thick, lusty sauce was stippled with mustard seeds.

Paradis Barcelona is a good place to become familiar with some of the singular bargains offered by Spanish wines. The generally well-informed waiters can help you sort them out. Producers like Raimat, Masia Bach, Pesquera, and Marques de Riscal make some charming reds and whites. While markups are high, there are still plenty of good selections available in the $20-to-$25 category.

Caution is advised in ordering appetizers. Three strong choices are the refreshing marinated salmon with white kidney beans and a good olive-oil dressing; sautéed chanterelles and shiitake mushrooms with chives; and the mixed cold plate of roasted peppers, eggplant, and buttery Serrano, the aged Spanish ham.

Befitting Spanish tastes, most desserts are extremely sweet. The best are Catalan cream, a Spanish version of crème brûlée, and tuile flowers filled with pistachio ice cream. A caramelized apple with custard has a glassy sugar crust; chocolate cake is dense and sweet but otherwise unsatisfying.

# PARIOLI, ROMANISSIMO

★ ★

*24 East 81st Street, 288-2391.*

*Atmosphere: Luxurious town-house setting.*

*Service: Generally professional and formal.*

*Price range: Expensive.*

*Credit cards: American Express and Diners Club.*

*Hours: Dinner, 6 to 11 P.M., Tuesday through Saturday.*

*Reservations: Necessary.*

*Wheelchair accessibility: Five steps at the entrance. Restrooms on same floor.*

Strand for strand, Parioli, Romanissimo is probably New York's most expensive Italian restaurant. A three-course meal with the most humble wine easily tops $80 a person before tax and tip, and if your blood runs hot for appetizers like risotto with wild mushrooms ($26) and such entrees as rack of veal ($64 for two), tack another digit onto the total. And what do you get for these prices? An urbane setting, pampering service, and Italian fare that is generally pleasing but hardly provocative.

Parioli, Romanissimo is in an airy town house on East 81st Street. You enter through a hushed little bar and proceed down a corridor to the main dining room, a stately parlor with a fireplace and a high, ornately molded ceiling. The mottled ocher walls are warm and soothing—but not the clownish paintings all about, made even more obtrusive by their harsh illumination. Beyond a leafy atrium is a smaller back room.

The menu carries five regular appetizers and a half dozen pastas. The pastas are not served in half portions, our captain informed us, "but the portions are not large."

The best pasta sampled was the remarkably light homemade ravioli stuffed with wild mushrooms in a frothy cream sauce. The aforementioned mushroom rissotto was a paragon of this northern Italian staple—light, creamy, and boldly flavored. Another subtly good starter is the carpaccio of lamb. Little petals of lamb are seared outside, raw in the middle, and served with a mild red-pepper-and-cream sauce.

The captains and waiters here go through their ministrations with cool solemnity. They know how to pamper their well-heeled patrons, many of whom are regulars. The only irksome flaw is that often dishes arrive at different times, so that one diner sits awkwardly while others at the table politely watch their food get cold. The wine list boasts some of Italy's best producers; whites are more reasonably priced than reds.

The entrée roster is like a rushed bus tour of Rome: you are exposed to a plethora of images but remember few details. Nine veal dishes are offered, including veal Valdostana, a thick, tender chop stuffed with Fontina cheese with an oversalted stock sauce with truffles; and bland veal Milanese, in which the same cut is pounded, breaded, and sautéed. A dish called veal birds provided some speculation about flying cows at my table but not much flavor when the dry, chicken-liver-stuffed rolled veal in brown sauce arrived. The best of the lot is the roasted rack of veal in a lovely reduced sauce of pan drippings. Garlic-encrusted rack of lamb is succulent and delicious, too.

Parioli, Romanissimo has an impressive cheese cart, a first-rate selection of French, Italian, and American cheeses in excellent condition. They are wonderful with a glass of port. Fruit tarts are uniformly pleasing, raspberries comes with a frothy zabaglione, and chocolate cake is intense.

# PARK BISTRO

★ ★ ★

*414 Park Avenue South, between 28th and 29th streets, 689-1360.*

*Atmosphere: Inviting and lively, tightly arranged but not cramped.*

*Service: Quick and unobtrusive staff, highly professional.*

*Wine: Well matched to the food, sensibly priced.*

*Price range: Moderately expensive.*

*Credit cards: American Express and Diners Club.*

*Hours: Lunch, noon to 3 P.M., Monday through Friday; dinner, 6 to 11 P.M., daily.*

*Reservations: Necessary.*

*Wheelchair accessibility: Dining room and restrooms on one level.*

With bistromania raging through New York City like a winter flu, it may be time to consider what constitutes a real bistro. A struggling French restaurant that knocks 20 percent off entrée prices certainly does not. Nor does a place that simply adds cassoulet to the menu and hires a svelte hostess with a French accent.

To my mind, Park Bistro exemplifies the best this genre of restaurant can offer: consistently pleasing, down-to-earth food; intelligently chosen, affordable wines; a snappy and knowledgeable staff; and an easygoing, convivial setting that has what the roving epicure Joseph Wechsberg called "a glow of happiness about the place."

Park Bistro's success springs from the experienced triumvirate at the helm. Philippe Lajaunie, the original owner, struggled on his own for several years before teaming up in early 1989 with two seasoned professionals from the former Hotel Maxim's de Paris (now the Peninsula Hotel): Max Bernard, the maître d'hôtel, and Jean-Michel Diot, the chef.

Park Bistro is an inviting spot with a small bar up front, long red banquettes, pale gray walls, framed film posters, and gentle lighting. The kitchen is partly visible behind a window in the back. Mr. Diot, who trained in the South of France, has a masterly sense of balance with the aromatic ingredients of Provence. The obvious joy he experiences when cooking is evident on the plate. This is happy food.

One example is his brandade de morue, which is essentially shredded codfish blended with potatoes and seasoned with garlic and mixed herbs. Others are his seafood soup, anchored by a stout shellfish stock and tinted with tomato, and the unusual but scintillating cannelloni filled with eggplant and sardines. A loosely bound terrine of tender rabbit is sublime with fresh artichoke hearts, tomato, and eggplant. One appetizer that seemed a bit muddled was the terrine of foie gras, mashed potatoes, and duck confit: I would have preferred the three ingredients separately. Potatoes were put to better use in a warm salad in which they were sliced and topped with creamy goat cheese and black olives in a thyme-scented vinaigrette.

Waiters are quick on their feet and unobtrusive. What's more, they have a thorough understanding of the food and wine. I was particularly impressed with our waiter who, upon seeing us debating a suitable wine to match a wide range of dishes, suggested a chilled red Sancerre. It was perfect. Half a dozen pleasant wines from Burgundy, the Côtes-du-Rhône, and the Loire are available at $25 or less. Among reds, you might try a gutsy bottle from Cahors or Corbières in the southwest of France, or a zesty Château Montus from Madiran, in the Armagnac region.

You know you are in a real bistro when onglet (sometimes called hanger steak or butcher's steak) is on the menu. French butchers used to keep this cut from the flank for themselves; hence the name. It needs hanging and should be cooked rare. The version here was as succulent as any I have had in France, served at dinner with garlic-perfumed eggplant, carrots, and a fine sauce choron (a béarnaise sauce blushed with tomato). Braised lamb shank is exceptional, too, tender and gelatinous, set over fennel and sautéed apples, and with a sauce sweetened with dried fruits. Another standout is succulent stuffed breast of guinea hen with a port-wine sauce, sliced turnips, and a cabbage packet holding foie gras and couscous. When I asked Mr. Bernard what the terrific stuffing was, he replied sheepishly, "Pigs' feet, but I don't write it on the menu because some people might go, 'Yuk!'"

Seafood excels here: herb-infused skate with garlicky white beans and a lovely sauce of red-wine vinegar and fish stock; crisp-skinned striped bass on a bed of eggplant with a purée of olives, basil, and a touch of cream; and roasted monkfish with a heady Provençale sauce combining fennel, tomato, carrots, and chervil. One evening, codfish was substituted for coalfish (or hake), roasted and served with a basil sauce and ratatouille garnished with deep-fried leeks. The only dish that left me cold was slightly tough lobster meat surrounded by a basil-accented pumpkin purée.

Desserts were not a strong point here on my earlier visits, but they have improved. Chocolate mousse cake is light yet intense, and moist, dense bread pudding benefits from a dousing of crème anglaise. I have sampled a half dozen different fruit tarts, and all but one (which had a leathery crust) were winners. And finally there is the exceptionally light napoleon—well, as light as any eight-hundred-calorie dessert can be.

Park Bistro has opened a carryout and catering facility just around the corner, at 47 East 29th Street. It has a handsome room upstairs that can be reserved for private parties.

# PATSY'S

**SATISFACTORY**

*236 West 56th Street, 247-3491.*

*Atmosphere: Clean and comfortable 1950s ambiance; aqua-blue room downstairs, gold upstairs.*

*Service: Matter-of-fact veterans, good-natured and professional.*

*Price range: Moderately expensive.*

*Credit cards: All major cards.*

*Hours: Noon to 10:30 P.M., Sunday and Tuesday through Thursday, noon to 11:30 P.M., Friday and Saturday.*

*Reservations: Necessary.*

*Wheelchair accessibility: Dining on street level; restrooms downstairs and upstairs.*

Restaurant warning signal No. 5: The quality of food is in inverse proportion to the number of signed celebrity photographs on the walls. Where do all these black-and-whites glossies come from? Are they actually tokens of gratitude from stage and screen stars, or does some photo lab simply churn them out and peddle them by mail?

I frequent these photo-festooned establishments, yet never have I spotted Frank Sinatra, Joey Bishop, or Joe Namath. And if one believes these are authentic testimonies —"To Mo, a great host!"—then Joey Heatherton must be the greatest roving gastronome since Escoffier.

Patsy's, the forty-seven-year-old theater-district institution, is a veritable Smithsonian of celebrity souvenirs, which hardly inspires confidence. It's a shame the southern Italian food is so mundane and overpriced, for there is something endearing about this cocky anachronism. The dining rooms are marvelous time capsules of New York circa 1953. Joseph Scognamillo and his nephew Frank DiCola, the owners, seem to know every customer in the place. Patsy's attracts a mostly older, formally attired crowd that has been coming here for lobster fra diavolo and veal piccata since the days when they were prepared with finesse.

Soups are probably the best appetizers—either the tart escarole in a good chicken stock, or lentils and macaroni, a Saturday special. The hot antipasto resembles something you would get on a paper plate at the San Gennaro festival in Little Italy but not so tasty. We did not fare any better with the fatigued steam-table artichoke heaped with dry bread crumbs. Mozzarella in carrozza was cleanly fried and tasty, though.

Pastas sampled were consistently muted in flavor, sometimes simply from undersalting—the linguine with pesto, and fettuccine Alfredo—other times from lack of balance, like the pasta in an anemic clam sauce that sorely needed more garlic and herbs. The only interesting pasta sampled was fettuccine in a gutsy Bolognese sauce with porcini. Seafood, while fresh, suffered from the blahs too, whether it was papery swordfish in white-wine-and-garlic sauce or diner-quality broiled sole with a gummy potato fritter.

The safest haven here is meat. The manly veal chop was tender and well cooked, although the vinegary sauce with shards of garlic did little for it. Lamb chops were plump, well trimmed, and cooked to order.

Desserts taste like the experiments of a high-school home-economics class, among them gluey napoleon with rubbery pastry, and soupy tiramisù.

The loyal cadre of Patsy's patrons must find something there that I missed while working through the menu systematically. If I ever meet Joey Heatherton, I will surely ask her.

# PERIYALI

★ ★

*35 West 20th Street, 463-7890.*

*Atmosphere: Trim and clean whitewashed walls and wooden floors.*

*Service: Amiable and efficient.*

 373

*Wine: Moderately priced list; Greek wines best bargains.*

*Price range: Moderate.*

*Credit cards: American Express, MasterCard, and Visa.*

*Hours: Lunch, noon to 3 P.M., Monday through Friday; dinner, 5:30 to 11 P.M., Monday through Thursday, 5:30 to 11:30 P.M., Friday and Saturday.*

*Reservations: Necessary at lunch and dinner.*

*Wheelchair accessibility: Four steps at entrance; everything on one level.*

Periyali is a long, clean, whitewashed spot with cushioned wooden banquettes along one wall, a Mediterranean cornucopia and photographs of Greece on the walls, and a long polished wood bar in front. Billowy fabric between the rafters adds a soft edge to the room—without doing much for the noise, though, which can be rattling. Two smaller back rooms are more tranquil.

While the setting is upscale, the food is down to earth. A standout appetizer is the red-wine-marinated octopus grilled over charcoal. The slightly blackened tendrils are delightfully chewy and full of the herby marinade flavors. White beans tossed in a garlic-infused vinaigrette are simple and tasty, as is the tossed salad with cleanly fried calamari and, an occasional special, golden deep-fried smelts with lemon wedges.

The wine list carries some uncommon and pleasing Greek wines, most under $20.

Among the entrées, lamb, naturally, is a highlight. I much preferred a daily special, succulent oregano-dusted leg of lamb with roasted potatoes, over the skimpily seasoned and slightly overcooked chops. Another special at lunch was terrific: buttery braised lamb shank in a garlic-powered tomato sauce with orzo on the side. Rabbit stew sounded promising, but the meat was on the dry side and the tomato-based sauce, while flavorful, had a floury texture. Moussaka, the layered casserole of eggplant and ground lamb, is seductive under its blistered lid of béchamel.

Seafood entrées change daily. Grilled porgies swathed

with olive oil, along with couscous flecked with sweet red peppers, are fresh and delicious, as is the baked red snapper in a tomato-onion-and-garlic sauce.

Baklava is relatively light, made with toasted almonds instead of walnuts. Moist and minimally sweet lemon semolina cake is worth trying, too, as is galaktobouriko, a semolina custard pie wrapped in phyllo pastry. The house Greek coffee is so thick with sediment you could plant a flag in it.

# PETER LUGER

★

*178 Broadway, Brooklyn, (718) 387-7400.*

*Atmosphere: Old New York charm in a century-old landmark.*

*Service: Lighthearted and chatty veteran waiters who perform their duties in a casually efficient manner.*

*Price range: Moderately expensive.*

*Credit cards: Peter Luger charge cards.*

*Hours: Lunch, 11:30 to 3 P.M., Monday through Saturday; dinner, 3 to 9:45 P.M., Sunday through Thursday; until 10:45 P.M., Friday and Saturday; 1 to 9:45 P.M., Sunday.*

*Reservations: Required.*

*Wheelchair accessibility: One step at entrance; everything on one level.*

For nearly a century this landmark in the Williamsburg section of Brooklyn, in the shadow of the Williamsburg Bridge, has been a crowded, no-frills, elbows-on-the-table steakhouse.

Menus are strictly for the tourist trade, offered to those who insist upon seeing one. The first time I requested a menu, the waiter replied with the same quip that has been drawing chuckles since the McKinley Administration. "Sure you can see a menu, but first I'll ask you how you want your steak done." Your choices are juicy slabs of broiled porterhouse steaks in portions serving one to four, and fist-thick double lamb chops. Both are nicely encrusted from high-fire broiling and succulent.

Leaning on the long, worn oak bar at Peter Luger while waiting for a table, you feel as if you are a thousand miles from Manhattan. In one corner of the room, four white-haired local cronies chew on thick stogies and debate politics in Brooklyn accents as thick as Peter Luger's lamb chops. Couples in sports clothes banter with the bartender and sip bloody marys while businessmen in pinstripes from "the City" belt down martinis and swap jokes.

The main dining room is vaguely Teutonic, with its exposed wooden beams, burnished oak wainscotting, brass chandeliers, and scrubbed beer-hall tables. The veteran waiters are a jocular bunch if you get them going, and are casually efficient. On our first visit we ordered a porterhouse for three and lamb chops for one. The formidable cut of singed steak had been sliced in the kitchen and placed on a hot platter. Our waiter set a small dish under one end of the platter to let juice run into a corner while commenting, probably for the hundredth time that week, "If you don't like this steak you don't like steak!" He then portioned out enough beef to sate a tugboat crew. The beef was cooked rare as ordered and had a good meaty flavor and plenty of juice for bread dipping.

The lamb chops were equally flavorful and profited from the same skilled broiling. The perennial salad of sliced onions and tomatoes is only worth ordering during peak tomato season; the dreary horseradish-tomato sauce slathered over it could be done without. Shrimp cocktail is available, but chances are the waiter won't tell you about it unless you are a regular. When I noticed a couple eating shrimp at the next table, I asked why we were not offered some. Our waiter laughed and replied, "I didn't want to confuse you."

The staff is a bit less secretive about the wine selection, offering you a peek if you ask nicely. The small list has a token Bordeaux selection, two California reds, two Italian reds, and an equal number of whites. On the lunch menu, in addition to steaks and chops, daily specials are served, such as corned beef and cabbage, knockwurst and sauerkraut, and assorted sandwiches.

Among the side dishes, German fried potatoes were burned around the edges and underseasoned on two occasions. They also showed telltale signs of having been prepared in advance and reheated before serving. The bland creamed spinach would prompt a groan in a prep-school dining hall, though the steak fries were better than average.

If you finish all this and still want dessert, there is sweet pecan pie that is brought to the table with a bowl filled with enough fresh whipped cream to paint a stripe across the Williamsburg Bridge, as well as a lightweight chocolate mousse and good dense creamy cheesecake.

# PIERRE AU TUNNEL

★

*250 West 47th Street, 575-1220.*

*Atmosphere: Homey French bistro feeling with well-spaced tables and good noise control.*

*Service: Waitresses are professional.*

*Price range: Moderate.*

*Credit cards: American Express, MasterCard, and Visa.*

*Hours: Lunch, noon to 5 P.M., Monday through Saturday; dinner, 5:30 to 11:30 P.M., Monday, Tuesday, Thursday, and Friday; 4:30 to 11:30 P.M., Wednesday and Saturday.*

*Reservations: Necessary for pretheater.*

*Wheelchair accessibility: Three steps down at the entrance; restrooms down a long flight of stairs.*

Nearly forty years on the scene, Pierre au Tunnel can be recommended as a homey theater-district French bistro that can easily become habit forming—that is, if you know your way around the menu. Mellow peasant-style dishes and Gallic classics are the specialties here, so stick with those and you will be happy.

The setting is warm and familiar, with a cozy little bar up front and a rustic French feeling in the dining room. Tables are well spaced and noise is muted, making this a fine spot for business lunches. French waitresses in black-and-white outfits can be either matter-of-fact or endearing, but they are nearly always efficient.

The most dependable appetizers are the moist and rich pork terrine, robust onion soup, and pâté de tête (a well-seasoned gelatin-bound headcheese). Salads are prepared with care, especially such occasional specials as the combination of rare-sautéed salmon with green leaf lettuce in a mild vinaigrette, and the mixed green salad crowned with broiled disks of goat cheese.

Leek tart was flavorful and fresh but the crust was undercooked, while carrot soup was pale and mussels ravigote lacked the aromatic herb flavor they should have. The dinner menu carries an exceptionally light and vivid scallop mousse glossed with chive butter. The wine list sensibly matches the food, and at relatively modest prices.

If you are an aficionado of the classic French country dish tête de veau, this is one of the best places in New York to have it—a mélange of brain, tongue, cheek, boiled potatoes, and carrots with a zippy mustard vinaigrette bolstered with capers and eggs. Less intrepid diners would be happy with the juicy lamb chops with sautéed potatoes or the lusty beef à la Bordelaise. Seafood is not always so successful. The two best dishes sampled were poached grouper in a lovely beurre blanc sauce and swordfish steak in a rosemary-perfumed broth; simple sole à la meunière, on the other hand, was leathery from overcooking, and what the menu calls scampi Escoffier was nothing more than chewy little shrimp in a thick brown sauce. The Friday bouillabaisse was generous with cod, mussels, clams, and eel, but the broth was watery and the flavors were not integrated.

Desserts are generally attractive and pleasing—raspberry tart with an airy puff pastry crust, peach tart layered with coconut cream, and crème caramel among them. Pierre au Tunnel is a survivor in a dwindling genre of family-owned French restaurants in the theater district. For a pretheater meal or a sedate business lunch, it's worth keeping in mind.

# PIG HEAVEN

★ ★

*1540 Second Avenue, corner of 80th Street, PIG-4333.*

*Atmosphere: Barnyard motif. Fun for kids.*

*Service: Competent, amiable, and well-informed.*

*Price range: Moderate.*

*Credit cards: American Express and Diners Club.*

*Hours: Noon to 11:30 P.M., Sunday to Thursday, until 12:15 A.M., Friday and Saturday. On weekends a special Shanghai-style brunch is served from noon to 3 P.M.*

*Reservations: Necessary.*

*Wheelchair accessibility: Everything on one level.*

When Pig Heaven opened in 1984, its barnyard motif, complete with dozens of little piggies prancing along the pink barn-board walls, even included loose hay strewn on the floor. Shortly afterward, the hay was removed —the city Department of Health failed to see the humor— but otherwise this ebullient Chinese restaurant remains the same, serving some of the better Cantonese and Sichuan fare uptown.

Pig Heaven is part of the David Keh empire, which also includes David K's, Third Avenue at 65th Street, and i' casual annex, David K's Café. Uptown Chinese restaur are often accused of being overpriced, but Pig Heaven appetizers in the $3-to-$9 range and most main under $15, is quite reasonable.

Despite its name, Pig Heaven is not totally though pork dishes are the menu's strength dles are always bright and fresh, as is the cold hacked chicken swathed in a zesty combination of sesame paste and hot oil. A light and unusual starter is the duck salad: shredded duck tossed in a haystack of bean sprouts, puffed rice noodles, and sliced scallions, all in a sesame dressing.

Spring rolls are nothing more than dense, doughy egg rolls in disguise. Instead, get some dumplings (pork, vegetable, or seafood), preferably the golden pan-fried crescents that are habit forming with their soy dipping sauce, or the clean and light boiled variety.

Other vivid starters to consider are the thin, crenulate slices of cold pork in an eye-opening garlic sauce or the brittle deep-fried squid rings generously laced with black pepper, a special. And if you can get over the image of digging into a salad of cartilaginous shredded pig's ear, you may enjoy this delicacy combined with chopped scallions and seasoned with a sparkling sesame-oil vinaigrette.

Pig Heaven is a good place to go with large groups, and children, too, for the service staff is amiable and prompt. If you ask to have dishes arrive in progression, the staff complies, unlike in Chinatown, where such a request yields a quick nod by the waiter, who returns fifteen minutes later with a procession of buddies lugging ten platters.

I don't even like to contemplate the chemical reaction in the stomach when a Fuzzy Navel cocktail meets sliced cold pork in a spicy garlic sauce. For those of a scientific bent, controlled studies could be attempted with other house libations, like a peaches-and-cream concoction or something called a Pink Pig. A small wine selection is available as well.

Among the nearly twenty pork entrees, Cantonese-style suckling pig is still a house favorite. This dish will never make the Surgeon General's list of cholesterol-lowering foods—the brittle, caramel-colored skin covers a thin layer of fat that adds a luxurious richness to the meat—but it is worth a splurge. Shredded pork with pepper-and-garlic sauce is lively and succulent, too (a similar dish made with beef is equally appealing), while a good, mildly seasoned alternative is minced pork sautéed with corn, bell peppers, and pine nuts. Try a side dish of dry-cooked string beans with ground pork and garlic.

Among seafood entrées, sautéed flounder, an occasional special, is on the bland side, though fresh and colorful with carrots, snow peas, and straw mushrooms. Another special, jumbo shrimp in black-bean sauce, can be enticing, just salty enough to keep you coming back. Not to be missed are the flattened shrimp served in their shells with a peppery scallion sauce.

The Western-style desserts are humdrum.

# POIRET

★

*474 Columbus Avenue, at 82nd Street, 724-6880.*

*Atmosphere: Moderately noisy, closely arranged dining room.*

*Service: Sometimes overtaxed and slow.*

*Wine: Well-priced list appropriate to the food.*

*Price range: Moderate.*

*Credit cards: All major cards.*

*Hours: Brunch, 11:30 A.M. to 4:30 P.M., Sunday; dinner, 6 to 11:30 P.M., daily.*

*Reservations: Necessary.*

*Wheelchair accessibility: Everything on one level.*

The unwavering popularity of two-year-old Poiret attests to the paucity of competent, moderately priced restaurants on the Upper West Side. This lively bistro is the least institutional-looking link in the Ark Restaurants chain, which also includes Ernie's, America, and B. Smith's. Some of the food tastes as if it were conceived in a central commissary, but considering the neighborhood alternatives, the locals don't gripe.

A visit to Poiret several months after it opened was more notable for its din than for dinner: the room was shatteringly loud and overcrowded. Since then, management has muffled the noise considerably by adding carpet. Votive candles and indirect lighting make for a more relaxed scene. One problem with some chain restaurants, or at least places with absentee owners, is the lack of an easily identifiable leader, someone with authority and a long-term interest in the restaurant's survival. In two out of three visits, my party arrived and stood unacknowledged inside the entrance for several minutes, like a foursome that had just wandered into the wrong office party. On a third visit, an exceptionally cordial hostess apologized for the backlog in reservations and offered us a glass of wine—which we drank standing off in one corner of the room.

The pace of the kitchen and the service staff can be erratic as both struggle to keep up with mounting orders. The food at its best is satisfying but not memorable. Among the more reliable options are a somewhat chewy but flavorful steak au poivre with a mildly peppery brandy sauce, bland mashed potatoes, and brussels sprouts; nicely charred, juicy lamp chops with dry couscous; and a moist roast chicken with golden shoestring potatoes. The kitchen stumbles when it attempts bistro classics like navarin of lamb and carbonade of beef. The navarin was not lacking flavor, but the lamb had been cooked to stringy dryness and came with more of that Sahara-dry couscous. Carbonade, a Flemish dish in which cubes of beef are browned and then cooked with beer, onions, and vegetables, suffered the same fate as the navarin; in fact, the two dishes even looked the same on the plate—with the same couscous.

Among seafood offerings, salmon paillard is moist and tasty, served over mixed greens, tomato, spinach, and fresh chervil. Sole meunière is competently done, too, with green beans, brussels sprouts, and more of that couscous. Two entrée salads sampled were the nicely grilled shrimp over curly chicory and grilled red peppers in a light vinaigrette, and the salade Niçoise, slightly dry cubes of grilled tuna atop sliced potatoes, black olives, greens, and hard-boiled eggs.

Poiret keeps its wine prices in line with the entrées, and the selection is varied.

Except for a subtle cream of asparagus soup, sweet steamed clams, and grilled Bleu de Bresse with lettuce and tomatoes, appetizers are forgettable.

If you are a fan of paper-thin, buttery apple tart, save room for this one. Otherwise, the crème caramel is fine, as is what the menu calls marjolaine cake: layers of génoise, praline, and chocolate. A hot raspberry soufflé is more air than flavor. You would be better off with fresh strawberries and Devon cream (when they're in season).

# POSITANO

★

*250 Park Avenue South, at 20th Street, 777-6211.*

*Atmosphere: Dramatic three-tiered dining room. Deafeningly loud.*

*Service: Pleasant but often overburdened. Long waits at busy times.*

*Wine: Appealing, mostly Italian, moderately priced list. Few bargains.*

*Price range: Moderately expensive.*

*Credit cards: All major cards.*

*Hours: Lunch, noon to 3 P.M., Monday through Friday; dinner, 5:30 to 11:30 P.M., Monday through Thursday, 5:30 P.M. to 12:30 A.M., Friday and Saturday.*

*Reservations: Necessary.*

*Wheelchair accessibility: First level accessible; restrooms on same level but very small.*

"Hi-yaaa!" hails the young waiter dressed in all black, a pastel tie tucked rakishly inside his shirt. "Whaddalya have to drink?" The din on a weeknight at Positano could wilt basil. We bellow our orders immediately, knowing from experience that once a waiter disappears it may be a long dry wait before he visits again.

Positano, which was in the front line of the nouveau Italian invasion of New York in the mid 1980s, seems still to be rolling along at a brisk clip. The three-tiered dining room with a bar on midlevel attracts a substantial business crowd after work, and a younger, casual clientele later.

Positano occupies a pre–World War II building with neo-Gothic accents on Park Avenue South. The tiered dining room with its lofty ceilings and soaring columns makes for a dramatic setting. It is surprising, though, that the management has never dealt with the acoustic problem.

A fine twist on chicken salad proves a good starter, the warm, boned white meat set over a bed of carrots, cubed potatoes, zucchini, and strips of Fontina cheese. A salad combining chicken sausage with watercress, tomato, and mushrooms had lots of flavor, but the sausage was raw.

A special of linguine with sweet baby clams in the shell and a delightful garlic-scented broth with a sharp boost of pepper is so good it should be added to the regular lineup. Another exceptional special was a light and firm spinach cannelloni stuffed with ricotta, mozzarella, and ground veal in a zesty Bolognese sauce. Salmon-filled ravioli had no discernible seafood flavor. Cavatelli is a firm, bullet-shaped pasta that was delicious in a light tomato sauce dressed up with fresh peas, mushrooms, and sausage. While the pastas are almost uniformly pleasing, risotto was hit and miss.

While pastas are as good as ever, several entrées over three visits missed the target: grilled breaded tuna, a special, was dry; grilled red snapper with grilled vegetables was fresh but anemic; and veal scaloppine with garlic and capers was tough once, perfectly cooked the next time.

Among the recommended items are skillfully grilled sweetbreads arranged on a toasty slice of grilled eggplant, sautéed boneless quail in a light tomato sauce with just the right amount of salt from olives and capers, and salmon with Pernod over slices of faintly crunchy fresh fennel.

Two desserts that were memorable several years ago but have lost their edge are tiramisù, which no longer is stout with espresso but rather is sweet with zabaglione, and torta bebe, a cherry-and-cream sponge cake that is now sugary sweet. Espresso granité was pallid, too.

# THE POST HOUSE

★ ★

*28 East 63rd Street, 935-2888.*

*Atmosphere: Sophisticated and masculine steakhouse setting with Americana theme.*

*Service: Prompt and knowledgeable.*

*Wine: Superior all-around list; prices on high side.*

*Price range: Expensive.*

*Credit cards: All major cards.*

*Hours: Lunch, noon to 3 P.M., Monday through Friday; dinner 3 to 11 P.M., Monday through Thursday, until midnight Friday, 5:30 P.M. to midnight, Saturday, 5:30 to 11 P.M., Sunday.*

*Reservations: Necessary.*

*Wheelchair accessibility: Four steps down into the bar area from the street, then three steps down into the dining room. Restrooms at the bar level.*

This classy East Side steakhouse has a long bar up front, beyond which is a polished and warm room with parquet floors, commodious tables, leather armchairs, and decorative American artifacts. It has a virile feeling: with so many men in conservative dark suits, the scene can resemble an American Bar Association convention. You find less locker-room jocularity here than at its sister restaurant, Smith & Wollensky, on East 49th Street. Both are owned by Alan Stillman, a wine aficionado who also owns the Manhattan Ocean Club on West 56th Street and La Cité on West 51st Street.

The Post House is expensive, but the quality of steaks and seafood is top notch, and Andrew Papas, the chef, does them justice. The service staff is brisk and professional but never pushy.

You would be hard pressed to find a better aged rib steak

in town, its crust blackened and well seasoned, the meat richly flavored and juicy. The same Brobdingnagian cut is also prepared Cajun-style with a moderately peppery coating. The monstrous veal chop could not be more tender or flavorful; ditto the lamb chops. Most of the former shotputters who eat here get hash browns (crispy and good) or potato pie (needs seasoning) on the side. Other options include simple but tasty creamed spinach, broccoli with hollandaise sauce, or fried onion rings (all vegetable dishes, which easily serve two, are à la carte, from $6 to $6.50).

Most seafood is equally compelling, whether the broiled or steamed lobster (sizes vary daily), lovely cold poached salmon with a mustardy vinaigrette-style sauce and tomatoes, or the lobster-oyster-scallop pan roast (a Friday special) in a heady cream-based shellfish-stock sauce. The only disappointment was an overcooked tuna steak. Even something as simple as roast chicken is done with a special touch, its skin puffed and crisped and rubbed with lemon rind and ground black pepper. At lunch recently, I sampled the best roast beef hash in town, chunky with potatoes and onions and crowned with a poached egg.

The Post House is becoming a haunt for sophisticated wine drinkers, owing to the broad and provocative (but not budget-priced) list compiled by Raymond Wellington, who is wine director for all of Mr. Stillman's restaurants. Pay particular attention to what is called the California cache, which features sixteen wines from small producers that are sold in New York exclusively by the Post House.

Recommended appetizers include the sweet, plump crab cakes, sautéed shrimp in a thyme-bolstered shellfish-stock sauce with tomatoes and cucumbers, and perfectly sautéed sea scallops on a nest of mixed greens ringed by a tomato concassée. Another winner is called cedar-planked salmon, in which a strip of fillet is cooked over a plank of cedar until just pink inside and infused with a woody nuance, then served with a chive beurre blanc with tomato. If you want something lighter, Caesar salad is the real item.

Desserts are not as uniformly enticing. Among those worth trying are the intense black and white chocolate mousses served in a molded chocolate box garnished with raspberries, a superb blueberry cobbler, and heavy-duty cheesecake with passion fruit and strawberry sauce. Lemon tart was frothy and pallid, and pound cake on the dry side.

# PRIMAVERA

★

*1578 First Avenue, corner 82nd Street, 861-8608.*

*Atmosphere: Formal and urbane.*

*Service: Uneven, depending on whether you are known.*

*Price range: Expensive.*

*Credit cards: All major cards.*

*Hours: Dinner, 5:30 P.M. to midnight, Monday through Saturday, 5 to 10 P.M., Sunday.*

*Reservations: Necessary.*

*Wheelchair accessibility: Dining room on one level; restrooms downstairs.*

This dark, clubby, and expensive Italian restaurant has the looks of a confident winner: burnished mahogany walls, a coffered wood ceiling, soothing paintings, tulip-shaped lamps, waiters in black tie, a well-dressed and lively crowd. My experiences there have been mixed, though, and except for a few notable dishes, Primavera offers a fairly predictable curriculum.

If you start with the seafood appetizer, you get a generous amount of baby squid along with tiny chunks of octopus in an oregano-scented vinaigrette. In my experience the seafood was a bit overcooked but otherwise flavorful and fresh; baked clams are rubbery and stuffed mushrooms are a stodgy concoction of bread crumbs and a tasteless brown sauce.

Better choices are the hearty minestrone soup, blushing-fresh carpaccio with a basil-lemon mayonnaise, and any appetizer featuring the creamy-textured and slightly nutty buffalo mozzarella from Italy. On my last visit steamed mussels were tasty, as was a half order of fettuccine with vibrant pesto sauce. Other pastas sampled were uneven. Among the best are the tortellini with peas and prosciutto. The tortellini were resilient and tasty, while the cream sauce had a delightful smoky tinge. The penne in a fresh and lively tomato sauce with bits of bacon can be good, too.

Service can be as crisp and attentive as you'll find anywhere. Primavera's wine list is a pretentious document unsuited to the cuisine. There are many expensive and prestigious Bordeaux and Burgundies running into the hundreds of dollars but scant choice for those looking for a pleasant drinking wine under $20.

Sautéed veal with prosciutto and spinach was flaccid when I tried it, and paillard of beef was thick and without flavor. A house special, roasted goat with paprika and rosemary, was dry and underseasoned. Simple grilled meats, such as veal or lamb chops, are the best options. Grilled seafood, like salmon or tuna, is generally reliable.

One nice touch is the huge and varied assortment of fresh fruit that is presented at the end of the meal. Among sweets the caramelized apple tart and the winy tiramisù, made with lady fingers, mascarpone cheese, and heavy cream, are the best desserts.

# PRIMOLA

*1226 Second Avenue, near 64th Street, 758-1775.*

**Atmosphere:** *Simple, cheerful room with moderate noise level and good lighting.*

**Service:** *Highly professional.*

**Wine:** *Good standard Italian list; moderate prices.*

**Price range:** *Moderately expensive.*

**Credit cards:** *American Express, MasterCard, and Visa.*

*Hours: Lunch, noon to 3 P.M., Monday through Friday; dinner, 5 P.M. to midnight, Monday through Saturday, until 11 P.M., Sunday.*

*Reservations: Necessary for dinner.*

*Wheelchair accessibility: Dining on main level; restrooms downstairs.*

Primola is a paradigm of a well-managed restaurant, with a dining room that hums like a well-tuned BMW. Juliano Zuliani, the host and co-owner with Franco Iacoviello, the chef, thrives on pressure. Their deftly professional Italian waiters are exceptionally controlled and organized. And except for one evening when the chef seemed to have misplaced his spice rack, the food is as beguiling and consistent as always.

The dining room is good looking in a spare sort of way, with light oak wainscotting under white walls holding pastel sketches and Italian posters, benign lighting, scattered palms, and neighborly tables. Most nights the room buzzes with the tolerable white noise of conversation, which is preferable to the blaring radio on one unusually slow evening. The most serene time is at lunch. Nibble on some moist, herby focaccia while studying the menu: it's much better than the unexpectedly boring bruschetta topped with cottony, tasteless tomatoes.

The written menu is not appreciably different from those at a dozen other northern Italian restaurants in the neighborhood. Most of the standards, though, are exceedingly well executed: chicken with prosciutto and herbs, greaseless veal Milanese, veal Abruzzese (veal scaloppine with prosciutto and peas in a thick veal-stock sauce), and the like. My favorites here are the countrified dishes, like the cut-up chicken sautéed with lots of rosemary and parsley and sweetened with balsamic vinegar. Or the pan-browned quails—the herb dusting embedded in the skin—which are best eaten with the fingers to extract the last morsels of meat. They come with creamy, Parmesan-glazed polenta and a pork sausage that is reminiscent of the gutsy French andouillette.

Cornish hen, a special one evening, was nicely roasted, moister and more flavorful than chicken, with a mildly sharp green-peppercorn sauce and polenta. Chicken breast with fatigued truffles and fontina cheese was a letdown, as was underseasoned sautéed fillet of sole. A better seafood selection is the mixed grill. The players change with the season, but usually include halibut, salmon, scallops, and shrimp over a light yet ripe tomato sauce.

Pasta dishes sampled were prepared with finesse and restraint, from orecchiette (ear-shaped pasta) in a simple but boldly flavored sauce of tomato, zucchini, and warm cubes of mozzarella, and exceptionally fresh linguine with clams and mussels, to black taglierini with shrimp, tender baby squid, and tomato. Billowy pillows of spinach gnocchi were excellent, too, on a palette of fresh tomato sauce with splotches of melted mozzarella. If the one risotto sampled is any indication, that, too, is a felicitous choice: arborio rice, firm to the bite, combined with perfectly cooked baby clams and mussels, scallops, shrimp, and calamari.

Pastas and polenta can be split as appetizers, an option many Italian restaurants do not offer these days. Fine lighter starters include sparkling marinated salmon over slices of fennel with a caper-flavored vinaigrette, a fresh mushroom salad with fennel and shaved Parmesan, and the sautéed porcini mushrooms with garlic. Considering the quality of food and service here, it is puzzling that the wine list is so pedestrian.

Desserts are modest but generally pleasing. They include the homemade gelati (try the excellent ricotta version enhanced with grated lemon rind, or the intense hazelnut) and the moist, rich chocolate almond torte.

# PROVENCE

★ ★

*38 Macdougal Street, at Prince Street, 475-7500.*

*Atmosphere: Casual, stylish country bistro with romantic backyard garden.*

*Service: Overburdened and rushed at times. Often mobbed.*

*Wine: Fine French selection, especially among southern wines.*

*Price range: Moderate.*

*Credit cards: American Express.*

*Hours: Lunch, noon to 3 P.M., Tuesday through Friday, noon to 3:30 P.M., Saturday and Sunday; dinner, 6 to 11:30 P.M., Tuesday through Thursday, 6 to midnight, Friday and Saturday, 5:30 to 11 P.M., Sunday.*

*Reservations: Necessary.*

*Wheelchair accessibility: Dining area on one level; restrooms downstairs.*

Michel Jean does not use the term Provençale carelessly. A native of the Provence region whose roots run deep in the sun-bleached soil, he opened his own restaurant in the summer of 1986 with his wife, Patricia, to celebrate the area's foods and wines. Provence has been a hit from opening day, largely because of its reasonably priced, fresh, and spirited foods that include such specialties as salt cod sautéed with garlic and mixed vegetables, anchovy-and-onion tart, herb-perfumed fish soup, rabbit with basil sauce, oceanic bouillabaisse, and more.

The only clouds over this beguiling terrain are in the form of service. The place is often overbooked, and things can get slow and confused. The ambiance is pleasing and unpretentious. Pale yellow walls hold scallop-shaped sconces, dried flowers add a countrified accent, and tables are neighborly but not cramped. In the back is a romantic little garden with a stone fountain.

Surprises that add an authentic touch abound on the menu, whether an intriguing giveaway called poutargue, croutons coated with the roe of gray mullet; crunchy little salad greens called purslane; or the Jeans' terrific homemade peach wine.

A wonderful introduction to Provençale fare is the morue St. Tropez, a fillet of salt cod sautéed with a lusty combination of tomato, anchovies, bay leaves, black olives, and garlic. It is superb along with some of the chewy country bread. Eggplant purée, fortified with fistfuls of garlic, is a tantalizing choice too, accompanied by three rounds of toast, one slathered with tapenade of black olives, the others with prosciutto and diced tomato, and puréed egg yolks blended with mustard and chickpeas. Other sure-fire starters are the sweet and buttery sea scallops nested on mixed greens in a delicate vinaigrette, and a well-seasoned terrine of rabbit in aspic.

Pissaladière is sort of a Provençale pizza topped with onions, anchovy, and tomato. It can be deliciously light and herbaceous, although the version here was doughy and dry. Raw tuna marinated in lime, basil, and minced peppers is an invigorating way to start the meal, as is the excellent cold cauliflower soup, a special.

Mr. Jean's authentic approach extends to the well-priced wine list, which offers a sampling of Provence labels. The crisp white Cassis is delightful (about $25); among reds, the Bandol is a ripe and pleasing bargain for about $20.

Dezso Szonntagh, the Hungarian-born chef who came over from Le Cirque, is not diffident with seasonings, as can be seen in the tarragon-bolstered veal medallions in lemon sauce, a serendipitous combination; tender strips of lamb alongside a thyme-and-garlic-haunted ratatouille; and the gusty bouillabaisse, replete with mussels, clams, eel, and snapper in a rich tomato-tinged fish stock.

A heady specialty from the Mediterranean coast that is rarely found in restaurants here is called bourride, which is a fish stew bound with garlic mayonnaise. This rendition ranks right up there with those I have had in France—a garlic-fueled combination of lotte, squid, and cod.

After all this garlic, your staggering taste buds will yearn for something sweet and revivifying. Homemade fruit sorbets doused with eau de vie will do the trick; light and semisweet orange terrine with white-chocolate sauce is a winning combination, too. Those who believe that Le Cirque serves the best crème brûlée in the galaxy will be amazed by the perfect clone here, which Mr. Jean obviously has studied meticulously. If you really want to be Provençale, have some of that peach wine, sit back, and peel a fresh peach.

# PRUNELLE

*18 East 54th Street, 759-6410.*

*Atmosphere: Handsome, understated room with burled-maple walls, gentle lighting, and lavish flower displays.*

*Service: Staff is professional and pleasant.*

*Wine: Sizable list but few bargains.*

*Price range: Moderately expensive.*

*Credit cards: All major cards.*

*Hours: Lunch, noon to 3 P.M., Monday through Friday; dinner, 5:30 to 11 P.M., daily.*

*Reservations: Suggested.*

*Wheelchair accessibility: Everything on one level.*

For six years, Prunelle, owned by Jacky Rhuette and his chef, Pascal Dirringer, has been the Chicago Cubs of big-time French restaurants, slugging it out with the best but never quite garnering the pennant. It is an alluring place, cloaked in polished burled maple, with Art Deco etched-glass partitions, luxuriant flowers, well-spaced tables, and soft, indirect lighting. And the decorous service staff is well schooled in the food and wine. The restaurant's trappings, attitude, and menu bespeak grandeur; the food overall is very good, too, though at times it seems a little formulaic.

An example of the kitchen's shortcomings among appetizers is a near-miss of shrimp with angel-hair pasta with a sauce of olive oil and tomatoes. The shrimp were a bit overcooked, and the sauce was ladled around the pasta rather than on it: attractive but illogical. Big, fluted ravioli filled with lobster had little flavor themselves but came in a pool of lovely lobster stock. Crab cakes are better, meaty and well browned, served with mixed greens and asparagus in a creamy vinaigrette.

Few bargains can be found on the good-sized wine list, especially at the lower end.

Entrées are more consistent, particularly seafood. Giant sea scallops are crisply seared and teamed up with spaghetti squash and blinis garnished with different caviars. Salmon is deftly grilled and set over spinach with a cleansing herb-and-lemon-accented vinaigrette. I had hoped that the two-sauce phenomenon had vanished along with kiwi garnishes and the silver-dollar portions of nouvelle cuisine, but it came back to haunt me here: a fine fillet of halibut, moist and with a crisp golden crust, was flanked by julienne potatoes and carrots and, flowing along the banks of the plate, two rivers of sauce, one of basil butter, the other a red-pepper coulis. Not a bad dish, really, but what's the point? The only fish that really sank was the dry and unevenly seasoned swordfish with ginger.

You get a nice portion of venison loin here, well peppered, with snow peas and spaetzle, and a homey rack of lamb with turned vegetables. Simple roast chicken with tarragon, though, was a letdown: no tarragon flavor, in fact not much flavor at all. At lunch, a hefty and satisfying dish was veal, liberally peppered, with spaetzle and wild mushrooms.

A new pastry chef is turning out some dizzying creations. Two that disappeared fast at my table were an airy caramel mousse and the fabulous chocolate mousse layer cake. Gratin of crème brûlée is another worthy indulgence.

# QUATORZE

★ ★

*240 West 14th Street, 206-7006.*

*Atmosphere: Casual and comfortable bistro; can be loud when full.*

*Service: Capable and efficient.*

*Wine: Paragon of a bistro wine list; well matched to food and moderately priced.*

*Price range: Moderate.*

*Credit cards: American Express.*

*Hours: Lunch, noon to 2:30 P.M., Monday through Friday; dinner, 6 to 11:30 P.M., Monday through Saturday; 5:30 to 11:30 P.M., Sunday.*

*Reservations: Necessary, especially for dinner.*

*Wheelchair accessibility: Two steps down to dining room; all facilities on one level.*

Quatorze's modest setting is as guileless as the food—a long, pale-yellow-toned room with maroon wood trim, Art Deco sconces that cast even light, French posters, and neighborly banquettes. Waiters minimize banal chatter and get right down to business in a genial, professional manner. On busy evenings, the gregarious crowd can be distractingly loud; lunch is a much more tranquil affair.

When Quatorze opened in late 1985 along West 14th Street, a Latin-flavored commercial strip of bodegas, cut-rate clothing emporiums, and bilingual driving schools, it seemed as incongruous as Yves Montand in a salsa band. Yet the restaurant was an immediate hit. This is the sort of place you go to for sustenance, not surprises.

On a slushy winter evening when your bone marrow feels like sorbet, a lusty bowl of cabbage-and-white-bean soup is so restorative it should be delivered around the neck of a Saint Bernard. Follow that with a grilled sirloin steak with an herby béarnaise sauce, a woodpile of brittle french fries, and a glass of robust red wine, and spring seems just around the corner.

The menu is concise, supplemented by several daily specials. Among the reliable starters are pristine oysters on the half shell (varieties depend on the season), mildly livery terrine enlivened with green peppercorns, and sweet marinated herring with onions. The classic French salad called frisée aux lardons (chicory with bacon and croutons in a warm bacon vinaigrette) is nicely turned out here, almost a meal in itself. The regular house green salad, though, was harsh with too much vinegar. An inviting special one evening was bay scallops wedged between sheets of airy puff pastry ringed with a red-pepper purée; beef barley soup rich with a good stock was bracing, too.

The wine selection at Quatorze is a paragon of what a bistro wine list should be—it complements the food perfectly and is priced right.

When I want something homey and straightforward, I get the grilled half chicken with french fries, for its herb-seasoned meat and crisp skin will be cooked to a turn. Green beans and carrots come on the side. Grilled fillet of salmon comes with a fine choron sauce (a béarnaise sauce blended with puréed tomatoes). Quatorze makes much ado about its choucroute garnie, the Alsace specialty of sauerkraut with pork and assorted sausages, but I could never warm to it. On more than one occasion, the sauerkraut was limp and tasted as if it had been reheated repeatedly; except for the snappy garlic sausage, the rest of the meats were humdrum.

A special one day of pork chops stuffed with prunes sounded compelling, but was dried out. Duck is prepared in an interesting way. The breast is grilled rare, and the sinewy leg is braised to succulent tenderness, served with pan juices and roast potatoes.

The dessert of choice is still the thin, buttery apple tart, followed by an excellent crème caramel and a deadly rich flourless chocolate cake.

As of this writing, Quatorze is opening a branch at 323 East 79th Street, 535-1414.

# THE QUILTED GIRAFFE

★ ★ ★ ★

*550 Madison Avenue, at 55th Street, in the AT&T arcade, 593-1221.*

*Atmosphere: Modern, mini-amphitheater with stainless-steel walls, leather banquettes, and candlelight.*

*Service: Excellent.*

*Wine: Wide, expensive American and French selection, prices more varied among California labels.*

*Price range: Expensive.*

*Credit cards: All major cards.*

*Hours: Lunch, noon to 1:30 P.M., Tuesday through Friday; dinner, 5:30 to 10 P.M., Tuesday through Saturday.*

*Reservations: Necessary well in advance.*

*Wheelchair accessibility: Dining room and restrooms on one level.*

Many consider the Quilted Giraffe synonymous with farcical New York prices. But it also happens to turn out exquisitely original food, making each experience there an intellectual and gustatory epiphany. Four years ago, when Barry and Susan Wine, the owners, offered menus of $75 and $100 (plus an 18 percent service charge), many people were shocked. Enough insouciant expense-account types came in to fill the room, but the stock-market crash in October 1987, among other factors, ended that binge. Only in the last year or so has business come back to near precrash levels, the Wines say, thanks in part to a sizable international clientele.

As other Manhattan luxury restaurants approach the $60 prix-fixe plateau, $75 no longer seems so outlandish for this level of excellence. (The tasting menu is now $110.) When the restaurant moved to the AT&T arcade on East 55th Street from its intimate town house on Second Avenue in

1986, the new room's stainless-steel walls, black granite tables, and "Star Trek" lighting columns left many customers cold. The room has been softened considerably with tablecloths, candlelight, abstract Japanese art, and prodigious flower clusters. The food is served on a magnificent array of Japanese ceramics that contrast with the colorful ingredients.

For example, little pizzas combining pink hickory-smoked salmon with crispy fried capers and a layer of mashed potatoes (but a tough crust) are served on stark black plates. A more successful assembly is pan-seared sweetbreads with a soy sauce sweetened with caramel and decorated with crunchy antennae of deep-fried soba noodles. Sour cherries are an inspired match for warm morsels of peppered duck with spaghetti squash and translucent ravioli filled with Swiss chard. Tuna fillet, also sharpened with pepper, is tempered with a mild wasabi cream.

As sublime as the house signature beggar's purses (beluga caviar gift-wrapped in thin crêpes with a touch of crème fraîche) are, at $50 extra a pop (on the $75 menu) they give me heartburn. One of the more winsome new appetizers is called potato risotto, which is really potatoes cut to resemble rice cooked in cream and sprinkled with bacon bits and oven-crisped shiitake mushrooms.

No small part of the blissful experience here is the able and reserved service staff, which keeps a trained eye on your table but from a comfortable distance. The wine list is extensive across the board. California chardonnays and cabernet sauvignons are priced at nearly twice retail level, which is standard; the Bordeaux selection is elitist, with most in the three-digit bracket.

Picking wines for some of the entrées may require skilled help. What do you drink with two wonderful but challenging dishes like grilled Norwegian salmon with a sweet-hot mustard glaze and deep-fried beets, and sublime sautéed sea bass with sake sauce and cooling cucumber? Less tricky are the delicious grilled sweetbreads with purée of Provençale herbs, and a five-fish platter holding kisu, a Japanese delicacy that looks like a large smelt; syori, a needle-nose species with tender mild flesh; briny red shrimp from Maine; scallops in warm vinaigrette sauce; and sea urchin. One entrée that worked visually but failed to excite the palate was giant sea scallops with nearly raw braised celery and an unmemorable sweet-potato cream sauce.

If your spirit and wallet are propitious, you might go for the $135 Western version of a kaiseki dinner, a tradition-bound ten-course Japanese meal built around seasonal ingredients and personally served by the chef. Mr. Wine goes all out for this, trotting out of the kitchen beaming like a ten-year-old carrying Mom's breakfast-in-bed on Mother's Day. The ever changing repertory, in which the chef alternates Western and Eastern tasting portions, is as spectacular as it is culturally illuminating: ours started with beggar's purses and the best vichyssoise I've ever tasted; swordfish and wasabi pizza; sizzling baby squid with ginger-scented enoki and shiitake mushrooms; smoked salmon over pickled seaweed; and beef seared on one side, nearly raw on the other, with confetti of corn kernels and mashed potatoes. The polymorphic parade rolls on, ending with an assortment of the house's superlative desserts.

One of my favorites from the early days is phyllo crumple, a pleated disk of fragile dough encasing apples and raisins, served with vanilla ice cream. Pecan squares with warm whipped cream are a revelation, as is the astoundingly good vanilla custard served with homemade cookies.

The controversial Quilted Giraffe is one of those institutions that embody this city of excess and risk taking. The Wines have cut their own sometimes rocky path for fifteen years, and their dedication to excellence can only be admired.

# THE RAINBOW ROOM

*30 Rockefeller Plaza, 65th floor, 632-5000.*

*Atmosphere: Sumptuous Art Moderne dining room with panoramic views and revolving dance floor.*

*Service: Waiters professional and pleasant, but the pacing of the meal is slow.*

*Wine: Large international list; good selection in $20–40 range.*

*Price range: Expensive.*

*Credit cards: American Express.*

*Hours: Brunch, 11:30 A.M. to 1:30 P.M., Sunday; pretheater dinner, 5:30 and 6 P.M. seatings, Tuesday through Saturday; dinner, 6:30 to 10:30 P.M., Tuesday through Saturday, 5:30 to 9:30 P.M., Sunday; supper, 11 P.M. to midnight, Tuesday through Saturday.*

*Reservations: Required well in advance.*

*Wheelchair accessibility: Gradual terraced dining room that could be negotiated with help; restrooms down a long corridor with several steps.*

The two-year, $25-million facelift of this two-story complex, whose cynosure is the Art Moderne ballroom called the Rainbow Room, has been a rousing success. The gracefully terraced room wonderfully evokes another era in New York: wraparound views of the city and beyond, aubergine silk walls, cast-glass balusters, a tiered bandstand, period outfits on the service staff, and a giant crystal chandelier poised over the revolving dance floor. The renovation, overseen by Joseph Baum, the restaurant consultant, does not make the Rainbow Room feel like a new or, heaven forbid, trendy place. It's as if ghosts of the prewar years have been jitterbugging up there all along—and they just recently invited us to join in.

The food soothes but never distracts, just like the mollified pop and show music performed by a tag-team of bands (one a twelve-piece brass-and-keyboard ensemble, the other a bloodless salsa group). André René, the chef whom Mr. Baum recruited when he created Windows on the World in the late 1970s, turns out a fine Black Angus sirloin with an herby béarnaise sauce, juicy rack of lamb for two, and rosy venison steak in a grand veneur sauce touched with red currants—the meat entrées come with festive pommes soufflés. Or you can nibble down memory lane with lightened renditions of such culinary artifacts as lobster thermidor or tournedos Rossini, a rare-cooked (and rather bland) filet mignon under a slab of foie gras and set in a truffle-enriched stock sauce.

Pigeon en cocotte is a solid winner: succulent braised squab in a lustrous stock sauce flanked by fresh green peas and pearl onions. Dried-out grilled swordfish cannot be rescued by its pretty diadem of baby carrots and marrow-enriched red-wine sauce, and roulade of red snapper and salmon is tasteless unless you dredge it in lots of the roasted-red-pepper purée—a timbale of eggplant and tomato alongside is bright and tasty, though.

Out on the wooden turntable, couples who for years have been looking for a place like this where they could dance, are spinning in blissful unison. Women weighted down with jewelry parade their most showy lamé and sequined gowns; many men dress up in tuxedos just for fun. An evening at the Rainbow Room runs on for at least three hours. You can't really fault the enthusiastic and well-trained waiters; one suspects that either the kitchen is slow or the meal is paced that way for dancers. (A $15-a-person music charge is imposed nightly).

Appetizers are almost uniformly good. The shellfish extravaganza is a diverting way to start, an iced platter heaped with mussels, oysters, clams, lobster, crab, and more (depending on the season). Two starters that seem appropriate in this setting are the excellent steak tartare crowned with iced sevruga caviar, and oysters Rockefeller, the shells lined with blanched spinach and slivers of fennel, all under a light glaze. The Rainbow Room's international wine list offers something for every taste and budget, with decent selections starting under $25.

For dessert, an intensely nutty frozen praline soufflé is scooped out in the center and lubricated with hot chocolate sauce; chocolate sorbet is sharp and refreshing as part of a trio that also includes mango and lemon. Skip the boring pear charlotte for the crumbly crusted fruit tarts. If you are in a particularly nostalgic or silly mood, order the baked alaska and marvel at the flaming volcano of meringue-covered sponge cake and ice cream.

The Rainbow Room is a musical time machine that blasts off nightly with a crew of insouciant mirthmakers (at about

# RENÉ PUJOL

★

*321 West 51st Street, 246-3023.*

*Atmosphere: Old World French background with timbered walls, stucco, and fireplace.*

*Service: Can be haphazard and slow at lunch; better at dinner.*

*Price range: Moderately expensive (dinner prix fixe, $30–35).*

*Credit cards: All major cards.*

*Hours: Lunch, noon to 3 P.M., Monday through Friday; dinner, 5 to 11:30 P.M., Monday through Saturday.*

*Reservations: Suggested during theater hours.*

*Wheelchair accessibility: Three steps at entrance; all facilities on one level.*

René Pujol is among the few survivors on the endangered-species list of family-run French restaurants in the Broadway theater district. As so many in this aging fraternity succumb to old age or indifference, René Pujol has remained relatively vigorous. The menu is built upon the culinary crossbeams of classic bourgeois fare, with just a few nods to contemporary tastes.

The dining rooms have period stucco-and-timber walls holding copper knickknacks and an oversize mural of the home country, a fireplace and red plaid rugs. At lunchtime the place is jumping, while at night it languishes.

Upon being seated you are served a ramekin of pork rillettes, a lusty blend of shredded and aggressively seasoned meat moistened with—dare I say it?—pure fat. It is delicious smeared over French bread. Lunch and dinner menus are essentially the same except for specials. Onion soup, steaks, simple sautéed seafood, stews, and such are the path to satisfaction. Sauces, especially those made with cream and eggs, are mighty rich for contemporary tastes.

The appetizer list offers no surprises. Duck terrine is rustic and tasty, generously spiked with cognac. Lean fresh salmon perfumed with dill and served with a dill mayonnaise is more interesting than plain smoked salmon. An example of the chef's heavy hand with cream is the cloyingly rich fish mousse, an outer ring of scallop and pike mousse surrounding a core of lobster dotted with pistachio shards. As the cold weather comes on you can't go wrong with the intense and soothing old-fashioned onion soup.

Service at lunch can drag when the pace gets frenetic; on slow evenings the operation is smoother. The wine list has much of historic interest, with many fine old vintages in the three-digit category; at the same time, you can find a few pleasing lesser Bordeaux and Burgundies in the $20 range.

Square meals, not adventurous ones, are what you should seek among the entrées. Rack of lamb for two with pan juices and assorted tiny vegetables cannot be faulted. A special, steak with four kinds of peppers—black, white, red, and green—sets off an intriguing volley of sensations (but the regular steak au poivre with black pepper that's on the menu is muted under a stodgy thick sauce). Pink sautéed veal kidneys are fresh and assertive in their red-wine sauce.

A lunch special, roast chicken in tarragon sauce, was more compelling than a similar dish in a pale Calvados cream sauce garnished with apple slices. For fish, go with the Dover sole meunière, which is undramatic but fresh, or the poached salmon with a good lemony hollandaise sauce. Grilled tuna prepared Provençale style with sun-dried tomatoes and peas, a lunch special, was lively but overcooked by about two minutes; on a second sampling it was better.

Several desserts are arresting: a coal-black slab of chocolate marquise set in a pool of crème anglaise, pear charlotte in a multicolored fresh fruit sauce, and bright fruit sorbets. Orange cake is gelatinous and overly sweet; a sugary glaze also mars the apricot fruit tart.

René Pujol holds the torch of classic French food in this once solidly Gallic neighborhood. While there are ample good dishes to satisfy theatergoers, some updating in the kitchen would make the torch burn brighter.

# THE RIVER CAFÉ

★ ★ ★

*1 Water Street, Brooklyn, (718) 522-5200.*

*Atmosphere: Romantic dining room on a barge with stunning views of Manhattan and the East River.*

*Service: Professional if sometimes mannered.*

*Wine: Excellent international list, especially strong among older California vintages; prices vary.*

*Price range: Expensive (prix-fixe dinner, $55).*

*Credit cards: All major cards.*

*Hours: Brunch, noon to 2:30 P.M., Saturday, 11:30 to 2:30 P.M., Sunday; lunch, noon to 2:30 P.M., Monday through Friday; dinner, 6 to 11 P.M., daily.*

*Reservations: Necessary a week or more in advance.*

*Wheelchair accessibility: Ramps into the dining room. All facilities on one level.*

The River Café, on a barge on the Brooklyn shore of the East River under the Brooklyn Bridge, remains one of the most spellbinding settings in New York. The vista of lower Manhattan across the busy waterway is stirring any time of day but especially at dusk, when the sky deepens to silvery indigo and the lights begin flickering in the glass towers. The dining room—with a piano bar on one side and rows of well-spaced tables, all with good views—attracts a blend of special-occasion revelers, out-of-town visitors, and well-heeled New Yorkers. Despite the festive nature of the place, noise is rarely bothersome.

The River Café has seen three chefs in the last six years: first Larry Forgione, who established it as one of the premier all-American restaurants in the country; then Charles

Palmer, who added his own distinctive touch until quietly moving on last December to open his own place. Since early 1988, the chef has been twenty-six-year-old David Burke, an inventive former sous chef at the café who spent most of 1987 training in France with such luminaries as Gaston Lenôtre, Georges Blanc, and Marc Meneau.

Mr. Burke obviously has fun with food presentation, and many of his winsome creations leave diners loath to disassemble them. The pristine carpaccio of yellowfin tuna comes with a dome of salmon tartar on top pierced with two corrugated potatoes and a ruffle of crème fraîche speckled with black olives; bright green snow peas ring the dish. Quail legs are stuffed with foie gras, enveloped in pasta, and served so the bones form little handles; the legs and sautéed quail breasts are set in a clear, heady mushroom broth flecked with pistachios.

A starter called warm pastrami-cured salmon belly was too provocative to pass up. This eccentric twist on the New York deli staple is cured in coriander, salt, pepper, and sugar overnight, then brushed with a mélange of peppery spices and smoked. The ruddy strips of salmon are pleasingly salty and leave a piquant echo on the palate. They are served with creamy mashed potatoes and artichoke sections rubbed with mustard oil.

The café's service staff is well informed and highly proficient. The recently updated wine list, which includes a special selection of older California vintages, reflects considerable care.

Mr. Burke is a flashier chef than his predecessor, sometimes a bit too flashy. Some of the best entrées are the least cerebral: superb aged Black Angus sirloin, grilled over fruitwood and served with a lusty red-wine sauce and rosti potatoes, or the perfectly sautéed salmon steak embedded with cracked pepper and ginger, over an invigorating red-wine-and-butter sauce perfumed with ginger. Tuna steak also is masterly prepared, under a thin golden roof of sautéed potatoes. Sweet, buttery sea scallops are set in the center of the plate and ringed with a vegetable-bouillon-based sauce scattered with minced black olives, carrots, white beans, and broccoli florets.

One effort that failed to excite my intrepid crew of tasters was the overproduced grilled chicken breast that came with a staggering supporting cast: mushroom sausage, morels, black-olive pasta, and tomato sauce, all of which muddled the plot.

Several desserts are worth rowing across the East River for: the incredibly light timbale-shaped banana-and-chocolate parfait with light and dark chocolate sauces; an assortment of sublime chocolate pastries, ice creams and cookies; and sharp, moist cinnamon pudding with crème anglaise. Plum tart is a distant runner-up, although the lemon cream accompanying it is great, and crème brûlée is a winner.

# ROGERS & BARBERO

**SATISFACTORY**

*149 Eighth Avenue, near 17th Street, 243-2020.*

*Atmosphere: Comfortable and genial spot in natural wood and teal blue.*

*Service: Likable but not very vigilant.*

*Price range: Moderate (prix-fixe dinner, $19.95).*

*Credit cards: American Express, MasterCard, and Visa.*

*Hours: Brunch, noon to 4 P.M., Sunday; lunch, noon to 3 P.M., Monday through Friday; late lunch, 3 to 5:30 P.M., Monday through Friday, 4 to 5:30 P.M., Sunday; dinner: 5:30 to midnight, Monday through Saturday, 5:30 to 11 P.M., Sunday.*

*Reservations: Suggested.*

*Wheelchair accessibility: Dining facilities available on ground level; restrooms downstairs.*

Rogers & Barbero is an inviting and genial spot with a natural wood bar up front flanked by high-backed booths and a cluster of tables; another dining area in the back is done in cool teal blue with a high ceiling and wood trim. Soft jazz adds to the easygoing charm of the room: it's the kind of place you would go to with a close friend for a long, soul-baring conversation.

As for the contemporary American food, it has many peaks and valleys that are hard to comprehend: success or failure has little to do with level of difficulty, ingredients, pressure on the kitchen, or any of the normal variables. Virtually all the preparations sound appealing; it's just that many don't work.

A good way to start is with the warm salad of sliced chicken breast with balsamic vinegar, nubbly wild rice sweetened with black currants, and roasted peppers. Another good choice is the roasted vegetables (eggplant and red peppers) paired with firm-cooked lentils moistened with a sherry vinaigrette.

Onion tart with sun-dried tomatoes was a harmonious combination except that the crust was tired and soggy, while angel-hair pasta with smoked salmon and scallions was tasteless. Slightly more interesting was the spinach-filled ravioli glossed with a spinach-flecked butter sauce.

Rogers & Barbero takes its wines seriously, and the well-chosen list has plenty of good selections under in the $20 neighborhood.

The old reliables on this menu are the crunchy and moist Southern fried chicken with mashed potatoes and gravy, as well as the flank steak tenderized in a marinade of dark beer, ginger, and garlic. The sinewy slices of medium-rare beef were exceptionally tender and full of flavor. Considering those successes, it is difficult to understand why the kitchen turns out a dry, bland pot roast that is reminiscent of a high-school cafeteria, or red snapper that is so overcooked it curls up on both ends. The chef cannot get enough of sun-dried tomatoes; they show up in the grilled chicken breast with shiitake mushrooms, a pleasing combination, and a less successful shrimp-and-cucumber match with a bland butter sauce. One house specialty that has been on the menu almost since the restaurant opened is thinly sliced calf's liver in a warm garlic vinaigrette sweetened with maple syrup: if you have a sweet tooth, you will like it.

The dessert list is supplemented by a large selection of sherries, ports, and other sweet wines. Homemade ice creams are the most reliable of the desserts, especially the intense hazelnut.

# ROSA MEXICANO

★ ★

*1063 First Avenue, at 58th Street, 753-7407.*

*Atmosphere: Lively grill room up front, slightly more subdued back room done in shades of rose and pink.*

*Service: Well-informed staff, but not as vigilant as it should be.*

*Wine: Token list; beer and margaritas preferable.*

*Price range: Moderately expensive.*

*Credit cards: All major cards.*

*Hours: Lunch, noon to 3:30 P.M., Monday through Saturday; Sunday buffet, noon to 3:30 P.M.; dinner, 5 p.m. to midnight, daily.*

*Reservations: Necessary.*

*Wheelchair accessibility: One small step up at entrance; restrooms on same level.*

Most Mexican restaurants here are American-owned margaritavilles that churn out cliché food characterized by mountains of shredded iceberg lettuce, indigestible deep-fried tacos, and more starch than a Chinese laundry. Rosa Mexicano is one of the rare exceptions. Josephina Howard, the chef and co-owner, is a diligent researcher of Mexican regional cooking. Her menu is relatively light, emphasizing grilled meats and fish as well as casseroles seasoned with mole sauces, various chili combinations, and herbs. This is not a place for thrill seekers with asbestos palates. Virtually all dishes are mildly spiced.

The front room, with a long, open kitchen, is the livelier and louder of the two dining areas. The back room, done in warm rose-colored stucco, is ringed by high-backed pink banquettes and has dramatically illuminated tropical greenery in the center. You might want to start off with the house special margarita made with pomegranate, or the traditional version: both catch up with you fast. Mexican beer is the other beverage of choice with this food.

Rosa Mexicano has become justly renowned for its superior guacamole, which is prepared at tableside to your specification: mild, moderately hot, hot, or bring-me-a-garden-hose-with-it hot. Another favorite starter is called taquitos de moronga, good grainy corn tortillas rolled around blood sausage, onions, and fresh coriander; also recommended are the taquitos de tinga poblana, tortillas filled with shredded pork, smoked jalapeño chilies, onions, and tomato.

On glacial winter evenings, the sopa de bolitas is welcome, a rich chicken broth with fat corn dumplings, bits of tomato, and grated white cheese.

A creation called ostiones enchilados, or sautéed oysters in cold marinade of chilies and spices, was not as satisfying as I remember from previous visits, primarily because the oysters were overcooked. Better seafood selections are the meaty lump crabmeat sautéed in a zesty combination of onions, fresh coriander, celery, and mild chilies, served cool.

Waiters are well informed about the food and helpful in recommending dishes, although they are not always as attentive as they should be when it comes to follow-up duties. One entrée that is an unqualified winner is tamal en cazuela, a lusty casserole of cornmeal similar to polenta, with chicken in an earthy dark mole sauce sprinkled with melted fresh cheese. Budin Azteca is another casserole-style dish, this one made with layers of tortillas holding shredded chicken, white cheese, and a mildly spicy chili poblano sauce. Sliced duckmeat is rolled in tortillas along with a faintly sweet, rough-textured pumpkin-seed sauce.

Nearly half the main courses are grilled. Grilled whole red snapper with rice and beans was overcooked on two samplings (a baked fillet of grouper was better, well cooked and delicate in its warm coriander vinaigrette). Shell steak is satisfying, but rather plain with just a few strips of sautéed chili poblano on top.

Flan is as much a part of Mexican life as the siesta. The firm, eggy custard here comes with an espresso sauce that was rich and aromatic one evening, unpleasantly harsh another time. Coconut ice cream with raspberry sauce is a fine alternative, as is pink-fleshed cactus pear.

# ROSE CAFE

★

*24 Fifth Avenue, at Ninth Street, 260-4118.*

*Atmosphere: Lively setting with glass-enclosed terrace on Fifth Avenue.*

*Service: Friendly and efficient.*

*Wine: Good French and American selection at sensible prices.*

*Price range: Moderate.*

*Credit cards: American Express, MasterCard, and Visa.*

*Hours: Brunch, 11:30 A.M. to 3:30 P.M., Saturday and Sunday; lunch, 11:30 A.M. to 3:30 P.M., Monday through Friday; dinner, 5:30 P.M. to 12:30 A.M., Monday through Thursday, until 1:30 A.M. Friday and Saturday.*

*Reservations: Necessary.*

*Wheelchair accessibility: Two steps at front door, restrooms on lower dining-room level (one step from main level).*

If you have any doubts that New Yorkers are in a thrifty mood these days, just drop into the teeming dining room of Rose Cafe, an upbeat American restaurant on lower Fifth Avenue that serves single-digit appetizers and main courses that peak at $19. The success of this place is even more impressive considering it occupies a sauce that has seen two higher-priced flops in the past four years, Mosaico and 24 Fifth Avenue.

Rose Cafe is owned by Richard Krause, the former chef and co-owner of the defunct Melrose in Greenwich Village, and two partners, Stewart Rosen and Philip Scotti. The three dining areas can be somewhat close and at times loud, but not excessively so. The flamboyant tiles and bold colors of the late Mosaico have been replaced by soft eggshell-toned walls and simple cylinder-shaped sconces. A glass-enclosed sidewalk terrace affords an animated urban panorama.

Mr. Krause's menu carries at least one hit reminiscent of Melrose: irresistible little potato pancakes with a dollop of crème fraîche and three kinds of caviar. One gutsy starter is the beanless duck and venison chili, which has a nice delayed kick of cayenne. Clam chowder is emboldened with lightly smoked bacon, leeks, and corn, and two bright, fresh salads can be recommended: the enormous mound of chicory with smoked bacon and crumbled goat cheese, and the warm new potato salad with string beans, strips of lightly smoked sturgeon, and bacon in a mustardy vinaigrette.

One alluring-sounding starter is a salad of lentils and tempura of red onions. The lentils are delicious, aromatic of rosemary and enlivened with red-pepper oil, but the onion tempura (essentially onion rings) is on the greasy side.

The genial staff here has to hustle to keep up with the crowds, and only occasionally do they or the kitchen fall behind. Rose Cafe has assembled a wide-ranging wine list —mostly French and American—at sensible prices.

As a graduate of the California school of grilling, Mr. Krause has a deft touch over the coals. This can be seen in the grilled chicken with a subtle mustard cream sauce flanked by well-seasoned spring vegetables. Light, cleanly fried shoestring potatoes on the side didn't last long at our table. Two other grilled items excel: salmon steak that is nicely blackened outside and deep pink in the center, along with a similar vegetable medley; and charred tuna with a zesty vinaigrette combining sweet mango, tomato, and green onions.

A flavorful shell steak came off the fires a bit more cooked than requested, and with a pallid green peppercorn sauce. Watery and bland mashed potatoes provided little compensation. A better bet would be the terrific brittle-skinned Peking duck with plum sauce and thin sheets of scallion pancakes, or tender roasted saddle of rabbit paired with linguine in a basil and tomato cream sauce. Spaghetti with a leek and cream sauce was memorable mostly for the portion size. The morel-flavored sauce had a pleasing subtle flavor, but the veal meatballs standing guard around the plate were exceedingly dry.

For dessert, three superlative choices are the raspberry tart, light but intense chocolate soufflé cake, and plum-raspberry crisp with crème fraîche. Two all-American options are the crusty apple crisp sweetened with raisins and currants, and the run-of-the-mill strawberry shortcake.

# ROSEMARIE'S

★

*145 Duane Street, 285-2610, between West Broadway and Church Street.*

*Atmosphere: Romantic brick-walled dining room with well-spaced tables.*

*Service: Affable and casual. Can be slow.*

*Wine: Well-chosen, moderate-size list.*

*Price range: Moderately expensive.*

*Credit cards: American Express, MasterCard, and Visa.*

*Hours: Lunch, noon to 3 P.M., Monday through Friday; dinner, 5:30 to 10:30 P.M., Monday through Thursday, until 11 P.M., Friday and Saturday.*

*Reservations: Suggested.*

*Wheelchair accessibility: Small step at entrance; restroom doors narrow.*

Rosemarie's is one of those enchanting out-of-the-way restaurants you immediately want to love. I tried it twice in its early days, but never swooned over the kitchen's unpredictable output. In the past year, though, I heard murmurings of improvements there, which three more samplings confirmed.

Rosemarie Verderame, a physical therapist turned restaurant manager, opened her own establishment in Tri-BeCa months ago after having lived in Italy. Finding reliable chefs turned out to be her biggest challenge, thus the uneven food for so many months.

The dining room is brick walled with a photo-mural of an Italian cloister covering one wall. Display cases hold pretty ceramics. Tables are widely spaced to allow privacy and comfort. Rosemarie's gets a young Wall Street crowd as well as some of the newer residents of this increasingly popular downtown residential area.

Pastas are by far the best bets here. Among the winners is the saffron fettuccine in what is called a seafood Bolognese sauce, a vibrant shellfish stock loaded with scallops, shrimp, and onions. Another contender is the stracci, folded triangles of thin pasta, with moist boneless chicken, sliced artichoke hearts, snow peas, and wild mushrooms.

Among starters, a special of nice veal sausage and wild mushrooms was marred only by a portion of oversalted polenta. Fried calamari rings were clean and crunchy, and sautéed wild mushrooms seasoned with sage, garlic, and pancetta were a rustic delight. Perhaps the best appetizer is the lusty salt-cod soup, thick and peppery, into which you stir some serious garlic-infused aïoli. One fancy dish that didn't work was basil-cured salmon set over a burned potato crust and crowned with crème fraîche and salmon caviar.

The best main courses are the least complicated, such as the roast chicken with buttery mashed potatoes garnished with strips of prosciutto; rosemary-scented roast loin of lamb with eggplant purée and red-pepper sauce; veal chop with glazed carrots and chive sauce; and osso buco over a richly flavored base of garlic and white beans. For seafood, roasted snapper over fennel with a saffron vinaigrette was the best.

Desserts are hit and miss. The tiramisù laced with Kahlúa was not as sweet as one might expect. Hazelnut ice cream was good, too, as was the chunky chocolate mousse cake (although the espresso sauce was filled with coffee grounds).

# ROUMELI TAVERNA

★

*33-04 Broadway, Astoria, Queens, (718) 278-7533.*

*Atmosphere: Festive and informal dining room with illuminated vines on the walls and ceilings and a buoyant Greek clientele.*

*Service: Glum and workmanlike.*

*Price range: Moderate.*

*Credit cards: American Express.*

*Hours: 11:30 A.M. to 1:30 A.M., daily.*

*Reservations: Suggested.*

*Wheelchair accessibility: Dining room on one level; restrooms in the basement.*

Distinctive Greek cuisine is difficult to come by in New York City, even in Astoria, Queens, our own little Peloponnesus just over the East River. The restaurant scene there is just as volatile as in Manhattan, with reputations rising and falling like the river tide. One of the more reliable and diverting spots in the neighborhood is Roumeli Taverna along bustling Broadway (just two blocks from the N subway stop).

It's always Christmastime inside the Roumeli Taverna, where the stucco walls are hidden behind a jungle of leafy vines ablaze with hundreds of tiny bulbs. At the entrance, a glass counter displays the evening's provender, everything from glistening whole porgies to ruddy lamb livers, calf brains, and huge coiled octopus. The dining room is convivial and casual, packed nightly with Greek couples and families stabbing mounds of lamb and polishing off bottles of retsina wine to the background of bouzouki music.

Waitresses here, pen in mouth and notepad in apron, are, shall we say, somewhat lacking in the fine art of hospitality. Sullen and uncommunicative, their conversational skills are confined to "Ready yet?," "Anything else?" and "Don't have it."

The menu carries the familiar Greek standards—fat and flaky spinach pie, tasty stuffed grape leaves, crisply fried eggplant, a rather heavy and grainy taramosalata (red-caviar-and-potato dip purée), and vibrant hummus (chickpea-and-garlic purée)—as well as more exotic fare. Octopus marinated in lemon, olive oil, and oregano is delicious, as are deep-fried tiny Mediterranean fish similar to smelts (they are misidentified as smelts on the menu). Deep-fried calamari hacked into the size of napkin rings are tasty with a drizzling of lemon. The appetizer of broiled kasseri, a salty hard cheese, was burned.

If you are not a fan of retsina wine, two dry whites that go well with this food are Demestica and St. Helena by Chaia (both under $15).

The best entrées are simple grilled fish, either porgies, snapper, or mullets, which are served whole, on the bone, with lemon halves (and a festive maraschino cherry). Lamb is prepared in myriad ways. The best is a frequent special of roasted baby leg of lamb with potatoes, which is a slab the size of a sneaker, moist and rich, served room temperature, and sitting in a pool of oil—Greeks cook everything with oil, so you have to roll with it. Barbecued lamb, however, was oddly flavorless, and the house special, mezeli à la Greek, was a muddled mess—overcooked gray meat suffocating under a layer of salty melted cheese and broiled tomatoes.

Beef sweetbreads, more assertive than those from veal, are nicely deep fried. I never had the chance to sample barbecued goat, suckling pig, or something called "the secret of Platon" (I assume he is the cook).

"Don't have it," our waitress grumbled.

When the time came for dessert I asked, diffidently, what was available.

"Nothin'," she said matter-of-factly.

"Nothing at all?" I replied, thinking perhaps she misunderstood.

"Nothin'," she repeated.

In a weird way, I really love this place.

# THE RUSSIAN TEA ROOM

★

*150 West 57th Street, 265-0947.*

*Atmosphere: Exuberant holiday feeling with tinsel-draped chandeliers, bright colors, and celebrity crowd.*

*Service: Generally cordial but sometimes slow.*

*Price range: Expensive.*

*Credit cards: All major cards.*

*Hours: Brunch, 11:00 to 4:15 P.M., Saturday and Sunday; lunch, 11:30 to 4:15 P.M., Monday through Friday; dinner, 4:30 to 9:30 P.M., daily; supper, 9:30 to 11:45 P.M., daily.*

*Reservations: Recommended.*

*Wheelchair accessibility: Restrooms are on the second floor.*

One thing you can say about the Russian Tea Room is that it is consistent—not always good, but consistent. The setting is uplifting, though, and it still attracts a star-studded clientele. Maybe they come for the Christmas-in-July ambiance: pine-green walls, bright red banquettes, tinsel-draped chandeliers decorated with gleaming Christmas-tree balls; "Russian" waiters named Salvador and Bob decked out in festive red tunics; and stargazing and Stolichnaya in abundance?

The food, at least in recent years, has been secondary to the ambiance. Regulars who know the menu stick to a few well-executed dishes—chicken à la Kiev, lamb chops, blini with caviar—and sit back and enjoy the show. More extensive expeditions into the menu can be risky and expensive.

The Tea Room still sizzles at lunch in the main downstairs room; the after-theater crowd enlivens the place about 10:30 P.M. A large upstairs room, dubbed Siberia by regulars and celebrity spotters, is less kinetic than downstairs, but it is commodious. Service is generally cordial but can be slow, so make it clear if you must leave at a certain time for a concert or play.

The cold borscht is delightful, a creamy pink broth chunky with sweet beets and cucumber and amply seasoned with fresh dill; the warm borscht is built on a good beef stock and garnished with a cloud of sour cream. A special soup of leeks, watercress, and potatoes, though, was saltier than the Black Sea.

Follow-up visits have found the zakuski, a Russian appetizer plate, falling in quality: commercial-tasting smoked salmon and capers, dry chicken livers, overly sweet marinated herring, good salmon caviar and sour cream, scallop seviche that is also too sweet. If you are feeling extravagant, blini and caviar are always a treat. The buckwheat blini are light-textured and delicious with a coating of melted butter, a dollop of sour cream, and some caviar.

Reliable entrées include the chicken à la Kiev, which seems lighter than it used to be, a rolled, breaded chicken breast that spurts herb butter when the waiter cuts into it. Grilled chicken breast, an occasional lunch special, is moist and flavorful, too, set over semolinalike grain enhanced with currants, saffron, and almonds. Another light lunch option is fresh salmon swathed in a mayonnaise dressing over radicchio.

Lamb dishes are a mixed bag: the simple lamb chops can be good, as can the karsky shashlik supreme, a fillet paired with a piece of kidney; on the other hand, luli kebab, a traditional ground lamb dish from the Caucasus, tastes like a bad version of diner meatloaf. Duck is well roasted, although its unappetizing sweet sauce is studded with hard unripe cherries.

The best dessert is still cranberry kisel, which is essentially a purée of cranberries, cream, and sugar. It is refreshing and both tart and sweet. Kasha à la Gourieff was described accurately by our waiter: "It's kind of like Cream of Wheat, with some apricots and almonds in it." It was nostalgic, all right, and not bad.

The Russian Tea Room has made some changes for the better, although it is still recommended as much for its fanciful mood as its food.

# SABOR

★

*20 Cornelia Street, 243-9579.*

*Atmosphere: Small, cramped dining room with a casual Latin atmosphere.*

*Service: Capable and matter-of-fact.*

*Price range: Moderate.*

*Credit cards: American Express, MasterCard, and Visa.*

*Hours: Dinner, 5:30 to 11 P.M., Sunday through Thursday, until midnight Friday and Saturday.*

*Reservations: Recommended.*

*Wheelchair access: Rather confined quarters, although all facilities are on the main level.*

The narrow dining room of this popular Greenwich Village spot, with its cream-colored brick walls brightened with woven baskets, is designed for limber ectomorphs. You reach your seat by inhaling deeply, standing on tiptoe, and wedging yourself sideways into the allotted slot. A fresh lime margarita makes it all seem a bit more comfortable—and three of them make the place seem absolutely palatial.

A good introduction to the zesty Cuban and Caribbean fare here is frituras de malanga, deep-fried balls of a neutral-tasting Caribbean root vegetable that are enlivened with generous amounts of garlic and parsley. Tamales are engrossing, too, the packed mass of cornmeal and spices cooked inside a corn husk that keeps the mixture moist and lends it a smoky sweet aftertaste. Crescent-shaped empanadas were filled with lean, spizy chorizo, but the pastry was burned.

Among entrées, you can get a whole baked snapper cooked to a turn and blanketed with a piquant green sauce made with parsley, garlic, and capers. The zarzuela de mariscos is a rather tame choice, although fresh and nicely presented; it is a combination of mussels, clams, and scallops in a pulpy red sauce touched with saffron. A more distinctive preparation is an occasional special, shrimp cooked in a sweet-sharp sauce made with coconut milk, curry, and onions. It comes with delicious and exotic-tasting rice flecked with mustard seed, turmeric, coriander, and lime.

Several earthy meat dishes are appealing, including braised oxtail in a garlicky tomato sauce and the ropa vieja, or old clothes, shreds of well-braised flank steak in a red sauce aromatic of cloves and cinnamon. Good black beans come with entrées. Two other side dishes worth ordering are the cleanly fried sweet plantains or the potatolike yucca (another root vegetable) dabbed with lime-sharpened olive oil and garlic. Sabor will prepare a complete feast around a roast suckling pig for groups of eight or more for $40 a person.

Sabor's Key lime pie does not have the tart citric edge I remember, but it is still pleasing. Another winner is the coco quemado, a thick, hot coconut custard with a blistered coconut crust. It's flavored with sherry and cinnamon and is served under a melting glacier of fresh whipped cream. Sharp, semisweet chocolate ice cream is a fine palate cleanser.

# SAN DOMENICO

★ ★ ★

*240 Central Park South, 265-5959.*

*Atmosphere: Luxuriant, spacious room; low noise level.*

*Service: Vigilant and professional.*

*Wine: Extravagant Italian and American list; few bargains.*

*Price range: Expensive (Prix fixe, Monday through Friday: lunch, $32.50; pretheater dinner, $37.50; dinner, $50).*

*Credit cards: All major cards.*

*Hours: Lunch, 11:45 to 2:30 P.M., Monday through Friday; dinner, 5:30 to 11 P.M., Monday through Saturday, 4:30 to 10 P.M., Sunday.*

*Reservations: Recommended.*

*Wheelchair accessibility: Several steps down to dining room; restrooms on same level.*

This luxurious venture on Central Park South owned by Tony May (of Palio, Sandro's, and La Camelia) is modeled after the original San Domenico in Imola, a small town in Emilia-Romagna. The consulting chef, Valentino Marcattili, who garnered two stars from the *Michelin Guide* in 1979, came to New York to start the branch and now spends most of his time in Imola with occasional trips to New York.

Most of the northern regional cuisine here is faithful to tradition yet at the same time exquisitely refined and beautifully presented. It is expensive—count on $70 and up per person with wine, tax, and tip—but unlike so many places in this price range, San Domenico delivers food that is as original as it is delightful.

When you enter the extravagant 130-seat dining room (the former Alfredo's restaurant), the price tag is understandable: terra-cotta floors imported from Florence, ocher-tinted stucco walls applied by artisans sent from Rome, scalloped glass sconces on marble columns, rich leather chairs, orange tablecloths, and matching doilies on silver plates. Waiters in screeching-red blazers are urbane and vigilant; waitresses in prim black dresses with white bonnets look as if they just emerged from an Amish prayer meeting.

Among the more titillating antipasto selections are perfectly steamed sea scallops and potatoes sliced into translucent disks and garnished with scallop roe and a chive-flecked olive oil dressing. Pan-roasted sweetbreads came in a sublime garlic-enhanced tomato sauce enriched with smoked bacon (unfortunately, they were slightly overcooked), and saline-cured tuna roe was appealing in its nest of mixed greens and lemony dressing, although the salty black olives were redundant.

Pastas elevate San Domenico above the pack. You would have to go to Genoa to find a dish as authentic as the potato-filled spinach ravioli swathed in a sunny pesto sauce with lacy young string beans. Seafood ravioli is sublime, too, in a sauce of garlicky broccoli, olive oil, and white wine. Even the most homespun dish can be an epiphany here, such as the pasta from Abruzzi called spaghetti alla chitarra—fresh pasta dough rolled by hand over a guitarlike device—in an explosively fresh basil and tomato sauce. A similar contraption is used to form the tiny curls of pasta called garganelli, a specialty of Imola. They are served in a whimsical butter-based sauce stippled with beluga caviar and chives. And if you are tired of restaurant gnocchi that is better suited to slingshots than to sauce, try the lovely rendition here with melted fontina cheese and sage leaves.

San Domenico has a nine-hundred label wine list, primarily Italian and American, but don't expect any bargains. As for entrées, overcooking diminished the lamb chops in a rousing rosemary and balsamic vinegar sauce and, on one occasion, the squab with braised radicchio and excellent polenta (the second sampling was superb). Guinea hen braised with savoy cabbage and mushrooms was a good, gutsy choice, as were roasted rabbit in a rosemary-infused rabbit-stock sauce and succulent Muscovy duck with black olives.

The kitchen respects fresh seafood, never obscuring its flavor by oversaucing. Good examples are the light and herby lobster fricassee with sliced artichoke hearts and the swordfish with olive oil and tomato compote. Roasted porgy in an orange-scented sauce, however, was hopelessly overcooked.

A refreshing punctuation to this cuisine is any of the velvety fruit sorbets, brandy-soaked prunes with chilled lemon cream, or vanilla ice cream drenched in expresso. If you have a weak spot for tiramisù, the mascarpone el caffé is virtually the same thing with a different name and is terrific.

# SAY ENG LOOK

**SATISFACTORY**

*5 East Broadway, near Catherine Street, 732-0796.*

*Atmosphere: Red-felt-and-dragon theme.*

*Service: Indifferent management, unattentive service.*

*Price range: Inexpensive.*

*Credit cards: All major cards.*

*Hours: 11 A.M. to 10 P.M., Sunday through Thursday, until 11 P.M., Friday and Saturday.*

*Reservations: Suggested.*

*Wheelchair accessibility: Dining room on street level; restrooms down a flight of stairs.*

Part of the adventure in going to Chinatown is that you can never be sure if the place you so enjoyed the last time will bear any resemblance in décor or food to what you find today—or if it will even exist. Say Eng Look, which received three stars in 1982, has undergone dramatic, and lamentable, changes.

Not only has the Shanghai-style food sunk to a mediocre level, but to make matters worse, management seems indifferent about the whole operation. When I arrived at the half-empty restaurant one evening at 8:30 in a group of four, we were greeted with the warmth usually accorded Internal Revenue Service auditors. At 9:30 P.M. on two occasions, in the middle of our meal, we were asked if we wanted anything else because the kitchen was about to close. "What do you have for dessert?" I asked. "We don't emphasize that," the manager said, which hardly seemed a vote of confidence for the Italian spumoni and tortoni listed on the menu. Meanwhile, the staff was sitting at a round table off in a corner wolfing down dinner.

The red felt dining room is done up in gold dragons, ornate mirrors, and other Chinese ornamentation; I never saw the upstairs. The menu carries 122 dishes, plus about 40 specials. When faced with such a staggering array, I believe the prudent course is to rely on the specials or solicit the help of a waiter. Since our waiter was rather sullen and uncommunicative on the first visit, we rolled the dice and went with an assortment of specials.

Fried wontons were dusty and insipid little doughballs that needed more help than the sweet plum sauce could provide them; shrimp toast was much better, puffed to golden-brown and tasty, while cold noodles in sesame sauce were totally bland. From that inauspicious start we moved on to one of the best specials encountered, paper-thin sheets of bean curd wrapped around fish fillets and cleanly deep fried. You dip the rolls in salt as you eat them. Beef with scallops and snow peas, which was recommended by a waiter one evening, could have come from a can for all the flavor it had.

Few of the regular entrées received more than lukewarm response from my table, including the sweet-and-sour fish (more sweet than sour), so-called crisp aromatic duck (it was crisp but virtually unseasoned) with gummy steamed dumplings, and nondescript beef with scallions. The only dishes sampled that had any zip were the combination of peppery shredded pork and pleasantly salty chicken accompanied by sautéed watercress, and the tai chi chicken fortified with stir-fried black mushrooms. The kitchen does a creditable job with roasted whole carp presented in a pool of richly flavored fish broth along with scallions and assorted Chinese vegetables.

# THE SEA GRILL

★ ★

*19 West 49th Street, Rockefeller Center, 246-9201.*

*Atmosphere: Handsome and roomy space facing the ice-skating rink and outdoor garden.*

*Service: Efficient and knowledgeable about the wine and food.*

*Wine: Excellent regional American selection; average prices.*

*Price range: Expensive (pretheater dinner prix fixe, $37).*

*Credit cards: All major cards.*

*Hours: Lunch, noon to 3 P.M., Monday through Saturday; dinner, 5 to 11 P.M., Monday through Saturday. Closed Saturday lunch from mid-May to early October.*

*Reservations: Recommended, especially for lunch.*

*Wheelchair accessibility: Elevator access to the restaurant. All facilities on ground level.*

The Sea Grill went through some major changes as this book went to press. The capable young chef, Stefano Battistini, was hired away by The Four Seasons, and at the same time The Four Seasons's chef, Seppi Renggli, came over to the Sea Grill. Changes in the menus at both places are undoubtedly in the works, but judging from the reputation of the two chefs, the restaurants' respective ratings should hold.

The Sea Grill is the most ambitious operation in a three-restaurant complex—including the humdrum American Festival Cafe and an annex called the Bar Carvery—and until recently it was more alluring for its fancy address than its fish.

You descend to the restaurant from street level in a little glass capsule and enter a long wood-paneled dining room with gurgling illuminated pools, pretty flower displays, and floor-to-ceiling wine racks along one wall. Outside, the gushing fountains surrounding the gold sculpture of Prometheus seem to have gone psychedelic—every minute or so the water changes from after-shave blue to lollipop red to eerie green. In warm months, tables are set up outside under expansive umbrellas and a Texas barbecue is featured, complete with a live band. At lunch The Sea Grill is a masculine lair of expense-account business types; at dinner, when a pianist is in residence, a well-dressed mix of local people and out-of-towners fills the room.

As of this writing the menu has not changed substantially. One of the more enticing starters is called medallions of lobster tartar. The barely steamed lobster meat is coarsely chopped and arranged over spokes of endive and garnished with strips of sun-dried tomatoes and fresh tarragon, then drizzled with extra-virgin olive oil and lemon. Another visual and textural delight is the trio of sea scallops gift-wrapped in strips of zucchini and set over a crayon-yellow bell-pepper coulis flecked with fresh chervil.

Among hot starters, crab cakes are plump and vibrantly seasoned, with two assertive sauces (one made with lobster essences, the other a chive sauce); al dente fettuccine is particularly good tossed with sweet little fresh shrimp from Maine and a faintly smoky roasted-red-pepper sauce.

The Sea Grill boasts an excellent all-American wine list at relatively modest markups. Waiters have a good working knowledge of the wines and can guide you in the right direction. In fact, the service is thorough and professional in all respects.

Nearly all the seafood entrées are appealing. Tops on my list are the rare-grilled tuna steaks in a light ginger butter sauce paired with curls of brittle deep-fried ginger, and the salmon steak poached in sparkling wine and court bouillon. The bluish-pink salmon is surrounded by little balls of carrots and zucchini afloat in the chervil-scented sauce. Grilled swordfish is superior, too, escorted by plum tomatoes, capers, and scallions in a light parsley-butter sauce.

For dessert, go with the bright Key lime pie, velvety Prometheus chocolate cake, or the assortment of ripe tropical fruit mousses. What's billed as bittersweet orange custard is neither bitter nor custardy (rather soupy), and cappuccino flan is a dud, although the mocha sauce with it is good.

# SEVILLA RESTAURANT AND BAR

★

*62 Charles Street, 929-3189, 243-9513.*

*Atmosphere: Tavernlike setting with a lively, informal crowd.*

*Service: Efficient and pleasant.*

*Price Range: Moderate.*

*Credit cards: All major cards.*

*Hours: Lunch, noon to 3 P.M., Monday through Saturday; dinner, 3 to midnight, Monday through Thursday; 3 P.M, to 1 A.M., Friday and Saturday; 1 P.M. to midnight, Sunday.*

*Reservations: Not accepted.*

*Wheelchair accessibility: Everything on one level.*

The dining room of this venerable Greenwich Village hangout has a long, well-worn bar, red vinyl booths, ersatz Tiffany lamps, red-and-white tablecloths, bullfight posters, and, watching over the proceedings, a giant bull's head. The place is packed nightly with everyone from corporate types out for a quick, cheap meal to the Village flannel-shirt set.

You can settle in with a pitcher of sangria, which is delightfully fruity but not too sweet, or a bottle of hearty Spanish wine for under $15.

The menu appears enormous at first, but a lot of it involves basic dishes with minor twists. Grilled shrimp are dressed up in a half dozen ways, and if they don't overcook them—the odds are slightly in your favor—most are pleasing. The version with hot garlic sauce makes a zippy starter. Actually, no matter how you order shrimp (with white-wine sauce, green sauce, or simply grilled), they come with garlic, and lots of it. Another good starter is the steamed mussels, which float in on a high tide of garlic-infused broth.

A touchstone of Spanish restaurants is the tortilla. Not the tortillas found in Mexican restaurants, but rather a densely layered potato-and-egg omelet. Sevilla turns out the real thing, lightly browned and encrusted, studded with sweet peas and onions. The tortilla is listed as an entrée, but I like it as an appetizer shared among four or more diners. On frigid evenings when even macho matadors don long johns, try the caldo Gallego, the Iberian answer to Mom's chicken soup. A real blood warmer, it is so thick as to mimic a stew, combining white beans, pork, ham, potatoes, and greens.

Hearty fills, not Spanish thrills, are what you can expect from the entrées. Chicken dishes are the most reliable meat courses. Chicken Riojana comes in a big metal crock, the meat succulent and tender in its thickened red-wine sauce. It is served with heaps of mildly seasoned yellow rice. The simple chicken with hot garlic sauce will assure a wide berth on the bus ride home. Shrimp with green sauce (olive oil, parsley, garlic, and onions) arrives in the same well-used container, the sauce not as robust as I would like, but that didn't stop my table companions from polishing the metal crock with garlic bread.

The three versions of paella—one with just seafood; another with seafood, sausage, and chicken; the third with lobster added—vary in quality depending on when you order them. In my experience, the rice is moister earlier in the evening, and the ingredients fresher tasting. Late at night, the chicken can be tired and dry. More consistently satisfying is the mariscada, or mixed shellfish with green sauce, a garlic-blasted assembly of mussels, clams, shrimp, and scallops.

Predictably, flan (caramel custard) is the dessert of choice here, and it is one of the best renditions in New York—firm and rich yet not too eggy, glazed with caramel sauce. Cheesecake, from Miss Grimble, has a nice tart edge, too. Vanilla custard comes in a distant third.

# SFUZZI

★

*58 West 65th Street, 873-3700.*

*Atmosphere: Jarring neoclassical meets high-tech, multilevel room. Loud.*

*Service: Exceedingly friendly and diligent.*

*Price range: Moderately expensive (brunch prix fixe, $16.95; pretheater dinner prix fixe, $29.95).*

*Credit cards: All major cards.*

*Hours: Brunch, 11:30 to 3:30 P.M., Saturday and Sunday; lunch, 11:30 A.M. to 3 P.M., Monday through Friday; pretheater dinner, 5:30 to 7 P.M., daily; dinner, 5:30 to 11:30 P.M., Monday and Tuesday; 5:30 to midnight, Wednesday through Saturday, 5 to 11:30 P.M., Sunday.*

*Reservations: Recommended.*

*Wheelchair accessibility: Two steps up into restaurant; dining available on ground floor; restrooms on ground level.*

The hip Sfuzzi design concept began in Dallas before the New York branch opened in 1988, then another in Washington, D.C.'s Union Station. It's difficult to figure out what the designers are trying to say, if anything, with their motif for this sprawling multilevel establishment. The trompe l'oeil ancient Rome setting is juxtaposed with flashing overhead video monitors, pulsing pop music, and bizarre triangular-shaped steel-and-rubber chairs that look more appropriate to the space shuttle than a dining room.

While the setting is outlandish, the menu is conventional: pizzas, pastas, grilled meats, and seafood. Some of the pizzas make nice starters to split, their crusts puffed and yeasty and the toppings generally harmonious: two good ones are the smoked salmon with pancetta and mascarpone cheese, and the mildly spicy sausage, roast peppers, and fontina cheese. Pastas can be split as appetizers or ordered as main courses. The best is penne tossed with a beautifully balanced combination of smoked salmon, mascarpone cheese, and fresh basil. Fettuccine with prosciutto, peas, and Parmesan cream has a nice contrast of sweet and sharp, while rigatoni with a vodka-laced marinara sauce and mozzarella is pale by comparison.

Among the appetizers, deep-fried pinky rings of calamari are addictive with their mustard aïoli, and pine-nut-coated warm goat cheese is a lovely match for mixed greens in a mustard vinaigrette.

The sometimes overly chummy waiters are well trained and exceedingly cooperative. They could use a sartorial consultant, though—several looked as if they had been mugged on the way to work, wearing rumpled old shirts and jackets. But they explain the menu knowledgeably—if sometimes a bit too passionately—and keep on top of their details, including who gets what. The staff strives to please. For example, when we sent back a partly eaten veal chop for a bit more cooking, an entirely new chop was substituted, perfectly cooked. The mostly Italian and California wine list is well chosen and priced reasonably.

Among main courses, seafood seems to be the kitchen's strength. The seared salmon fillet was indeed good. The fillet was crisp outside, buttery within, and moistened with a warm lemon-and-lime vinaigrette. It was set over sautéed leeks and garnished with laces of deep-fried leeks. Grilled salmon with a whole-grain mustard sauce was deftly cooked, simple and good. Only swordfish, while moist, was lacking in seasonings. The kitchen relies too heavily on demiglace-based sauces (heavily reduced stocks) for most meat dishes, a shortcut that can be monotonous.

The rack of lamb is juicy and flavorful, served with creamy polenta, but the one-dimensional sauce had been so reduced that it began to congeal on the plate. The same occurred to the otherwise excellent grilled tenderloin with roasted garlic cloves and shiitake mushrooms.

The best desserts are the ricotta gelato (espresso gelato filled with ice shards) and the unremittingly rich chocolate mousse. Cheesecake was likewise so rich that more than a few bites could keep you anchored to those triangular chairs for some time; apple crumb was good but served too cold.

# SHUN LEE

★ ★

*43 West 65th Street, 595-8895.*

*Atmosphere: Dramatic black-and-white design scheme; comfortable banquettes, and acceptable noise level.*

*Service: Congenial, friendly, and eager.*

*Wine: Modest list available.*

*Price range: Moderately expensive.*

*Credit cards: All major cards.*

*Hours: Noon to midnight, daily. Dim sum, Saturday and Sunday.*

*Reservations: Required for dinner.*

*Wheelchair accessibility: Two small steps lead into the dining room.*

Over the years I have found Shun Lee to be a culinary conundrum, harder to get hold of than mercury balls from a broken thermometer. I have had some unforgettable meals here, and others that I would like to forget. The variation from one visit to the next, or even one dish to the next, has baffled me. Of course restaurant reviews are based on the law of averages. After three or more visits and a sampling of some forty dishes, I look at the kitchen's overall performance, then assign a star rating.

In 1981, shortly after it opened, Shun Lee was flying at two-star altitude; by 1987, it had dropped to one star. Recent visits indicate that the kitchen has refined its act markedly. Better yet, there seems to be a newfound consistency in the menu.

Shun Lee is certainly among the more elegant and comfortable uptown Chinese restaurants. Patrons enter through the bar, where playful papier-mâché monkeys frolic overhead. The amphitheaterlike dining room is done in black, creating a dramatic background for the tongue-thrashing, red-eyed dragons overhead.

Appetizers, which used to be as precarious as some stretches of Eighth Avenue, have improved dramatically. You can start with light steamed scallop or pork dumplings (the scallop dumplings are heady with fresh coriander); crispy Peking-style pan-fried pork dumplings; or sweet prawns in a lovely black-bean sauce. Even the pork ribs, which can be so humdrum in many places, are meaty and have a light honey glaze. Other good starters are the cool hacked chicken in a vibrant sesame sauce with a peppery afterburn; the exceptionally delicate, thinly sliced kidneys in a snappy sauce combining ginger, hot peppers, and soy, and cold slices of duck breast in a Hunan-style hot-pepper sauce fragrant with fresh coriander. The only two dishes that did not excite were the doughy spring rolls and underseasoned, slightly greasy, deep-fried soft-shell crabs.

The kinetic waiters could not be more vigilant or eager. They hustle out with dishes in the order you request them and happily prepare plates, unless you prefer to dine family style. And talk about steaming hand towels—I haven't seen so many towels passed out since the last swim meet at my health club.

A modest wine list is available, as well as domestic and imported beers.

The cooks here are seasoning dishes with more zest than before, so if you are pepper shy make it known. Two sizzlers to watch for are the dry shredded crispy beef, which comes on sweet and crunchy and builds to a fiery crescendo, and Sichuan scallops, in a sauce of garlic, ginger, scallions, and hot pepper. Among the tamer selections is a satisfying combination of sliced chicken breast with black mushrooms, water chestnuts, and snow peas.

Orange beef, one of those touchstone dishes, had a nice bittersweet flavor from preserved orange rinds, but unfortunately the meat was chewy. Smoked duck tasted like ham (which is all right, I guess, if you are in the mood for ham) and came with a gummy hockey puck called a scallion pancake. If you want duck here, get either the sliced duckling with a ginger-root-and-hot-pepper sauce, or the well-executed Peking duck. Side dishes sampled excelled: bean curd with scallions and garlic, peppery Chinese broccoli with garlic and lemon, and soothing cold sesame noodles.

Somewhere along the line Shun Lee decided to serve fancy French desserts, which is about as befitting as Amtrak trying to dish out shabu shabu. Forget the sodden, sweet profiteroles and the cloying ganache; go instead for the fruit sorbets, fresh pineapple, or—what else—vanilla ice cream.

For spirited food, zealous service, and the best diners' hygiene program in town, Shun Lee can be recommended enthusiastically.

# SHUN LEE PALACE

*155 East 55th Street, 371-8844.*

*Atmosphere: Luxurious, spacious room with Chinese murals and soft lighting.*

*Service: Professional and friendly.*

*Wine: Small selection available, but beer usually preferred.*

*Price range: Moderately expensive.*

*Credit cards: American Express and Diners club.*

*Hours: Lunch, noon to 3 P.M., Monday through Friday; dinner, 3 to 11 P.M., Monday through Thursday, until 11:30 P.M., Friday and Saturday, noon to 11 P.M., Sunday.*

*Reservations: Suggested.*

*Wheelchair accessibility: Everything on one level.*

This two-decade-old institution, the sister restaurant to Shun Lee on West 65th Street, is as close to Chinatown as many Upper East Siders ever get. Staying uptown is no great loss, really, for the food here is more refined than at 90 percent of the places downtown—as long as you are willing to pay three to four times as much.

Shun Lee Palace has all the creature comforts East Siders seem to desire: plenty of room, benign lighting, bucolic Chinese murals, cushy high-backed chairs, thick rugs, and prodigious flowers. An army of grinning waiters in spiffy uniforms is under the command of the urbane owner, Michael Tong. The menu spans several regional cuisines, and most are executed with authority and élan.

The best way to start is with an assortment of fried and steamed dumplings. The fried dumplings are thick-skinned, crisp, and filled with ginger-seasoned pork. The translucent steamed version is stuffed with either pork, shredded vegetables, or scallops.

On the cold side of the appetizer menu is drunken chicken, which is ineffably moist white meat that has been poached in bouillon and rice wine. It is delicious with various dipping sauces. Also recommended is fiery pepper-laced shrimp with ginger and scallions. When we asked our waiter for something light and nonspicy, he recommended mock duck. It's an intriguing dish: essentially layers of fried tofu skin that resemble the texture of duck skin (but not necessarily the flavor), served with hoisin sauce and scallions, like Peking duck. It's a peculiar sensation that people love or loathe (I fall in the first category).

A welcome aspect of the service is that waiters will bring

out food in any order you wish. I have asked waiters in Chinatown countless times to bring dishes two by two, to no avail. They invariably nod, return to the kitchen, and come back a little later with eight platters.

One of my favorite dishes here from years ago is still drawing raves from the crowds. Smoked duck has a caramelized skin as fragile as thin glass, and succulent meat. It comes with thick scallion pancakes that can be used to make a small sandwich. Fans of Peking duck should be ecstatic about the version here, too. It is filled with perfectly cooked meat and has the same irresistible skin. Sweetbreads are not usually associated with Chinese cuisine, but the rendition here is arresting, stir fried in a wok with scallions, black mushrooms, and water chestnuts in a mildly piquant sauce.

Orange beef, a classic that is too often sweet and sticky, comes out of the kitchen acrid from burned orange rind. A better beef option is the dry shredded beef cooked until crisp and sprinkled with a tangy sauce of vinegar, soy, and spicy Sichuan paste.

Shun Lee Palace offers a roster of dishes low in sodium and calories and without sugar. The vegetable dishes sampled were healthful all right, but as bland as porridge. Only the giant prawns with garlic have a modicum of flavor.

Other seafood items of note are the spicy crispy whole bass, which is deftly fried and served with a pepper-laced sauce, and fried gray sole. The sole is filleted and the bone is deep fried so that it curls up and forms a basket. The cooked fillet is placed inside with mixed vegetables—a fine concept, but the vegetables sorely needed seasoning.

Evidently, Mr. Tong has decided that Chinese desserts just don't make the grade in this neighborhood, so he has supplemented his list with trendy crowd pleasers like tiramisù (just average), honey apple fritters dusted with sesame seeds (sweet, but well fried and tasty), and assorted fruit sorbets. One of the best Oriental selections is almond-flavored tofu in almond water with pineapple, strawberries, and oranges.

# SIAM INN

★

*916 Eighth Avenue, at 54th Street, 489-5237.*

*Atmosphere: Informal, dimly lit dining room with Thai artwork on the walls.*

*Service: Friendly and competent.*

*Price range: Inexpensive.*

*Credit cards: American Express and Diners Club.*

*Hours: Lunch, noon to 3 P.M., Monday through Friday; dinner, 5 to 11:30 P.M., Monday through Saturday, 5 to 11 P.M., Sunday.*

*Reservations: Suggested for pretheater.*

*Wheelchair accessibility: Everything on one level.*

Siam Inn, a dimly lit, pleasantly appointed restaurant, is fairly typical of the genre of Thai restaurants in town, perhaps a notch better than average. It turns out several bright dishes that reflect the exotic allure of this cuisine.

Start with an appetizer called curry puffs, inflated crescents of light pastry stuffed with a sweetish combination of curried ground chicken, potatoes, and onions. It comes with a vinegar-based cucumber sauce that foils the sweetness nicely. Another good preliminary is spicy fish cakes made with ground kingfish, which are crusty and browned outside yet moist within.

The best entrée is the steamed seafood combination. It comes to the table enclosed in aluminum foil that is molded into the shape of a swan. Inside are mussels, shrimp, squid, cubes of salmon, fermented black beans, and ginger in a pool of aromatic fish broth enlivened with fresh lemon. You could round out this meal with a platter of Bangkok duck —the meat is rich and succulent, the skin crisp, and the mildly sweet sauce tinged with tamarind and curry. So much for the menu's A-team; now for a tour of the dugout.

If the kitchen has one overriding flaw that debases some otherwise good preparations, it is a relentless sweet tooth. The cold spring-roll appetizer, for instance, is a cool combination of bean sprouts, Thai sausage, bean curd, and minced vegetables wrapped in rice paper—but a lollipop-sweet sauce overwhelms it. Thai salads—lettuce, cucumber, bean sprouts, and bean cake—suffer the same fate under a shower of sweet coconut-milk and peanut dressing.

Even the most famous Thai dish of all, pla lad prig, is marred by a sucrose attack. The deep-fried red snapper set over a bed of spinach is surrounded by thick sauce that is both aggressively sweet and aggressively hot at the same time—the ensuing battle on the palate leaves the fish all but lost. Another familiar preparation, beef saté, was disappointing. The strips of meat had been overmarinated before grilling, leaving them unpleasantly mealy. You would be better off with the shrimp in mild curry sauce cut with coconut milk and red peppers.

Two satisfying entrées are the broiled salmon with a garlic-and-scallion sauce and frogs' legs in a straightforward garlic sauce. At lunch the sautéed shrimp in garlic sauce was drenched in oil. The best side dish is pad thai, a tasty mélange of minced shrimps, egg, dried bean cake, and bean sprouts.

Probably the most suitable beverage with this assertive cuisine is beer; wine fanciers will find a tiny but relatively decent selection. The staff at Siam Inn is accommodating and efficient in a laconic sort of way, and the setting is usually tranquil enough for easy conversation. Don't bother with the commercial-tasting desserts—carrot cake, assorted pies, and the like.

# THE SIGN OF THE DOVE

★ ★ ★

*1110 Third Avenue, at 65th Street, 861-8080.*

*Atmosphere: Romantic grand grotto effect with brick arches, soft lighting, and generously spaced tables.*

*Service: Staff polite and professional, but exceedingly long delays occur between courses.*

*Wine: Superior international list at affordable prices.*

*Price range: Expensive.*

*Credit cards: All major cards.*

*Hours: Brunch, 11:30 A.M. to 3:30 P.M., Sunday; lunch, noon to 2:30 P.M., Tuesday through Saturday; dinner, 6 to 11 P.M., Monday through Saturday, 6 to 10 P.M., Sunday; caviar menu, 10 P.M. to midnight, daily.*

*Reservations: Recommended.*

*Wheelchair accessibility: A separate ground-floor entrance on 65th Street accommodates the handicapped. Restrooms, however, are up five steps.*

The Sign of the Dove continues to fly high under the culinary guidance of its chef, Andrew D'Amico. And the romantic setting makes it a favorite among New Yorkers for special occasions.

A piano bar near the entrance, done in brick and marble and rose-tinted wood, is a soothing place to pass the time if your companion is fashionably late. The main dining rooms, separated by brick arches with wrought-iron filigree, are enchanting with eruptions of flowers, skylights, soft indirect lighting, and well-separated tables.

Virtually every appetizer sampled can be recommended. Aside from the superb oyster casserole, another superior dish is the gossamer oversize ravioli stuffed with mellow slices of duck confit and shiitake mushrooms flanked by a lusty fricassee of wild mushrooms; another is roasted sections of tender quail on a cushion of sautéed spinach with artichoke hearts, chanterelle mushrooms, and a poached quail egg.

Something for every taste can be found among the entrées. Winning seafood dishes include a deftly grilled salmon fillet over a zesty ragout of winter greens, and goujons (finger-size strips) of impeccable red snapper and bass that form spokes around a core of rosemary-flecked pasta, all ringed by a subtle zinfandel wine sauce bound with veal stock. Mr. D'Amico's twist on the garlicky Provençale seafood stew called bourride, however, lacks the gutsy rusticity of the original. Scallops, prawns, and medallions of lobster ride a tide of ultra-light chervil-and-tomato sauce thickened with a timid aïoli.

Meat and game preparations are more straightforward. Sections of roasted baby pheasant, golden and succulent, are ineffably good over braised lentils sweetened with caramelized onions; another stellar choice is medallions of fork-tender veal matched with wild mushrooms and a helium-light garlic custard. It takes pluck to serve boiled beef in such a luxury restaurant, yet a ruddy chunk of tenderloin achieves aristocratic stature in the company of firm-braised carrots, onions, artichokes, snow peas, and leeks, especially when dabbed with some horseradish cream sauce. The broth is rather bland, but a pinch of the coarse salt that comes on the side does the trick.

An after-dinner cheese plate deserves plaudits for its all-American emphasis, but, truth be told, the domestic Brie is a pale cousin to its French counterparts. The sweets are not quite up to the standard of the rest of the menu: a rich layered bittersweet (more sweet than bitter, really) terrine in a lovely orange cream sauce, buttery apple and pear tarts, exceedingly sweet raspberry mousse cake, and terrific homemade ice creams—prune Armagnac, vanilla, and toasted almond.

# SIRACUSA

★ ★

*65 Fourth Avenue, near 10th Street, 254-1940.*

**Atmosphere:** *Homey, spacious room with soft lighting and good noise control.*

**Service:** *Low-key and professional.*

**Wine:** *Well-rounded Italian list with fair prices.*

**Price range:** *Moderately expensive.*

**Credit cards:** *American Express.*

**Hours:** *Lunch, noon to 3 P.M., Monday through Friday; dinner, 5:30 to 11 P.M., Monday through Thursday, until 11:30 P.M., Friday and Saturday.*

**Reservations:** *Suggested.*

**Wheelchair accessibility:** *Everything on one level.*

Five years ago, a friend and I wandered into a little Italian delicatessen near Astor Place and noticed several Formica tables in one corner. From under a door came the deep, rich aroma of something simmering on the stove. When I asked what was cooking, the man behind the counter said his mother was making pasta sauce, and asked if we would like some lunch.

We sat on the flimsy chairs and ate ourselves silly on fettuccine with fresh porcini and ground veal, spaghetti all'amatriciana, fresh mozzarella with sun-dried tomatoes, caponata, glasses of Barbera d'Alba and, for dessert, four kinds of gelati. The bill was under $35. Since then, the Cammarata family—Gino, his mother, Maria, and father, Giuseppe, all of whom share kitchen duties, and Enzo, the maître d'hôtel—has built a cozy forty-seat restaurant in the back room, complete with a long, well-stocked wine bar, antique cupboard, well-spaced tables, and soft lighting. The pastas still excel, and, naturally, prices have inflated. But Siracusa is still as warm and genial as ever.

The best way to start is with a sampling from the changing appetizer platters that are on display near the bar. One evening, the platters could have squares of light fennel-filled pastry; wonderful caponata; asparagus wrapped in prosciutto; and tender baby octopus in a peppery fresh tomato sauce. Another time, the assortments might feature glistening broccoli di rape in strong olive oil and flecked with prosciutto, mozzarella with sun-dried tomatoes, mussels on the half shell stuffed with rice and peas, and a simple but sublime Sicilian specialty called panelle, which is chickpea-flour bread filled with ricotta and baked until toasted. Every tidbit is not a winner, though: swordfish carpaccio, which comes with the assorted appetizers, is so swamped in capers and vinaigrette that the fish is undetectable. Two specials to watch for are scacciata, a delicious thin-crusted pie filled with fresh spinach, sun-dried tomatoes, and capers, and the cleanly fried codfish fritters.

It seems that half of the customers are on a first-name basis with the Cammarata family, which makes for a neighborly atmosphere. Waiters are sincere and professional. Siracusa has a well-rounded Italian wine list, starting at $18.

Main courses are restricted to pastas. Outstanding winter specials include fettuccine with a thick, lusty lamb-and-potato ragu, and curri curri, which is simply homemade pasta tossed with a clean, fresh sauce of tomato and prosciutto. The seafood pasta is noteworthy, too, combining baby octopus, squid, shrimp, and a changing roster of other ingredients in a light, oregano-scented tomato sauce.

Mrs. Cammarata still makes the tiramisù, and it is relatively light and dusted with chocolate powder. Lemon sorbet is a fine palate cleanser, but most regulars go for the marvelous homemade gelati, either ricotta, hazelnut, espresso, or vanilla (Siracusa sells its gelati to many Italian restaurants in town and has a gelateria next door that is open from spring to fall).

# SMITH & WOLLENSKY

★

*201 East 49th Street, 753-1530.*

*Atmosphere: Bustling, masculine rooms decorated with Americana.*

*Service: Low-key, efficient.*

*Wine: Exceptionally strong selection of California cabernet sauvignons and red Bordeaux.*

*Price range: Moderately expensive.*

*Credit cards: All major cards.*

*Hours: Lunch and dinner, noon to midnight, Monday through Friday, 5 P.M. to midnight, Saturday and Sunday.*

*Reservations: Recommended.*

*Wheelchair accessibility: Everything on one level.*

There is something extraordinarily uplifting about a bustling New York steakhouse: the animated camaraderie of urban warriors back from corporate combat, the snappy pace of the staff, the aura of abundance, the refreshing lack of pretension. Smith & Wollensky, a paean to protein in midtown, exudes that winning feeling by the magnum.

This may not be the best steakhouse in town, but it is probably the busiest. You will not find many carpaccio-and-seafood-salad social lunchers here, and at night trend-chasing foodies are as rare as vegetarians. The prosperous citizens who fill these sprawling dining rooms daily are what mothers call good, healthy eaters.

Smith & Wollensky is an efficient feeding machine. As you enter, a man in a gray suit, built like a linebacker, peremptorily takes your name and dispatches you to one of two dining arenas. The main floor, all wood and brass and starched white tablecloths, seems designed to appeal to the largely masculine clientele, at least those men with a fondness for duck decoys, ornithological prints, brass lanterns, weather vanes, and other Americana. By day, the upstairs dining room is bathed by sunlight filtering through skylights. It is nice to see waiters who are over twenty-seven years old and not aspiring to be the next Kevin Costner, and this place is full of such unassuming veterans. For a place that churns out more than seven hundred meals daily, Smith & Wollensky maintains a comfortable pace. And soundproof ceilings keep the din lower than at many midtown bistros with fifteen tables.

In his book *The Physiology of Taste,* Jean Anthelme Brillat-Savarin noted that in medieval times it was believed that a man's appetite was in direct proportion to his importance, and that a man "to whom was served no less than the whole back of a five-year-old bull was served his drink in a cup almost too enormous to lift." By such measure, Smith & Wollensky is a den of kings. The steaks are grand, cooked as requested, but not always with the intensity of flavor one would expect from a place that dry-ages its own meat. Filet mignon au poivre is a blackened Gibraltar, mildly peppery, more notable for tenderness than for flavor. Similarly, the Cajun rib eye, a special one evening, had no more punch than the timid filet au poivre, although the meat itself was pleasing. The thick broiled sirloin has more character, darkly encrusted and with some hint of beefiness from aging.

Other variations include sliced steak Wollensky, with onions and mushrooms, and an occasional special called Colorado rib eye, which is said to be aged for three weeks to give it a more pronounced flavor. No one at my table could perceive any difference, though.

One of the most succulent veal chops I have had in a long time is served here, as are fat, rosy lamb chops. Hash browns are de rigueur, our waiter said, and they are good, nicely crisped and well seasoned; not so the slightly greasy onion rings. Thick silver-dollar-sized cottage fries are an alternative. The deep-fried zucchini sticks are not bad, but they make for heavy going with either of the potato dishes. And vegetables—spinach or asparagus—were devoid of seasoning.

Smith & Wollensky probably serves more fish than many seafood houses in town, but I have not had much luck with it. Lemon-pepper tuna, for example, a daily special, came out parched, stringy, and bitter from too much lemon. Grilled sole was more gently treated but nondescript; ditto the grilled salmon. Probably the best bet is lobsters, from four pounds to creatures approximating the size of those kiddie automobiles sold at F.A.O. Schwarz.

The wine list here is among the finest in town, with an extraordinary selection of California cabernet sauvignons and red Bordeaux. It also stocks an interesting selection of oversize bottles: magnums, double magnums, and imperials (six liters) that can be fun for large groups.

Appetizers are slightly more enticing than they were several years ago. Particularly good are the thick, subtly hammy pea soup, and the fresh, sweet lump crabmeat salad. When stone crabs are in season, they are respectably presented here, accompanied by a mild mustard mayonnaise. I would pass on the turbid, commercial-tasting beef barley soup, the marginally better chicken-vegetable soup, and the pale logs of $7 asparagus.

Desserts are about as dainty as the New York Giants front line. Of course, there is cheesecake, and it is dense, creamy, and expensive enough (at $6) to satisfy swaggering aficionados. Lemon, pear, and Alsace-style apple tarts ride on thick pavements of pastry, but each is tasty and not too sweet. Not so the sugary white chocolate mousse in a dark chocolate shell.

Smith & Wollensky feeds the battered urban psyche as well as the manliest of appetites in equal measure. It is not a flawless formula, but it is a successful one.

# SPARKS STEAKHOUSE

★ ★

*210 East 46th Street, 687-4855.*

*Atmosphere: Bustling and masculine steakhouse ambiance in large wood-lined dining rooms.*

*Service: Briskly efficient.*

*Wine: One of the best lists in the city, particularly among California cabernet sauvignons and red Bordeaux.*

*Price range: Expensive.*

*Credit cards: All major cards.*

*Hours: Lunch, noon to 3 P.M., Monday through Friday; dinner, 5 to 11 P.M., Monday through Thursday, 5 to 11:30 P.M., Friday and Saturday.*

*Reservations: Required.*

*Wheelchair accessibility: Everything on one level.*

Anyone who thinks the health craze is turning American men into Perrier-sipping, radicchio-nibbling rabbits should experience the nightly scene at Sparks Steakhouse, where brawny gangs of buttoned-down carnivores devour slabs of charred beef with primordial gusto. Sure, there are women scattered around the various dining rooms, and some of them attack steaks with fervor, but for the most part this is a masculine, two-fisted, pass-the-hashbrowns kind of place. It also happens to serve the best steaks in New York City.

The dining rooms have a burnished glow, with rich wood paneling alternating with red fabric wall covering adorned with bucolic oil paintings, gentle lighting, and thick, sound-absorbing rugs. The place runs at a brisk, efficient pace. However, diners with reservations at peak hours may have to wait up to an hour for a table. Waiters are not big on personality or the fine points of service, but they get their jobs done with no-frills efficiency.

Appetizers are more or less formalities, something to kill the time while your steak is broiling. The lump crabmeat-and-scallop starter is fresh tasting, buttery, and not overcooked. Cold lump crabmeat cocktail is fine and certainly generous. Bluepoint oysters on the half shell are in peak condition.

The menu carries an adequate selection of fish, most of it broiled. Swordfish steak and salmon were nicely done, if minimally seasoned, while halibut steak with a dusting of paprika was inedibly dry. Lobsters come in three sizes, from three and a half pounds to something the size of a child's bicycle. Split and broiled with butter, they are delightful, from $48 for a three-and-a-half pounder to $64 for a five-and-a-half pounder.

As for steak, my favorite has always been the unadorned prime sirloin—broiled exactly to order with a terrific salt-edged crust, incredibly tender and intensely beefy. Close runners-up are the thick and buttery rib lamb chops and the thick, flavorful veal chop. Filet mignon, which so often is a bore, excels here: juicy, firm, and richly flavored. Sauce making is not the kitchen's forte. Sliced beef "Bordelaise" is made with the same excellent cut of meat, but the sauce tastes like little more than beef drippings garnished with mushrooms.

The best side dish is crusty hash browns. Spinach and broccoli are cooked with care but served without even butter or salt and pepper.

Sparks's wine list is one of the best in the city, particularly strong in California cabernet sauvignons and red Bordeaux. Unless you want to go for high-price prestige labels, some good selections are available in the $20-to-$30 range among California pinot noirs and zinfandels.

The staff engages in a bit of showmanship between the entrée and dessert. With a great flourish, a waiter folds the used tablecloth and unrolls a crisp new one. If this compels you to have dessert, you might try the good creamy cheesecake or the even more profligate chocolate cheesecake. Berries and a mountain of whipped cream or the baseball-size chocolate-covered tartufo are considered light selections here.

# SUKHOTHAI

*149 Second Avenue, between 9th and 10th streets, 460-5557.*

*Atmosphere: Pub atmosphere with brick walls, brass rails, long bar, and high ceiling. Noise level moderate.*

*Service: Slow and confused when the restaurant is more than half full.*

*Price range: Moderate.*

*Credit cards: American Express, MasterCard, and Visa.*

*Hours: Dinner, 5 to 11 P.M., Sunday through Thursday; until midnight, Friday and Saturday.*

*Reservations: Suggested on weekdays, required on weekends.*

*Wheelchair accessibility: Flight of stairs up to entrance.*

Sukhothai is on the second story of an aging building in a former English-style bar and grill. The Thai family that took over did not try to Orientalize it. Instead, they left intact its long wooden bar, brick walls, brass railings, and garish multicolored glass ceiling panel. The air-conditioning system leaves much to be desired at times, so dress lightly on warm days.

Most of the wooden tables are a bit wobbly—and so is the service. The small staff, besides having difficulties with English, becomes easily overtaxed.

These inconveniences aside, there are several good reasons to visit Sukhothai. It offers some zesty hot and spicy dishes as well as a few nicely fried tidbits. Foremost among them is the appetizer of deep-fried minced shrimp with Thai spices wrapped in bean curd. The cooks are deft at frying, and these flavorful little dough pockets are light, mildly seasoned, and strong with the flavor of shrimp. They come with an invigorating sweet-and-sour sauce. Exotic and equally tasty starters are the kingfish dumplings perfumed with curry. They are served with sliced cucumbers soaked in a tart fermented fish sauce that has just a hint of sweetness. The kingfish has a chewy texture and a flavor not unlike pork.

Both of the satés—char-broiled morsels of marinated chicken or beef swabbed with peanut sauce—are moist and delicious. Another pleasing offering is a deep bowl of plump mussels steamed in peppery broth flavored with scallions, green peppers, bay leaf, lemon, and lime. The fried bean cakes are greaseless and crisp but devoid of flavor, and Thai salad is a lackluster mound of pale greens and sprouts.

Thai food embraces diverse taste sensations—hot, spicy, citric, sweet, herbaceous—so when you order, remember to choose dishes that span the flavor range to get the full effect. This is easier said than done at Sukhothai because some of the asterisks printed on the menu, which supposedly indicate dishes that are hot and spicy, seem to be tossed around at random.

Soups are accurately labeled, and some are exceptional. The hot-and-sour shrimp soup, redolent of fragrant lemongrass, combines fish sauce with Oriental mushrooms, chili, and lime to achieve just the right balance between hot and sour, pushing you right to the threshold of peppery pain, then backing off and soothing the palate with fresh lime. Another multidimensional taste sensation is set off by the exotic chicken soup that combines coconut milk, lime juice, chili paste, and loads of fresh coriander. The coriander imparted a dry edge that foiled the sweet coconut.

The entrée list looks impressively large at first, but upon closer inspection one realizes that many of the preparations are the same, only the main ingredient is different. Seafood seems to be the best bet. Aside from the aforementioned grilled shrimp, deep-fried whole sea bass under a blizzard of garlic is a good rendition of this standard Thai dish. Another good selection is the seafood combination with Thai spices. The food came out in an inflated foil bag the size of a football. When pierced, it releases a cloud of saline steam. When the air clears, it reveals the familiar Thai cast of characters—shrimp, squid, mussels, and scallions tossed with rice noodles and stoked with whole red chili pods. The combination is fresh, evenly cooked, and resting in a pool of broth that is dotted with explosive mines of hot chili pods. Navigate around them at all cost. While Sukhothai has limited ambitions, it does enough things well to give you a taste of Thailand's intriguing cuisine at budget prices.

# SUSHIDEN

**SATISFACTORY**

*19 East 49th Street, 758-2700.*

*Atmosphere: Attractive wood-and-marble dining room with five tatami rooms upstairs.*

*Service: Fast but forgetful.*

*Price range: Moderate.*

*Credit cards: All major cards.*

*Hours: Lunch, noon to 2:15 P.M., Monday through Friday; dinner, 5:30 to 10 P.M., Monday through Friday, 5 to 9 P.M., Saturday.*

*Reservations: Recommended.*

*Wheelchair accessibility: Everything on one level.*

Every few years a new wave of Japanese restaurants washes over Manhattan, usually in the midtown area and aimed at the fast-paced expense-account crowd. Sushiden is one of the more attractive of the recent crop, part of an eighty-two-outlet restaurant chain in Japan that is gaining a foothold in Manhattan with plans to expand. The establishment is packed daily with a largely Oriental clientele, supposedly a good omen, so I decided to give it a try.

The long, rectangular main room has a clean, fast look: blond wood and marble, a high ceiling, symmetrically arranged Formica-topped tables, and two big sushi bars. Spacy new-age synthesized music slows the pulse—if you can hear it over the clatter at busy times. Five pretty, private tatami rooms on the second level can be reserved.

I had the unsettling feeling here that Westerners, or people not perceived to be sushi connoisseurs, receive routine treatment and less-than-prime quality food, while the best is reserved for regulars. Over three visits, food and service fluctuated so wildly it seemed like three different restaurants. The workmanlike service staff in general is fast but occasionally forgets spoons for soups or serves the wrong dishes.

On one occasion, the sashimi assortment featured glistening fresh tuna, yellowtail flounder, and sweet baby shrimp; a second time, the fish was slightly mealy and bland. Futomaki, the big seaweed rolls filled with egg, minced fish, vegetables, and rice, was sprightly once, limp and tired another time. All the soups sampled were vibrant, especially lobster miso and regular miso.

The cooks here have an affinity for sweetness, which leads to some bizarre combinations. While the futomaki can be good, I could do without the pinkish flakes that were added. Described as fish flakes by our waiter, they resemble Fiberglas insulation and taste like spun sugar. This awful substance also showed up in the chirashi entrée. The unconventional chirashi served here comes in two decorative lacquered boxes, one holding assorted well-vinegared rice with some of that sugary asbestos, pickled vegetables, mushrooms, and cucumbers, the other with assorted fish. This was the first time I had encountered a plastic fern for garnish with raw fish. It's a scary prospect. The best dish we sampled was takosu, disks of clear, resilient octopus in a slightly sweetened vinegar sauce with cucumber garnish. Another winner here is uzaku, or eel and cucumber in rice vinegar.

The menu offers several combination dinners, an unmistakable tip-off to the staff that you are a greenhorn in sushiland. Don't expect more than the safe and standard tuna, fluke, and salmon assortments, with perhaps a briny uni (sea-urchin roe) roll tossed in for color.

Tempura, either à la carte or as part of a set dinner, is a bit sodden, as if the frying oil was not hot enough. Cooked entrées—broiled salmon or chicken teriyaki style—were moist and pleasing once, dry the next.

You don't expect much in the way of dessert at a Japanese restaurant, just the standard green-tea (pale) and ginger (better) ice creams.

# SYMPHONY CAFE

★

*950 Eighth Avenue, at 56th Street, 397-9595.*

*Atmosphere: Grand café done in dark mahogany dominated by a giant mural of Carnegie Hall.*

*Service: Somewhat inexperienced but extremely sincere.*

*Wine: Good selection of inexpensive French and California labels.*

*Price range: Moderate (pretheater dinner prix fixe, $23).*

*Credit cards: All major cards.*

*Hours: Brunch, 11:30 A.M. to 3 P.M., Saturday and Sunday; lunch, 11:30 A.M. to 3:30 P.M., Monday through Friday; pretheater dinner, 5 to 6:30 P.M., daily; dinner, 5 P.M. to midnight, Monday through Saturday, until 9 P.M., Sunday.*

*Reservations: Recommended.*

*Wheelchair accessibility: Two steps down to dining room; restroom for handicapped is on street level.*

The metamorphosis of Eighth Avenue between 50th Street and Columbus Circle is most evident in the fast-changing food scene. Once a tawdry strip of dim bars and dingy storefronts, the street is sprouting spiffy cafés, colorful fruit markets, and an ethnic smorgasbord of restaurants, from Mexican, Thai, and Italian to its latest and most stylish resident, called Symphony Cafe.

This grand expanse was designed by Jeffrey Beers, who also created China Grill in the CBS building on the Avenue of the Americas. Symphony Cafe is similarly colossal in scale, yet unlike the marmoreal and glacial China Grill, it extends warmth and a sense of neighborhood congeniality. The unpretentious menu and relatively moderate prices—most entrées at dinner are under $20—have made it a popular pre- and postperformance dining spot among Carnegie Hall patrons.

Situated on the ground level of the Symphony House apartment complex at 56th Street, the café is a vast open space with dark mahogany walls, a sixteen-foot-high ceiling, banks of soft amber lights, pine-green banquettes, and a striking floor-to-ceiling mural of Carnegie Hall from the performers' perspective. Memorabilia from the stage and screen fills glass-enclosed shelves: gold and platinum records, original scores, even Gene Kelly's shoes from *Singin' in the Rain*.

The kitchen gives several performances that merit standing ovations, while others receive reserved and polite applause. Starting from the top is a knockout roast chicken with mashed potatoes and carrot purée, and a first-class New York strip steak, richly charred and juicy, with sizzling golden french fries. Filet mignon with a mild pepper sauce is a worthy alternative. Pan-seared salmon is another hit, buttery and crisp outside, rosy and succulent within, garnished with golden globules of salmon roe and moistened with a basil-butter sauce.

Lamb chops are nicely prepared with a thyme-perfumed port reduction. The roast duck with brandied apples sounded tempting, but it arrived dryish and sauceless. Both of the scallop dishes I tried were unmemorable: sea scallops with leeks in an anemic champagne sauce, and a timidly seasoned grilled seafood medley that also included chunks of tuna and swordfish.

The hard-working service staff makes up in sincerity what it lacks in polish. The wine list harmonizes well with the menu, with ample choices under $20 among California chardonnays and sauvignon blancs and French muscadets and Mâcons. A half dozen wines are available by the glass.

The best appetizers are the grilled shrimp with mustard sauce and thyme and a mixed green salad threaded with duck confit. Crab cakes are cleanly fried but need a dose of pepper, and a layered terrine of eggplant, red peppers, and tomatoes, while pretty and fresh, is lackluster.

If you need a blast of sugar to keep you awake during the Carnegie Hall concert, this is the place. Unfortunately, though, some desserts are overloaded with it, like the nearly inedible chocolate cake and the marzipan-based raspberry tart. Apple tart is the best choice, a light-crusted disk with buttery browned apples over a layer of apple sauce, along with a scoop of sharp cinnamon ice cream. Crumbly pecan pie is a runner-up.

Symphony Cafe is well poised to ride the wave of gentrification rolling up Eighth Avenue. With just a little refinement in the food, its appeal could spread well beyond the neighborhood.

---

# TAORMINA

★

*147 Mulberry Street, between Hester and Grand streets, 219-1007.*

*Atmosphere: **Spacious and clean, with brick walls, wood, and brass. Moderate noise level.***

*Service: **Welcoming and amiable; not always vigilant.***

*Wine: **Undistinguished and spotty list.***

*Price range: **Moderate.***

*Credit cards: **All major cards.***

*Hours: **Lunch, noon to 3 P.M., daily; dinner: 5 to 11 P.M., Sunday through Thursday, until midnight, Friday and Saturday.***

*Reservations: **Necessary on weekends.***

*Wheelchair accessibility: **Everything on one level.***

As the physical dimensions of Little Italy have diminished over the years, slowly squeezed by swelling Chinatown and other neighbors, so, too, has the quality of food there. While Mulberry Street's fading Old New York image still lures the tourists, New Yorkers from other parts of town no longer consider it the epicenter of authentic Italian cuisine.

In recent forays to Mulberry Street, I found Taormina to be one of the more consistent and congenial spots on the block, serving a spirited medley of primarily Sicilian fare. This hardly looks like a typical Little Italy restaurant. The big open room resembles a suburban fern bar minus the ferns, with light wood, natural brick, brass rails, and plenty of elbow room. Lighting is gentle and the sound level is merciful.

Appetizers are generally clean and light, like the tender little clams oreganato, exceptionally good mozzarella in carrozza, and zuppa di clams in a well-seasoned shellfish broth heady with garlic. Carpaccio of beef, which is often made by freezing the meat so it is easier to slice thin, can at times be still icy cold and smothered in so much sauce and cheese that it is all but lost. The Piedmontese-style risotto is a winner, properly firm textured and potent with the flavors of chicken stock, sharp Parmesan, and porcini mushrooms. The seafood risotto, made with converted rice rather than the arborio of the Piedmontese, has a much lighter texture. Texture isn't the problem, though: it is simply bland.

Several pastas can be recommended highly. One of the best is a special made with al dente penne swathed in a beautifully balanced sauce of tomato, prosciutto, cognac, and just a touch of cream: the saltiness from the ham plays off the sweet cognac in a magical way. Penne with bits of smoked salmon and shallots in a light cream sauce is seductive, too. The spaghetti alla carbonara is much lighter than the conventional version yet richly flavored with bacon and onions. Linguine with white clam sauce is fresh and vibrant with garlic and herbs.

As amiable as service can be, waiters tend to disappear for long stretches, leaving you to fend for yourself. The wine list is undistinguished and unreliable.

Quality veal is served here, so many main courses using it can be recommended, including veal chop stuffed with mushrooms along with sautéed escarole and potato croquettes, and a Milanese-style chop with a light breading served under a salad of tomato and red onions, simply broiled or with a strong, rich Marsala sauce. One disappointment is the version with garlic and a light tomato sauce; the chop is not seasoned before cooking. Filet mignon is the favored beef here, and it receives a needed boost of flavor from a pleasing Madeira sauce.

When you inquire about seafood, waiters run through the various preparations with much gesticulation, then usually recommend some variation featuring white wine, garlic, and tomato. This works fine with the fresh, nicely cooked red snapper as well as with the sea bass. Chicken dishes are prosaic.

Desserts are not a strength here. You can get a run-of-the-mill cannoli or a good, espresso-packed tiramisù.

# TATANY

★ ★

*388 Third Avenue, near 28th Street, 686-1871.*

*Atmosphere: Trim and informal restaurant with a pleasant sushi bar and two dining rooms.*

*Service: Relatively fast-paced and efficient despite the crowds.*

*Price range: Moderately expensive.*

*Credit cards: All major cards.*

*Hours: Lunch, noon to 2:30 P.M., Monday through Friday; dinner, 5:30 to 10:30 P.M., Monday through Thursday, 5:30 to 11:30 P.M., Friday and Saturday, 5:30 to 10:30 P.M., Sunday.*

*Reservations: Not accepted.*

*Wheelchair accessibility: One step at entrance; everything on one level.*

Tatany is a relentlessly popular Japanese restaurant on Third Avenue near 28th Street—and for good reason. The fish is among the freshest around. Every evening a legion of seafood aficionados invades this animated, moderate-size restaurant with its simply appointed sushi bar and dining area in front and a more densely populated room in back.

Waiters are impressively vigilant about removing used dishes and glasses even at the busiest times. Overflow customers pass the time with warm sake or cold Kirin at a tiny bar near the entrance. An unflappable host in a Tatany

T-shirt does his best to direct the flow smoothly. Reservations are not accepted, and you may wait up to forty minutes for a table at peak hours. For the most part, though, the wait is worth it.

For instance, five Japanese pasta dishes are offered. My favorite, called shrimp and wakame, combines fettuccine-shaped noodles, nuggets of shrimp, and resilient seaweed in a deliciously concentrated fish broth. Another pasta, called yaki-udon, is not so successful. Its noodles are mired in a viscous and excessively sweet sauce holding mixed vegetables and beef. Yosenabe, described on the menu as a Japanese bouillabaisse, is an evocative creation based on a flavorful and crystalline fish broth embellished with fresh clams, chicken, shrimp, assorted fillets of fish, and crinkly saline seaweed.

Purists contend that the touchstone of a Japanese restaurant is its raw fish. The trio of seafood samurai behind this sushi bar turns out an exemplary array of sashimi, sushi, and assorted maki (seaweed rolls). The mixed sushi platter includes tuna, salmon, fluke, shrimp, and maki, usually made with tuna. The fish here is uncompromisingly firm and fresh. Yellowtail flounder in particular was astoundingly pristine and buttery. An important element sometimes overlooked in sushi bars is the rice, which is critical. At Tatany, it is just right, moderately sticky and neither too sweet nor too vinegary.

An exceptional maki worth trying is the toasted salmon skin, which is brittle and oceanic, packed in rice with minced green onions and rolled in a lightly toasted seaweed sheet, all crowned with a sprinkling of tiny red lumpfish caviar. It makes an arresting composition of texture and flavor. Frying is done well, too, as evidenced in the puffed and golden tempura of shrimp with vegetables, fried eggplant with sweet miso paste, and golden cubes of bean curd. A staple in New York Japanese restaurants, negimaki, the scallion-stuffed beef rolls, is relatively inelegant and bland.

The ginger-flecked ice cream is a sprightly palate cleanser; vanilla with red-bean sauce is sweeter but equally good. A special one evening was tempura ice cream, which is an intriguing dish, essentially a ball of vanilla ice cream coated in tempura batter and quickly deep-fried to the point at which the crust becomes hot and crisp yet the ice cream remains intact.

# TAVERN ON THE GREEN

★

*Central Park West at 67th Street, 873-3200.*

*Atmosphere: Festive, lavish setting featuring two main dining rooms with views of illuminated trees and outdoor patios.*

*Service: Generally professional, if brisk and businesslike.*

*Wine: Significantly improved international list.*

*Price range: Moderately expensive.*

*Credit cards: All major cards.*

*Hours: Lunch, 11:30 A.M. to 3:30 P.M., Monday through Friday; pretheater dinner, 5:30 to 6:15 P.M., Monday through Friday; dinner, 5:30 to 11 P.M., Monday through Thursday, 5 to 11:30 P.M., Friday and Saturday, 5:30 to 10 P.M., Sunday.*

*Reservations: Recommended.*

*Wheelchair accessibility: Everything on one level.*

As this book was going to press Tavern on the Green was about to install a new chef, Marc Poidevin, whose contemporary yet classical French cooking had elevated Maxim's on Madison Avenue to a two-star level. He replaces the capable George Masraff, who performed about as well as anyone could at a five-hundred-seat restaurant that churns out fifteen hundred meals a day. Mr. Poidevin is expected to maintain that level.

The glass-enclosed, often loud Crystal Room is a circus of lavish chandeliers, balloon clusters (given to birthday parties), and snugly arranged tables. The smaller Chestnut

Room is more subdued. A leafy outdoor courtyard is a delight in the warm months.

Some of the more successful dishes on the menu as of this writing are buttery sautéed sea scallops presented over faintly tart Chinese cabbage in a vinegar-edged sauce, a clever contrast of textures and flavors. Seafood sausage (made with fish and shellfish) is fresh and delicious, too, along with basil-perfumed potato salad. Crab cakes enriched with chunks of fresh lobster are moist and well seasoned; and lobster bisque is a pure and oceanic winner.

Certain pitfalls can be expected in a restaurant of this size. For instance, pheasant terrine anchored with foie gras is sometimes served dry and too cold. Tuna carpaccio can be fresh and pretty with its garnish of scallions, red onions, and lime, but lackluster. And the last time I tried the saffron-tinted shrimp risotto it was undercooked.

Don't expect to get too chummy with the service staff, for the workload here requires a hit-and-run strategy; for the most part, though, the waiters and waitresses are professional and accommodating. The formerly pretentious and haphazard wine list was significantly improved in 1988, and now good selections can be found in all price ranges, as well as in by-the-glass offerings.

In any restaurant of this size, a wise strategy is to order the least elaborate fare. One such winner is sautéed salmon steak in a white-peppercorn-stoked sauce, along with taglierini cooked with fresh peas and bacon in a rich red-wine sauce. Ginger-perfumed shrimp in a light, clean shellfish sauce with scallions, carrots, and artichokes is a felicitous combination, as is simple sautéed sea bass accompanied by translucent slices of barely cooked fresh fennel and a peppy black-bean-and-sweet-pepper relish.

Other good choices are the thick, juicy veal chop served with braised endive and roasted potatoes set in a lovely veal broth; rack of lamb bolstered with garlic; and tender venison in a concentrated red-wine sauce freckled with piquant pink peppercorns and truffles.

Desserts have always been exuberant here, and they still are. Crème brûlée, with a brittle sugar glaze, is exceptionally light; the assertive hazelnut mousse is drizzled with warm chocolate and set in a pool of coffee sauce.

# TEN TWENTY-TWO

★

*1022 Lexington Avenue, at 73rd Street, 737-1022.*

*Atmosphere: Snug and clubby, with dark wood wainscotting and pressed-tin ceiling.*

*Service: Often overburdened and slow.*

*Wine: Small, well-priced list that goes well with the food.*

*Price range: Moderately expensive.*

*Credit cards: All major cards.*

*Hours: Breakfast (coffee, juice, pastries), 9 to 11:30 A.M., Monday through Saturday; lunch, noon to 3 P.M., daily; dinner, 6 to 10:30 P.M., daily.*

*Reservations: Necessary for dinner.*

*Wheelchair accessibility: Two small steps at entrance. One table on ground floor; main dining room inaccessible because of winding staircase.*

If one were to study up-to-date restaurant-industry consumer research, read all the media soothsaying about dining in the 1990s, and then go out and build a new restaurant, it would probably resemble Ten Twenty-two. Christopher Idone, the owner (and the co-founder of the caterer Glorious Foods), is nothing if not canny about popular taste.

You say diners are returning to homey food? He gives them homey food. They're tired of three-digit dining? Most of his entrees are under $25. They want low-key, commodious settings? No problem, this place could pass for a bankers' clubhouse. Even the name, or I should say lack of one, bespeaks gentility and intimacy.

You enter a long, narrow, softly lighted room with a handsome mahogany bar, and your elevated pulse rate from the kamikaze taxi ride immediately subsides. To reach the dining room, guests ascend a tight spiral staircase to a space of similar proportions. It's a cozy if somewhat tight space with dark-wood wainscotting, pale gray fabric-covered walls, a pressed-tin ceiling, and wooden Venetian blinds.

Everything on the menu sounds appealing. Big, buttery sea scallops are perfectly grilled and set over cool green beans in a mild ginger-spiked vinaigrette. Soups are standouts, especially the earthy black bean with corn sticks, and the thick ham-bolstered pea soup with a rich ham-bone base. Kumamoto oysters from the Pacific Northwest are plump and reminiscent of sea foam, but I could do without the oversalted lamb patties served with them. This is said to be a combination favored in Bordeaux, but I don't get the logic.

With Mr. Idone's experience as a caterer to New York's elite, it is surprising to find such scattered service at his restaurant. The dining room is sometimes understaffed, resulting in lots of hand waving on the part of customers. The restaurant has a small French and American wine list well matched to the food; ample good selections are available for less than $25.

It's unfortunate that there are so many near-misses among entrées. Best choices among main courses are the most homespun: juicy roast chicken in pan juices comes with buttery mashed potatoes strewn with threads of fried leeks. And I sampled one of the best chicken potpies in New York here at lunch, moist white meat and barely al dente vegetables with a hint of tarragon under a mushroom cloud of Cheddar cheese puff pastry. Rare-grilled lamb chops are fine, although a potato pancake with them is oily and devoid of even salt and pepper.

One would expect to get a good steak at a place like this, but the entrecôte with herb butter, while well cooked, is remarkably anemic. Marinated grilled tuna is nicely turned out, paired with a corn, pepper, and tomato salsa. A Long Island version of bouillabaisse with assorted local fish, white beans, and spicy rouille is a commendable effort, too.

I'm not a fan of the pale chocolate sorbet, but all other desserts prompt guilt-ridden grins: sharp citrus tart with a light, thin crust; custardy chocolate bread pudding with a rum-laced créme anglaise; and a tasty if tastelessly dubbed chocolate caramel crack mousse. It's kind of a chocolate mousse under a carapace of phyllo and caramel with chocolate sauce.

# THE TERRACE

★ ★

*400 West 119th Street, 666-9490.*

*Atmosphere: Romantic, spacious room with sweeping views of the city and beyond.*

*Service: Professional and caring.*

*Wine: Respectable French and American selections at average prices.*

*Price range: Expensive.*

*Credit cards: All major cards.*

*Hours: Lunch, noon to 2:30 P.M., Tuesday through Friday; dinner, 6 to 9:30 P.M., Tuesday through Friday, until 10 P.M., Saturday.*

*Reservations: Suggested.*

*Wheelchair accessibility: Several steps at the entrance (ramp available for those who call in advance).*

For several years so much attention has focused on Manhattan's downtown dining scene that one could forget there is anyplace to eat above 79th Street. While it is true that most gastronomic tributaries flow south, it is reassuring to paddle upstream and find some places holding their own.

It is always a pleasant surprise to return to the Terrace, a beguiling rooftop dining room in a Columbia University residence hall with a stellar view and exceptionally good food. The Terrace changed from an unremarkable campus restaurant—the kind of place where students buttered up their parents for a bigger allowance—to a significant player in the French dining scene in the early 1980s under Dusan Bernic, a resourceful Yugoslav-born chef. Mr. Bernic's

▷ 459

death in 1984 left the Terrace's future in doubt. However, his wife, Nada, took over and, with the help of three successive chefs, managed to maintain its quality.

The Terrace is an unabashedly romantic spot: soft lights, candles, a solitary rose on each table, spacious armchairs, even a harpist. The view from the main dining room, depending on your table, takes in much of the West Side of Manhattan and nearby New Jersey all the way up to the sparkling spires of the George Washington Bridge; eastward, on a clear night, you can see all the way to the mouth of Long Island Sound. This is a big spot for birthdays, anniversaries, and (one supposes) tenure celebrations. In clement weather, a rooftop terrace is open for drinks.

The current hearty but not heavy menu roughly follows the classically inspired path of its predecessors. For starters, a thin disk of puff pastry is smothered with sea scallops, lobster morsels, and mussels in a lustrous champagne butter sauce. Our only problem with the moist grilled quail in a warm sherry vinaigrette studded with raisins was that there was not enough to survive a pass around a table for four, although everyone did taste some of the grilled leeks and red cabbage on the side. A salad built around a ring of smoked salmon holding underseasoned mashed avocado was forgettable, but white-bean-and-lobster soup had the kind of heady, long-simmered stock that evokes summers in Kennebunkport. The unstintingly seasoned duck terrine is another good choice.

As an oyster purist, I believe that fresh oysters should be served on the half shell or perhaps in a chowder, but otherwise not cooked or gussied up with sauces. But judging from the enthusiastic reception at my table, the bluepoints poached in champagne and served with a frothy lobster-stock sauce that managed to retain some brine was a noteworthy effort.

The chivalrous dining-room captains here are about as far as you can get from the ponytailed plate-slammers downtown. The whole staff at the Terrace has a highly tuned sense of pacing and a respect for privacy that is rare today.

One main course from Mr. Bernic's tenure, in a slightly modified version, is red snapper Adriatic style. The garlicky sautéed fillet is served under a mound of brittle deep-fried parsley and accompanied by red beets, green beans, boiled potatoes, and fennel purée. Another recommended seafood dish is medallions of steamed salmon in a faintly tart sorrel-butter sauce with three kinds of caviar. The only disappointment was a well-cooked sea bass that was marred by a bland chardonnay sauce.

Our captain had little trouble selling steamed lobster meat served in a Pernod-butter sauce. What came out was well cooked and elegantly presented, but the only seasonings detected were shallots and a few sprigs of tarragon. Tarragon was used to better effect with a special of roast baby chicken served with tasty little slivers of deep-fried potatoes and roast shallots. Breast of Muscovy duck had a surprisingly assertive flavor that was counterbalanced by a mildly sweet sauce of port and figs, along with wild rice, beets, and carrots. A bitter, scorched flavor ruined a saffron-and-watercress sauce that came with tender medallions of veal. A more reliable choice is the herb-encrusted rack of lamb.

The Terrace has a respectable French and American wine list with some good buys starting at about $25.

Except for a showy Grand Marnier soufflé that is nearly all egg white and little flavor, and an overly sweet chocolate mocha cake, desserts are superior. Among those to watch for are the chocolate mousse laced with Grand Marnier, plump tarte Tatin with homemade vanilla ice cream, and an exceptionally light napoleon with raspberries and whipped cream.

# TOMMY TANG'S

★ ★

*323 Greenwich Street, between Duane and Reade streets, 334-9190.*

*Atmosphere: Long, spare room with skylights in back; can be very loud.*

*Service: Prompt and helpful.*

*Wine: Small California list at reasonable prices.*

*Price range: Moderate.*

*Credit cards: All major cards.*

*Hours: Lunch, 11:30 A.M. to 3 P.M., Monday through Thursday; dinner, 6 to 10:30 P.M., Monday through Thursday, 6 to 11:30 P.M., Friday and Saturday. Bar opens at 5:30, Monday through Saturday.*

*Reservations: Suggested, especially at dinner.*

*Wheelchair accessibility: Two small steps at entrance; restrooms downstairs.*

Manhattan still awaits a great Thai restaurant. There are a dozen or so places around town that turn out a striking dish or two—and there are some solid family-run places in Brooklyn and Queens—yet no place has captured in a big way the delicacy and diversity of this underrated cuisine. If pressed to recommend Thai food, I usually mention the Los Angeles import Tommy Tang's on Greenwich Street. Not because it has the most authentic food around—it is really a winsome hybrid that might be called Cali-Thai—but because it is a jaunty place with food that is generally fresh and aggressively seasoned.

Mr. Tang, who has developed a following on the West Coast, ricochets between California and New York overseeing his restaurants, promoting his videos, and giving cooking demonstrations. His Lower Manhattan establishment is a popular lair for corporate cubs from the nearby financial district. The place can get obstreperous about 8 P.M., when rep ties and blazers slide off, the music cranks up, and the Oriental cocktails spark a bull market in sociability.

The long, two-level dining room, with a bar up front, gets its resonance from hardwood floors, pale yellow walls adorned with bold modern art, and high ceilings with saucer-shaped lights up front and skylights in the back. Your first hint that some liberties have been taken with Thai tradition is the chopsticks on the table, something not generally found in Thailand. Then again, how many restaurants in Bangkok serve arugula duck salad and Santa Fe chili pasta?

Most of the menu comprises familiar Thai specialties, though. Satés—morsels of chicken or beef marinated in coconut cream, curry, and spices, then grilled on skewers—are moist, and pleasantly sweet. They are delicious with two dipping sauces: ground peanuts blended with curry and olive oil, and a cooling cucumber-and-vinegar combination. Thai toast—crispy disks of minced pork and shrimp—benefits from both of the dips. So do the boned chicken wings stuffed with chicken, bamboo shoots, onions, and mushrooms. Crab rolls, a special one evening, were fresh and zippy with hot pepper, but the dough was too thick and a bit oily.

The Cali-Thai duck salad with arugula, garlic, sun-dried tomatoes, and honey vinaigrette is a good palate soother if you have overdone it with the hot sauce. If you have a sweet tooth, try the mee krob, which combines brittle sweet noodles with tidbits of shrimp, pork, and eggs garnished with bean sprouts, scallions, and coriander.

The young waiters and waitresses, in stylish starched chef's jackets, manage to keep a brisk pace even when the house is full. A small wine list is offered if you prefer that to Thai beer. Crisp, acidic whites go best with this food, perhaps a 1987 sauvignon blanc from Simi ($20) or St. Clement ($22).

One of my favorite dishes from visits more than a year ago is called Tommy duck, a crisp-skinned and succulent creation in which the meat is marinated in ginger and soy, then roasted. At the end, the duck is flash-deep-fried and glazed with a sweet plum-and-ginger sauce. This time around it was satisfying but lacked the textural contrast I remember and was a bit on the dry side. The outstanding dish recently was a special: grilled giant prawns, firm and sweet, under a frothy cilantro-champagne sauce. Other winners include perfectly cooked sea scallops with hot chili sauce, and a fine, moderately spicy chicken curry with potatoes, carrots, and coconut cream. A good side dish is the pan-fried noodles with pork that are spiked with chili and tossed with bean sprouts and mint leaves; in comparison, the vegetarian noodle plate seems flat. Instead, get the fried rice filled with crunchy duck.

The Western desserts are less than exciting. Skip the carrot cake that is one-quarter icing, and the humdrum black-and-white chocolate mousse cake. The chocolate torte is one of those near flourless killers that come with raspberry sauce, but some nights a chocolate macadamia torte, which is less severe, is available.

# TOSCANA RISTORANTE

★ ★

*200 East 54th Street, 371-8144.*

*Atmosphere: Ultra-stylish modern décor reminiscent of a luxury liner.*

*Service: Generally competent and well-intentioned.*

*Wine: Good Italian wine list; average prices.*

*Price range: Moderately expensive (pretheater dinner prix fixe, $30).*

*Credit cards: All major cards.*

*Hours: Lunch, noon to 3 P.M., Monday through Friday; pretheater dinner, 5:30 to 7 P.M., Monday through Saturday; dinner, 5:30 to 10:30 P.M., Monday through Saturday.*

*Reservations: Suggested.*

*Wheelchair accessibility: Everything on one level.*

Toscana Ristorante, the Tuscan-style Italian veteran that moved into striking new quarters on the 54th Street side of the oval-shaped "lipstick" building on Third Avenue in 1987, is a dynamic new spot worth visiting, both for its evocative design and for the food, some of which is outstanding.

The restaurant is owned by the Bitici brothers—Sergio, Michael, John, and Joseph—who also operate Minetta Tavern (113 Macdougal Street), Chelsea Trattoria Italiana (Eighth Avenue near 16th Street), and the Grand Ticino

Restaurant (228 Thompson Street). The new Toscana is by far the largest and most ambitious, not to mention most pricey.

You enter through a classy café, all marble and pearwood and copper, where light meals are served all day. The main dining room is a sweeping curvilinear affair reminiscent of a great luxury liner, almost Scandinavian looking in its spareness and use of light wood. Rippled waves of blue glass hang from an overhead faux skylight, reinforcing the oceanic theme. The asymmetrical molded wooden armchairs are befuddling at first—one armrest extends farther than the other—but once you get the hang of it, they are fine. My one gripe with the room is the uneven lighting. Tables at center stage are under the spotlights, but those around the rim are lost in the shadows and a miner's helmet is needed to read the menu.

While the kitchen has its peaks and valleys, all in all the odds are well in your favor at Toscana. Two dependable appetizers are the exceptional vitello tonnato, thin sheets of cold veal under a refined tuna-and-anchovy sauce, and pristine carpaccio of beef garnished with sharp slivers of Parmesan cheese and white mushrooms. On the disappointing second visit, we sampled overly salty smoked swordfish and a clashing creation called warm shrimp and artichokes in two sauces, one fresh tomato and the other lemon and pepper—the sauces were rivals, not partners.

Another evening our capable and congenial captain, a James Caan look-alike, suggested a special of shrimp paired with Tuscan white beans, called borlotti, and mixed greens in an olive-oil vinaigrette; it was a splendid match. Two soups tried were sublime, too, the turbid and flavor-packed shellfish broth holding perfectly cooked scallops, shrimp, oysters, and clams, and a fresh vegetable soup enhanced before serving with herb-flavored extra-virgin olive oil that contributed a haunting woody flavor.

The service staff tries hard to please and, for the most part, succeeds. When I asked our captain if we could taste a sliver of cured goose along with our appetizers, he came back with four beautifully garnished mini-servings—and didn't charge us (it was buttery and delicious, by the way).

Several of the pastas, which can be had in half portions as starters, excel. If it's available, try the occasional special of taglierini smothered in a voluptuous lamb ragù, the next best thing to renting an Italian grandmother. One of the most luxuriant dishes is the thin cheese-filled ravioli arranged around zucchini flowers, baby zucchini, and diced vegetables in a clear aromatic broth.

Fettuccine with shrimp and radicchio in a smoky tomato sauce was a bright winner, as were two specials: angel-hair pasta tossed with eggplant, tomato, fresh basil, and resilient little cubes of mozzarella; and green fettuccine with scallops and spinach. Sail past the dry and tasteless fish ravioli in an elusive saffron sauce and the gummy gnocchi (an occasional special); opt instead for the boldly seasoned risotto blended with smoked provola Tuscan cheese and escarole.

Few of the entrées were as memorable as the best pastas. My favorites were the firm and well-crisped sweetbreads under a subtle asparagus sauce along with roasted potatoes and haricots verts. The assorted mixed grill was simple yet compelling, an assortment of shrimp, snapper, and sea scallops brightened with fresh herbs. Red snapper with diced tomatoes and thyme was fresh and skillfully cooked, although the herby tomato-and-olive sauce seemed to overpower the delicate fillet.

When desserts come rolling around the bend, you might punctuate the meal with the good cheese and fruit selection, a lush peach tart, nutty Linzer torte, or the exemplary créme caramel. The rest is not very exciting, including the soupy and too-sweet tiramisù.

# TRASTEVERE

★ ★

*309 East 83rd Street, 734-6343.*

*Atmosphere: Tiny candlelit room with brick walls and oil paintings. Romantic though cramped.*

*Service: Good. Leisurely pace.*

*Wine: Run-of-the mill, expensive list.*

*Price range: Moderately expensive.*

*Credit cards: American Express.*

*Hours: Dinner, 5 to 11 P.M., daily.*

*Reservations: Necessary.*

*Wheelchair accessibility: One step at entrance; everything on one level.*

The candlelit dining room, slightly larger than a bus shelter, is adorned with old prints and oil paintings. Trastevere is a romantic little Roman-style restaurant on the Upper East Side owned by the indefatigable Lattanzi family—they also have Trastevere 84 a block away, as well as Erminia's on East 83rd Street and Lattanzi on West 46th Street. The menu is traditional, and generally well executed.

You would do well to start with one of the better appetizers, such as the lightly fried and tasty spiedino alla Romana made with prosciutto, mozzarella, and anchovy sauce, or the bright vegetable salad for two combining green beans, artichoke, zucchini, roasted potatoes, broiled tomato wedges, and red peppers.

Many patrons split a portion of pasta as a first course. Linguine with white clam sauce is a model of how the dish should be done. It is made with aromatic basil leaves, lots of garlic, and good olive oil. The sparkling little clams are cooked to tender perfection and arranged, still in the shells, over the pasta. Trastevere's version of capellini primavera is a welcome change from the run-of-the-mill preparation, which is so often filled with woody hunks of underseasoned vegetables; this one blends al dente capellini with firm, steamed morsels of broccoli florets, zucchini, and fresh peas in a vibrant tomato-and-basil sauce.

One expects a much better wine list in a restaurant of this caliber and price range. Some of the commonplace Italian whites and reds are significantly overpriced.

Among meat entrées a nod goes to the vitello Trastevere, a pummeled piece of top-quality veal that is breaded and nicely fried, then served under a knoll of tomatoes and lettuce in a subtle vinaigrette—it makes a fine warm-weather dish. That old Italian workhorse veal piccante benefited from the same tender breaded veal in a lemony wine-and-butter sauce. Of the chicken dishes sampled, pollo alla Romana—moist chicken nuggets in a tomato-wine sauce bolstered with green peppers, onions, and rosemary—packs plenty of flavor; not so the pollo alla Gaetano, which features the same chicken—this time dried out—in a nondescript garlic-and-mushroom sauce.

Shrimp are exceptionally well prepared, whether in the scampi Angela (sautéed with garlic and wine), or as part of the excellent zuppa di pesce replete with white fish, clams, mussels, lobster, and squid in a lively tomato-based broth.

And for dessert? Just what you might expect—a fist-size tartufo with a dark chocolate crust enclosing chocolate ice cream. The surprisingly light and flaky napoleon is a winner, while the leaden, fudgelike chocolate mousse is guaranteed to energize you for the evening.

# TRATTORIA DELL'ARTE

★

*900 Seventh Avenue, 245-9800.*

*Atmosphere: Brightly lighted, boldly colored dining rooms with oversize anatomical renderings on the walls.*

*Service: Chatty and casual but generally efficient.*

*Wine: Moderately priced list well matched to food; inventory spotty.*

*Price range: Moderately expensive.*

*Credit cards: All major cards.*

*Hours: Lunch, noon to 3 P.M., daily; café menu, 3 to 5 P.M., daily; dinner, 5 P.M. to midnight, daily.*

*Reservations: Necessary.*

*Wheelchair accessibility: Steps up to dining room; restrooms downstairs.*

One-shtick restaurants, like one-shtick comedians, can be amusing for a while, but their routines soon wear thin. That was my impression after repeated visits to Trattoria dell'Arte, a restaurant designed by Milton Glaser with an anatomical theme that is about as subtle as Pee-wee Herman.

At first the loud (aurally and visually) peach-toned main dining room adorned with giant renderings of everything from noses to derrieres is fun, even though the lighting is harsh. But on subsequent visits the art, like a bad comedian, just doesn't let up. The oversize drawings do not adorn, they attack. And the colors—a smaller side dining room is sort of an eerie chlorophyll shade—seem more suited to interrogation than dining. An upstairs dining room, which is comfortable except for its oppressively low ceiling, is a virtual nasal hall of fame, with sketches of famous proboscises, from Joe DiMaggio's to Mussolini's.

It is the food, not art, though, that is of primary concern here, and some of it is worth highlighting. Shortly after being seated, you are presented with a big silver tray of savory-looking appetizers. This is the antipasto platter, which waiters promote with such zeal that I suspect they receive bonuses for each one sold. That aside, the $8.50 platter, which easily feeds two, carries some tasty morsels: a delicious white-bean-and-shrimp salad, baby artichokes with olive oil, well-seasoned grilled eggplant, sautéed broccoli di rape, zesty caponata, sheets of prosciutto wrapped around thin breadsticks, and more. The Caesar salad is freshly prepared but so showered with Parmesan that you barely taste the anchovy or garlic. The thin-crusted pizzas sampled are light enough to enjoy without getting full. The version with fennel sausage, roasted peppers, and garlic disappeared quickly at my table. I can't say the same for the pallid so-called Tuscan tomato stew, which tasted like a bowl of watered-down marinara sauce.

The staff members at Trattoria dell'Arte could not be more pleasant or accommodating: they actually appear pleased that you came in, and they say so. Waiters are chatty but generally efficient and eager to please. As for the wine, cone-shaped wineglasses may be pretty, but they are impractical: they hold little and you can't swirl the wine to aerate it. The wine list is appropriate for trattoria food, starting at about $15, but unevenly stocked, with many vintages missing.

Pastas, which can be ordered in half portions as starters, are among the best options here. On the lighter side are pinci, little handmade dumplings, tossed with al dente broccoli and zucchini along with roasted garlic cloves in a nice olive-oil-based sauce, and penne with salmon and radicchio.

Among other main courses, odds are in your favor with three charcoal-grilled options: steak garnished with garlic and rosemary (along with a haystack of good french fries), lamb chops, and the swordfish presented over sautéed radicchio with garlic.

Grilled sea bass, a special, is deftly cooked, but our waiter's bumbling boning job left it looking as if it had collided with a boat's propeller. A tempting winter dish called claypot-roasted chicken is little more than a dry bird heaped with fresh rosemary (obviously the chef's favorite herb), with onions and roasted potatoes.

Desserts are not worth the guilt. There is the obligatory tiramisù, which is merely a bland custard; undistinguished cherry-flavored chocolate tartufo; and an equally boring chocolate-hazelnut square with vanilla sauce.

# 20 MOTT STREET RESTAURANT

★

*20 Mott Street, 964-0380.*

*Atmosphere: Bright, bustling three-tier restaurant.*

*Service: Prompt, pleasant.*

*Price range: Moderate.*

*Credit cards: American Express, MasterCard, and Visa.*

*Hours: 8 A.M. to midnight, daily.*

*Reservations: Suggested.*

*Wheelchair accessibility: Several steps up to main dining room; restrooms down two flights of stairs.*

My most vivid memory of 20 Mott Street is its extraordinary roast duck, which comes with a glossy, caramelized skin and dark, juicy meat. Revisits confirm that has not changed. Nor has the setting, a clattering three-story mirrored-and-marbleized palace with lighting that would make an all-night deli seem romantic.

It is clear after a broad sampling of the endless menu here that you should concentrate on the house specials, which are listed, all forty-nine of them, in a supplementary pamphlet. Here one finds superior cleanly fried soft-shell crabs, salt-baked shrimp served in the shell, fresh eel with a crunchy taro-root breading and black-bean sauce, and an interesting combination of shredded beef with scallions and fresh mango served in a deep-fried taro-root basket. The highly recommended octopus is one of the off-menu (or maybe Chinese menu) specials that you have to ask for. It is crisp, as tender as young squid, and served with a spicy dipping condiment of minced hot peppers, ginger, and scallions. Other dishes to watch for are the salt-baked lobster, shrimp with hot peppers (mildly hot; ask if you want more fire), and sliced chicken with black beans served on a roaring hot plate with sizzling onions.

The daunting main menu features many run-of-the-mill Cantonese standards, like shredded pork with garlic sauce, and chicken with Chinese vegetables. Waiters here tend to steer non-Asian customers toward bland, unadventurous fare, like shrimp with lobster sauce, and shredded beef with Chinese vegetables; one evening we dined with a Chinese friend and the scenario was completely different.

If you want to sample something while waiting for main courses, skip the doughy fried dumplings and instead get the puffed, light stuffed crab claws or one of the soups. Mixed seafood soup with sizzling rice, and minced chicken soup with fresh corn are two winners.

# "21" CLUB

★ ★

*21 West 52nd Street, 582-7200.*

*Atmosphere: Formal upstairs dining room is clubby and comfortable; famous wood-paneled barroom downstairs noisy and masculine.*

*Service: Generally professional although sometimes slow when the restaurant is crowded.*

*Wine: Excellent international list; moderately high prices.*

*Price range: Expensive.*

*Credit cards: All major cards.*

*Hours: Lunch, noon to 3 P.M., Monday to Friday (closed for lunch on Saturday in July and August); dinner upstairs, 6 P.M. to 10:30 P.M., downstairs until 11 P.M., Monday to Saturday (no dinner on Saturday in July and August); supper menu downstairs, 11 P.M. to 12:30 A.M., Monday to Saturday (no supper on Saturday in July and August).*

*Reservations: Necessary.*

*Wheelchair accessibility: Several steps down at the entrance; barroom and restrooms on ground floor.*

It's a delicate balancing act, preserving the old while introducing the new. And "21" has tried to be something to everyone in recent years, with only marginal success. Its shift toward haute French fare several years ago was met with a yawn, and since then the menu has veered back to a mix of its traditional steaks, chops, burgers, and chicken hash, elevated with a few French-style specialties.

The patrician town house is as beguiling as ever. The celebrated bar was taken apart several years ago, with each of the hundreds of toys that are suspended from the ceiling cleaned and replaced precisely where it was. The big red leather banquettes are still the best seats in the house.

The menu carries a number of golden oldies: the dandified version of chicken hash, which is really a deliciously seasoned creamed chicken ringed by a rampart of wild rice, and the oversize hamburger, which is lean and nicely charred. You can get an invigorating seviche of red snapper aromatic of coriander for starters, pristine oysters or satisfying black-bean soup. The salmon and lobster terrine, however, was mealy and humdrum; the cold terrine of beef and root vegetables in aspic needed a touch of seasonings.

The upstairs dining room has the warm and welcoming feeling of a country cabin after a day of skiing. The thick carpet with its "21" insignias, fabric panels above the glowing wood wainscoting (the wood is painted to look more textured than it is), and floor-to-ceiling curtains muffle noise well. Brass chandeliers, leather banquettes, and tables with plenty of elbow room add to the pampering ambiance.

Among the specials might be Black Angus steak in a hot mustard crust or sweetbreads sautéed to golden-brown perfection along with delicious roasted tomatoes and the heady truffle-freckled potatoes.

Among the other entrées, red snapper fillet atop lustrous creamy risotto was an extraordinary match; so, too, was roasted monkfish crowned with beef marrow and set in light red wine fumé with spinach. Wild duck stew is deliciously assertive, garnished with pearl onions and string beans.

Desserts are worth exploring. Pecan maple pie is not as gooey sweet as you get down South, but I prefer it the "21" way. The chestnut dacquoise, with its chewy crust, is terrific, as are the assorted souffles. Only the dainty rice pudding was disappointing, not even close to a lumpy diner version.

The renowned wine list has ample selections in the $20 to $30 range, although it really gets impressive a few notches above that.

# UMEDA

★ ★

*102 East 22nd Street, 505-1550.*

*Atmosphere: Relaxed and gracious space with a dining bar and two tatami rooms. Low noise level.*

*Service: Casual pace but efficient and helpful.*

*Price range: Moderately expensive.*

*Credit cards: All major cards.*

*Hours: Lunch, noon to 2:30 P.M., Monday through Friday; dinner, 6 P.M. to midnight, Monday through Friday, 6 to 11:30 P.M., Saturday, 6 to 10:30 P.M., Sunday.*

*Reservations: Necessary.*

*Wheelchair accessibility: Three steps down to dining room; restrooms on same level.*

Umeda is a peaceful little haven near Gramercy Park where the clamor of the city gives way to bucolic strains of the flute, where gentle Japanese women always have a reassuring smile, and where the food is as pure and clean as a Pacific dawn. This is as close as you can get to a health spa without breaking into a sweat.

The step-down dining room is softer and more relaxing than most Japanese restaurants. For one, it lacks the traditional sushi bar. Behind the dining counter, on an elevated platform, several waitresses crouch on mats and serve patrons.

Waiters tend to the tables, which are adorned with pretty ceramics designed for the restaurant by Richard Bennett of Great Barrington Pottery. The room is done in soothing shades of green and tan, with woven bamboo panels in the ceiling and gentle indirect lighting. Two tatami rooms—as a Western concession they have little wells for the legs—accommodate up to six people each. Most evenings there is unobtrusive music played on the flute or the koto.

The pace here is casual, and the staff is patient and helpful. Chances are you will need some help with the long and somewhat confusing menu. Aside from the regular listing of entrées, there is a sheet of otsumami, or appetizer-size dishes. Meals can be assembled from either or both; moreover, the chef will make a tasting banquet for $30, $40, $50, $60, and up.

I took all three roads on different visits. Adventurous diners might want to give the chef free reign with a tasting dinner. The $50 spread began with strips of duck breast that had been marinated in sweet miso paste before roasting. The meat, with a thin rind of fat, was succulent and tender. Next came a small sashimi assortment: excellent tuna, salmon, and fluke, and a little crab the size of a quarter that you eat shell and all (more memorable for texture than flavor). The kitchen is deft at frying, as evidenced by the superb tempura of eel; after that came delicate grilled squid legs with a mirin-and-soy sauce.

Ankake is the term for a strong clear broth mixed with mountain potato, a white tuber whose texture when grated can be most accurately, if infelicitously, described as slimy. When added judiciously to a broth, as in amadai no ankake —a tilefish-and-shrimp combination—the potato adds a slight gelatinous texture that can be pleasing. Taken straight with some raw tuna on top, it can be off-putting to Western palates. A traditional finale to this kind of meal is a rice dish. Tai meshi is a fine punctuation, a tasty and multitextured blend of toasted scallions, raw eggs, and strips of red snapper.

From the à la carte menus, sushi and sashimi are lavishly presented on handmade lavender platters ($20 for the assorted sushi or sashimi main course). The fish is impeccably fresh and the rice is expertly seasoned with vinegar and sugar. Particularly good were fluke, salmon, tuna, eel, and octopus. Vegetable tempura is clean and light, as are the soba noodles in a rich fish broth with scallions and wasabi. A similar soup that has tempura of shrimp seems ill designed because the crispy tempura immediately becomes soggy in the broth.

One of the house specials worth trying is amadai kashirazake, or grilled head of tilefish drowned in hot sake. If you can get over the idea of staring down a big fish head, pick out the sake-sweetened flesh with chopsticks; it is a delight.

"You can pick up the dish and drink," our waiter pointed out, gleefully offering to hold the platter for us while we sipped the broth.

If you don't get enough sake that way, there are fifteen kinds of sake and shochu (a distilled grain spirit) from which to choose. If that doesn't relax you, nothing will.

# UNION SQUARE CAFE

★ ★ ★

*21 East 16th Street, 243-4020.*

*Atmosphere: Well-spaced tables in countrified, comfortable main dining room; back room louder.*

*Service: Eager and enthusiastic.*

*Wine: Excellent, well-priced selection from Italy, France, and California.*

*Price range: Moderately expensive.*

*Credit cards: All major cards.*

*Hours: Lunch, noon to 3 P.M., Monday through Friday, noon to 2:30 P.M., Saturday; dinner, 6 to 10:45 P.M., Monday through Thursday, until 11:45 P.M., Friday and Saturday.*

*Reservations: Necessary.*

*Wheelchair accessibility: Dining available on main level. Restrooms down a narrow staircase.*

Union Square Cafe has a well-deserved national reputation as a paragon among a new breed of restaurants that might be called international bistros. Danny Meyer, the engaging young American owner, studied in Italy and France, but clearly his soul resides in Tuscany. Both his original chef and a recent replacement come from orthodox French backgrounds. Yet while the culinary compass here has fluttered back and forth over the years, the ship has never strayed off course.

The restaurant has three distinct dining areas, each with

a different mood. Past the long mahogany bar at the entrance, where solitary diners like to perch for oysters and light lunches, is a convivial and often loud cluster of tables in an area with a soaring ceiling and playful wall murals. Overhead is a balcony seating eighteen. The step-down main dining room, with windows at sidewalk level, is inviting and countrified, with hunter-green wainscoting, off-white walls, and colorful artwork. Tables are spaced well to allow easy conversation, and the young, eager staff is thoroughly trained.

The menu by Michael Romano, who came here from La Caravelle, is cleverly balanced, and considering the quality, reasonably priced. One can start with such light titillations as a sparkling chicory-and-lamb's-lettuce salad with a disk of baked goat cheese atop a delicious purée of flageolets, or sautéd mushrooms in a vivid blend of olive oil, lemon, and garlic. The mushrooms come with matzoh polenta, which to my taste is a gastronomic oxymoron. Good polenta has a subtle graininess from cornmeal; moistened matzoh turns to paste.

An excellent way to start is with pasta or risotto. A smashing dish from the earliest days is bombolotti (tubular pasta) tossed in a sublime combination of crumbled sweet fennel sausage, cognac, and cream: a flash of hot pepper sweeps across the palate in the aftertaste, priming you for more. Risotto is prepared in masterly ways here, whether it is the version with spinach, prosciutto, and crispy fried sage; with escargot; or with radicchio, red wine, and duck confit. Another terrific special is fillet of salmon over lentils and bacon.

Mr. Meyer has assembled one of the city's premier wine lists, offering more than seventy selections from France, Italy, and California. Many uncommon treasures are to be found, with ample selections around $20. Ports, cognacs, Armagnacs and grappa are well represented, too.

Among main courses, standouts include the roast chicken with excellent creamy polenta and a sourdough panzanella, which is a sprightly Roman bread-and-tomato salad. A smoked Black Angus shell steak is deliciously fibrous yet tender, accompanied by mashed potatoes garnished with deep-fried julienne of leeks. If you are ending a long fast, try either the thick, succulent veal chop along with a crusty torte of sliced zucchini, eggplant, and Parmesan, or the two meaty lamb shanks braised in a rich red-wine sauce and tasty flageolets. Round it off with a side order of terrific mashed turnips topped with fried shallots.

The best seafood dish sampled was red snapper braised in a casserole with potatoes, thyme, tomatoes, and fish stock. When the lid is removed at the table, the steamy aromas are intoxicating. One dish I enjoyed on earlier visits but found lacking since then is the grilled filet-mignon-shaped tuna steak. It was dry outside and gray in the center, with little flavor other than the pickled ginger on top.

For dessert, semifreddo, the Italian chilled, whipped light custard, is well made here, whether flavored with banana and chocolate sauce or fresh fruit. Chocolate torte is exquisitely light yet intensely rich, even better with homemade pistachio ice cream. Crème brûlée flavored with fresh raspberries, and the light, ripe pear crisp are exceptional, too.

Like a good red wine, Union Square Cafe is only improving with age.

# VICTOR'S CAFÉ 52

★

*236 West 52nd Street, 586-7714.*

*Atmosphere: Festive nightclub ambiance. Skylight in the back room creates a sunny, cheerful setting at lunch.*

*Service: Amicable. Capable at lunch and on weeknights, slow and harried on busy weekends.*

*Wine: Limited international selection without vintages listed; fair prices.*

*Price range: Moderate.*

*Credit cards: All major cards.*

*Hours: Noon to midnight, Sunday through Thursday, noon to 1 A.M., Friday and Saturday.*

*Reservations: Suggested.*

***Wheelchair accessibility:** All on ground floor; restrooms several steps down.*

The granddaddy of Cuban cuisine in New York is Victor del Corral, who opened the original Victor's Café twenty-five years ago on Columbus Avenue. I have fond memories of that steamy and colorful spot in its heyday, before yuppification washed over the neighborhood, when exuberant Latin couples packed the place late at night sharing pitchers of fruity sangria and excavating earthenware crocks overloaded with arroz con pollo. Mr. del Corral sold the café in 1982, although it retains his name, and he now concentrates on his second, larger establishment opened seven years ago in the Broadway theater district, called Victor's Café 52.

The dramatic midtown Victor's looks like the kind of palmy nightclub you would find in Miami, a glittering expanse of mirrors, greenery, tile, and celebrity photos. The back room is crowned by an expansive skylight, which makes for a cheerful, sunny setting at lunch. Many of Victor's original Cuban customers, now older and more rakishly attired, fill the tables and the dance floor on weekends. A pianist is always on hand, sometimes supported by strolling tuxedoed violinists.

How about the food? A revamping of the menu in the last year has led to marked improvements, with some lusty Latin specialties added. Start off with some tamal Cubano, seasoned cornmeal flecked with red peppers steamed in a corn husk. Hacked chunks of tender chicken in a spirited sauce of garlic and red peppers prime the palate, as do three superior soups: a hammy chickpea-and-cabbage combination, earthy black bean, and restorative garlic soup with a poached egg floating in the middle.

The fried chorizo, or Spanish-style sausage, is rather mundane, reheated not fried; clams in green sauce are on the chewy side and the sauce is overthickened. If you have never eaten fried yucca, a root vegetable with a potatolike texture also known as cassava and manioc, try it here. The tuber is sliced into finger-size strips and golden-fried, then served with a bright coriander-vinaigrette dip.

Waiters are for the most part cheerful and eager; service is adequate on weeknights, frenzied and slow on weekends.

The limited international wine list fails to mention vintages, which makes it more difficult to select bottles, but prices are fair. You can't go wrong with the simple and appealing Marques de Caceres, red or white, for about $16.

Many patrons in Cuban restaurants go immediately for the paella. Victor's is acceptable—a heaping portion of lobster, clams, sausage, rice, and vegetables—but nothing to bang the congas over. More distinctive options include the sopon de pollo, a savory chicken-and-rice stew bolstered with green olives, red peppers, and fresh peas. Grilled pork chops strewn with garlic slivers and paired with sweet fried plantains is a delight, too. The Argentine-style marinated flank steak, called churrasco, is exceedingly tender and delicious when drenched in chimichurri sauce, the garlicky vinaigrette. Fried chicken sounded exotic—described on the menu as marinated in garlic and bitter orange juice—but what came out, while crisp and moist, had neither of those flavors. Fresh ham described in a similar way was a bore, too—and as dry as parched palm leaves.

A typical peasant dish, ropa vieja, which combines shredded flank steak with garlic, tomato, onions, and green peppers, was tasty but tepid. The best seafood entrées sampled were a meaty red snapper baked over a bed of sweet peppers and sliced potatoes, and shrimp in a mildly seasoned creole-style sauce.

Desserts include a flan, which was light and semisweet, and a sugary mound of rum-sprinkled bread pudding. If you don't know how to rumba, learn a few steps before you go—you'll need the exercise after all this.

# VOULEZ-VOUS

★ ★

*1462 First Avenue, at 76th Street, 249-1776.*

*Atmosphere: Glass-fronted, contemporary design; comfortable and relatively quiet.*

*Service: Friendly and capable.*

*Wine: List well chosen and budget-priced.*

*Price range: Moderate (pretheater dinner prix fixe, $17.95).*

*Credit cards: All major cards.*

*Hours: Brunch, 11:30 A.M. to 4 P.M., Sunday; lunch, 11:30 A.M. to 3 P.M., Monday through Friday; pretheater dinner, 5:15 to 6:30 P.M., daily; dinner, 5:15 P.M. to midnight, daily.*

*Reservations: Strongly suggested.*

*Wheelchair accessibility: Everything on one level.*

When the wind chill hammers the thermometer into single digits, one of the most effective human antifreezes is a bracing stew along with a slab of rough country bread and a glass of husky red wine. To the French, that translates as pot-au-feu, and one of the best around is ladled out at Voulez-Vous.

Pot-au-feu is just one of the enticements at this moderately priced French bistro on the Upper East Side. The glass-fronted contemporary dining room gives scant hint of the rustic fare within. It is comfortable and mercifully muted by acoustic tile and has tinted-mirror walls, stout cushioned chairs, and a sleek bar in the back. Jacques Rameckers, the genial owner, is a no-nonsense host who keeps tabs on his young, earnest staff.

As for that pot-au-feu, a Tuesday special, it arrives in a capacious bowl steaming like a manhole cover in February. Contents include a meaty beef shank, with a dollop of custardy marrow oozing from the bone, submerged in a clear full-flavored broth strewn with carrots, potatoes, and leeks.

Wednesday is couscous day at Voulez-Vous, but the version here needs some beefing up before it can be recommended. A stingy portion of the nubbly semolina grain cushions an assortment of spicy merguez sausage, stewed chicken, meat patties combining lamb and beef, and chickpeas—but no other vegetables—all moistened with a broth stoked to your specification with fiery harissa sauce. If you show up on Thursday, navarin of lamb with orange zest is available; Friday is bouillabaisse; and Saturday, rack of veal with truffle sauce. You can also get a garlic-bolstered cassoulet brimming with moist duck, country sausage, and lamb.

The Alsatian staple, choucroute garnie, prepared daily, is a mellow assembly of smoked sausages, pork chops, smoked chicken, sauerkraut, and potatoes, enlivened by sharp juniper berries. Have it with a glass of crisp Sancerre.

Three other notable dishes are the aggressively seasoned filet mignon au poivre and french fries, the first-rate steak tartare, and a lovely seafood special, red snapper layered with tomatoes and zucchini in a light, lemony butter sauce.

Befitting the prodigious main courses, appetizers are lightweight primers. Billi bi, a velvety cream-of-mussel soup tinged with saffron, is a lustrous starter here; equally good is the mussel salad, which is not really a salad but rather wine-steamed mussels in a terrific broth laced with julienne of red and yellow peppers. Caesar salad was too timid for my taste, and three-layered vegetable terrine needed a jolt of seasonings.

For dessert, go with profiteroles—ice-cream-filled puff pastry under an avalanche of whipped cream and chocolate sauce—the excellent crème brûlée, sharp-edged frozen cappuccino soufflé, or the light yet intense chocolate mousse cake.

# THE WATER CLUB

★ ★

*On the East River, at 30th Street, 683-3333.*

*Atmosphere: Glass-enclosed barge on the water with sweeping views of the river and city.*

*Service: Highly professional and congenial though sometimes slow.*

*Wine: Impressive domestic selection; prices slightly high.*

*Price range: Moderately expensive.*

*Credit cards: All major cards.*

*Hours: Brunch, noon to 2:15 P.M., Saturday, 11:30 A.M. to 2:45 P.M., Sunday; lunch, noon to 2 P.M., Monday through Friday; dinner, 5:30 to 11 P.M., Monday through Friday, 5:45 to 11 P.M., Saturday, 5:45 to 10 P.M., Sunday.*

*Reservations: Necessary.*

*Wheelchair accessibility: Wheelchair ramps available; restrooms on ground floor.*

The Water Club is an exuberant spot that offers sweeping views of the city as well as sophisticated American cuisine under its chef, Richard Moonen. It is owned by Michael O'Keeffe, who also owns the French-influenced River Café just downstream on the Brooklyn shore.

You enter the Water Club via a nautical-looking bar with a long shellfish display on one side. In warm weather, the top deck is an al fresco cocktail area. The two-tier main dining room, wrapped in glass, has views of the river and industrial Queens (it looks much better at night). When the lights are low, the effect can be romantic, as long as the landlubbers who pack the place nightly don't get too obstreperous, as often happens.

Mr. Moonen, a spirited young chef who trained in France and worked here in such diverse kitchens as La Côte Basque, Le Cirque, and Le Relais, turns out a menu that is vibrant and contemporary yet rarely strays far from the shores of American traditional food.

For starters, you would do well with either of the gutsy soups on the menu: crab-and-corn chowder that is richly flavored but not heavy, or the seafood gumbo in a small cast-iron crock combining mussels, clams, and vegetables in a snappy shellfish stock laced with pepper. Other good choices are the multitextured terrine of game birds—partridge, grouse, pheasant, wood pigeon, and wild duck—that was lean, moist, and delicious (a special); the superb crusty crab cakes; the moist, well-seasoned duck confit on salad greens; and the silken, ginger-cured smoked salmon with black bread.

Waiters here have all the fine points covered, and they know the menu down to every sprig of thyme and exotic garnish, but the pace can drag on busy nights. The wine list is impressive, especially among domestic labels, if slightly pricey.

For entrées, you can find such homespun winners as rack of lamb with a lovely balsamic-vinegar-edged stock sauce along with rosemary-and-mustard-flavored pasta and a macho one-pound Black Angus steak that is sublimely tender and flavorful. The same cannot be said for the pan-seared rib steak, which tasted pale; it was served with a barbecued short rib on the side and terrific corn bread presented in a tiny cast-iron skillet. But the roast baby chicken is superbly juicy and crisp, along with a corn-and-wild-mushroom risotto.

As for seafood, the nod goes to steamed halibut over a bed of fresh fennel and bell peppers with a zesty ginger-citrus vinaigrette. Swordfish in a simple but fresh tomato vinaigrette is a nice combination (along with one jumbo shrimp and ribbons of al dente carrots); red snapper fillets are prepared in a compelling way, first coated with herbs and seared in a pan, then run under the broiler and served over mixed vegetables. The Water Club is justifiably renowned for its mashed potatoes O'Keeffe, the kind of lusty fare that could sustain a tugboat crew for a three-day shift. It combines whipped potatoes with scallions, onions, and lots of fresh black pepper.

Desserts have improved considerably since the last time this restaurant was reviewed. The flourless chocolate mousse cake is superb, as are the ginger-pear ice cream and the sliced glazed bananas over pecan shortbread.

# WATER'S EDGE AT THE EAST RIVER YACHT CLUB

★

*East River Yacht Club, 44th Drive at the East River, Long Island City, Queens, (718) 482-0033, (212) 936-7110.*

*Atmosphere: Formal yacht-club ambiance with wonderful views.*

*Service: Polite and eager but at times slow.*

*Wine: Limited international list with reasonable prices.*

*Price range: Moderately expensive.*

*Credit cards: All major cards.*

*Hours: Lunch, noon to 3 P.M., Monday through Friday; dinner, 6 to 11 P.M., Monday through Saturday.*

*Reservations: Suggested.*

*Wheelchair accessibility: Access to the boat is difficult; several steps in dining room.*

One can spend weeks in the concrete labyrinth of Manhattan and never have a hint that it is a seaport. To the average resident, the closest thing to an island experience is an occasional mai tai. During the warmer months, Water's Edge, on the East River in Long Island City, Queens, offers not only a sweeping nautical view, but also a delightful boat ride to and from Manhattan.

The restaurant, on a barge in the East River, has a large dining room on the lower level and a banquet room above. The main dining room is rather formal for a yacht club, with dark wood panels, scalloped sconces, gray rugs, and tuxedo-clad captains.

This is a celebratory place, where starry-eyed couples from Queens—he in white jacket, she in ruffled, low-cut dress—mingle with good-time tourists and wide-eyed Manhattanites. The ferry to the restaurant leaves from the 23rd Street Marina on the East River hourly between 6 and 11 P.M. and returns on the half hour.

The English-born chef Mark French has a well-honed sense of textures and flavors, but with his wide-ranging menu he seems to have cast a net that is too big to haul in smoothly. Appetizers that work best include the velvety, dill-accented scallop-and-shrimp mousse, sparkling gravlax with a dilled cucumber salad, and nicely seared foie gras cut with a subtle Grand Marnier sauce and tangerine garnish. When there are shortcomings, they are accidental rather than systematic. Shrimp in a delicate sesame sauce came with twirls of overcooked pasta; seviche of scallops with melon and ginger was ruined by a puckering excess of lemon; and one bad oyster spoiled the fun in an otherwise well-assembled plate of poached oysters under a chive beurre blanc.

The service staff can be overly mannered, but it is earnest. On busy nights, though, the pace can be laggard. The wine list touches all the bases and is reasonably priced.

Among main courses, you can't go wrong with the excellent, fist-thick veal chop in a light sherry-spiked tomato sauce with roasted potatoes and carrot purée or the roulade of grilled salmon with a well-balanced herby vinaigrette sauce. Lobster is excellent, too, with its aromatic herb beurre blanc and spaghetti squash.

Some of the more enterprising dishes do not work so well. Grouper cooked in a banana leaf was woefully dry, and almond-coated soft-shell crabs tasted only of nuts.

The elaborately displayed desserts look better than they are. Raspberry layer cake and fruit tarts are too sweet, as is chocolate layer cake. Better bets are prune clafoutis (really a torte), banana mousse with apricot sauce, and ice creams.

# WILKINSON'S SEAFOOD CAFÉ

★ ★

*1573 York Avenue, north of 83rd Street, 535-5454.*

*Atmosphere: Welcoming, casual café setting in brick and wood.*

*Service: Professional and unobtrusive.*

*Wine: Quality selection, at slightly high prices.*

*Price range: Moderately expensive.*

*Credit cards: All major cards.*

*Hours: Dinner: 6 to 10:30 P.M., Monday through Saturday, 5:30 to 9 P.M., Sunday.*

*Reservations: Recommended.*

*Wheelchair accessibility: Dining on main level; restrooms downstairs.*

Wilkinson's Seafood Café needs more publicity about as much as lobsters need mittens. On weeknights this inviting little neighborhood spot has an easygoing cadence: it is busy enough to be sociable, yet calm enough to offer intimacy. If it were not my job to blow the cover on such places, I'd keep it to myself.

Aside from the setting, what lures Upper East Side regulars here is sprightly seafood cooking and smart, unobtrusive service. Andrew Tun, the Thai-born chef, has an affinity for Oriental preparations, which, when successful, can be light and spirited. His few failures are attributable to creativity at the expense of cohesion.

The dining room, behind a friendly little bar, would not win any interior design awards—it is a jumble of brick grotto and pastel-shaded contemporary, with medieval-looking art hanging next to country trompe-l'oeil murals—but somehow the composite is still appealing. A casually well-dressed Yorkville crowd drifts in nightly about 8.

My favorite starter here has always been the tender ring-sized fried calamari with a side of tarragon-tomato sauce. Instead of the undistinguished seafood salad, try the heaping plate of tart arugula in a good vinaigrette garnished with big grilled shrimp, or the same greens with delicious little slices of sweet Chinese pork sausage. Soups are uniformly good, from the visually dramatic purée of roasted red peppers with mussels in their shells to a combination of salmon and meaty Manila clams in a creamy seafood stock. Fans of New England clam chowder might find the rendition here a bit precious—the clams are arranged around the plate in their shells—but the light broth is packed with flavor. One of the chef's more inventive successes is called scallop hash, a thick patty of golden cubed potatoes and rare-cooked scallops infused with fresh thyme.

The kitchen's best efforts among main courses are traditional preparations rather than the nouvelle Oriental ones. Skillfully grilled halibut, moist and smoky, is arresting over a bed of lentils sweetened with minced carrots. A special of pompano one evening was equally well turned out, set atop a sweet-tart blend of onions and cabbage with a mild mustard sauce. Peppered salmon benefits from the same harmonious pairing, this time with a sweet, ripe tomato sauce and earthy duxelles.

One of the Oriental preparations that did not work was poached red snapper over a sauce of sake and black beans. The powerfully salty fermented beans blew the delicate salmon right out of the water. Grilled marinated swordfish came out thicker than a Michener novel and woefully overcooked.

Portions here are colossal, so dessert may be problematic. Warm chocolate mousse cake with raspberry sauce is splendidly decadent, and the creamy vanilla-scented cheesecake is rich enough to sink a dolphin. Maple crème brûlée is a nice twist on this omnipresent classic, and the kitchen turns out a fine, pulpy apple tarte Tatin.

# WINDOWS ON THE WORLD

★

*1 World Trade Center, 107th floor, 938–1111.*

*Atmosphere: Wide, glass-enclosed, wraparound restaurant with stunning views of New York City and the harbor.*

*Service: Professional and reasonably prompt.*

*Wine: One of the best lists in the city.*

*Price range: Moderately expensive (pretheater dinner, $37.50; Saturday and Sunday buffet, $22.50).*

*Credit cards: All major cards.*

*Hours: Breakfast, 7 to 10 A.M., Monday through Friday; à la carte brunch in Grill Room, noon to 2:30 P.M., Sunday; lunch, noon to 2:30 P.M., Monday through Friday (private club at lunch, $7.50 entrance charge for nonmembers); buffet lunch, noon to 2:30 P.M., Saturday; buffet lunch and supper, noon to 7:30 P.M., Sunday; dinner, 5 to 10 P.M., Monday through Saturday; pretheater dinner, 5:30 to 6:30 P.M., Monday through Saturday.*

*Reservations: Required.*

*Wheelchair accessibility: Special entrance for wheelchairs, restrooms accessible.*

Windows on the World, on the 107th floor of the World Trade Center, is one of the most dramatic settings in New York. While the food may not be as stimulating as the view, it is certainly respectable.

The Continental-style menu is nicely balanced and contemporary without lapsing into trendiness. Stocks are homemade, the quality of provender is top-notch, and seasonings are generally employed with skill. When the kitchen stumbles, it is usually a consequence of trying to feed the estimated four thousand customers who pass through weekly—similar sauces show up in a variety of dishes, and a few items must be prepared in enormous quantities a bit too long in advance.

Windows offers good value for the dollar, with a four-course dinner as well as à la carte options. The prix-fixe menu has considerable appeal. It might begin with a platter of sparkling Cotuit oysters on the half shell paired with a tart mignonette sauce, or the lovely chilled pea soup suffused with fresh mint. A double beef consommé is clear and intense, garnished at the last minute with strips of scallion-laced pancakes—an unlikely but winning combination. Only the salmon-and-leek terrine fell short because of dryness.

The expanded à la carte offerings include sheets of bright mint-marinated fresh salmon with an Indian-style yogurt-and-cucumber sauce.

Two pleasing entrées on the prix-fixe menu are succulent roast baby chicken with an intensely reduced veal-stock sauce garnished with miniature vegetables, and pale slices of buttery veal in the same stock sauce bolstered with white mushrooms—this veal stock, albeit good, is the fuel that propels most of the kitchen's meat dishes.

Best bets on the regular menu include most steaks and chops, such as the pink-roasted rack of lamb for two, the double-thick lamb chops with savory gratin potatoes, and a crusty and beefy sirloin steak for two in a heady red-wine-and-stock sauce sweetened with shallots and beef marrow.

Soft-shell crabs do not fare so well; the dizzying ascent to the 107th floor left them pale and lifeless. A fricassee of lobster and crayfish is better.

The army of service personnel somehow manages to keep this three-ring circus moving right along, and with relatively good cheer. The complexion of the multitiered dining room changes dramatically on weekends, when it is inundated by tourists who are forever jumping out of their seats to press their faces against the windows while trying to illuminate the entire island of Manhattan with flash cameras. At such times the noise level can be jarring.

The wine list at Windows is justly famous, not only for its wide selection of French and American brands, but also for its prices, which are among the lowest I have encountered anywhere in town—in some cases only 25 percent above retail.

The best desserts are the luxurious frozen raspberry soufflé, a rich and creamy hazelnut dacquoise, and a classic New York–style cheesecake that is so weighty you may not need the elevator to sink to ground level. Floating islands must react badly to heights, for they are more like flaccid islands, and the white chocolate mousse is gelatinous and pallid.

# ZARELA

★ ★

*953 Second Avenue, near 51st Street, 644-6740.*

*Atmosphere: Pleasant brick and wood-paneled former wine bar with Mexican touches.*

*Service: Pleasant and knowledgeable, but there can be long waits between courses.*

*Price range: Moderate.*

*Credit cards: American Express and Diners Club.*

*Hours: Lunch, noon to 3 P.M., Monday through Friday; dinner, 5 to 11:30 P.M., Monday through Thursday, 5 P.M. to midnight, Friday and Saturday, 5 to 10 P.M., Sunday.*

*Reservations: Necessary.*

*Wheelchair accessibility: Bar and small dining area on street level; main dining room and restrooms upstairs.*

The cooking of Zarela Martinez is aggressive yet refined without lapsing into cuteness, and varied enough for all tastes, from the macho asbestos-palates to those who prefer low-voltage spiciness. This is arguably the best Mexican restaurant in town.

The long tiled bar up front serves peppy citric margaritas that you tend to drink faster than you should while dipping nacho chips into a pepper-stoked salsa. Ms. Martinez has added Mexican touches here and there to the brick-walled publike downstairs dining room, including a trio of mariachis. The wood-paneled upstairs room is less raucous and more comfortable.

Virtually all the appetizers are recommended, including the moist and soothing tamales, which are little cigar-shaped rolls of corn masa and chicken steamed in corn husks and brightened with sharp-edged mole sauce, and chilaquiles, which are fried tortilla strips overlaid with shredded chicken, tart sour cream, and white Cheddar cheese baked until molten and bubbly—they come with either hot ranchero sauce or bright green tomatillo sauce. Those with sensitive palates can feel safe with the flautas, chicken-filled tacos served with fresh guacamole; lightly puffed fried calamari rings that you dip in a mild tomato sauce; and the enchiladas de mole in a sweet and pungent mole sauce.

When Zarela cranks up the BTU's, look out. Twice I tried the poblano relleno, believing from experience that the poblano chile is among the least explosive of its family. The bulbous pepper is stuffed with diced chicken and dried fruits and set over a roasted tomato sauce. The first sensations in the mouth are of the sweet fruit and the smoky sauce, then a hint of cinnamon, followed by a gradual attack of heat that, within ten seconds, breaks out into a battle of the Alamo on the palate.

Most entrées are winners. Two of the best are the fajitas, slices of sinewy but fork-tender barbecued skirt steak served with guacamole, hot tomato salsa, and soft tortillas; and the grilled pork tenderloin under strips of smoky and sweet ancho chilies and poblano chilies in a roasted-tomato-and-garlic sauce. It is delicious with a side of frijoles charros, a crock of pinto beans cooked with tomatoes, onions, pickled jalapeños, and beer. Two seafood entrées are superior: lovely seared tuna, rare in the middle, dabbed with mole sauce, and shrimps sautéd with garlic and two kinds of chilies.

One does not normally think of exciting desserts south of the border, but the praline-hazelnut flan is worth dropping a few pesos, as is the terrific bread pudding studded with dried fruit and doused with applejack-brandy–butter sauce. Cinnamon-spiked apple pie has a wonderfully brittle crust (it comes with ice cream or melted Cheddar cheese); only the white almond cajeta torte went unfinished—a fluffy and sugary creation not worth the calories.

# DINER'S JOURNAL

# AL AMIR

The exotic and economical menu at Al Amir, a Middle Eastern restaurant on Second Avenue near 74th Street, has so many tantalizing choices we had trouble reaching a consensus at my table. "Let me put together a plate of appetizers for you," offered the chef, Radwan Rammal, who worked in the Paris sister restaurant before opening Al Amir in Manhattan in March 1989.

Within minutes, our table was laden with Middle Eastern tidbits, many of them Lebanese, with glasses of arak, an anise-flavored liqueur similar to Pernod. Besides the familiar and exceptionally well-done baba gannoush; hummus; lemony tabbouleh, crunchy with crushed wheat; and falafel (all under $4), there are specialties like the complimentary rose-colored batons of marinated turnips, and a fabulous Lebanese version of moussaka, a cold eggplant stuffed with chunks of garlic and minced onions.

One of the most arresting appetizers is called arayess, pita stuffed with seasoned lamb, onions, and cinnamon, then baked until the bread turns dark and crispy. Among the entrées I sampled were the succulent charcoal-grilled baby lamb chops and a grilled lemon-marinated chicken, which, while tasty, had been left on the fires just a minute too long. Entrées are under $20.

Al Amir, at 1431 Second Avenue, between 74th and 75th streets, is a sparkling, spacious restaurant with white marble floors, mirrored columns, and well-separated tables. Dinner is served from 6 to 11 P.M., Monday through Saturday; Sunday from noon to 11 P.M. All major credit cards accepted. Telephone: 737-1800.

# ALGONQUIN HOTEL

When the eighty-nine-year-old Algonquin Hotel was sold to a Tokyo corporation two years ago, there was speculation that the two dining rooms, long known for stodgy Continental fare, would be upgraded. Three lunches in the Oak Room and the former writers' haunt off the lobby called the Rose Room squelched that rumor. The venerable charm of both rooms still attracts a woolly, vaguely literary crowd. As for the food, it would have been faster to walk to Gristedes, buy lettuce, rinse it in the bathroom sink, mash the anchovies with the dull end of a pen, and grate the Parmesan against the table leg than to get a Caesar salad ($11.50).

Breaded chicken breast with chopped walnuts and honey might have made a good dessert with a different main ingredient, and pasta with a salmon-and-dill sauce was a sodden mess. If you want salmon—or any other fish for that matter—have it broiled, like the satisfying salmon with lemony hollandaise. Veal scallopine was well cooked, but the accompanying pasta in a peppercorn sauce was tasteless. The best bet might be simple roast prime rib. Count on about $35 per person for lunch, $40 to $50 for dinner.

The Oak Room in the Algonquin Hotel, 59 West 44th Street, serves lunch from noon to 2:30 P.M., Monday through Friday; pretheater dinner from 5:30 to 6:45 P.M., Tuesday through Saturday; at 8 P.M. there is a seating for the cabaret and dinner. All major credit cards accepted. Telephone: 840-6800.

# ARCOBALENO

This casual, romantic Greenwich Village spot with its white walls, wood trim, and abstract pastel-shaded paintings, is refreshingly unpretentious. And some of the food can be enticing.

Among the best dishes is the zesty pasta puttanesca, the

sauce melding two types of olives, capers, tomato, nubbins of garlic, and bouquet of fresh basil. Another is the paglia e fieno (thin green and white strands of noodles) in a light cream sauce brightened with peas and prosciutto (pastas are under $14). A main course of snapper, mussels, and clams in a summery broth tinged with tomato and parsley was as tasty as it was copious; it was better than the slightly gritty mixed seafood assortment.

Arcobaleno, 21 East 9th Street, serves lunch from noon to 3 P.M., Monday through Friday; dinner, 5 to 11 P.M., Monday through Saturday; until 10 P.M., Sunday. All major credit cards accepted. Telephone: 473-2215.

# ARIZONA 206 CAFE

This fast-paced, casual annex to Arizona 206 restaurant is done in clean desert tones of stucco and bleached wood, with firm, fabric-covered banquettes, little tables scattered about, and an exposed kitchen behind a tile service counter.

Provocative options include the Arizona desert salad, a combination of cactus, mixed greens, pumpkin seeds, and goat cheese in a well-balanced vinaigrette; pasta with a strange-sounding but delicious sauce of corn, fennel, beets, black beans, chicken stock, and cream. Other options might include tender sheet of cold beef marinated in dried chilies, cumin, and coriander with roasted red peppers; grilled sweet onions in a smoldering mole sauce; and deliciously smoky grilled vegetables accompanied by a snowy goat-cheese croquette. Wines by the glass are served, and desserts are as good as ever.

Arizona 206 Cafe, 206 East 60th Street, serves from noon to midnight, Monday through Saturday; 5 to 11 P.M., Sunday. All major credit cards accepted. Telephone: 838-0440.

# AU GRENIER CAFÉ

Upper Broadway in the Columbia University neighborhood abounds with little ethnic storefront restaurants catering to student tastes and budgets. One that is worth investigating even if your diploma is getting yellow around the edges is Au Grenier Café, a sunny walk-up French-bistro-like place at Broadway near 111th Street, where lunch fare includes some tasty soups, salads, and pâtés—and at bargain prices.

The clean and simply appointed dining area with its brick walls, lacquered wooden tables, and tall windows overlooking the avenue attracts a casual crowd of students and area businesspeople. A chalkboard lists a dozen wine specials by the glass. Lunch might begin with a beefy and sweet-edged onion soup gratinée and chewy rye bread. Various pâtés, which come from the reputable Les Petit Cochons, are reliably fresh and well-seasoned—a country blend flecked with green peppercorns, rabbit with Armagnac, duck with port wine, and more.

The changing selection of salads makes for an engaging light lunch (prices range from about $3 to $5 for a chunky chicken version). The hands-down best is firm and sprightly lentil salad in a vinaigrette blended with red pepper, scallions, red onions, and parsley. The others are invariably fresh, although a few needed an extra shot of seasonings. The dinner menu, which has not been sampled, offers the same salad selection as well as steaks, chops, fowl, and other straightforward fare in the $10-to-$16 range.

Au Grenier Café, one flight up at 2867 Broadway, between 111th and 112th streets, is open for lunch Monday through Friday, 11 A.M. to 4 P.M., and dinner every day, 6 to 10:30 P.M. All major credit cards accepted. Telephone: 666-3052.

# AUNT SONIA

Aunt Sonia is not a matronly relative who loves to cook. It's a down-home, no-frills restaurant in the Park Slope section of Brooklyn—named for the nearby Ansonia Clock Building—that turns out some engaging fare at budget prices. The chef and co-owner, Michael Schrieber, is a self-taught cook who took over a bric-a-brac shop in a landmark building two and a half years ago and with his partner, Wayne Perez, turned it into a spare but pleasant neighborhood spot. The dining room has a bar on one side, a black-and-white tile floor, a high pressed-tin ceiling, and blue-speckled Formica tables.

The menu changes often. Among the dishes I enjoyed was a terrific starter of blackened chicken croustades, essentially moist slices of pepper-coated chicken breast set over toast slathered with a good garlicky mayonnaise. Chicken is a soothing main course, too, if you get it "smothered"—that is, braised along with bacon, celery, carrots, and onions—and served with moist cornmeal dumplings the size of tennis balls. Blackened jumbo shrimp are hot enough to melt a snowbank and come with mixed greens and zestily seasoned "dirty rice." Blackened tuna is deftly done as well, along with a nice semisweet tahina-based sauce. Dinner runs about $25 to $30.

The restaurant has a good little all-American wine list featuring some fine selections from the Pacific Northwest.

For dessert, burnt coffee custard is light, with just a nice sharp edge from the coffee.

Aunt Sonia, 1123 Eighth Avenue, at 12th Street in Brooklyn, serves dinner from 5:30 to 11:30 P.M., Monday through Thursday, until midnight Friday and Saturday, until 11 P.M. Sunday; Saturday and Sunday brunch, 11 A.M. to 3 P.M. MasterCard and Visa accepted. Telephone: (718) 965-9526.

# BACI

Fresh and vibrant pastas are the specialty of this spiffy little café owned by the Sindoni family, who also own Azzurro on 84th Street and Second Avenue. The selections change daily, but among those I have enjoyed are the penne with eggplant-garlic-and-tomato sauce; spaghetti tossed with a light Sicilian-style sauce of marinated black olives and tomato; and linguine in a tuna-and-tomato sauce. Pastas run between $11 and $13 at dinner, a bit less at lunch.

Be forewarned that Baci can be shatteringly loud at night; lunch or off-hours are much more peaceful. Appetizers are pure and simple, and desserts are purely fattening, especially the terrific tiramisù that oozes with mascarpone cheese.

Baci, 412 Amsterdam Avenue, between 79th and 80th streets, serves lunch noon to 3 P.M., daily; dinner, 5:30 to 11 P.M., Monday through Thursday, until midnight Friday and Saturday; 5 to 10:30 P.M., Sunday; prix-fixe brunch ($15), Saturday and Sunday. No credit cards. Reservations only for parties of five or more. Telephone: 496-1550.

# BARROW STREET BISTRO

The California grill called Melrose, in the West Village, dropped its prices by about 20 percent in early 1990 to become a solid economy-priced spot called Barrow Street Bistro. The setting has been modified slightly—sponged ocher walls, paper tablecloths, soft lighting—and the food by Lynn McNeely, formerly of the now-defunct Alex Goes to Camp, on Third Avenue, is an appealing blend of down-home country French and subdued California. Fine starters included ricotta-filled ravioli in a fresh tomato sauce potent with garlic and basil; leek-and-goat-cheese tart with an exceptionally delicate crust, and crisp rosti potatoes served with salmon tartare, crème fraîche, and sevruga caviar.

For main courses, there are a delicious rib-eye steak in a shallot-sweetened green-peppercorn sauce, with Swiss chard and gratin potatoes; fresh, mild calf's liver with pearl onions and raisins; and grilled lamb chops with terrific green lentils cooked with balsamic vinegar and smoked bacon ($19). The only flub was grilled chicken that got too close to the flames, leaving it acrid.

Barrow Street Bistro, 48 Barrow Street, at Seventh Avenue South, serves dinner 6 to 11 P.M., Tuesday through Thursday; 6 to 11:30 P.M., Friday and Saturday; 5 to 10 P.M. Sunday; brunch, Sunday, 11 A.M. to 3 P.M. American Express, MasterCard, and Visa accepted. Telephone: 691-6800.

# BELLA LUNA

Bella Luna is a generically good-looking place with white walls, bold, colorful artwork, indirect lighting, paper-draped tables, and waiters in black T-shirts and matching pants. At this point the restaurant is more style than substance. The service staff can be dizzy and inelegant, although I must admit it was a nifty trick when our waiter managed to pile plates from a table of five along one outstretched arm (he dropped only one on the way to the kitchen).

Prices are moderate, though quality is uneven. Best starters are the sautéed wild mushrooms with olive oil and garlic and the sliced cured salmon with capers and dill. The carpaccio of beef tasted like deli roast beef and was much too thick, and seafood salad was tasty in its lemony dressing but the shrimp was rubbery. Recommended entrées are the juicy grilled veal chop with rosemary, garlic, and julienne of carrots, ricotta-filled tortellini in a light sage cream sauce, and manicotti with a simple but ripe tomato-and-basil sauce. Grilled chicken breast was papery dry, and the Bolognese sauce with the green tagliatelle tasted like hamburger sauce.

Bella Luna, 584 Columbus Avenue, at 89th Street, serves

from noon to 11:30 P.M., Sunday through Thursday until midnight, Friday and Saturday; Saturday and Sunday prix-fixe brunch ($8.95), noon to 4 P.M. No credit cards. Telephone: 877-2267.

# BENNY'S BURRITOS

Both outlets of this burrito parlor are cramped, boisterous, and brusque, but the foot-long burritos rolled in soft charred-flour tortillas are fresh and tasty. At $4.50 (filled with beans, rice, Monterey Jack cheese, guacamole, and sour cream, with lettuce and tomato on the side) to $5.25 (with either chicken or beef), this is one of the cheapest fill-ups in the Village. Tacos, made with soft tortillas, are $4, and zesty black-bean chili is $4 to $5.25, depending on what is heaped onto it.

Benny's Burritos are at 113 Greenwich Avenue, at Jane Street (telephone: 633-9210); 93 Avenue A, corner of 6th Street (telephone: 254-2054). Open 10:30 A.M. to midnight, Monday and Tuesday, until 2 A.M., Wednesday through Friday, from 11:30 A.M. to 2 A.M., Saturday, and 11:30 A.M. to midnight, Sunday. No credit cards.

# BORDER CAFE

Early evenings the curved wooden bar at Border Cafe, 244 East 79th Street, resembles a Dodge City saloon on payday as young East Siders drift in after a long day on the corporate range. The setting is urban cowboy, with oversize black-and-white photos of Marlboro men and, framing the walls, neon tubes that give the desert-toned walls a dusty twilight patina. Tequila-based drinks are big movers here, especially the heady margaritas ($4.50 and $6.50). Recommended dishes include the coriander-laced guacamole, spicy chicken wings, fajitas (strips of chicken, beef, or shrimp rolled in flour tortillas and served with various sauces), and the lemon-pepper chicken with avocado mayonnaise. Dinner for two runs between $40 and $50, lunch about 20 percent less. Serves from 4 P.M. to midnight, Monday through Friday, from noon to midnight, Saturday, noon to 11 P.M., Sunday. All major credit cards accepted. Telephone: 535-4347.

Another Border Cafe is at 2637 Broadway, at 100th Street. This is essentially a larger version of the East 79th Street location, but more family oriented. Kids love the video monitors overhead and the friendly, casual staff. The menu is essentially the same. Serves noon to midnight, daily. All major credit cards accepted. Telephone: 749-8888.

# BRASSERIE

It's not easy to find comfortable places to dine after midnight in New York, aside from clattering delicatessens or oppressively illuminated pizza parlors. The recently renovated Brasserie, in the Seagram's Building on East 53rd Street, is a spot to keep in mind for its clean, casual ambiance and plain but agreeable food served around the clock. The fare hardly rivals La Coupole in Paris, but the kitchen turns out a creditable steak with good french fries and a decent chicken paillard (if they don't overcook it) with herb butter. Start off with the cheesy onion soup and top it all off with a fruit tart or crème caramel. Entrées are generally under $17. The espresso packs a Mike Tyson punch. Sunday brunch is a particular bargain at $16.95, including a glass of sparkling wine.

Brasserie, 100 East 53rd Street, is open twenty-four hours daily. All major credit cards accepted. Telephone: 751-4840.

# BROADWAY DINER

Broadway Diner, 1726 Broadway, at 55th Street, falls somewhere between the far West Side's gritty blue-collar roadhouses and the fatuous 1950s-theme diners around town. The food is not to swoon over, just wholesome and satisfying: nicely grilled chicken breast with avocado salsa and a volcano of real mashed potatoes, good homemade coleslaw, satisfying club sandwiches, and a wide range of homemade desserts. It's easy to fill up here for under $15. The tile-and-steel surfaces can amplify noise to piercing levels, though.

Serves from 7 A.M. to midnight, Sunday through Thursday, from 7 A.M. to 1 A.M., Friday and Saturday. No credit cards. Telephone: 765-0909.

The Broadway Diner at 590 Lexington Avenue, at 52nd Streeet, is a slightly larger, glitzier version of the Broadway outlet, with similar food. Serves from 7 A.M. to 11 P.M., Monday through Saturday; until 4 P.M., Sunday. No credit cards. Telephone: 486-8838.

# BROADWAY JOE

Broadway Joe, 315 West 46th Street, has suffered an identity crisis among its increasingly Italian neighbors on Restaurant Row. The dining rooms here are tired and rather lugubrious—dim, superficially renovated, and plain. The kitchen specializes in high-fire torching of steaks and chops until they are carbonized outside and medium-well inside; vegetables are unsullied by any seasonings. Open 11:30 A.M. to midnight, daily. All major credit cards accepted. Telephone: 246-6513.

# CABANA CARIOCA

If you are the type who measures food bargains by the pound, this has to be the heavyweight champ of Manhattan, a gutsy Brazilian dining room where hulking portions keep happy patrons coming back for more. Cabana Carioca is an amiable two-story establishment, with a colorful bar upstairs and tight communal tables; downstairs is less cramped and less animated.

Every Wednesday and Saturday Cabana Carioca at 123 West 45th Street (581-8088) and its less-cluttered sister restaurant, Cabana Carioca II, just down the block at no. 133 (730-8375), discount the Brazilian national dish, feijoada: $9.95 Wednesday, $10.95 Saturday ($12.95 other days). You get an individual Dutch oven heaped with black beans, ham hocks, smoky sausage, and shoulder of beef—a rich and boldly seasoned combination. Other lusty stews, seafood casseroles, and simple chops and steaks are in the $10-to-$15 range.

A buffet lunch is offered downstairs—eight cold dishes, twelve hot dishes plus dessert—for $8.95. Upstairs the same buffet costs only $5. "You have paper placemats so we charge less," the owner explained, "and there is less variety." Cabana Carioca is open from noon to 11 P.M., daily. All major credit cards accepted. Cabana Carioca II serves from noon to 11 P.M., Monday through Friday, from 4 to 11 P.M., Saturday. All major credit cards accepted.

# CAFE BETWEEN THE BREAD

Cafe Between the Bread, at 145 West 55th Street, is a cool and casual place that serves a light selection of salads and sandwiches. The dining rooms tumble back from a bar to a pretty trellised courtyard with skylights, a tile floor, and drooping ivy.

The lunch menu carries a light, peppery gazpacho, grilled shrimp seasoned with coriander and lime, and herbed mozzarella with roasted peppers and sun-dried tomatoes. Pastas are uneven, such as the fettuccine with basil, pine nuts, and tomatoes that sorely needed seasoning. All the salads are attractive, particularly in the combination of grilled shrimp, swordfish, white beans, carrots, and mixed greens. Entrées range from $9 to about $17. Desserts to watch for are the peach tart with a lovely buttery crust and a citric lemon tart with a hazelnut crust.

Cafe Between the Bread serves lunch from noon to 3 P.M., Monday through Friday, from 11 A.M. to 3 P.M., Saturday; dinner 5:30 to 10 P.M., Monday, until 11 P.M., Tuesday through Friday, 5 to 11 P.M., Saturday. All major credit cards accepted. Telephone: 582-9589.

# CAFÉ DE PARIS

New York City is filled with unassuming little neighborhood haunts that rarely if ever get press attention, and they get along just fine without it. Café de Paris is one such place, an inviting little pine-and-brick bistro. The menu features a three-course dinner, including a mixed salad, entrecôte (actually a shell steak) served with a special house sauce, and dessert for $25.50 (cash only).

The shell steak, which comes on an oval chafing dish with candles underneath, is tender and cooked rare as ordered, under a "secret" herb butter sauce. The raspberry cocotte for dessert is more fluff than flavor, but there are seven other sweets to consider. The menu carries other entrées in the $12.95-to-$20 range. We sampled a steak au poivre, which was stoked with lots of crushed black peppercorns and had a nice cognac-and-cream sauce. Too bad the steak was chewy and pale-tasting. Two entrée-size salads worth trying are the frisée au lardons, which is chicory with croutons and bacon, and the goat cheese and mixed greens with walnuts, olives, and tomatoes.

Café de Paris, 924 Second Avenue, at 49th Street, serves lunch from noon to 3 P.M., Monday through Friday; dinner, 6 to 11 P.M., daily. Prix-fixe dinner, $25.50; prix-fixe lunch,

$15.50; pretheater menu, 6 to 7 P.M., $22. Special menus, cash only; otherwise American Express, MasterCard, and Visa accepted. Telephone: 486-1411.

# CAFE NICHOLSON

Cafe Nicholson may not be the most chic or ambitious restaurant in town, but if a prize were awarded for eccentricity, it would win spatulas down. John Nicholson has been in the food business since 1952, first as a partner in an American café with Edna Lewis, the author of several books on Southern cooking, and since 1967 on his own at a fanciful little spot tucked under the entrance to the Queensboro Bridge. The bespectacled, chatty Mr. Nicholson is literally a one-man show: cook, dishwasher, floor washer, maître d'hôtel, and waiter (although he brings in service help when the pace is busy). Don't expect to just walk into Cafe Nicholson—the restaurant, which seats about thirty-five, opens according to Mr. Nicholson's personal schedule. If things are slow or he has something better to do, he just locks up and takes off. In the winter he may decide to take an extended trip through Costa Rica or Mexico. "This summer I may be away for a couple of months, too," he warned. "For the moment I'm trying to be open for dinner Tuesday to Saturday."

If you can catch him in residence, you are in for a singular experience. The romantic main dining room, covered with ornate nineteenth-century handpainted tiles, looks as if it belongs in a Spanish nobleman's villa. Handsome antique furniture, artwork, and pottery have been collected by Mr. Nicholson on his jaunts around the globe.

Mr. Nicholson's cooking repertory is limited but satisfying: cheese soufflé, roast chicken with herbs, filet mignon, pork chops, fillet of sole, and chocolate soufflé. Dinner is prix fixe at $40, including a mundane house wine. An equally ornate private room is available for parties. Cafe Nicholson, at 323 East 58th Street, between First and Second avenues, is open for dinner from 6 to 9 P.M., Tuesday through Saturday. Hours erratic; be sure to call ahead. All major credit cards accepted. Telephone: 355-6769.

---

# CA'NOVA

This attractive newcomer to Madison Avenue is owned by Corrado Muttin, formerly of the restaurant Corrado on Avenue of the Americas near 55th Street. His new venture is subdued, woody, and elegant, with bucolic tapestries covering one wall, oak wainscotting, and comfortable upholstered chairs.

Based on a limited sampling, some of the Mediterranean fare is invigorating. A special called cima genovese is a fine alternative to the ubiquitous carpaccio: cold, thinly sliced roasted veal coated with an herby vinaigrette under a tomato salad. Ricotta-filled ravioli in a pesto sauce mellowed with a bit of cream is a fine course (pastas run about $15 to $19), as is a Venetian regional specialty of rigatoni with luganega, piquant lean sausage that is crumbled to make a rustic sauce.

Fish entrées are uneven: we sampled a well-cooked salmon with a tomato-dill sauce, and dryish swordfish with an acidic caper sauce. If you have room, the cheesecake is exceptionally creamy and relatively light.

Ca'Nova, at Madison, near 62nd Street, serves lunch from noon to 3 P.M. and dinner, 5:30 to 11 P.M., Monday through Friday, noon to 1 A.M., Saturday, 5:30 to 9:30 P.M., Sunday. All major credit cards accepted. Telephone: 838-3725.

# CARIBE

Caribe, a funky, moderately priced tropical restaurant in the West Village, looks more like a florist than a restaurant, with its jungle of palms thriving in both dining rooms, one with flamingo-pink walls and wicker furniture.

Among the more satisfying dishes here are a huge portion of braised fork-tender oxtail in a brassy broth that is delicious when soaked up with bread. Along with the chewy golden disk of fried plantain, the dish features sautéed bananas, yams, and rice with beans. Most dinners here are under $12.

You can start with a gutsy black-bean soup aromatic with onions and bay leaf along with a giveaway starter of innocent-looking steamed green cabbage that detonates on the tongue with hot pepper.

Other menu regulars are Jamaican-style curried goat; churrasco, the steak in batter from "Little Havana" in Miami; and "jerked" chicken. Caribe, at 117 Perry Street, at Greenwich Street, serves from 11:30 A.M. to 11 P.M., Sunday through Thursday; until midnight, Friday and Saturday. No credit cards. Telephone: 255-9191.


# CARNEGIE DELI

New York City is synonymous with the clattering and chattering institution known as the delicatessen. To devotees of corned beef, pastrami, chicken dumpling soup, and "a bagel with a schmeer!" there is no place like the Carnegie Delicatessen.

The atmosphere is something right out of a Woody Allen parody of New York Jewish culture—in fact, the Carnegie played a large role in the movie *Broadway Danny Rose*.

The reason Carnegie's corned beef is superior—remarkably tender and lean yet intensely flavorful—is that big slabs of brisket are cured in house and hand trimmed. The Carnegie also prepares its own peppery pastrami in a slow smoker that was specially made for it in Canada. A sandwich of either is served on the best-quality rye bread, weighs in at a pound and three-quarters, and stands five inches high on the plate, fairly daring you to finish it. Perpetual lines outside the door at lunchtime attest to the Carnegie's reputation as one of New York's best. The Carnegie Deli, 845 Seventh Avenue, at 55th Street, is open from 6:30 A.M. to 4 A.M., daily. No credit cards. Telephone: 757-2245.

# CENTURY CAFE

The food has improved at this animated, theatrical American-style bistro just off Times Square. Drop in before theater for a drink and a platter of oysters on the half shell (prices vary), brightly seasoned little Vietnamese spring rolls, vodka-cured gravlax, or grilled marinated shrimp. A group of two or more may want to split the excellent shellfish-packed gumbo. Be forewarned, service can be slow here, so allow plenty of time and make your schedule known to the service staff. Century Cafe, 132 West 43rd Street, serves from 11:30 A.M. to midnight, Monday through Saturday; bar menu served after 5 P.M. All major credit cards accepted. Telephone: 398-1988.

# CHEZ MOMO

Chez Momo, at 48 Macdougal Street, is a trim little Moroccan restaurant with paper-covered tablecloths, folding chairs, wood floors, and soft Middle Eastern background music. Not everything is notable, but prices are right and some dishes are worth noting. For starters, hummus, the mashed chickpeas with sesame butter, is well seasoned and good with some pita bread for dipping, as is the baba gannoush, or mashed eggplant. But the merguez, which is supposed to be a spicy lean lamb sausage, is bland and mushy.

Tagines—herb-and-vegetable stews made with lamb or chicken (both under $10)—are among the better bets for main courses. Another good choice is the pastilla, a Moroccan specialty that traditionally is a pigeon pie made with ground almonds, sugar, and cinnamon. The version here, made with chicken and phyllo dough, onions, raisins, and almonds, is tasty and has a good flaky texture. Couscous "royale," though, is a disappointment: dry and underseasoned. The restaurant has no liquor license, so many customers bring their own wine and beer.

Chez Momo serves dinner from 5 P.M. to midnight, Tuesday through Sunday. American Express accepted. Telephone: 979-8588.

# CORNER BISTRO

If Greenwich Village leaves you weary and hungry, an inviting little spot to recuperate with a bowl of chili or a fist-size hamburger is Corner Bistro. Slide into one of the high-backed wooden booths across from the long mahogany bar where neighborhood regulars hang out and watch sports events on the overhead television. The brick-walled back room is snug and romantic in a bohemian sort of way.

The juicy "bistro burger" should come with dry cleaning instructions, for if you try to take a bite out of this monster —wrapped with bacon and topped with tomato and lettuce— it will fight back to the death, squirting and sliding all over the place. It comes with a woodpile of excellent rust-colored french fries. The preferred beverage with this all-American duo is McSorley's ale on tap. The chili is fresh but meekly seasoned for my taste, but you gets lots of it. Corner Bistro, 331 West 4th Street, is open from 11:30 A.M. to 3 A.M., Monday through Saturday, and noon to 3 A.M., Sunday. No credit cards. Telephone: 242-9502.

# COURTYARD CAFÉ AND BAR

This handsome restaurant in the Doral Court Hotel is a popular spot, particularly at lunch, among the local business crowd. The main part of the café resembles an English inn with subdued pastels, landscape oil paintings, handsomely appointed tables, and a lively bar off to one side. A glass-enclosed terrace looks over the outdoor café, where a waterfall gurgles and white latticework and pretty flower clusters create a tranquil retreat in bustling midtown.

The lunch menu features a wide assortment of soups, salads, pastas, pizzas, and grilled entrées. Cream of asparagus soup is rich and well seasoned; salad Niçoise is made with slices of cool, fresh tuna over green leaf lettuce, and radicchio along with new potatoes, green beans, cucumber, and hard-cooked egg. The ingredients were fine but the combination cried out for a dressing of some sort. Spaghetti with mussels and clams was cooked al dente and was redolent of olive oil and oregano. Lunch runs about $20 to $25. The service staff is green and sometimes bumbling, but if you sit back and enjoy the setting, such shortcomings can be overlooked.

The Courtyard Café and Bar, in the Doral Court Hotel, 130 East 39th Street, serves, breakfast from 6:30 to 11:30 A.M., daily; lunch, 11:30 A.M. to 3:30 P.M., daily; prix-fixe brunch ($21.95, 11:30 A.M. to 3:30 P.M., Sunday; dinner, 5 to 11 P.M., daily. All major credit cards accepted. Telephone: 779-0739.

# COWGIRL HALL OF FAME

Cowgirl Hall of Fame is a restaurant started by a native of Texas, Sherry Delamarter, who is a partner in Tortilla Flats, Gulf Coast, and Sugar Reef. It is named for the actual Hall of Fame in Hereford, Texas.

The restaurant is a rough-edged place, with a loud, woody bar and a dining room adorned with antelope chandeliers, leather saddles, cowhide, and Western memorabilia. Some of the modestly priced chow is tasty, especially the superior fried chicken with authentically glutinous cream gravy and well-seasoned vegetables. A meaty mound of smoked pork ribs is satisfying, too, with two kinds of sauce (mildly hot and sweetish), homemade potato salad, beans, and good coleslaw. Entrées are under $15. For starters, I sampled a spicy (but not hot) black-bean-and-potato soup and overcooked barbecued shrimp.

Cowgirl Hall of Fame, 519 Hudson Street, at 10th Street, serves lunch from 11:30 A.M. to 3:30 P.M., Monday through Friday, until 4 P.M., Saturday and Sunday; dinner, 5 P.M. to midnight, daily. American Express accepted. Telephone: 633-1133.

# CRÊPES SUZETTE

The smiles are as genuine as they are wide when you are welcomed by the Frenchwomen who run this stucco-and-brick bistro. While the food is predictable, much of it is assertively seasoned and soothing. Cassoulet, full-flavored with sausage and duck, is a winner; other suggestions are rack of lamb for two, beef bourguignon, and coq au vin.

Crêpes Suzette, 363 West 46th Street, serves from noon to 10 P.M., Monday through Thursday, until 11:30 P.M., Friday and Saturday. During the winter it is open noon to 4 P.M., Sundays; prix-fixe dinners, $11 to $13. All major credit cards accepted. Telephone: 974-9002.

# DOMINICK'S

Dominick's, the pint-size, wildly popular Italian institution on Arthur Avenue in the Bronx, has expanded by about a third, but that doesn't seem to alleviate the lines outside this thirty-six-year-old Bronx institution. About a half dozen more communal tables have been added by moving the kitchen farther into the back of the building.

At 3 P.M. on a typical Sunday, customers are lined up in the foyer while inside gleeful diners, packed tighter than a jar of Italian peppers, dig into oval platters of homemade lasagna, stuffed shells, ziti in red sauce, bresaola, pork chops, and more.

Affable waiters in kitchen whites still approach your table and ask, "Whadda' you guys want?" There are no menus, no reservations, no credit cards, no wine list, no desserts, and no checks (they just tell you the price at the end of the meal, which can vary from visit to visit depending on the waiter's math and mood).

The food is still as homespun and copious as ever. A dainty Sunday repast for two began with a large mixed salad, slabs of terrific home-baked bread, a bottle of Corvo (a dry Italian white wine from Sicily), and a platter combining shells stuffed with ricotta cheese in red sauce and splendid ravioli. Next came a softball-size portion of bresaola (the dried salt beef in a tomato-and-parsley sauce). It seems that everyone punctuates the Dominick's experience with an espresso and Sambuca—they plop the bottle on the table so you can help yourself. Dinner for two costs from $35 to $45.

Dominick's, 2335 Arthur Avenue, between East 186th Street and Crescent Avenue, serves from noon to 10 P.M., Monday, Wednesday, Thursday, and Saturday, noon to 11 P.M., Friday, 1 to 9 P.M., Sunday. No credit cards. Telephone: 733-2807.

# DONALD SACKS

The awesome World Financial Center in lower Manhattan has finally unveiled its myriad food outlets. Among those is the American bistro called Donald Sacks in the soaring lobby of the American Express building. The 160-seat dining area under a brass gazebolike structure has marble café tables and a semiexposed kitchen. Fans of Mr. Sacks's Prince Street shop will find similar homespun fare here: lusty kale-and-sausage soup, hammy split-pea soup, crisp rotisserie-roasted duck with chutney and (limp) fried potatoes, good roast chicken, and a wide variety of bright and tasty salads and sandwiches (most under $10). Lunch runs about $20 to $25. The bar offers wine by the glass and beer.

Donald Sacks, World Financial Center Courtyard, 220 Vesey Street, serves from 11 A.M. to 10 P.M., Monday through Friday, 11 A.M. to 6 P.M., Saturday and Sunday. All major credit cards accepted. Telephone: 619-4600.

# EL CID

El Cid is a welcoming and modest little Spanish restaurant and tapas bar at 322 West 15th Street. On most weeknights the bar, under a Mediterranean tile roof, is filled with neighborhood regulars—Spanish-speaking all—nibbling on cured ham and cubes of hard sharp cheese along with glasses of red wine. The dining area has fewer than a dozen closely clustered tables, but everything in this tidy, spare place is done with care, down to the candlelight and fresh carnations on each table.

The food is homey and generally satisfying at budget prices. Tapas are a fun way to start: country sausage in red-wine sauce that you stab with toothpicks, marinated octopus aromatic of paprika, roasted eggplant and peppers. Actually, the portions are larger than traditional Spanish tapas, which are mere tidbits; these appetizer portions are called raciones in Spain.

Other dishes I tried were lusty if not always adequately seasoned. Oxtail in red beans with smoky bacon needed some salt to pull it together. Roast chicken with a potent garlic sauce was better. For dessert, there is a perfect flan ($3.50) and powerful coffee.

El Cid serves dinner from 5 to 11 P.M., Tuesday to Sunday. American Express accepted. Telephone: 929-9332.

# THE "11" CAFE

The "11" Cafe is a tidy and welcoming little Venezuelan restaurant in the East Village that offers some lusty national specialties at budget prices. Its compact dining room and bar with a dozen colorful tables sports a buoyant tropical décor; a tape deck near the coffee machine pours out big-band Ricky Ricardo Latin tunes, which prompt an occasional South American customer to break into a few samba passes.

The phone-booth-size kitchen in back produces a wide range of tasty arepas, which are thick cornmeal tortillas filled with a variety of fillings and eaten as snacks or appetizers. I can highly recommend the smoky and succulent roast pork, which is terrific with a sprinkling of the liquid fire they call hot sauce. The shredded beef is delicious, too. The same pork is served as part of an entrée, called pabellon de pernil, flanked by white rice, brassy black beans, and sautéed sweet plantains. Another good choice is called la hallaca, which is essentially a Venezuelan tamale made with cornmeal-encased bits of pork, beef, and chicken steamed in banana leaves. Beer, sangria, and Spanish wines are available, unless you are in a political frame of mind and opt for the house Cuba libre (rum, Coke, and bitters). You can have a three-course meal here for well under $20.

The "11" Cafe, 170 Second Avenue, at 11th Street, is open from 3 P.M. to midnight, Monday through Friday, noon to midnight, Saturday and Sunday; American Express and Diners Club accepted. Telephone: 982-4924.

# FERRIER

The ravenous demand these days for casual dining at fair prices is vividly demonstrated at Ferrier, a gleaming little bistro on 65th Street just east of Madison Avenue. Owned by Alain Chevreaux, who also has Chez Ma Tante in Greenwich Village, Ferrier has a lively little bar up front and a neighborly rectangular dining room in the back with colorful French prints on the walls and a bank of mirrors to minimize claustrophobia. At peak lunch and dinner hours, the mob here can make Ferrier's chic neighbor, Le Cirque, look underbooked. Early or late reservations are recommended.

At lunch you can start with a heady bisque filled with cubes of lobster meat and a chunky, full-flavored pork terrine. The ample house salad is bathed in an excellent creamy tarragon vinaigrette. A big mover at lunch is the sparkling oversize warm salad with shrimp and scallops. In the evening you can't go wrong with the sirloin steak and crunchy french fries or the picture-perfect rack of lamb. At Sunday brunch we sampled perfectly cooked asparagus vinaigrette, nicely done leeks vinaigrette, and scrambled eggs with salmon. The boudin noir, however, had good seasoning but a rubbery skin, and the mashed potatoes with it were watery and tasteless.

Ferrier, 29 East 65th Street, serves noon to midnight, Monday through Thursday, until 1 A.M., Friday and Saturday, until midnight, Sunday. All major credit cards accepted. Telephone: 772-9000.

# FLORENT

It's an Edward Hopper painting come to life, this World War Two coffee shop turned French bistro in the heart of the gritty West Side meat-market area. Formerly the R & L Restaurant, a stainless-steel-and-Formica hash house that catered to butchers and truck drivers in the market's heyday, it was taken over by a genial young Frenchman, Florent Morellet. The new owner changed the name to Florent while leaving the period décor largely intact.

The menu has abandoned "Adam and Eve on a raft" (poached eggs on toast) for French onion soup gratinée, duck mousse, couscous, sweetbreads, grilled calf's liver, and other homey Gallic fare. Not only is much of the food surprisingly well prepared, it's also a bargain—a three-course meal runs about $30, or a bit more with wine.

Duck liver mousse is freshly made, creamy and well seasoned; and rillettes of pork are appropriately rough-textured and peppery. Although I had heard good reports about the tripe, my waitress steered me instead to the fresh, golden sautéed sweetbreads with thin, crunchy french fries. Two dining companions enjoyed the inky and oniony boudin noir and a nicely poached monkfish swathed with onions and leeks. Florent is a good spot for a leisurely weekend breakfast.

Florent is at 69 Gansevoort Street, a half block west of Greenwich Street. Open twenty-four hours daily. No credit cards. Telephone: 989-5779.

# FRANK'S

This seventy-five-year-old steakhouse in the heart of Manhattan's wholesale-meat district, with its pressed-tin ceiling, languid overhead fan, sawdust-strewn tile floor, and long, elbow-worn mahogany bar, is as comfortable as an old flannel shirt. It has been known to generations of butchers and truck drivers as a place to start the day with coffee and rolls at 2 A.M. and, after the cooks come in at 4 A.M., virile breakfasts of everything from steak and eggs to kidneys, liver, pancakes, and bacon.

Frank's has a sizable and satisfying seafood selection and a changing roster of pastas. The steaks are better than average quality. The ambiance is terrific.

Frank's, 431 West 14th Street, is open for lunch noon to 3 P.M., Monday through Friday; dinner, 5 to 10 P.M., Monday through Thursday, until 11 P.M., Friday and Saturday. All major credit cards accepted. Telephone: 243-1349.

# GIRASOLE

One would think that the Upper East Side needs another rakish Italian restaurant about as much as the Park Avenue mall needs mobile homes. But here is Girasole, at 151 East 82nd Street, a sleek, compact, neutral-toned space with a vaguely neoclassical décor, packed nightly with a soignée crowd that devours pasta as if a national noodle-rationing program were to begin tomorrow.

Girasole, on the site of the short-lived Da Nanni, is run by Juliano Zuliani, the fastidiously professional co-owner of Primola on Second Avenue at 64th Street, with his partners, Franco Iacoviello, the chef at Primola, and Michele Maritato.

The same qualities that have made Primola such an enduring success are being applied to Girasole. The dining room is efficiently run by sharp, knowledgeable waiters, and the menu, consisting mostly of northern Italian dishes, is contemporary and appealingly diverse. Dinner can begin with penne in a delightfully complex sauce of tomato, mushrooms, pancetta, shrimp, and arugula, a special, and a brightly seasoned grilled vegetable plate of eggplant, zucchini, sweet peppers, baby artichokes, endive, and a round of warm goat cheese. Another pasta that can be recommended is an exceptionally good combination of spaghetti with mussels, clams, and squid moistened with a lusty garlic-scented shellfish broth. Seafood is also well turned out as a main course, judging from a deft version of swordfish Livornese, in a light tomato sauce with black olives, capers, and garlic. For dessert there is a relatively light pear-and-marzipan tart, strawberry tart, and (unexceptional) gelati.

Girasole serves lunch from noon to 3 P.M. and dinner from 5 to midnight, daily. American Express accepted. Telephone: 772-6690.

# HAMBURGER HARRY'S

This sleek grillery has two locations: downtown on Chambers Street and near Times Square, on West 45th Street. They sport violet walls, neon highlights, blond wood tables, and open charcoal-mesquite grill. Their thick hamburgers are made with good quality semilean ground beef and are served on sesame-seed buns. You can get everything from the "naked burger" (served without a roll) to a caviar-and-sour-cream burger or the "ha ha burger" (chili, Cheddar cheese, chopped onion, guacamole, and pico de gallo hot sauce). Coleslaw is freshly made and tasty, although french fries are sometimes soggy.

Hamburger Harry's at 157 Chambers Street serves from 11:30 A.M. to 10 P.M., Sunday through Thursday, until 11 P.M., Friday and Saturday. American Express, MasterCard, and Visa accepted. Telephone: 267-4446. Hamburger Harry's, 145 West 45th Street, serves from 11:30 A.M. to 11 P.M., Monday through Saturday. American Express, MasterCard, and Visa accepted. Telephone: 840-0566.

# HAROLD'S

One of the better recent additions to the Murray Hill neighborhood is tucked away in the Dumont Plaza Hotel, at 150 East 34th Street. Called Harold's, it is a trim, smart-looking place done in blond wood with bright red fabric-covered chairs, high-backed booths, and clusters of orchids and lilies.

Louisiana-born chef Tony Najiola honed his style of urbane American cooking at the River Café, La Réserve, and the Village Green.

Some of his dishes are reminiscent of the cooking that garnered him two stars at the Village Green: grilled leeks with pecan-coated goat cheese, grilled leg of lamb with marinated butternut squash and savoy cabbage, mustard-coated chicken with grilled vegetables, and seared tuna over spinach with roasted tomatoes and Dijon-mustard-cream dressing. Not everything is on target yet—seasonings are hit and miss—but a quality effort is evident. Don't miss the smashing plum-apple crisp with vanilla ice cream. One shortcoming has been the bumbling, amateurish service.

Harold's, in the Murray Hill Hotel, 150 East 34th Street, serves breakfast 7 to 10 A.M., daily; lunch, noon to 3 P.M., Monday through Friday; dinner, 6 to 10 P.M., daily; brunch ($12.50), 11 A.M. to 3 P.M., Saturday and Sunday. All major credit cards accepted. Telephone: 684-7761.

# THE HEALTH PUB

Considering the sizable demand for vegetarian fare in New York, there are few places around that make an effort to be distinctive in either ambiance or food. A happy exception is the Health Pub, a cheerful vegetarian café on Second Avenue. The two large dining rooms are crisp and tidy, done in soft beige with butcher-block tables.

The menu sounds so appealing that even hard-core junk-food addicts might be tempted. Cold soba, the Japanese buckwheat noodles, with snow peas is an attractively arranged appetizer laced with julienne strips of carrots, cucumber, and Chinese radish, all in a dynamic sesame sauce. Soups, which change daily, are well seasoned, such as the vegetable soup (butternut squash, carrots, rutabaga, parsnips) sweetened with miso.

Two sandwiches to watch for are the tofu-sunflower burger, a combination of mashed tofu, sunflower seeds, brown rice, and onion on a whole-wheat English muffin and another made with baba gannoush (roasted eggplant and garlic mashed with chickpeas and olive oil) on thick slices of sourdough bread.

For dessert there are seasonal fruits in tasty almond cream and a moist poppy-seed cake with lemon sauce. No alcohol is served, but all sorts of freshly made fruit and vegetable drinks are available.

The Health Pub, 371 Second Avenue, at 21st Street, is open from 11 A.M. to 10:30 P.M., daily. American Express accepted. Telephone: 529-9200.

# HSF

The little dim sum carts roll by endlessly, and a couple can eat until they fall over on the simulated leather banquettes without spending $50—individual plates from the carts generally range from $2.50 to $3.50. The steamed shrimp dumplings and fried pork dumplings are nicely seasoned and fresh; other highlights are the hacked-up steamed spare ribs, sesame-sprinkled chicken patties, stuffed green peppers, and stuffed eggplant. Wine by the glass and Chinese beer are available. The room is trim and comfortable, with beige tablecloths and soft lighting. Most of the waiters' and waitresses' English is incomprehensible to Americans, but just point to things that look good and you'll do fine.

HSF, 578 Second Avenue, at 31st Street, serves 11:30 A.M. to 11:30 P.M., Sunday through Thursday, until 12:30

A.M., Friday and Saturday. All major credit cards accepted. Telephone: 689-6969.

# HSF (CHINATOWN)

HSF's original and larger site, at 46 Bowery, south of Canal Street, offers a similar range of food. The setting is louder and brighter, filled with dozens of Chinese families. The show starts rolling at breakfast and continues to midnight. Serves from 7:30 A.M. to 2 A.M., daily. No credit cards. Telephone: 374-1319.

# INDIAN CAFE

Yogurt-tenderized chicken roasted in a tandoor, lentils spiked with ginger and garlic, and earthy Indian breads make a blood-warming delight at this pint-size café. The kitchen is not afraid to season—sometimes it gets carried away with the hot pepper, though—and the food, while not terribly refined, is generally fresh and appealing. Lean goat meat cooked in the tandoor in a snappy curry sauce with slivered almonds is another good bet.

Indian Cafe, 201 West 95th Street, serves from 11 A.M. to 11 P.M., daily. American Express, MasterCard, and Visa accepted. Telephone: 222-1600.

The Indian Cafe at 2791 Broadway, at 108th Street, is a larger, prettier version of the 95th Street original. It has a glass-enclosed sidewalk café, soft lighting, and gray banquettes in the intimate back room.

Serves from 11:30 A.M. to midnight, daily. American Express, MasterCard, and Visa accepted. Telephone: 749-9200.

# ISTANBUL KEBAP

English is a minority language at this compact, family-run Turkish restaurant. It's a clean and well-organized place, with carnations adorning the paper-draped tables, Turkish rugs on the walls, and hanging plants. Lamb is the foundation of the Anatolian cooking: dishes include adana kebap, minced lamb seasoned with peppers and grilled on skewers; sis kebap, cubed marinated leg of lamb grilled on skewers; etli bamya, okra, lamb, tomato, and onions; and yogurtlu kebap, a hearty casserole of pita triangles, chopped lamb, onions, yogurt, paprika, and tomato. Appetizers are under $3; main courses are under $11.

Istanbul Kebap, 303 East 80th Street, serves 1 P.M. to midnight, daily. No liquor is served. American Express accepted. Telephone: 517-6880.

# LA BONNE SOUPE

Customers line up outside the door of this rustically humble French bistro in midtown, attesting to the singular bargains within; lunch is a real crush, dinner less so. As the name promises, the soups are indeed good—particularly mushroom barley with lamb, and lusty cheese-encrusted onion both of which come with good French bread, a green salad, and dessert ($7). Watch for other specials, such as the brandade de morue daily during the cool months, a garlicky purée of codfish and potatoes that you can scoop up with toasted French bread, or the little crock of fragrant bouillabaisse ($14.95). The downstairs dining room is lined with neighborly banquettes, two dining rooms upstairs are festooned with a fabulous collection of colorful Haitian primitive-style paintings. Keep this spot in mind for late dining. La Bonne Soupe, 48 West 55th Street, serves from 11 A.M. to midnight, Monday through Saturday, until 11 P.M., Sunday. American Express accepted. Telephone: 586-7650.

# LA FUSTA

Parrillada is the Spanish term for mixed grill, which in the Argentine tradition usually means a mini-charcoal barbecue presented at a table heaped with T-bone steak, marinated skirt steak, morcilla (blood sausage), sweetbreads, kidneys, calf's liver, and sausage. At La Fusta, a popular neighborhood Argentine restaurant in the Elmhurst section of Queens, the lusty and well-cooked parrillada (sans kidneys and liver) comes with a jar of chimichurri, a piquant sauce made with garlic, parsley, and olive oil. The parrillada is about $15 per person.

For starters, try the thick-crusted empanadas de carne, redolent of garlic and minced olives, or the typically Argentine salad of sharp, fresh watercress with onions. La Fusta is a casual and congenial spot with stucco-and-timber walls festooned with horse-racing memorabilia—*la fusta* means rider's crop—red checkered tablecloths, a friendly staff.

I was pleasantly surprised by the Argentine wines sampled, including the clean, crisp Navarro Correas white and the easy-drinking red from the same house (both under $20). For dessert, flan with dulce de leche, the sweetened caramelized milk, is a must if you want to be truly Argentine; another good choice is the thin apple pancake flambéed with rum.

La Fusta, 80-32 Baxter Avenue, Elmhurst, Queens, serves dinner daily except Tuesday from noon to midnight. No credit cards. Telephone: (718) 429-8222.


# LA KASBAH

Vegetable couscous is one of the menu highlights at this bustling kosher restaurant. Another good option is the combination platter, holding smoky roasted eggplant purée called baba gannoush, falafel, tabbouleh, Tunisian-style eggplant salad, and mixed Moroccan salad. This engaging glatt kosher restaurant has two simply appointed peach-and-white dining rooms that are often full but not intolerably loud.

Actually, there are three varieties of couscous—chicken, lamb, and vegetarian (all under $20)—all prepared in the traditional way, letting the ingredients cook slowly over a double steamer to meld their flavors. Portions are enormous. Tagine, the lamb stew made with prunes, celery, pine nuts, raisins, and rice, is also full flavored and thoroughly satisfying. From the grill come highly seasoned lamb and chicken kebabs. For starters, there is a deliciously smoky baba gannoush, the Middle Eastern eggplant dip, as well as hummus, tahina, and falafel. Several simple kosher table wines are available for under $20.

La Kasbah, 70 West 71st Street, serves 5 P.M. to 11 P.M., Monday through Thursday, 6 P.M. to 1:30 A.M., Saturday, winter only, 6 P.M. to 1:30 A.M., Sunday, year-round; prix-fixe brunch ($13.50), 1 to 3:30 P.M., Sunday. All major credit cards accepted. Telephone: 769-1690.

# LA MÉDITERRANÉE

It will never make anybody's list of Manhattan's ten most chic restaurants, nor will you see it mentioned in the society columns accompanied by photographs of insouciant celebrities clinking glasses and pecking cheeks. La Méditerranée, on Second Avenue at 50th Street, is about as voguish as spats—but considerably more comfortable. Quite simply, it is a wonderfully homey and neighborly spot that gives you a warm feeling upon entering, with its timber-and-stucco façade, faux wooden shutters, colorful murals of France, and cozy banquettes.

The moderately priced menu is just as familiar and soothing, running from hot sausage and potato salad to calf's liver with raisins, lamb chops, and assorted daily stews and roasts, such as a poached stuffed chicken and winter vegetables.

Prix-fixe lunch is $24, prix-fixe dinner $26.50. The food is generally wholesome and satisfying (specials are the best bets). On Sunday evenings, a beaming Frenchwoman strolls through the dining room singing "La Vie en Rose" and other nostalgic hits, occasionally joined by the owner, Robert Chamou.

La Méditerranée, 947 Second Avenue, serves noon to 10 P.M., Monday through Friday, 5 to 10:30 P.M., Saturday and Sunday; pretheater dinner ($24), 5 to 7 P.M., Monday through Saturday. All major credit cards accepted. Telephone: 755-4155.

# LA MÉTAIRIE

La Métairie on West 10th Street is one of the tiniest restaurants in Manhattan, having just sixteen seats. It is also one of the most romantic, with white barn-board walls, dried flowers, candlelight, Provençale fabrics on the banquettes, and a pair of doves in an overhead bird cage. The rustic French fare is light and herb infused. Two fine starters are ravioli filled with oysters and celery root in a clarified duck-stock sauce touched with soy sauce and rich, pepper-encrusted gravlax over a bed of yellow lentils, a special. Less successful was an overchilled terrine of lobster, salmon, and scallops over a sun-dried tomato coulis.

Among main courses, grilled salmon steak is delicious over slices of fennel with a light tomato-and-fish-stock sauce, as is the Black Angus steak in red-wine sauce sweetened with confit of shallots, along with braised endive and sautéed mushrooms.

Tarte Tatin is puffed and nicely glazed, and the same good puff pastry makes a napoleon of strawberries sublime. La Métairie is no bargain—count on at least $50 a person —but worth keeping in mind when you want refuge from the crowds.

La Métairie, 189 West 10th Street, serves dinner from 6 to 11 P.M., Monday through Saturday. American Express, MasterCard, and Visa accepted. Telephone: 989-0343.

# LANDMARK TAVERN

Dating to 1868, this West Side spot has a splendid Old New York feeling with its burnished wood bar, huge brass wood-burning stove, uneven floors, and smoke-smudged ceiling. This is a great place for a drink, although don't expect much from the food. Strip steak with pommes soufflés is pleasing, and simple burgers and grilled items are reliable if not exciting. The kitchen has an aversion to seasoning of any kind, so vegetables, stews, and shepherd's pie come out utterly bland. The bar stocks a fine old selection of single-malt Scotches and cognacs.

Landmark Tavern, 626 Eleventh Avenue, corner of 46th Street, serves lunch from noon to 4:30 P.M., Monday through Friday; brunch, noon to 4:30 P.M., Saturday and Sunday; dinner, 5 P.M. to midnight, Monday through Thursday, 5 P.M. to 1 A.M., Friday and Saturday. American Express, MasterCard, and Visa accepted. Telephone: 757-8595.

# LA VIEILLE AUBERGE

Comfort and tranquillity are the two major assets of this enduring Restaurant Row institution, which is showing its mileage—the off-white banquettes have become off-off-white from years of friction. The food is unreconstructed 1950s fare. Vichyssoise is light, creamy, and brightened with chives; saucisson en croute is hearty and filling with a brown stock sauce; and for main courses, stick with roast poultry, rack of lamb with rosemary, and steak with red-wine sauce. The seafood I have sampled there was given heavy-handed treatment.

Lunch is prix fixe, $14.50 and $18.75; dinner, $21 and $29.

La Vieille Auberge, 347 West 46th Street, serves lunch from noon to 2:30 P.M., Monday through Friday; dinner, 5 to 9 P.M., Monday through Thursday, until 11 P.M., Friday and Saturday. All major credit cards accepted. Telephone: 247-4284.

# LE LUCKY STRIKE

Le Lucky Strike, opened in late 1989, is a moderately priced bistro in SoHo that looks as if it has been there forever. In fact, this creation of Keith McNally (the Odeon, Cafe Luxembourg, and Nell's) and four partners is in the former La Gamelle, a bohemian hangout that had the mistiming of being a rough-and-tumble bistro before rough-and-tumble bistros became the rage.

Le Lucky Strike has the congenially grungy feeling of an ancient haunt in Les Halles in Paris: a derma of pallid yellow paint, a bonhomous bar, tightly arranged tabloid-sized tables, vinyl banquettes, and overhead fans. The minuscule menu is scrawled on mirrors in the dining room—an amusing idea, but from our distant table the pale lettering and glare from room lights made it about as legible as billboards from a DC-9.

Some of the appetizers soar; many entrées sputter. Among the enticing starters are an earthy lentil-and-arugula salad ($5.50), crunchy corn-flour-dusted calamari, and fennel with Parmesan salad. An entrée of strip steak was humdrum, along with sodden french fries. Grilled chicken with sweet peppers is pleasant, and lamb chops are succulent and well seasoned, although the roasted potatoes served with both were tired and oily. Pasta with anchovies and capers was a sorry excuse for puttanesca ($10.50).

Thick-crusted fresh apple tart and custardy bread pudding with strawberry sauce are fine finales.

Le Lucky Strike, 59 Grand Street, serves breakfast, lunch, dinner, and late supper, from noon to 4 A.M., daily. American Express, MasterCard, and Visa accepted. Telephone: 941-0479.

# LE MADELEINE

Le Madeleine, an engaging little French bistro on West 43rd Street near Ninth Avenue, is often overlooked as a moderately priced dining option in the theater district, although it shouldn't be. It is a lively spot at night, where theater people gather at the long bar to leaf through issues of *Variety* and talk shop. The dining room is low-key and charming, with brick walls, wooden banquettes, and butcher-paper-covered tables. During the warm months, a backyard garden is open for dining.

The menu is straightforward bistro fare with more than a few appealing dishes. Mussels marinière are plump and well cooked in their flavorful white-wine-and-herb sauce— they make a good light lunch along with a salad and some French bread for dipping in the broth. Soupe au pistou, while thicker than the traditional version, is tasty and well seasoned. Simple grilled fish are usually nicely done as well.

Not everything is so successful, but you should do well by sticking to homey soups, stews, and salads. Dinner entrées range from $10 to $20. Le Madeleine, 403 West 43rd Street, serves brunch (prix fixe, $12.50) from noon to 3:30 P.M., Saturday and Sunday; lunch, noon to 4 P.M., Monday through Friday; dinner, 5 to midnight, Monday through Sunday. American Express, MasterCard, and Visa accepted. Telephone: 246-2993.

# LE STEAK

There are not many places in midtown where you can have a satisfying three-course dinner for $21.95, at least not sitting down. Le Steak has been a fixture on Second Avenue for twenty-five years, and it is still going strong. The room has a warm and cozy feeling, with a Tudor-style stucco-and-wood-beam façade, lipstick-red banquettes, and a small bar up front. We recently started with the romaine salad tossed in an exceptionally well-balanced vinaigrette and the house onion soup, one of those cheese-encrusted crocks with a big crouton inside (the broth was on the pale side, though).

The steaks are good sirloins, full of flavor; they would have been better seared on both sides instead of one. The thin, light french fries are delicious. Swordfish, too, is pleasing: moist, well seasoned, and served with carrots and green beans. For dessert, there is a fine crème caramel, a decent chocolate mousse, and a boozy rum parfait that comes in one of those tall metal dishes that drugstore soda fountains used to have. A bottle of Beaujolais ($18) pushes the tab for two to about $55.

Le Steak, 1089 Second Avenue, near 58th Street, serves from 5:30 to 10:30 P.M., Sunday through Thursday until 11 P.M., Friday and Saturday. All major credit cards accepted. Telephone: 421-9072.

# LOTFI'S COUSCOUS

West 45th Street is becoming a miniature Restaurant Row for the budget-minded with the recent opening of Lotfi's Couscous, a welcoming Moroccan spot that serves zesty fare at remarkable prices. The second-story dining room is trim and clean, with airline travel posters and paper flowers the salient design elements. The menu carries a fine array of Moroccan specialties, including spicy harira, a chickpea-and-lentil soup ($2.50); zaalouk, which is puréed eggplant ($3); chicken or lamb kebabs ($8.95 to $10.95); couscous ($8.95 lunch, $9.95 dinner); tagine, a stew made with chicken or lamb ($9.95, $10.95); and pastilla, a phyllo dough holding squab, chicken, or seafood with almonds, eggs, and spices ($11.95 for squab or chicken, $13.95 for seafood, at lunch and dinner).

Lotfi's Couscous, 135 West 45th Street (one flight up), serves from noon to midnight, Tuesday through Friday; until 11 P.M., Monday; 4 P.M. to midnight, Saturday; 4 to 11 P.M., Sunday. No credit cards. Telephone: 768-8738.

# MADELINE'S

The former Patisserie Lanciani in SoHo has expanded to a full-service restaurant called Madeline's, under the same ownership. The new menu carries everything from poached calamari with black angel-hair pasta to braised chicken chasseur with couscous (both $15.50). I have not had the opportunity to sample much of that menu, but recent late-night dessert binges have reassured me that some of the best sweets in town can still be found here.

One specialty is an astoundingly good boule noire, a Grand Marnier–splashed chocolate cake filled with chocolate mousse and decorated with curls of chocolate ribbons ($5). A custardy cornerstone of warm bread pudding in caramel sauce is another sublime choice ($4). Some fine dessert wines are available by the glass.

Madeline's, 177 Prince Street, serves from 9 A.M. to 11 P.M., Tuesday through Saturday; brunch (prix-fixe $10.95 to $12.95), 11:30 A.M. to 4 P.M., Saturday and Sunday; Sunday dinner, 6 to 9 P.M. American Express accepted. Telephone: 477-2788.

# MANDARIN COURT

Following the rise and decline of dim sum restaurants in Chinatown requires the vigilance of a stockbroker. And a little insider information never hurts, either. On a tip, I had lunch at the Mandarin Court Restaurant on Mott Street, a clean and contemporary spot with pastel walls, sparkling tiles, sleek black tables, and an open kitchen up front. Don't be alarmed by the piped-in country-and-western music: this place is authentic. You get two long menus upon arriving, one listing specials. No sooner have you grappled with that than a woman strolls by pushing a cart of dim sum specialties.

From the cart (all items under $2), all the dumplings sampled were light and delicious, particularly the firm, sweet shrimp and the heartily seasoned pork. Turnip cake with Chinese sausage was a lively combination, while three chunks of roasted eggplant in sweet sauce were nice palate teasers before moving on to the main event: six skewers holding shrimp and scallops surrounded by a snappy black-pepper sauce ($9.95), easily enough for two. Fried scallops come with the same good sauce for $12.95.

Mandarin Court, 61 Mott Street, serves 7:30 A.M. to midnight, daily. Dim sum served between 7:30 A.M. and 3:30 P.M., daily. All major credit cards accepted. Telephone: 608-3838.

# MANHATTAN CHILI COMPANY

The combustible "Texas chain-gang chili" here has fueled many a New York University student through frigid winter nights. This upbeat, fast-paced chili parlor has friendly service and congenial prices (chilies about $7 to $9). Most of the chilis can be recommended: ground beef with beans, onions, cumin, and garlic; Texas-style beef chili with no beans, laced with two kinds of chili powder; and lamb-and-hominy chili with nutmeg, ginger, and plenty of black pepper. Fajitas of chicken and steak are recommended, too.

Manhattan Chili Company, 302 Bleecker Street, serves from noon to midnight, Sunday through Thursday, until 1 A.M., Friday and Saturday. American Express, MasterCard, and Visa accepted. Telephone: 206-7163.

# MARY ANN'S

Dainty plate design is not the specialty here: some of the heaping dishes look like chuck-wagon rations. Aesthetics aside, much of the Mexican food is fresh and tasty, with entrées under $10. Try chimichanga, beef-filled burritos with guacamole and sour cream, or pollo Yucatan, chicken breast sautéed with scallions, garlic, chili, and Cheddar cheese. The wine-marinated slices of grilled beef for fajitas are exceptionally succulent, but the tortillas can taste of steaming.

The brick-and-stucco setting with plain wooden tables and south-of-the-border paraphernalia on the walls jumps daily at lunch and dinner. Mary Ann's, 116 Eighth Avenue, at 16th Street, serves from noon to 10:30 P.M., Sunday through Thursday, until 11:15 P.M., Friday and Saturday. No credit cards. Telephone: 633-0877.

# MENCHANKO-TEI

Japanese noodle parlors, of which there are dozens in midtown Manhattan alone, are ideal for the rushed dip-and-run luncher. Many are clean, satisfying, and unquestionably cheap, if not much on atmosphere. For a step up in comfort but not in price, consider Menchanko-Tei, a sleek, forty-four-seat restaurant on West 55th Street with an eight-seat dining bar and a dozen black-lacquered tables.

The specialty here is "home-style soups," our waitress explained. Judging from the portions, the home she is referring to must have something to do with sumo wrestlers. At a recent lunch, a soup called Menchanko came out in a deep brass bowl—a bucket might be a more accurate term—and was a richly flavored broth filled with pressed bean curd, soba noodles, cabbage, sweet balls of fish cake, bean sprouts and other vegetables, all cooked until just al dente ($7.50).

Another soup, called Kikuzo Ramen, is made with squiggly fresh noodles, scallions, bamboo shoots, fish cake, and delicious slices of lean roast pork ($6.50). All soups are served with big, black bamboo spoons and chopsticks. Rice and Japanese pickles are traditional accompaniments.

Menchanko-Tei, 39 West 55th Street, serves from 11:30 A.M. to 12:30 A.M., Monday through Saturday, until 11:30

P.M., Sunday. All major credit cards accepted. Telephone: 247-1585.

# MEZZALUNA

This charming little Italian trattoria has been much imitated since it came on the scene in 1984. Mezzaluna—Italian for half moon, or in this case for a semicircular chopping blade with a handle at each end—is designed with whimsy and style, with colorful drawings and collages that cover one wall, a painted-sky ceiling, designer plates and chairs, and marble tables. What's more, the food is very good.

The menu specializes in pastas and, after 10 P.M., pizzas, which are cooked in a wood-fired brick oven. For starters, there are some bright versions of carpaccio. You might want to try the seared tuna carpaccio with a lovely black-olive sauce. Another is tissue-thin slices of beef resting on a bed of glistening arugula with slices of Parmesan cheese as garnish. Drizzled with olive oil and dusted with fresh pepper, it is a tasty and invigorating appetizer.

Almost all the pastas are winners. Two favorites are the maccheroni (thin, ribboned tubes) with slices of artichoke and fennel, plum tomatoes, and black olives; and orrechiete tossed with crumbled fennel sausage, broccoli, and plum tomatoes. The pizzas, which can serve as an entrée for one or be split in a multicourse meal, are bright and fresh, with a thin, slightly puffed crust. Among the toppings are tomato and fresh basil, eggplant and black olives, basil pesto and a combination of zucchini, carrots, tomato, peppers, and leeks. A sorbet of grapefruit with pink peppercorns is a good after-dinner refresher. The tiramisù, which I used to like, was too sweet the last time I tried it; don't bother with the pale chocolate Italian version of chocolate pudding.

Mezzaluna, 1295 Third Avenue, near 74th Street, serves lunch from noon to 3 P.M., Monday through Friday, until

3:45 P.M., Saturday and Sunday; dinner, 6 P.M. to 1 A.M., Monday through Friday and Sunday, 6:30 P.M. to 1 A.M., Saturday. No credit cards. Telephone: 535-9600.

# MOROCCAN STAR

Some of the best dining bargains in New York can be found along Brooklyn's Atlantic Avenue, home of about a dozen Middle Eastern and North African restaurants. One of these is Moroccan Star, a simple, tidy restaurant that serves a mélange of Arabic and European dishes for prices so low you can't help suspecting they are a mirage.

The kitchen of this family-run restaurant is presided over by Ahmed Almontaser, formerly of Luchow's, the Four Seasons, and the Brasserie in Manhattan, which explains the Continental accent on the menu. However, forget the beef stroganoff and crêpes, and head right for the lamb steak, a juicy, intensely flavorful slab of meat that makes you wonder why this dish is not generally served in Manhattan steakhouses. The best side dish is al dente baby okra.

Other good choices on the menu are pastella (sometimes spelled pastila or bastila), traditionally a semisweet pigeon pie in paper-thin pastry, and tagine. The pastella is made with chicken, raisins, garlic, and spices, and is served in a large wedge, like a thick slab of pizza.

The tagine, while different from the version served in Morocco, is nonetheless satisfying. It is a savory lamb stew with carrots, prunes, and dried almonds, and it is meant to be eaten in large pockets of pita bread. Moroccan Star does not serve beer or wine, so you may provide your own. Moroccan Star, 205 Atlantic Avenue in Brooklyn, is open 11 A.M. to 11 P.M., daily. All major credit cards accepted. Telephone: (718) 643-0800.

# NEW PROSPECT CAFE

Standing-room crowds nightly attest to the good food at bargain prices offered by this neighborly little restaurant on bustling Flatbush Avenue. The small gray-and-white dining room with its chalkboard specials and budget-priced wine list attracts a gregarious flannel-shirt-and-corduroy clientele. The food is imaginative and consistently good—not to mention remarkably inexpensive by Manhattan standards. Among the winning starters: sesame-coated chicken wings in a soy-based sauce, a tasty zucchini timbale with roasted red-pepper sauce, Parmesan-laced polenta accompanied by roasted whole garlic. Entrées range from a fresh and bright bouillabaisselike concoction to crisp-skinned and succulent game hen with apples and green peppercorns and eggplant rollatini with polenta and roasted peppers.

New Prospect Cafe, 393 Flatbush Avenue, at Eighth Avenue, serves brunch from 10:30 A.M. to 3 P.M., Sunday; lunch, 11:30 A.M. to 4:30 P.M., Tuesday through Saturday; dinner, 5 to 10 P.M., Monday through Thursday, 5 to 11 P.M., Friday and Saturday, 3 to 10 P.M., Sunday. American Express accepted. Telephone: (718) 638-2148.

# OLLIE'S NOODLE SHOP AND GRILLE

This clean, bustling Chinese restaurant near the Columbia University campus, with closely assembled tables and watercolor paintings on the wall, offers a little bit of everything, starting with omelets and Oriental soups and moving on to deli fare, burgers, and Cantonese dishes. Based on my experience, I would recommend sticking to the Orient.

The best items sampled were the sweet-skinned and juicy roast duck ($4.95 for a quarter of a duck, $7 for a half, and $14 for a whole) and an equally good soy-brushed roast chicken ($4.75, $6.50, and $13). Get a side order of the pepper-laced sautéed green beans with squiggles of chicken ($4.50 lunch, $6.50 dinner).

For starters, the steamed dumplings are tasty but a tad undercooked. Chicken-filled buns have delicious insides, but the hamburger-size buns are too sweet for my taste. Ditto for the pork buns. Ollie's serves no alcohol.

Ollie's Noodle Shop and Grille, 2957 Broadway, at 116th Street, serves from 7 A.M. to 2 A.M., Monday through Saturday, until midnight, Sunday. American Express, MasterCard, and Visa accepted. Telephone: 932-3300. A second Ollie's opened in May 1990, at 2315 Broadway, at 84th Street. Telephone: 362-3712.

# PALM COURT

Sunday brunch in the fabled Palm Court in the Plaza Hotel has been a New York institution since this magnificent Edwardian landmark was erected in 1907. Under the ownership of Donald and Ivana Trump the setting and food have returned to a level of splendor worthy of F. Scott Fitzgerald. The three-tier Palm Court is still one of the grandest Old World spaces in the city, with its towering mural-covered wood ceiling, lavish chandeliers, and lilting chamber music.

All this sumptuousness comes at a stiff price: $39 a person without beverages. But if you are showing off the town to a visitor or just in a celebratory mood, the experience can be dazzling. The endless buffet is opulently presented and impressive for its diversity and freshness. I barely put a dent in the selection, which includes copious cheeses, fruits, breads, terrines, smoked fish (try the exceptionally rich and delicate Nova Scotia salmon and the pepper-encrusted smoked trout), omelets, daube of lamb, and much more. One could gain three pounds just looking at the dessert table.

Palm Court at the Plaza, 59th Street and Fifth Avenue, serves brunch (prix fixe, $42) from 10 A.M. to 2:15 P.M. Tea served from 3:45 to 6 P.M., Monday through Friday, 4 to 6

P.M., Sunday. All major credit cards accepted. Telephone: 546-5350.

# PANEVINO

Patrons of Lincoln Center have another dining option before and after performances: Panevino, a Restaurant Associates creation in Avery Fisher Hall. It is a moderately priced Italian trattoria said to be designed after a Tuscan farmhouse—although I've never seen a Tuscan farmer eating on little faux-marble tables and sleek leather-and-steel chairs surrounded by a gallery of abstract pastel drawings. Simple starters like mozzarella with eggplant, tomato, and basil and grilled shrimp with zucchini can be pleasing, although you may need to boost them with some salt and pepper. Pastas sampled were unevenly seasoned: tagliolini with shrimp and radicchio was a tad overcooked but otherwise tasty, while fusilli came in a searing, unharmonious hot-pepper-and-sun-dried-tomato sauce. Pizzas range from $8.75 for buffalo mozzarella, tomato, and roasted peppers to $11.50 for shrimp and artichokes. For dessert, tiramisù was nothing but a sugar blast, so gelato is probably the best bet. A short wine list has eleven selections by the glass.

Panevino, at Lincoln Center Plaza, 65th Street and Columbus Avenue, in Avery Fisher Hall, serves lunch and dinner daily (hours vary with performances). All major credit cards accepted. Telephone: 874-7000.

# PAOLA'S

The proverbial hole-in-the-wall restaurant—owned and run by a well-intentioned, indefatigable chef in a space decorated with heirlooms—is an endangered species. One engaging survivor is Paola's, on East 85th Street near First

Avenue, where the owner, Paola Marracino, offers some homespun Italian fare at affordable prices. The slender rectangular dining room looks like a truncated Victorian parlor, with a stamped-tin ceiling, burgundy walls, lace curtains, candlelight, and tulip clusters. A Sunday dinner featured a lusty pasta puttanesca, potent with garlic and black olives, a platter of succulent boned chicken with fennel sausage, and an enormous but tender veal chop with rosemary. Faithful renditions of tiramisù and chocolate mousse rounded out the meal. Service can be brusque.

Paola's, 347 East 85th Street, serves dinner from 5 to 11 P.M., Monday through Saturday, 4 to 10 P.M., Sunday. American Express accepted. Telephone: 794-1890.

# PASTA & DREAMS

This cheerful and compact little spot at 1068 First Avenue (near 58th Street, telephone: 752-1436) is done in bright yellow and pink with yellow cane chairs and a clay-colored tile floor.

The lunch menu carries a number of prix-fixe meals, mostly under $20. You will find combinations such as a sparkling salad of arugula, green leaf lettuce, and radicchio; spaghetti with fresh tomato sauce and basil; a glass of wine, beer, or mineral water and coffee.

A la carte choices include summery dishes such as tagliatelle with asparagus, farfalline with salmon and spinach, and penne with zucchini and mozzarella. The inexpensive wine list offers some reliable Italian labels by the glass and the bottle. Pasta & Dreams also has outlets at 2161 Broadway (at 76th Street, telephone: 724-4324) and 1675 Third Avenue (between 93rd and 94th Streets, telephone: 348-8477). All are open daily for lunch and dinner. All accept all major credit cards.

# PASTA PRESTO

You don't go to Pasta Presto for gastronomic enlightenment, but you do go for satisfying bargain-priced fare in an upbeat setting. Pastas are in the $8-to-$11 range.

The two dining rooms, with white brick walls, café tables, and bent-cane chairs, are filled nightly with a mixed informal crowd. Among the fresh and appealing appetizers are eggplant-and-zucchini salad in a light creamy vinaigrette sauce and fresh green beans and tomato salad; the cottony winter tomatoes, though, could have been left out.

The menu carries about sixteen pastas and one or two daily specials. Penne with prosciutto, firm-cooked broccoli, and garlic is vibrant and light, spaghetti with chunks of chicken and eggplant in marinara sauce is nicely seasoned and al dente, and daily specials, such as farfalle with a dill-accented cream sauce, shrimp, and crab, hit the spot. Not all pastas are unqualified successes, but at these prices you can afford to experiment and get to know the best offerings. Simple Italian wines run $12 or so.

Pasta Presto is at 613 Second Avenue, near 34th Street (889-4131), 959 Second Avenue, near 51st Street (754-4880), 93 Macdougal Street, near Minetta Lane and Bleecker Street (260-5679), 37 Barrow Street, near Bleecker (691-0480). All accept all major credit cards.

# PEKING DUCK HOUSE RESTAURANT

The name says it all. If you are looking for a succulent rendition of Peking Duck, try this unassuming and lively second-story restaurant at 22 Mott Street, where the art has been honed to a reliably satisfying science. A whole duck, which feeds up to six as part of a multicourse meal, costs $24. Serves from 11:30 A.M. to 10:30 P.M., Sunday through

Thursday; 11:30 A.M. to 11:30 P.M., Friday and Saturday. American Express and Diners Club accepted. Telephone: 227-1810.

# PUNSCH

Punsch, at 11 West 60th Street, bills itself as a French restaurant with Scandinavian accents. At first glance, it looks like a Brian McNally trend-o-mat uprooted from SoHo: stark monochromatic walls, cool teal-blue banquettes, a sleek bar, and ashen waitresses who make Keith Richards look like a chestnut-skinned Malibu lifeguard. Punsch is the hippest spot uptown at the moment, although dizzy, erratic service keeps me from recommending it as a pretheater option.

For starters, there is a tasty example of the open-faced shrimp-and-dill sandwich called toast skagen garnished with golden whitefish caviar. Tender morsels of boneless rabbit over white beans in a bacon-enriched tomato sauce were so succulent I would have happily had another plate for the main course.

Among the main events are a decent rack of lamb with green beans and what was called dauphine potatoes (but were actually just sautéed potatoes), tender roast duck over mustard greens and lentils, and run-of-the-mill roast chicken with papery mashed potatoes.

At lunch, ten types of Scandinavian open-faced sandwiches are served, including sologa (matjes herring, capers, onion, and red beets) and gravlax.

Punsch serves lunch noon to 3 P.M., Monday through Friday; dinner, 6 P.M. to 12:30 A.M., Tuesday through Saturday; until 11:30 P.M., Sunday and Monday. American Express accepted. Telephone: 767-0606.

# RIO MAR

From the outside, Rio Mar looks like a frayed Latin shots-and-beer bar catering to butchers in the old West Side wholesale-meat district. "It's a great place," a usually sensible friend assured me. "Nobody knows about it." With more than a little skepticism, I gave it a try.

The downstairs bar of this family-run establishment is a convivial place. Upstairs, a small L-shaped room is clean and functional, with yellow walls holding a haphazard gallery of bullfight paintings and assorted posters. The waiters are warm and friendly, although their English can be spotty. As for the food, it is fresh, pure, authentically Iberian, and remarkably cheap.

Caldo gallego, a foggy bowl of kale, white beans, potatoes, and assorted meats, rivals the best I have had in Spain. Homemade chicken soup is the real item, made with chicken carcasses, gizzards, and vegetables. The more adventurous might sample the pristine octopus salad with sliced onions in a zippy red sauce (most appetizers are under $5). A limited wine list carries some of Spain's better-known labels.

Shellfish is lovingly prepared, too, whether in the aromatic paella loaded with shrimp, chicken, sausage, and mussels or the terrific mariscada Rio Mar, a cornucopia of shellfish in a garlic-powered broth. The garlic-strewn T-bone steak with french fries will assure you a wide berth at a movie theater afterward. Perhaps the best bargain is the succulent chuletas de puerco (extrathick pork chops) smothered with onion gravy. If you clean your plate, the strolling guitarist may dedicate "Malagueña" to you. Entrées are under $15.

Rio Mar, 7 Ninth Avenue, at the corner of Little West 12th Street, is open daily from noon to 3 A.M. No credit cards. Telephone: 243-9015. A sister establishment, called **Riazor,** at 245 West 16th Street, carries similar food. Telephone: 929-9782.

# ROETTELE A.G.

This cozy, brick-lined nook is one of those places you always fantasize about stumbling across in your neighborhood but never do. The German-born Ingrid Roettele, the owner, and her young chef, Robert Rusak, dabble in four national cuisines: German, Italian, Swiss, and French. On a recent evening, they prepared a terrific mustard-swabbed smoked pork chop with crispy spaetzle and red cabbage and a delicate plate of veal in a light mushroom cream sauce with Swiss-style rosti potatoes. For starters, there was raclette, the pungent cheese from Switzerland served melted in a baking dish with boiled potatoes, cornichons, and pearl onions. You might try it with some viande de Grison, the air-dried cured beef from Switzerland. Linzer torte, made with raspberry jam and a latticework crust, is delightful, as is the apple-pomegranate tart.

The narrow dining rooms, with pretty faux grape vines creeping along the celing, have paper-draped tables and votive candles. A small garden is open in warm weather. The restaurant does not have a liquor license as of this writing.

Roettele A.G., 126 East 7th Street, serves dinner from 5:30 P.M. to 11 P.M., Tuesday through Thursday, until midnight, Friday and Saturday, 5:30 to 10 P.M., Sunday. MasterCard and Visa accepted. Telephone: 674-4140.

# RUSTY STAUB'S ON FIFTH

A sports-theme restaurant on Fifth Avenue owned by the former New York Mets slugger Rusty Staub seems like an unlikely place to find one of New York's better American-wine lists. The handsome two-level establishment, called Rusty Staub's on Fifth, has a long brass-and-wood bar upstairs with paintings and photographs from Mr.

Staub's major-league career. The downstairs room is casual and contemporary, with rare bottles of wine in glass cases.

The grill-style American menu is complemented by an impressive roster of wines from California—including fifty-seven chardonnays, nineteen fumé blancs and eighty-three cabernet sauvignons—as well as smatterings from other American wine regions, France, Australia, and Italy. In addition, the restaurant offers a fine selection of wines by the glass.

Mr. Staub, whose major-league career began in 1961 with Houston and ended in 1985 with the Mets, became enamored of wine in 1969 while playing for the Montreal Expos, owned by Charles Bronfman (co-chairman of the Seagram Company). Mr. Staub opened his first pub-style restaurant, called Rusty's, 1271 Third Avenue, at 73rd Street, in 1977.

The menu at his new restaurant is more ambitious. Several lunches found the food to be simple, tasty, and generally well prepared. The best dishes were paillard of chicken with roasted garlic and herb butter, grilled mahimahi with black-bean sauce, and pasta with sautéed scallops and fennel.

Rusty Staub's on Fifth, 575 Fifth Avenue, at 47th Street, serves from 11:30 A.M. to 11 P.M., Monday through Friday, noon to 11:30 P.M., Saturday, 1 to 9 P.M., Sunday. All major credit cards accepted. Telephone: 682-1000.

# SAIGON

This tidy, step-down dining room enhanced by mirrors and greenery serves some of the best Vietnamese fare in town. Lemongrass chicken is addictive, the delicate sensation of lemongrass combining with a sweet glaze on morsels of meat; purée of shrimp molded around stalks of sugarcane, then barbecued, is an enticing starter, as are the exotic soups like shredded chicken and bean with vermicelli. Pork-filled spring rolls are crispy but need some sauce to give them flavor.

Saigon, 60 Mulberry Street, serves from 11:30 A.M. to

10:30 P.M., Sunday through Thursday, until 11 P.M., Friday and Saturday. All major credit cards accepted. Telephone: 227-8825.

# SARABETH'S KITCHEN

As a lifelong pancake aficionado, I usually eschew the floury, leaden, manhole-cover versions served in many restaurants in favor of making them at home. It had been several years since I had tried the pancakes at Sarabeth's Kitchen, but a revisit was a delightful surprise.

The whole-wheat pancakes with wheat berries sounded inviting on a bitter-cold morning, and they were exceptional. The puffed, faintly nutty wheat berries add a delightful texture, not to mention a dose of salubrious fiber. The pancakes also come ringed with sliced bananas. Among other winter-morning jump starts are pumpkin waffles with sour cream, raisins, pumpkin seeds, and honey and apple-cinnamon french toast with bananas (on weekends only).

Judging from conversations heard over the classical music in the background, the 10 A.M. weekday scene at Sarabeth's includes actors and actresses disparaging casting directors, mothers on midmorning hegiras from the children, and an assortment of leisurely shoppers. This would be a great place to start a day of playing hooky from work.

Sarabeth's Kitchen, 423 Amsterdam Avenue, near 80th Street, serves breakfast and lunch from 8 A.M. to 3:30 P.M., Tuesday through Friday, from 9 A.M. to 4 P.M., Saturday and Sunday; tea service 3:30 to 5 P.M., Tuesday through Friday, 4 to 5 P.M., Saturday and Sunday; dinner 6 to 11:30 P.M., Monday through Thursday, until 12:30 A.M., Friday and Saturday. All major credit cards accepted. Telephone: 496-6280.

# SARANAC

The rough-hewn stone fireplace, rustic caned chairs, deer-antler chandeliers, and mounted fishing poles are reminiscent of a vacation cabin in the woods. Saranac, named for the Saranac Lakes region of the Adirondacks, is in many ways just that, an easygoing, unpretentious restaurant serving all-American food at accessible prices.

The menu starts off with a thick, intense tarragon-laced shrimp bisque and delectable fried rings of calamari with lemon and homemade tartar sauce. Entrées include everything from turkey club sandwich and lobster roll ($11.50) to grilled salmon steak. The rare-cooked salmon needed just a shake of salt to bring out the flavor the last time I had it, but was otherwise fine. Crab cakes are well seasoned and come with good crunchy coleslaw.

Saranac betrays its name by not offering any New York State wines, but a good little selection of California labels is available, many under $20. Two desserts to try are the excellent strawberry shortcake with crumbled shortbread atop a bluff of sweetened whipped cream and sliced berries, and a hearty glazed apple tart with a thick crust.

Saranac, 1350 Madison Avenue, at 94th Street, serves from noon to 11:30 P.M., Monday through Friday; on Saturday and Sunday lunch runs from 11:30 A.M. to 3:30 P.M.; Saturday dinner from 5:30 P.M. to midnight, Sunday dinner until 11:30 P.M. A special children's menu is served from 5:30 to 6:30 P.M. Reservations for six or more only. American Express accepted. Telephone: 289-9600.

# SETTE MEZZO

Sette Mezzo bears a cookie-cutter resemblance to a score of smart-looking little Italian trattorias in town: white walls adorned with black-and-white photographs, tile-topped tables, splashes of colorful flowers, and stylishly attired waiters who are sometimes hard to distinguish from the stylishly attired customers.

The restaurant was opened in April 1989, by Gennaro Vertucci and Antonino Esposito, the owners of Vico on Second Avenue near 83rd Street. Sette Mezzo, or Seven and a Half, is a card game in Italy, and the theme is reflected in framed playing cards on the walls.

Pastas are nicely seasoned, but the chef seems to have extremist views on the subject of al dente texture. An otherwise enticing combination of black fusilli with scallops and arugula in a saffron-tinged broth was sent back for further cooking: it was fine on the rebound ($16, or $9 as an appetizer). The linguine with clam sauce was exceptional, made with good olive oil, lots of garlic, and garnished with sweet baby clams on the half shell. A main course of whole roasted snapper was lovely, drizzled with a blend of olive oil and mint. Broccoli on the side was done with care, too. Another fine light lunch was the grilled paillard of chicken, moist and nicely seared, which came with a mixed green salad.

Unable to face another tiramisù that week, I tried a dessert called zuccotto, a génoise soaked in cognac and rum encasing vanilla and chocolate ice cream, chocolate chips, and nuts, with a mountain of whipped cream and berries on the side for good measure.

Sette Mezzo, 969 Lexington Avenue, near 70th Street, serves lunch from noon to 3 P.M., daily; dinner, 5 P.M. to midnight, daily. Closed for Sunday lunch between July 4 and Labor Day. No credit cards. Telephone: 472-0400.

# SIDEWALKERS'

You are hit with a blast of a familiar aroma upon entering the sprawling dining room, a blend of sea air and hot spices. All over the room, animated diners wearing plastic bibs are hammering away at mounds of steaming red crabs, sending shards in all directions. Sidewalkers', at 12 West 72nd Street, is about as close as you'll get to the eastern shore of Maryland without leaving Manhattan Island.

Its specialty is steamed and liberally spiced hard-shell crabs, the kind that make a mess of your hands, napkin, bib, the table and floor. The crabs are generally fresh, the meat snowy and sweet, and the spices just piquant enough to keep you rubbing your lips against an icy beer mug in between bites. The size of the crabs depends on availability; a dozen of the medium-size cost about $25, a dozen large about $30.

The dining room has a free-wheeling, down-home atmosphere conducive to such inelegant consumption—wooden plank floors, rust-colored walls, paper-covered tables, and a young good-time crowd. In addition to the hard-shell crabs, you can get nicely sautéed soft shells with tarragon butter and some of the best crab cakes in town.

Sidewalkers' serves from 5 to 11 P.M., Monday through Thursday, until 11:30 P.M., Friday and Saturday, 4 to 10 P.M., Sunday. All major credit cards accepted. Telephone: 799-6070.

# SIDO ABU SALIM

Middle Eastern food has great appeal during the hot summer months, with its cooling vegetable purées, lemony salads, and aromatic grilled meats. Sido Abu Salim, run by a Palestinian family, has always been one of the more reliable spots in town for this kind of cooking—and a real bargain. The restaurant recently relocated to more commodious quarters on Lexington Avenue at 26th Street, a few blocks south of its former home.

The new setting is spare and clean, with tile floors, wood wainscotting, white walls adorned with botanical prints, and glass-topped tables. A recent lunch began with a sampling of sprightly tabbouleh combining minced parsley, wheat germ, onions, and tomato; excellent hummus, the chickpea-and-sesame-oil purée; the sesame spread tahina; and a wonderfully smoky rendition of baba gannoush, the roasted eggplant purée. A mean-looking hot sauce set out on the table can send you wailing out the door in search of an open fire hydrant.

Cumin-scented falafel, made with chickpea flour, is fresh and crisp ($2.95), as are the ground lamb-and-onion-filled croquettes called kibbee ($1.50). The best entrée sampled was the heaping portion of moist, delicious chicken couscous, replete with carrots, chickpeas, zucchini, and celery ($9.50). An all-vegetable couscous is also good ($7.50). One letdown was the Sido mixed grill, which combined tough, dry cubes of lamb, seasoned ground meat, and vegetables ($12).

Sido Abu Salim, 81 Lexington Avenue, serves from noon to 11 P.M., Monday through Thursday, until 11:30 P.M., Friday, 1 P.M. to 11 P.M., Saturday and Sunday. All major credit cards accepted. Telephone: 686-2031.

# SIRACUSA GELATERIA

The gelati wave that washed over New York in recent years has given New Yorkers a kaleidoscopic selection of this Italian ice cream. Some of the best gelati I have tasted is served at a sparkling little spot called Siracusa Gelateria, 65 Fourth Avenue, near 10th Street. It makes a half dozen or so flavors in $4, $3, and $2 sizes. My favorites are the nutty hazelnut and ricotta. Open spring to fall, 5 to 11 P.M., Sunday through Thursday, and 4:30 P.M. to 12:30 A.M., Friday and Saturday. Telephone: 505-0243.

# SYLVIA'S

To call Sylvia's the most popular ribs and fried chicken restaurant in Harlem, if not in the entire city, would be a gross understatement. This congenial spot, operated by Mrs. Sylvia Woods and her family, is an institution where local politicians meet over braised short ribs, and an ever-growing roster of celebrities from near and far stop by for some restorative soul food that has its origins in Mrs. Woods's hometown of Hemingway, South Carolina.

Sylvia's has a pleasantly appointed dining room for leisurely meals and a long bonhomous counter for those who want to eat and run—waddle is more like it—after one of these rib-sticking repasts. Friday night is braised ribs night, and they can be ordered with peppery collard greens and moist cornbread. The congenial waitresses tend to address customers as "honey" and to encourage them to eat more than they should. Save room for the sweet potato pie, which is so good it could stop a Baptist preacher in mid-sermon. Sylvia's, 328 Lenox Avenue, between 126th and 127th streets, serves 7:30 A.M. to 10:30 P.M., Monday to Saturday, 1 to 7 P.M., Sunday; prix-fixe brunch ($6.95), 1 to 3 P.M., Sundays. Reservations accepted for eight or more. No credit cards. Telephone: 996-0660.

# TERRACE FIVE

One of the more delightful lunch spots in Fifth Avenue's shopping district is a little-known restaurant perched on the fifth floor of the Trump Tower. Called Terrace Five, this charming bistrolike place offers engaging salads and entrées as well as a superior little wine list with many selections available by the glass. On clement days, you can sit on a tiny outdoor terrace that affords a striking view down the avenue; even from the indoor seats, the view through the wraparound windows is inspiring.

Among the bright and tasty salads you might find are steamed vegetables with brown rice and miso; a copious seafood combination featuring large, pearly white sea scallops, squid rings, shrimp, tomatoes, and mixed greens in a pleasantly tart lemon vinaigrette; and chicken salad with sliced poached chicken breast, lettuce, and sections of oranges and grapefruit. Sautéed shrimp in mustard sauce is fresh and piquant, while good starters included the salmond carpaccio marinated in lime and fresh mint and slices of mozzarella and tomatoes marinated in fresh herbs. Waiters and waitresses wear white shirts, black bow ties, and welcoming smiles, conveying a real enthusiasm for their jobs—maybe it has something to do with the altitude.

A small wine bar is open from noon until closing. Terrace Five, Fifth Avenue and 56th Street, in the Trump Tower, serves from noon to 5 P.M., Monday through Saturday. All major credit cards accepted. Telephone: 371-5030.

---

# TRIXIE'S

Don't be surprised if you walk into Trixie's, as I did one evening, and see a man wearing a silver-sequined jacket and no shirt standing on a table in front of the piano belting out "Tutti Frutti." Customers were bouncing off the walls, as waitresses right out of a James Dean movie were pirouetting behind the Formica counter; Mr. 1965, a waiter in a tie-dyed shirt with a giant peace medallion around his neck, led a dozen revelers in a loose-limbed tribal dance. A roving spoon player was tapping syncopation on a customer's arm. Most of the crowd is young here—fraternity-party age—and this is the wildest time they have had since the highschool weekend when Mom and Dad went off to Saranac Lake and left behind a stocked liquor cabinet and a new stereo.

You don't go to Trixie's for gastronomic enlightenment: the food is down-home diner-style and generally satisfying. Buffalo chicken wings made nice nibblers with a cold beer (sold in quart bottles). The grilled rib-eye steak could use some of the promised black pepper, but the french-fried sweet potatoes are irresistible. A cold chicken salad sprinkled with sesame is sprightly, but ravioli in pesto sauce is anemic. Dinner runs about $25 to $30 per person.

Trixie's, 307 West 47th Street, serves lunch from 11:30 A.M. to 3 P.M., Monday through Friday; dinner, 5 P.M. to midnight, Monday through Saturday, 11:30 A.M. to 4 P.M., Sunday. American Express, MasterCard, and Visa accepted. Telephone: 582-5480.

# TROPICA BAR AND SEAFOOD HOUSE

Metro-North meets Margaritaville at Tropica Bar and Seafood House, adjacent to Grand Central Terminal in the concourse of the Pan Am Building. This latest creation of Restaurant Associates, in the former Charlie Brown's, sports a Key West theme complete with tropical murals, colorful tiles, and beach-bungalow architecture. The chef is Edward G. Brown, formerly of Marie-Michelle and Maurice in Manhattan and Lucas Carton in Paris.

Seafood, naturally, is emphasized here, and you can get off to a good start with a plate of meaty, tender mussels under a zesty pesto enlivened with fresh coriander; excellent crab cakes with mustard sauce, and robust black-bean-and-sausage soup under a swirl of crème fraîche. Conch chowder was light on the conch, but it was an engaging soup nonetheless, made with a lime-brightened seafood stock and full of okra and christophene, a pear-shaped squash.

About a dozen types of grilled fish are available, along with side orders of fried plantains or steamed rice and beans. Among the chef's specialties are perfectly roasted monkfish, served with wilted kale and a delicious garlic flan, and well-herbed, moist mahi-mahi with a refreshing relish of plum tomatoes. Sea scallops steamed in a banana leaf with sweet-earthy mashed plantain was a provocative combination, although the dish might have worked better texturally with shrimp. Barbecued shrimp with just a hint of tamarind came with rice and mango relish. The beach theme carries through dessert with orange flan, passionfruit mousse, and an incredible Key lime pie.

Tropica Bar and Seafood House, 200 Park Avenue, at 44th Street, serves lunch from 11:30 A.M. to 3 P.M.; dinner 5 to 11 P.M., Monday through Friday. All major credit cards accepted. Telephone: 867-6767.

# VUCCIRIA

Vucciria is the name of a well-known food market in Palermo. It is also the latest Sicilian-style trattoria in Manhattan opened by the Sindoni family, who also own Azzurro on Second Avenue and Baci on Amsterdam Avenue. The setting, formerly the Wine Bar on West Broadway between Prince and Spring streets, is larger (eighty-five seats) and more artsy looking than its predecessors, but the vibrant, moderately priced fare is just as good.

Befitting its trendy neighborhood, Vucciria's dining room sports all the latest design fancies: faux marble columns, a cloud mural ceiling, sponged yellow walls. With so much emphasis on details, it is surprising to get paper napkins. Those who still associate Sicilian food with mountains of pasta under buckets of thick tomato sauce will be delighted by the subtlety in such house specialties as linguine with chunks of fresh tuna in a light tomato-tinted broth with fresh basil and penne with ricotta and ripe tomatoes.

Several of the appetizers sampled could use some refinement, like the excessively oily grilled eggplant and a mozzarella en carrozza that was overloaded with capers. The best starter sampled was grilled endive drizzled with olive oil and set over fresh basil and arugula.

Hackneyed though it may be, tiramisù can be a delight when it is made by the Sindonis. This one is robust with espresso flavor and rich with chocolate and mascarpone ($5).

Vucciria, 422 West Broadway, serves from noon to midnight daily. American Express accepted. Telephone: 941-5811.

# YELLOWFINGERS DI NUOVO

This lively trattoria and bar at the busy corner of Third Avenue and 60th Street is one of the better bargains on the East Side. One of my favorites here is the terrific roast chicken salad: warm slices of white meat nestled in a thicket of fresh greens with pine nuts and sweet peppers. Also good are the bright and herb-scented pizzas that they call fa' vecchia that include everything from salt, herbs, and extra-virgin olive oil to arugula, prosciutto, and Parmesan. There is also an appealing little selection of grilled fish and meat, with most entrées under $20.

Yellowfingers di Nuovo, 200 East 60th Street, is open noon to 1 A.M., Monday through Saturday, until midnight Sunday. All major credit cards accepted. Telephone: 751-8615.

# YELLOW ROSE CAFE

You know this is serious Southwestern food when you see chicken-fried steak on the menu, a Texas-Oklahoma oddity in which a slice of well-pounded cube steak is dipped in a flour-and-buttermilk batter, then fried like chicken. It might not be everyone's idea of an elegant steak dinner, but for aficionados of this culinary hybrid, the Yellow Rose version, which is greaseless, crispy, and smothered with cream gravy, is better than most served in the Lone Star state.

Owned by a Fort Worth native, Barbara Clifford, this is a real down-home restaurant, as honest as a country preacher and as comfortable as an old saddle.

Fried chicken, all puffed and brittle outside and moist within, is an archetype for all would-be Southwesterners around town. Side dishes are prepared with care as well, particularly butter beans laced with small cubes of ham, fried okra, and potato salad. For starters, try the lumpy guacamole, the hot tomato-scallion sauce with nacho chips, or the beanless chili with molten Monterey Jack cheese and chopped onions. A couple can eat like ranch hands for under $40.

Yellow Rose Cafe, Amsterdam Avenue at 81st Street, serves from noon to 11 P.M., Monday through Thursday, until midnight Friday; brunch, 10:15 to 3:30 P.M., Saturday and Sunday; dinner, 5:15 to midnight Saturday, 5:15 to 11 P.M., Sunday. All major credit cards accepted. Telephone: 595-8760.

# ZULA

Adventuresome bargain hunters in the Columbia University neighborhood may want to stop by Zula, a tidy and friendly little spot specializing in Ethiopian food, specifically that of the province of Eritrea, which is on the Red Sea. Zula, which is owned by Yohannes Tecle and Kidane Tesfay, is a spare, wood-paneled space with folk art and photographs on the wall and a bar in the back. It is a popular student hangout on weekends.

Meals traditionally begin with a clove tea called shai: I didn't like it at first, but it tasted better with the food, much of which is scented with the same spice. The menu is divided into lamb, chicken, beef, and vegetables. My table sampled two lamb stews: zegenie, with a mild pepper sauce of onions, garlic, and sweet peppers; and alitcha, which is similar but milder and somewhat silken with butter. Both were served atop injera, the pizza-size round of thin, spongy bread that you tear and use to scoop up ingredients. We also sampled a vegetarian assortment that included tasty lentils in a highly seasoned sauce; shiro, which is mashed chickpeas blended with butter, onion, and berbire (a peppery blend of cayenne and assorted spices); and sweet sautéed onions. Ethiopian cooking combines so many spices that it is difficult to single them out, except sometimes clove and cumin.

When I inquired about the Ethiopian wine listed on the menu, the owner provided a sample of the white. Mondavi chardonnay it is not: it took all my willpower to swallow it politely. And one whiff of the malodorous red was enough. African beer is a better bet.

Zula Restaurant, 1260 Amsterdam Avenue at 122nd Street, serves from noon to midnight daily. All major credit cards accepted. Telephone: 663-1670.

# BEER

New York City is often touted today as one of the wine capitals of the world. Long before the wine boom came to this country, however, it was a mecca for beer drinkers—more than seventy breweries existed in the five boroughs at the turn of the century. That era is long gone, but there are still a good number of taverns and restaurants that stock a wide range of domestic and imported beers. Among them are:

**American Festival Cafe,** Rockefeller Plaza, Fifth Avenue at 50th Street, 246-6699.

**Empire Diner,** 210 Tenth Avenue, at 22nd Street, 243-2736.

**First Avenue Restaurant,** 361 First Avenue, at 21st Street, 475-9068.

**Fleming's,** 232 East 86th Street, 988-1540.

**Gage & Tollner,** 372 Fulton Street, Brooklyn, (718) 875-5181.

**Joe Allen,** 326 West 46th Street, 581-6464.

**Landmark Tavern,** 626 Eleventh Avenue, at 46th Street, 757-8595.

**Manhattan Brewing Company,** 40–42 Thompson Street, between the Avenue of the Americas and West Broadway, at Broome Street, 219-9250. Five draft beers as well as a half dozen or more microbrewery products are available in this brewery setting complete with giant copper fermenting vats. Texas barbecue is featured nightly.

**North Star Pub,** 93 South Street, in the South Street Seaport, 509-6757.

**Peculier Pub,** 145 Bleecker Street, corner of LaGuardia Place, 353-1327. Have a craving for a frosty beer on a hot summer day? How about a bottle of Kulmbacher Schweizerhofbräu from Bavaria, or Tooth's Sheaf Stout from Australia, Tiger from Singapore, Chihuahua from Mexico, or EKU 28 from West Germany, billed as "the strongest beer in the world."

These and about two hundred other domestic and imported brews can be found at a remarkable bar in the West Village called the Peculier Pub (the unorthodox spelling comes from Old Peculier Ale from England, the manager's favorite brew).

The pub has a two-page beer list; daily beer specials are listed on a chalk board. The day I dropped in specials included Peking, a Chinese beer, O.B. from Korea, and Taj Majal from India.

The pub's manager, a former chemist, who identifies himself only as Tommy, is a walking encyclopedia of brewing lore. Prices range from about $2 for domestic beers (fifteen of them) to $6 and more for special imports such as St. Sixtus Trappist Ale, a wonderfully creamy and flowery dark brew from Belgium. The Peculier Pub is strictly a burgers-and-sandwiches spot, presumably to keep the spotlight on the beers.

**P.J. Clarke's,** 915 Third Avenue, at 55th Street, 759-1650.

**Rathbone's,** 1702 Second Avenue, between 88th and 89th streets, 369-7361.

**Ryan McFadden,** 800 Second Avenue, at 42nd Street, 599-2226.

**SoHo Kitchen and Bar,** 103 Greene Street, between Prince and Spring Streets, 925-1866. This remarkable bar, a soaring warehouse of a place, is well known for its staggering wine-by-the-glass selection: some one hundred in all. Recently it boosted its beer list, offering about a half dozen draft beers and ales, as well as many more in bottles—everything from Anchor Steam Ale from San Francisco to Lindeman's Framboise Cork Finish (a Belgium top-fermented ale to which fresh raspberries are added in the brewing process. Draught beers can be tasted in flights, just like wine, for about $9.

**White Horse Tavern,** 567 Hudson Street, at 11th Street, 243-9260.

# BEST DISHES

NOTE: *Because menus change unexpectedly it is always wise to call ahead to inquire about the availability of special dishes.*

| | |
|---|---|
| Angulas (Spanish-style eels) | Harlequin, Paradis Barcelona |
| Apple pandowdy | An American Place |
| Apple pie | The Coach House, the Oyster Bar and Restaurant in Grand Central Station |
| Apple pie, deep dish | The Oyster Bar and Restaurant in Grand Central Station |
| Apple tart | La Tulipe, Quatorze |
| Baba gannoush | Al Amir, the Health Pub, La Kasbah |
| Baked Alaska | The Rainbow Room |
| Baklava | Anatolia |
| Beef brisket | Gage & Tollner |
| Beef, cooked over hot stones | Chikubu |
| Beef with orange | Auntie Yuan, Chin Chin, Fu's |
| Beef, prime ribs | The Coach House |
| Beef, prime ribs, blackened | K-Paul's New York |
| Beef ribs, grilled | Rosa Mexicano |
| Beignets | Madeline's |
| Black-bean soup | The Coach House, Union Square Cafe, Victor's Café 52 |
| Blueberry cobbler | The Post House |

▷ 561

| | |
|---|---|
| Bouillabaisse | La Colombe d'Or |
| Boudin noir (blood sausage) | Chez Josephine, Florent |
| Brandade de morue | La Bonne Soupe, Le Périgord, Provence |
| Bread pudding | Arcadia, Barocco |
| Bruschetta | Barocco, Paper Moon Milano, Union Square Cafe |
| Cajun popcorn | K-Paul's New York |
| Calf's liver | Bellevues, Cafe Luxembourg, Il Cantinori, the River Café |
| Calamari, fried | Barocco, the Odeon, Wilkinson's Seafood Café |
| Caponata | Azzurro |
| Carpaccio | Le Cirque, Palio, Paper Moon Milano |
| Cassoulet | Café des Artistes, Crêpes Suzette, Florent, La Côte Basque, Voulez-Vous |
| Cheesecake | Palm, the River Café, Peter Luger |
| Cheese plate | Chanterelle, Le Régence, Felidia, Palio, the Quilted Giraffe |
| Chicken, drunken | Shun Lee Palace |
| Chicken, fried | Cowgirl Hall of Fame, Yellow Rose Cafe |
| Chicken, grilled | Michael's |
| Chicken, roasted | Arizona 206, Gotham Bar and Grill, the Quilted Giraffe |
| Chicken, salt-baked | The Nice Restaurant |
| Chicken, tandoor-baked | Bukhara |
| Chicken paillard | Cafe Luxembourg |
| Chicken potpie | The Coach House, Ten Twenty-two |

| | |
|---|---|
| Chicken salad | Yellowfingers di Nuovo |
| Chili | Arizona 206, Manhattan Chili Company |
| Chinese hot pot | Great Shanghai |
| Chocolate cake | The Coach House, Eze, Gotham Bar and Grill, Le Refuge |
| Chocolate pudding | An American Place |
| Choucroute garnie | Voulez-Vous |
| Clam chowder | Coastal, Docks (both locations) |
| Conch chowder | Claire |
| Corn bread | The Coach House, Jezebel, Sylvia's |
| Corned-beef sandwich | Carnegie Deli |
| Couscous | La Kasbah, La Mirabelle, Lotfi's Couscous |
| Crabs, steamed | Sidewalkers' |
| Crabs, soft shell | Bridge Cafe, Chanterelle, the Manhattan Ocean Club |
| Crab cakes | The Coach House, Cafe Luxembourg, the Odeon |
| Crème brûlée | Le Cirque, Le Cygne, Provence, Voulez-Vous |
| Crème caramel | La Bonne Soupe |
| Crostini | Union Square Cafe |
| Desserts (overall) | Bouley, Gotham Bar and Grill, La Tulipe, Le Cirque, Madeline's, the Quilted Giraffe, the River Café |
| Duck, Peking-style | Auntie Yuan, Peking Duck House, Shun Lee Palace |
| Duck, roasted | La Bohème |
| Duck, roasted, Chinese style | The Nice Restaurant, 20 Mott Street Restaurant |
| Duck confit | La Colombe d'Or, La Tulipe, Prunelle |

| | |
|---|---|
| Duck à l'orange | The Terrace |
| Dumplings, Chinese | Auntie Yuan, Great Shanghai, Mandarin Court, Pig Heaven, Shun Lee |
| English trifle | John Clancy's |
| Espresso | Il Cantinori, Mezzaluna |
| Fajitas | Zarela |
| Feijoada | Cabana Carioca, Cabana Carioca II |
| Fish (overall) | Le Bernardin |
| Fish, grilled/broiled | John Clancy's, Periyali, Wilkinson's Seafood Café |
| Flan | El Cid |
| Foie gras, sautéed | La Caravelle, Lafayette, Prunelle |
| Frisée aux lardons | The Manhattan Ocean Club, Le Refuge, Quatorze |
| Gelati | Positano, Siracusa, Siracusa Gelateria |
| Goat, roasted | Paradis Barcelona |
| Gravlax | Aquavit |
| Guacamole | Rosa Mexicano |
| Guinea hen | Alison on Dominick Street |
| Gumbo | K-Paul's New York |
| Hamburger | Hamburger Harry's, Union Square Cafe |
| Hash, corned beef | Broadway Diner |
| Hash, roast beef | The Post House |
| Herring | Aquavit |
| Hummus | Al Amir, Sido Abu Salim |
| Ice cream | Chanterelle, Rose Cafe |
| Ile flottante | La Tulipe |
| Key lime pie | Café des Artistes, the Oyster Bar and Restaurant in Grand Central Station, Sabor, Tropica |
| Lamb | Bukhara |

| | |
|---|---|
| Lamb chops | Peter Luger, Sparks Steakhouse |
| Lamb shank | Alison on Dominick Street, Anatolia |
| Lamb steak | Moroccan Star |
| Lentil soup | Lotfi's Couscous |
| Linguine with clam sauce | Trastevere |
| Lobster, broiled | Palm, the Post House |
| Lobster, steamed | Dock's (both locations), John Clancy's, the Post House |
| Lobster club sandwich | Arcadia |
| Mozzarella en carrozza | Taormina |
| Mud cake (chocolate) | Dock's (both locations) |
| Mutton chops | Keen's Chop House |
| Napoleon | Café des Artistes, the Terrace |
| Octopus | Periyali, Rio Mar, 20 Mott Street Restaurant |
| Osso buco | Felidia, Il Cantinori, Park Bistro |
| Oxtail | Caribe |
| Oysters on the half shell | Docks (both locations), the Oyster Bar and Restaurant in Grand Central Station |
| Oyster pan roast | The Oyster Bar and Restaurant in Grand Central Station |
| Paella | The Ballroom, Harlequin, Rio Mar |
| Pancakes | Sarabeth's Kitchen |
| Pasta (overall) | Arquà, Azzurro, Baci, Barocco, Bice, Mezzaluna, Mezzogiorno |
| Pastrami | Carnegie Deli |
| Pea soup | Ten Twenty-two |
| Pecan pie | K-Paul's New York |
| Pizza | Mezzogiorno, Orso |
| Polenta | Palio, Union Square Cafe |

| | |
|---|---|
| Pork chops | Roettele A.G. |
| Potatoes, french-fried | Michael's, the Odeon |
| Potatoes, mashed | K-Paul's New York |
| Potatoes, roasted | Barocco |
| Potatoes, sautéed | Maxim's |
| Pot-au-feu | Café des Artistes, Voulez-Vous |
| Prosciutto | Felidia |
| Quail, barbecued | Arizona 206, Auntie Yuan, Chin Chin |
| Quail, grilled | Orso |
| Quail, roasted | La Réserve, Gotham Bar and Grill |
| Rabbit, roasted | Alison on Dominick Street, Gotham Bar and Grill, Lutèce |
| Ribs, beef | Sylvia's |
| Rillettes of pork | Brandywine, Florent |
| Risotto | Chelsea Trattoria Italiana, Malvasia |
| Salads | Aquavit, China Grill, Gotham Bar and Grill, Mezzogiorno, Michael's, Yellowfingers di Nuovo |
| Salmon, grilled | The Quilted Giraffe, Aquavit, Rose Cafe |
| Salmon, sautéed | Prunelle, Union Square Cafe |
| Salmon terrine | Le Cygne |
| Satés, chicken or beef | Tommy Tang's |
| Saucisson chaud | La Bohème |
| Scallops | Le Bernardin |
| Sea urchins | Le Bernardin, La Cité, Mitsukoshi |
| Semifreddo | Felidia, Palio, Union Square Cafe |
| Shabu shabu | Mitsukoshi |
| She-crab soup | Gage & Tollner |
| Shrimp, grilled on sugarcane | Cuisine de Saigon |
| Shrimp, salt-baked | The Golden Unicorn |

| | |
|---|---|
| Sole, Dover, grilled | John Clancy's Restaurant |
| Sole, Dover, meunière | La Côte Basque |
| Soupe au pistou | Le Périgord |
| Spaetzle | Roettele A.G. |
| Spareribs, Chinese | Fu's |
| Spring rolls | Indochine, 20 Mott Street Restaurant |
| Squab | Gotham Bar and Grill, La Tulipe, Montrachet |
| Steak | Michael's, Peter Luger, the Post House, the River Café, Sparks Steakhouse |
| Steak au poivre | Chez Josephine, the Coach House, the Odeon |
| Steak pommes frites (steak with french fries) | Cafe Luxembourg, Chez Josephine, La Bonne Soupe, the Odeon, Symphony Cafe |
| Steak tartar | Café Un Deux Trois, Voulez-Vous |
| Strawberry shortcake | An American Place |
| Suckling pig | The Nice Restaurant, Sabor |
| Sushi | Hatsuhana, Mitsukoshi |
| Sweetbreads | Lutèce, the Quilted Giraffe |
| Sweet potato pie | Sylvia's |
| Tabbouleh | Al Amir, Sido Abu Salim |
| Tacos | Rosa Mexicano |
| Tempura | Inagiku, Mitsukoshi, Umeda |
| Terrines (overall) | The Four Seasons, La Caravelle |
| Tiramisù | Arquà, Il Cantinori, Mezzogiorno, Palio, Primola |
| Tomato soup | La Tulipe |
| Tortilla, Spanish-style | The Ballroom |
| Tripe | Orso |

| | |
|---|---|
| Truffles | Le Cirque |
| Veal chop | Le Régence, the Post House |
| Vegetable platters, steamed | Akbar (Park Avenue), Auntie Yuan, Felidia, The Four Seasons |
| Venison | Aquavit, Arcadia, Chanterelle |
| Vichyssoise | The Quilted Giraffe |
| Wine bar | SoHo Kitchen and Bar |
| Wine list, American | The Oyster Bar and Restaurant in Grand Central Station, Windows on the World |
| Wine list, French | La Côte Basque, Le Cirque |
| Wine list, Italian | Le Cirque, Sparks Steakhouse |
| Wine list, overall | Le Cirque, the Quilted Giraffe, the River Café, Windows on the World |

# RESTAURANT INDEX

*Map numbers appear in parentheses.*
*Map section begins on page 2.*

Adele, 55
Adrienne (1), 57
Akbar (49th Street) (5), 59
Akbar (Park Avenue) (6), 60
Al Amir (7), 495
Alcala (1), 63
Algonquin Hotel (2), 496
Alison on Dominick Street (4), 65
Alo Alo (6), 67
Ambassador Grill (5), 69
American Festival Cafe (1), 557
American Harvest (4), 71
An American Place (5), 73
Amsterdam's Bar and Rotisserie (1), 75
Amsterdam's Grand (4), 77
Anatolia (7), 78
Andiamo! (1), 80
Aquavit (1), 82
Arcadia (6), 85
Arcobaleno (5), 496
Arizona 206 (6), 86
Arizona 206 Cafe (6), 497
Arquà (4), 89
Au Grenier Café (1), 498
Auntie Yuan (6), 91
Aunt Sonia, 499
Aureole (6), 93

Au Troquet (3), 95
Azzurro (7), 96

Baci (1), 500
The Ballroom (2), 98
Bangkok House (7), 100
Barbetta (2), 102
Barocco (4), 103
Barrow Street Bistro (3), 500
Bella Luna (1), 501
Bellevues (2), 105
Bellini by Cipriani (1), 107
Benny's Burritos (Avenue A) (5), 502
Benny's Burritos (Greenwich Avenue) (3), 502
Bice (6), 110
Border Cafe (Broadway) (1), 502
Border Cafe (79th Street) (7), 502
Bouley (4), 112
Brandywine (5), 115
Brasserie (6), 503
Bridge Cafe (4), 117
Broadway Diner (Broadway) (1), 504
Broadway Diner (Lexington Avenue) (6), 504

▷ 569

Broadway Joe (2), 504
B. Smith's (2), 119
Bukhara (5), 121

Cabana Carioca (2), 505
Cabana Carioca II (2), 505
Cafe Between the Bread (1), 505
Café de Paris (5), 506
Café des Artistes (1), 123
Cafe Greco (7), 126
Cafe Luxembourg (1), 128
Cafe Nicholson (6), 507
Café Pierre (6), 130
Cafe San Martin (7), 132
Café Un Deux Trois (2), 134
Cameos (1), 135
Ca'Nova (6), 508
The Captain's Table (5), 137
Caribe (3), 509
Carnegie Deli (1), 509
Cellar in the Sky (4), 139
Century Cafe (2), 510
Chantal Café (1), 141
Chanterelle (4), 142
Chelsea Central (2), 144
Chelsea Trattoria Italiana (2), 146
Chez Josephine (2), 149
Chez Louis (6), 151
Chez Momo (3), 510
Chikubu (5), 153
China Grill (1), 155
Chin Chin (5), 157
Christ Cella (5), 160
City Cafe (7), 161
Claire (2), 163
The Coach House (3), 165
Coastal (1), 167
Contrapunto (6), 169
Corner Bistro (3), 511
Corrado (1), 171

Courtyard Café and Bar (5), 512
Cowgirl Hall of Fame (3), 512
Crêpes Suzette (2), 513
Cuisine de Saigon (3), 173

Darbar (1), 174
Da Tommaso (1), 177
da Umberto (2), 179
David K's (6), 181
Dāwat (6), 183
Docks (Broadway) (1), 185
Docks on Third (5), 188
Dominick's, 514
Donald Sacks (4), 515

East (7), 190
Ecco! (4), 192
El Cid (2), 515
The "11" Cafe (5), 516
Empire Diner (2), 557
Erminia (7), 193
Eze (2), 195

Felidia (6), 197
Ferrier (6), 517
First Avenue Restaurant (5), 557
Fleming's (7), 557
Florent (3), 518
44 (2), 199
The Four Seasons (6), 201
Frank's (2), 518
Fu's (7), 203

Gage & Tollner, 205, 558
Gallagher's (1), 207
Gaylord (5), 209

Girasole (7), 519
Gloucester House (6), 210
The Golden Unicorn (4), 212
Gotham Bar and Grill (5), 214
Great Shanghai Restaurant (4), 216
Greene Street Restaurant (4), 218

Hamburger Harry's (Chambers Street) (4), 520
Hamburger Harry's (45th Street) (2), 520
Harlequin (3), 220
Harold's (5), 521
Hatsuhana (5), 222
The Health Pub (5), 521
HSF (Chinatown) (4), 523
HSF (Second Avenue) (5), 522
Huberts (6), 224
Hudson River Club (4), 226

Il Cantinori (5), 229
Il Mulino (3), 231
Inagiku (5), 233
Indian Cafe (Broadway) (1), 523
Indian Cafe (95th Street) (1), 523
Indochine (5), 235
Istanbul Kebap (7), 524

Jane's Bar and Grill (6), 237
Jane Street Seafood Cafe (3), 239
Jezebel (2), 241
Joe Allen (2), 244, 558
John Clancy's (3), 246

Keen's Chop House (2), 247
King Fung (4), 249
K-Paul's New York (5), 251

La Bohème (3), 253
La Boîte en Bois (1), 255
La Bonne Soupe (1), 524
La Caravelle (1), 257
La Cité (1), 259
La Colombe d'Or (5), 262
La Côte Basque (6), 264
Lafayette (6), 267
La Fusta, 525
La Gauloise (3), 269
La Grenouille (6), 271
La Kasbah (1), 525
La Méditerranée (6), 526
La Métairie (3), 527
La Mirabelle (1), 273
Landmark Tavern (2), 528, 558
La Petite Ferme (7), 275
La Réserve (2), 277
Lattanzi (2), 279
La Tulipe (3), 281
La Vieille Auberge (2), 528
Le Bernardin (1), 283
Le Chantilly (6), 285
Le Cirque (6), 288
Le Cygne (6), 290
Le Lucky Strike (4), 529
Le Madeleine (2), 530
Le Madri (2), 293
Le Périgord (6), 295
Le Refuge (7), 296
Le Régence (6), 298
Le Steak (6), 530
Le Zinc (4), 300
Lola (2), 302
Lotfi's Couscous (2), 531
Lusardi's (7), 304
Lutèce (6), 305

Madeline's (4), 532
Malvasia (6), 308
Mamma Leone's (2), 310
Mandarin Court (4), 532
Manhattan Brewing Company (4), 558
Manhattan Chili Company (3), 533
The Manhattan Ocean Club (1), 313
Marie-Michelle (1), 315
Mary Ann's (2), 533
Maxim's (6), 317
Memphis (1), 319
Menchanko-Tei (1), 534
Mezzaluna (7), 535
Mezzogiorno (4), 321
Michael's (1), 323
Mickey Mantle's (1), 325
Mitsukoshi (6), 327
Mon Cher Ton Ton (French) (6), 329
Mon Cher Ton Ton (Japanese) (6), 331
Montrachet (4), 333
Moroccan Star, 536
Mortimer's (7), 335


New Prospect Cafe, 537
The Nice Restaurant (4), 337
Nippon (6), 340
North Star Pub (4), 558


The Odeon (4), 342
Ollie's Noodle Shop and Grille (1), 537
Omen (4), 344
150 Wooster Street (4), 346
Oriental Pearl (4), 348
Oriental Town Seafood Restaurant (4), 350

Orso (2), 352
The Oyster Bar and Restaurant in Grand Central Station (5), 354


Palio (1), 357
Palm (5), 359
Palm Court (1), 538
Pamir (7), 361
Panevino (1), 539
Paola's (7), 539
Paper Moon Milano (6), 363
Paradis Barcelona (6), 365
Parioli, Romanissimo (7), 367
Park Bistro (5), 369
Pasta & Dreams (Broadway) (1), 540
Pasta & Dreams (First Avenue) (6), 540
Pasta & Dreams (Third Avenue) (7), 540
Pasta Presto (Barrow Street) (3), 541
Pasta Presto (Macdougal Street) (3), 541
Pasta Presto (613 Second Avenue) (5), 541
Pasta Presto (959 Second Avenue) (7), 541
Patsy's (1), 372
Peculier Pub (3), 558
Peking Duck House Restaurant (4), 541
Periyali (2), 373
Peter Luger, 375
Pierre au Tunnel (2), 377
Pig Heaven (7), 379
P. J. Clarke's (6), 559
Poiret (1), 381
Positano (5), 383
The Post House (6), 385
Primavera (7), 387

Primola (6), 388
Provence (3), 391
Prunelle (6), 393
Punsch (1), 542

Quatorze (2), 395
The Quilted Giraffe (6), 397

The Rainbow Room (2), 399
Rathbone's (7), 559
René Pujol (1), 402
Rio Mar (3), 543
The River Café, 404
Roettele A.G. (5), 544
Rogers & Barbero (2), 406
Rosa Mexicano (6), 408
Rose Cafe (3), 410
Rosemarie's (4), 412
Roumeli Taverna, 414
The Russian Tea Room (1), 416
Rusty Staub's on Fifth (5), 544
Ryan McFadden (5), 559

Sabor (3), 418
Saigon (4), 545
San Domenico (1), 419
Sarabeth's Kitchen (1), 546
Saranac (7), 547
Say Eng Look (4), 421
The Sea Grill (2), 423
Sette Mezzo (5), 548
Sevilla Restaurant and Bar (3), 425
Sfuzzi (1), 427
Shun Lee (1), 429
Shun Lee Palace (6), 431
Siam Inn (1), 434
Sidewalkers' (1), 549

Sido Abu Salim (5), 549
The Sign of the Dove (6), 436
Siracusa (5), 438
Siracusa Gelateria (5), 550
Smith & Wollensky (5), 440
SoHo Kitchen and Bar (4), 559
Sparks Steakhouse (5), 442
Sukhothai (5), 444
Sushiden (5), 447
Sylvia's (1), 551
Symphony Cafe (1), 449

Taormina (4), 451
Tatany (5), 453
Tavern on the Green (1), 455
Ten Twenty-Two (7), 457
The Terrace (1), 459
Terrace Five (6), 551
Tommy Tang's (4), 461
Toscana Ristorante (6), 464
Trastevere (7), 466
Trattoria dell'Arte (1), 468
Trixie's (2), 552
Tropica Bar and Seafood House (5), 553
20 Mott Street Restaurant (4), 470
"21" Club (1), 472

Umeda (5), 474
Union Square Cafe (5), 476

Victor's Café 52 (1), 478
Voulez-Vous (7), 480
Vucciria (4), 554

The Water Club (5), 482

Water's Edge at the East River Yacht Club, 484
White Horse Tavern (3), 559
Wilkinson's Seafood Café (7), 486
Windows on the World (4), 488

Yellowfingers di Nuovo (6), 555
Yellow Rose Cafe (1), 555

Zarela (6), 490
Zula (1), 556